D1297586

MY LIFE WITH THE ESKIMO

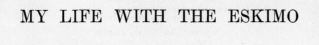

THE MACMILLAN COMPANY
NEW YORK · BOSTON · CHICAGO · DALLAS
ATLANTA · SAN FRANCISCO

MACMILLAN & CO., Limited
LONDON · BOMBAY · CALCUTTA
MELBOURNE

THE MACMILLAN CO. OF CANADA, Ltd.
TORONTO

COPPER ("BLOND") ESKIMOS

Here were not remains of the Stone Age, but the Stone Age itself:
men and women, very human, entirely friendly, who welcomed us to
their homes and bade us stay.

MY LIFE WITH THE ESKIMO

BY

VILHJALMUR STEFANSSON

FOREWORDS BY

HENRY FAIRFIELD OSBORN

PRESIDENT, AMERICAN MUSEUM OF NATURAL HISTORY
NEW YORK

AND

REGINALD WALTER BROCK

DEAN, COLLEGE OF APPLIED SCIENCE, UNIVERSITY OF
BRITISH COLUMBIA

WITH A NATURAL HISTORY APPENDIX

BY

DR. RUDOLPH M. ANDERSON

ILLUSTRATED

New York

THE MACMILLAN COMPANY

1924

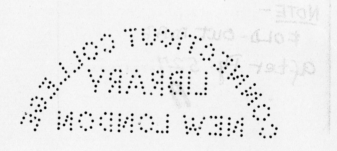

Norwood Press
J. S. Cushing Co. — Berwick & Smith Co.
Norwood, Mass., U.S.A.

NOTE

THE publishers regret that owing to Mr. Stefánsson's departure on his new expedition to the far North he was unable to read the final proofs of this volume.

FOREWORD

IN a late autumn month of the year 1907 there came into my office at the American Museum a young man of earnest and serious personality who said he desired to explore in the Arctic region, not in search of the still undiscovered Pole but in a region still untouched by any competent explorer. He asked nothing for his own expenses and very little money for outfitting the expedition, something a little over two thousand dollars for the outfit and supplies. I was not very much impressed with this financial estimate; I felt that it was far under the probable outlay. Nor did I carefully consider the scientific features of the plan, because I was deeply impressed with the personality and subdued enthusiasm of the young man himself — in short, it was the personality of Vilhjalmur Stefansson rather than his project which attracted me. Here, I thought, might be another Nansen or Peary or Shackleton, only awaiting a fair opportunity to put his potentiality into actual service. In the hope of perhaps discovering or revealing another born Arctic explorer I felt that the American Museum should take the risk even of increased financial expenditure and the possibility of negative or barren results. Stefansson had been prepared for leadership by his expedition of 1906–1907, in which he was accidentally separated from the large party under Leffingwell and Mikkelsen and was compelled to act independently.

Accompanied by a very able zoölogist, Rudolph Martin Anderson, Stefansson started with these slender promises of support. It was not long before the mother institution, the American Museum, which ever watches over its young explorers with maternal solicitude, began to feel very great anxiety about the two men. We had expended the original amount of $2,000 for the outfit and supplies, which were duly forwarded to a destination arranged beforehand but which we were informed did not reach them. A few months after Stefansson's visit to me I was elected President of the Museum and with the efficient aid of my secretary, George H. Sherwood, we embarked on an apparently fruitless endeavor to reach Stefansson and Anderson with fresh supplies. From first to last these efforts cost us upwards of $14,000, more than seven times the original estimate. Still no word from either explorer; every day we became more anxious; finally the Arctic silence was broken and there came over the wires the news of the extraordinary success achieved by these two young men, the successful exploration of an entirely unknown country and the discovery of Eskimos with supposed traces of Nordic blood, the so-called "blond Eskimos," about whom there is much supposition and many attempts to explain, although Stefansson himself now considers that of Norse-Greenlandic ancestry the most probable.

Thus apparently in a moment, but actually as a result of the splendid hereditary equipment of both Stefansson and Anderson, the expedition achieved world-wide fame. And how could this be acquired with the absence of the provisions and all the supplies forwarded with such care and at such great expense? Because in the meantime Stefansson had made one of the most interesting discoveries in the whole history of polar exploration — a discovery reflected in the title of his later book — the *friendly* Arctic, signifying that to those who know how to live there, to those who keenly enjoy life there, this region of the long Arctic night and of the bitter cold is not hostile but friendly.

This is one of the bright and happy episodes in my long life as head of the American Museum of Natural History, which sends young explorers into every part of the world. I have learned that there are very few men who are really fitted for exploration, among the many who desire to explore or who think they are fitted to explore. Exploration brings out all the highest human virtues; it also lays bare all the human weaknesses. Few natures are sufficiently well balanced to stand the stresses and strains of the Arctic and the Antarctic, no matter how friendly these regions appear to men of the caliber of the writer of this book.

I have often wondered why men desire to explore, and in this connection I am reminded of a second interview with Stefansson some time after he returned from this most successful expedition. I asked him a question I should have asked him in the first place; namely, where he was born and who his parents were. He responded, "I was born on a Manitoba farm and brought up on a North Dakota farm until I became a cowboy at fourteen." Then I asked him a second question, "Your father and mother were immigrants to this country. Where did they come from?" "From Iceland," he replied, "the farthest north civilized island in the world." Doubtless the same impulses which had driven Stefansson's remote ancestors to Iceland were still ebbing in him, with those which impelled him to overcome all difficulties and all obstacles to discover and know the Life of the Eskimos and, later, the Friendly Arctic.

HENRY FAIRFIELD OSBORN, President,
American Museum of Natural History, New York.

AMERICAN MUSEUM OF NATURAL HISTORY,
NEW YORK CITY,
December 28, 1923.

FOREWORD

MR. STEFANSSON, in the winter of 1907–08, told me of his proposed overland expedition from the Mackenzie River to the Coppermine and Victoria Land and kindly offered to do anything he could, while there, for the Geological Survey of Canada. There was much in that inaccessible portion of Canada of prime interest to us. A short conversation confirmed the impression I had formed from his previous expedition, that he was a man who was likely to get into that country, where he could do a great deal for the Survey. Geographical information would be of value; mineralogical information, especially of occurrences of copper that might be obtained from the Eskimos, would be of value; but most valuable of all would be ethnological investigation in Canada proceeding under the auspices of the Survey.

This expedition promised to afford a golden opportunity to reënter the field, if Mr. Stefansson and the American Museum of Natural History would permit the Geological Survey to coöperate in a small way.

The expenditure involved would be so small, and the geographical and mineralogical information likely to accrue so valuable, that it would surely prove too great a bargain for the watchdogs of the Treasury to resist. Mr. Stefansson strongly supported the proposal, President Osborn and Director Bumpus of the American Museum were glad to encourage in any way the study, under Canadian Government auspices, of the native races of Canada, and generously agreed to make the expedition a joint one of the American Museum and the Geological Survey, although it was virtually financed by the former, the Survey contributing a purely nominal sum. The Canadian Government got a bargain but created the precedent of expenditure for ethnological work.

The situation was described in my Summary Report of the Survey for 1908 as follows:

" ETHNOLOGY

"In the new Museum one of the most popular sections is likely to be the ethnological exhibit.   Very little investigation has been made in Canada of the native races, and what has been done has been under the auspices of foreign institutions.   The opportunities for such studies are fast disappearing.   Under advancing settlement and rapid development of the country, the native is disappearing, or coming under the influence of the white man's civilization.   The older people who are familiar with the folk lore or traditions of the tribe are dying off, and the rising generation under the changed conditions is acquiring a totally different education.

"If the information concerning the native races is ever to be secured and preserved, action must be taken very soon, or it will be too late.   It is a duty we owe to the Canada of the future to see that such material is saved.

"The work on the Eskimo of the Arctic, undertaken this year in conjunction with the American Museum of Natural History, it is hoped will prove only the beginning of a serious effort to acquire the valuable ethnological data that are yet to be had."

Our hopes were fulfilled, for in 1910 an Anthropological Division was created in the Survey, and by 1911 it was hard at work with an ethnologist, an assistant ethnologist, an archæologist and a stenographer on its permanent staff and with six parties, in addition to Mr. Stefansson's, engaged in field work.   This Division has already achieved excellent results, it has preserved valuable records of the native races that even to-day are no longer available, and it will prove still more valuable in the future.

All this may be credited truly, if indirectly, to the Expedition, described in such an interesting way in this volume.   While the Survey did not contribute extensively toward the cost of the expedition, it rendered service that enabled Mr. Stefansson to achieve success.   He had sent to both the American Museum and the Geological Survey an account of the hard winter of 1909–10 and the ill luck that had dogged the party up to this time.   On its receipt the American Museum informed me that they were recalling the expedition and asked the Survey to do the same.   In my reply I expressed the opin-

ion that the party had suffered from hard luck only, such as was often
experienced in exploratory work in Canada; that they had done exceptionally well under the circumstances; that it was greatly to their
credit that they were not discouraged but were planning to proceed;
that they had endured and overcome, and now that success seemed
almost within grasp it would be cruel to deprive them of their opportunity; consequently I would instruct Mr. Stefansson to proceed and
would meet the entire cost of the expedition if the American Museum
wished to withdraw.

In view of this opinion the American Museum countermanded their
letter of recall and continued to furnish their strong encouragement
and support.

How thoroughly this confidence was justified the reader may see
for himself. The expedition returned with most interesting and valuable information, and the best collections ever brought back from
the North; Mr. Stefansson adapted himself perfectly to the conditions
obtaining in that region, which made him the outstanding traveler and
hunter of all who have worked in the Canadian Arctic, and furthermore he has presented to the public the most vivid and readable description of the country, of its inhabitants, and of life within the
Arctic.

(Signed) REGINALD WALTER BROCK

Dean, College of Applied Science,
University of British Columbia.

ILLUSTRATIONS

Copper ("Blond") Eskimos . . . . *Frontispiece*

FACING PAGE

York Boat going over Cascade Rapid, Athabasca } 8
Scow running Boiler Rapid, Athabasca }

Fleet of Scows and "Model Boats" going down Athabasca, 1906 } . . 12
Funeral of Herbert Bray, May, 1906 }

Cooking with Driftwood, Mackenzie Delta } 32
Skinning a Bearded Seal }

Ruins of Amundsen's House at King Point, occupied 1905–06 } . . 36
Grave of Wiik at King Point }

Sunday, July 26, 1908, at Shingle Point 40

Most Northerly White Man's Dwelling on the Continent 44

Mackenzie River House in Summer }
A Woman dancing to the Accompaniment of Singing and Drum Beat- } 60
   ing — Flaxman Island, 1908 }

Sledging over Barren Ground in Summer 70

Camp on Sea Ice when Open Lead prevented getting Ashore } . . 80
Camp in Woods of Horton River }

A Dead Caribou } 102
Natkusiak shooting a Sleeping Seal }

The Adaptability of the Skin Boat 112

Tracking Umiak by Dog Team near Langton Bay 124

Mud Volcano between Darnley Bay and Langton Bay } . . . 140
Our Camp, Langton Bay, in Summer (1911) }

"Rosie H." in Winter Quarters } 150
Wreck of Steam Whaler "Alexander" }

When we shot a Seal during the Day he was dragged along behind the
   Sled till Camp Time 162

Our Sled at a Permanently Deserted Snow Village } 170
Temporarily Deserted Village }

Village, Dolphin and Union Straits, Early May } 174
A Stone House of Unknown Origin }

Watching the Arrival of Visitors } 180
Bowmen hunting Ptarmigan }

Mamayauk 184

A Group of Victoria Land Eskimo 194

Our Camp in the Interior of Victoria Island }
Coming Home from a Successful Bearded Seal Hunt — Each Dog drag- } 200
   ging a Segment of the Seal }

FACING PAGE

Ekalukpik 206

Cooking with Heather in Spring }
Cooking with Dwarf Willows in Spring on the Shore of a Frozen Lake } 210

Yearly Migration of the Caribou 224

Scene crossing Victoria Island 226

Rough Ice on Coppermine }
Eskimo wearing Snow Goggles } 238

Traveling on the Coppermine River in Spring 240

Meat Caches and Traps set to guard them 246

Three-roomed Dwelling, Coronation Gulf 256

Boys of Eight and Six Years, Coronation Gulf 260

Eskimo skinning the First Caribou they had seen shot with a Rifle }
Spring Tent of Eskimo, South Shore of Coronation Gulf, Late April } . 266

Coronation Gulf Hunters with Bows and Arrows }
Palaiyak and Nogasak } 268

On Sea Ice 272

Crowd at our Tent, June 14, 1913 }
The Largest Copper Eskimo Village we ever visited — Twenty-seven } 274
   Snow Houses and Tents }

Three Women of Prince Albert Sound 276

A Village of Twenty-seven Deserted and Three Occupied Houses . . 278

Prince Albert Sound Young Women 280

Prince Albert Sound Women and One Man 282

Hitkoak, Alunak and Pamiungittok }
A Coronation Gulf Family } 284

Prince Albert Sound Men and One Woman 292

Prince Albert Sound Group, all of whom show Blond Tendencies . . 296

Prince Albert Sound — Spring House, Sled, and Dogs . . . 300

Beacon built on Bell Island }
Coronation Gulf Eskimo Men's Styles in Dress } 306

Skinning a Large Bear
The Part that went to waste because our Party was too Small to eat or } 312
   haul the Meat

The Story of a Forgotten Tragedy }
Skinning a Seal for Supper } 314

Richardson's Drawing and Three Photographs of the Same Place . . 316

Water on Top Solid Sea Ice in June }
Loose Ice Cake forming Bridge across Lead } 322

Sledging across Barren Ground in June is Hot Work . . . 324

Drying Clothes and Ethnological Specimens after traveling over Water- }
   covered Ice } 326
The Cache

Bringing Ashore a Bearded Seal at Langton Bay 332

The " Teddy Bear " 336

The March across Barren Ground }
Camp Breaking and preparing Packs for Travel } 338

FACING PAGE

Frame of Coal Creek House, 1911–12
Dease River House, February, 1911 } 346
Dease River House, May, 1911
Ruins (1910) of House occupied in 1908–09

Coal Seam, Coal Creek } . . . 360
Smoking Mountains (Burning Coal Mines), Franklin Bay

Sections of Underground Ice Bowlders exposed in Cutbank, Pitt Point } 384
One Method of Formation of Underground Ice

Searching for Archæological Specimens at Cape Smythe 388

Columnar Basalt underlaid by Stratified Limestone
A View of Two Islands from the Southwest, the Nearer One a Half- } 442
    mile distant

Setting Fish Net underneath the Ice in Spring, Mackenzie Delta,
    June 7, 1910
Setting Gill Nets in Summer, Richard Island, Mackenzie Delta, Sep- } 450
    tember 18, 1909
A Day's Catch on the Hula-Hula River, Alaska (mostly Salmon Trout)

Male Willow Ptarmigan in Early Plumage, Dease River, May, 1911
Female Rock Ptarmigan, Coronation Gulf } . 460
Nest of Rock Ptarmigan, near Franklin Bay, June 17, 1911

Leaving our Winter Sheep-hunting Camp, Hula-Hula River, Alaska,
    March, 1909
Male Barren Ground Bear, Horton River, N. W. T. } 518
Head of Northern Mountain Sheep (Ram), Hula-Hula River, Endicott
    Mountains, Alaska, 1909
Polar Bears swimming at Sea near Cape Parry, August, 1911

Map of the Arctic Coast of Alaska and Northwestern Canada, showing
    the Route of the Stefánsson–Anderson Expedition, 1908–12.

Map of Victoria Island and Adjacent Regions, with Approximate Addi-
    tions and Corrections, and Eskimo names, by V. Stefánsson.

FACING PAGE

Frame of Coal Creek House, 1911-12
Dease River House, February, 1911   314
Dease River House, May, 1911
Ruins (1910) of Houseway, led in 1905-06

Coal Seam, Coal Creek   360

Smoking Mountains (Burning Coal Mine), Franklin Bay
Sections of Underground Ice, Bowlders exposed in Cutbank, Elt Point   362
One Method of Formation of Underground Ice

Searching for Archaeological Specimens at Cape Smythe   368
Eskimo Bread analyzed by Esoterical Laboratory

A View of Two Islands from the Southwest, the Nearer One a Half   474
    mile distant

Setting Thin Net underneath the Ice in Spring, Mackenzie Delta,
    June 5, 1910
Setting Gill Nets in Summer, Richard Island, Mackenzie Delta, Sep-   484
    tember 15, 1909

A Day's Catch on the Hula Hula River, Alaska (mostly Salmon Trout)
Male Whitefish in Breeding Coloration, Dease River, May, 1911   490
Female Rock Ptarmigan in Winter Plumage, Coronation Gulf
Face of Rock Formation near Franklin Bay, June 17, 1911

Passing on a Winter Sheep Leather Carpet, Hula Hula River, Alaska,
    March, 1909
Male Barren Ground Hair, Horton River, N. W. T.   ??
Head of Northern Mountain Sheep (Ram), Hula Hula River, Endicott
    Mountains, Alaska, 1909

Polar Party embarking at Sea near Cape Crozer, August, 1911
Map of the Arctic Coast of Alaska and Northwestern Canada, showing
    the Route of the Stefansson-Anderson Expedition, 1908-12
Map of Victoria Island and Adjacent Regions, with Approximate Addi-
    tions and Corrections, and Estimate of V. Stefansson.

MY LIFE WITH THE ESKIMO

CHAPTER I

THE plans of my second expedition took gradual shape during the years 1906–1907, while I was still north of the Arctic circle engaged in the work of my first expedition.

It was once intended that I should be the ethnologist of the Leffingwell-Mikkelsen Arctic Expedition, sometimes known as the Anglo-American Polar Expedition, which sailed from Victoria, British Columbia, in the spring of 1906. When the proposal was made to me I found it an attractive one in everything except this: that the expedition's schooner, the *Duchess of Bedford*, was unprovided with auxiliary motive power, and my book knowledge of Arctic conditions made me fear that she would never reach the proposed site of operations, the west coast of Victoria Island. Mr. Leffingwell and I therefore agreed that I should not join the expedition in Victoria as did its other members, but should go overland and down the Mackenzie River to meet them at Herschel Island, which lies about eighty miles west of the Mackenzie delta. My reason was that if the expedition failed to get so far east I should be able to occupy my time profitably in the study of the scientifically unknown Mackenzie Eskimo. On the other hand, if nothing obstructed the expedition I should be able to join it in early August and proceed with it eastward toward Victoria Island. It turned out that the *Duchess of Bedford* had good fortune until she reached Point Barrow. At that point the ice blocked her further advance until the season had become late and she was finally overtaken by winter on the north coast of Alaska at Flaxman Island. She was never able, therefore, to pick me up, and I consequently never became a member of the expedition. From the point of view of the ethnologist, this was a very fortunate circumstance. Although I had always doubted that the ship would come to pick me up, I had nevertheless intrusted my entire outfit to her, for I wanted, if

I lived with the Eskimo at all, to live exactly as one of them, in their houses, dressing like them, and eating only such food as they did. I now found myself, in accord with my own plan, set down two hundred miles north of the polar circle, with a summer suit of clothing, a camera, some notebooks, a rifle, and about two hundred rounds of ammunition, facing an Arctic winter, where my only shelter would have to be the roof of some hospitable Eskimo house.

These were ideal conditions for me. Had I had my own party and my own house I should have lived near the Eskimo instead of with them. I should have seen them as an outsider, a stranger. If I had visited them now and then, I should have found them wearing their company manners and should have obtained no better insight into their lives than does the ordinary missionary or trader. Now my very poverty was my greatest advantage; I was not rich and powerful like the whaling captains or mounted policemen, so there was no reason why they should flatter me or show me defer-ence. I had no visible means, and therefore what they did for me was without hope of reward. They took me into their houses and treated me hospitably and courteously, but exactly as if I were one of them. They gave me clothes to wear and food to eat, I helped them in their work and joined in their games, until they gradually forgot that I was not one of them, and began to live their lives before my eyes as if I were not there. This gave me a rare oppor-tunity to know them as they are.

The details of that winter are not a part of the present story, although the things I learned have not only been useful to me since, but have also furnished the incentive to five years of further ex-ploration. To begin with, I found that the Eskimo language, although exceedingly difficult for a European to learn, was not impossible of acquisition, for at the end of a winter in the house of the Mackenzie Eskimo I already had a good foundation in it. The people, too, were agreeable. They were not only interesting from a scientific point of view, as all primitive people must be to the student of mankind, but they were cheerful, self-reliant, and admirable companions. They are people among whom you might possibly have enemies and among whom you were certain to make friends; people very much like you and me, but with the social virtues developed rather more highly than they have been among our own race. In a difficult struggle for existence under hard natural conditions they have acquired the ability to live together in peace and good will.

But what led most definitely to the planning of my second expedition was that I learned that to the eastward of Cape Bathurst the Mackenzie Eskimo were unaware of the existence of any people. The coast of Dolphin and Union Straits had been mapped by Dr. John Richardson in 1826, but he had seen none of its inhabitants. My knowledge of the habits of the Eskimo led me to suspect that his finding no people was in itself no proof of the non-existence of people on this portion of the mainland, for he had skirted the coast in summer when the natives were likely to be inland caribou hunting. Further, the English explorers had seen Eskimo on Coronation Gulf and on Victoria Island in the first half of the eighteenth century, and these people had not been visited since. It would be interesting to revisit them after sixty years. At Herschel Island I happened to meet Captain Amundsen on his way west from his now famous voyage of the Northwest Passage, and I found that he also had sailed past these shores without seeing any people and in fact without opportunity of seeing any.

A whaling ship also brought news of interest. The schooner *Olga*, commanded by Captain Klinkenberg, had wintered somewhere to the eastward, and had seen Eskimo. The captain, when he landed at Herschel Island, announced that he had spent the winter on Banks Island. But this I think was believed by few of the whaling captains, and seemed entirely improbable to me, for his own description of the country in which he had wintered showed clearly that it could have been no portion of Banks Island, unless indeed Banks Island were very different from the descriptions and charts we have of it. While no one could be certain, therefore, just where the *Olga* had wintered, it was generally agreed that it must have been somewhere on Victoria Island, and the majority favored Minto Inlet, to which Captain Klinkenberg himself later on agreed. I shall not here take time by the forelock to say just where it eventually turned out that he had wintered, for we did not discover that interesting fact until May of 1911, but the important thing was that wherever it might have been, Captain Klinkenberg had there seen Eskimo who were armed with bows and arrows, who used copper implements, and who evidently had therefore been in no contact with white men in recent years. The white men and Eskimo of the crew of the *Olga* brought back many semi-fabulous stories which they had got from these Eskimo; their divergence from actual truth is to be explained partly by the inability of the Alaskan Eskimo on the ship to understand the dialect of their eastern countrymen with whom they associated for only a few days all together.

Shortly after my return from the first expedition in the early winter of 1907, my plans for scientific exploration in the Arctic were laid before Dr. Herman C. Bumpus, Director of the American Museum of Natural History. It seemed possible that there might exist on the north shore of the continent of America, and possibly on Banks Island and Victoria Island, people who had not seen a white man, either they or their ancestors, and there almost certainly were other people who themselves had not seen white men, although the ancestors of some of them might have seen explorers of Franklin's own party or else men of the Franklin Search. True, some prominent authorities on the Eskimo did believe that the islands west of King William Island were uninhabited. One of these men told me that I should certainly find no people on the west coast of Victoria Island, for all the Eskimo seen there by Collinson and M'Clure (1852–1853) had long ago moved east to Hudson Bay to trade with the whalers. Acting on these opinions, the Canadian Government had issued in 1906 a map on which the word "Uninhabited" is printed in red letters across the face of Victoria Island, where we eventually found a dense population, as Eskimo go.

The scientific importance of the study of these people by an ethnologist was clear to Dr. Bumpus and appealed no less strongly to Dr. Clark Wissler, the Museum's curator of anthropology. They both assured me at once of their interest in my plans, and from that point on it was merely a question of financial detail to make the expedition a certainty. The funds were not available to support a large expedition; the purchase of a ship and its equipment with the customary paraphernalia of Arctic exploration were out of the question — neither did it seem necessary to have such complex equipment for so simple a task as that of ascertaining whether or not human beings live in a certain stretch of country. Our thesis was this: that we were not looking for any waste places, but for land occupied by human beings; if those human beings were there at all, they must be Eskimo supporting themselves by the most primitive implements of the chase; and it seemed clear that if Eskimo could live there, armed as they must be with bows and arrows, and not only live there but bring up their children and take care of their aged, then surely we, armed with modern rifles, would be able to live in that sort of country as long as we pleased and to go about in it as we liked. Of course the thesis was bound to prove out.

I had at first considered going north alone, relying entirely on the support of the Mackenzie River Eskimo for my journey toward the eastward in the search of their hypothetical countrymen, but one day a letter came which changed my plans at once. I had often considered the possibility of taking some one with me, and in thinking over all the available men whom I knew, I had always felt that one of them was qualified before all others, and the letter I got was from that very man, Dr. R. M. Anderson, a classmate in the University of Iowa and a friend of mine for many years. I had known him in the University as one of those exceptional men who won honors both through scholarship and athletic ability. He had been captain of track teams; he held various athletic records; he was a crack rifle shot; he was experienced in roughing it in various places, and had also been a soldier in the Spanish-American war; he held the degree of Doctor of Philosophy and had written learned books and articles on birds and animals, and was now tired of civilization and eager for a chance to go north with me. As soon as I showed his letter to the Museum authorities it was agreed that we must do everything to get him to go along, for they knew him by reputation and it was at once clear to all of us that by his going the scope of the expedition could be doubled; for whereas I was but an ethnologist, a student of men and their works, he could study the animal life also of the little-known and unknown districts we expected to traverse. Besides, his being with me would double my

own chances of success, for it is often difficult to get Eskimo to leave
their own country for the exploration of, to them, unknown districts,
and if there were two of us together we could at all times, if we
desired, be independent of the assistance of the Eskimo, could do
what we liked and go where we pleased; whereas a man who is alone
cannot safely make long journeys on an uninhabited Arctic
coast.

Our equipment was the simplest possible. It consisted merely
of two cameras that used films of the same size; a supply of films
for these cameras; a pair of rifles that were the best that money
could buy, and a thousand rounds of ammunition for these rifles;
half a dozen ordinary rifles and shot guns for the use of the Eskimo,
and ammunition for these; two pairs of six-power field glasses, also
the best that the market afforded; writing materials, pens and pen-
cils; two silk tents; a little tobacco for the use of our prospective
Eskimo employees; some aluminum cooking utensils, and very little
else. The outfit we took down the Mackenzie River weighed less
than a ton, and yet with one exception—to be later noted—it
contained all the essentials for Arctic exploration of the sort that we
had planned. We considered that carrying food to the Arctic was
carrying coal to Newcastle.

The first laps of the journey were very simple. I left New
York April 22d, 1908, and joined in Toronto Dr. Anderson, who
had preceded me there by a few days, for we had arranged with
Mr. R. F. Stupart, Director of the Dominion Meteorological Service,
to establish for him six Meteorological stations along the Mackenzie
River between Edmonton and the Arctic coast, and Dr. Anderson
had gone to Toronto to take charge of the instruments and equipment for these stations. From here we went to Winnipeg and thence
to Edmonton, over the new line of the Canadian Northern Railway,
which had just opened up vast tracts of fertile farm lands lying
well to the north of the older Canadian Pacific road.

In Edmonton, as everywhere else along the line of our travel,
people took the kindliest interest in our plans, and did everything to
help us on our way. The private individuals who did us services
are too many to mention, but of greater value to us than any one
thing was the good will of the Hudson's Bay Company, extended

through its commissioner, Mr. C. C. Chipman of Winnipeg. There was a time when the Hudson's Bay Company owned Canada, and still more recently they were in such absolute control of vast districts that their friendly support was an essential to any one who traveled in the country. To-day along the Mackenzie system their competitors in the fur trade have planted their stations every few hundred miles, yet even now the great Company is a power whose sphere stretches to the Polar Sea.

We had at first intended to transfer our equipment to the Arctic in a York boat belonging to the Church of England. I had made arrangements for doing this with my friend and former fellow-traveler, Bishop Reeve, previously of the Mackenzie diocese but now stationed in Toronto. But it turned out on our arrival in Edmonton that this boat had not yet been built; nor was there immediate prospect of its being built. We therefore accepted the kind offer of Mr. Christie, Chief Clerk of the Mackenzie district, to become his guests on the first boats of the Company to go down the Athabasca River that spring. Civilization is continually making further inroads into the wilderness of the North. Since that time a railroad has been built from Edmonton ninety miles north to Athabasca Landing, but when we went north this was a two-days journey by stage. At Athabasca Landing was the most northerly post office and telegraph office, and from it we sent out our last messages and bade good-by to civilization — in the form in which that word is understood by the majority of men. Of course the two thousand miles of the Mackenzie Valley to the north of us were occupied at intervals by white men. These were the trappers and traders who from the point of view of the city dweller and the farmer are living in the wilderness, although I must confess that from the point of view of the Arctic explorer they seem to be dwelling in the heart of civilization.

The three scows over which Mr. Christie had immediate command left Athabasca Landing at two in the afternoon of May 7th. The Athabasca had been ice-free for but a few days, and huge blocks of ice were even now piled along its banks in windrows. The mosquitoes, the plague of the northern forest, were not yet out in any numbers, and the down-river journey was a pleasant one. Generally we floated with the current, but occasionally our Indian crews would take the oars and row awhile.

As this is to be a story of Arctic exploration we shall give but little space to the northward journey, although it is picturesque in itself and although it leads one through land strange to the ordinary traveler. The trading posts of the Hudson's Bay Company were located along the river's northward course, at distances averaging about two hundred miles apart. The first one hundred and sixty-five miles of the Athabasca River, from the Landing to the "Grand Rapids," form a stretch of shoal water nevertheless navigable by flat-bottomed steamers of light draft, and although we now traveled in the typical eight-ton spruce-wood freight scows of the Hudson's Bay Company, I had two years before traveled the same section of the journey aboard the steamer *Midnight Sun*. Although the *Midnight Sun* carried no freight but instead pushed several loaded freight scows in front of her, her fourteen inches or so of draft were too many for the depth of the river and we had kept running aground, bumping into rocks and having various accidents. At one time we stove a hole in the steamer's bottom and sank, but as the sinking only meant the settling of a few inches, it was a serious matter only from the point of view of delay. I have forgotten just how we went about the repairs. I am not sure but they may have raised her with jackscrews — at least that is a method which would seem practical enough in most cases of shipwreck on the Athabasca.

We made the one hundred and sixty-five miles in 1906 at an average speed of thirteen miles per day, which is very likely a low record for downstream steamboat navigation. On our present journey we got along much faster and reached "Grand Rapids Island" on May 12th. The river here has a considerable fall; the rapid on the west side of the island is impassable for any craft, while on the east side it may be run with comparative safety with unloaded or lightly loaded boats. This is risky business, however, in freighting, and the Hudson's Bay Company have built a tramway the full half mile of the island's length, and over this all the freight and some of the boats are usually transported while a few of the empty boats are run down the eastern channel.

From Grand Rapids for a hundred miles to Fort MacMurray the

York Boat going over Cascade Rapid, Athabasca.

Scow running Boiler Rapid, Athabasca.

stream is here and there interrupted by rapids, none of them serious for good canoe men, although the big freight scows when heavily loaded occasionally come to grief. The freight carried in the boats is always insured and accidents therefore do not mean any great loss of money, but it is a very inconvenient thing for that particular Hudson's Bay post to which the stores of the sunken boat had been consigned. It happens occasionally that a boat carrying most or all of the consignment to a certain post is wrecked and that the post is then compelled to go a year without such articles as tea, tobacco, prints, ribbons, chewing gum, and other things which the Indians nowadays consider the necessaries of life. It would seem that the Company might distribute the loss so as to make it fall less heavily on any particular post, but for some reason they do not generally do this.

Each freight scow has a crew consisting of three or four rowers, a bowsman, and a steersman. The bowsman knows the rapids fairly well and is a good judge of water; he stands in the front end of the boat with a pole raised above his head, which he manipulates so as to indicate to the steersman the direction that the boat should take. The steersman, however, is the most important member of the crew. He is the man of the greatest experience, resourceful, and has a reputation for knowing these particular rapids. When the boat approaches a rapid the steersman gives the word and all the oarsmen row as hard as possible so as to keep steerage way on the craft. With the speed of the water at anything from six to nine or ten miles an hour, and with an additional weight on the boat of perhaps a mile and a half or two miles due to the rowing, one's progress through the rapids is somewhat spectacular, although the real danger does not seem to be great; for although boats are wrecked and cargoes sunk, I never heard of a single man losing his life. Still, the thing is considered dangerous locally, and a steersman who has an accident usually loses his nerve so completely that he never conducts a boat through the rapids again. Yet this is not a universal rule, for some steersmen whom I know have had several accidents.

Some of the rapids are dangerous only in periods of low water. These low periods are irregular and cannot be predicted, for they depend apparently chiefly on the rainfall and the melting of the snow in the mountains of British Columbia. Such a rapid as the Cascade may even disappear in really high water; in stages of phenomenally low water it becomes impassable for boats, for it is but a plunge of water over a sharp ledge with a knifelike edge that may catch the boat's bottom and balance the boat so that it can go neither down nor back.

Coming down the river we continually had before our eyes examples of how a new country, careless of its rich natural resources, allows them to go to waste. The value of the spruce forests of Canada is apparent to those who theorize about it, but here day after day we traveled through a haze of forest fires, some of them burning at unknown distances from the river, others coming down to its very banks, with the flames licking the water.

Sometimes these fires start no one knows how; sometimes people know and do not tell and sometimes they are started intentionally by Indians, who consider that the hunting is made better by clearing the land so that they can see the game from greater distances. To do this is as shortsighted a policy for the Indian as it is for the government to allow its being done. True, there are forest rangers, but these I suppose exist to fulfill the letter of some law and to draw a salary. There is one who plies over two hundred and fifty miles from Athabasca Landing to Fort MacMurray, and another a somewhat shorter distance from Fort MacMurray to Smith Landing. But even he who has the shorter beat makes but three trips a year and these are perfunctory. One of these rangers was a fellow passenger with us and did exactly as we did, — sat in his boat and lazily watched the flames as we drifted down the river. No doubt he reported the occurrence and presumably it was somewhere tabulated, to become a part of a useful body of statistics.

On my previous trip down the river, in 1906, there was in our company Mr. Elihu Stewart, Forestry Commissioner for the Dominion of Canada, and as he has made a report on the forest resources of the Mackenzie Valley, there is far less reason than otherwise for my dwelling on the extent of its natural wealth — vast even yet in spite of the periodic fires. It will give some idea to say that there were in 1908 two sawmills near the south shore of Great Slave Lake that made lumber suitable for the building of steamboats, and that trees twelve inches in diameter, six feet above the ground, grow tall and graceful in the Mackenzie delta less than a hundred miles south of the tidewater of the Polar Sea.

The thing that impresses a stranger in the country, and one to which a person of any feeling or imagination does not soon grow callous, is the cruelty and thoughtlessness with which dogs are treated in the north. It is a common thing that they are not fed all summer, and some therefore die of starvation, while most of them survive only as living skeletons until the approach of fall makes it necessary to feed them up in order that they may have some strength for the coming winter. And it is not merely that they are never fed — to show kindness to a dog is an unheard-of thing. If he merely passes your tent door, walking along and minding his business, it is good form for you to seize a hatchet or a hammer or anything that is near and throw it out to see if you can hit him. If you happen to knock an eye out or break a leg, it is considered an excellent joke, unless the dog's particular owner should be near, in which case he is offended; not because he feels for the dog, but merely because he thinks that showing offense may give him some chance of recovering damages. Some of the white men treat the dogs a little better than the average Indian or half-breed, but a dog used to kindness is nevertheless a thing that I do not remember seeing. The result is that the poor dogs, who always expect a kick, will always receive your approach with a snarl. By buying some of these dogs and using them myself, I have found that even after this sort of bringing up they quickly become under kind treatment as friendly as our house dogs at home.

Most of the men who composed our crews owned dogs, and when we left Athabasca Landing these to the number of twenty or so followed us along the banks of the river. The river frequently curves, and the boat channel generally lies now along one bank of the stream and now along the other. The poor dogs seemed to think each time our boat swung to one side of the river that we were about to land there, and those on the far side would accordingly take the water and swim over to us and land; but soon the boat channel would take us across the stream again, and again the dogs would take the water. The poor animals were weak from hunger, but had they known how to husband their strength they could probably have followed us a good many days; as it was, one by one they began to drop out and be left behind, many of them, no doubt, eventually to die of starvation. A thing that made the road of the dogs all the more difficult was that as we proceeded downstream the quantities of drift-ice stranded along the river's edge became greater and greater; the broken blocks were piled in windrows from twelve to twenty feet high, and to climb over these quickly tired the dogs out.

Our first accident occurred on Sunday, the 10th of May. We had passed Pelican Portage at noon and at three o'clock we were running a small rapid. Our boat and the second one went through safely, but the last, occupied by Mr. Christie and Mr. Bremner, was stove on a rock and was a third full of water before they succeeded in running it aground. We put our scows immediately ashore and went to the rescue, but before we were able to empty the boat it had sunk in shallow water, and some sugar, tea, and other goods got spoiled. Still, the accident was not a very serious one, and by 6.30 in the evening we were on the road again. Our Indian steersman commented upon the fact that this was a Sunday accident, and pointed out that his long experience on the river showed him that accidents often occur to boats that run on Sundays.

The following day we came to the Grand Rapids of the Athabasca, but stopped for a little while two or three miles south of the rapids at a place where two years before I had helped to bury an unknown Englishman, — unknown to all of us except that we knew his name was Herbert Bray. He had been cook on the *Midnight Sun,* had been taken sick a few days before we reached the rapids, and had been abused and maligned by everybody because he was supposed to be playing sick on account of being too lazy to do his own work. Nobody thought that there was anything serious the matter with him until one evening he died quietly. The next day we dug him a grave above high-water mark among the thick spruce trees. Mr. Stewart, the Forestry Commissioner, carved his name on a blazed tree, and I climbed the tree to make him the memorial of the North — the lop-stick. This consists in taking a tall and preferably isolated spruce tree and lopping off its branches for a dis-

FLEET OF SCOWS AND "MODEL BOATS" GOING DOWN ATHABASCA, 1906.

FUNERAL OF HERBERT BRAY, MAY, 1906.

tance of a few feet about three quarters of the way up the trunk. Usually the North forgets slowly. When a lop-stick is made to commemorate the killing of a fat moose or the giving of a great feast, the story is long remembered, but such a thing as the death of a stranger in a far country is apparently less impressive. Herbert Bray's grave was now in two years so nearly forgotten that I had to refer to Mr. Stewart's carving to prove that my opinion was more correct than two or three divergent ones as to where the grave actually was.

May 9th was the first really hot day of the year. Along our route so far we had seen the willow catkins and some buds but no green leaves, but on the 10th a green tinge began to spread over all the woods, showing especially on the poplar bluffs. The nights were cool; there was a slight frost between the 9th and 10th, but by the 11th the deciduous woods were fairly uniformly green.

CHAPTER II

MAY 12th we arrived at the Grand Rapids of the Athabasca River, one hundred and sixty-five miles north of Athabasca Landing. By the use of push carts on the tramway which the Hudson's Bay Company has built along the center of the island, it took two days to get our freight down to the eddy below the rapids. The empty boats were some of them run down the east channel and others let down by bow and stern lines. Our three boats were not the only ones here, for traders, prospectors, and adventurers are always on their way north into a country that each year attracts greater and greater numbers of such folk. One party of three men reminded us of a tragic story we had heard on the river two years before. I think it was in 1902 that two brothers by the name of MacLeod, the sons of an old Hudson's Bay factor in the Mackenzie Valley, came from the Pacific coast east across the Rockies to the head of the Liard River and descended it safely to the Mackenzie at Fort Simpson. Two years later one of these same brothers, accompanied by two other white men, went up the Liard again with the notion of retracing his former route to the Pacific, and none of the three had been heard of since. For a year or two no particular alarm was felt, for communications are slow in that country, but by now it was four years since they had disappeared into the mountains, and most people had given up hope of their ever being heard from again. There were various speculations: there might have been accidents; they might have been murdered by the "bad Indians" whom many of the Mackenzie traders fear, and who are said to be located about the headwaters of the Liard. There were even rumors, which could have had no solid foundation, to the effect that the party had found a rich gold mine and that one of them had killed the other two so as to make himself sole possessor of the secret and that he was now lying low until he could safely develop the supposed gold mine. Two of the MacLeod brothers, one of them the same that had come

14

from British Columbia six years before, and one other man, had now set out with the intention of tracing the lost travelers as carefully as possible, with the hope of finding out at least where and how they had died.

May 14th we left the Grand Rapids. The river was still falling and the rapids that lay between us and Fort MacMurray were therefore getting more dangerous every day. We had no serious mishaps, however, although now and again we struck a rock and sprung a slight leak. Our boats were built of spruce lumber, a material which has its disadvantages, but which seems to make the toughest and most flexible boats possible under the circumstances. At the Cascade Rapid we found the water so low that most of the boats preferred not to risk running over, and the freight was therefore portaged a dozen or fifteen yards and the boats lowered over the rapid by a rope.

As we approached Fort MacMurray a strong, all-pervading odor began to be noticeable — the smell of tar which here and there trickled down the cut-banks of the river and which soiled our clothes when we went ashore. We had for some time been running through a belt of land supposed by many to be rich in oil, and one hundred and twenty miles north of the Athabasca Landing at the Pelican Rapids we had passed a burning gas well. Some years before, the government in prospecting for oil had struck a flow of natural gas. This stopped the boring operations and some one lit the torch which is still burning. It is a stimulating and in a way romantic thing, when a boatman drifts at night into the circle of its flickering light. It is the torch of Science lighting the way of civilization and economic development to the realms of the unknown North. Both the government and individuals have followed up the promise of the tar-sands and considerable boring has been done, some of it showing a good prospect of oil production when sufficient capital shall be enlisted and suitable laws passed to enable investors to recover, if successful, the large sums that must be spent in prospecting.

A short distance above Fort MacMurray the boats came rushing out of the last rapid into quiet and deep water that extends from there on north to Athabasca Lake. The steamer *Grahame* would at a later season of the year have met us at this point and carried us north, but she was just now occupied on Peace River, and we therefore proceeded in our scows. All along the river we saw numerous traces of game, especially the tracks of moose and of black bears. Now and then we would see a frightened bear running up the hillside from the river and occasionally a small cub would climb a tall spruce tree and be silhouetted against the skyline — a black knob near the top of the tree. It is probable that had it not been for the few straggling dogs which still followed us along the bank we should have seen several moose, but as it was there was scarcely a chance of it.

The 21st of May was the first day of our journey that the mosquitoes were out in great numbers. From now we had continuous swarms of them every day, until more than two months later when we reached the Arctic Ocean. There are just as many mosquitoes in the Arctic as anywhere on the Mackenzie, but the difference is that the Athabasca River season for them runs from May to September, while on the Arctic coast it is only from about the 20th of June till the 10th of August.

When we reached Athabasca Lake, May 22d, we found that the main body of the ice had been cleared out of the west end of the lake by a westerly wind a few days before, but still we had to shove our way through considerable belts of mush-ice now and then, while we were crossing from the mouth of the Athabasca to Fort Chipewyan, near the northwest corner of the lake. We stopped for a few days at the Fort, and while we were there a change of wind brought the ice back again from the east and drifted much of it into the head of Slave River.

It is a curious thing that the Peace River, which, by the way, is a stream about the size of the Missouri and three times the size of the Danube, has two mouths, one into Athabasca Lake and one into Slave River. At seasons when the Peace is low this gives Athabasca Lake two outlets, for its water flows not only into the head of the Slave but also upstream, as it were, into the Peace. When again the Peace is high the process is reversed, and a considerable volume of its water flows into Athabasca Lake.

The Athabasca River, through which we had been traveling, is a stream comparable in size to the Ohio or the Danube, and flows most of its way through a valley of considerable proportions both as to width and depth; but the Slave, from Athabasca Lake to Smith Rapids, flows through nearly level country, so far as one can see from the river. On the Athabasca there are outcrops of limestone and sandstone, but on the north shore of Athabasca Lake and about the head of Slave River the formation changes and granitic rocks become conspicuous. The current is sluggish and the river shows magnificent straight reaches, miles in length and the greater part of a mile in width, shining like mirrors in the sunshine, which at this season of the year is continuous and brings terrific heat. At noonday on our boats thermometers placed in the shade occasionally went above the hundred mark. We suffered considerably from the heat, but this is not peculiar to the Slave River. Even north of the Arctic Circle, whenever you get a hundred miles from the sea-coast you have temperatures running into the nineties in the sun.

We arrived at Smith Landing June 5th, and had to delay there for several days while our freight was being transferred to Fort Smith, sixteen miles downstream below the Smith Rapids. This is a series of rapids, each of which has its name. Some of them can be run when special precautions are taken, but others require portages from a few yards up to several hundred yards.

We got to Fort Smith in time to see an event of great interest — the launching of the steamer *Mackenzie River*. This is not the first steamer by any means that has plied on the lower Mackenzie. Her immediate predecessor was the screw-propelled *Wrigley*, and there had been others even before her. Most of the boats have been built north of the Smith Rapids, but one of them, Hislop and Nagle's *Eva*, was built on the upper river and taken down through the rapids and portages — a task which apparently no one believed possible of accomplishment except Mr. Nagle himself, at the time that he undertook it. There probably never has been a more dramatic surprise in the history of the Mackenzie River than when the *Eva* floated into the view of the Hudson's Bay officers at Fort Smith, out of the gorge below the last rapid.

On my first journey to the Arctic we went thirteen hundred miles down the Slave, across Slave Lake, and down the Mackenzie aboard the *Wrigley*. That the Mackenzie is a good river is well shown by a comparison of it with the Yukon. The Yukon has long ago demon-

c

strated its tremendous importance in the economic development of Alaska, yet in spite of the most expert piloting and the most careful buoying of its channel I have been stranded on the Yukon flats for two days in a steamer drawing only four feet of water, and progress up the river was finally possible only by unloading and abandoning on the riverbank practically all the freight we had on board. The contrast with the Mackenzie is striking, for the *Wrigley* drew six and one half feet against the Yukon boat's four, was screw-propelled instead of being a stern-wheeler, ran over an unbuoyed course all the way, and had for a pilot a man who did not know the river particularly well but was merely a "good judge of water," and yet we had no serious trouble. Of course we ran aground now and then, but that was merely because we got out of the channel. In anticipation of these frequent groundings we carried all the lead and shot consigned to the North packed in 200-pound sacks in the bow of the *Wrigley* so as to make her down by the bow; then whenever she ran her nose into a sand bar, the passengers and crew would turn to and carry all the lead back to the stern, and we floated free again.

The *Mackenzie River* had been built under the supervision of a veteran of the northern rivers and lakes, Captain J. W. Mills, from lumber sawed in the Company's own sawmill near by. The old *Wrigley* had had but scant accommodations for six passengers; the *Mackenzie River* provides for thirty-six. Of course she is not a large boat, but still she is a decade in advance of all other craft on the Mackenzie and would be a creditable boat even on the Yukon.

The ice breaks out of the western end of Athabasca Lake usually about the middle of May and out of its east end a week or two later, for the seasons seem a good deal colder as you go east. In 1907 Slave River opened May 24th, at Smith Landing, which was considered a late spring, while in 1908 the ice broke off May 12th. There are usually tremendous ice jams in the rapids between Smith Landing and Fort Smith, and these retard the open water of the upper river so that it takes it several days to make the sixteen miles. The break-up is therefore about a week later at Fort Smith.

Here, as in many other places on the river, we saw examples of the improvidence of the Indians. Even in winter they dress in imported cloth garments which are far more expensive and not half so warm as the clothing they could make out of the skins of the animals they kill. But similar things occur the world over. Perhaps it should not be regarded as strange, but rather as a proof of the universal brotherhood of man, that the Northern Indian would rather shiver in fashionable attire than be comfortable in the furs which are cheap and therefore unaristocratic. On Bear Lake I have known them to sell caribou skins at fifty cents apiece to buy a duck coat at eight or ten dollars, when two caribou skins would have made a much warmer garment. An Indian woman at Smith Landing, while we were there, traded twenty suckers, which was food enough for a week, for one pound of tinned salmon, which did not make even a meal for her, and this at a time when she had been on short rations for several days on account of the want of fish, and when the twenty fish were all she had caught. Chocolate, imported English jams and marmalade, candies, and ribbons are the staple wares of these posts nowadays. It must be said that it was a part of the generally wise policy of the Hudson's Bay Company not to encourage among the Indians the development of these expensive tastes which it is so difficult for them to find the means to satisfy, but of late years the Company has had to follow where other traders have led them and now, instead of taking into the country what they consider good for the Indian, they are forced to take in anything that the Indian will buy. It is only the wise laws of the land that have determined that these articles shall be candies and sweetmeats instead of brandies and gin.

Here, to the west of Smith Landing, in the woods, is the only herd of wild buffalo now in existence in the world. These are the so-called "wood buffalo," of which there are several hundred. It is an easy walk from the river to the district they frequent, and any one can see them who has two or three days to spare and the money to hire an Indian guide. At present there is some effort being made to protect them from the extermination that has been the fate of the buffalo elsewhere. In connection with this general policy of the government, Major W. H. Routledge had been detailed to "look into the buffalo question," and we found him now at Smith Landing on his way out. During the winter he had made the trip westward across the Salt River and had photographed one of the bands. He gave it as his guess that there were at least three hundred of the animals and probably more.   There were many stories of the Indians having gone out and shot buffalo since the protective laws were passed, but these it was rather difficult to sift to the bottom, for some declared stoutly that it had been done within a year, and others declared with as great conviction that the thing had not been done at all.

After staying for a few days at Smith Landing, where Dr. Anderson and I were the guests of the factor, Mr. Maxfield Hamilton, we drove in a horse stage sixteen miles to Fort Smith.   The road is through a forest and little has been done to improve it, but still it is very passable, for it leads chiefly through sandy land.   Dr. Anderson, who continually interested himself in such things, collected here a number of specimens of rare birds, and investigated the most northerly known pelican rookery on one of the islands of the Smith Rapids.   The young of these were already hatched on June 9th.

Up to this time we had been traveling with the transports of the Hudson's Bay Company.   None of them were going forward beyond Fort Smith for some time to come.   Dr. Anderson and I would have been compelled to proceed north alone had it not happened that some friends of ours were at Fort Smith, bound on a voyage to Bear Lake. They were the Englishmen C. D. Melvill and John Hornby, and with them was perhaps the best known of all the Hudson's Bay men of the North, Mr. James Mackinlay, who had been factor at several posts, and whose name is well known in the literature of the North through his connection with the journeys of David Hanbury, Warburton Pike, Edward A. Preble, Gordon Cumming, and A. H. Harrison. They had a York boat and a scow, neither heavily loaded, and were therefore easily able to take aboard our small outfit and us.   They accordingly invited us to be their guests on the down-river journey as far as the mouth of Bear River.

We started from Fort Smith June 11th and that afternoon stopped at the mouth of the Salt River to buy salt from the Indians, which they get nearly pure in a bed exposed a few miles upstream. They bring it down to the mouth of the Salt River, where they keep it for trading purposes, supplying the entire Mackenzie district with salt.

The Indians everywhere along the river are dressed in general like white men. Many of them speak English, often with a broad Scotch accent, for most of the Hudson's Bay factors, through a whole hundred years or more of the continuous occupation of the Mackenzie valley, have been Scotchmen and Orkneymen. Although practically unknown to science, these Indians are thoroughly sophisticated and have to a large extent forgotten the manners and customs of their ancestors. They are all Christianized, with the exception of one small tribe who live in the mountains westward from Fort Providence.

It is a remarkable thing, as we have it from the stories of James Mackinlay and Joseph Hodgson and others who know them well, that this one tribe keep with jealousy the customs, religion, and language of their ancestors. They come down to Fort Providence to trade every summer, but they have nothing to do with the Christianized Indians, nor with the white men, except in so far as they are compelled to in the mere matter of trading. These Indians are said by the Hudson's Bay men to differ strikingly from the rest of the natives in being more enterprising, more honorable, and thoroughly self-respecting. Up to four years ago, at least, they had constantly refused to take presents from the Canadian government, a thing which all the other Indians do under the name of "treaty money." An arrangement was made a few years ago by which all the Indians, with the one exception noted, as far north as Fort Providence, signed away their "tribal rights" in consideration of the payment to them every year by the Canadian government of five dollars in money, and small presents of tea, flour, and other articles of trade.

This is an arrangement which for the present at any rate does not seem to be doing the Indians any good, for they lose much valuable time in coming from great distances to the trading posts to wait for the "treaty parties" of the Indian Department; but the arrangement at least furnishes employment, no doubt both pleasant and profitable, to a few white men who come each year bearing gifts and who make the annual round of the tribes. There is with them a doctor, usually, who takes a glance at whatever sick and maimed there may be in the Indian villages, and who no doubt picks up information of interest about the condition of the natives; but he could scarcely be supposed to do them much good, directly, by this one visit a year. It would be much more to the advantage of the Indian if the Cana-

dian government would do as the Danish government does in Greenland, and instead of sending these expensive parties on perfunctory
visits, should station a medical man every two hundred or three
hundred miles so that his services could be available when needed.

We proceeded without adventure to the mouth of the Slave River,
where through the kindness of Mr. Nagle we were taken in tow by
one of his steamers and helped across Slave Lake. This is a great
body of water, larger in area than Lake Erie, and the crossing of it
would have been a fairly serious matter in the sort of craft we had.
Before entering upon the real crossing of the Lake, we coasted west
along its south shore from the mouth of the Slave to the mouth of the
Hay River, where there is located a flourishing mission of the Church
of England. Here we purchased, from the Rev. Mr. Vale, a whale
boat perhaps twenty years old, which ten or more years ago had been
secured by Bishop Reeve from the whalers of Herschel Island and
had been brought up the river to be used on Slave Lake. It turned
out that no one on Slave Lake was used to the manipulation of such
craft, and this boat, which on the ocean is accustomed to weather
severe gales, was here considered unsafe and none cared to use it.
The boat was so leaky that after Mr. Nagle took her in tow behind
the *Eva* it took constant bailing to keep her from being swamped.
Every one not connected with the mission cautioned me against this
purchase, saying the boat was rotten with age, but my opinion differed from theirs and it turned out that she gave us several years of
good service in the Arctic.

On my first visit to Hay River, in 1906, the mission was in charge
of Rev. Mr. Marsh, an excellent man in many ways, and remarkable
as one of the first missionaries in the North to realize the deadliness
to the Indian of the white man's house. Few things are more common in missionary conferences than to have those who have just
returned from work in distant fields show with pride the photographs of the native communities at the time of the coming of the
missionaries, and again a few years later. Typically the first picture
shows a group of tents or wigwams, while twenty years later the
missionary is able to point with pride to how, year by year, the number
of cabins increased until now the last tipi has gone and a village of
huts has replaced them. They do these things and we listen and

applaud, in spite of the fact that we ourselves have come to realize that the way to deal with tuberculosis, which is deadly among us but far more deadly among the primitive peoples, is to drive the affected out of the house and into tents in the open air; and while charitable organizations in New York are gathering money to send the invalids of the city into the open air, there are also in New York missionary organizations gathering money to be used in herding the open air people into houses. While the missionary shows on the one hand a series of pictures indicating the growth of his village of civilized looking dwellings, it would be interesting to ask him if he happens to have also a series of photographs illustrating the growth of the graveyard during the same period. No dwelling could be more sanitary and more likely to forestall tuberculosis than the tipi of the Indians of the Mackenzie Valley. It is not only always filled with fresh air, but it never becomes filthy, because it is moved from place to place before it has time to become so; but when a house is built it cannot be moved. The housekeeping methods which are satisfactory in a lodge that is destined to stand in one place only two or three weeks at a time, are entirely unsuited for the log cabin, which soon becomes filthy and remains so. Eventually the germs of tuberculosis get into the house and obtain lodging in it. The members of the same family catch the disease, one from the other, and when the family has been nearly or quite exterminated by the scourge, another family moves in, for the building of a house is hard work and it is a convenient thing to find one ready for your occupancy; and so it is not only the family that built the house that suffers but there is also through the house a procession of other families moving from the wigwam to the graveyard.

Mr. Marsh saw these conditions and attempted to remedy them, but the Indians had become used to the warmth of the house and refused to go back to their old tenting habits. One family in particular had a daughter grown to womanhood who showed in the spring the symptoms of tuberculosis. In the fall when they wanted to move back from their summer camp into their filthy cabin, Mr. Marsh gave the father a lecture on the unsanitariness of the house and on the necessity of their living in a tent that winter if they wanted to save their daughter's life. But the arguments did not appeal to the Indian. He could not see the germs that the missionary talked about, and did not believe that the cabin had anything to do with it. He announced that he knew better than to freeze in a tent if he could be comfortable in a house and therefore he would stay in the house. But it happened that Mr. Marsh had been a heavyweight prize fighter before he became a missionary, and so he walked into the Indian's house one day and threw him and his family bodily outdoors and their gear after them, nailed up their doors and windows, and told them that he did not want to see them around the village until the next spring. There was some loud talk among the Indians and several threats of shooting and other violence, but eventually the family moved out into the woods and stayed away all winter as directed. In the spring they came back with their daughter apparently cured, and when I saw her she looked as well as any woman there. Mr. Vale and Mr. Johnson have since taken up Mr. Marsh's work along lines he had set for them and apparently with good results. In some other places, however, tuberculosis has made a nearly clean sweep of the population. This is noticeably true at Fort Wrigley, where we were told that only nineteen hunters are left in all the territory belonging to that post.

The ice in Slave Lake usually breaks up the first part of July. The earliest crossing of it known took place some years ago on June 23d. For two weeks or so before the lake can be actually crossed, the ice in it will be broken up and in motion. In 1908 the ice off Resolution began to move June 12th, and off Hay River on June 15th. Hay River itself usually breaks up about a month ahead of the Lake.

From Slave Lake north to the Arctic Ocean there are no interruptions to navigation and our travel proceeded smoothly and without adventure. Here and there we passed Indian lodges on the shore and Indian cabins, and on an average every two hundred miles a Hudson's Bay post, where a mission is also located.

The two churches that have workers in the field are the Roman Catholic and the Church of England, both of them doing considerable useful work. The Church of Rome has a much stronger hold upon the people, partly, no doubt, because of its earlier introduction into the country, and because also of its greater resources it is doing more work. After many years of observation of the labors of missionaries

I am inclined to the view that with the other churches the excellence of the results depends primarily upon the individual at any particular place, but that the Church of Rome has a system which produces results to some degree independent of the personality of the man. One weakness of other missionaries in general is that they come from cities and other places with crystallized notions of exactly what must be done and exactly how every one must live and act under no matter what conditions. The fundamental precepts of Christianity apparently seem to many of them to be linked with certain purely local customs of the city from which they happen to come, and they emphasize both equally. The three commandments, "Love thy neighbor as thyself," "Thou shalt keep the Sabbath holy," and "Thou shalt eat thy potatoes with thy fork," impress themselves with equal vividness upon the aborigines and are likely to be considered by them to be means of grace of coördinate value. But the missionaries of the Church of Rome seem less concerned about these inessentials. They are no less concerned than the missionaries of other churches about getting the Indian to change his religious views, but they seem less inclined to waste their strength in trying to persuade him to change the color of his coat. The net result of this difference is shown to be entirely in favor of the Roman Church. These natives have, through the evolution of centuries, been ground into such perfect adjustment to their environment that the more you disturb this adjustment the more disastrous the result will be to the physical welfare of the native.

Both the English Church and the Roman have schools in the Mackenzie district — the English at Hay River and the Roman at Fort Providence. At both places are men and women doing conscientious and self-sacrificing work, and at both places numbers of Indians are learning to read and write, but nevertheless it seems to most observers that the labor and expenditure of money are scarcely justified by the results. You have everywhere the Indians of the old type, who are ignorant of book learning but who still retain some of the integrity and self-respect of their ancestors. These men on the whole seem to be more self-confident and self-reliant than the educated ones, and are more likely to be making not only a living but also an honest living. Somehow it seems that one of the first things an Indian learns in school is contempt for the ways of his ancestors; but after all, the ways of his ancestors are the only ways that can prevail in that country. Hunting and fishing are the necessary occupations of every man, and the sewing of clothes and the preparation of food are equally the inevitable work of the women. When a man who has no occupation other than that of hunter open to him gets to feel that he is above that occupation, the community has lost much and no one has gained anything.

There are many people in the Mackenzie district who have given me much valuable information about their country, the greater part of which, however, has to be omitted here, but few men perhaps know the country better than Father Giroux, formerly stationed at Arctic Red River but now in charge of Providence. He says it is true in the Mackenzie district, as it is among the Arctic Eskimo, that measles is the deadliest of all diseases. There have been several epidemics, so that it might be supposed that the most susceptible had been weeded out, and yet the last epidemic (1903) killed about one fifth of the entire population of the Mackenzie Valley. He had noticed also a distinct and universal difference in health between those who wear white men's clothing and who live in white men's houses, as opposed to those who keep the ancient customs in the matter of dress and dwellings. These same elements I have since found equally harmful among the Eskimo, although among them must be added the surely no less dangerous element, the white men's diet, which is no more suited to the people than white men's clothing or houses.

Grains and vegetables of most kinds, and even strawberries, are successfully cultivated at Providence. North of that, the possible agricultural products get fewer and fewer, until finally the northern limit of successful potato growing is reached near Fort Good Hope, on the Arctic Circle. Potatoes are grown farther north, but they do not mature and are not of good quality.

In certain things the Mackenzie district was more advanced the better part of a century ago than it is now; the explorers of Franklin's parties, for instance, found milk cows at every Hudson's Bay post and were able to get milk and cream as far north as the Arctic Circle and even beyond. At that time, too, every post had large stores of dried

meat and pemmican, so that if you had the good-will of the Company
you could always stock up with provisions anywhere. Now this is
all changed. Game has become so scarce that it would be difficult
for the Company, even if they tried, to keep large stores of meat on
hand. The importation of foodstuffs from the outside, on the other
hand, has not grown easy as yet, and it is therefore much more difficult
to buy provisions now than it was in Franklin's time. The trading
posts are located now exactly where Franklin found them, so that taking this into consideration, and the decrease of game all over the
northern country, it is clear that exploration on such a plan as ours —
that of living on the country — is more difficult now than it was a
hundred years ago. Another element that makes the situation more
risky is that while then you could count on finding Indians anywhere
who could supply you with provisions, or at least give you information
as to where game might be found, now there are so few of the Indians
left alive, — and all of those left are so concentrated around the trading
posts, — that you may go hundreds of miles without seeing a camp or
a trail, where seventy-five or a hundred years ago you would have
found the trails crossing each other and might have seen the camp
smokes rising here and there.

The food supplies of the different posts vary according to location.
In general the trading stations are divided into "fish posts" and
"meat posts." Fort Smith is a typical meat post, for caribou are
found in the neighborhood and moose also; and the Indians not
only get meat enough for themselves and for the white men, but
the fur traders even find the abundance of the meat supply a handicap in their business, — for the Indian who has plenty to eat does not
trap so energetically as do others who must pay in fur for some of
their food. Resolution, Hay River, and Providence, on the other
hand, are fish posts, while at any of the northern trading stations
potatoes nowadays play a considerable part in the food supply, even
as far up as Good Hope. In certain places and in certain years
rabbits are an important article of diet, but even when there is an
abundance of this animal, the Indians consider themselves starving
if they get nothing else, — and fairly enough, as my own party can
testify, for any one who is compelled in winter to live for a period of
several weeks on lean meat will actually starve, in this sense : that there

are lacking from his diet certain necessary elements, notably fat, and it makes no difference how much he eats, he will be hungry at the end of each meal, and eventually he will lose strength or become actually ill. The Eskimo who have provided themselves in summer with bags of seal oil can carry them into a rabbit country and can live on rabbits satisfactorily for months. The Indian, unfortunately for him, has no animal in his country so richly supplied with fat as is the seal, and nowadays he will make an effort to buy a small quantity of bacon to eat with his rabbits, unless he has a little caribou or moose fat stored up from the previous autumn.

June 30th, we had our first sight of the Rocky Mountains, about four hours after leaving Fort Simpson. These are spurs of the Rockies which approach nearer and nearer to the river, until at Fort Wrigley the river skirts the foothills, while at Fort Norman, at the mouth of Bear Lake River, the mountains have even thrown a chain of high hills across the Mackenzie. The highest of these is Bear Rock, standing north of Bear River in the angle between it and the Mackenzie.

We were told at Fort Wrigley that the Mackenzie River broke open May 22d, and had not been frozen solid until November 18th of the fall before. These were considered average seasons. At Fort Good Hope, near the Arctic Circle, the Mackenzie may frequently be crossed on the ice as early as November 1st. The Mackenzie freezes a few days ahead of Bear Lake River, on account, no doubt, of the swiftness of the latter, and also because of the comparative warmth of the water where it comes out of Bear Lake. The very head of Bear River, where it emerges from the lake, never freezes over all winter.

At Fort Norman game conditions have undergone great changes during the last fifty years. The mountain sheep (Ovis dalli) were then, as now, confined to the mountains west of the river, but the moose were also west of the river then, while since that time they have crossed the river and have gradually moved toward Bear Lake and encircled it until, in the summer of 1909, the first moose were seen by the Eskimo on Coronation Gulf near the mouth of the Coppermine River (a fact which, of course, was unknown to the Hudson's Bay traders and which we learned from the Eskimo in the summer of 1910). The caribou fifty years ago were abundant around Fort Norman and used to pass on their seasonal migrations in vast herds between Fort Norman and Bear Lake; but for the last decade or two practically no caribou have been seen west of the lake, and the hunters have to go to the eastern end of it to get any. The Indians meantime have become not only few through disease, but have also lost their enterprise because of the ease with which they can make their living by sponging on the missions and the traders, and by catching a little fish in the Mackenzie; very few of them, therefore, ever go to the eastern end of the lake for caribou unless some white man goes there too. For years there had been no Indians around the mouth of the Dease River, but now that Melvill, Hornby, and Mackinlay were going in there, a number accompanied them.

Another animal the migrations of which are of interest is the muskrat. It has been spreading northeast at about the same rate as the moose. We found in 1910 that even the young men among the Eskimo of Coronation Gulf can remember the time when first they saw muskrats on the upper Dease, while to-day these animals are found much farther north than that, even going close down to the Arctic coast. The beaver, too, are said to be spreading northeastward, although they are not yet so near the ocean as to be seen by the Eskimo.

We arrived at Fort Arctic Red River July 5th. This is the most northerly "fort" of the Hudson's Bay Company on the Mackenzie River proper. It is, perhaps, a little late in the day to explain what we should have explained in our first reference to the institution known as a "fort" in the North. A Hudson's Bay "fort" is typically a small group of log cabins consisting of the factor's residence, a store in which he trades with the Indians, and possibly a small house in which he keeps dried fish or other provisions. In the early days among the Indians to the south some of the Hudson's Bay trading posts used to have stockades about them, and were, therefore, more deserving of the title of fort; in the Mackenzie River district there is nothing to suggest special suitability for defending the trading posts against attack. In fact, there has never been any danger of attack, for a simple reason which may be worth pointing out.

In the fertile lands of the United States and Canada a saying grew up that "the only good Indian is a dead Indian," because the Indian encumbered the land which the farmer needed for cultivation of crops, and the miner for his digging and delving. The Indian was in the way and had to go, for we could not let questions of mere humanitarianism and justice restrain us from taking possession of the valuable lands that the Indian had inherited from his ancestors. In the South, economic and humanitarian interests were diametrically opposed, and the economic had their way. In the North, economic and humanitarian interests happened to coincide. The northern land was valueless to the farmer, and the country was of value to the trading companies only in so far as it produced fur; and furs could best be secured by perpetuating the Indian and keeping him in possession of the lands, because dead men do not set traps. The only good Indian in the North was the live Indian who brought in fur to sell. No doubt it is largely the result of this economic fact that the Hudson's Bay Company has always treated the Indian so well that it has never been to the Indian's interest to quarrel with the Company, any more than it was to the Company's interest to quarrel with the Indian. And now that civilization, with its diseases, is making inroads into the country, and the Indian seems in danger of disappearing, it is not only human lives but also dollars and cents that the Company sees disappearing before its eyes. When they controlled all the North, they handled its problems a great deal more wisely than the Canadian government has done since, although the Canadians have been both wiser and cleaner-handed than the people of the United States. But the Company no longer own Canada, and they are powerless to check the evil tendencies which they recognize more clearly than any one else.

CHAPTER III

WE found on reaching the head of the Mackenzie delta that the river at this point had broken open May 22d, and so had the Arctic Red River. This was a rather late spring, for we have since known the Mackenzie two hundred miles farther north, where it enters the ocean, to open up before the 20th of May.

From the Arctic Red River we descended to the head of the delta, termed Demarcation Point, and ascended the Peel River for eighteen miles to Fort Macpherson. Here I found many whom I knew well from my previous expedition — my old friend John Firth, who has been in charge of northerly trading posts for the Company for the better part of half a century, the four officers and men of the Royal Northwest Mounted Police, the Reverend and Mrs. C. E. Whittaker, and Miss Florence Hamilton, their assistant. The police detachment was under the command of Major A. M. Jarvis. It consisted of Sergeant Selig and two constables, the brothers Pearson. Although I had never met Major Jarvis before, it turned out that we had several mutual friends.

Dr. Anderson had remained behind at Fort Norman for the purpose of carrying on his investigations at that zoölogically interesting locality, and I expected him to arrive with the steamer *Mackenzie River*, which was due now in a few days. My idea in hurrying so much to reach the mouth of the Mackenzie had been to make sure that I would not miss certain of the Eskimo whom I had it in mind to try and hire for the coming year. Since leaving Fort Norman I had traveled in the whale-boat purchased at Hay River, which was towed behind Mr. Nagle's steamer. This was Mr. Nagle's first trip down the river and his steamer had never before gone farther than Arctic Red River, although the Hislop and Nagle Company had a trading

post at Fort Macpherson.   His company had found that the fur trade
for the last few years had not been paying them well and Mr. Nagle
had therefore come down the river a week or two earlier than usual
in order to close up his trading establishment at Fort Macpherson.
This had been good fortune for me and had brought me to Macpherson before the coming of the first Eskimo from the North.   The
Indians will always make a point of waiting at their trading post for
the coming of the steamer, but the Eskimo occasionally come up to
Fort Macpherson and leave again before the steamer arrives, for
they are in a hurry to go back to the Arctic coast, both on account of
their summer fishing and because they want to intercept the whaling
ships at Herschel Island for trading purposes.

During my stay at Fort Macpherson I was the guest of Major
Jarvis.   The rest of the policemen occupied the barracks on top of
the high bluffs that here flank the eastern side of the Peel, but the
Major preferred a tent by himself down by the riverside.   Soon after
our arrival, the Eskimo boats began to come from the North and the
Major's tent became the center of a village of their tents.   Most of
the Eskimo were old friends among whom I had lived on my previous expedition.   There was much talking and laughter, and apparently they were very glad to see me, but no more glad, I am sure,
than I was to see them, for I had reason to consider some of them
among my best friends in the world.   Under their communistic
system of living the Eskimo have developed the social virtues to a
considerably higher degree than we have; they are therefore people
easy to live with, and one readily makes friends among them, but,
of course, they differ individually as we do.   Of all those who came
here this summer the finest, in my estimation, was Ovayuak, a man
who had been my host for several months during 1906–1907.   The
Hudson's Bay Company had recognized in him the same qualities
which were apparent to me, and had accordingly made him a "Chief,"
which merely means that he is the Company's accredited representative among his countrymen, and acts, in a sense, as the Company's
agent.   In talking with Ovayuak I found that many of my acquaintances of a few years before were dead, some of them of consumption,
some of unknown diseases, and a group of eight had been poisoned by
eating the meat of a freshly killed white whale.   It happens every

COOKING WITH DRIFT-WOOD, MACKENZIE DELTA.

SKINNING A BEARDED SEAL.

now and then that a whole party of natives is killed by eating white whale meat. This sort of thing is referred to by the whalers ordinarily as ptomaine poisoning; but it can scarcely be that, as I have seen tons of semi-decayed whale meat eaten and have never known a single case of sickness or death connected therewith, while the poisonings always occur at feasts which are held immediately after the killing of a whale, or else from whale meat that has been cut up promptly after the killing and stored so as to largely or entirely prevent its decay.

On the lower posts of the Mackenzie River and here at Macpherson we had gradually been picking up such dogs as were for sale, and now had eleven all together. So as to put in operation as early as possible our principle of living on the country, we began here to set our fish nets to get food for ourselves and the dogs, but there were so many other nets in the water that we got very little, and I had to buy a few hundred pounds of dried fish to eke out.

July 14th the steamer *Mackenzie River* arrived, bringing, besides the officers and men of the Hudson's Bay Company, Dr. Anderson and two women travelers, Miss Agnes Deans Cameron and Miss Jessie Brown. Miss Cameron had come to get material for a book on the Mackenzie River and listened eagerly to all the stories she heard about the North. Most of these were picturesque, but judging from the ones which I personally heard related to Miss Cameron I should say that a considerable portion of them were scarcely gospel truth. I happened to be, besides the missionary Mr. Whittaker, the only person present who spoke any Eskimo at all, and I therefore volunteered my services to Miss Cameron as her interpreter, but she declined them graciously, saying she preferred to get her impressions at first hand. She went into a considerable number of Eskimo tents for the purpose of securing information and local color. I have since heard what it was that the Eskimo thought she asked them, but I have not yet learned what it was that she thought they told her in reply.

On my first trip down the Mackenzie River all of the affairs of the Company had been under the direction of Mr. Thomas Anderson, an energetic and capable officer of the old school. He was a man generous to a fault with his own property, as I have good reason to

D

know through being with him in Winnipeg and Edmonton, but as
soon as he got into the North where everything he handled belonged
to the Company rather than to himself, he became parsimonious
even to niggardliness; and much of his talk concerned the degenerate
later days when people insisted on living on such imported things as
beans, canned corn, and tomatoes, whereas in his day they lived
entirely on fish and caribou meat. Now everything was changed.
Not only had the modern *Mackenzie River* replaced the old-fashioned
Wrigley, but Thomas Anderson had died, and the affairs of the Company were under the no less energetic but completely modern
direction of Mr. Brabant. I remember how, in 1906, Mr. Anderson
boiled with indignation at having to carry one of the servants of the
Hislop & Nagle Trading Company as a passenger for sixty miles from
Red River to Macpherson, and he spoke with suppressed fury of the
degenerate officials at Winnipeg who compelled him to countenance
such things; and now we had in his stead Mr. Brabant, who would
have been the better pleased the more of his rivals' men he could have
carried, providing, of course, they paid him fares for transportation
which yielded a profit to the Company. The change had been
gradually taking place, but with the coming of Mr. Brabant the
transformation was complete, from the old policy of exclusion of
competitors to the modern one of unrestricted competition.

Mr. Whittaker, who had no intention of discontinuing his labors
at Macpherson, found that through some miscarriage the supplies
intended for him had failed to make connection at Fort Smith with
the *Mackenzie River*. He and his family, therefore, found themselves
with nothing to live on for the winter at Macpherson, and had to
take passage upstream to Hay River. This ill wind blew me considerable good, for I was able to rent a good whale-boat for the use
of my party from Mr. Whittaker, and to buy from him three excellent
young dogs, the faithful work of which through the coming four years
was one of the factors in such success as we had on our sledge exploration. Three good dogs are worth thirteen poor ones, and a great
deal more.

July 16th Dr. Anderson and I in our two whale-boats set out from
Macpherson for the Arctic coast, distant about two hundred miles
as the river runs. We were accompanied by two Eskimo boys,

whose services with us were temporary, and by Ilavinirk, whom I had known well upon my previous expedition and whom I now engaged, together with his family of wife, daughter of seven, and adopted son of about eighteen. The family were on the seacoast and Ilavinirk alone joined us here, for he had come south in the service of a white man named Chris Stein, a retired whaleman who is now a trader and trapper in a small way in the Mackenzie delta. Mr. Stein was also an old friend whom I knew well during the winter of 1906–1907, when he lived at Shingle Point on the Arctic coast.

In traveling down the river we sailed when the wind was fair, and occasionally tried to tack against a head wind, but in this we were usually not successful, for when the wind blows against the river current there is soon produced a choppy sea, which is too much for a loaded whale-boat. In head winds and calms, therefore, we used to "track" the boat. This process consists in fastening a long line to the boat mast about five feet up, and attaching either men or a dog team to the other end of the line to tow the boat along the beach.

We reached the open ocean July 23d, but were delayed here somewhat by strong winds, for, like the delta flats of any other river, the Mackenzie mouth is an exceedingly dangerous place in a high wind, when mountainous breakers roll in from the open sea. On the 24th we reached the first Eskimo camp on the coast, at a place called Niakonak, just after the sudden death of a woman and young girl from white whale poisoning. This is another of the cases I have since heard referred to by mounted policemen and whalers as ptomaine poisoning. But the Eskimo explain it by saying that the women died because they made some caribou skin into garments the day after they ate white whale. In other words, they had broken a taboo. Personally, I agree neither with the policemen nor the Eskimo. It seems to me the poisoning could scarcely have been ptomaine, because the meal after which the women sickened took place within three or four hours after the animal was killed; in fact, the pieces of meat were put right into the pot the moment they were cut from the animal.

We reached the harbor behind the Shingle Point sandspit July 24th. We were now less than sixty miles from Herschel Island, and found ourselves in company with something like twenty whale-boats, all of them as eager as we to get to Herschel Island, for we feared the whaling ships might come in from the west any day. The vessels when they come in usually run behind the Herschel Island sandspit for a few hours or a day, and then keep on with their whaling cruise to the northwest, returning to Herschel Island again only in September. It was therefore imperative for all of us to get there ahead of the vessels, for the Eskimo wanted to trade, and some wanted to go east along the coast, while we wanted to get certain supplies that had been shipped to us through San Francisco. We were also in hopes of getting a ship to carry us as far at least as Cape Bathurst on our road to Coronation Gulf. It was our plan to spend the coming winter near Cape Parry, about one hundred miles east of the most easterly known settlement of Eskimo, from which point we wanted to start the following spring on our search to the eastward for Eskimo who had not seen a white man. These we hoped to find, if we found them at all, about two hundred miles east of Cape Parry.

But though we were all in a hurry to get to Herschel Island, we had to remain at Shingle Point several days on account of strong head winds. Then one day when I awoke in the morning I could see by the way in which the wind bulged in the east side of my tent that the hoped-for fair wind had come at last. I lost no time in awakening my companions, but before we had breakfast prepared, a number of the other Eskimo came to see us and asked whether we intended starting for Herschel Island that day. My answer was that of course we did, at which they seemed very well pleased and returned to their respective camps, struck their tents and got everything ready for the start. When breakfast was over I said to my Eskimo that we would start now, but they replied that they could not be the first to start, but would be glad to start if some other boat led off. They explained to me then that they were no longer heathen, as they had been two years ago when I was among them; that they now knew God's commandments and were aware of the penalties which awaited the Sabbath-breaker. I asked them what difference it would make who started first. The reply was that God punished those who took the lead in evil-doing, and if some one else was willing to take the lead and risk the punishment, they were perfectly willing

RUINS OF AMUNDSEN'S HOUSE AT KING POINT, OCCUPIED 1905–06.

The sea has since carried off every vestige. The ship is the whaler *Bonanza* of San Francisco, stranded in September, 1905.

GRAVE OF ——— WIIK AT KING POINT.

to take advantage of the fair wind and sail along behind. Dr. Anderson and I at once suggested that we could sail the first boat, and our Eskimo could come in the second; but they said that a subterfuge of that sort would avail nothing, that they were members of my party, and the punishment would fall on the party as a whole. They suggested, however, that I go around to the tents of the other Eskimo and see if I could not induce some of them to start out so that we could follow. I accepted this suggestion, but in tent after tent I got everywhere the same answer: "We are no longer heathen; we know the punishment that awaits the Sabbath-breaker. We were hoping that you would sail first, but as for us, none of us are willing to take the responsibility." And so we sat there all day through a fair wind, all of us eagerly willing to go, but all of us unwilling to lead off in any "evil-doing." Finally, towards sundown, a whaleboat was seen coming from the east. It turned out to be the boat of the Royal Northwest Mounted Police, under command of Sergeant Selig. We signaled to them. I told Sergeant Selig our predicament, and found, as I expected, that he was willing to help us out by stopping to eat a meal with us, and thus becoming one of our party, and then leading off in such a way that it became evident he took all responsibility upon himself and his boat. As soon as this fact was made known, there was great rejoicing in camp. Every tent was quickly struck, and all the boats loaded, and when Sergeant Selig set sail we all followed him. But it was now near evening, and the wind fell with the sun. We had sat through a fair wind that could easily have taken us to Herschel Island, and now instead we had to row a large part of the way and finally, toward morning, to tack against head winds. Monday morning we passed King Point, where Amundsen wintered 1905–1906, and photographed the ruins of his house which the sea has since completely swept away, and the grassgrown grave of Wiik, the magnetician whose painstaking work brought so much credit to Amundsen's expedition. We reached Herschel Island at noon on Wednesday, to find, however, that the whaling ships had not yet arrived.

This was our first conflict with Christianity, and we had come off second best, as many others have done who have set themselves against the teachings of religion. The Eskimo had of course, when

I was with them two years before, a religion, but it had not been Christianity. One frequently hears the remark that no people in the world have yet been found who are so low that they do not have a religion. This is absolutely true, but the inference one is likely to draw is misleading. It is not only true that no people are so low that they do not have a religion, but it is equally true that the lower you go in the scale of human culture the more religion you find, and that races on the intellectual level of the Eskimo have so much religion that a man scarcely turns his hand over without the act having a religious significance. Every event in life, every possible circumstance, has its appropriate religious formula.

When I was with the Eskimo in 1907, they had not yet been Christianized, although Mr. Whittaker and other missionaries of the Church of England had been working among them for the better part of fifteen years. It was then said by Eskimo and whites alike that there were perhaps half a dozen Alaskan Eskimo living in the Mackenzie district who had been converted, besides one Mackenzie Eskimo who was married to an Alaskan Christian woman. That was the condition when I left the Mackenzie in September, 1907. When we returned in July, 1908, we found every man, woman, and child converted.

This seems a rather sudden thing, especially as the missionaries had had so little influence for the many years preceding. But it appears that the spread of Christianity among the Eskimo was as the spread of a habit or a fashion, much indeed as it was in certain of the northern European countries, the history of which is well known to us. In a general way it seems true that Christianity first got its foothold in Kotzebue Sound, Alaska, due largely, I have been told, to the work of the Moravian Mission. From there the fashion seems to have spread both northward along the coast to Point Hope and northeastward up the Kuvuk and Noatak rivers, thence across the Arctic Mountains and down the Colville to the coast. Christianity, then, came to the Eskimo of Point Barrow from two sides; they heard of it from the Point Hope Eskimo to the west and from the Colville Eskimo to the east, and they, although missionaries had been laboring among them for many years, seem to have been suddenly converted. Apparently they felt this way about it : if it is good enough for the Point Hope people and the Colville people, it ought to be good enough for us. And when in the winter of 1907–1908, the Mackenzie River Eskimo heard that all of the people to the westward had accepted the faith, they seem to have felt that it was about time for them to do so too, and they were converted in a body.

When we reached Herschel Island, we did not go to the village in the northeast corner where the mounted police barracks are situated as well as the Eskimo village, both of which are there because of the sandspit that makes the whalemen's harbor. This is not only an excellent harbor in summer, but also a nearly ideal wintering place for the whaling vessels which are shielded by the sandspit from the pressure of the ocean ice. We pitched our camp on Flanders Point on the southeast corner of the island, for that is the best fishing place in the neighborhood, and we were here able to get not only fish enough for ourselves and our dogs, but also were able to lay by a considerable store for our expected boat journey.

The first whaling ship reached Herschel Island in 1889, and for a few years thereafter the industry prospered greatly. It was immensely profitable, and at times as many as fourteen ships wintered in the Arctic at one time. This had a sudden effect on the fortunes of the Eskimo. Before that time they had been in the habit of making summer trading voyages up to Fort Macpherson to buy a few small things, but now, when this large whaling fleet came, all their conditions of life were changed. All of the articles which they had been used to buying, they could now get cheaply or for nothing from the whalers, and they soon learned the use of a great many other articles, the very names and appearances of which were unknown to them before — articles which even the Hudson's Bay factor at Macpherson had been compelled to do without. The ships brought, too, an abundance of provisions. At first the Eskimo would have nothing to do with any of these ; but in the course of a few years they learned the use of flour, molasses, sugar, etc., which became first luxuries and then necessities. It was important for the whaling ships to get plenty of fresh caribou meat to keep their crews from getting scurvy, and they employed practically the whole population in the pursuit of caribou, fish, and ptarmigan. Such things as flour, hard bread, sugar, canned meats and vegetables, butter, etc., they gave with a free hand to the Eskimo, urging them to use them and to save meat. The Eskimo of course preferred meat as an article of diet, and now they were further impressed with the fact that the white man seemed to consider meat of priceless value and the other food articles of little value or none. Meat, therefore, came to have a fabulous price compared with other commodities, and during the time of my experience in the North, a pound of meat has been worth more than a pound of any article of civilized diet except tea.

It would be a matter of too great detail to enter here into the minute causes of the change in the Eskimo's habits of life, but the net result is that although the time from 1889 to 1906 is but a few years, still there has been greater change wrought among the Eskimo during that time than the Hudson's Bay Company has been responsible for among any of the northern Indians in a hundred years. The condition was now, therefore, serious, for the whaling industry was beginning to show the signs of a gradual breakdown, which has since terminated in a complete collapse of the industry. The winter of 1907–1908, only one ship, the *Karluk*, commanded by Captain James Wing, had wintered at Herschel Island, and he had been so short of provisions and trading articles that the Eskimo considered themselves to be suffering for want of many things to which they were used. It is true, as experience has since shown, that in the absence of whalers the Eskimo of the Mackenzie River are able to live perfectly well on the game and fish of the country; but they did not think so themselves the summer of 1908, any more than those of us used to high living think we can get along on the simple fare of the poor. The mounted police agreed with them in this, and every one therefore considered that they were facing a critical winter. Whaling ships had been expected, but none came. Finally, August 15th, the *Karluk* came in sight from the east, returning from the Banks Island summer whaling cruise. I went over to see Captain Wing and found that he was very short of stores; indeed he was completely out of sugar and potatoes and many other articles, and had only a little flour left, but plenty of meat.

My opinion agreed with that of no one else with regard to the prospects for the coming winter. It seemed to me the condition was nowise

SUNDAY, JULY 26, 1908, AT SHINGLE POINT.
Eskimo whale-boats loaded and with sails up ready to start.

serious. I had lived with the Eskimo the year before and had seen what an abundance of fish there was in the eastern channels of the Mackenzie delta, and I knew that fish and caribou were also plentiful farther east. But the whalers had never seen Eskimo living anywhere except around whaling ships and dependent on them; neither had the mounted police, and, consequently, it seemed to all of them that the district was facing a period of starvation. For myself and my party I did not worry however, except for one thing, — that I had no matches. When by the 15th of August it began to seem likely that no ships would come, I went to the mounted police and explained to them that I had everything that I considered necessary for making a living for myself and my party in the country with the exception of matches, and asked them to give, lend, or sell my party a sufficient quantity to do us the winter. This the commanding officer, Sergeant Fitzgerald, refused to do. He told me that if I would discharge all my Eskimo (I had then engaged a party of nine all told), and if Dr. Anderson and I would live for the winter in a small house which he would assign to us near the barracks, then he would supply us with not only matches, but also everything that we needed to eat. It was in vain I explained to him that we had not come to the country for the purpose of spending a winter at Herschel Island. His point of view was that he did not know or care why we had come, but he did know that we were now destitute and likely to die of starvation, and it was his duty to supply us, in a way that suited him, with sufficient food to keep us from actual want. We could not agree on the possibility of a white man making a living in the country. I told him that I needed but matches to be safe and independent, but he believed that a white man needed twelve months' provisions of white man's food in order to live twelve months in the country. He pointed out that according to his view one of two things was sure to happen if he gave us matches : either we should go to the eastward as far as the most easterly civilized settlement, four hundred miles to the eastward at the Baillie Islands, and there become a charge upon those natives, — in other words, we were incompetent to look after ourselves, and so would have to be taken care of by the Baillie Islands Eskimo, — or, in the other event, if we unwisely left the Baillie Islands settlement behind and went into the uninhabited district, we should surely starve to death, and he did not want, as an officer of the Government, to be a party to either event. He further informed me that the laws of the Yukon gave him a right to ship Dr. Anderson and me out of the country because we had no visible means of support. But, he said, seeing he could accomplish the same result by refusing us matches, he would prefer that method, and let us go west to Point Barrow for them. He knew that we would then winter at Point Barrow, where the whaling station has abundant stores, and where we should be in no danger of starving.

I had previously gone to Captain Wing and tried to get matches, but he had none, or at least so few that none could be spared. He offered me, true enough, a package said to contain a thousand matches, and it seemed to me that we could go a long way on that, but this was quickly vetoed by Dr. Anderson and the Eskimo of our party, who were all of them smokers and did not like the prospect of facing a winter without knowing they would be able to light a pipe whenever they felt like it. There was nothing for it, then, but to turn west along the coast towards Point Barrow, four hundred miles away. We knew it would take all the summer to get there, but Dr. Anderson and I quickly readjusted our plans and made up our minds we would, after getting the matches, attempt to spend the winter near the mouth of the Colville River, a district which from the point of view both of zoölogy and of ethnology was an attractive field of work.

Captain Wing told us that eventually he intended to try to get to Point Barrow, but he did not know how long he would stay at Herschel Island. He promised, however, that on his way west along the coast he would keep a lookout for our boats, and if he overtook us he would take us aboard and give us a lift as far as Point Barrow. It turned out that three days after we started, Captain Wing overtook us some forty miles west of Herschel Island, for we had made slow progress on account of head winds. We decided then to divide our party. Dr. Anderson would proceed west along the coast in one of our whale-boats with the Eskimo men, Akpek and Natkusiak, and the woman Sungauravik, all of whom were Alaskans, while I took the other whale-boat and the Alaskan man Ilavinirk, his Mackenzie River wife, Mamayauk, and their daughter Nogasak aboard the *Karluk* with me to Point Barrow.

My favorite thesis is that an adventure is a sign of incompetence. Few have disputed the Greek, or whoever it was, that said, "Blessed is the country whose history is uninteresting," and no one (unless it be some journalist) will dispute the statement that "blessed is the exploring expedition the story of which is monotonous." If everything is well managed, if there are no miscalculations or mistakes, then the things that happen are only the things you expected to happen, and for which you are ready and with which you can therefore deal. Being thoroughly alive to the truth of this principle, I am also thoroughly ashamed of owning up to such adventures as we have had, for they always reflect either on me, or the companions whom I have chosen, and therefore on me indirectly. By keeping steadily in view the two maxims, "Better be safe than sorry" and "Do in Rome as the Romans do," Dr. Anderson and I managed to conduct for nearly five years a satisfactorily monotonous expedition, and one the interest of which, so far as it has any interest, is in having attained the results which we set out to attain.

But we did have some adventures, and the star part in one of them fell to me, August 16th, just after I had separated from Dr. Anderson's party, and when I was attempting to board the *Karluk*. It was a raw day, and we had all been sitting in our boats for hours, bundled up in as many clothes as we could possibly put on. When the *Karluk* came in we stood out to meet her. Within two hundred yards of us she shut down her engines, but was still moving with considerable speed when we brought our boat up alongside. I was standing in the bow and threw the painter over the gunwale of the *Karluk* to a group of men who were standing there to catch it. But they were apparently numb with cold, as I was, and fumbled the rope before getting hold of it. I forgot everything else and was staring at them, wondering if those fellows were ever going to get hold of the rope, when suddenly my boat bunted the *Karluk*, my foot caught in something and I made a clean dive overboard, going down almost vertically, head first. One thinks of many things in moments such as that, and I realized at once that I could not swim, bundled up as I was, and especially wearing hip wading boots of sealskin. I kept my eyes open of course, and could see the moment I struck the water a bight of my painter, perhaps twelve or fifteen feet down, and fortunately I was making straight for it. When I got as far down as the rope I got hold of it with both hands, and then I knew the question was as to whether or not the men who had been fumbling the rope end when last I saw them had by now succeeded in making it fast to the ship. If it were fast, it was problematic whether I could hold on or not, for the ship was still moving with considerable speed. There was also the possibility, which I realized fully, that the Captain might reverse his engine with the idea of stopping the ship quickly, and that my rope might be long enough to get me tangled in the propeller. It turned out that the rope end had been made fast. The rope quickly came taut, and for a moment until I reached the surface it took all my strength to hang on. As soon as I came up to where my Eskimo could see me, they hauled up on their end of the rope until the boat came up to me and then pulled me into the whale-boat. A few moments later the Captain welcomed me on deck with the remark that this was "a hell of a way to come aboard a man's ship," and then handed me over to his engineer, Mr. Carpenter, who took me down to the warm engine room and dressed me up in a dry suit of his own clothes.

The day after this little adventure we passed Flaxman Island, which lies a little less than halfway from Herschel Island to Point Barrow. Two years before, there had been wrecked at this point Leffingwell and Mikkelsen's exploring schooner, and Mr. Leffingwell had been living there ever since to do geological and other scientific work of an intensive character in the district around about, and especially in the Endicott Mountains, which here lie about twenty miles inland to the south. When we approached the island Mr. Leffingwell hailed the *Karluk* with the desire of taking passage in her for San Francisco. I made here another attempt to get matches, but although Mr. Leffingwell had some he did not consider he could let me have any without breaking faith with certain Eskimo among whom he had promised to divide them. Thus disappeared my last hope of not having to go all the way to Point Barrow to get matches.

On our way west from Flaxman Island we kept seeing more and more ice, until we got within about thirty miles of Point Barrow, when our way was completely blocked by apparently impenetrable floes. Here we had the explanation of why the whaling vessels this year

MOST NORTHERLY WHITE MAN'S DWELLING ON THE CONTINENT.

Thomas Gordon and his house six miles southwest of Point Barrow.

had failed to come in to Herschel Island. There was an ice blockade at Point Barrow which none of them had been able to break through. Although the progress of the *Karluk* was arrested, it appeared that near shore, between the land and the ice, there was a narrow channel of shoal water. This is often the case on the Arctic coast, and that is why a vessel of shallow draught can often get along better than the most powerful ice-crusher, by simply hugging the coast and going in water too shoal for the bigger vessel.

I was in a hurry to reach Point Barrow, so I bade good-by to Captain Wing and his officers and crew, all of whom had shown us the greatest kindness, and lowered the whale-boat to try to reach the whaling station along the shore. Mr. Leffingwell was also in a hurry and therefore took passage with us, to get as quickly as possible into communication with the whaling vessels which we felt sure would be lying tied up to the ice, or anchored just beyond Point Barrow.

With the small boat we had no trouble. Part of the time we proceeded through lagoons, and part of the time along the beach between the deep grounded ice and the land. At Point Barrow, much to our surprise, we saw no vessels, and as there is nothing but a native village at the Point itself, we rounded it and stood nine miles down the coast to the house of Mr. Thomas Gordon, a man who has for many years held the distinction of living farther north on continental America than any other white man. Here again we were disappointed, for Mr. Gordon was not at home. Mrs. Gordon could give us only discouraging news,—no whaling vessels had yet been sighted this year, and the ice blockade continued along the coast, so far as they knew. Mr. Gordon had taken the small boat and gone down the coast with the idea of possibly finding the whaling fleet, thinking they might be in the ice in the neighborhood of the Sea Horse Islands. Three miles farther on we found Mr. Charles D. Brower, and were received by him into the (for that country) sumptuous establishment of the Cape Smythe Whaling and Trading Company. The village of Cape Smythe, which coincides on the map with the post-office of Barrow, Alaska, is a town of a population in winter of over four hundred Eskimo, besides the white whalemen, the missionaries, and the school teachers. At this time the whalemen consisted of (besides the already named Mr. Gordon and Mr. Brower) Mr. John Hadley and Mr. Fred Hopson. The missionary was Dr. H. R. Marsh, with his wife and four children, while in a government schoolhouse we found Mr. and Mrs. Charles Hawkesworth, with their assistant, Miss Annie Koodlalook, a returned Carlisle student of Eskimo parentage.

CHAPTER IV

THE ice conditions, Mr. Brower told us, were worse this year than they had ever been before since 1884, when he first came to Point Barrow. In the worst previous seasons the ice had always been in motion parallel to the coast, even when it did not move away from the land enough to allow the coming of ships; but this year it did not seem to be moving at all in any direction. The spring had been an early one, so far as the disappearance of snow from the land was concerned, but after all, temperature has practically nothing to do with the navigability of the Arctic Ocean north of Alaska. It is entirely a matter of the prevailing winds. When westerly winds blow, the ice is blocked solidly against the land, while with easterly winds the ice goes abroad, leaving no obstructions to navigation. Four years later, in the summer of 1912, I saw the Polar Sea west of Point Barrow apparently as open as the Atlantic off Sandy Hook, — in spite of the fact that the summer of 1912 was the coldest of thirty years.

Up to the 23d there was no change in the condition of the ice which lay offshore, white and apparently solid as in winter. Before the 24th, the wind changed to a northeaster, which blew steadily for three days. There were signs of motion in the ice on the second day. The third day there was a wide channel of clear water between the ice and the land. This channel widened until the ice was out of sight, and the fourth day the whaling ships came in, — the *Beluga*, *Belvedere*, *Bowhead*, *Jeanette*, *Narwhal*, and *Thrasher*. They had fought ice ever since rounding Point Hope, but had been longest delayed at Icy Cape. The U. S. Revenue Cutter *Thetis* had followed them as far as the Sea Horse Islands, but had turned around there with the timidity characteristic of revenue cutters. It cannot be that naval officers are essentially more timid than ordinary men, and the reason that the stoutly built and powerful government vessels turn tail when comparatively weak freighting and whaling ships

47

keep on into the ice, is no doubt the result of the general instructions under which the different craft sail. A whaler has to take risks and to get there at all costs. A whaling captain is justified in risking his ship, and even losing it, in an attempt to get to his destination; whereas the commander of a government vessel always finds ample excuse for failure but no excuse if he loses his vessel.

The whalers that had arrived were all steamers, but they reported several sailing vessels to be following them close behind, — the *Rosie H.*, under Captain Fritz Wolki, bound for the eastward trade; the schooner *Challenge*, Captain Theodore Pedersen, intending to sail around Point Barrow and to winter there; and besides these, freighting vessels carrying goods to Mr. Brower, the Mission, the Government School, and to certain wealthy Eskimo who now carry on whaling on such a large scale that they buy groceries and other commodities by the tens of tons, wholesale. Several of the whalemen were old friends: Captain Jim Tilton of the *Bowhead* I had first seen at Herschel Island in 1906, and Captain Porter of the *Jeanette*, at Herschel Island in 1907; Captain Steve Cottle and Mrs. Cottle, who always accompanies him on his whaling voyages, I had met several times, and last in July, 1907, when they found me doing archæological work on an uninhabited island near the Colville and carried me thence east to Herschel Island, from which point I struck south across the mountains on my journey home from my first expedition; Captain George Leavitt of the *Narwhal* had entertained me aboard his ship in winter quarters at Herschel Island several times during the winter of 1906–07, and had now brought me a consignment of ammunition, kerosene, alcohol for the preservation of scientific specimens, and various things of that sort, sent North in his care by the American Museum of Natural History.

I had been compelled to come to Point Barrow for the lack of matches, but now that I was there I needed a great many other things, for the season was so short that I could not possibly get east to the Mackenzie River before the freeze-up. Instead of being able to winter in a region well supplied with fish and game, as I should have been had I obtained matches at Herschel Island, I was now compelled to winter on the northern coast of Alaska, where ten years before there had been vast herds of caribou, but where there now is practically no game at all.   The let-alone policy of the Government, the cupidity of traders, and the ignorance of the Eskimo themselves have practically destroyed the caribou as the buffalo was destroyed in our own West.   The situation here, however, was fundamentally different.   In the West the destruction of the buffalo was a necessity, for he cumbered the land which the farmers needed for the planting of crops; but the caribou graze on lands where no crops will ever grow.   Shooting buffalo for their hides and for sport destroyed them a few years before they would have had to go anyway; but the shooting of the caribou for the same reasons cannot be similarly extenuated, for had no more been killed than were needed for food and clothing for the population of the country itself, they would have lasted indefinitely, and would have been forever an economic resource not only for the Eskimo but for the country at large.

As there could be no hope of our party "living on the country" the coming winter, I had to buy from the whaling vessels food enough to take us through twelve months.   I had no money, for I expected to buy nothing in the Arctic, but fortunately, several of the whaling captains knew me and realized the circumstances; I had therefore no trouble in getting what I needed.   But perhaps of greater service to me than anything else was the generosity of Mr. Gordon, who put at my disposal a small sloop capable of carrying about five tons of freight.   Without the use of this boat I should have been unable to transport to the eastward as many supplies as my party needed.   And now that I had her my crew was insufficient.   I therefore engaged Mr. Storker Storkerson, an energetic man whom I knew well, for he had been the first mate on the schooner *Duchess of Bedford*, of the Anglo-American Polar Expedition.   He had come to the North aboard the *Narwhal*, intending to come into the service of Mr. Leffingwell, but now that Mr. Leffingwell was going home, he willingly conceded to Storkerson his freedom, and I was thereby enabled to secure a competent sailor and an ideal man for the work I had in hand.

We loaded the sloop and our whale-boat to their full capacity with about five tons of our own goods and a ton and a half of Mr. Leffingwell's, which we promised to try to deliver to the Eskimo who were working for him at Flaxman Island, about two hundred and fifty miles to the eastward.   We also carried an Eskimo named Kunaluk, who

E

worked for Mr. Leffingwell. It was four o'clock in the afternoon of
the 30th that we set sail from Mr. Brower's place at Cape Smythe,
heading northeast through a thick fog for Point Barrow, which
was about twelve miles distant. The wind was easterly, so that we
were able to steer almost a straight course along the beach. Every
two or three miles we would get too far offshore, and would have to
tack in again. Of course each time we tacked we lost that much
time, and Storkerson, who was in charge of the sloop, was keeping
her up into the wind as much as possible. This circumstance was
the cause of an adventure which came near being disastrous.

I was in the bow of the boat, keeping a careful lookout ahead
in the fog, for we expected that possibly we might suddenly run
into grounded ice. The fog cleared a little, so that we had at least
three hundred yards' warning of our approach to a small cake of
grounded ice which lay about two hundred yards offshore. As
Storkerson was a sailor and I was not, I did not presume to command
the sloop, but merely suggested to him that we had better go to
leeward of the cake of ice. We had plenty of time to discuss the
matter, and I pointed out to him that I had always found it "better to be safe than sorry," and better to lose half an hour than
to run the chance of an accident. But Storkerson said that there
was no chance of an accident, that we would easily be able to
clear the cake to windward. The sloop was making more leeway,
however, than he thought, and when we were about twenty-five yards
away from the cake Storkerson realized we were going to be unable
to clear it, and therefore tried to tack ship; but the sloop refused to
go about, and before we knew it we had crashed at full speed into
the ice and carried away our mast and rigging. Both of us thought
that the boat was probably stove also, but this did not turn out to
be the fact. She was so solidly built that she did not even spring
a leak. I immediately jumped upon the cake of ice, carrying the
painter of the sloop, and made her fast to the ice; but the wind was
blowing so hard offshore that it was hopeless for us unaided to try
to get the crippled sloop ashore.

The fog was still thick, and we expected no one to come along,
for our whale-boat, manned by our Eskimo, had disappeared an
hour before into the fog ahead of us, and we thought they

would be at Point Barrow by now. No doubt they would eventually come back to look for us, but that was not likely to happen for twelve or fifteen hours. As long as the wind continued strong northeasterly we should be comparatively safe, although unable to get ashore; but as soon as the wind changed to any other quarter the tide would immediately rise and our grounded cake would float off and be carried out to sea by the strong currents which continually sweep this coast. We had made up our minds to spending a few inactive hours on this cake of ice, waiting for something to turn up, when all of a sudden there came out of the fog behind us our own whale-boat which had, because of the fog, been going closer to the shore than we, and had found some friends camped on the beach with whom they had stopped to drink a cup of tea. This was great luck for us. We got our ropes out, and found that these were long enough for the whale-boat to take to a second cake of grounded ice that lay halfway between us and the shore. When this was done, all of us landed on the second cake of ice, and then hauled the sloop hand over hand up to us. From this cake in turn the rope was run to the beach, and the second lap of the journey ashore was completed in the manner of the first. As soon as we reached solid land we got out the carpenter's tools, most of which had been in our whale-boat, and Storkerson went energetically at the repairs of the sloop. The mast had not broken close down to the deck, but within about ten feet of the top, so that after fifteen hours of hard work we had it spliced and were ready to put to sea again.

The loss of this fifteen hours had been a serious blow to us, for no sooner had we gone ashore than the wind changed to a steady southwest breeze. Had we been in a position to sail, these fifteen hours of fair wind would have taken us at least sixty miles beyond Point Barrow. As it was, however, we lost not only fifteen hours, but about six hours more through the running away of our dogs, and the consequent search for them. When we finally rounded Point Barrow the fair wind had slackened to a gentle breeze which later on died down completely. The sloop was so heavy that she could not be rowed, and so we had to camp on a sandspit known to the Eskimo as Iglorak, which seems to be the same as that set down on the charts as Cooper's Island. We went ashore here and camped, but soon a strong northeaster blew up so suddenly that something had to be instantly done to save our heavily laden boats from being swamped in the breakers or crushed in the ice which was sure to come in within the next two or three hours. It took us but a few moments to bundle our camp gear into the boats, but unfortunately our dogs — some of them — had gone off on the island squirrel hunting, and we could not get them quickly. I did not dare to leave them alone on the island for fear they might get fighting and tear each other to pieces, so I let the boats go without me, telling them to run into shelter, if they could, behind the westerly end of the second island west of us, where we knew there was a channel where the Point Barrow lagoon could be entered. As soon as they had succeeded in getting into shelter, they were to unload the whale-boat and to come back with it to fetch me.

The boats should have been back in two hours at the most, had all gone well; but all did not go well, for they found the channel so crooked that they dared not run into it, and preferred to anchor on a lee shore under the shelter of a big cake of grounded ice. The chief danger here was that small cakes of ice might float in behind the big sheltering cake, and might break the boats in that way; but as only small cakes could possibly do this, the boats were rendered comparatively safe by having a man with a long pole standing on guard. When a cake of ice came floating along he would not be able to stop it, but he might push it aside enough so that it would miss the boat. Storkerson and Kunaluk undertook this work while Ilavinirk landed the camping gear from our whale-boat and came back to fetch me. He got to me in about eight hours instead of two, as I had expected, and it was already nearly dark. We both of us got wet nearly to the neck in the breakers when carrying the dogs out into the boat, and then we had perhaps the most exciting sail in which I have ever taken part. We used a storm sail reefed down close, but the wind was fairly strong, and the speed of the boat must have been seven or eight miles per hour. It was dangerous work scudding along like this through the darkness in a fragile cedar boat, with cakes of ice floating around you everywhere. We had several narrow escapes but no accident, and landed on the beach behind the grounded cake where Storkerson was guarding the sloop.

It was a bad night for Storkerson and Kunaluk, but fairly comfortable for the rest of us who slept ashore. The next morning the wind had moderated enough so that it seemed safe to try running into shelter behind the island, and we did so successfully. The chief trouble with our sloop was that she was too heavily laden. She carried about a ton more than she had ever carried before, and had only about six inches of free-board. For that reason we devoted the next day to carefully battening down the manhole and generally getting her deck so waterproof that the waves might wash over the craft without danger of her filling.

The ice had been on the coast all summer, and possibly this was the reason why we now had the indications of an extraordinarily early fall, which worried us considerably, for although we had no hope of being able to reach the Mackenzie River, we still had fully expected to be able to get to or beyond the Colville, where we should be fairly well situated for the pursuit of ethnological and zoölogical studies in the winter, and for archæological work in the spring. But thick ice was now forming on shallow water every night. It was with considerable relief, therefore, that on the morning of September 5th we sighted the schooner *Rosie H.* going eastward. We headed offshore to her, told her our troubles, and got her to take Mr. Leffingwell's ton and a half of freight off our hands, for it seemed that her chances were really better than ours of being able to land the stuff at Flaxman Island. Captain Wolki also kindly took along some of my own gear, promising to try landing it at Flaxman Island.

The afternoon of the 5th of September was the beginning of serious troubles for us, — troubles that were caused partly by untoward weather, but chiefly through the inaccuracy of the chart. We had been working eastward from Point Barrow along a continuous line of islands which the chart represents as ending near a place named Point Tangent, east of which the chart sets down a deep bay about five miles across. We came to the end of our island chain, and then followed the land along until, sure enough, we came to a bay. The chart was so perfectly definite in this quarter that we had no doubt this was the bay set down east of Point Tangent. We therefore steered southeast true, expecting to sight land in less than an hour at the furthest. But we kept going for several hours, and still no sight of land. Then it occurred to us that possibly the abundance of iron aboard our boats might have set our compasses wrong, and so we headed inshore, steering first south, and later on even southwest, but in spite of this we saw no land. After about six hours of sailing, and after going some fifteen or eighteen miles in crossing a bay that should have been only five miles wide, the sloop all of a sudden went aground in four feet of water. We had been having a southwesterly wind with a high tide; now all of a sudden the wind changed to northeast, and the tide went down perhaps two feet, — as it always does on this coast upon such a change of wind. The result was that not only was the sloop aground, but even the water through which she had come was now so shallow that she could not possibly get back over the same course. All the indications were that we must have gotten on to the mud flats of Smith Bay, but Smith Bay is the third and not the first bay east of Point Tangent, according to the charts. We know now that the two bays between Point Tangent and Smith Bay are purely mythical. Had we had the faintest suspicion that we were crossing the mouth of Smith Bay, we should have held our southeasterly course for twenty or twenty-five instead of ten or twelve miles and should have made Pitt Point easily before the change of wind.

It blew cold from the northeast, and it snowed a little, — all together our night on the shoals was a very unpleasant one. Shortly after going aground in the evening, Kunaluk and I had got out of the boat with the idea of being able to push her off the sand bar where she stuck. We had been able to do this, only to find that she floated in a small depression, surrounded everywhere by sand banks that she could not cross to get out. We waded about here and there, gauging the depth of the water by about how far up it came on us as we waded. Mushy ice was already forming. I was wet well above the waist, and Kunaluk, being smaller, was wet nearly to his shoulders, so that he rather had the worst of it. Mamayauk, who usually kept her nerve under trying circumstances, was irrational and hard to get along with, and did not sleep all night, continually complaining that she did not see why we did not put ashore so that we might have a chance of making a fire and getting something warm to eat. We all joined in pointing out to her that we had waded in complete circles around the sloop and that there was no way of getting anywhere until the tide should rise on the change of wind. "But," she argued, "if we stay here the wind is likely to blow up and the breakers will swamp us." We appreciated that point quite as well as she did, but the fact remained that there was nothing to be done.

The following day was clear and calm, with a slight rise of water. Low land was visible four or five miles to the south. Our exploration in the whale-boat that morning revealed the curious fact that while everything seemed hopelessly shoal out to seaward, we would be barely able to float the sloop landward into the channel of a river, in the delta of which we were evidently entangled. There was nothing to do but go ashore, — seeing we could, — for we knew that we could at any time, on a rise of the water, come back along the same channel to the place where we now were. By careful work we got the sloop within half a mile of shore, anchored her there, and all went ashore in the whale-boat. We pitched a tent, had a comfortable warm meal, and went to sleep.

The next morning there was glare ice all over Smith Bay, and winter had set in. Three days later we took an improvised sled out to the sloop where she lay, solidly frozen in the ice, and began hauling our stuff ashore. Had either myself or any of my Eskimo been required to name the place along the whole coast where we were least willing to be overtaken by winter, we should have agreed in naming the foot of Smith Bay where we now were. There were no people near, there was practically no game, there was less driftwood than anywhere else, — the place had no redeeming features; it was the deadliest, most desolate place on the whole coast. But of course we had to make the best of it.

We hunted in all directions and got what game there was. Had we been just east to the mouth of Colville, where we should have preferred to be, we should have been able to get a few deer, the meat of which we did not need as much as we did the skins for clothing. In Smith Bay our game list for the entire time reads monotonously:

September 9th: 6 marmots, 5 ptarmigan, 3 ducks.

September 10th: 3 ptarmigan, 1 gull, 1 loon, 1 marmot, etc.

The only variant came when on Sunday, the 30th, we got a solitary young swan.

We employed much of our time in wishing for a chance to get away, and in making preparations to that end. Driftwood was scarce and of poor quality, but still we managed to find sticks fairly suitable for sledge runners, and a sledge was constructed. Dog harness was made of sailcloth, and a stove and stovepipe out of some empty kerosene tins.

The ethnologist has this advantage over other scientists who go to the polar regions, that he has a good field for investigations wherever he is not alone. The navigator is hampered by the winds and seasons; the secrets that the geologist tries to decipher are covered up in winter by a blanket of snow; but the ethnologist can learn something about human nature wherever he has companions, and strange and unpleasant situations are likely to bring out peculiar and interesting phases of character. For our Eskimo our present situation was not essentially peculiar, however; they are used to being overtaken by winter in places that do not suit them, and they simply put up with it as a matter of course. Their life goes on in the ordinary way, in the search for and the preparation of food, in the making of clothing, and in the exercise of their religious observances. My notebook for this period is therefore not barren. I recorded folk-lore stories which my Eskimo told each other in the evenings when the day's hunting for marmot was over. I noted that Nogasak's milk teeth were pulled out by her mother with a piece of sinew and that they were not thrown away but were put carefully inside of pieces of meat and fed to dogs. It is a matter of wise forethought to do this, for were some evilly disposed man to get hold of one of your teeth, he could practice magic on you by practicing it on the tooth. This is the sympathetic magic known to many primitive peoples. You freeze a man's tooth, or a paring of his finger nails, or a lock of his hair, and you give him chills; you put these, or any other parts from his body, near a fire, and he suffers with a fever; you let them drop, and he is likely to have a fall in the mountains and to break some of his bones if not to kill himself. Some Eskimo therefore will burn a tooth, put it into a marmot hole, or throw it into the sea; but the Mackenzie River Eskimo believe the safest way is to feed the tooth to a dog.

I learned also why it is that animals allow themselves to be killed by men. The animals are much wiser than men, and know everything in the world, — including the thoughts of men; but there are certain things which the animals need, and which they can get only from men. The seals and whales live in the salt water, and are therefore continually thirsty. They have no means of getting fresh water, except to come to men for it. A seal will therefore allow himself to be killed by the hunter who will give him a drink of water in return; that is why a dipperful of water is always poured into the mouth of a seal when he is brought ashore. If a hunter neglects to do this, all the other seals know about it, and no other seal will ever allow himself to be killed by that hunter, because he knows he is not going to get a drink. Every man who gives a seal a drink of water, and keeps this implied promise, is known by the other seals as a dependable person, and they will prefer to be killed by him. There are other things which a seal would like to have done for it when it is dead, and some men are so careful to do everything that seals want that the seals tumble over themselves in their eagerness to be killed by that particular man. The polar bear does not suffer from thirst as much as the seal, for he can eat the fresh snow on top of the ice. But polar bears are unable to make for themselves certain tools which they need. What the male bears especially value are crooked knives and bow-drills, and the female bears are especially eager to get women's knives, skin scrapers, and needle cases; consequently when a polar bear has been killed his soul (tatkok) accompanies the skin into the man's house and stays with the skin for several days (among most tribes, for four days if it is a male bear, and for five days if it is a female). The skin during this time is hung up at the rear end of the house, and with the skin are hung up the tools which the bear desires, according to the sex of the animal killed. At the end of the fourth or fifth day the soul of the bear is by a magic formula driven out of the house; and when it goes away it takes away with it the souls of the tools which have been suspended with it and uses them thereafter.

There are certain manners and customs of humanity which are displeasing to polar bears, and for that reason those customs are carefully abjured during the period when the soul of the bear is in the man's house. The bear, in other words, is treated as an honored guest who must not be offended.   If the bear's soul has been properly treated during his stay with the man, and if he has received the souls (tatkoit) of implements of good quality, then he will report those things in the land of the polar bears to which he returns, and other bears will be anxious to be killed by so reliable a man.   If the wives of certain hunters are careless about treating the souls of the bears properly while they are in their houses, this will offend the bears quite as much as if the man who killed them had done it, and this may cause an excellent hunter to get no polar bears at all.   Certain women are known in their communities for this very undesirable quality, and if a woman becomes a widow, her reputation for carelessness in treating the souls of animals may prevent her from getting a good second husband.

This and similar things the ethnologist who understands the language of the people he is among continually learns by merely being an observant member of the family.   Direct questions seldom bring such things out, both because one does not know what to ask for, and because the Eskimo have a very definite idea of what sort of things it is that a white man believes in and approves of, and what sort of things he disbelieves in and ridicules, and they will in response to questions tell exactly the things that they think will be approved of by the questioner.   But one who is a member of the family, as I was, learns everything as the children around him learn, by observation, and by listening to the conversations of everyday life, and especially to the folk-lore stories that are told whenever any one has leisure to listen.

We learned also (a thing which has for generations been well known to the Eskimo) that Smith Bay is the delta of a large river hitherto unnoticed by map-makers.   It is probably the largest river west of the Colville in northern Alaska.   It is too large to have a name as a whole, apparently, but one of its mouths is known as the Mayoriak, from the circumstance that the Point Barrow Eskimo on their trading voyages to the Colville in the spring ascend this river for some distance, until they come to a large lake known as Tasirkpuk, or "the big lake."   From the eastern end of this lake there is a short portage to another river, which has its mouth just west of the mouth of the Colville.   This eastward route is pursued by the Point Barrow traders because it opens up earlier than the sea route along the coast. On their return journeys in the fall they never follow it, but come back by the sea.   Going east, they carry skin boats (umiak) on their sleds as far as Smith Bay, where they take the water at the mouth of the Mayoriak.

CHAPTER V

ON September 17th we considered that the sea ice was probably strong enough for sled travel. The ice of Smith Bay had been strong enough for several days, but we feared — and with good reason I am sure — that east of Smith Bay the coast would still be open. In the afternoon of the 17th Ilavinirk and I took a small sled-load with the idea of going to Point Pitt at the eastern end of the Bay, to cache it there and to find out if conditions were propitious. We did not get quite that far, for about ten miles southwest of Point Pitt, well within Simpson Bay, we saw an Eskimo camp pitched on ground that rises about twenty feet above the sea at the mouth of a small creek that comes out of a well-known fishing lake lying a few miles inland.

This camp turned out to be returned traders who had been to the Colville and even to Flaxman Island to exchange ammunition, flour, tea, cloth, and other commodities — which they get cheaply at Point Barrow — for skins of caribou, mountain sheep and foxes. At Point Barrow these men work for the Cape Smythe Whaling & Trading Company, and for other white and Eskimo whalers. Some of the Eskimo at Point Barrow now carry on whaling on a large scale, maintaining as many as five or six boat crews. Irrespective of whether their employers are white or Eskimo, these men get each year as wages about two hundred dollars' worth of supplies. This means that the Point Barrow community leads an easier life than any other community does as a whole in any land where I have ever traveled. The whaling season in the spring is six weeks, and it is six weeks of fairly easy work at that. For all the rest of the year the men have nothing to do, — are their own masters, and can go wherever they like, while their employers must not only pay them a year's wage for six weeks' work, but also furnish them houses to live in, usually, and rations for the entire year. Of course the men are expected to get their own fresh meat, which they do by seal and wal-

MACKENZIE RIVER HOUSE IN SUMMER.

The doorway to the forty-foot alleyway is at the left of the picture.

A WOMAN DANCING TO THE ACCOMPANIMENT OF SINGING AND DRUM BEATING —
FLAXMAN ISLAND, 1908.

rus hunting, and by cutting in the whales, — only the bone (balleen) of which goes to their employers. The employer supplies them with cloth for garments, and such suitable provisions as flour, tea, beans, rice, and even condensed milk, canned meats and fruits. Each man each year gets, among other things, a new rifle with loading tools and ammunition. The result is that firearms are probably nowhere in the world cheaper than they are at Point Barrow (or at least were, up to 1908). When I first came to Point Barrow you could buy a new Winchester rifle of any type, with loading tools, five hundred rounds or so of smokeless powder ammunition, and a considerable quantity of powder, lead, and primers for five dollars in money; had you bought the same articles wholesale at the factory in New Haven, the price would have been in the neighborhood of twenty dollars. There are few Eskimo who will use a rifle more than one year. They will no more think of using a last year's rifle than our well-to-do women will consider wearing a hat of last year's fashion, and you see rifles and shotguns, which our most fastidious sportsmen would consider good as new, lying around on the beach, thrown away by Eskimo who have no realization of their value because of the ease with which they have always obtained them in the past. The reason for all this is that whaling was, until a few years ago, so fabulously profitable an industry that the whaling companies cared scarcely at all what they paid for services as long as they got the whales. But now that the price of whalebone has suddenly gone down through the invention of a substitute, the Eskimo are facing a new era and the change will be hard on them.

The pay-day of the Point Barrow Eskimo comes in the spring, and their employer hands them out rifles, ammunition, cloth, provisions, and various things which the people scarcely know what to do with. So they load them into their skin boats and take them east along the coast, to sell them at any point in the Colville or at Flaxman Island. To give some idea of the scale of prices it is worth while to say that one of the men whom we met returned with ten deerskins, which was all he had received in the Colville River for a boat-load of supplies consisting of two new rifles, two cases of smokeless powder ammunition for these, twenty-five pounds of powder and a corresponding supply of lead and shot, three bolts of cloth, a case of carpenter tools, some camp gear, three hundred pounds of flour, sixty pounds of good tea, two boxes of tobacco, and various other articles too numerous to mention. The ten caribou skins were of varying quality. The best of them were worth that year about five dollars apiece, and the total value of the ten skins could not have been more than thirty dollars. In other words, had this same Eskimo stayed at Point Barrow during the summer and been able to board a whaling ship with thirty dollars in his pocket, he could have bought ten deerskins of a corresponding quality, had they been carried by the ship, — although of course the ships carry only fairly good skins, averaging much better than the ten which he had secured in the Colville.

These Eskimo told us that they had been overtaken by the freeze-up just east of Point Pitt and that they had come overland to this fishing lake where they were catching quite enough fish for themselves and their dogs. Most of them expected to proceed to Point Barrow in a day or two, but two families intended to spend the winter living on the fish they could catch.

We returned home the same day and remained in camp, waiting for this band of Eskimo to call on us on their way to Point Barrow, for we wanted to buy from one of them a set of whalebone sled-runners to use on our improvised sled. The next evening when they came they camped beside us, and immediately made preparations for setting fish nets. We had several excellent fish nets in our boat, and I had said to my Eskimo in the beginning that I thought we ought to put them out to see if we could catch any fish; but they said very definitely that there were no fish here. At that time I had had no experience with Eskimo in a country new to them. I had dealt only with Eskimo near at home, and my experience with them was that they knew exactly where to put nets, and knew also what places were hopeless as fishing localities. I know now that the Eskimo temperament is that they never expect to find anything in any place where no one has found it before, so far as they know, and never having heard of any one catching fish in Smith Bay they had felt sure there would not be any. Now when these local Eskimo put out their nets, my Eskimo wanted to put out nets also, and argued vehemently our delaying our departure for a week or so, for they were fish-hungry. I, however, insisted on starting in the morning, and we put none of our own nets out, although we shared in the fish which the visitors caught in considerable numbers right at our very door. This was a valuable lesson to me, and has on many occasions encouraged me to go into districts that the Eskimo considered devoid of game and in which I have usually found plenty.

The following day, accordingly, we left Smith Bay for the east. We had long before carried ashore everything from the sloop, and had erected a platform cache, which is a safe cache in this country, for there are no wolverines, and polar bears will seldom go into the bottom of a deep bay, depending for their food on the seals which they find in the open leads that only occur outside a straight line tangent to the points of the coast.

Our journey was at first entirely without incident. We found no Eskimo and we had expected to find none, although of course the old, ruined houses which indicate the large population that has vanished are scattered along the coast; but at Cape Halkett, on the 23d of September, a surprise awaited us. We saw the masts of a ship evidently frozen into the ice a few miles offshore from Halkett. The next day we went out to investigate, and found that this was the gasoline schooner *Olga*, commanded by Captain William Mogg. The *Olga* had been attempting to get out to the Pacific from her whaling and trading voyage in the east. They had passed the *Rosie H.* just east of the mouth of the Colville, and were of the opinion that she, with my goods and Leffingwell's, would be frozen in behind the Jones Islands, just east of the Colville. On September 11th the *Olga* had run aground on a shoal about three miles off Halkett; but for this misadventure she might have reached Point Barrow, but it took them so long to get her off with kedge anchors that a sudden spell of calm weather allowed the ice to freeze, and there they were, fast for eight months at least. The vessel was evidently in danger of two sorts: a strong on-shore wind was likely to crush up the ice, in which case it would crush the vessel with it; or a strong offshore wind might carry the ice abroad, likewise taking the vessel with it. Captain Mogg had therefore wisely sent most of his more valuable stuff ashore on Cape Halkett Island. As he did not have provisions enough to winter, he was now preparing to abandon the *Olga* and to take his crew to Point Barrow, where Mr. Brower would be abundantly able to take care of them.

Captain Mogg entertained us aboard with great hospitality for a day, and urged us to stay longer; but we could not, for we suspected that Dr. Anderson with his party of Eskimo must be frozen in somewhere east of Flaxman Island, and there was need that we should get together to formulate our plans for the winter. Moreover, I was not sure how he was getting along. I had faith in their ability to get fish and ptarmigan, even if caribou failed them, and in the mountains south of Barter Island, sixty miles east of Flaxman Island, mountain sheep were at that time known to be fairly numerous. Still, there is "many a slip" as the saying goes. We could not be completely at ease until we found out certain news of him, and I suspected he would feel similarly about us.

In going eastward, September 27th, we found the ice off the mouth of the Colville still too thin for safe travel, and we had to go along the shore, thus nearly doubling our traveling distance, for the land has many and deep bights. We were able to shoot a few seal, and to get a ptarmigan, gull, or a duck now and then. We were in no danger of shortage of food, for our load consisted of over two hundred pounds of provisions, besides the ammunition and camp gear. The ducks and gulls, we noticed, were all traveling west parallel to the coast.

Just east of the Colville, at a point known to white men and Eskimo alike as Oliktok, but which on charts is called Beachy Point, we had luck in seeing a band of caribou. There were nine of them, and between Ilavinirk, Kunaluk, and me we got seven. This was the first time in my experience that I had shot at caribou with Eskimo, and it was probably the first time in the experience of these Eskimo that they had ever seen a caribou killed by a white man. Ilavinirk and Kunaluk, accordingly, had some amusing arguments about the matter later on. They had agreed that neither one of them would shoot at a big bull caribou until the others had been killed, because he was sure to be poor and his skin would be less valuable than that of the younger animals; nevertheless the bull was dead now, and Ilavinirk said that I had killed it; but Kunaluk said that could not be, and that one of them must have killed it by a stray shot, although admittedly neither of them had aimed at it. Ilavinirk and Kunaluk had never hunted caribou together before, and we learned later that Kunaluk considered he himself had killed most of these caribou, and that I had certainly killed none — and it was doubtful whether Ilavinirk had killed any or not. But it was Eskimo custom — and by it he was willing to abide — that when three men shoot at a band of caribou, the booty shall be divided equally among the three. This did not suit me particularly, however, as I had been feeding and taking care of Kunaluk for some time, and I pointed out to him that by white men's custom all the animals belonged to me. I told him, however, that I was willing to concede the point only in the matter of the skins and would keep all of the meat.

We stopped a day to make a platform cache for the meat, and that day Kunaluk, unaided, killed another caribou, so that we had the meat of eight to leave behind in cache. Three of the animals were skinned as specimens, and are now, with many others, in the American Museum of Natural History in New York. These are the first skins of caribou taken for scientific purposes on the north coast of Alaska east of Point Barrow.

On October 8th, just west of the mouth of the Kuparuk River, I went inland alone and killed a young bull caribou which even Kunaluk did not dispute had been shot by me. We had seen a band of caribou in another direction in the morning, and Ilavinirk and Kunaluk had gone after them, but with no success. In the afternoon, however, the three of us together killed another bull caribou, so that at the mouth of the Kuparuk also we were able to leave behind a cache of meat. These we expected to be useful some time later in the winter when we should come back over the same trail.

The low, coastal plain of northern Alaska is triangular in shape, with its apex at Point Barrow, perhaps two hundred miles north from the base, which is formed by the east and west running Alaskan spur of the Rocky Mountains, which comes within a few miles of the coast in eastern Alaska at the international boundary and meets the ocean in western Alaska at Cape Lisburne. This plain is so nearly level that in most places it is not possible, in going inland, to determine offhand whether you are going up hill or down. The rivers are all sluggish, but thirty or forty miles inland most of them

F

run between fairly high banks, which shows that the land does slope
up, even though imperceptibly, towards the foothills. Just east of the
Colville River at Oliktok, the mountains are probably about eighty
miles inland. As you proceed eastward along the coast they become visible from near the mouth of the Kuparuk. Continuing eastward they get steadily nearer the coast, and apparently higher, until
their distance from the sea is not more than six or eight miles at
Demarcation Point, while their highest places are probably about
ten thousand feet in elevation and lie southward from Flaxman and
Barter islands, where they contain a few small glaciers.

This whole coastal plain was a few years ago an immense caribou
pasture and inhabited by hundreds of Eskimo who lived mostly on
the meat of the caribou. Of late years the country has been de-
populated through the disappearance of the caribou. This fact
explains the United States census returns as to the population of
northern Alaska. To any one ignorant of the facts, the census figures
seem to prove that the population of northern Alaska has remained
stationary during the last two or three decades. This is so far
from being true that I am certain the population is not over ten per
cent now of what it was in 1880. The trouble arises from the fact
that the census covered only the coastal strip. The village of Cape
Smythe contained probably about four hundred inhabitants in 1880,
and contains about that to-day. But only four persons are now living
who are considered by the Eskimo themselves to belong to the Cape
Smythe tribe, and only twenty or twenty-one others who are descended
from the Cape Smythe tribe through one parent. The fact is that
the excessive death rate of the last thirty years would have nearly
wiped out the village but for the fact that the prosperity of the
whaling industry there year by year brought in large numbers of immigrants; so that while thirty years ago it was safe to say that seventy-
five per cent of the four hundred Eskimo at Cape Smythe must have
been of that tribe, no more than seven per cent can now be considered
to belong to it. The difference is made up by the immigrants, who,
according to their own system of nomenclature, belong to a dozen
or more tribes, and hail from districts as far apart as St. Lawrence
Island in Bering Sea, and the mouth of the Mackenzie River in Arctic
Canada, while the majority come from inland and from the headwaters

of the Colville, Noatak, and Kuvuk rivers. It seems that the inland Eskimo, who by their head-form and other physical characteristics show clearly their admixture of Alaskan Indian blood, are more hardy than the coast people, or at least are less susceptible to the half dozen or so particularly deadly diseases which the white men of recent years have introduced. But hereafter the census figures will begin to be more truthful, for now the northern interior of Alaska is all deserted, and no recruits can come down from the mountains to fill in the vacant places left by diseases among the coastal Eskimo.

It was the vanishing of the caribou from the interior coastal plain that drove down the Eskimo to the coast, and now it seems that the caribou are having a slight chance, for in large districts where formerly they had to face the hunter, their only enemy is now the wolf. Temperamentally, the Eskimo expects to find everything next year as he found it last year; consequently the belief died hard that the foothills were inexhaustibly supplied with caribou. But when starvation had year after year taken off families by groups, the Eskimo finally realized that the caribou in large numbers were a thing of the past; and they were so firmly impressed with the fact, that now they are assured that no caribou are in the interior, as they once thought they would be there forever.

One result of this temperamental peculiarity was this, that during the winter of 1908–1909 there were numerous families huddled around Flaxman Island (where, as it turned out, the *Rosie H.* was wintering) with the idea that it was impossible for them to get caribou for food or for clothing, while we went inland to where every one said there was no game, and were able to live well. Our own small party that winter in northern Alaska killed more caribou than all the rest of the Eskimo of the country put together, because we had the faith to go and look for them where the Eskimo " knew " they no longer existed.

At the Kuparuk River, after we had killed the two bull caribou spoken of above and cached the meat safely, we saw an abundance of tracks, and there is no doubt that had we stayed there to hunt we could have secured a comparative abundance of meat. But our chief anxiety now was to communicate with Dr. Anderson, and so we hurried on down the coast. Traveling at this time of the year on this portion of the northern coast of America is comfortable enough, for every few miles, — and in some cases every few hundreds of yards, — you find an abundance of driftwood for fuel. We therefore carried a sheet-iron stove which we used in our tent, and which made it a very cosy place indeed, even in stormy weather. In the fall, however, sledging is often heavy on account of the salt water which, curiously enough, remains unfrozen, even in cold weather, on top of the ice in many places. Because of this water on the ice one is compelled in the early fall to wear boots with waterproof soles. The snow also cakes between the dogs' toes, rendering them footsore. The hauling weight of the sleds is doubled or trebled by the inch or so of soaking wet snow on top of the ice. In looking over an expanse of icy sea the snow everywhere looks white and dry, but the feet of men and dogs and the runners of loaded sleds break continually through this dry and soft upper layer into the salty slush below.

We reached Flaxman Island October 12th, to find the *Rosie H.* there in winter quarters, and Dr. Anderson staying in Mr. Leffing-well's house, which he did at the invitation of Mr. Ned Arey, an American miner of Mayflower descent who has lived in the northern country for the last fifteen or twenty years, and who, during Mr. Leffingwell's stay in the region, had been associated with him continually, and now, in a manner of speaking, represented him locally. Mr. Storkerson, whom I had found in every way an excellent man, quit our service at this place. My chief reason in engaging him in the beginning was that I wanted him to sail the sloop. Misfortunes had prevented our getting the sloop any distance to the eastward, and I now no longer needed his services. He, for his part, considered himself under obligations to Mr. Leffingwell, and told me that he believed Mr. Leffingwell's outfit at Flaxman Island, which consisted not only of his dwelling house there, but also of valuable gear such as chronometers and other expensive scientific instruments, as well as books, firearms, and other property, were likely to be stolen during the winter by Eskimo and might even be misappropriated by white men. The reasons Mr. Storkerson gave were perfectly satisfactory to me, especially as I wanted to decrease the size of my party, and he accordingly took possession of Mr. Leffingwell's house and lived in it that winter on the stores which he found already there and on others which he purchased from Captain Wolki of the *Rosie H*.

Dr. Anderson told me that his party had been able to reach by open water Barter Island, which lies about sixty miles east of Flaxman Island. At this point they were overtaken by the frost September 6th, the same day we were in Smith Bay, over two hundred miles farther west. They tried to feed themselves and their dogs by setting fish nets along the coast, but met with little success, and were therefore compelled to abandon their coast camp temporarily and to go inland up the so-called "Oolahoola" River, where they were more successful in the capture of brook trout and other fish, as well as in the killing of ptarmigan and marmot. They had also secured half a dozen caribou, but having over twenty dogs, they had not much more than made their living.

At Flaxman Island Dr. Anderson and I talked over plans for the winter in detail. From a zoölogical point of view it seemed most important for him to go into the mountains south of Barter Island in search of the scientifically unknown mountain sheep, which would probably prove to be a variety of the *Ovis dalli*, and which, by native account, were fairly abundant. He would later on, if everything went well, go still farther south, beyond the mountains and the mountain-sheep country, into the Yukon Valley, where he hoped to take some specimens of the also scientifically unknown caribou of northern Alaska. These plans of his eventuated very well. During the four months that intervened between this and our next meeting he secured numerous specimens of sheep, caribou, and other far northern mammals, and incidentally had his first experience of "living on the country." In fact the caribou proved much more abundant than we had hoped for; so abundant that had it not been for a shortage of tobacco, Dr. Anderson would have found considerable difficulty in inducing the Eskimo to leave the fleshpots and comfortable forest camps of the Yukon slope for the Arctic coast, where they could look forward to nothing better than living on the provisions we had purchased at Point Barrow; and living on "white men's grub" is always a hardship to an Eskimo. It was, incidentally, Dr. Anderson's first experience of living without salt, an ordeal which he had much dreaded, for he shared the common belief that salt is a necessary article of diet. But it turned out, as I knew from experience it would, that he did not mind it seriously.

Most people are in the habit of looking upon the articles of our accustomed diet, and especially upon salt, as necessities. We have not found them so. The longer you go without grain foods and vegetables the less you long for them. Salt I have found to behave like a narcotic poison — in other words, it is hard to break off its use, as it is hard to stop the use of tobacco ; but after you have been a month or so without salt you cease to long for it, and after six months I have found the taste of meat boiled in salt water distinctly disagreeable. In the case of such a necessary element of food as fat, on the other hand, I have found that the longer you are without it the more you long for it, until the craving becomes much more intense than is the hunger of a man who fasts. (The symptoms of starvation are those of a disease rather than of being hungry.) Among the uncivilized Eskimo the dislike of salt is so strong that a saltiness imperceptible to me would prevent them from eating at all. This circumstance was often useful to me later in our travels about Coronation Gulf, for whenever our Eskimo visitors threatened to eat us out of house and home we could put in a little pinch of salt, and thus husband our resources without seeming inhospitable. A man who tasted anything salty at our table would quickly bethink him that he had plenty of more palatable fare in his own house.

The experience of Dr. Anderson's party during the time they spent in the mountains of Arctic Alaska were as interesting as any during our whole expedition, and he has often told them to me, but they are his story and it is his place to tell it.

Dr. Anderson took with him of our party of Eskimo only Ilavinirk and Mamayauk, with their eight-year-old daughter Nogasak, but several other Eskimo voluntarily joined his fortunes and accompanied him south. My own chief interests were in the people of the country rather than in its sheep and caribou; I accordingly turned west along the coast with the intention of spending some time on the Colville River, which I supposed to be inhabited by a few families of inland Eskimo. My companions were a man who had been born in the Colville River district named Akpek, with his wife Sungauravik and a Port Clarence man named Natkusiak. I had engaged Akpek

SLEDGING OVER BARREN GROUND IN SUMMER.

Making use of ice foot of small lake. Man has stripped and dog lies in ice water on account of heat.

SLEDGING OVER BARREN GROUND IN SUMMER — SLED ON TOP OF RIDGE.

and his wife on Ilavinirk's recommendation. Ilavinirk had known Akpek some six or eight years before when he had been an energetic and successful hunter, but his wife Ilavinirk did not know at all. She was a strong-looking and prepossessing woman, and I had said to Ilavinirk when he recommended Akpek to me that I would take him on his recommendation, but that I would take his wife on my own judgment, for she was, as any one could see, a capable and competent person. It turned out that Akpek had been taken, since Ilavinirk knew him, with the common complaint of the country — tuberculosis — and was so weakened by it that his prowess as a hunter was largely gone ; while his wife turned out to be the laziest and most slovenly person that I have dealt with among the Eskimo, proving incidentally that I am no better at reading Eskimo character than I am at reading that of my own countrymen. Poor Akpek was willing enough had he had the strength to hunt, but his weakness kept him to the camp and the result was that he did much of the cooking and housework. The more difficult tasks of all kinds fell upon Natkusiak and me. The lady Sungauravik seldom turned a hand to anything useful.

The three Eskimo and I with two sleds and eleven dogs left Flaxman Island, going west, October 20th. On our arrival there, ten days before, we had reported the fact that caribou were to be found in some numbers to the westward, and a man by the name of Oyarayak had gone west with his family to try his fortune. Our second day out we met him coming back east to Flaxman Island with a small sled-load of caribou meat which he intended to sell to Captain Wolki of the Rosie H. He had killed six deer, it seemed, and had left his wife and two children to take care of the greater part of it while he went to Flaxman Island to sell some of it for ammunition and tea. He invited us to proceed to his camp and pitch ours beside it, for there was plenty of meat for all (for a day or two) and his wife would be glad of a neighbor while he was away. Accordingly we headed for the place indicated, reached it in two days, and hunted south from it for two days, but with no success. We saw on the first day a few deer, it is true, but through mismanagement were unable to get near enough to them to shoot. Oyarayak's meat supply was getting noticeably smaller on the third day, so we decided it was better for Oyarayak's wife and family to be neighborless than hungry, and proceeded west toward the meat cache we had made October 8th near the Kuparuk River and hunted from there again, likewise without success. The few caribou tracks we found seemed to be about two weeks old.

At most seasons of the year one is considerably troubled with mirages; perhaps more in summer than in winter, but in winter also. On my hunts at this time I was frequently deceived not so much by the mere appearance of objects out of all natural proportion, but more especially by their apparent motion and their disappearances and reappearances on the level snow surface. Where the only game to be expected is caribou you take it for granted that whatever black speck you see is probably a caribou and the probability ordinarily becomes a certainty if you see the thing move. I was a little inexperienced in these matters and during the three or four days we camped near the Kuparuk River I several times allowed myself to be deceived by black specks moving on the distant horizon, exactly after the manner of caribou. That there could have been no living thing was always eventually shown by the fact that there was no trail left in the spotless snow. The mountains inland were visible and were continually changing their shapes but they seldom looked like real mountains. More frequently they simulated the water-front appearance of New York sky-scrapers, even to chimneys and whiffs of smoke. They would continually change their shape and order, and at times seemed to be marching in single file either to the east or west.

I think it is David Hanbury who tells of mistaking a lemming for a musk-ox, and Lieutenant Gotfred Hansen speaks of being astounded by the courage with which his dogs attacked a polar bear, and of being dumfounded not only at seeing them killing the bear but more especially at one of the dogs bringing the bear back in his mouth. It turned out, of course, that the polar bear had been an Arctic fox. In things of this sort there is always a certain amount of suggestion; Hanbury had his mind centered on musk-oxen, and Hansen was expecting to see a polar bear. On one occasion when I had strongly in mind the scientific value, as well as the food value, of the grizzly bear, I discovered a grizzly sitting on a hill slope outside of his den, for it was October and they had already "holed up." I was surprised to find the bear awake so late in the season, but delighted at my opportunity not only of securing meat and a valuable skin but also of seeing the animal's habitation ready for its winter occupancy. After giving an hour or so to a lengthy detour by which I was enabled to approach the animal from behind under cover of the hill in the slope of which his den was located, I found nothing but a few marmot tracks and a small heap of earth upon which the marmot had been sitting an hour before. Such things happen continually.

The main reason for such cases of self-deception is that one sees things under circumstances that give one no idea of the distance, and consequently one has no scale for comparison. The marmot at twenty yards occupies as large a visual angle as a grizzly bear at several hundred, and if you suppose the marmot to be several hundred yards away you naturally take him for a bear. There is, under certain conditions of hazy Arctic light, nothing to give you a measure of the distance, nothing to furnish a scale to determine size by comparison.

After a few days of vain hunts and mirage-chasing, we started west along the coast again, and on October 30th we saw caribou. When we caught sight of the band they were about to disappear behind a hill, and we could not tell exactly what direction they would take. Natkusiak and Akpek therefore went one way and I another to try to head them off. It turned out that I missed the animals, but the Eskimo came up with the band, and in a fusillade of thirty or forty shots at fairly close range they secured two caribou. The poor shooting was no doubt due chiefly to a slight fog which made them overestimate the distance. The animals were really much closer than they appeared; under the impression they were far off, the hunters raised their rifle-sights and consequently shot over. It is the great advantage of such a rifle as the Mannlicher-Schoenaur that it has a comparatively flat trajectory and one does not have to worry so much about judging distances as one has to with an ordinary rifle such as my Eskimo used.

October 31st Oyarayak and his family overtook us, coming from the east. We had been moving slowly, partly with the expectation of Oyarayak's coming, for he had, when we met him before, expressed a desire to accompany us to the Colville, to visit his daughter, who was being brought up by a Colville River family.   November 1st, while our two sleds and Oyarayak's were moving west along the sea ice, I hunted, according to my usual custom, parallel to the coast a few miles inland.   I was looking for caribou or their tracks, but on this day, somewhat to my surprise, I found not what I was looking for but the recent trail of a polar bear instead, leading directly inland. The Eskimo had seen the tracks also on the coast, and I could see through my glasses that they had stopped to consult over them. Clearly this was the trail of a female going inland to hibernate, a thing which the male polar bears never do, so far as I know.   It seemed to me likely that we could overtake the animal if we made pursuit at once, so I hurried down to where the Eskimo were and told them to make camp, while Natkusiak and I with a light sled took the trail.

We followed the trail inland all the rest of that day and all the next.   It had been the opinion of the Eskimo that half a day's journey would surely bring us to where the animal had stopped to dig a hole in some soft bank to spend the winter there; but in this, as in many other opinions about the habits of animals, the Eskimo were wrong. We followed without result the first day and all of the second.   It was bitterly cold and the snow drifted a little, but we should probably not have given up the chase even on the third day except for the complication that arose that morning in finding all of our dogs missing when we emerged from our tent after breakfast.   The probability was that a band of caribou had passed us to windward in the night; the dogs had probably scented them and had gone off on a hunt of their own.   Natkusiak and I accordingly went out in different directions, not so much caribou hunting as dog hunting.   I happened upon a band of caribou, however, of which I secured only one.

There seemed to be no prospect of overtaking the bear, for evidently she had been moving not only in a direct line for the mountains, which were visible to the south from our turning point, but she had never stopped more than a moment at a time and then only to dig up a little moss on which she had been feeding.   We decided, therefore, to load on our sled the meat of the deer killed and start for the coast, which we did even though our best dog had not returned; the rest had straggled home to camp during the day, and one had been following by scent the caribou I killed and had come up to us where we were skinning it.

It took us two days to get back to the coast where we had left our Eskimo in camp. We found only a vacated camp site, however—they had evidently moved on to the west with the intention of reaching Oliktok, where we had cached the meat of eight caribou about a month before. Although we reached the coast only after dark, the trail of our party was plainly to be seen and we followed it, getting to their camp about midnight to find that our lost dog Lindy had preceded us by a few hours. He had evidently been lost and wandering about inland for two days. He was more tired than the dogs that had had the work of hauling our sled, and hungrier, poor fellow. I thought he looked as if he were sorry — not so much sorry, I fancied, that he had missed his meals, but sorry that he had not been there to help us with the heavy loads. I had not the slightest suspicion that he had run away from us to escape from hauling. That was not his way. During the two years we worked together he never shirked a pound in fair or foul weather. He seemed to consider doing his part a privilege as well as a duty. He had come into our service on the Mackenzie River four months before the time of which we are writing, and we were just beginning to know each other. He was an Indian's dog but with a white man's self-respect and stability of character. During the two years that followed we grew closer and closer together. I do not know which of us was fonder of the other. When he came to die I lost my best friend in the world, whom I shall never forget.

The last few miles of our road home from the bear hunt, the evening of November 6th, we had a head wind of about fifteen miles an hour — just enough so the snow was drifting along the ground. Although we had had winter for about two months none of us had suffered a frost bite, but this evening Natkusiak froze his face considerably. It is one of the common superstitions about the North that Eskimo as a class can stand more cold than white men. As a matter of fact the readiness with which a man's face freezes is an individual rather than a racial characteristic. It depends, no doubt, partly at least, on the blood circulation. It happened that although Natkusiak could stand the cold in a general way better than any other member of our party, white or Eskimo, he was always each year the first to freeze his face, and kept freezing it continually all winter. Of course a frozen cheek or nose is no more serious than a sunburn, if you thaw it out with your warm hand promptly so soon as it begins to freeze.

It is curious how many an Arctic explorer has carried with him through lengthy experience in the North superstitions about cold which have grown up among his ancestry in warm climates. One of these superstitions is that when your face or any other part of your body begins to freeze you must thaw it out with an application of snow. Few things could be more absurd. Any high-school pupil could tell us offhand what would happen if liquid air were applied to a man's cheek or nose; of course the part would freeze instantly. The same would be true of the snow of carbon dioxide, and the same is true of the snow of water except, of course, that the freezing will not be so nearly instantaneous.

Nothing I have read in the literature of the Arctic ever impressed me more than the account of one of the famous explorers of half a century ago who tells how he dealt with a frost bite. The story runs substantially as follows: A sledge party was traveling along one day when the commander of a sudden noticed a small spot of white the size of a ten-cent piece upon poor Mr. So-and-So's cheek. With promptness upon which he prides himself in the narrative, he immediately ordered a halt and camp to be pitched, and while the other men of the party were thus occupied the commander rubbed poor Mr. So-and-So's cheek with snow, but "so intense was the cold," he tells us, that before camp was finally pitched the wretched man's entire face was frozen.

Such ignorance of elementary things as this story shows can be justified only by pointing out that a great many other Arctic explorers have known no better. Even in a warm room it would be possible to freeze a man's whole face by rubbing it with snow which was brought in from out-of-doors when the temperature was anything below minus 40° F. The whole secret of dealing with frost bites is to keep your hands warm, and (when the weather is severe) to run your hand over your face every few minutes to see if any part of it be frozen. Usually you can also keep yourself fairly well informed of the condition of your face by continually wrinkling it and "making faces." If a spot of skin on your cheek or chin the size of a twenty-five-cent piece becomes stiff you can always detect it by making a grimace. Then all you have to do is take your warm hand out of your mitten and press it on the frozen spot for a moment until the whiteness and stiffness are gone. In the very coldest of weather our method of taking care of the face is a little different, however. When a man is properly dressed for winter his coat is a loose-fitting one with the sleeves cut so that any time he likes he can pull his arm out of the sleeve and carry his hand on his naked breast inside his coat. The neck of the coat is made loose, and whenever any part of his face refuses to wrinkle up he pushes his hand up through the loose-fitting neck of the coat and presses it for a moment on the stiffened portion of the face. So soon as the frozen spot is thawed out he pulls his hand in upon his breast again. In this way one can walk all day facing a steady breeze at − 35° or − 40° F., which is the worst kind of weather one ever gets in the Arctic, for when the temperature falls to − 50° or below − 50° there is always a dead calm. Apparently the friction of air in motion raises the temperature, for if there be a calm at − 50° and the wind begin to rise, then the temperature rises as the wind rises until at sixty miles an hour the temperature will generally be up to + 10° or + 15° F. at any time of winter. A sixty-mile wind at 0° F. feels colder and does more damage than a fifteen-mile wind at − 30° or a calm at − 50°.

One more thing is essential to keep the face from freezing; it must always be clean shaven. For if you wear a beard the moisture of your breath congeals on it and makes for you a face mask that is separated by an air space of a quarter of an inch or so from the skin of your face. If then you begin to freeze you cannot get at your cheek or chin to thaw it out with the warm palm of your hand, as you could do in a twinkling if your face were smooth shaven. On my first expedition, before I fully realized this fact, I once traveled against a rather warm blizzard all day, and not only my breath froze on my beard but also the snow which struck my face melted and formed ice, until a mask covered my whole face. I tried at first to thaw the ice off with my hands, but I soon saw I had to choose between having my face freeze and having my hands freeze, and of course there is no choice; your hands and feet you must protect at all costs. The result was that when I got into camp in the evening the ice mask I wore must have weighed several pounds. It covered all my face except that I had kept one eye open, allowing the other to freeze over. A day or two later the skin began to peel off all the way from above my eyebrows to my "Adam's apple." The weather had not been very cold and the freezing proved to be only skin deep, but had I been smooth shaven my face would probably not have frozen at all. On another occasion when I got lost alone, and had to build a snow house (without a fire) in which to sleep overnight, my beard had frozen so solidly to the hood of my coat that it took me several hours of thawing away with my hands after I got into camp before I could pull my coat off, with the result that there thawed on me and made me soaking wet some snow which had blown in between my outer and inner coat through a rent in the outer one, and which I could have shaken out in a moment had I been able to pull the outer coat off. But it would not come off — my beard and the lining of the hood were welded by a mass of ice.

The most elementary thing, then, to keep your face from freezing, is to keep it smooth shaven. A face mask of skin or cloth is of no avail. It protects you for half an hour or so in the morning, but then ice forms upon it, and no matter what the material may be to begin with, the mask becomes an ice mask and gives you no further comfort. By actual trial I have found also that the hood you wear should not come close around the face. The typical Eskimo hood merely covers the ears and leaves the whole forward half of the head unprotected. The first improvement that a white man usually tries to make on Eskimo clothing is that of having the hood come farther forward so as to "fit snug about the face" and leave but a small part of it exposed. The result is that if the hood comes out to the cheek bones and to the point of the chin, a circle of hoarfrost forms on the face along the edge of the trimming of the hood, and presently the skin under the hoarfrost ring freezes. On the other hand, if the face is completely bare there is a sufficient distance between the nose and mouth on one side and the trimming of the coat on the other so that the breath in very cold weather freezes before it reaches the trimming of the coat and settles upon it in the form of snow which can be brushed off, rather than in the form of ice, as when the trimming is only an inch or two from one's mouth.   Every few minutes, then, with your mitten you brush the snow from your hood trimming and keep your face free of ice, giving your warm hand opportunity to thaw out any frost bite that may appear.

The Eskimo, although physically no better fitted for withstanding cold than we, know so much better than most of us how to deal with cold that they give the uninitiated the impression of greater hardihood, but a white man who keeps his eyes open soon acquires all the winter lore that is of great value and becomes quite the equal of the Eskimo in taking care of himself.   There is no art in keeping your hands and feet from freezing — it is merely a matter of dress.   The foot-wear is the more important, for if your mittens are cold you can take them off entirely, pull your arms inside your coat and thus keep warm, unless, of course, you have some work with the hands to do, in which case the hands will have to be exposed, with or without mittens as the circumstances dictate.   The Eskimo foot-gear consists of a caribou skin sock with the fur turned in, and a caribou skin boot with the fur of the sole turned in also and the fur of the leg turned either in or out.   This makes ideal foot-wear not only in the matter of warmth but also in lightness and comfort.   On such little jaunts as the bear hunt we have just described one may freeze chin or cheek or nose, but — barring accident — there is no danger to other parts of the body.

CHAPTER VI

NOVEMBER 9th we arrived at an Eskimo village of five houses near where the Itkillik River empties into the head of the Colville delta. Most of the people belonged to one or another of the Colville River tribes, but a few of them hailed from across the mountains in the Kuvuk and Noatak valleys and elsewhere. Their houses were of the typical inland Eskimo type — a dome-shaped frame, of stout willows covered with moss and earth to a thickness of six or eight inches, with doors about three feet high in the wall, closed with flaps of bearskin or heavy caribou hides. Most of these people had sheet-iron stoves which they had bought from the Point Barrow Eskimo, about whose trading operations we have already spoken, but some of them had open fires built on the center of the floor, with holes in the roof which served the purposes alternately of a chimney and a window. When the fire was going these openings in the roof were kept uncovered, and when the fire was extinguished they would be covered with transparent membranes made in some cases of the thin skins of summer-killed caribou or of fresh-water codfish, after the manner of the inland dwellers; in other cases the windows had been purchased from the Point Barrow Eskimo and were made of the intestines of bearded seals or walrus according to the custom of the coast. These people had made the summer caribou hunt inland and had killed a large number of caribou but had made no use whatever of the meat. One man, who six weeks before we saw him had killed about one hundred and twenty-five caribou, was now living on fish entirely and had only a few days' provisions ahead, for the caribou had been killed a long way from where he intended to winter and he had taken only the skins as he could not haul the meat home. This camping ground, which a dozen families had selected for their winter home, was at a fairly good fishing place and every one was catching

CAMP ON SEA ICE WHEN OPEN LEAD PREVENTED GETTING ASHORE.

CAMP IN WOODS OF HORTON RIVER.

enough to eat for the time being. Still, it was a foregone conclusion that they would starve more or less before spring.

Although white men do not frequent the Colville district, most of these Eskimo were familiar with the ways of white men and all of those who were full grown had seen white men once or oftener. But many of the children had never seen a white man until they saw me, even those who were thirteen or fourteen years of age. Nevertheless they were all Christians and had been for several years. Christianity had come to them, spreading up the Kuvuk and Noatak rivers from Kotzebue Sound, where it had been started by Moravian missionaries. When we came to the village we were invited, according to Eskimo custom, to come in and have something to eat, but contrary to Eskimo custom a wash dish and towel were placed before us, and after the water had been blessed with a lengthy prayer we were directed to wash our hands and faces. My Eskimo did as they were told, and after the washing was over the water in the bowl was again blessed before it was spilled out. A lengthy grace was then said over the food and a separate grace over the tea which came after. Finally at the end of the meal thanks were returned. All of this was of course in Eskimo. When the ceremonies were over we were asked whence we came; and when it turned out that my Eskimo had been to Herschel Island, where there was known to be a missionary, the local people inquired eagerly whether we had brought any new prayers with us. Natkusiak, who was at that time scarcely a Christian as yet, although since then he has become exceedingly devout, did not know any prayers, but Akpek knew a great many. For that reason Natkusiak was from the beginning treated with little consideration by the community, while Akpek gained their highest respect at once and retained it to the end. During our entire stay he was much sought after and continually invited around to the various houses to eat and to teach the community new prayers.

What the people especially wanted, they told us, was a new prayer for caribou. Three years before, they said, they had obtained an excellent prayer for caribou from Kotzebue Sound. It had worked so well for the first two years that they had secured plenty of caribou through the use of it, not only during the summer season when the skins are good for clothing, but also (so efficient was the prayer)

G

during the winter, when under ordinary circumstances they would not have been able to get any. But this year the prayer did not seem to be working so well. They supposed that white men's prayers, like their rifles and other things, no doubt deteriorated with age, and now they were anxious to secure a new and more efficient prayer. Akpek told them that he had a very good one, and he at once proceeded to teach it to them. I refrained from much comment on all these things for I had come to the country to learn rather than to teach, but it was difficult for me to restrain myself from pointing out to our hosts that unless they had better success with this prayer than Akpek himself had had with it during the time he had been in our service, they would probably find it a weak reed to lean upon in time of emergency.

The most prominent man of the village, Panniulak, had a large package of pictures concerning which he wanted my opinion. Most of them had evidently been clipped out of cheap American magazines and embraced subjects of all sorts. A considerable number were sacred pictures from the Old Masters, but not a few were pictures of actors and actresses of all nationalities. Panniulak said to me he understood fully that all the pictures where there was a circle around the head were pictures of Good Dead Men (which was his name for a saint). He knew further that some of those that did not wear a halo were Good Dead Men also, and he wanted my opinion on certain pictures as to whether they did or did not belong to this class. The first picture he inquired about with reference to the sainthood of the original happened to be one of Anna Held, and after her came Hall Caine and Joan of Arc. It was an interested circle that watched me classify the pictures into two packages, on the basis of my idea of the comparative sanctity of the subject of each.

Although Point Barrow is the nearest place from the Colville River at which there is a missionary station, very little of the Colville River Christianity comes from there. The reverse is in fact true, for Dr. Marsh, the missionary at Point Barrow, has told me that each fall when the Point Barrow natives return from the Colville they bring with them to Point Barrow a varied assortment of new prayers and some of the most astounding beliefs. Most of these seem to come across the mountains from Kotzebue Sound, although no doubt they undergo considerable metamorphosis on the way over.

It seems that in Kotzebue Sound the fishing is chiefly done with nets. The missionary, in teaching his flock to keep the Sabbath holy, has prohibited the use of nets on Sunday, saying nothing about other methods of fishing, for he found no others in use. The news of this prohibition spread not only northwest along the coast to Point Hope and thence to Point Barrow, but also northeast up the Kuvuk and Noatak rivers and across the mountains to the Colville, where we were trying to lay up a winter store of fish, chiefly by netting but also by the use of the hook, which we found a less productive as well as a more laborious method. When the commandment reached us it appeared in the form: "God has said, you shall not use fish nets on Sunday" (the implication being, of course, that if you did you would be liable to eternal damnation). Being good Christians and anxious to do nothing which could possibly endanger their eternal welfare, the Colville River natives accordingly pulled their fish nets out of the water on Saturday night, fished with hooks all day Sunday, and put their nets back on Monday morning.

It soon became evident to me that we could not stay long in the Colville district on account of the insufficiency of the food supply. Two families who were living there had commenced fishing in the summer-time and had laid up several tons of fish, but against these two families were a dozen others who had been hunting caribou for their skins all summer and accordingly had nothing of their own to eat. They had, however, according to the communistic ways of the country, been gladly received by the provident families and had turned to with a will to make short work of their fish piles. Clearly this was not a place in which we would do well to tarry long. Akpek and his wife, however, wanted to stay, and I was glad they did. I wanted a chance to get away from them, for I thought they might make some attempt to take care of themselves if they did not have Natkusiak and me to look out for them. Accordingly, after staying a few days and taking a series of physical measurements of all the people and finding out whatever I could about them in that short time, Natkusiak and I, with one sled, proceeded west along the coast to Point Barrow. We were accompanied by one Colville River family who, like us, felt sure that starvation was not far distant and wanted to get away in good time. This family had a considerable supply of fish which they gave to those whom we left behind.

Our journey was without incident until we came to Cape Halkett, where Captain Mogg's *Olga* was frozen in three or four miles offshore. Captain Mogg had given me certain things when I was aboard of him two months before and we accordingly went out to the ship to get them. We expected to find it deserted, but much to our surprise we saw fresh tracks of men all around the ship and aboard it we discovered Leighton, a colored man who had been Captain Mogg's first mate. It turned out that when Captain Mogg and his crew had left the ship Leighton had considered himself insufficiently clad for the journey to Point Barrow and had refused to leave, or rather had started off with Captain Mogg and his party, had dropped behind gradually, and without Captain Mogg's noting it had returned to the ship. Captain Mogg, knowing that there were plenty of provisions on board, had not concerned himself further about the man and had kept on to Point Barrow, and Leighton had been alone for two months. I offered to take him along with us the eighty miles or so to Point Barrow where he would find housing and plenty of food and company. He preferred to remain with the ship, however, so we put in a day with our dog teams hauling him drift-wood from the shore to his ship. He had been almost out of fuel when we came and would have found it very hard work to haul it without the aid of dogs upon the crude hand-sled which he had made.

From Cape Halkett we proceeded to Smith Bay, where we found our cache and our boats in good order. Here we were struck by such a terrific southwester that for three days we camped right beside the cache, living on short rations within fifty feet of an abundance of food, for the wind was blowing so hard that we did not dare to open the cache for fear of the lighter articles being carried away by the wind, were we to remove the tarpaulin which was lashed down over our pile of goods.

November 28th, after the storm had abated and we had been able to get at our stores, we set out from our cache toward Point Barrow, and on December 1st we arrived aboard the schooner *Challenge*, Captain Pedersen's ship. She was wintering inside the Point Barrow lagoon about three miles east of Point Barrow proper. The next day we proceeded eight miles southwest to Tom Gordon's house and the day after that to Cape Smythe village, where we stayed the following two months as the guests of Mr. Brower.

Mr. Brower, although he lives far from civilization, lives well. The Cape Smythe Whaling & Trading Company have, besides numerous storehouses, a commodious and substantial building known as the "station," which contains not only their workshops where boats, sleds, and other needed articles are made and repaired, but also living rooms, of which Mr. Jack Hadley and myself were the sole occupants, and a well-equipped kitchen, presided over by a man who is the master of his profession. Mr. Morgan had once, he told us frequently (and his cooking bore him out), been a chef on one of the Fall River steamers. But it was not so much the excellence of the table and the comfort of the house that made Cape Smythe attractive, but rather the quality of the few white men and women who were gathered there together. My time was spent not only pleasantly but profitably. I was as yet but a beginner in Eskimo linguistics, and received considerable help both from Mr. Brower, who is the one whaleman I have ever known who has command of real Eskimo speech, and from Dr. Marsh, who speaks the Point Barrow dialect with readiness. Mr. and Mrs. Hawkesworth, at the government school, also took the greatest interest in my work and put their house completely at my disposal. Miss Annie Koodlalook, who had acquired perfect command of English in her nine years of residence in the United States, still retained a fair knowledge of her mother tongue and was therefore able to be of the greatest service to me as an assistant in recording folk-lore.

During these two months, therefore, I wrote down a vocabulary of over nine thousand words of the Point Barrow dialect, compiled originally by Dr. Marsh and by Mr. Spriggs, who had been at Point Barrow for several years but who had left before I came there. This vocabulary was now revised to some extent by myself, with the assistance of Dr. Marsh. I also wrote down several hundred thousand words of Eskimo folk-lore in English translation. This was the last folk-lore I recorded in English, for thereafter my greater command of Eskimo enabled me to record directly in the original dialects of the narrators each tale as it was told me; so that while the folk-lore gathered at Point Barrow is of interest only as folk-lore, that gathered in the three following years has its linguistic value also.

The week between Christmas and New Year's Dr. Marsh, in his capacity as government physician, made a trip southwest along the coast two hundred or so miles to Icy Cape, and I accompanied him as his guest about two thirds of the way through to Wainwright Inlet, where I spent a few days visiting my old schoolmate, J. E. Sinclair, who with his wife was staying at Wainwright Inlet as government school teacher. When Dr. Marsh came back from Icy Cape I returned with him to Point Barrow. This trip is a very simple one to make, for Eskimo houses are scattered along the beach every twenty miles or so, which makes travel almost as commonplace there as it is in the mining districts of Alaska, where one can count on reaching a "road-house" every night.

The fuel problem has, of recent years, become a difficult one everywhere in the vicinity of Point Barrow. Up to thirty or so years ago the beach was thickly strewn with drift-wood, for the Eskimo used only oil for heating, cooking, and lighting purposes, and whenever a stick of wood was thrown on the beach it remained there until it decayed, which in the cold North is a matter of centuries. The houses the people lived in then were of such a type that not much fuel was needed in order to keep them warm. They were not underground dwellings, but the wooden frames of which they consisted were covered with earth to such a thickness that the houses were practically cold-proof. These houses were entered through a long alleyway by a door that was never closed all winter, and the ventilating hole in the roof was always open, so that a current of air circulated through the house at all times. For this kind of a house two or three seal-oil lamps were abundantly sufficient to keep the temperature uniformly at from 60° to 70° Fahrenheit the twenty-four hours through, and the winter through. With the white men of the last half century there came to the Arctic the white men's lofty and commodious frame dwellings. Although these are thoroughly ill-adapted to the country they soon became the fashion, and the Eskimo began to build their poor hovels in the best imitation they could make of the pretentious homes of the foreigners. The flimsy walls of these new dwellings admitted cold by conduction so that the seal-oil lamps were no longer sufficient for keeping them warm, and even the sheet-iron stoves in which drift-wood could be burned had difficulty in keeping them at a comfortable temperature. Drift-wood lay in apparently inexhaustible windrows along the seashore, but these were the accumulations of centuries, which the Eskimo, having no use for wood as fuel, had allowed to grow. Now, instead of being used as formerly only in the construction of the house frames and in the making of sleds and implements, the drift-wood was used for fuel in an attempt to keep the flimsy new-style houses warm. The result was that the drift-wood disappeared so rapidly that in thirty years, by the use of stoves, all of it is gone, from Point Hope to thirty miles east of Point Barrow. With the increasing scarcity of fuel the ventilation of the houses had to be curtailed gradually, so that the modern Eskimo house is practically hermetically sealed against fresh air. If there is a key-hole in the door you will find it stuffed with chewing gum.

Not only is the fuel problem serious from an economic point of view, it is even more serious as a question of sanitation. Although a few of the Eskimo are able to import coal from Seattle, and others can get it through difficult labor from the coal mine at Wainwright Inlet, the majority have not the means to secure fuel of any sort sufficient to keep the new-style houses warm. Instead of the comfortable, well-ventilated, and therefore healthful dwellings of a few years ago, we now have hoarfrost-coated and unventilated frame houses which look well in photographs to those used to frame houses in temperate climates, but which are among the chief causes of the high death rate among the Eskimo, through their encouragement of pulmonary consumption and other diseases that flourish in filth and foul air.

At the same time that Dr. Marsh and I went southwest to Icy Cape, there also went from Point Barrow something like fifteen or twenty Eskimo sleds to a native dance at Icy Cape. The white men call it a "dance," but really it is the most northeasterly variant of the British Columbian "potlatch." Formal invitations had been sent by certain men at Icy Cape to certain men at Point Barrow to visit them. These invitations had included a statement of what sort of present the host expected to receive from his guest on his arrival. The messengers from Icy Cape when they returned home from Point Barrow carried in turn not only the acceptances or regrets of the people who had been invited, but in case of acceptances they carried also an intimation of what sort of present the visitors would expect in return for the presents which their hosts demanded. I did not see the dance at Icy Cape, but have seen a number of similar ones and the procedure is always the same. The visitors camped a few miles before reaching the Icy Cape village and a messenger was sent ahead in the evening to announce their coming. Several young men then came from Icy Cape to the camp of the visitors, and the following morning when everything was ready, these and a few of the young men from among the visitors ran a race back to Icy Cape. Each man who runs a race does it not for himself but as the representative of some prominent man who is going to take part in the ceremonies. Each racer as he arrives in the village goes to the dance-house, where he is met by the wife of his master, or other woman of his household, who brings him a warm drink of water and something to eat. Later on, the main body of visitors arrive and either pitch their own camps or move into the houses of their friends in the village.

That evening the dance begins. A local man will dance first, singing songs, recounting his own achievements and telling whatever is in his mind to tell. Following this his wife or some one of his household hands him the articles which he intends to present to his guest. When the presentation is over the guest arises, and in some cases dances and sings in the manner of his host, but in others merely makes a brief speech and hands over the articles with which he pays for the present he has received. Sometimes the initial presents, or else the counter presents that pay for them, are not material, but apparently one of them must be, for I never saw a pledge of supernatural assistance paid for in kind. At one of these dances at Point Barrow I have seen a man give two cross fox skins to an old "medicine man" in return for the promise that the shaman would see to it that he got two whales the following whaling season. Incidentally it may be stated here that the man who gave the two fox skins really did get the two whales which were promised in return for them. This somewhat strengthened at Point Barrow the general opinion that while Christian prayers are very good in ordinary things, the old-fashioned whaling charms are much more effective when it comes to catching whales.

At such a dance or potlatch as this one at Icy Cape the visitors usually remain for several days, although the ceremony of exchanging presents is commonly accomplished within twenty-four hours after the arrival of the party. There is a good deal of feasting, singing, dancing, and story-telling, and every one has a good time.

On this trip of ours to Wainwright Inlet and Icy Cape we kept getting new sidelights on the forms the new religion is taking in northern Alaska. One of the first things that an Eskimo learns when he becomes Christian is the importance of refraining from work on Sunday. In general the Eskimo's own religion consists mainly in a series of prohibitions or taboos, and the prohibitions of Christianity are therefore, of all the new teachings, the things he most readily understands. Under the old religion it used to be believed that sickness, famine, and death were caused by such trivial things as the breaking of a marrow bone with the wrong kind of hammer, or the sewing of deerskin clothing before enough days had elapsed from the killing of the last whale or walrus. To avoid breaking these taboos meant prosperity and good health, and the gaining of all the rewards (or rather the escape from all the penalties) provided for by that system of religion. Similarly, now that they know about salvation and damnation it seems but logical to them that one may be gained and the other avoided by the mere observance of such simple prohibitions as that against working on Sunday.

Dr. Marsh, who is a man of university education and of broad views in religious matters, often tried to explain to his congregation at Point Barrow that while the keeping of the Sabbath was in general an estimable thing, there were certain circumstances under which it was not called for, nor even desirable. To try to make clear this idea he preached again and again from the text of how Our Lord gathered the ears of corn on the Sabbath, but failed completely in getting them to see the matter from his point of view. I suggested to Dr. Marsh, therefore, that possibly his own example would do more good than his preaching in showing the Eskimo how Sunday might safely be treated. Accordingly, in order to give the people an example, we traveled on two occasions upon Sunday. But the example availed nothing except further to lose Dr. Marsh his standing in the community. I heard many comments, most of which were to the effect that if Dr. Marsh was willing to endanger his temporal and eternal welfare, they nevertheless were not. They knew of old how dangerous it was to break taboos; they could see now that undoubtedly many of the past misfortunes and accidents of their people were no doubt due to the fact that they had broken the Sabbath taboo before they knew of its existence. Now that they knew it, no man who took thought of his own interests or those of the community would break the taboo. Possibly Dr. Marsh and I had some charm by which we could evade the effect of our transgression, but the punishment would surely fall on some one.

It has been true in Greenland, and wherever Christianity has long had root among the Eskimo, that it has taken upon itself developments such as those just indicated, which are strange to our European ideas, and which the European missionaries are entirely powerless to check. So it was with Dr. Marsh at Point Barrow. He tried to combat certain doctrines, which to his mind were narrow-minded and which were certainly of local growth, with the result that his own congregation judged him a man who was opposed to the Kingdom of God and one whom they did not desire to have as a missionary. The case is interesting, and although the ending of it does not fall at this point of our narrative chronologically, it may be as well to take it up here, seeing that I, in a measure, deserve the blame for urging Dr. Marsh into a conflict in which I might have known he was sure to be defeated.

Some of Dr. Marsh's more serious difficulties with his flock grew out of matters pertaining to whaling. The whaling season at Point Barrow in the spring is about six weeks long, beginning generally the first of May. At that time northeasterly winds usually blow, with the result that a lead opens up, commonly somewhere between a half and five miles offshore. This lead may be anything from a few yards to several hundred yards in width, and extends southwest along the coast to Bering Straits, forming a path of open water along which the whales come in the spring on their annual migration from the Pacific to the Beaufort Sea. Whether the land-floe be half a mile or five miles wide, the whalemen must go to the outer edge of it with their boats and whaling gear and wait there for the coming of the whales. There is no regularity about the migration of the animals, and often at the height of the whaling season the crews may be encamped for a week at a time without seeing any; and then, all in one day, scores of whales may come along and pass on to the eastward. This day of opportunity is, according to our modern way of thinking, as likely as not to be a Sunday. When the Eskimo learned that God had forbidden work upon the Sabbath they took the point of view that it does not profit a man that he gain the whole world if he lose his own soul, and although the catching of whales was the one thing in the world which all of them most desired, nevertheless they agreed that the loss of one's soul was too great a price to pay for even a bow-head whale. Accordingly they would commence on Saturday afternoon to pull back their boats from the edge of the ice and get everything ready for the Sabbath observance. Saturday evening the men themselves would abandon temporarily their boats and gear, on the outer edge of the shore ice, to go ashore and remain there all day Sunday. It usually took them half of Monday to get everything ready for work again. In this manner they lost two days out of every seven from a harvest season of only six weeks in the year.

It was in vain that Dr. Marsh expostulated with the people, and pointed out that not only were they losing the chance of getting whales but that they also ran a serious risk of losing their boats and whaling gear in case a strong northeaster should happen to blow up while they were ashore. This would carry all of their belongings out to sea in the break-up of the ice that was sure to occur under a strong offshore wind. "But can't you see to it," they asked him, "that the whales do not come on Sunday and that a northeaster does not blow too hard while we are away from our boats? God controls the winds and the movements of the whales; can't you ask Him to have the whales come on week days only, and can't you ask Him to keep our boats and gear safe?" Dr. Marsh explained to them that, according to his view, the Lord governed the earth by certain laws with the operation of which he was not likely to interfere even in response to the most heartfelt prayers. He explained further in the most modern way the subjective efficacy of prayer and how, if they prayed rightly and sincerely, a balm would descend upon their souls and make them stronger and better men. But they did not want a balm — they wanted a change of wind, and they began to mutter among themselves that this was a fine sort of missionary to have, who was unable to control the winds and help them in whaling. They reminded themselves how their own medicine men had been able not only to control the comings and goings of the whales, but had even been able to make the whales willing to be killed. They also inquired from their countrymen in other districts, who reported that the missionaries whom they had assured them that, if they prayed to God in the right way, He would do for them whatever they asked Him. That was the kind of missionary to have, and why could not they, too, have such a missionary? And so they formulated charges, which were written down by the scholars among them and forwarded to the Board of Home Missions of the Presbyterian Church, in New York. There were a good many counts in the charges, but the ones of the greatest importance to the Eskimo mind were these: that Dr. Marsh encourages Sabbath-breaking; that Dr. Marsh teaches that prayers are of no avail; and that Dr. Marsh encourages immodesty by taking off his coat in the Eskimo houses.

With reference to the last charge it may be said that it was the Eskimo custom for men and women, whenever they entered their superheated dwellings, to take off their coats and sit naked to the waist, while children were commonly allowed to go entirely naked up to the age of six years. The fact that the human form is essentially vile and must be kept from sight was not known to the primitive Eskimo, but was accepted unquestioningly by them, along with the other truths of Christianity, so soon as they heard of it.

When a missionary or any one connected with the church tells the Eskimo anything, they always take it as coming directly from God, or else as a downright falsehood. It had been so with the shamans before the missionaries — the good and honorable ones spoke the simple truth as they received it from the spirits; the bad shamans were merely liars, who pretended to represent the spirits but did not. The missionary, who in the mind of the Eskimo is a new and in certain ways a superior kind of shaman, does not, therefore, speak as a private individual; he is in their eyes but the mouth-piece of the Lord. When some missionary somewhere in Alaska had said that sitting stripped to the waist was wrong, the Eskimo had understood it as one of the things which if done would lead to dam-nation. When Dr. Marsh had failed to fall in with this view, but on the other hand considered taking off his coat the only sensible thing to do in the overheated houses, they believed him in error either through malice or lack of knowledge of the taboo in question, and considered he was encouraging a practice that endangered the eternal welfare of those who might follow it.

I have no information at hand to indicate why the Board of Home Missions in New York dismissed Dr. Marsh from his post at Point Barrow, as they eventually did the summer of 1912. But I do know why his congregation thought him dismissed. The Eskimo at Point Barrow consider that it was done on the basis of the complaints which they themselves had sent to the Mission Board, the vital points of which, to their minds, are the three cited above; and I do know that they expressed great satisfaction in securing a missionary, in 1912, who believed with them that prayers would have a material and immediate answer of the sort they desired.

But while the Point Barrow Eskimo rejoiced that they were getting a missionary with more orthodox views and whose influence with the Lord was more immediate and effective than that of Dr. Marsh, they also realized their loss in being compelled, in the future, to go without his constant medical care as a doctor. There was many a chronic invalid at Point Barrow whom I saw him visit every day for months on end, and many a woman whose life he had saved at childbirth. Especially when the day of his leaving had come, when they saw their minister's family packing up their things in preparation for departure, this aspect of the case began to strike the people more forcibly, and on that day (when I was about to take the revenue cutter at Point Barrow in 1912) a number of them came to me saying that they were the ones who had signed the complaint against Dr. Marsh and that they were now sorry they had done it. They wanted me to inter-cede with the captain of the revenue cutter, whom they supposed all-powerful, to get him to permit Dr. Marsh to stay after all. Of course I had to tell them that the revenue cutter had nothing to do with it — that Dr. Marsh was going, never to return, and that they would now have to depend upon the efficacy of prayer for the cure of their ailments as well as for the success of their whaling.

After Dr. Marsh's return and mine from our journey southwest, I remained at Cape Smythe another six weeks, chiefly engaged in the recording of folk-lore. On March 6th Natkusiak and I finally set out eastward hoping to connect with Dr. Anderson; for I considered he would by now have had plenty time to get his mountain sheep and caribou specimens in the Endicott Mountains south of Barter Island and would probably have returned to the coast where I could find him, and where we could begin to get ready for our eastward journey of the coming summer. The first lap of the journey was a short one, for we went only twelve miles to Captain Pedersen's *Challenge*. Mr. and Mrs. Hawkesworth and Miss Koodlalook accompanied us that far with their own dog team, but returned the same evening. The *Challenge* was lying only about three miles east of the Point Barrow village, and I stayed there a day with the idea of purchasing some dog feed from the Eskimo. Captain Pedersen and I went to the village with my sled, and as he had plenty of trade goods on the ship he expected to buy the dog meat for me, but it turned out that I could get all I wanted for nothing. Gratitude for services or gifts is practically unknown among the younger generation of the Alaskan Eskimo, but it was not so formerly, and, as I now found out, there are a few men still left at Point Barrow whose ideas in such matters are still those of their ancestors.

During the preceding September, when Storkerson and I were on our way east with our two boats loaded with provisions, we had met the boat of the Point Barrow Eskimo, Akowak, on one of the barren sandspits where they were detained by a head wind and were out of provisions, and I had given them a sack of flour and a few other things. When Akowak now learned that I was wanting seal meat for my dogs he at once sent me word that he would see to it that I got as much for nothing as I cared to haul. He himself gave me a whole seal, and several other people in the village sent me presents of meat, saying that certain relatives of theirs had been hungry in Akowak's boat at the time I gave them the flour and that they also wanted to show their appreciation. Such incidents are, in my experience, typical only of the men of the older generation, whose characters were thoroughly formed under the system of their own people before civilization had wrought the distressing changes which are now everywhere apparent. In this my experience does not differ from that of any white man whom I know whose experience with the Eskimo is sufficient to entitle him to an opinion.

On March 10th we finally left the *Challenge*, going east, and on March 13th we reached the Eskimo houses at the fishing lake near the southeast corner of Smith Bay. Here we were storm-bound for four days, together with an Eskimo family who were going in a different direction and who had arrived here a day or two before us. This couple brought to mind a story which I must now go back a few weeks to narrate.

Early one Saturday afternoon about Christmas time a man and his wife arrived at Cape Smythe with a few caribou skins to sell. The word that they had skins for sale and sinew passed around quickly, and I heard of it the same day because my Eskimo, Natkusiak, came and asked me whether I wanted to buy any of the skins. The couple reported that they had been spending the autumn on the upper Colville River, that game had become scarce there, and that they had struck across country, a distance of perhaps two hundred miles, toward Cape Smythe. This was the substance of all they told until about midnight of the day of their arrival, when they added the further detail that on the Colville with them had been another Eskimo family, the woman of which was the sister of the man who had arrived at Cape Smythe. The two families with their two dog-sleds had left the Colville together, but the man now at Cape Smythe had had his sled loaded with caribou meat and the other family had none. With great magnanimity the man who had the meat fed his sister and her husband, but would not give their dogs anything to eat, although he fed his own dogs well. The result was that the dogs of the second couple got weak with hunger and finally froze to death. When the dogs were all dead the second family were no longer able to keep up, and so were left behind about forty miles east of Cape Smythe.

When the Cape Smythe people heard this story they immediately set about organizing a search party and were about to start off when somebody pointed out that it was now already Sunday (for Sunday, according to Cape Smythe opinion, begins at twelve o'clock Saturday night). When those about to start on the search for the abandoned couple realized it was Sunday they saw at once that nothing could be done, for no work must be done on the Sabbath, and especially no journey must be started on the Sabbath day.

Curiously enough, although all the white men at Cape Smythe had heard at noon on Saturday the story of the arrival of the couple with the skins to sell, none of us happened to hear until late Sunday evening the story of the other couple who had been left to starve thirty or forty miles to the east of us. We found out later that the case had been the subject of continuous conversation among the Eskimo for the last twenty-four hours, but for some strange reason none of us happened to hear of it. Dr. Marsh conducted his Sunday evening service that night in the ordinary way, but when it was over he was surprised to find that the people, instead of going home at once as they commonly did on Sunday nights, all lingered about the church. When he asked them what they were waiting for they told him they were waiting for Sunday to be over, so they could start out to the rescue of a man and his wife who were starving and probably freezing to death. As soon as Dr. Marsh realized the facts he did everything possible to get the search party started, but it was already after midnight and the Sabbath well over when they finally got off.

In following the trail eastward they found evidences to show that the couple who had arrived at Cape Smythe had been traveling with great speed, taking turns sitting on the sled while the other ran ahead of the dogs. In other words, had they so desired they could very easily have brought home the other couple instead of abandoning them, for both they and their dogs had evidently been in full strength.

A blizzard came up on Monday morning before the searching party had got far enough east to discover the place where the couple had been abandoned. The Sunday which they had wasted in inactivity had been a day of excellent weather, but that was all changed now, for the snow was drifting so thick that the searchers were unable to find the abandoned couple and returned empty-handed on the second day. But the same morning on which the searchers returned empty-handed to Cape Smythe, Mr. Thomas Gordon, who lives three miles north of the Cape, heard a faint noise outside his door. He took it for the noise made by the scratching of a dog, but a few minutes later when the door was accidentally opened by some member of the household they found outside it an unconscious man. When the warmth of the house had restored him it turned out that he was the man of the couple who had been abandoned. He had barely had the strength to drag himself to Mr. Gordon's house and had collapsed two or three times within the last two hundred or three hundred yards before reaching it. Mr. Gordon at once sent out a search party, who followed the man's trail through the snow and found his wife, with her hands and feet slightly frozen, in a fireless camp a few miles to the east.

During the next few weeks I often saw the abandoned man and his wife, but the couple who abandoned them I now met here in Smith Bay for the first time. When we took our meal together on the first evening I noticed that this man was the one who took it upon himself to say grace, and as the circumstance interested me I inquired carefully of him about his religious views and how long he had been a Christian. He had been a Christian for about ten years, he said, and knew more prayers than any other Eskimo and was very particular not to break any of the commandments of the Lord. For many years he had done no work on Sunday; for many years he had never eaten a meal without saying grace; and in every other way he lived according to the law as he understood it. I asked him whether he had never heard that such things as leaving his sister to starve to death were also against the law of the Lord. He replied that he never had heard anything about that. His Christianity, he told me with evident regret, might not be the best and most up-to-date kind, for he had never himself had the chance to get any first-hand from a missionary. He had learned his Christianity entirely from the converted Eskimo of the Kuvuk River, who, he said, might not be well informed about all the prohibitions necessary for salvation.

It may be worth a passing note that the abandoned family were also Christians. During the several weeks that they were being nursed back to health by Mr. and Mrs. Gordon they noticed Mr. Gordon never said grace at meals, and they many times expressed to my Eskimo companion, Natkusiak, their strong abhorrence of

H

their host's irreverent ways. After they finally left his house and
began to live with some Eskimo relatives in the Cape Smythe village
I questioned them as to what they thought of Mr. Gordon and got
some frank criticisms, but no expression of gratitude. The following spring when Mr. Gordon needed some help in whaling he asked
this man to work for him, but he preferred to work for some one
else at the same salary offered by Mr. Gordon.

We were not in any hurry to leave this Smith Bay fishing place,
for I was learning many interesting things from the Colville River
Eskimo with whom we were camping, so it was not until March
17th that we finally started. As Leighton had been removed some
time before from the *Olga*, there was no one for us to visit at
Cape Halkett, and neither did we care to go out of our way in the
Colville delta to look for our former employee, Akpek, and the rest
of the people whom we had left there in the autumn, for we thought
they had probably moved to other parts before now; and if they were
there we feared they might be so short of food that visitors would
not be particularly welcome. We therefore took the sea route
outside the Colville delta for Oliktok, where we had cached the
meat of the eight caribou killed in October. We found that Akpek
had been there ahead of us, and had eaten up most of the meat.
I had hired him in the fall with the idea that he would hunt for me
and that his wife would sew me clothing; but it turned out that she
made for me, all together, one boot; and as for Akpek, he was present
at the killing of a single caribou while he participated in the eating
of more than a dozen that Natkusiak and I had killed. Both in
the fall, while we had him with us, and later on in the spring after I
allowed him to join us again, we had to look after him and his wife
continually. I was paying Ilavinirk and his wife two hundred
dollars a year, besides furnishing them with tobacco, ammunition,
and other necessities, and Akpek was to have received the same.
When I finally severed connections with the family after looking out
for them for several months, he felt, and so did all the Eskimo of the
country, that I owed him two hundred dollars for having had the
privilege of looking after him for half a year; and if ever I go
back to the Arctic I expect to find that no one has forgotten how I
cheated him out of half his wages, for I did give him about one

hundred dollars' worth of gear to pay for the entertainment of his company. Originally the Eskimo had among themselves nothing corresponding to the institution of service, and although in Arctic Alaska they are now frequently hired by white men, they do not seem to grasp the idea that the pay they get is a return for the work they do. The industrious ones you hire remain industrious, the lazy ones continue lazy, but neither the industrious nor the lazy seem to have any idea that the lazy deserve less pay than the most skillful and tireless workers.

Although we saw recent traces of Akpek at Oliktok he had left there before we arrived. Two days later, near the mouth of the Kuparuk River, we saw several caribou tracks and of a sudden noticed three dark objects moving ahead of us. We were badly in want of meat and both of us eagerly began to study them through our field glasses. Much to our satisfaction we were able to decide that these were two large caribou and a fawn. We took our dogs ashore and tied them up to a log, seized our rifles and ran ahead, only to find when we rounded the next point that our two big caribou had changed into two sleds under sail, for it was blowing steadily from the east, which gave them a fair wind. The fawn had become a man running ahead of the dog teams. This party proved to consist of Kunaluk, who had accompanied Storkerson and me in the fall, and with him were his family, another man, and Akpek's wife. They informed us that they came from the cache just east of the Kuparuk River, where we had stored the meat of three caribou, shot in October. They had just finished eating the last remnant of our meat and were now without food, but were on their way up the Kuparuk River to where they expected Akpek and some other Eskimo would be catching fish in considerable numbers. They inquired how much meat there was left in our cache at Oliktok. After I had truthfully answered that there was still considerable, they did not seem so keen about continuing up the Kuparuk. They said they were going up the river to Akpek's camp, but they said it with far less conviction than they had shown before, and from that time on I had forebodings about the Oliktok cache which were destined to prove themselves justified about a month later. We gave the party about a day's rations of food and advised them strongly to proceed up the

Kuparuk River, suggesting that we ourselves might sometime find use for our own meat at Oliktok if they did not eat it up.

Three days after parting with these Eskimo we arrived at Flaxman Island to find that Dr. Anderson had not yet returned from the mountains. We stayed for a day or two, however, to visit with Captain Wolki of the *Rosie H.* and with Storkerson. When we were on the point of setting out in search of Anderson, a sled arrived with the news that he was due to follow in the course of a day or two. According to report he had been successful in his winter hunt and he and his party had returned to the coast, partly for want of tobacco, and partly also because the time had come which was set by him and me for a meeting at Flaxman Island.

For several days after this I waited impatiently for Anderson to appear and finally set out to look for him. But we did not have to go far, for we met him about eighteen miles east of Flaxman Island. He had been delayed partly by heavy going, for he was hauling big loads of mountain sheep and caribou heads and skins, and partly also by the hospitality of Ned Arey, who for the time being was living at Barter Island.

CHAPTER VII

APRIL 16th we left Flaxman Island again, bound this time for Point Barrow. Dr. Anderson had some work to do at Flaxman Island, and I expected to make a quick trip to Point Barrow and return thence to Smith Bay, by which time Anderson, who would leave Flaxman Island about a week after us, would be able to reach Smith Bay also and meet us there. In my party this time were Ilavinirk and his family. Storkerson also accompanied us, bound for Point Barrow where he intended to try his luck at whaling. We now had daylight the twenty-four hours through, and at first we traveled at night with the idea that the nights were cooler than the days and therefore better suited for travel, and the days better adapted for comfortable camping. We found the nights were too cool, however,—as low as − 35° in some cases; not that this interfered at all with our physical comfort, but hauling sleds is much easier in warm weather than in cold, for the friction of the sled runners against the snow increases as the temperature falls, until at − 50° F. it is almost as if one were sledging on sand. After traveling for two nights and finding the sleds dragged we decided to travel only daytimes thereafter. At noon the bright sun brought the mercury up to fifteen or even twenty degrees above zero, at which temperatures the sled runners glide so easily over the snow that although the dogs incline to laziness in warm weather, this is more than compensated for by the improved going.

On April 22d we reached our meat cache at Oliktok, to find, as we had feared, that Kunaluk's party and Akpek's had been there more than two weeks ahead of us. They had gone at the matter energetically and between them and their dogs they had, about four days before we arrived, so nearly finished our provisions that they were able to load the rest on their sleds and carry it off with them. Akpek had stayed behind, however, and it was only Kunaluk and his son-in-law with their two sleds who were concerned in the direct

101

theft of our provisions, for in that country one does not consider it a theft to merely camp beside a food cache and eat it up.

Besides the meat there had been cached here fifty pounds of rice which belonged to Kunaluk. In the fall I had tried to buy this sack of rice from Mr. Leffingwell, but he felt that he had to give some white men's provisions to poor Kunaluk, who was working for him. I had told Leffingwell that Kunaluk would not appreciate the rice, but of this he had remained unconvinced. I now felt in a measure repaid for the loss of my caribou meat through learning, from Akpek, that Kunaluk had fed the entire fifty pounds of rice to his dogs while he himself and his family lived on my deer meat, which showed precisely how much he thought of the rice that would have been nearly priceless to us. I could now, when I saw him next, tell Leffingwell exactly how much "poor Kunaluk," who "must have some white men's food for a delicacy now and then," valued the delicacy when he had it.

On our journey west along the coast this time we found fewer traces of caribou than ever before and only old ones at that, although Dr. Anderson and Natkusiak, when they came along two weeks later, were able to secure three cow caribou near Oliktok.

When I found Akpek at Oliktok I saw at once that I would have to do something for him, for he was so evidently helpless that to abandon him would have been tantamount to murder. I had tried to shirk the responsibility of looking after him earlier in the winter by leaving him with his relatives on the Colville, but now I saw the only thing to do was to take him to Point Barrow where the laziest and most improvident Eskimo can make a good living. He was not feeling very well and his wife was also sick (or else she played sick very successfully, for she was so exceedingly lazy that one always suspected her motives whenever she had some excuse for not working). But whether she was sick or not we treated her as if she were, and hauled her on our sleds three fourths of the time, while Akpek himself was on the sled about half the time, a thing which delayed us considerably, especially as our dogs were poorly fed and consequently not pulling very hard.

When we finally got to Smith Bay Akpek's troubles were augmented by a severe case of snow-blindness, so we left him and his

A Dead Caribou.

Natkusiak shooting a Sleeping Seal.

family behind at our food cache, telling them they might stay as long as they liked, and then moved on the fifty or so miles to Point Barrow. We could leave them without fear that they would stay to eat all our provision store, for although there were plenty of white men's provisions at our cache there was no fresh meat to be had in Smith Bay, and it does not take an Eskimo long to get thoroughly tired of white men's food. They were sure therefore to follow us as soon as they could to Point Barrow.

April 30th we arrived at Point Barrow to find whaling in full progress. Captain Pedersen was off on the ice and his schooner, the *Challenge*, was deserted except for the colored steward who remained on board as caretaker. A half mile south of the *Challenge* in the same lagoon was another schooner, the *Ivy*, owned by Captain Charles Klinkenberg, to whale with whom Storkerson had come to Point Barrow. Accordingly Storkerson and I parted company there, while I proceeded south to Cape Smythe, to find of course that all the white men were five miles or so away on the sea ice engaged in whaling. Under ordinary circumstances Mr. Brower's house at Point Barrow has been my home whenever I have been there, but it was deserted now, and so I accepted the kind invitation of Mr. and Mrs. Hawkesworth to stay with them at the government school the few days we should remain at Cape Smythe.

On our arrival at Cape Smythe we heard distressing news. The night before we came, there died, under tragic circumstances, one of the most promising young Eskimo women of the village. But this was almost forgotten by every one except her most immediate relatives in the suspense caused by an accident of a few days before. A strong northeasterly wind had suddenly sprung up. The whalemen, both Eskimo and white, were five miles from shore on the edge of the floe and they, together with about four miles of ice, were all carried out to sea, for the ice broke off no more than a mile from the beach. Most of the boats had immediately realized their danger, although it was by no means self-evident, for it is difficult to tell about so huge a mass of ice whether it is in motion or not, if it floats off in one body. Most of the boats had immediately been loaded on the sleds, hauled landward across the four miles of ice, and launched on the landward side before the lead between the now detached ice mass and the land had become too wide for safe crossing. Two of the boats, however, did not come to land, and both of these belonged to Mr. Brower's party; one of them was commanded by an Englishman, Jack Hadley, the other by an Eskimo; the crews of both were entirely Eskimo. By morning, after a few hours of the strong northeasterly wind, all the ice had been driven out of sight, and it was evident that in that state of weather it would be impossible for Mr. Hadley's boats to reach land against the wind. Although the wind blew from the northeast the ocean currents along the shore flowed strongly from the southwest, so that the presumption was that the boats had been carried in a direction that was the resultant of these two forces, or in other words, in a northwesterly direction, away from all land.

As the days lengthened into weeks hope for the return of the boats grew less and less, until by May 16th when we left Cape Smythe Mr. Brower had nearly given up all hope and the Eskimo were mourning their relatives for lost. It was several months after this that we heard the outcome, which was not tragic after all, and which brought out incidentally the interesting scientific fact that the ocean currents which are so steadily and constantly from the southwest at Point Barrow are merely local within a few miles offshore.

When the storm that drove the ice away struck them, Mr. Hadley and his two boats' crews were just engaged in cutting in a large whale. They realized their danger no less than did the other boats, but they did not want to lose the $10,000 worth of whalebone which they had just secured. By the time the bone was all safe in the boat it was too late to attempt getting to shore against the wind, and they merely had to bide their time until a change of wind should make the attempt feasible. They thought, exactly as we did on shore, that the current was sweeping them steadily to the northwest, so they expected to be carried far out beyond all land. They had no sextant or similar instrument with them and were therefore unable to determine their position even when the sun shone brightly, and so, reasoning on the basis of all they knew, they steered southeast from ice cake to ice cake, expecting that if they ever saw land again it would be at Point Barrow, whence they had been carried away.

The party had some ammunition and a rifle and were able to kill both seals and polar bears, but were nevertheless on short rations for several days; but what they suffered from most, and especially the Eskimo, was the want of tobacco, for all of them were tobacco users, the Eskimo from infancy. When they finally saw land, much to the surprise of all of them it turned out to be Cape Lisburne, about four hundred miles southwest of where they expected to be. In other words, when the offshore wind drove the floe on which they were out to sea, they were carried out of the northeasterly current into a southwesterly one, which had, in the course of two weeks, carried them something like four hundred miles to the southwest. As soon as they recognized the land everything was simple, for they knew where the Eskimo villages were and their journey back to Point Barrow was merely a matter of a few days of rowing and sailing.

Shortly before our arrival the spring mail had come, bringing letters from Seattle dated as late as January 24th. The news we got from San Francisco was discouraging news for every one. The price of whalebone, it was said, had fallen, and no whaling vessels were coming up the following season. This meant financial loss and inconvenience to all those engaged in the whaling business, and affected my plans in so far that we were now evidently compelled to rely upon our own resources entirely on going east along the coast, whereas in an ordinary whaling season we might have boarded a whaling vessel at Point Barrow to be carried by her as far east as Cape Bathurst. There was nothing for it then but to commence at once moving our gear east.

The sloop which Mr. Gordon had so kindly lent us the fall before was in the ice in Smith Bay, in considerable danger of being broken up if stormy weather should accompany the spring thaws. One had to take those risks, however, and I engaged an Eskimo to go down and look after the sloop, so far as he could, during the break-up of the ice and to bring her back to Mr. Gordon at Point Barrow as soon as there was open water. Our whale-boat also had to be disposed of. We could not possibly afford to wait in Smith Bay until a thaw should enable us to sail her out, and she was far too heavy for hauling on a sled. The Point Barrow Eskimo, however, value whale-boats very highly, so I took the expedient of trading her off for an Eskimo skin-boat, which was really much more serviceable to us. One of these skin-boats will carry a ton and a half of freight in calm weather, which is more than a whale-boat will carry, and yet they are so light that two men can carry them overland and they can conveniently be hauled on dog sleds any distance. Besides this, the skin-boats (which are made of the hides of six bearded seals, sewed together and stretched over a frame of drift-wood) are much stronger and less liable to accident than the expensive cedar-wood whale-boats, and being flat bottomed they go in shallower water and can be beached anywhere, even in fairly rough surf, in the manner of a dory. They are also the best craft known to me for the navigation of shallow rivers. Their one defect is that you have to dry them every few days to prevent the skin from rotting. This does not necessitate much delay in fine weather, for it merely means unloading the boat and propping it up on edge on the beach alongside the camp overnight; but in damp or rainy weather it becomes almost impossible to dry the boats and they will then go to pieces in one season, whereas a boat properly taken care of and dried every few days will last three or four seasons.

It was evidently going to be slow work to haul eastward the large outfit we had at Smith Bay. The outfit was in fact much larger than I approved of theoretically, but having it I lacked the moral courage for throwing it away. One of our troubles was evidently going to be to secure meat for the dogs to enable us to haul, without consuming it too fast, the flour and other white men's food in our cache. I accordingly borrowed from Dr. Marsh his excellent team of dogs, and with them and my own dogs hauled to Smith Bay about a thousand pounds of whale meat of which Mr. Brower had made me a present from one of the whales he had just killed. This took Ilavinirk and me five days, and it was not until May 16th that we finally left Point Barrow for good, hauling our new skin-boat along with us.

In traveling eastward we soon found that although the skin-boat is light it is so big and takes on so much wind that traveling with it on top of the sled is impracticable in windy weather. It was like towing against the wind a square-rigged ship with all sails set.

This did not cause serious delays, however, as we had to "double-trip" all of our hauling. When it was too windy to haul the boat we could usually occupy our time in sledging forward our provisions and gear.

Dr. Anderson had, according to our expectations, reached our cache on Smith Bay a few days before we got there with the skin-boat from Point Barrow, and had already hauled everything that belonged to us east beyond Pitt Point, where we overtook him May 25th.

The story of our journey eastward for the next two or three weeks is merely a story of hard labor and heavy freighting. We would move our camp and three sled-loads of stuff ahead about eight or ten miles and pitch camp; then it would take us two extra trips to haul the rest of the gear up to the camp; then we would move camp ahead another ten miles and in two more days we would haul the freight up to it again. This meant slow travel. Had I possessed the moral courage to throw away our flour and other provisions and to depend entirely on the country for food, we should have made treble speed and have been much better off in the end. To depend on the country had been our plan from the first; I now excused to myself the deviation from that plan by saying it had never been our intention to follow it in Alaska, where white men had nearly exterminated the game upon which we counted on living in the more easterly districts, for which our programme was originally made out. In the spring season we could have lived on the country even in Alaska, however, as we later had occasion to prove (in May, 1912).

By the end of May signs of the coming of spring began to multiply. The snow in large patches was gone from the land, geese and ducks had come, and there was water in places on the sea ice. Dr. Anderson and his party had, the fall before, abandoned our second whale-boat and considerable gear with it at Barter Island, two hundred miles east of Cape Halkett, where we now were (May 30th). Somebody would have to be at Barter Island to look after the boat and gear during the spring thaws and we therefore decided to send Ilavinirk ahead. He left us the morning of May 30th and, as we learned later, reached Barter Island safely in about two weeks, although this was the very latest time for safe travel, as the rivers were already opening and the ice was rapidly breaking up.

After Ilavinirk left us, things moved even more slowly than before. We had had three sleds and three dog teams and now we had only two. We could see at once that it would be impossible for us to cross the Colville River on the ice, and the best we could hope for was to reach the western edge of the delta so as to be ready to launch our boat and cross it by the first open water. But even in this we had no success. The water and slush became too deep on the sea ice. Further moving of heavy loads became impracticable June 12th, when we were as yet some fifteen miles west of the most western mouth of the Colville. This was hard luck, for it would have been very desirable to cross the Colville while as yet it only (and not the sea off its mouth) was open, for the solid ice to seaward would have sheltered us from the on-shore winds and dangerous breakers which make navigation of river deltas the terror of boatmen in all parts of the world. However, there was nothing for it but to wait until the ice melted away and to hunt as energetically as possible meantime, to keep our stores of food up to the level.

It was at this time that I first became familiar with the psychology of seals. Arctic explorers of some experience have said in print that a white man may learn to hunt caribou as well as an Eskimo, but no white man can ever learn to hunt seals successfully on top of the Arctic spring ice. This is so far from being true in my experience that I should say it is much easier to stalk seals than it is to stalk caribou. All you have to know is one or two elementary facts about the seal's habits and mental processes. One day Dr. Anderson and I were out on the sea ice and happened to notice a seal basking in the sun. As a matter of scientific interest one of us watched him through the field glasses, while the other held a watch in one hand and a pencil in the other, and noted down the length of the naps the seal was taking between his short periods of wakefulness. Like other seals at this time of year, he was lying beside his hole, enjoying the warm sun. After each short nap he would raise his head about twelve inches above the level of the ice, take a survey of the horizon, and drop to sleep again. From his movements we took down the following series of observations:

AWAKE	ASLEEP		AWAKE	ASLEEP
5 seconds	70 seconds		4 seconds	20 seconds
2 "	10 "		5 "	30 "
10 "	10 "		2 "	5 "
1 "	30 "		3 "	18 "
8 "	2 "		5 "	90 "
7 "	7 "		2 "	60 "
8 "	48 "		3 "	4 "
2 "	15 "		4 "	48 "
6 "	45 "			

From this we deduced the interesting fact that the ratio of the lengths of his periods of wakefulness to those of his periods of sleep was as 1 : 6.6, and further, that the average length of his periods of wakefulness was 4.5 seconds, and the average length of his naps was 30.1 seconds.

Another day, watching another seal, we got the following results:

AWAKE	ASLEEP		AWAKE	ASLEEP
8 seconds	60 seconds		7 seconds	50 seconds
8 "	22 "		3 "	25 "
4 "	100 "		4 "	18 "
6 "	14 "		4 "	20 "

This seal was evidently somewhat more somnolent than the first, for his sleeping time was to his waking as 1 : 7.02. He was awake on an average 5.5 seconds at a time and his naps averaged 35.6 seconds each.

The whole principle of successfully stalking a seal is just in realizing from the first that he is bound to see you and that your only hope is in pretending that you also are a seal. If you act and look so as to convince him from the first that you are a brother seal, he will regard you with unconcern. To simulate a seal well enough to deceive a seal is not difficult, for, to begin with, we know from experience that his eye-sight is poor. You can walk up without taking any special precautions until, under ordinary conditions of light, you are within two hundred and fifty or three hundred yards. Then you have to begin to be more careful. You move ahead while he is asleep, and when he wakes up you stop motionless. You can safely proceed on all fours until within something less than two hundred yards, but after that you will have to play seal more faithfully. Your method of locomotion will then have to be that of the seal, which does not differ very materially from that of a snake, and which therefore has its disadvantages at a season of the year when the surface of the ice is covered with puddles of water anywhere from an inch to twenty inches in depth, as it is in spring and early summer. You must not only crawl ahead, seal-fashion, but you must be careful to always present a side view of your body to the seal, for a man coming head-on does not look particularly like a seal.

Until you are within a hundred yards or so the seal is not likely to notice you, but somewhere between the hundred yard and the seventy-five yard mark his attention will suddenly be attracted to you, and instead of going to sleep at the end of his ordinary short period of wakefulness, he will remain awake and stare at you steadily. The seal knows, exactly as well as the seal hunter knows, that no seal in this world will sleep continuously for as much as four minutes at a time. If you lie still that long, he will know you are no seal, and up will go his tail and down he will slide into the water in the twinkling of an eye. When the seal, therefore, has been watching you carefully for twenty or thirty seconds, you must raise your head twelve or fifteen inches above the ice, look around seal-fashion, so that your eyes will sweep the whole circle of the horizon, and drop your head again upon the ice. By the time he has seen you repeat this process two or three times in the space of five or six minutes he will be convinced that you are a seal, and all his worries will be gone. From then on you can proceed more rapidly, crawling ahead while he sleeps and stopping while he remains awake, never doing anything unbecoming a seal. In this way you can crawl within five or ten yards of him if you like, and as a matter of fact I have known of expert seal hunters who under emergencies would go after a seal without any ordinary weapon and crawl so near him that they could seize him by a flipper, pull him away from his hole, and club or stab him. My Eskimo companions generally used to crawl within about fifteen or twenty yards; but I have found under ordinary circumstances that fifty yards is close enough for a man with a rifle. The animal lies on a slippery incline beside his hole, so that the shot that kills him must kill him instantly. It must shatter the brain or break the spinal cord of the neck; the slightest quiver of a muscle will send him sliding into the water and all your work will have been to no purpose.

Seals were not common in this locality, and although we got a few we were anxious also to get some caribou. The second day after our enforced halt Natkusiak and I accordingly went off in different directions looking for caribou. It was a long hunt for both of us. I returned in about eighteen hours with a young fawn for a back-load, which was one of two animals I had seen, while Natkusiak returned six or eight hours later with the story of having killed two caribou out of three that he saw. Evidently this was no paradise for big game. Ducks, however, were very abundant.

As our main food supply at this time was waterfowl, we expected our dogs as well as ourselves to live on ducks, but this did not suit them very well at first. Our experience with dogs shows that their food prejudices are very much like those of men. It is the common opinion of those who keep hotels and boarding schools that they can tell much about a man's bringing up from the things he objects to eating. The son of wealthy parents who is used to eating fifty different articles of food in a week will take readily to the fifty-first; but a farmer's son who from one year's end to another has lived on nothing but fat pork, potatoes, bread, and tea, is likely to be so wedded to the idea that nothing but pork and potatoes is fit to eat that when he meets with a new dish, the fifth or sixth one of his experience, it strikes him as an unheard-of thing and unfit for food. It is common knowledge among guides in such out of the way places as Iceland that the wealthy travelers who visit the country will readily and with enjoyment adapt themselves to the food of the peasant, while the servants who accompany their wealthy masters have to be specially looked after by the guides and insist on being fed on provisions such as they are used to having in their own country.

The same principle applies to our house dogs, which are used to eating all the varied things that we eat. They are used to so many different flavors that they take readily to one more that happens to be strange. The white man's dog that comes to the Arctic is likely to eat seal meat or any other meat of local growth the first time it is offered him, but take an Indian's dog, that has been brought up inland on nothing but caribou meat, and bring him to the coast, and he will starve for a week before he is willing to swallow the first mouthful of seal. Similarly, I have known Eskimo dogs brought up on seal meat, which when taken inland would have to be starved for a week or more before they would eat the first mouthful of caribou.

We now had with us dogs which we had brought from the Mackenzie River and which it had taken several days of starvation to teach to eat seal; we also had with us dogs of Eskimo bringing up which had similarly been forced to eat caribou meat, but now all of these were simultaneously brought face to face with a new diet (ducks), and it took long periods of abstinence from food to enable them to get up an appetite for the new dish. An interesting observation in this connection is that we have invariably found the conservatism of the females to be greater than that of the males. Out of any pack of dogs that are compelled to learn to eat a new kind of food, the last to give in are the female dogs.

Numerous travelers have pointed out that dogs will not eat dog meat, and have considered this a proof that dogs have an inherent aversion to cannibalism. We have seen nothing to substantiate this view, for a dog that has been brought up on seal meat will eat dog meat quite as readily as he will caribou, and a dog brought up on caribou meat will learn to eat dog meat quite as readily as he will learn to eat seal or duck. There is prejudice against the new but no disinclination to cannibalism.

In the summer season eggs usually form some part of our diet, and this year we got the first on June 16th, for Natkusiak found the nest of a willow ptarmigan. Although we have spent four summers in a country frequented by ptarmigan in large numbers, we have not found over a dozen nests all together, for the male continually stands guard on some eminence near the nest and gives ample warning to the female of the approach of danger, so that the spot where the female flies up is never an indication of the location of the nest. But if for some reason the male be unable to give warning in season, the female will remain on the nest without stirring until you are about to step on it. The protective coloration both of the bird itself and the eggs is so nearly perfect that to discover them is almost

THE ADAPTABILITY OF THE SKIN BOAT.
(1) Umiak being hauled on sled.   (2) Umiak under paddles in narrow shore lead.
(3) Umiak raised on edge to shield goods from rain.

impossible. A very different matter is the swan's nest, of which
we found some in the Colville delta, although they are not nearly
so numerous there as in certain other districts such as the vicinity
of Cape Parry. You cannot see the ptarmigan until you are about
to step on them, but a swan sitting on a nest is the most conspicuous
thing in the animal life of the North, for the nest is on the barren
shore of some lake and consists of a dun-colored heap of straw the
size of a bushel basket, upon the top of which the snow-white bird
can be seen much farther than either the caribou or the grizzly
bear. From the point of view of food supply a swan's nest is a find
of some importance, for there are as many as six eggs, and each of them
is double the size of a goose egg.

In saying that the ptarmigan eggs of June 16th were the first of
the season, I am refraining from an encroachment upon Dr. Anderson's special field as an ornithologist. Of course, he had found nests
of snow buntings, Lapland long-spurs, sandpipers and other small
fry of that kind much earlier in the season.

On June 23d we launched the umiak, loaded all our gear into it,
and paddled away eastward along the coast, through the narrow
lane of open water between the land and the as yet immovable sea
ice. On the 24th the first mosquito of the year appeared. We
saw only a single one that day, but three days later we had them in
millions. The 25th we entered the western edge of the Colville delta
proper and the day after that we fell in with a camp of the Colville
Eskimo, consisting of three families. They told us that during the
winter all of them had starved more or less, but none to death,
although they had lost a good many dogs. Now the main body
of the people were camping at the trading site of Nirlik, about six
miles to the east, where they would wait for the arrival of the Point
Barrow traders.

Rare caribou tracks were to be seen here and there in the delta,
but none of the Eskimo had killed any so far. On the evening of the
28th I happened to see a small black dot on the landscape and pointed
it out to one of the Eskimo, who said it was undoubtedly a mound
of earth. I let it go at that, for I appreciated the social value of being
in a position to give away meat rather than to receive it from others;
and accordingly Dr. Anderson, Natkusiak, and I set out, when the

I

others were not looking, toward this object, which my glasses had shown to be a deer. There turned out to be three of them — all very restless on account of the plague of mosquitoes. Dr. Anderson and Natkusiak therefore approached them from one side, and myself from the other. Apparently they must have either seen or winded them for they came running toward me. They turned out to be all skin poor, as was to be expected on account of the season of the year, for in June no caribou except the oldest bulls have any traces of fat on them whatever in this district. The Colville Eskimo consider themselves the greatest caribou hunters in the country and to them venison is the one palatable and satisfactory article of diet. It was something therefore to be able to show our prowess greater than theirs, and to feed them in their own country on caribou meat, of which they had not had a taste for several months.

July 31st we arrived at Nirlik and found thirty-eight people there. They were catching numbers of fish in nets set in the river, and were sun-drying some of them. A party of eighteen, we were told, had gone to the southeastern edge of the Colville delta near Oliktok, where they were hunting seal to get skins for their water boots for the summer, and oil for their lamps for the coming winter.

We remained at this village a few days, making various inquiries about the country, and the habits and customs of the people, as well as taking physical measurements of them. They and their ancestors were mostly Colville River people as far back as they knew, which in no case was more than four generations, but some of them belonged to tribes from across the mountains toward Kotzebue Sound. Most of them had hunted, at one time or another, well south into the forests of the Yukon Valley, where they had always been in the habit of meeting the Indians and where of late years they had seen white men also. A young woman of the party had had her father killed five years before by an Indian, but this seemed to be looked upon as a murder rather than an act of war. In general their attitude toward the Indians was not different from that which they have toward strange tribes of Eskimo. Some of them knew they were of Indian blood, and others had relatives who had gone to live among the Indians.

We left the trading village of Nirlik on July 5th, and July 6th we reached the mouth of the Itkillik River, where we had spent some weeks the previous winter and where we had left behind some ammunition and other gear. We picked these up now, and then proceeded down the eastern arm of the Colville delta, reaching Oliktok July 14th. The slowness of our progress was due chiefly to the fact that the river we were following, although miles in width in many places, was so shallow that our boat kept going continually aground, in spite of the fact that it drew no more than a foot of water. Somewhere along the bottom of this river of magnificent expanses there wriggled a narrow boat channel of sufficient depth. From its crookedness we kept continually losing it, continually going aground, and we had to spend half of our time wading about the barely water-covered mud-flats in our water-proof sealskin boots, seeking to rediscover the mysterious channel which we had just lost and which we generally lost again as soon as we had found it. Although the water is fresh some distance out to sea off the Colville delta under ordinary conditions, there is a considerable rise of tide even as much as thirty or forty miles upstream when a strong southwest wind blows. One day when we had been dragging our boat for hours across mud-flats, and after all hope of further progress seemed to be gone, the water rose suddenly a foot or more and gave us plain sailing where an hour or two before the walking had been fairly good.

A few miles east of Oliktok our further progress was stopped for a day by an on-shore wind which brought the lagoon ice in dense masses against the shore. The coast line proper is here fenced off from the ocean by a series of outlying sand bars or islands, running from the Colville delta to the mouth of the Kuparuk River. It was therefore none of the sea ice we were facing, but only a comparatively thin ice formed in these inclosed waters. The obstruction was therefore not serious and the minute the wind slacked up the ice was sure to drift off again.

It is a fact not generally understood that old salt-water ice is always fresh. When ice forms in the fall it is as salty as the water out of which it is made, and if you take a chunk of it and melt it you get brine unfit for the ordinary uses of water. The ice remains salty all winter, but the following spring, so soon as the warm weather comes, it begins to freshen, and even though the cake be of considerable size it will freshen enough for use in tea-making or other cooking by the end of the summer. But the lagoon ice, which has never been over six feet thick to begin with, thins down to a few inches by July and cakes of it are perfectly fresh by that time, as we abundantly proved at Oliktok. I had known for two years about the freshness of old sea ice, but it was not until this experience that I knew that the water from even this year's ice could, under certain circumstances, be used for cooking or drinking.

On the way from the mouth of the Itkillik to Oliktok I had hunted inland several times while the boat was trying to pick its way downstream over the shoals, but I had seen only four caribou, all of which I had shot. Proceeding east from Oliktok we did not hunt much till we got to the mouth of the Kuparuk River. We were now short of meat again, and besides, it blew a head wind; so we ran the boat into the mouth of the river in search both of shelter and of caribou. We were in luck, for we found just east of the Kuparuk the largest caribou herd we had seen up to that point. Dr. Anderson, who prides himself on his conservatism and always estimates numbers at about half what he thinks they really are, considered this herd to be about four hundred. We shot eight of them, which was all we cared for. Most of the deer seen up to now had been young bulls, but this herd seemed to consist of a mixture of young bulls and cows with calves.

Eight deer were really more than we should have killed, for our boat, after picking up our caches in the Colville delta and at Oliktok, was already overloaded. It was out of the question to try to carry green meat along, so we camped for a few days, drying the meat to make it lighter and easier to haul as well as to insure its not being spoilt.

It was now time for the Eskimo of Point Barrow to be coming along from the west on their annual trading voyage to Flaxman Island. On account of our heavy load it was dangerous for us to attempt the sea passage outside of the shoals which lie off the mouths of the larger rivers, such as the next one east of us, the Sagavanirktok. We were wishing, therefore, that our delay in drying the meat of the caribou we had killed would enable these traders to overtake us, so we could get some of them to lighten our boat as far as Flaxman Island. I knew they would appreciate the deer meat we had to give them, and while no formal payment is as yet needed to induce even the most civilized Eskimo to do you a service when he finds you in trouble cn a journey, yet it would not be amiss to put them in good humor through a gift of meat. In fact, it had been largely with that end in view that we had shot so many caribou to begin with.

On the morning of July 28th we saw a boat-sail out at sea, but strangely enough it was coming from the east. We had been expecting boats from the west only. It turned out that this was Mr. Ned Arey and his son, Gallagher, who were on their way to Point Barrow to buy some provisions for the coming winter. They had had head winds and were short of provisions, and caribou meat had not been abundant with them during the year, so they enjoyed our feast of meat as much as the Eskimo would. The next day the Point Barrow boats arrived and, as we expected, took on some of our freight, which made the remainder of the journey to Flaxman Island a simple one.

At Flaxman Island on August 5th we met our Eskimo Ilavinirk, who had come with the whale-boat to meet us from Barter Island. We stopped for three days at the Flaxman Island trading village, and then continued eastward in company with several Eskimo boats that had come up from Herschel Island for trading purposes. We stopped now and then for fishing and went occasionally ashore to look for caribou; and now and again we were delayed by head winds — sometimes for a few hours and sometimes for a few days — until finally, when a protracted calm stopped us some thirty miles west of Herschel Island, I made up my mind to hurry ahead in our skin-boat, leaving Dr. Anderson with our whale-boat and the other Eskimo boats to follow later. I took with me my favorite companion, Natkusiak, and an elderly countrywoman of his named Pannigabluk, whose husband had died the year before and who had been taken on with our party as a seamstress.

No sooner had we left Dr. Anderson than we sighted caribou inland. It was evidently a big bull and we were very anxious to get him, for the skins of the bulls about the middle of August are in ideal condition for winter boot-soles and the animals then are fatter than at any other season. We got within range of the bull, fired at him, and wounded him. Just as he started off for the mountains I happened to turn around, and saw a sail to the westward, the first of the incoming whaling ships, which, according to the news we received at Point Barrow, we had not expected to come at all. I therefore left Natkusiak to follow the wounded bull while I ran as fast as I could the six miles to the coast to make a smoke signal for the whaler, and if necessary to put out in our boat to intercept her, for I recognized even from the mountains that the ship was Captain Pedersen's schooner the *Challenge*, which had been wintering at Point Barrow, and I knew Captain Pedersen would be willing to go out of his way to do us a service. When I got down to the coast the faint breeze of the morning had given out completely and the *Challenge* lay becalmed a mile or so offshore just a little west of our camp. It turned out that Natkusiak had plenty of time to kill the wounded bull he was following, but on account of his fear that the wind might come up again and take the ship away, he brought back with him only the skin and forty pounds or so of back-fat, abandoning all the meat to the wolves and foxes. It was a great pity to waste over two hundred pounds of prime venison, especially as we had for several months been living on lean, flavorless meat. It took a good while for all of us to get over thinking about the feast of which accident had deprived us, and later when we boarded the *Challenge* and told Captain Pedersen about it he was scarcely less regretful, for he and his men were without fresh meat.

It took the *Challenge* about half a day to cover the six or eight miles between the place where we first saw her and our camp, but when she came abreast of us we signaled her, loaded our boat and went aboard. It was about midnight then. We had a calm for several hours after that, but before noon of the next day the wind freshened up and we made good speed. We dropped anchor in the harbor of Herschel Island, August 18th.

Captain Pedersen told us that one whaler at least, Captain Cottle with the *Karluk*, was coming into the Arctic and might be expected at Herschel Island any day. Captain Cottle arrived, as a matter of fact, the 19th of August, and kindly offered to take me and my party eastward to Cape Bathurst.

It was one of our serious misfortunes that Dr. Anderson and his section of our party were not at Herschel Island also to take advantage of this offer. As I learned later, they had spent too much time in caribou hunting and had besides been delayed a day by allowing the dogs to get away inland chasing caribou. They were of course forced to wait for them until their hunting desires had been quenched and they straggled one by one back to the coast again, for one cannot at the beginning of winter afford to lose his dogs. Up to the last moment I hoped that Anderson might turn up before the *Karluk* would have to set sail. It was not to be, however, for the *Karluk* hove anchor the morning of August 24th and carried us off on a short whaling cruise toward Banks Island.

Captain Cottle had intended to land us at Cape Bathurst before going on the Banks Island cruise, but while crossing the mouth of the Mackenzie River (where, by the way, we sailed for a whole day through fresh water although no land was in sight), a gale blew up which increased so in violence that when we approached the harbor at the Baillie Islands, just off Cape Bathurst, Captain Cottle did not consider it safe to try entering through the somewhat devious channel and we were forced therefore to sail past. Under other circumstances I should not have regretted the delay much, for the cruise gave us the chance to see the taking of a bow-head whale, an unusual spectacle nowadays anywhere in the world, and one which not many are likely to see hereafter, for the whaling industry as carried on by the big ships is a thing of the past in the Arctic.[1] Now, however, we were anxious to get ashore somewhere near Cape Parry, to commence, while yet there was time, the autumn hunt for caribou to supply us with skins for clothing for the coming winter. We were now in a locality where we could put into operation our principle of "living on the country," and we had to live on the country, not only in the matter of food but also in the matter of clothing.

August 26th the *Karluk* finally put in at the Baillie Islands and we transferred from her to Captain Wolki's *Rosie H.* which we found waiting there for us. The *Rosie H.* was going down to Cape

[1] A commercial substitute — an imitation whalebone — has recently been invented. This is so cheap and so satisfactory a substitute for whalebone in most of its uses that the market for whalebone seems permanently gone. The winter of 1905–1906 there were eleven whaling vessels in the western Arctic ; of these in the winter 1912–1913 the *Belvedere* alone remained, and the summer of 1913 she goes north for trading purposes only.

Parry to try to get some coal from a wrecked whaling ship, the *Alexander*, which went ashore there in a fog in August, 1906, and which was still lying solid upon the rocks where her crew had left her. August 29th the *Rosie H.* tied up alongside the wreck of the *Alexander*. The *Rosie H.* was able to go all around the *Alexander* where she lay hard aground, for although a ship of something like eighty tons, she is flat-bottomed and draws less than six feet of water, while the *Alexander* drew sixteen in her day. She is now aground in nine feet of water forward and thirteen at the stern, which gives some idea of the force with which she was driven upon the rocks by the combined power of her engine and of all her sails, for she was at the time making nine knots before a fresh breeze. The rocky shore sprang so suddenly out of the fog that there was no time to reverse the engines or to give an order to the man at the wheel.

CHAPTER VIII

IN a way, the real work of the expedition began with our landing at Cape Parry. Hitherto we had been in a country frequented by white traders and whalers and by semi-civilized Christian Eskimo, but now we had left all that behind. Cape Parry is about one hundred miles east as one travels by sled in winter from the Baillie Islands and Cape Bathurst, the most easterly settlement of the civilized Eskimo. The country to the eastward was known to us only through having been skirted twice in summer by Sir John Richardson's exploring parties, first in 1826 and again in 1848. Their boats had usually stood along well offshore, traveling in fog and all sorts of weather, so that the information their account gives us of the coast is necessarily fragmentary and inconclusive. We had already learned, and were destined to learn more fully later, that while the Cape Bathurst Eskimo had no doubt, a century or so ago, had frequent and continuous communication with the Eskimo to the east, the country was entirely unknown to the present generation; and as for us, we had no means of telling whether it was inhabited or not. True, we knew from the records of the English explorers that Coronation Gulf was peopled by Eskimo, and Victoria Island also, as late as 1852, but no one had ever seen people on the stretch of coast running from Coronation Gulf west three hundred miles to Cape Parry. The evidence, so far as we had any, was negative, for Richardson on his two voyages through Dolphin and Union Straits had seen no people. But my reasoning was that this did not prove the non-existence of people, for he had touched the coast only at rare intervals, and that at a season when a migratory population like the Eskimo would be expected to be absent from the seashore, inland hunting caribou, or spearing fish.

When the *Rosie H.* landed us at Cape Parry she put ashore also that portion of our gear which Dr. Anderson did not have in his whale-boat when we separated, and provisions equal to about three months' rations for four men.   Most of these I had secured from Captain Cottle and Captain Pedersen, and Captain Cottle had given me also several hundred pounds of whale blubber from the whale which he had taken while I was aboard his ship.   All these things we stored in an old house which had been built on shore near the wreck of the *Alexander* by Baillie Islands Eskimo who had come down during the winter of 1906–1907 to plunder the vessel, after the news had come to them of her being wrecked and deserted by her crew.

We had no expectation of finding many caribou on the Cape Parry peninsula.   It was our intention therefore to load our skin-boat with a selection of things we thought we might need, and sail south toward Langton Bay.   But the *Rosie H.* had landed our outfit on an exposed rocky beach, and it took two trips for our boat to transfer it to the deserted house where it was to be stored.   We had installed the first load safely and were loading up the boat for the second trip when a northwest wind suddenly blew up, making the exposed bit of coast on which we were working a very unsafe place for us.   If the wind had blown up half an hour sooner, while our boat was yet empty, we could have run it ashore and pulled it up on the beach out of reach of the waves; or had the wind come half an hour later we should have had the boat unloaded and our stores safely within doors.   But it came at just the wrong moment.   The surf instantly increased to a dangerous one for landing, so that an attempt to make one would have resulted both in the wrecking of the boat and the loss of many of the things in it.   Half a mile away was the entrance to a deep fjord, and our only course was to run for shelter there, which we did.   The wind kept blowing steadily from the northwest for several days, and while at first we landed within the fjord, expecting to be able to get back, we eventually gave this up and started south toward Langton Bay with a bigger load than we had intended to carry, consisting chiefly of articles for which we had no immediate need, while others that we needed remained behind at Cape Parry.

The northern portion of the Cape Parry peninsula consists of rocky hills running up to an extreme height of perhaps six hundred feet.   It is nearly cut into many islands by the deep fjords which run into the land from both sides. This peculiarity of topography was of use to us, for the weather continued stormy, and in one case we found it advisable, in order to get a sheltered route to the south, to portage our boat and its contents across a neck of land about a hundred yards wide, which separated a fjord some five or six miles in length from another still larger to the south of it.

In our hunting excursions, and such walks as we took across the land for purposes of investigation, we began to find here and there the same type of human remains which we were destined to continue finding for more than a year to come in all the country between Cape Bathurst and Coronation Gulf. They had been, those vanished men, a people who did not make their camps down by the seashore, but only on the tops of high hills. Evidently they had used wood for fuel in summer. They had, in their excursions inland, been in the habit of carrying it with them from the beach, so that on any high hill-top we were likely to find a few sticks of decayed wood, as well as tent-rings of stone and stone fire-places where they had done their cooking. Later on, after we discovered people to the east, we found them using exactly such fire-places at camps pitched on exactly such hills. Long before we found people we had learned to recognize in the most casual glance at a landscape the hills upon which ruins were likely to be found, although why just such hills were chosen we did not fully understand until we found people occupying them and were able to ask about whys and wherefores.

Of course these that we speak of are only summer camps. The ruins of the permanent dwellings where the people had lived in winter are found down on the sea beach in just the locations which the Eskimo of to-day would choose for carrying on sealing. These houses had long ago fallen into ruins, and while there is no scale by which we can judge their age archæologically, I am now convinced, on the basis of a collation of various kinds of evidence, that none of them are very old, although none of them can be more recent than about 1840.

Besides the house ruins and the camp-sites we found also the graves of the people, containing broken sleds upon which the bodies had been hauled to the graveyard, as well as property which the relatives of the dead had left with them. These things we collected, and they have their scientific interest, but a discussion of them is somewhat too technical for our present purposes.

Head winds and violent gales are frequent at this time of year, and we made slow progress toward Langton Bay, partly on account of the gales and partly because the country was strange to us; so that we spent much time in looking for caribou in a district where we now know they are not to be found at this time of year. We had good luck in sealing, however. One day, for instance, as we were sailing along, Natkusiak shot from our boat a bearded seal, which promptly sank. We camped about five miles away, and the next morning a gathering of gulls about two hundred yards from our tent led us to the spot where the dead seal had floated ashore during the night. On another day, while I was looking for caribou, a polar bear that I should under ordinary circumstances not have seen took it into his head to hunt me, with the inevitable result.

We had been talking over various plans, and all of us agreed that the thing to do at this season of the year was to find a river and ascend it inland as far as possible, for it was clear that the caribou had already left the coast. The reasons for following a river inland, instead of striking across country, are mainly two: first, a boat of shallow draft can be taken upstream a considerable distance along most of the Arctic rivers; and secondly, one may expect a river valley to be stocked with a heavy growth of willow suitable for fuel, even in places where spruce trees are not to be found.

I had with me the same chart which had misled us the fall before and had been the direct cause of our losing a year through getting tangled up in Smith Bay. I considered, however, that by the laws of chance some portion of the chart ought to be in fair accordance with the facts, and here we were now near the place where a large river, known as the "River la Ronciere," is drawn across the map with great detail as heading to the southeast several hundred miles away, near Bear Lake, and entering the Arctic Ocean at the foot of the Parry peninsula. The day we came to that part of the coast where the mouth of the river is laid down on the chart, we found, sure enough, that there was every appearance to indicate that this was the delta of a considerable river. There was a big bight filled with many low alluvial islands and the shores of these

Tracking Umiak by Dog Team near Langton Bay.

were strewn with willows and small spruce drift-wood, all of which might reasonably be supposed to come from such a river as the "la Ronciere" is on the map.

On the evening of September 8th I made the following entry in my diary: "We are exactly to-night where Petitot's River la Ronciere le Noury should be, and we seem to be in the mouth of a river — a strange thing if true, for it shows that Arctic maps cannot be relied upon to be invariably wrong." The following day, however, September 9th, my diary has this entry: "River la Ronciere does not seem to be the exception that I took it to be; yesterday we found the mouth of a small river and followed it up a few miles but it turned out to come from a lake about 4 or 5 miles inland. The lake is about 2 miles wide and 4 or 5 miles long, and it seems to be the head of our river." Further investigations showed us that in reality this creek is about thirty miles long instead of three hundred, as the "River la Ronciere" is represented to be on the chart, and that the "River la Ronciere" is in fact non-existent.

The consequences of following our chart were not as serious here as they had been in Smith Bay the year before, but still the detour lost us two days of fair weather with a light offshore breeze that would have taken us to Langton Bay September 8th. We got there, however, all safe, September 11th, after a good deal of hard rowing in a rough sea against adverse winds.

The characteristics of Langton Bay deserve a paragraph and perhaps more than that, for circumstances kept bringing us back to it, and it was, more nearly than any other place, the base from which we conducted most of our operations for three years. The bay itself is roughly triangular in shape, with each side of the triangle ten miles or so in length, and with an opening of about two miles at its western angle or apex, through which it can be entered from the main body of Franklin Bay, the southeast corner of which it forms.

Langton Bay as a whole is very shallow, and it is probable that no ship of any size can enter it, but just outside of its mouth is a sand-spit half a mile long that joins the mainland at an angle of about 30°. This sandspit and the harbor it forms were first seen by Sir John Richardson, who incorrectly states that the mouth of it is so shallow that the harbor would be of no use to vessels of any size.

As a matter of fact, the entrance around the point of the sandspit is so deep that vessels of sixteen-feet draft can safely run within twenty yards of shore and have done so, for Langton Bay has at three different times, for a winter each time, been the harbor of whaling ships.

This is the most easterly outpost of the whaling industry, and the place has not been visited since 1897(?). One of the whale ships when wintering at Langton Bay built a small house ashore for the occupancy of the Alaskan and other western Eskimo who formed part of the crew. This house is still standing, and during three years we used it as the storehouse for our steadily growing scientific collections, as well as for ammunition and anything else which we needed to keep there.

As a wintering place, Langton Bay has two main defects: first, that drift-wood for fuel is scarce in the neighborhood; and second, that Franklin Bay is so deep that polar bears seldom come so far south as Langton Bay, for they follow the open water, which is found chiefly outside a line drawn from the tip of Cape Bathurst to that of Cape Parry; and neither do the caribou come near, for the country is not suitable as a feeding ground for them in winter. Such an expedition as ours, which lives on the country, may therefore use Langton Bay only as a point of departure; and although we considered it home for a period of three years, we did not stay there three months all together.

We had no sooner landed at the Langton Bay harbor than we began preparations for going inland hunting, and, with us, to begin preparations was to be ready in a few hours. Although talkative by nature, Pannigabluk did not mind being alone for a day or a few days, so we left her to fix up camp as well as she could on the coast, while Natkusiak hunted southeast and I southwest in the hope of finding caribou.

At Langton Bay the Melville Mountains, about a thousand feet high, are three miles inland. They are really the sea-front of a plateau that slopes almost imperceptibly south from their crest to Horton River, ten miles farther inland. Each of us climbed the mountains by a separate ravine, and each reached a commanding peak at about the same time. We were three miles apart, but could see each other clearly with the glasses. It was evident to me that Natkusiak soon got his eye on game to the south of him, for he spent but little time on his peak — there is always something decisive and unmistakable about a hunter's actions when he sets out toward a distant band of caribou. I read the signs clearly and with satisfaction, but I knew my man and that he needed no help, so, although I saw nothing from my point of vantage (except scenery, which at the approach of an Arctic winter has no attractiveness save as a fitting background for caribou), I started southwest in the hope of picking up something.

The afternoon developed for me into a profitless twenty-mile tramp over the spongy tundra. There were few tracks of caribou, none very fresh, and all going east — evidently we were a little too late to intercept the few animals that had spent the summer toward Liverpool Bay and were now moving to other pastures. I had given up hope of game for the day and had turned home, for the dusk of the short night was approaching, when I saw over a small ridge what I took to be the flutter of a raven. A little farther on, and I thought I saw four ravens. They were not quite in my line of march down the mountain toward the sea, so I turned my glasses on them, thinking to see if it was the carcass of a caribou they were feeding on. It was fortunate for me and for the American Museum that I was inquisitive, for this proved my first sight of the Barren Ground grizzly, *Ursus arctos richardsoni*, perhaps the rarest of the large land carnivoræ of the world in museums and the least known scientifically; but my inquisitiveness was unlucky for the bear, for he became the nucleus of our collection, which finally grew to number nineteen specimens. It was his four paws I had taken for four ravens; for he had been lying on his back, pawing the air like a fat puppy — and fat he was, in truth. On the rump the blubber layer was about four inches thick, for he was an old male almost ready for hibernation. In the hurry of skinning him, a good deal of the fat remained with the hide; I allowed the paws and head to go with the skin for mounting purposes, and the matted, woolly hair was wet, all of which went toward making that skin one of the heaviest back-loads I ever carried to camp — it must have weighed upwards of two hundred pounds. Natkusiak had seen several deer, but had been able to approach only three before it became too dark to shoot. He got those three, all fairly fat. In an Arctic existence ordered as ours the necessities of life are meat and skins; the luxuries are fat caribou meat and short-haired summer caribou skins. We had, therefore, begun well. In one day we had secured meat enough for perhaps three weeks, skins enough for one suit of outer clothes, and oil enough for light for a month.

The next day Natkusiak and I hunted together. There were no caribou near the coast, but about ten miles inland we saw seven, all of which we shot. Ten caribou and a bear made a pretty good showing for the first two days of hunting, but we found that we had come to the end of our rope. The animals we had secured had been the rear guard of the east-moving herd, and it soon became evident that we could reach no more game from a hunting base on the sea-coast. We therefore cached the meat of the bear and the three deer first killed at Langton Bay, and moved camp about ten miles inland to where we had buried the meat of the seven caribou — buried it with the double idea of keeping it fresh in the cool ground until the freeze-up (which was now only a few days distant) and of protecting it from foxes.

The second day after moving camp inland I had one of the pleas-antest surprises of my traveling experience. The 'general topog-raphy of the country led me to believe there should be a river at a greater or less distance to the southwest. To ascertain the truth of this I had gone about five miles southwest, when I suddenly came upon a deep ravine. Looking down this for half a mile to where it had its mouth into another and deeper ravine, I saw a small band of little Christmas trees struggling up the steep bank. I have never been half so glad to see the sun after its midwinter absence. I had intended to make an all-day hunt, but the news was too good to keep — the Eskimo were at home, I knew, and I had to go and tell them about it. The branch of evergreen I took to them carried an invitation not to be resisted. None of us had suspected that trees were anywhere near. We had been using small green willow twigs for fire. It was already autumn; ice formed every night on the ponds, and the drizzling rains of the season made comfort impos-sible on the shelterless barren ground. There were no two opinions, therefore, about moving camp; and the following night found us sitting by a crackling fire of dry wood in a sheltered spruce grove in my creek-bottom.   This creek proved to be a branch of Horton River, a stream about the size of the Hudson that it has been our privilege to add to the map of North America.

This was the harvest season on the Arctic tundra; the caribou were still short-haired, and their skins therefore suitable for clothing; they were still fat, and their meat therefore good eating; but we knew that the approach of cold weather was about to change all that.   We expected every day that Anderson's party would come to join ours, in which case — between men and dogs — our supply of meat would last less than a month.   The *Rosie H.* had, it was true, landed about three months' supplies for us, besides ammunition and other gear, at Cape Parry, about seventy-five miles to the north, but these supplies we hoped not to be forced to touch for a long time, for we had several years — it turned out to be three — of work ahead of us, and could count on no reinforcements.   We hunted, therefore, energetically every day from dawn till dark, but saw no caribou.   One day, however, I picked up two more grizzlies.   We were in the habit of considering a full-grown grizzly equal in food value to about two large bull caribou.   I also shot a fat white wolf, which gave us a good seventy-five pounds of excellent meat.

On September 29th we had the first heavy snowfall of the year. The snow and ice are one's best friends in the North, for they make travel easy.   Up to this time we had been forced to make beasts of burden both of ourselves and our three dogs; we carried our camp gear on our backs from place to place, and whenever we killed an animal we had to pack the meat and skin home.   Carrying a hundred-pound back-load of meat ten or fifteen miles home over boggy ground is more like work than sport, especially after an all-day hunt, when darkness overtakes you while you are skinning your game or cutting up the meat.   So soon, therefore, as there was sufficient snow on the ground we made a trip to Langton Bay to get our sled, and then proceeded southeast up Horton River in the hope of overtaking the caribou which, as we knew by their tracks, had gone in that direction about three weeks before.

Before starting we cached, as safely as we could, not only our store of meat, but most carefully of all, the grizzly bear skins, which we

K

considered priceless scientifically. We took little meat with us, and the first night out one of our dogs stole half of that. On the third day of the up-river journey we supped on the half of an Arctic fox I shot that day, and breakfasted on the other half. That morning, however, we came on the tracks of eight young bull caribou. Leaving Pannigabluk to pitch camp, Natkusiak and I followed these, overtook them about five miles away, and killed seven of the eight. We soon found that we had overtaken the rear guard of the caribou, and as we were anxious that Dr. Anderson's party should overtake us as soon as possible, we built here a permanent house of wood, sod, and moss, and prepared to spend the winter. During the remainder of October we shot sixteen more caribou and hauled their meat safely to camp.

At this point we made the first serious mistake of the year. I myself did not worry much about Dr. Anderson's not turning up, for I considered that he had probably been unable to get any farther than the Mackenzie delta by open water, and that he was, therefore, hardly overdue; but my Eskimo were of the opinion that his Eskimo might possibly have "struck" and refused, on account of fear of hunger, to accompany him farther east than the most easterly Eskimo settlement (at the Baillie Islands). They therefore advised that we should make the 150-mile trip to the Baillie Islands to let the news get out that we had found caribou. If we did not actually meet Dr. Anderson there, they argued, the news would eventually get to his party, and his Eskimo would then be all eagerness to come and help us eat our store of venison. I yielded to these persuasions unwisely; we should, of course, have stayed where we were to make hay while the sun shone — to kill more caribou while we yet had daylight enough for shooting purposes. Dr. Anderson was in no danger; for if he could not get his Eskimo to go where he wanted them to, he could always stay where they wanted to stay, as I had had to do myself on a former expedition — the winter of 1906 in the Mackenzie delta.

I let the arguments of my Eskimo prevail, and we accordingly left Pannigabluk to look after our camp and protect our meat caches from the wolverines while Natkusiak and I went to the coast to look for Dr. Anderson. We met him and his party on their way to join us; it was a pleasing thing to see him a fortnight earlier than we should have done; but this trip to the coast was the beginning of our misfortunes.

Inland on Horton River we were short of ammunition, tea, and tobacco — the first of which is a real necessity; the last two are considered necessities by the Mackenzie Eskimo. It was therefore decided that Dr. Anderson, Natkusiak, and Pikaluk (a man who had at his own instance joined Dr. Anderson's party) should make a quick trip to Cape Parry for a supply of these necessities, while I returned to our hunting-camp up the river with the remaining five of Dr. Anderson's party: Ilavinirk, his wife, Mamayauk, their nine-year-old daughter, Nogasak, and an eighteen-year-old boy, Palaiyak, whom they had adopted, and Kunasluk, a decrepit rheumatic old man, the father of Pikaluk.

When we parted with Dr. Anderson, November 23d, at the mouth of Horton River, we each had about two days' provisions. It was blowing a blizzard from the southwest and was very cold, but the wind was nearly fair for him, and he would be able, we thought, to make our meat cache at Langton Bay in three days (which he succeeded in doing). It would take us longer, we knew, to get home to our hunting-camp. It turned out that it took us thirteen days. The sun was gone, and there were blizzards more than half the time. We had counted on getting both ptarmigan and rabbits along the way, but on account of the snowstorms and darkness we got not a single rabbit and only seven ptarmigan.

On the beach near the mouth of Horton River we had discovered the carcass of a bow-head whale that had (we afterward learned) been dead four years. It would have been securely hidden from sight by the level three feet or so of snow that covered it had not the Arctic foxes smelled it out and by their tracks and burrowings given us the clue. After working half a day to shovel off the snow, we got at the carcass at last, and chopped off from the tongue of the huge animal about a hundred pounds of what we intended for dog feed. When fresh the tongue is mostly fat, but after four years of weathering there remained chiefly the connective tissues, so that what we cut off more resembled chunks of felt than pieces of meat. Of these one hundred pounds Dr. Anderson and I each had taken

half; he took no more because he expected to reach Langton Bay
with its cache of caribou and bear-meat in three days; I took no
more because I expected to find plenty of small game along Horton
River as we ascended it toward our main camp.

After Dr. Anderson left us we were kept in camp two days by a
blizzard so violent that our dogs would not face it. Whether your
dogs will or will not face the wind is the test of fit and unfit traveling
weather in the Arctic, for a properly dressed man will face a wind
that is too much for the Eskimo dog. These two storm-bound days
used up most of our ordinary food, and on the first day of actual
travel we were on half-allowance. The second day out we boiled up
some sealskins that we had intended for boots; the third day we ate
some more skins and boiled a little of the whale tongue. This last
all of us found unpalatable, for the tongue had been so long awash
on the beach that it had become thoroughly impregnated with sea
salts (other than sodium chloride). No doubt it was these salts,
too, that made us sick, so that two or three days farther on our journey, when — between men and dogs — we had finished the whale
tongue, we were really better off than while we had it. We had
tried slicing it thin and boiling it twice and even three times, but it
seemed impossible to get rid of the quinine-like bitterness.

I must not give the impression that we were really starving, or
even suffering much from hunger. We had plenty of seal-oil — a
sealskin bag full of it — and of this we ate all we wanted. All of us
found, however, that we could not take much of it "straight" —
the stomach needs bulky food; it craves to be filled with something.
For this reason we used to eat the oil soaked up in tea leaves, ptarmigan feathers, or caribou hair. Most commonly we used to take
long-haired caribou skin, cut it in small pieces, dip the pieces in oil,
and eat them that way. This is, too, the method we used in feeding
oil to dogs in an emergency; on this trip, as on many other occasions, we and our dogs fared exactly alike.

The tenth day out (December 4th) we camped near the place
where two months before we had cached our grizzly bear skins. I had
then been so profoundly impressed with their value to science that
I had spent a day in burying them safely in frozen ground; now their
food value impressed us so strongly that we spent a day in digging

them up to eat the heads and paws, though we destroyed thereby the scientific value of the skins. There was one ham of caribou cached at the same place, but that and the heads and paws of the bears all went in one day, as well as five Canada jays we had killed and kept as ornithological specimens, our dogs getting a share, of course. They were now so weak that we had to pull most of the weight of the sleds ourselves, though we were a little weak, too. I have noticed — and Dr. Anderson's experience has been the same as mine — that on a diet of fats alone one gradually loses strength, but that this symptom of malnutrition is not so conspicuous as sleepiness and a mental inability to call quickly into action such strength as one has.

After a day of high living on the one caribou ham, eight bear-paws, and five Canada jays we were down to a diet of skins and oil again. We also ate our snow-shoe lashings and several fathoms of other raw-hide thongs — fresh rawhide is good eating; it reminds one of pig's feet, if well boiled. It occurs to one in this connection (seriously speaking) that one of the material advantages of skin clothing over woolens in Arctic exploration is that one can eat them in an emer-gency, or feed them to one's dogs if the need is not quite so pressing. This puts actual starvation off by a week or so. As for eating one's dogs, the very thought is an abomination. Not that I have any prejudice against dog-meat, as such; it is probably very much like wolf, and wolf I know to be excellent. But on a long, hard sled trip the dogs become your friends; they work for you single-mindedly and uncomplainingly; they revel with you in prosperity and good fortune; they take starvation and hard knocks with an equanimity that says to you: "We have seen hard times together before, we shall see good times again; but if this be the last, you can count on us to the end." To me the death of a dog that has stood by me in failure and helped me to success is the death of a comrade in arms; to eat him would be but a step removed from cannibalism.

After finishing our bear-paws we had only two more days on deer-skins and oil, and it was lucky we had no more, for on the evening of the second day when we were about eighteen miles short of our camp, Ilavinirk, Mamayauk, and Kunasluk all complained of weakness and Mamayauk seemed so sick that we feared not being able to move camp the following day. For some days past the dogs had not been pulling much. They had been losing strength faster than we, for although they had about the same allowance as we of deerskins and oil, they were forced to sleep outdoors in the cold while we had always our cozy and cheerful camp, and the cold saps strength as quickly as does hard work. Ilavinirk and I had therefore been pulling the sleds with little assistance from the dogs, and now it seemed clear that if he were to cease work and Mamayauk's weight were to be added to the sled, it would be out of the question for me alone to try to move it. Evidently the one thing for me to do was to try to hurry ahead to where Pannigabluk was guarding our meat cache, to fetch a back-load of food for men and dogs.

Although I was both tired and sleepy I accordingly, at the end of the day's work on December 7th, shared with the rest my last meal of skins and oil, and then, between 8.30 P.M. and 4.15 next morning, I walked through a starlit night against a fairly strong wind the eighteen miles to our camp. I found Pannigabluk up and cooking over a cheerful open fire, for, like many other elderly people, she was an early riser. It was a pleasant home-coming. Contrary to what might have been expected, I did not sit down to a huge meal. I was too tired for that, and sleepy, and tumbled at once into bed. It was not until 10.30 o'clock in the forenoon that Pannigabluk, according to my directions, awoke me to eat. At 11.45 I was on the road back, with thirty pounds or so of dried meat. I met the party about five miles away from our camp, for Mamayauk had felt better in the morning and was able to travel. We made camp where I met them and by noon the next day we were all sitting around huge troughs of boiled venison in our comfortable winter house. Most of the meat we had killed in the fall was still on hand. Pannigabluk had of course eaten some while we were away, and a wolverine had stolen a few pieces from under her very nose — they are animals with a genius for thievery and mischief. For the time our prospects were not bad, except that out of the six Eskimo I now had with me three were more or less sick from the effects of the diet of deer hair and oil — or rather, perhaps, from the effect of overeating when they got where meat was abundant. We now had meat to do us about two months, we thought, but we were short of fat. Some blubber cached on the coast was one of the things Dr. Anderson had gone to get for us.

When we arrived at our home camp, December 7th, it seemed for the time being that all our troubles were over. We took a look the next day at our stock of caribou meat and it was an imposing pile. But then, frozen carcasses always do make a great showing. We agreed that there must be food enough there for two months for men and dogs, and fresh caribou tracks were numerous all around the house, so that it seemed we surely ought to be able to get plenty more fresh meat when the stock on hand was gone.

A band of caribou passed the house early in the morning of our second day at home and we saw their tracks an hour or two after. I took the trail and followed it a few hours, but my long walk home two nights before had chafed my feet badly and I was lame. There seemed no pressing need for getting these particular deer; had our meat pile been smaller I should not of course have returned without at least sighting the animals, but now seeing we had such abundance of meat at home, I turned about at noon and limped slowly homeward. For two days after that I stayed in the house to get my feet in proper condition. When I went out again hunting on the third day after that, there were no fresh tracks to be seen.

At the point on Horton River where our house was situated, there were woods not only in the valley proper, but also on top of the hill to the west, stretching unbroken three hundred miles to the Mackenzie, so far as we knew. To the east of the river, however, the Barren Ground is only a mile or two away. When there are caribou on the Barren Ground we much prefer to hunt them there, for with the aid of one's field glasses they are easily discovered, and stalking caribou without woods for cover is an easy enough thing for one who knows how. I therefore on three successive days made long hunts northeast and east and southeast into the Barren Ground, but without seeing anything except old tracks. Then I tried the forest to the west; there were plenty of old tracks but none quite fresh. Apparently the band I had followed so half-heartedly a few days before was the last band to visit those parts, and I now came to a not very comforting realization of the fact that I had allowed a few chafed toes to deter me from following up our only chance to replenish our failing stores of food in our home district. All the old tracks were going south, and it was evident that if we wanted to get meat we would have to go south too. It was now that I began to feel keenly the absence of Dr. Anderson and Natkusiak, the two dependable men of our party. Of those whom we had with us Kunasluk was too old and decrepit anyway, and Ilavinirk was seriously ill as the result of his hard experiences of the last month. Palaiyak, although a bright and willing boy, lacked self-reliance and was entirely inexperienced as a hunter.

One has to do with what there is, however, and on December 17th I set out to the south with Palaiyak and Pannigabluk. The plan was that we would follow Horton River south for a day and then strike west along the branch of the Horton known to us as West River, and follow wherever it led, with the idea that we might find caribou and possibly even moose. Their business was to travel upstream along the fairly smooth river ice and make camp on the river bank when twelve or fifteen miles had been covered, while I would hunt on top of the hill parallel to the river during day and when the hunting twilight was over at night I would pick up their trail in the river bottom and follow it to camp. It was one of our chief troubles that the hunting light was insufficient. The sun had been long gone, of course, but on a clear day there was light enough for about three hours at noon for shooting or for reading a newspaper out of doors (if we had had a newspaper). On a cloudy day, however, and especially when there was snow falling, there was practically no shooting light whatever.

The first day of this journey, and also the second, I hunted to no purpose, although toward evening of the second day we met with some encouragement in finding the old tracks of a moose. That evening, however, Pannigabluk was taken sick and we were therefore unable to move camp. So far as the hunting went, that did not make much difference, for the country south of West River was unknown to me as yet, and I employed the time in exploring it. It snowed thickly that day and I found neither deer nor the signs of any.

That evening when I came home I found that Palaiyak also, as well as Pannigabluk, was sick. Evidently it was the diet that was telling on them. On our journey up river from the sea we had lived on oil straight, and we had eaten so much of it that by the time we reached our camp we had only a pint or two left in a bag of oil that should, under ordinary circumstances, have lasted us for several months. The meat we had was all lean; we had therefore for some time been living on a diet of exclusively lean meat, which had aggravated the diarrhœa from which Ilavinirk suffered and which had now brought down my two companions.

Evidently, with two invalided out of three, it was not possible for us to proceed farther with our hunt, and we decided to return home. It was not only the illness of my companions that prompted this, but also the belief that Dr. Anderson and Natkusiak must surely have arrived by now, and I felt that with them to help me, the chances of success in the hunt to the south would be immeasurably greater.

On our return home, however, there was no sign of Anderson, which caused us worry of two sorts; for something must have gone wrong with him to keep him away so long, and something was likely to go wrong with us, if he did not come back, with only one able hunter to take care of seven people and six dogs in a country which the caribou seemed to have temporarily abandoned. And the tantalizing thing was to feel that the caribou could not be far away and that if we only had one or two able-bodied men to make up a sled party we were sure to overtake them. Inaction was not to be thought of, however, and Ilavinirk, although he was sick, realized this as keenly as I did, so he urged that we make another attempt to hunt upstream, in which he himself and Palaiyak would follow the river, making camps for me, while I hunted the east bank of the river into the Barren Ground, as I had hunted the west bank through the forest on the first attempt made with Pannigabluk and Palaiyak.

On December 22d I happened to think that Natkusiak had, two months before, set some dead-fall traps and baited them with pieces of blubber. I now revisited these traps and found that in some of them the blubber bait was still there. I picked these up and brought them home, and that evening all of us had some fat along with our meat, which did us a considerable amount of good.

December 24th Ilavinirk, Palaiyak, and I set out on our hunt upstream. On the first day, only a few miles southeast of our home camp I came upon the tracks of caribou, and half an hour later

I saw them grazing quietly about a mile east of the bank of Horton River. I did then the sort of foolishly conservative thing one is liable to do in an emergency — I decided not to take the responsibility of approaching these caribou alone, but to go and fetch Ilavinirk, with the idea that the two of us would be twice as sure as one to get them. This is just what I should not do now, for my experience has taught me since that you must take whatever chance offers, for you can never be sure that a second chance will present itself. I spent an hour of precious daylight in fetching Ilavinirk, and when we came back to where the caribou had been they were gone, and Ilavinirk himself was so spent with the running and the excitement that it was hard work for him to get back to the river again, unaided, where Palaiyak alone was pitching camp.

When we had seen that the caribou were gone from the place where I had seen them, Ilavinirk had gone back to camp alone, saying that he thought he had strength to do that but had not strength for anything more; and I spent another half hour in looking for the animals, at the end of which time it was already too dark to shoot. There was nothing for it but to go back to camp and try the next day. It is human nature to cry over spilt milk, and I slept little that night, thinking of the opportunity which I had foolishly let slip through my fingers. One of the features of Eskimo character is that they are far less liable than we to the tendency of indulging in vain regrets, or of saying, "I told you so," at every opportunity; and although Ilavinirk was sick, he spoke cheerfully of the probability of my finding these caribou again the next morning and getting them all.

The next day turned out to be an ideal day for hunting. The sky was clear to give us a maximum amount of light, and the wind was blowing about fifteen miles an hour, which is sufficient to keep the caribou from hearing you as you try to approach them up the wind. As always at this time of year we got up about four hours before daylight, and an hour before daylight I was on the road. The first gray of the dawn appeared about 7.30, and by 8.30 I was sitting on top of the highest hill in the neighborhood of where the caribou had been seen, and was looking around with my excellent glasses in the hope of seeing the animals by the first light. It was not clear enough for seeing much, nor for shooting, until about ten o'clock. By then I could be sure that no caribou were near, within the field of vision of my glasses, so the next thing was to pick up the trail of the evening before and follow it wherever it led. I had the trail by 10.30, and by eleven I had seen the caribou, which had moved only a little way from where they had been the evening before, and were now grazing upon the slope of a hill not more than two miles from the post of look-out, from which I had been searching the skyline for two hours with my field glasses. They had been hidden by the crest of a hill.

I did now what I should have done the day before — approached the animals directly, got within two hundred and fifty yards and secured them all. They turned out to be two young bulls and a cow with a calf. I did not stop to skin them, but covered them hastily with snow so as to prevent their freezing quickly, and made for the river as fast as I could, hoping to overtake Ilavinirk before he had moved camp far; for we had agreed in the morning before I left that he was to proceed up river on the presumption that I would be unsuccessful in the day's hunt and get as far south as possible, — we thought the farther south we got, the better our prospects.

Ilavinirk had gone about the programme energetically, and it was only after about ten miles of hard running that I overtook him getting ready to pitch camp in the mouth of a small creek. Daylight was gone and both Ilavinirk and Palaiyak were played out, so that we had to camp where we were and take the chance of wolverines and wolves stealing our precious meat during the night. The next day, when we went to fetch the meat, we found that a wolverine had eaten up a portion of one of the caribou. We shot the wolverine, and as its meat was much fatter and juicier than the caribou meat, it paid us well for the little it had stolen.

Our hunt had begun well. There is a saying that "well begun is half done." In our case well begun was four fifths done, for another week of hunting gave us only one caribou, which I shot by moonlight one early morning — the only caribou I have ever shot by moonlight, although since then I have killed more than one wolf by night.

This hunt, like the one before, I broke up rather sooner than I otherwise might, with the idea that Anderson must surely have

returned by now and that I would get him and Natkusiak to help
me.   Considering how sick and weak he was, Ilavinirk's conduct at
this time was worthy of the highest admiration, but of course he
could not do the work of a well man.   We had hunted south about
forty miles without finding the caribou there any more numerous
than they were near home.   Our return journey took us two days,
and we got home on the evening of January 5th, to find that Anderson had not yet arrived.

On the days between December 28, 1909, and January 8, 1910,
there are no entries in my diary, for on every one of those days I was
off hunting during the hours of daylight and we had no light in the
house at night by which diary entries could be written.   We had now
been nearly a month without oil or fat of any kind, either for food or
for light.   But on January 8th the women, after gathering together
all the old bones and breaking them up, had succeeded in boiling
a little tallow out of them, and by its light I made the diary entries
for the past ten days from memory, while the women mended clothes
and did other sewing they had been unable to do before for want of
light.

Of our entire seven I was now the only one not actually sick,
and I felt by no means well.   Doing hard work in cold weather on a
diet nearly devoid of fat is a most interesting and uncommon experi-
ment in dietetics, and may therefore be worth describing in some
detail.   The symptoms that result from a diet of lean meat are
practically those of starvation.   The caribou on which we had to
live had marrow in their bones that was as blood, and in most of
them no fat was discernible even behind the eyes or in the tongue.
When we had been on a diet of oil straight, a few weeks before, we
had found that with a teacupful of oil a day there were no symptoms
of hunger; we grew each day sleepier and more slovenly, and no doubt
lost strength gradually, but at the end of our meals of long-haired
caribou skin and oil we felt satisfied and at ease.   Now with a diet
of lean meat everything was different.   We had an abundance of it
as yet and we would boil up huge quantities and stuff ourselves
with it.   We ate so much that our stomachs were actually distended
much beyond their usual size — so much that it was distinctly
noticeable even outside of one's clothes.   But with all this gorging

MUD VOLCANO BETWEEN DARNLEY BAY AND LANGTON BAY.

OUR CAMP, LANGTON BAY, IN SUMMER (1911).

we felt continually hungry. Simultaneously we felt like unto bursting and also as if we had not had enough to eat. One by one the six Eskimo of the party were taken with diarrhœa.

By the 10th of January things were getting to look serious indeed. It was apparent not only that we could not go on indefinitely without fat, but it was also clear that even our lean meat would last only a few days longer. We had on December 11th estimated that we had two months' supplies of meat, and now in a month they were gone. Our estimate had not been really wrong, for if we had had a little fat to go with the meat, it would no doubt have lasted at least sixty days, but without the fat we ate such incredible quantities that it threw all our reckoning out of gear. It was not only that we ate so much, but also the dogs. They had been fed more meat than dogs usually get and still they were nothing but skin and bones, for they could not, any more than we, get along on lean meat only.

The caribou in the neighborhood were increasing in numbers now and I saw them almost every day, but I had the most outrageous luck. One day, for instance, I saw a band in clear, calm weather; it was one of those deathly still days when the quietest step on the softest snow can be heard by man or beast for several hundred yards. As the animals were quiet I did not dare to attempt approaching them, thinking that the next day might be cloudy or windy or in some way more suitable to deer-stalking, for it is a noticeable fact that even though the day be practically still, the condition of the air when the sky is clouded is such as to muffle any noise and to make the approach to deer within, say, a hundred yards feasible. The next day was windy, but altogether too windy, for it was one of those blinding blizzards when it is impossible to see more than forty or fifty feet. Because our condition was desperate, I nevertheless hunted that day and walked back and forth over the place where the caribou had been the day before, knowing that it was possible, although unlikely, that I might fall in with the animals. I did not fall in with them, however, and the next day was a blizzard of the same kind and my hunt had the same result. The third day Ilavinirk and I went out together and found the caribou still, strange to say, in the same spot, but a half mile or so before we came up to them a fawn suddenly appeared on the top of a hill near us and saw us. It is the nature of a frightened caribou to run toward any caribou that are in the neighborhood and to frighten them away also, so that there was nothing for us to do but to shoot this fawn, although we knew that the shooting would scare the large band away, which it did.

January 11th Ilavinirk and I were again out looking for caribou. He used to accompany me in the morning on the chance of our seeing something near home, but as his strength did not allow a long day's hunt he would return early while I went on as much farther as the daylight allowed. On this day we saw simultaneously to the north of us a caribou on top of one hill and three men on top of another hill. These must be Anderson, Natkusiak, and Pikaluk, we thought, and evidently they were hunting the same caribou that we saw. It was one of those still days, however, so that the chance of shooting him was not great for either party. We headed towards the caribou and so did the three men, but the caribou ran away long before we got near it.

It turned out that these three men were not the ones we had expected, however, but three Eskimo, one of whom, Memoranna, is well known under the name of Jimmie to those who have read Amundsen's account of the Northwest Passage voyage. The others were Okuk, a Baillie Islands man, and a Mackenzie River "boy," Tannaumirk, who was really about twenty-five years of age but who has an appearance and a disposition that preclude his being considered as grown up. They had come the 200-mile journey from the Baillie Islands to visit us with the hope of being able to get some caribou skins for clothing. They had had no particular luck so far in their hunts, but they had with them a little seal oil which they immediately offered to share with us. That night, therefore, we had lights again in our house and plenty of oil to eat. It was only a matter of two or three days from that time until all of us were in good form again.

CHAPTER IX

MEMORANNA was unable to tell us anything about Dr. Anderson, and now that our party was in fair health again I decided to go at once in search of him. We also needed to replenish our store of oil somehow, for the supply that Memoranna had brought with him was sufficient for a week or two only. There were three places where we had fat cached away; the nearest was about thirty miles downstream, where we had covered up with stones the fat of three grizzly bears killed in the fall, amounting to about a hundred and twenty-five pounds; teh miles farther, at Langton Bay, was the fat of one grizzly bear, one polar bear, and about half of a bearded seal, all together something over two hundred pounds; while at Cape Parry was the blubber which Dr. Anderson had gone to fetch, consisting of three or four hundred pounds that Captain Cottle had given us from the whale killed on the Banks Island voyage.

I took with me the boy Palaiyak of our own party and engaged Tannaumirk of Memoranna's party to go with us. In three days we reached our first cache of blubber to find it thoroughly rifled by wolverines. A day farther north we found that at Langton Bay a wolverine had gnawed its way through a two-inch pine plank, had entered our storehouse and eaten all but fifteen or twenty pounds of the blubber. This wolverine had lived so well on our stores that he was the fattest animal of his species I have ever seen killed; his meat was correspondingly good eating.

We had found no traces of Dr. Anderson so far, except that we could see from the fact that certain articles were missing from Langton Bay that his party had stopped there on the way north, but it was clear that they had not yet returned from Cape Parry. Because I was seriously worried for fear that some misfortune might have befallen him, and also because we had no other possible source of getting blubber, we had to continue north to Cape Parry.

I spent much time in speculations as to the possible reasons for Dr. Anderson's failure to return from Cape Parry, and some of these I recorded in my diary, so that it illustrates well my fluctuating frame of mind. There were no new facts at hand one day beyond those which I had the day before, but still my opinion of what had probably happened varied materially from time to time, evidently for subjective reasons, for on evenings when I was sitting comfortably in camp writing up my diary after a sufficient supper, I was generally of the opinion that no doubt Dr. Anderson and his party would turn up safe and sound with some logical, although for the present unimaginable, excuse for their prolonged absence. At other times, when my physical condition and surroundings were not so satisfactory, I used to incline to the view that he or some of his party had probably gone too far to sea on a polar-bear hunt and had been carried off on drifting ice by an offshore wind; or else one or more of the party might have sickened and the others might have stayed to take care of the invalids; or possibly two might have been lost for one reason or another, and the third, being alone, might later on either have been frozen to death or might have decided that the safest thing was to remain where he was and try to make his living for the winter. Had Dr. Anderson been well and the others lost, I felt sure he would have tried to reach home, but my knowledge of Natkusiak's character led me to think that under similar circumstances he would probably make himself as comfortable as possible and wait for better weather and longer days for traveling. However, all of these things were soon to be settled, for it is a matter of three days' travel only from Langton Bay north to Cape Parry, where we were sure to find some traces of the party.

January 21st we arrived at the cabin built by the wreck of the *Alexander*, where we had stored our belongings in the fall, and found it occupied by our entire party. It was a great relief to find them all there and a great surprise too, at the time. I never realized until I actually saw them how strong had been my inclination to expect that I would never see them again. But although they were all there, they were by no means well, for Dr. Anderson and Pikaluk were both in bed convalescing from pneumonia. They had had a pretty hard time. Pneumonia is a serious thing under any circumstances and especially in such a place as they were in, for not only was the house unsatisfactory, but the food at their disposal was not such as is suited to sick men. Ever since their convalescence had begun they had been hungering especially for fresh meat, and this was a place where no fresh meat was to be had, except a few foxes, for which Natkusiak trapped energetically. On an average he was getting about one fox per day. A stray caribou had wandered out upon the cape about Christmas time, and Natkusiak had secured him also, which was a great help to them. Pikaluk had been taken sick first, and Dr. Anderson had nursed him for a week, after which he was himself taken sick.

It was clear that Dr. Anderson and Pikaluk would not be fit for traveling for a month at least, and there was immediate necessity that a sled go back to our people inland with a supply of blubber for them. I therefore dispatched Natkusiak and Palaiyak at once off inland, for now that I had found Dr. Anderson I did not care to leave him again while he was sick. Tannaumirk also stayed with us, for there was no special reason for his going inland.

It was a fortunate thing that Dr. Anderson, since he was to be taken sick at all, should have been taken sick at Cape Parry, the one place where we had considerable provisions stored up against an emergency. My idea in buying flour and other things which formed our depot there had been that we should probably never need them, but I bought them as an insurance against emergency. I had not thought of the particular emergency which actually befell, but it seems, humanly speaking, that had it not been for this store of provisions, or had Dr. Anderson been taken ill anywhere else than in that neighborhood, the result would have been fatal, for the whole vicinity of Cape Parry is a poor country for game in winter in certain seasons, and this happened to be one of the bad seasons. In other words, when there are plenty of easterly or southeasterly winds, there is open water off the cape and it is a good hunting place both for seals and polar bears, but for this particular winter the winds were not strong enough to break away the ice, and bears and seals were not to be had. The supplies were calculated in the beginning to be equal to about three months' rations for four men, and it turned out that they were only just sufficient for carrying Dr. Anderson and

L

Pikaluk up to the time that they were so fully recovered as to be able to travel.

The old house in which we were staying was about ten miles south from the tip of the cape proper, and as soon as the sick men were able to move we changed our camp location from there to the tip of the cape, with the idea that we would there have a better chance to get polar bears. Tannaumirk and I hunted every day, with the result that in a period of about six weeks I had a fleeting glimpse of one polar bear at a distance, and Tannaumirk killed one caribou.

The circumstances of Tannaumirk's caribou killing bring to mind one of the common beliefs about Indians, Eskimo, and other primitive people. There are few misconceptions about them more prevalent than the one that they have a sort of "sixth sense," which may be called the sense of direction or locality and which prevents them from being lost under any circumstances. This belief is particularly strong among the whalemen who winter in the Arctic and who have seen much of the Eskimo on board ship only. There is a common saying at Herschel Island and elsewhere to the effect that "an Eskimo has a compass in his head."

Tannaumirk saw the caribou in question early one morning, and went in pursuit of it. When I came home in the evening from my polar-bear hunt to seaward he had not yet returned When he finally got home it was late in the evening, and he brought with him the skin of the caribou and some meat. There was great rejoicing in camp and Tannaumirk was the hero of the hour. In the manner common to Eskimo, he recounted in great detail his various adventures that finally led up to the successful shooting. When the story had been told, I asked him, was it a long way to where the meat was, and had he cached it safely? His answer was that he had covered the meat with snow and set traps by it, and the place was a long way off. I volunteered to go with him the next morning to fetch the meat, but he said that it would not be necessary; if he were to start early in the morning he would without assistance be able to get the meat and be home by night. Accordingly, bright and early the next day he was off with the sled and dogs. He was away all day and it had long been pitch dark and was well in the night before he returned. In answer to my questions he said that he had hurried all the time; that it was a very long way; and that he had hastily loaded the meat on the sled, set by the deerkill two additional traps, making four all together, and had come right back home, the dogs trotting some of the way.

The next day I remained in camp with Dr. Anderson and Pikaluk, while Tannaumirk was off somewhere setting fox traps. About noon Dr. Anderson heard dogs howling and called my attention to it. We went out-doors and could then hear plainly that several dogs were howling and whining on the other side of a ridge, about half a mile from camp. The situation was clear. Evidently Tannaumirk had put some traps near the house and several of the dogs had been caught in them. Dr. Anderson was so well by now that he followed while I ran as fast as possible to get the dogs freed from the traps; for at a temperature of anything like 40° below zero it takes but a sort while to freeze a paw that is pinched in a steel trap, and the best dog can be rendered valueless in half an hour through freezing if the jaws of the trap catch him well up on the paw and stop the circulation into the toes.

When we got across the hill from behind which the howls were coming we found what we expected in that four of our dogs were caught in traps; but what we had not expected to find was that this was the deerkill where Tannaumirk the day before had shot the caribou. What had happened was this: when the caribou had approached near the house and Tannaumirk had seen it, he had started after and had followed it through a circle of over ten miles without noting at all in what direction the animal was going, and he had finally succeeded in approaching and killing it when it was scarcely more than a quarter of a mile away from our house, behind the nearest hill. After skinning and cutting up the animal, Tannaumirk, with no idea of how far from camp he was, had started back over the ten miles of his old trail which eventually led him home, of course; and the following morning when he set out with the dogs to fetch the meat he had again gone the ten miles over the old trail, and had gone over it the fourth time in returning, never discovering that the place he went ten miles to reach was less than half a mile from home.

Through long experience with Eskimo and Indians I have gathered a number of anecdotes of this sort, and a number of similar ones I have obtained second-hand from others whose experience with the Indians is more extensive than mine. The fact is that most people who deal with Indians deal with them in their own country, over which the Indian has hunted since boyhood, until he knows every stick, every stone, and every creek-bed, whether he sees them in the daylight or stumbles upon them in the dark. To a man unfamiliar with this locality who accompanies the Indian, it seems next to miraculous how easily the Indian finds his way about, but there is nothing of the miraculous about it. For an Indian to recognize a rock that stands a mile and a half from his camp requires no other gift than that by which the city dweller recognizes the street corners in the neighborhood of his home. But take the Indian or the Eskimo out of his habitual surroundings, and he is, as a general thing, far the inferior of the white man in finding his way about. He has not the general principles to guide him that are clear in the mind of the average white man, and this is one of the reasons why Indians and Eskimo alike are afraid to go into a strange country, and why every white man who wants to accomplish anything in the exploration of such districts as the Barren Grounds of North America must be his own guide and that of his party as soon as they get beyond the Indian's familiar haunts.

Most white men, even those of slight education, have a knowledge of the properties of angles, so that a white hunter who goes seven miles south, then three miles east, then four miles southwest, and two miles northwest, will have a fairly definite idea of how to draw a line that will take him thence to his original starting point. The Indian or Eskimo in my experience will have no such notion, and instead of going straight home will go back over the route by which he came, unless there are some landmarks in sight which he recognized earlier in the day. In December, 1910, for instance, when we were traveling along Horton River in a district unknown to my companion, Natkusiak, — who, by the way, is the best of all Eskimo hunters that I have known, — he was away from camp two days in the pursuit and killing of some caribou. When he came to camp he reported to me that he would have to go upstream about ten miles, which meant south in that case, until he would be opposite the place where the meat was. He would then have to go on top of the hill to the east of the river and it would take him the larger part of the day to go to the deerkill, and it would be only the next day he could return. He went off early in the morning, going south; in the afternoon, while sitting on a hill three miles east of our camp spying out the country with my glasses for caribou, I saw a sled coming from the south. At first this astonished me very much, for I had no sleds to expect in that country except our own. And sure enough, it was our own sled and Natkusiak coming almost directly toward me. I headed him off and found that he was following his own trail of the day before by which he had come home, which was also the trail of the day earlier yet when he was following the caribou which he eventually killed. It turned out that he had shot the caribou about four miles northeast of our camp and that he had gone something like twenty-five miles out of his way to follow the trail by which he had come home. So much for the idea of the Eskimo having a compass in his head.

Commonly "primitive" people are supposed to have certain mental qualities, designated as "instinctive," through which they vastly excel us along certain lines; and to make up for this excellence they are supposed to be far our inferiors in certain other mental characteristics. My own observations incline me to believe that there are no points in which they, as a race, are any more inferior to us than might be expected from the environment under which they have grown up from childhood; and neither have they any points of superiority over the white man, except those which are developed directly by the environment. Of course an Eskimo can find his way about in the wilderness better than the city dweller or the sailor, but he is likely to fall behind the white man of experience in just about the proportion you would expect from knowing the greater advantages of training in logical thinking which the white man has had. The European who keeps his head and looks about him can, in a year, pick up all the essentials of the lore of the open country.

Very much to his surprise Dr. Anderson had discovered, a few days before he became ill, that Captain Wolki's schooner, the *Rosie H.*, was wintering behind the Booth Islands, an easy half-day's journey from Cape Parry. The *Rosie H.* was not abundantly fitted out with anything, and still it was a source of material comfort to us to know that she was there, for we could have fallen back on her in case of extreme need. It was due to certain of Dr. Anderson's temperamental traits, and to the possession of similar ones by Natkusiak, that Captain Wolki, although only some ten miles away, had remained in ignorance for a month of the hard straits in which our party were. After my coming up I paid a visit to the *Rosie H.*, and got roundly scolded in Dr. Anderson's stead for allowing such things to happen. Had they known of Dr. Anderson's predicament they would have done for him all they could. But now we were happily through the worst of the trouble.

By the beginning of March Dr. Anderson and Pikaluk were so completely recovered that they volunteered to make the six days' trip south to Langton Bay for the purpose of depositing there the sled load of ammunition and other necessities. It was our intention, then, by the 10th of March to proceed inland from Langton Bay where we had wintered and to strike across country thence to the northeast corner of Bear Lake, with the purpose of thereafter working north in the summer down the Coppermine River until we should meet Eskimo. We know now that this would not have been a good plan to follow; it was made impractical by the arrival, March 6th, of Ilavinirk and others of the inland party.

Ilavinirk's party told a tale of hardships and starvation rather worse than anything through which we had been previously. It had taken Natkusiak and Palaiyak a long time to reach them with the sled load of blubber. I had explained to Natkusiak when he started from Cape Parry that there was every need for hurry, for Ilavinirk's and Memoranna's parties had had practically nothing to eat when I left them. But Natkusiak could not realize that there was any real danger, and I do not think that there would have been any danger had Natkusiak been in Ilavinirk's place. As it was, however, instead of hurrying, Natkusiak stopped here and there on the way, in one place to catch fish because he had been so long without fish, and in another place to set traps because the trapping was good. Meantime Ilavinirk's and Memoranna's parties had had hard luck in hunting. There were caribou in the country, but the weather was continually bad and their management was not the best. The

"Rosie H." in Winter Quarters.

Wreck of Steam Whaler "Alexander."

little food left on hand when I went away soon disappeared, and then followed the larger zoölogical specimens which I had preserved for Dr. Anderson in the fall. There were nine skins of caribou of both sexes and all ages, which I had taken off carefully with heads, horns, and leg bones, making also careful record of the measurements. These specimens were of great scientific value, for they represented in all probability a new variety of caribou, or if not that, at least caribou from a district where none had previously been taken for scientific purposes. One of these specimens especially was a rare thing. I have been present at the killing of a thousand caribou, and in all that number I have seen only three that were hornless in a season when they should have had horns. In other words, I have seen only three caribou upon the heads of which horns were destined never to grow. One of these I had carefully skinned for Dr. Anderson. In this period of scarcity the head of this rare muley caribou went for food along with the other scientific skins. The heads of all these animals and the leg bones went first and then the skins themselves, as well as other skins which we had intended for clothing.

It was a period of scarcity not only among the human beings of that district but also among the wolves, all of which were skin poor and two of which died of starvation near our house at a place where their carcasses were found afterwards and eaten by our Eskimo. Pannigabluk was the only member of our party to whom wolf meat was taboo. The rest of us considered wolf, under ordinary circumstances, to be excellent eating. In summer when they are fat and caribou poor, all of us much preferred wolf meat to caribou. But those who tasted them were unanimous in saying that the wolves that died of starvation were no delicacy.

When Natkusiak finally arrived at the camp on Horton River, the tide had just been turned by Memoranna's success in caribou hunting. From that time everything had gone well, but the two periods of starvation in one winter, which were the first of his entire life, had proved too much for Ilavinirk and his family, for they now came to me and told me that they felt sure that if we went farther east the coming spring, things would go still worse with them. In fact, they would not go east with me and had made up their minds to quit our service and go back to the Mackenzie River, where there was plenty of fish, where tea and tobacco could be had, and where they could attend church service now and then.

These were rather critical days for us, for we had now been in the North two years without as yet being able to make an attempt to reach the country in which our goal was placed, — the country which might possibly contain Eskimo who had never seen a white man and which certainly was unknown to science and needed investigation. The situation had to be dealt with carefully, and I began by separating Natkusiak from the rest of the crowd and getting him to agree with me that the starvation of the past winter would in neither case have occurred but for the sickness and incompetence of members of our party, which were adventitious circumstances and could with reasonable care be eliminated in the future.

As a general thing the desire for adventure is foreign to the Eskimo race. They do not care to go over the mountain for the sake of finding out what there may be on the other side — they will go only if the prospect for hunting seems better there than here. But Natkusiak was the one individual I have known among his people who seemed to have a slight rudiment of the spirit of the adventurer and investigator, who likes to see things because they are new, irrespective of what may be called their commercial value.

I got him, therefore, to agree that he was still willing to proceed eastward with me, and I then told Ilavinirk that all I would ask him to do would be to stay at Langton Bay for a year and take care of our base there. I showed him that we were much better situated this year than last, for last year we had arrived at Langton Bay only in the late fall and had thus been prevented from taking advantage of the summer hunting season, and that now if I left him there, with nothing to do but hunt, the chances were that he would have an abundance of food and valuable skins laid up against the winter. Dr. Anderson would meantime make a trip to the Mackenzie River to get our mail and any supplies he might be able to secure from whalers, as well as ammunition and photographic apparatus which the American Museum of Natural History intended to send us. We pointed out to Ilavinirk that the whaling industry was, so far as we knew, on its last legs, and there was no guarantee that any ship would come to Herschel Island. And if none came, the Herschel Island people would be worse off than we were at Langton Bay, because there is less game around Herschel Island. After several days of argument Ilavinirk was finally convinced, and announced himself willing to stay at Langton Bay if Dr. Anderson would go west to Herschel Island and try to secure tea, and other things which the Eskimo consider necessities, from any whaling ships that might come in.

This was in general for us a winter of misfortunes, perhaps the most serious of which, in its effect upon our plans, was the loss of more than half of our dogs and most of the best ones. We had had twenty-three in the fall, besides several that belonged to our Eskimo, and now there were ten left all together. Of these I would have to take six at least for my trip to the eastward, and Ilavinirk could hardly get along with less than the remaining four around Langton Bay, for a man cannot do successful hunting without a sled for moving camp. Dr. Anderson therefore had no dogs with which to make his thousand-mile trip to Herschel Island and back. Memoranna was going west, however, and volunteered to take Dr. Anderson's small baggage on his sled and to let Dr. Anderson accompany him as far as the eastern edge of the Mackenzie delta—where our whaleboat had been cached by Dr. Anderson's party the fall before and at which point he would endeavor to hire an Eskimo to help him sail the boat to Fort Macpherson, and thence to Herschel Island. The idea was that if any whaling ship came in, Dr. Anderson would board it at Herschel Island and be brought east by it to Cape Bathurst; but if none came in, he would work his way eastward in the boat as far as possible during the summer, and would come afoot the rest of the way to join Ilavinirk in the early winter at the latest.

Pursuant of all these plans we moved south to Point Stivens, about ten miles north of Langton Bay, a place known to the Eskimo as Okat, which, being translated, means "Codfish," or rather "Tomcod." There is a bight behind Point Stivens where tomcod can be hooked in unbelievable numbers at almost any time in winter. We spent several days here, and each member of the party who applied himself to the fishing was able to haul out several hundred tomcod per day, so that it was not long until we had about a ton of fish.

When this was accomplished, Memoranna loaded up his sled with all the fish it would carry, and Ilavinirk his sled also; for he was to accompany Dr. Anderson as far as the mouth of the Horton River, with the view of recovering some tents, traps, ammunition, and other things which we had abandoned about thirty miles upstream on Horton River, at the time that we ran short of food on our journey up that river in December.

During the last days together, Dr. Anderson and I had frequent long talks about the prospects of the coming year — which were none of the brightest. We had suffered sickness with its consequences of delay, starvation, and the growth of discontent and worry for the future among our Eskimo. There had been accidents from causes beyond human control, and our best dogs had sickened and died. The aggregate effect of these things was depressing, but Dr. Anderson quite agreed with me that our plans had to be carried out, irrespective of whether or not we had good excuse for failing, for failure can never be so excused as to be the equivalent of success. We had been two years gone from New York, and the Eskimo uncontaminated by civilization were still as problematic as when we left home, but we had faith that they were somewhere along the coast less than three hundred miles to the east, and the time had come to go and find them.

We both felt that my journey to the eastward might turn out seriously because of the handicap we were under. We still had faith to believe that a white man can live on the country wherever an Eskimo can do so; but we did not know for certain that there were any Eskimo where we were going, for no one had ever — so far as I know — seen Eskimo on the mainland shore between Cape Parry and Cape Krusenstern, a stretch of coast which, as has been said, the Baillie Islands people believed destitute of game. As Dr. Anderson would have to take action and to answer questions in case we failed to return, I gave him written memoranda of what my plans were, gave him a date up to which he need not worry for our safety, and told him what efforts I should count on his making to reach me in case we overstayed our time-limit, which I put at about nine months.

It was March 14th that Dr. Anderson left for the west, accom-

CHAPTER X

A LTHOUGH minutes are seldom of enough value with us in the North to waste ink in recording them, I have set down the fact that it was 1.45 on the afternoon of April 21st, 1910, that we finally made our long-planned start from Langton Bay on our trip towards Coronation Gulf.

We were now fairly started for the unknown, but no one but myself was very enthusiastic over the enterprise. The reluctance of my people was due in part only (and in less part) to their fear of finding the unknown country gameless — they feared to find it inhabited by a barbarous and bloodthirsty race of which the Baillie Islands Eskimo had been telling us grotesque tales whenever our party and they came together. These dreaded people were the Nagyuktogmiut, the people of the caribou antler, who lived far to the east, and who used to come in semi-hostile contact with their ancestors long ago.

"These people bear the name of the caribou antler," they had told us, "because of a peculiar custom they have. When a woman becomes of marriageable age her coming-out is announced several days in advance. At the appointed time she is made to take her place in an open space out-of-doors, and all the men who want wives form around her in a circle, each armed with the antler of a large bull caribou. The word is given, and they all rush at her, each trying to hook her toward him with the antler. Often the woman is killed in the scrimmage, but if some one succeeds in getting her alive from the others he takes her for a wife. As strength and the skill which experience gives are the main requirements for success, some of the Nagyuktogmiut have a great many wives, while most of them have none. Because so many women are killed in this way there are twice as many men as women among them. We know many stories, of which this is one, to show what queer people these Easterners are. They also kill all strangers." That was the way all stories of the Easterners ended. Like Cato's *delenda est Carthago*, "they kill all strangers" were the unvarying words that finished every discussion of the Nagyuktogmiut by the Baillie Islanders.

No matter how fabulous a story sounds, there is usually a basis of fact; when we at last got to these Easterners we found that the kernel of truth consisted in the fewness of women as compared with men, but the reason for this fact had nothing to do with caribou antlers, but was instead connected with the fact that they practice the Spartan custom of exposing new-born children, and especially female children, with the result that women among them are much fewer than men.

When we finally made our start for the east we were in many respects poorly equipped for spending a year away from any possible source of supplies other than those which the Arctic lands themselves can furnish. When I had planned this undertaking in New York, I had counted on having good dogs, but the good dogs were now dead. I had counted on Dr. Anderson's company and coöperation, but necessity (chiefly the lack of ammunition for our rifles for the coming year) had dictated that he should go west for supplies, and that I should depend on Eskimo companions alone. I had counted on having a silk tent and other light equipment for summer use, and the lightest and most powerful rifles and high-power ammunition, but during one of our winter periods of shortage of food I had been compelled to abandon many of these things at a distance from which they could not now be got. Instead of the ten-pound silk tent, I therefore had to take a forty-pound canvas one, old and full of holes; I had only two hundred rounds for my Mannlicher-Schoenauer 6.5 mm. rifle, and had to piece out with far heavier and less powerful black-powder rifles and ammunition. In all we had four rifles of three different calibers, and a total of nine hundred and sixty rounds of three kinds of ammunition, when the right thing obviously is to have but one kind of rifle and ammunition. Had one of our rifles broken we should have had to throw away the ammunition suited to that gun.

It is true that what is right in theory cannot be wrong in practice, and still I fancy there are few men so sure of a theory that they are free from a bit of nervousness when they come to stake their lives on its holding good.   When our little party of three Eskimo and myself were finally started for the east, they felt, and expressed it, and I felt, but tried to refrain from expressing it, that we had embarked on a serious venture.   At Cape Lyon, April 27th, we left behind the farthest east point of the mainland upon which any of the American whalers are known to have landed, though some have cruised as far east as the western end of Dolphin and Union straits in summer, standing well offshore, of course, and never seeing any people.   Cape Lyon is set down by Sir John Richardson, who coasted this shore in the twenties and again in the forties of the last century, as the eastern limit of former occupation by people who build permanent earth and wood houses, after the manner of the Mackenzie Eskimo, and as, coincidently, the eastern limit of the bow-head whaling industry as carried on by the prehistoric Eskimo.   We soon discovered to be a fact what we might have inferred, that it was Sir John's method of traveling — that of summer exploration by water, when the boats usually stood well offshore — which had prevented his finding traces of permanent occupation.   Following the coast as we did, we found every few miles the ruins of such permanent whaling villages as we already knew from Alaska and the Mackenzie.   If these were not actually inhabited at the time of Sir John's coasting voyage in 1826, they must have been then but recently abandoned.   The most easterly house ruin actually seen by us was near the mouth of Crocker River, though others farther east are almost certain to have escaped us, as the snow was deep on the ground.   Many ethnologists had considered that there was an area of isolation for two hundred or so miles east of Cape Parry, and that the Eskimo of the east and west had not had much contact with one another across this supposedly barren stretch; our work has shown that while this may be true for the last hundred years at the most, it was not true farther back.   We saw no reason to think that a hundred years ago this stretch of coast was any less thickly populated than any other stretch of the Arctic coast of America.

We had with us on starting from Langton Bay about two weeks' supplies.   These were neither here nor there as provisions for a year's exploration — we would have been quite as well off had we started with only two days' supplies.   From the outset, therefore,

M

we tried to provide each day food for that day from the animals of the land. In carrying out such a programme for a party of four each had to do his share. My main reliance was the Alaskan man Natkusiak, and the woman Pannigabluk; the Mackenzie River boy Tannaumirk, a boy in character, though perhaps twenty-five in years, was a cheerful and companionable sort of fellow, but without initiative and (like many of his countrymen nowadays) not in the best of health. Our general plan was that the three Eskimo took care of the sled, one, usually the woman, walking ahead to pick out a trail through the rough sea ice, and the other two steadying the sled from upsetting too often, and pulling in harness at the same time to help the dogs. If they saw a seal or a bear, one of them would go after him while the other two waited at the sled, cooked a lunch if it was near midday, or made camp if night was approaching. If by camp-time no game had yet been seen, the woman Pannigabluk would stay by the camp to cook supper, while the two men went off in different directions to hunt. That the two should go in different directions was wise, for it doubled the chances of seeing game, but it at times caused unnecessary waste of ammunition and the killing of more meat than was needed. The very first time that both men went out to hunt in this manner, for instance, Natkusiak killed two seven or eight hundred pound bearded seals in one shot, and Tannaumirk a big, fat grizzly bear in four shots. This was meat enough for several weeks if we had (Eskimo fashion) stayed there to eat it up; traveling as we were, heavily loaded through rough ice, we could not take along more than a hundred pounds of meat.

Although the Eskimo frequently killed an animal or two if they happened on them along the line of march, their chief business was getting the sled load as many miles ahead as convenient during the day, which was seldom over fifteen miles in a working day averaging perhaps eight hours. We were in no hurry, for we had no particular distance to go and no reason to hasten back, but expected to spend the summer wherever it overtook us, and the winter similarly in its turn.

My companions traveled along the coast, made camp, and cooked, while I took upon myself the main burden of the food-providing. With this in view I used to strike inland about five miles in the

WHEN WE SHOT A SEAL DURING THE DAY HE WAS DRAGGED ALONG BEHIND THE SLED TILL CAMP TIME.

morning, starting often a good while before the Eskimo broke camp, and then walking rapidly eastward parallel to the coast. With my snow-shoes I made easy and rapid progress compared to that of the sled along the coast, unless I happened on caribou. These had been in some numbers on the Parry peninsula before we left home. (We called the Langton Bay and Cape Parry district "home" for three years, for, no matter how many hundreds of miles of land and ice separated Dr. Anderson or me from it, we always had at least one Eskimo family there protecting what supplies we had and the scientific collections already made.) Crossing Darnley Bay on the ice, we had of course seen no caribou; at Cape Lyon the Eskimo saw one yearling, but were unable to get it; and at Point Pierce, five days out from Langton Bay, we were stopped by an easterly blizzard without having yet secured any. The Eskimo, who had "known" all along that we were going into a gameless country, felt sure that the fawn they had seen at Lyon was the most easterly member of the deer species inhabiting the coast; it would, therefore, be wisdom to turn about now, they argued, before the road got too long for the back journey and we got too weak from hunger — all this over huge troughs of boiled meat and raw blubber of the seals killed two days before, on which we were gorging ourselves, for much eating was always our chief pastime when delayed by a blizzard that the dogs would not face. As a matter of fact, what my Eskimo really dreaded was not so much hunger as the possibility of our success in the quest of what to me were the scientifically interesting "people who had never seen a white man," but to them were the dreaded "Nagyuk-togmiut, so called because they hook to themselves wives with the antlers of bull caribou; *they kill all strangers.*"

Generally it is only in times of extreme need that one hunts caribou in a blizzard — not that nine tenths of the blizzards in the Arctic need keep a healthy man indoors; it is merely that the drifting snow (even when you can see as far as two hundred yards) diminishes many times over the chance you have of finding game. If you do find caribou, however, the stronger the gale the better your chance of close approach without being seen, for these animals, though they double their watchfulness in foggy weather, seem to relax it in a blizzard. In the present instance my reason for looking for caribou was that I wanted to kill a few for the moral effect it would have on my party; for in the midst of abundance they would be forced to fall back on their fear of the Nagyuktogmiut as the only argument for retreat, and this they were a bit ashamed of doing, even among themselves. It was therefore great luck for us, although we were in no immediate need of meat, that after a short hunt through the storm I ran into a band of seven cows and young bulls about five miles inland, southwest from Point Pierce. I came upon them quite without cover, but saw them through the drifting snow at three hundred yards before they saw me — the human eye is a great deal keener than that of the caribou, wolf, or any other animal with which I have had experience. By stepping back a few paces till the drifting snow had hidden the caribou again, and then guardedly circling them to leeward, I found a slight ridge which allowed safe approach to within about two hundred yards of where they had been. The main thing in stalking caribou that are not moving is the ability to keep in mind their location accurately while you are circling and winding about so as to approach them from a new direction behind cover of irregular hills and ridges that are of course unfamiliar to you. In this case my plans came suddenly to naught through the caribou appearing on the sky-line two hundred yards off. I shot three of them, though we could not possibly use more than the meat of one. The moral effect on my Eskimo of having food to throw away would, I knew, be invaluable to me. Had I killed only one, they would not have believed it to be for any reason other than that I was unable to kill more. This was the only time in a period of fourteen months of continuous "living on the country" that I shot more animals than I thought we should need, although I often had to kill a single large animal, such as a polar bear or bearded seal, when I knew we should be unable to haul with us more than a small part of its meat.

We proceeded eastward along the deserted coast without adventure. "Blessed is that country whose history is uninteresting" applies to Arctic expeditions as well. Having an adventure is a sign that something unexpected, something unprovided against, has happened; it shows that some one is incompetent, that something has gone wrong. For that reason we pride ourselves on the fewness of our adventures; for the same reason we are a bit ashamed of the few we did have. An adventure is interesting enough in retrospect, especially to the person who didn't have it; at the time it happens it usually constitutes an exceedingly disagreeable experience. On May 2d, near Point Dease Thompson, through incompetence of my own, I came near having a serious one; that I did not actually have it was due to the incompetence of a polar bear. After completely outmaneuvering me at the start, he allowed a fondness for grandstand play to lose him the game at the critical moment.

The thing happened in the afternoon. As usual, I was hunting caribou eastward along the sea-front of the Melville Mountains that lie parallel to the coast a few miles inland. The sled and the Eskimo were traveling more slowly along the coast and were several miles behind — for one thing, the sled was heavy and the ice rough; for another, they used to stop an hour or so each day to cook a lunch at which I was seldom able to join them. I had seen no caribou all day nor the day before, and our meat was low; therefore I stopped whenever I came to the top of a commanding hill to sweep the country carefully with my binoculars. The land showed nothing but a white wolf or arctic fox now and then; ptarmigan there were, but they are too small game for a party of four that is going to go a year on nine hundred and sixty rounds of ammunition; the foxes, too, were beneath our notice, though their meat is excellent; but a wolf that came within two hundred yards seldom got by me, for a fat one weighs a hundred pounds, and all of us preferred them at this season to caribou, except Pannigabluk, who would not taste the meat because it is taboo to her people.

This day the wolves did not come near, and the first hopeful thing I saw was a yellow spot on the sea ice about three miles off. After watching it for five minutes or so I was still unable to determine whether or not the spot was yellow ice or something else than ice; had my party been abreast of me or ahead I should have given up and moved on, but as they were several miles behind I put in a half-hour watching this thing that was a bit yellower than ice should be; now and then I looked elsewhere, for a caribou or grizzly may at any time come out from behind a hill, a polar bear from behind a cake of ice, or a seal out of his hole. After sweeping the entire circle of the horizon perhaps for the sixth time I noted that the yellow spot had disappeared — it was, therefore, a polar bear that had been lying down; after sleeping too long in one position he had stood up and lain down again behind an ice cake.

A moment after noting this I was running as hard as I could in the direction of the bear, for there was no telling how soon he would start traveling or how fast he would go. I had, as soon as I began to suspect the yellow spot might be a bear, taken careful note of the topography behind me with relation to the spot's position out on the rough sea ice, for it is as difficult to keep a straight line toward an invisible object among the ice cakes and pressure ridges as it is in a forest. The mountains behind, however, could always be seen, and by their configuration I tried to guide myself straight toward the bear. Every three or four hundred yards I would climb a high pressure ridge and have a look around with the glasses, but nothing was to be seen. I did not, in fact, expect to see anything unless the bear had commenced traveling, in which case he would perhaps expose himself by crossing a high ridge. When at last I got to the neighborhood of the animal, according to my calculations, I climbed an especially high ridge and spent a longer time than usual sweeping the surroundings with the glasses and studying individual ice cakes and ridges, with the hope of recognizing some of those I had seen from the mountains to be in the neighborhood of my bear; but everything looked different on near approach, and I failed to locate myself to my own satisfaction. I had decided to go a quarter of a mile or so farther before beginning to circle in quest of the bear's tracks. My rifle was buckled in its case slung across my back, and I was slowly and cautiously clambering down the far side of a pressure ridge, when I heard behind me a noise like the spitting of a cat or the hiss of a goose. I looked back and saw, about twenty feet away and almost above me, a polar bear.

Had he come the remaining twenty feet as quietly and quickly as a bear can, the literary value of the incident would have been lost forever; for, as the Greek fable points out, a lion does not write a book. From his eye and attitude, as well as the story his trail told afterward, there was no doubting his intentions: the hiss was merely his way of saying, "Watch me do it!" Or at least that is how I interpreted it; possibly the motive was chivalry, and the hiss was his way of saying *Garde!* Whichever it was, it was the fatal mistake of a game played well to that point; for no animal on earth can afford to give warning to a man with a rifle. And why should he? Has a hunter ever played fair with one of them?

Afterward the snow told plainly the short — and for one of the participants, tragic — story. I had underestimated the bear's distance from shore, and had passed the spot where he lay, going a hundred yards or two to windward; on scenting me he had come up the wind to my trail, and had then followed it, walking about ten paces to leeward of it, apparently following my tracks by smelling them from a distance. The reason I had not seen his approach was that it had not occurred to me to look back over my own trail; I was so used to hunting bears that the possibility of one of them assuming my own rôle and hunting me had been left out of consideration. A good hunter, like a good detective, should leave nothing out of consideration.

On May 9th, nineteen days out from Langton Bay, we came upon signs that made our hearts beat faster. It was at Point Wise, where the open sea begins to be narrowed into Dolphin and Union straits by the near approach to the mainland of the mountainous shores of Victoria Island. The beach was strewn with pieces of drift-wood, and on one of them we found the marks of recent choppings with a dull adze. A search of the beach for half a mile each way revealed numerous similar choppings. Evidently the men who had made them had been testing the pieces of wood to see if they were sound enough to become the materials for sleds or other things they had wished to make. Those pieces which had but one or two adze marks had been found unsound; in a few places piles of chips showed that a sound piece had been found there and had been roughed down for transportation purposes on the spot. Prepossessed by the idea that Victoria Island was probably inhabited because Rae had seen people on its southwest coast in 1851, and the mainland probably uninhabited because Richardson had failed to find any people on it in 1826 and again in 1848, I decided that the men whose traces we saw were probably Victoria Islanders who had with sleds crossed the frozen straits from the land whose mountains we could faintly see to the north, and had returned to its woodless shores with the drift-wood they had picked up here. We learned later that this supposition was wrong; the people whose traces we found were mainland dwellers whose ancestors must have been hunting inland to the south when Richardson twice passed without seeing them.

The night after this discovery we did not sleep much. The Eskimo were more excited than I was, apparently, and far into the morning they talked and speculated on the meaning of the signs. Had we come upon traces of the Nagyuktogmiut "who kill all strangers"? Fortunately enough, my long-entertained fear that traces of people would cause a panic in my party was not realized. In spite of all their talk, and in spite of the fact that they were seriously afraid, the curiosity as to what these strange people would prove to be like — in fine, the spirit of adventure, which seldom crops out in an Eskimo — was far stronger than their fears. We were therefore up early the next morning, and soon out on the road.

All that day we found along the beach comparatively fresh traces of people, chiefly shavings and chips where the hewing and shaping of wood had taken place. None seen that day were of the present winter, though some seemed to be of the previous summer; but the next morning, just east of Point Young, we found at last human footprints in the crusted snow and sled tracks that were not over three months old. That day at Cape Bexley we came upon a deserted village of over fifty snow houses; their inhabitants had apparently left them about midwinter, and it was now the 12th of May.

The size of the deserted village took our breath away. Tannaumirk, the young man from the Mackenzie River, had never seen an inhabited village among his people of more than twelve or fifteen houses. All his old fears of the Nagyuktogmiut "who kill all strangers" now came to the surface afresh; all the stories that he knew of their peculiar ways and atrocious deeds were retold by him that evening for our common benefit.

A broad but three months' untraveled trail led north from this village site across the ice toward Victoria Island. My intentions were to continue east along the mainland into Coronation Gulf, but I decided nevertheless to stop here long enough to make an attempt to find the people at whose village we had camped. We would leave most of our gear on shore, with Pannigabluk to take care of it, while the two men and myself took the trail across the ice. This was according to Eskimo etiquette — on approach to the country of strange or distrusted people non-combatants are left behind, and only the able men of the party advance to a cautious parley. In this case the Mackenzie River man, Tannaumirk, was frightened enough to let his pride go by the board and to ask that he, too, might stay on shore at the camp. I told him he might, and Natkusiak and I prepared to start alone with a light sled, but at the last moment Tannaumirk decided he preferred to go with us, as the Nagyuktogmiut were likely in our absence to discover our camp, to surprise it by night, and to kill him while he slept. It would be safer, he thought, to go with us. Pannigabluk was much the coolest of the three Eskimo; if she was afraid to be left alone on shore she did not show it; she merely said that she might get lonesome if we were gone more than three or four days. We left her cheerfully engaged in the mending of our worn footgear, and at 2.30 P.M., May 13th, 1910, we took the old but nevertheless plain trail northward into the rough sea ice.

It was only near shore that the ice was rough, and with our light sled we made good progress; it was the first time on the trip that we did not have to pull in harness ourselves; instead we took turns in riding, two sitting on the sled at the same time and one running ahead to cheer the dogs on. We made about six miles per hour, and inside of two hours we arrived at another deserted village, about a month more recent than the one found at Cape Bexley. We were, therefore, on the trail not of a traveling party but of a migratory community.

As we understood dimly then and know definitely now, each village on such a trail should be about ten miles from the next preceding, and should be about a month more recent. The explanation of this is simple. The village of a people who hunt seal on level "bay" ice must not be on shore, for it is not convenient for a hunter to go more than five miles at the most from camp to look for the seal-holes, and naturally there are no seal-holes on land; the inhabitants of a sea village can hunt through an entire circle whose radius is about five miles; the inhabitants of a shore village can hunt through only half a circle of the same radius, for the other half of it will be on land. When the frost overtakes the seals in the fall, each of them, wherever he happens to be, gnaws several holes in the thin ice and rises to these whenever he needs to breathe. As the ice thickens he keeps them open by continuous gnawing, and for the whole of the winter that follows he is kept a prisoner in their neighborhood because of the fact that if he ever went to a considerable distance he would be unable to find a place to reach the air, and would therefore die of suffocation. By the aid of their dogs the Eskimo find these breathing-holes of the seals underneath the snow that hides them in winter, and spear the animals as they rise for air. In a month or so the hunters of a single village will have killed all the seals within a radius of about five miles; they must then move camp about ten miles, so that a five-mile circle around their next camp shall be tangent to the five-mile circle about their last one; for if the circles overlapped there would be that much waste territory within the new circle of activities. If, then, you are following such a trail and come to a village about four months old, you will expect to find the people who made it not more than forty miles off.

In the present case our task was simplified by the fact that the group we were following had not moved straight ahead north, but had made their fourth camp west of the second. Standing on the roofs of the houses of the second camp, we could see three seal-hunters a few miles to the west, each sitting on his block of snow by a seal-hole waiting for the animal to rise.

The seal-hunters and their camp were up the wind, and our dogs scented them. As we bore swiftly down upon the nearest of the sealers the dogs showed enthusiasm and anticipation as keen as mine, keener by a great deal than did my Eskimo. As the hunter was separated from each of his fellow-huntsmen by a full half-mile, I thought he would probably be frightened if all of us were to rush up to him at the top speed of our dogs. We therefore stopped our sled several hundred yards away. Tannaumirk had become braver now, for the lone stranger did not look formidable, sitting stooped for-

OUR SLED AT A PERMANENTLY DESERTED SNOW VILLAGE.

The dark openings are not windows, but are made for passing household goods out when house is abandoned.

TEMPORARILY DESERTED VILLAGE.

The people will return for their belongings left behind.

ward as he was on his block of snow beside the seal-hole; he accordingly volunteered to act as our ambassador, saying that the Mackenzie dialect (his own) was probably nearer the stranger's tongue than Natkusiak's. This seemed likely, so I told him to go ahead. The sealer sat motionless as Tannaumirk approached him; I watched him through my glasses and saw that he held his face steadily as if watching the seal-hole, but that he raised his eyes every second or two to the (to him) strange figure of the man approaching. He was evidently tensely ready for action. Tannaumirk by now was thoroughly over his fears, and would have walked right up to the sealer, but when no more than five paces or so intervened between them the sealer suddenly jumped up, grasping a long knife that had lain on the snow beside him, and poising himself as if to receive an attack or to be ready to leap forward suddenly. This scared our man, who stopped abruptly and began excitedly and volubly to assure the sealer that he and all of us were friendly and harmless, men of excellent character and intentions.

I was, of course, too far away to hear, but Tannaumirk told me afterward that on the instant of jumping up the sealer began a monotonous noise which is not a chant nor is it words — it is merely an effort to ward off dumbness, for if a man who is in the presence of a spirit does not make at least one sound each time he draws his breath, he will be stricken permanently dumb. This is a belief common to the Alaska and Coronation Gulf Eskimo. For several minutes Tannaumirk talked excitedly, and the sealer kept up the moaning noise, quite unable to realize, apparently, that he was being spoken to in human speech. It did not occur to him for a long time, he told us afterward, that we might be something other than spirits, for our dogs and dog harness, our sleds and clothes, were such as he had never seen in all his wanderings; besides, we had not, on approaching, used the peace sign of his people, which is holding the hands out to show that one does not carry a knife.

After what may have been anything from five to fifteen minutes of talking and expostulation by Tannaumirk, the man finally began to listen and then to answer. The dialects proved to differ about as much as Norwegian does from Swedish, or Spanish from Portuguese. After Tannaumirk had made him understand the assurance that we were of good intent and character, and had showed by lifting his own coat that he had no knife, the sealer approached him cautiously and felt of him, partly (as he told us later) to assure himself that he was not a spirit, and partly to see if there were not a knife hidden somewhere under his clothes. After a careful examination and some further parley, he told Tannaumirk to tell us that they two would proceed home to the village, and Natkusiak and I might follow as far behind as we were now; when they got to the village we were to remain outside it till the people could be informed that we were visitors with friendly intentions.

As we proceeded toward the village other seal-hunters gradually converged toward us from all over the neighboring four or five square miles of ice and joined Tannaumirk and his companion, who walked about two hundred yards ahead. As each of these was armed with a long knife and a seal-spear, it may be imagined that the never very brave Tannaumirk was pretty thoroughly frightened — to which he owned up freely that night and the few days next following, though he had forgotten the circumstance completely by next year, when we returned to his own people in the Mackenzie district, where he is now a drawing-room lion on the strength of his adventures in the far east. When we approached the village every man, woman, and child was outdoors, waiting for us excitedly, for they could tell from afar that we were no ordinary visitors. The man whom we had first approached — who that day acquired a local prominence which still distinguishes him above his fellows — explained to an eagerly silent crowd that we were friends from a distance who had come without evil intent, and immediately the whole crowd (about forty) came running toward us. As each came up he would say: "I am So-and-so. I am well disposed. I have no knife. Who are you?" After being told our names in return, and being assured that we were friendly, and that our knives were packed away in the sled and not hidden under our clothing, each would express his satisfaction and stand aside for the next to present himself. Sometimes a man would present his wife, or a woman her husband, according to which came up first. The women were in more hurry to be presented than were the men, for they must, they said, go right back to their houses to cook us something to eat.

After the women were gone the men asked us whether we preferred to have our camp right in the village or a little outside it. On talking it over we agreed it would be better to camp about two hundred yards from the other houses, so as to keep our dogs from fighting with theirs. When this was decided, half a dozen small boys were sent home to as many houses to get their fathers' snow-knives and house-building mittens. We were not allowed to touch a hand to anything in camp-making, but stood idly by, surrounded continually by a crowd who used every means to show how friendly they felt and how welcome we were, while a few of the best house-builders set about erecting for us the house in which we were to live as long as we cared to stay with them. When it had been finished and furnished with the skins, lamp, and the other things that go to make a snow house the coziest and most comfortable of camps, they told us they hoped we would occupy it at least till the last piece of meat in their storehouses had been eaten, and that so long as we stayed in the village no man would hunt seals or do any work until his children began to complain of hunger. It was to be a holiday, they said, for this was the first time their people had been visited by strangers from so great a distance that they knew nothing of the land from which they came.

These simple, well-bred, and hospitable people were the savages whom we had come so far to see. That evening they saw for the first time the lighting of a sulphur match; the next day I showed them the greater marvels of my rifle; it was a day later still that they first understood that I was one of the white men of whom they had heard from other tribes, under the name *kablunat*.

I asked them: "Couldn't you tell by my blue eyes and the color of my beard?"

"But we didn't know," they answered, "what sort of complexions the *kablunat* have. Besides, our neighbors to the north have eyes and beards like yours." That was how they first told us of the people whose discovery has brought up such important biological and historical problems, the people who have since become known to newspaper readers as the "Blond Eskimo."

CHAPTER XI

OUR first day among the Dolphin and Union Straits Eskimo was the day of all my life to which I had looked forward with the most vivid anticipations, and to which I now look back with equally vivid memories, for it introduced me, a student of mankind and of primitive men especially, to a people of a bygone age. Mark Twain's Connecticut Yankee went to sleep in the nineteenth century and woke up in King Arthur's time among knights who rode in clinking mail to the rescue of fair ladies; we, without going to sleep at all, had walked out of the twentieth century into the country of the intellectual and cultural contemporaries of a far earlier age than King Arthur's. These were not such men as Cæsar found in Gaul or in Britain; they were more nearly like the still earlier hunting tribes of Britain and of Gaul living contemporaneous to but oblivious of the building of the first pyramid in Egypt. Their existence on the same continent with our populous cities was an anachronism of ten thousand years in intelligence and material development. They gathered their food with the weapons of the men of the Stone Age, they thought their simple, primitive thoughts and lived their insecure and tense lives — lives that were to me the mirrors of the lives of our far ancestors whose bones and crude handiwork we now and then discover in river gravels or in prehistoric caves. Such archæological remains found in various parts of the world of the men who antedated the knowledge of the smelting of metals, tell a fascinating story to him whose scientific imagination can piece it together and fill in the wide gaps; but far better than such dreaming was my present opportunity. I had nothing to imagine; I had merely to look and listen; for here were not remains of the Stone Age, but the Stone Age itself, men and women, very human, entirely friendly, who welcomed us to their homes and bade us stay.

The dialect they spoke differed so little from the Mackenzie River speech which I had acquired in three years of living in the houses

VILLAGE, DOLPHIN AND UNION STRAITS, EARLY MAY.

Walls of snow, roofs of skins.

A STONE HOUSE OF UNKNOWN ORIGIN.

and traveling camps of the western Eskimo that we could make ourselves understood from the first. It cannot have happened often in the history of the world that the first white man to visit a primitive people was one who spoke their language. My opportunities were therefore unusual. Long before the year was over I was destined to become as one of them, and even from the first hour we were able to converse sympathetically on subjects of common concern. Nothing that I have to tell from the Arctic is of greater intrinsic interest or more likely to be considered a contribution to knowledge than the story of our first day with these people who had not, either they or their ancestors, seen a white man until they saw me. I shall therefore tell that story.

Like our distant ancestors, no doubt, these people fear most of all things the evil spirits that are likely to appear to them at any time in any guise, and next to that they fear strangers. Our first meeting had been a bit doubtful and dramatic through our being mistaken for spirits, but now they had felt of us and talked with us, and knew we were but common men. Strangers we were, it is true, but we were only three among forty of them, and were therefore not to be feared. Besides, they told us, they knew we could harbor no guile from the freedom and frankness with which we came among them; for, they said, a man who plots treachery never turns his back to those whom he intends to stab from behind.

Before the house which they immediately built for us was quite ready for our occupancy children came running from the village to announce that their mothers had dinner ready. The houses were so small that it was not convenient to invite all three of us into the same one to eat; besides, it was not etiquette to do so, as we now know. Each of us was, therefore, taken to a different place. My host was the seal-hunter whom we had first approached on the ice. His house would, he said, be a fitting one in which to offer me my first meal among them, for his wife had been born farther west on the mainland coast than any one else in their village, and it was even said that her ancestors had not belonged originally to their people, but were immigrants from the westward. She would, therefore, like to ask me questions.

It turned out, however, that his wife was not a talkative person, but motherly, kindly, and hospitable, like all her countrywomen. Her first questions were not of the land from which I came, but of my footgear. Weren't my feet just a little damp, and might she not pull my boots off for me and dry them over the lamp? Would I not put on a pair of her husband's dry socks, and was there no little hole in my mittens or coat that she could mend for me? She had boiled some seal-meat for me, but she had not boiled any fat, for she did not know whether I preferred the blubber boiled or raw. They always cut it in small pieces and ate it raw themselves; but the pot still hung over the lamp, and anything she put into it would be cooked in a moment.

When I told her that my tastes quite coincided with theirs — as, in fact, they did — she was delighted. People were much alike, then, after all, though they came from a great distance. She would, accordingly, treat me exactly as if I were one of their own people come to visit them from afar — and, in fact, I *was* one of their own people, for she had heard that the wicked Indians to the south spoke a language no man could understand, and I spoke with but a slight flavor of strangeness.

When we had entered the house the boiled pieces of seal-meat had already been taken out of the pot and lay steaming on a sideboard. On being assured that my tastes in food were not likely to differ from theirs, my hostess picked out for me the lower joint of a seal's fore leg, squeezed it firmly between her hands to make sure nothing should later drip from it, and handed it to me, along with her own copper-bladed knife; the next most desirable piece was similarly squeezed and handed to her husband, and others in turn to the rest of the family. When this had been done, one extra piece was set aside in case I should want a second helping, and the rest of the boiled meat was divided into four portions, with the explanation to me that there were four families in the village who had no fresh seal-meat. The little adopted daughter of the house, a girl of seven or eight, had not begun to eat with the rest of us, for it was her task to take a small wooden platter and carry the four pieces of boiled meat to the four families who had none of their own to cook. I thought to myself that the pieces sent out were a good deal smaller than the individual portions we were eating, and that the recipients would not get quite a square meal; but I learned later that night from my two companions that four similar presents had been sent out from each of the houses where they were eating, and I know now that every house in the village in which any cooking was done had likewise sent four portions, so that the aggregate must have been a good deal more than the recipients could eat at one time. During our meal presents of food were also brought us from other houses; each housewife apparently knew exactly what the others had put in their pots, and whoever had anything to offer that was a little bit different would send some of that to the others, so that every minute or two a small girl messenger appeared in our door with a platter of something to contribute to our meal. Some of the gifts were especially designated as for me — mother had said that however they divided the rest of what she was sending, the boiled kidney was for me; or mother had sent this small piece of boiled seal-flipper to me, with the message that if I would take breakfast at their house to-morrow I should have a whole flipper, for one of my companions was over at their house now, and had told them that I considered the flipper the best part of a seal.

As we ate we sat on the front edge of the bed-platform, holding each his piece of meat in the left hand and the knife in the right. This was my first experience with a knife of native copper; I found it more than sharp enough and very serviceable. The piece of copper (float) from which the blade had been hammered out had been found, they told me, on Victoria Island to the north in the territory of another tribe, from whom they had bought it for some good driftwood from the mainland coast. My hostess sat on my right in front of the cooking-lamp, her husband on my left. As the house was only the ordinary oval snow dome, about seven by nine feet in inside dimensions, there was only free room for the three of us on the front edge of the two-foot-high snow platform, over which reindeer, bear, and musk-ox skins had been spread to make the bed. The children, therefore, ate standing up on the small, open floor space to the right of the door as one enters; the lamp and cooking-gear and frames for drying clothing over the lamp took up all the space to the left of the door. In the horseshoe-shaped, three-foot-high doorway stood the three dogs of my host, side by side, waiting for some one to finish

N

the picking of a bone. As each of us in turn finished a bone we would toss it to one of the dogs, who retired with it to the alleyway, and returned to his position in line again as soon as he had finished it. When the meal was over they all went away unbidden, to curl up and sleep in the alleyway or out-of-doors.

Our meal was of two courses: the first, meat; the second, soup. The soup is made by pouring cold seal blood into the boiling broth immediately after the cooked meat has been taken out of the pot, and stirring briskly until the whole comes nearly (but never quite) to a boil. This makes a soup of a thickness comparable to our English pea-soups, but if the pot be allowed to come to a boil, the blood will coagulate and settle to the bottom. When the pot lacks a few degrees of boiling, the lamp above which it is swung is extinguished and a few handfuls of snow are stirred into the soup to bring it to a temperature at which it can be freely drunk. By means of a small dipper the housewife then fills the large musk-ox-horn drinking-cups and assigns one to each person; if the number of cups is short, two or more persons may share the contents of one cup, or a cup may be refilled when one is through with it and passed to another.

After I had eaten my fill of fresh seal-meat and drunk two pint cupfuls of blood soup, my host and I moved farther back on the bed-platform, where we could sit comfortably, propped up against bundles of soft caribou-skins, while we talked of various things. He and his wife asked but few questions, and only such as could not be considered intrusive, either according to their standards as I learned them later or according to ours. They understood perfectly, they said, why we had left behind the woman of our party when we came upon their trail, for it is always safest to assume that strangers are going to prove hostile; but now that we knew them to be harmless and friendly, would we not allow them to send a sled in the morning to bring her to the village? They had often heard that their ancestors used to come in contact with people to the west, and now it was their good fortune to have with them some men from the west, and they would like to see a western woman, too. It must be a very long way to the land from which we came; were we not satiated with traveling, and did we not think of spending the summer with them? Of course, the tribes who lived farther east would also be glad to see us, and would treat us well, unless we went too far to the east and fell in with the Netsilik Eskimo (King William Island), who are wicked, treacherous people who — strange to say — have no chins. Beyond them, they had heard, lived the white men (Kablunat), of whom, no doubt, we had never heard, seeing we came from the west, and the white men are farthest of all people to the east. They are said to have various physical deformities; they had heard that some of them had one eye in the middle of the forehead, but of this they were not sure, because stories that come from afar are always doubtful. The white men were said to be of a strangely eccentric disposition; when they gave anything to an Eskimo they would take no pay for it, and they would not eat good, ordinary food, but subsisted on various things which a normal person could not think of forcing himself to swallow except in case of starvation. And this in spite of the fact that the white men could have better things to eat if they wanted to, for seals, whales, fish, and even caribou abound in their country.

These and a great many other things I was told with friendly readiness; I had only to give them a hint as to what interested me, and they put all their information on that subject at my disposal; but on their own part they showed the greatest delicacy in asking questions. Were they not interested, I asked them, to know why I had come and where I was going? Yes, they were interested, but they knew that if I wanted them to know I would tell them. Asking many questions of strangers was not their custom, but they considered that I asked many because that was no doubt the manner of my people; it was to be expected that men coming from so great a distance would have customs different from theirs; and as for them, they were glad to answer my questions, and I would have to stay many days before they got tired of doing whatever they could to show they were glad I had come.

After the meal was finished we sat and talked perhaps an hour, until a messenger came (it was always the children who carried messages) to say that my companions had gone to the house that had been built for us, and that the people hoped I would come there, too, for it was a big house, and many could sit in there at once and talk with us. On arriving home I found that, although over half the village were already there, still we had plenty of room within doors for the four or five who had come along with me to see me home. The floor of the inner half of the house had been raised into the usual two-foot-high snow sleeping-platform, covered with skins, partly ours and partly contributed by various households for our comfort; a seal-oil lamp for heating and lighting purposes had been installed. It was a cozy place, heated by the lamp to a temperature of 60° Fahr. in spite of the fact that it was well ventilated by a door that was never closed day or night, and a hole in the roof that was also always open. On the bed-platform there was room for twelve or fifteen persons to sit Turkish fashion, and on the floor in front another fifteen could easily stand.

Although the house was full of guests at my home-coming, they merely stayed a few minutes, for some one suggested that we were no doubt tired and sleepy and would like to be left alone. In the morning, they said, we should have plenty of time for talking. When they were all gone, however, we did not go to sleep, but sat up fully half the night discussing the strange things we had seen. My Eskimo were considerably more excited over it all than I. It was, they said, as if we were living through a story such as the old men tell in the assembly-house when the sun is away in winter. What kindly, inoffensive-looking people these were, but no doubt they were powerful and dangerous magicians such as the stories tell about and such as my companions' fathers had known in their youth. My Mackenzie man, Tannaumirk, had, in fact, heard something to make this clear, for he had eaten supper in the house of a man who last winter had dropped his knife into a seal-hole through the ice where the sea was very deep, but so powerful was the spell he pronounced that when he reached into the water afterward the water came only to his elbow and he picked the knife off the ocean bottom. And this, Tannaumirk commented, in spite of the fact that the ice alone was at least a fathom thick and the water so deep that a stone dropped into it would no doubt take a long time to sink to the bottom.

Did they believe all this, I asked my men, though I knew what answer I would get. Of course they did. Why should I ask? Had they not often told me that their own people were able to do such things until a few years ago, when they abjured their familiar spirits

Watching the Arrival of Visitors.

Bowmen hunting Ptarmigan.

on learning from the missionary of the existence of heaven and hell, and of the fact that no one can attain salvation who employs spirits to do his bidding? It was too bad that salvation and the practice of magic were incompatible; not that such trivial things as the recovery of lost articles were of moment, but in the cure of sickness and the control of weather and ice conditions, prayers seemed so much less efficient than the old charms. Still, of course, they did not really regret the loss of the old knowledge and power, for did they not have the inestimable prospect of salvation which had been denied their forefathers through the unfortunate lateness of the coming of the missionaries? It was mere shortsightedness to regret having renounced the miraculous ability to cure disease, for God knows best when one should die, and to him who prays faithfully and never works on Sunday, death is but the entrance to a happier life.

We did not know, the next morning when we woke up and began to stir about within doors, that some one had been for a long time listening outside our snow house, waiting for signs of our being awake. From familiarity with their customs I now know that it was a signal from him that brought us our earliest visitors of the morning, the hunter whom we had first encountered the previous evening. He came from the village, walking slowly and singing at the top of his voice so that we might have ample warning of his approach. When he came to the outer door of our twenty-foot alleyway he stopped and announced himself: "I am So-and-so; my intentions are friendly; I have no knife. May I come in?" This was the invariable formula in our case; among themselves they would merely announce as they were about to enter a house: "I am So-and-so; I am coming in."

The talk that morning turned on various things. Who were their neighbors to the east and to the north? Had they ever come in contact with the Indians to the south? Had they any knowledge of white men visiting their country (for I considered it possible, though not likely, that some survivors of Franklin's luckless ships, wrecked more than half a century ago near the east coast of Victoria Island, might have lived for a time among these people). Although they were doubtless as curious concerning us as I was about them, still they asked few questions, even after I had given them an opening by asking many questions of them. Their admirable reticence and good breeding made me feel more nearly ashamed of my calling than I had ever been before, for an ethnologist must make inquiries, and impertinent ones at times; but they answered with greatest good humor. They had never seen white men, although they had heard about them the things they had told me last night; the Indians they had never seen, but they had seen traces of them on the mainland to the south where the musk-oxen are, and they knew by hearsay from the Coppermine River Eskimo that the Indians are treacherous, bloodthirsty people, wicked and great magicians — no greater magicians, it was said, than the white men, but more prone to use their power for evil purposes. To the east lived various Eskimo tribes (of whom they named over a dozen), all of whom were friendly. To the north, on Victoria Island, lived two tribes, their nearest neighbors and best friends.

And what did they think of me — to what people did they suppose I belonged? Oh, but they did not have to guess; they knew; for Tannaumirk had told them he belonged to the Kupagmiut, of whom they had heard many stories from their fathers, and my accent made it plain I belonged to the Kupagmiut also, and not to that more distant people to whom my other companion, Natkusiak, belonged, whose language was more strange than ours, and of whom they had never heard the name till told of them last night. But didn't they consider strange my eyes (which are blue), and my beard (which was light brown), and suppose that for that reason I belonged to a different people? Their answer was decisive: "We have no reason to think you belong to a different people. Your speech differs only a little more from ours than does that of some tribes with whom we trade every year; and as for your eyes and beard, they are much like those of some of our neighbors to the north, whom you must visit. They are our best friends, and they will never cease being sorry if you pass on to the east without seeing them." So it was arranged that on the morrow we should pay a visit to the people of Victoria Island, who were described to me in a way to make me think that likely I had found the descendants of some of the lost men of the Franklin expedition. We know now that the facts call for another interpretation.

One of the things that interested me was to see some shooting with the strong-looking bows and long copper-tipped arrows that we found in the possession of every man of the tribe. I therefore said that I would like to have them illustrate to me the manner in which they killed caribou, and I would in turn show them the weapons and method used by us. Half a dozen of the men at once sent home for their bows, and a block of snow to serve as a target was set up in front of our house. The range at which a target a foot square could be hit with fair regularity turned out to be about thirty or thirty-five yards, and the extreme range of the bow was a bit over one hundred yards, while the range at which caribou are ordinarily shot was shown to be about seventy-five yards. When the exhibition was over, I set up a stick at about two hundred yards and fired at it. The people — men, women, and children — who stood around had no idea as to the character of the thing I was about to do, and when they heard the loud report of my gun all the women and children made a scramble for the houses, while the men ran back about fifteen or twenty yards and stood talking together excitedly behind a snow wall. I at once went to them and asked them to come with me to the stick and see what had happened to it. After some persuasion three of them complied, but unfortunately for me it turned out that I had failed to score. At this they seemed much relieved, but when I told them I would try again they protested earnestly, saying that so loud a noise would scare all the seals away from their hunting grounds, and the people would therefore starve.

It seemed to me imperative, however, to show them I could keep my word and perforate the stick at two hundred yards, and in spite of their protests I got ready to shoot again, telling them that we used these weapons in the west for seal-hunting, and that the noise was found not to scare seals away. The second shot happened to hit, but on the whole the mark of the bullet on the stick impressed them far less than the noise. In fact, they did not seem to marvel at it at all. When I explained to them that I could kill a polar bear or a caribou at even twice the distance the stick had been from me they exhibited no surprise, but asked me if I could with my rifle kill a caribou on the other side of a mountain. When I said that I could not, they told me a great shaman in a neighboring tribe had a magic arrow by which he could kill caribou on the other side of no matter how big a mountain. In other words, much to my surprise, they considered the performance of my rifle nothing wonderful.

I understand the point of view better now than I did then. It is simply this: if you were to show an Eskimo a bow that would in the ordinary way shoot fifty yards farther than any bow he ever saw, the man would never cease marveling, and he would tell of that bow as long as he lived; he would understand exactly the principle on which it works, would judge it by the standards of the natural, and would find it to excel marvelously. But show him the work of the rifle, which he does not in the least understand, and he is face to face with a miracle; he judges it by the standards of the supernatural instead of by the standards of the natural; he compares it with other miraculous things of which he has heard and which he may even think he has himself seen, and he finds it not at all beyond the average of miracles; for the wonders of our science and the wildest tales of our own mythologies pale beside the marvels which the Eskimo suppose to be happening all around them every day at the behest of their magicians.

Perhaps I might here digress from the chronological order of my story to point out that the Eskimo's refusal to be astonished by the killing at a great distance of caribou or a bear by a rifle bullet whose flight was unerring and invisible, was not an isolated case. When I showed them later my binoculars that made far-away things seem near and clear, they were of course interested; when I looked to the south or east and saw bands of caribou that were to them invisible, they applauded, and then followed the suggestion: "Now that you have looked for the caribou that are here to-day and found them, will you not also look for the caribou that are coming to-morrow, so that we can tell where to lie in ambush for them?" When they heard that my glasses could not see into the future, they were disappointed and naturally the reverse of well impressed with our powers, for they knew that their own medicine-men had charms and magic paraphernalia that enabled them to see things the morrow was to bring forth.

At another time, in describing to them the skill of our surgeons, I told that they could put a man to sleep and while he slept take out

MAMAYAUK.

a section of his intestines or one of his kidneys, and the man when he woke up would not even know what had been done to him, except as he was told and as he could see the sewed-up opening through which the part had been removed. Our doctors could even transplant the organs of one man into the body of another. These things I had actually never seen done, but that they were done was a matter of common knowledge in my country. It was similar in their country, one of my listeners told me. He himself had a friend who suffered continually from backache until a great medicine-man undertook to treat him. The next night, while the patient slept, the medicine-man removed the entire spinal column, which had become diseased, and replaced it with a complete new set of vertebræ, and — what was most wonderful — there was not a scratch on the patient's skin or anything to show that the exchange had been made. This thing the narrator had not seen done, but the truth of it was a matter of common knowledge among his people. Another man had had his diseased heart replaced with a new and sound one. In other words, the Eskimo believed as thoroughly as I in the truth of what he told; neither of us had seen the things actually done, but that they were done was a matter of common belief among our respective country-men; and the things he told of his medicine-men were more mar-velous than the things I could tell of mine. In fact, I had to admit that the transplanting of spinal columns and hearts was beyond the skill of my countrymen; and as they had the good breeding not to openly doubt any of my stories, it would have been ill-mannered of me to question theirs. Besides, questioning them would have done no good; I could not have changed by an iota their rock-founded faith in their medicine-men and spirit-compelling charms. In spite of any arguments I could have put forth, the net result of our ex-change of stories would have been just what it was, anyway — that they considered they had learned from my own lips that in point of skill our doctors are not the equals of theirs.

It was near noon of our first day when some one asked me if there were not some way in which the western people celebrated the coming of visitors. I replied that usually all the village gathered in a great dance. That was just their way, my hosts told me, and, see-ing that our customs coincided, they would make to-day a dance-house, as large as if two large tribes had met to trade; we should see how they danced, and possibly we might dance for them, too. The idea was no sooner broached than a dozen young men ran off to their various houses to don their house-building coats and mittens and get their snow-knives. By mid-afternoon the dance-house was up, a snow dome nine feet high, and large enough to accommodate forty people standing in a circle around a five-foot open space in the center reserved for the dancers.

The conditions of life had for many years been hard in the tribe, I was told, and while their ancestors had danced often and had had many drums (the only musical instrument of the Eskimo), they themselves had of late years danced but seldom, and there was only one drum left among them. It was a sunshiny, warm day, and while the men were building the dance-house some one fetched the drum, and a young woman sang for us to its accompaniment. She handled it like a tambourine, and played it in a manner entirely different from that of the western Eskimo. The songs were different, too, and they sang them charmingly. One song had a rhythm resembling that of the ancient Norse scaldic poems. The girl who sang it was herself very fair for an Eskimo, and had the long, slim fingers I have seen only among half-bloods in Alaska. It was here I got the first definite suggestion that the blond traits which were observable in this tribe (though not to such a degree as among other tribes later visited) might have some direct connection with the lost Scandinavian colonists of Greenland.

The dance, which began as soon as the dance-house was built, continued the rest of the afternoon. None of the dances were identical with any known to my companions from Alaska or the Mackenzie, but there was a general similarity. The performers differed in some cases markedly among themselves; those especially whose ancestors were said to have come from the mainland coast to the west differed strongly from the rest. Many of the dances were performed without moving the feet at all, but by swaying the body and gesticulating with the arms. In some cases the performer sang, recited, or uttered a series of exclamations, in others he was silent; but all the dances were done to the accompaniment of the singing of all those present, who knew the song appropriate to each dance.

Some dances known to individuals could not be shown because no one was found who could sing the accompaniment.

At this time of year (the middle of May) there was no darkness at midnight, for summer was approaching. Nevertheless the people took three meals a day with fair regularity, and our dance ended about eight o'clock in the evening, when the women announced supper. After supper I sat awhile and talked with my host and hostess and one or two visitors, and then all of them walked home with me to our house, where about half the village was gathered as on the evening before. They stayed only a short while, and by eleven o'clock the last visitor had wished us a friendly good night and our first day among the Victoria Island Eskimo had come to an end.

CHAPTER XII

MAY 15, 1910, was the third day after our discovery of the Dolphin and Union Straits Eskimo. For two days they had entertained us with warm hospitality, and had already grounded firmly in my mind the impression which a year of further association with them was destined to do nothing to weaken — that they are the equals of the best of our own race in good breeding, kindness, and the substantial virtues. They were men and women of the Stone Age truly, but they differed little from you or me or from the men and women who are our friends and families. The qualities which we call "Christian virtues" (and which the Buddhists no doubt call "Buddhist virtues") they had in all their essentials. They are not at all what a theorist might have supposed the people of the Stone Age to be, but the people of the Stone Age probably were what these their present-day representatives are: men with standards of honor, men with friends and families, men in love with their wives, gentle to their children, and considerate of the feelings and welfare of others. If we can reason at all from the present to the past, we can feel sure that the hand of evolution had written the Golden Rule in the hearts of the contemporaries of the mammoth millenniums before the Pyramids were built. At least, that is what I think. I have lived with these so-called primitive people until "savages" and all the kindred terms have lost the vivid meanings they had when I was younger and got all my ideas at second-hand; but the turning blank of this picturesque part of my vocabulary has been made up to me by a new realization of the fact that human nature is the same not only the world over, but also the ages through.

I am not clear whether it was at my own instance or that of my hosts that we set out on the evening of the third day to visit the people of Victoria Island. The hospitality shown us up to this time had resembled that which I might have expected in my own country in most details, and also in this, that they had taken equal care to entertain us and not to weary us by too much entertainment; and now they seemed to get a great deal of satisfaction out of their opportunity of guiding us on a visit to their neighbors. No doubt it was a matter of pride to them to have the opportunity of introducing such unusual visitors, but I think they also thought they were doing us a service, and felt in that the same satisfaction we feel in doing a service to a friend.

At the point where we had discovered the Eskimo, Dolphin and Union straits are about as wide as the English Channel, and the village we had been visiting lay nearly in the middle of the straits, built on the six-foot-thick solid ice with which winter had covered the sea. If during one of the Ice Ages the English Channel was ever frozen over, the paleolithic Frenchmen of that day may have crossed afoot or by sleds, as we did, to visit their friends in Britain; they may even have stopped on the road from Calais to Dover at a fishing-village built on the ice halfway between, such a village as that of our hosts of the two days past, and then proceeded northward to their island neighbors. Like our Eskimo friends, too, they may not have known that Britain was an island, although Britain is far smaller than Victoria Island.

On the trip to Victoria Island I was accompanied by Natkusiak and one local man only, a man whose name sounds simple and natural to me through long familiarity, but which would look strange and unpronounceable if it were set down in English print. The afternoon before we started, there had been a dance in the snow assembly-house, followed first by a supper of boiled seal-meat and blood soup, and then by a conference on how we should go about finding the village we wanted to visit, for finding the nearest Eskimo village is not always the simple matter it is to go from the city to a suburban town. The villages, to begin with, are never permanent, nor are they built in any recognized places, and blizzards may nearly or quite obliterate the trails that show which way the traveling parties have gone. At first half the village wanted to accompany us, but common opinion overruled this proposal, for it was pointed out that if a large party went we should soon eat our hosts out of house and home if we happened to find them at a time when the hunt had not been particularly successful for the few days past, while they would no doubt be able to entertain a party of three as long as we cared to stay. Only one of them would therefore accompany us, a prominent man who had many relatives in Victoria Island, while the rest of my party remained in their village.

We started at 9 P.M., going east about five miles till we found some snow-houses that had been deserted perhaps six weeks before; the trail from here led north six miles to another deserted village, and then a trifle north of west five miles, where we found four inhabited houses, which was about half the number we should have found had the tribe of the Haneragmiut been all camped together. We had traveled sixteen miles to find a village seven miles distant from ours; but that was necessary, for the deserted village we first came to was the only point our guide had known at which he could be sure to pick up the trail. The houses as we found them were three of them of snow with skin roofs, and one entirely of snow, and were built on the sea ice about ten yards from the shore of Victoria Island. Every one was asleep, even the dogs, and no one noticed us as we stopped half a mile away while our guide alone ran up to the village to prepare it for our coming. We saw him disappear for an instant into the first house, and similarly into the second, third, and fourth. A few moments later men and boys, hastily dressed, began to come out of the houses and to gather around our guide, evidently asking excited questions. These he apparently answered satisfactorily, for it was only two or three minutes till we saw him come running toward us, while the men turned to look after their dogs to see that they were all securely tied, so there should be no danger of their getting into fights with our dogs later on. We started at once to meet our ambassador, who beckoned to us as he ran. The message he brought was one of welcome, to which he added his own assurance that the Haneragmiut were a straightforward people whose actions never contradicted their words.

Our reception at this village differed considerably from that at the one previously visited. We were told by our guide to halt about two hundred yards from the houses. As soon as we stopped, the nine men and boys started slowly toward us, walking abreast, with arms raised above their heads, saying: "We are friendly; we are as we seem; your coming has made us glad." By the instructions of our guide we, including himself, stood still, holding our hands above our heads, waiting for the others to approach. When they got within ten yards they stopped and stood in line, while I — still following instructions — walked up to within three paces of the man on the right of the line, stopped, and waited for him to tell me his name, and then told him mine in turn. I then moved to my left down the line, stopping before each, and receiving his name before giving my own. When my introductions were over, Natkusiak similarly presented himself; in the case of our guide there were no formalities. These proceedings had begun with an air of military precision which did not last quite through the ceremony, for the three boys (about ten, eleven, and twelve years old perhaps) broke ranks before I had reached them in my progress down the line, and were later informally introduced by their fathers, while some of the men had begun to talk with me or with our guide before the presentation of Natkusiak was over. There is among these people no custom corresponding to our ceremony of hand-shaking, nor are there any words or set forms of salutation or farewell in their language.

After the introductions were over everything went much as it had gone at the village previously visited, except that the women did not come out of the houses to be presented — they were too busy getting us something to eat, we were told. The men built us a snowhouse in which to live while we stayed, and when that was done they asked us to come to their houses to meet their wives and to get something to eat. As on previous occasions, each guest was taken to a separate house to be entertained. We found here the same unaffected kindliness that we were getting used to among these people, the same hospitality and good breeding. After we had eaten the boiled sealmeat and drunk the blood soup that were the best things they could offer us, they fed our dogs also with boiled meat, "for dogs like to be treated well, just as men do," they said; and then we went back to our house to sleep, for we had been up for nearly twenty-four hours, and they had been asleep but an hour or two before we came.

But before we went to sleep, and that in spite of being drowsy, as one always is in a snug and warm camp after a cold day's march, Natkusiak and I talked for hours about the extraordinary people among whom we found ourselves. We had been told by our guide that we should find the Victoria Islanders of a light complexion, with fair beards, but still we were not prepared for what we saw — we had believed what we had been told, but we had not realized it. Natkusiak kept saying, "These are not Eskimo; they merely dress and talk and act like Eskimo." And so it seemed to me.

It is hard, looking back over a gap of years, to call to memory even the intense feelings with which we meet a crisis in life. That morning, when the nine men and boys of the village stood before me in line on the ice in front of their huts of snow and skins, I knew I was standing face to face with an important scientific discovery. From childhood I had been familiar with the literature of the North; I knew that here a thousand and there a hundred men of Scandinavia and of England had disappeared into the Northern mists, to be hid by them forever from the eyes of Europe; and when I saw before me these men who looked like Europeans in spite of their garb of furs, I knew that I had come upon either the last chapter and solution of one of the historical tragedies of the past, or else that I had added a new mystery for the future to solve: the mystery of why these men are like Europeans if they be not of European descent. But although the situation appealed to whatever there was in me of the poet and the theorist, I had to remember that my supply of writing-paper was limited, and that the definite recording of my first impressions of facts was more important than filling the pages of my note-book with speculations. My diary entries are seldom verbose and often disjointed; they are never written with an idea that they will be published unchanged; there are cryptic abbreviations and missing verbs, — and yet I shall quote here a portion of my entry for May 16th, 1910, as being of more interest than a possibly better-phrased statement I might compose to-day, being written on the spot the day of my finding the "Blond Eskimo." The annotations that are absolutely needed to make the rest intelligible are supplied in parentheses.

"I now understand why the Cape Bexley people (the first Eskimo discovered by us) take me for an Eskimo. There are three men here whose beards are almost the color of mine, and who look like typical Scandinavians. As Natkusiak says: 'Three of them look like white foremast hands on a whaler, and aren't they huge! And one looks like a Portugee' ('Portugee' is the word used by the American whalemen for natives of the Cape Verde Islands). Among the Cape Bexley people I had noted that a large number of men have a few light hairs in their mustaches and, more rarely, in their beards. Some of them have mustaches to be described as dark brown, a thing I have never seen in the west (Mackenzie River or Alaska). Here (in Victoria Island), however, are men with abundant three-inch-long beards, a light brown in their outer parts, but darker toward the middle of the chin. The faces and proportions of the body remind of 'stocky,' sunburned, but naturally fair Scandinavians. They (the three bearded men) are very much alike, though no two of them have the same mother, and all resemble closely an Icelander I know, Sigurjón Sveinsson, of Mountain, North Dakota, as he looked about 1895. . . . The one that 'looks like a Portugee' has hair that curls a trifle — about as much as mine. One woman, of about twenty, has the delicate features one sees in some Scandinavian girls, and that I have seen in only one of the half-white girls to the westward (Mackenzie River), and in her to a less degree than here. I know over twenty half-bloods (in the Mackenzie district and Alaska), and none of them resemble a white man in particular — most of them could pass for Eskimo among either Eskimo or whites if no particular attention were drawn to them, but no one could fail to be struck by the European appearance of these people (the Victoria Islanders). . . . More will be written of their eyes, etc., after I have had better opportunities of seeing them."

The time-faded ink of such diary entries as this furnished me some comfort after my return to "civilization," when European cables and American telegraphs clamored "fake" so loudly that at times I almost doubted I had seen what I had seen. There were scientific weight and reverent age behind the names of many of those who argued conclusively on the basis of a judicious combination of what they knew and did not know, to the conclusion that what is could not be. They argued so deftly withal that I who came from the place they theorized about felt somewhat as I used to feel as an undergraduate in college when I listened to a philosophical demonstration of the non-existence of the matter that I had to kick to convince myself that what must be wasn't so. Now that the din has

o

quieted down, I am gradually coming to the conviction that I have really been telling the truth most of the time consistently, and that the facts regarding the "Blond Eskimo" are about as my note-books have them and as I originally stated them to the newspaper men, who did not always, however, quote me correctly, and who at times showed marked originality in their treatment of what I said.

The extract from my diary set down above was written on the first day of my meeting with the Victoria Island Eskimo. For a little more than a year from that time I lived in their country and that of their neighbors of Coronation Gulf, until I knew most of them by name and had had full opportunity to make up my mind as to what manner of men they are. Their physical characteristics as I saw them I am in the habit of summarizing as follows: Of something less than a thousand persons, ten or more have blue eyes, (no full-blooded Eskimo has a right to have blue eyes, as far as we know — his eyes should be as brown and his hair as black as those of the typical Chinaman); some of the men eradicate their beards (pull out the hairs by the roots, as many Indian tribes do also); but of those who have beards a good many have light-brown ones; no one seen has light hair of the golden Scandinavian type, but some have dark-brown and rusty-red hair, the redness being usually more pronounced on the forehead than on the back of the head, and perhaps half the entire population have eyebrows ranging from a dark brown to a light brown or nearly white. A few have curly hair.

It is, however, not only the blondness of the Victoria Islanders that suggests the European, but also the form of their heads, as shown by my measurements of adult males. Typically we think of the Eskimo as narrow of skull and wide of face; in other words, his face is wider than his head. This fact is scientifically expressed by a "facial index" of over 100; while if the face is narrower than the head, the index will be less than 100. The proportions of the head are considered by most anthropologists an excellent test to determine what race a group of individuals belong to. In a summary published by the American Museum of Natural History, Professor Franz Boas gives the following facial indices for (supposedly) pure-blooded Eskimo: Herschel Island, 101; Greenland, 105; Baffin Bay, 102; Alaska, 104; East Greenland, 102; Smith Sound,

A Group of Victoria Land Eskimo.

102. In the same paper he gives the following indices for persons of mixed Eskimo and European descent: Labrador, 96; West Greenland, 95. My own measurements of one hundred and four men of Victoria Island give an index of 97, which places the "Blond Eskimo," when judged by head form, exactly where it places them when judged by complexion — in the class with persons who are known to be of mixed Eskimo and white descent.

In other words, while they are Eskimo in language and culture, and while some of them are Eskimo in physical appearance also, there are among them a large number of individuals possessing greater or less resemblance to white men. These are people who in recent time have had no contact with whites that would change their physical type; then whence could these European-like characters have come? Can they be accounted for historically?

To understand the historic possibility of European contact with the central Eskimo we must go back a thousand years in the history of the Scandinavian countries. Shortly before 870 A.D. Iceland was discovered by Norwegian navigators, and a few years earlier some Irish monks had occupied a small island just south of Iceland. The rapid settlement of Iceland was favored by the conditions of unrest in Scandinavia, connected with the wars of conquest waged by Harald, who was making himself the first king of united Norway, and driving out the petty kings who formerly had been independent rulers of separate territories, and who now generally preferred exile to allegiance to Harald. As is well known, some of these went to France, where they became the Normans who conquered England. Others went directly to England, and established there the kingdom of Northumbria. War expeditions on a smaller scale got them footing in other parts of the British Isles, in the Orkneys, the Shetland, and the Faroe Islands. But perhaps the largest number of all were those who colonized Iceland, where the first settlement is considered to have been made in 872. Within a century from that time the entire coast line was peopled with seafaring men who spent their summers in piracy along the various shores of northern Europe, and returned to Iceland in the fall to spend the winter in the enjoyment of the fruits of their plundering.

Early in the last quarter of the tenth century a man named Eric the Red was outlawed from Norway for murder. He came to Iceland and settled there, but the habit of man-killing was too strong upon him, and in 982 he was outlawed from Iceland for a period of three years. At that time there was current in Iceland a belief that a certain sailor named Gunnbjorn, of whom little is otherwise known, had sailed to the west of Iceland, and seen there some reefs, on which he had not landed. The knowledge of this tradition, combined no doubt with the fear of returning to the Scandinavian countries where he would have been an unwelcome visitor, caused Eric at the beginning of his exile to sail west, to become the discoverer of Greenland, whose glacier-covered mountains rise from the sea before the peaks of Iceland disappear in the east. Like the navigators of the present day, Eric found the east coast blockaded with floes, so he sailed to the south around Cape Farewell, and landed upon the more inviting southwest coast, where he spent the three years of his exile. On his return to Iceland he gave a favorable account of the country, which he had named "Greenland," for, as the saga naïvely says, "he thought people would all the more desire to settle the country if it had a fair name." Eric advertised his discoveries with such success that in 985 a fleet of twenty-five vessels sailed from the west coast of Iceland for Greenland. Some of these were shipwrecked, some turned back, but fourteen reached their destination. There is no census of the original settlers, but it is probable that each ship carried not less than fifty people, and the number can therefore be safely put at from six hundred to seven hundred. Each ship carried all the household goods of the owners, including horses, cattle, and sheep, and a flourishing farming community soon sprang up.

One of the important results of the settlement of Greenland was the discovery of the mainland of North America. Leifr Eiriksson, the son of Eric the Red, sailed in the year 1000 from Norway to visit his father in Greenland. This was in the days before exact navigation, and in trying to find a direct route he sailed too far south, missed the south point of Greenland, and saw land for the first time in a much lower latitude than he had expected, where natural conditions showed him at once that he had struck another coast than that of Greenland. This was the first fully authenticated discovery of

America, and the story of his epoch-making voyage is therefore so well known that we shall not dwell upon it here. He returned the same summer to Greenland, and told the story of his discovery, which then spread to Iceland and the rest of Europe, and found lodgment not only in the minds of men, but also in documents in various parts of Europe.

About the year 1000 Christianity was brought to Greenland, and from that time on we find records of the colony, not only in the sagas and annals of Iceland, but also in the archives of the Holy See in Rome. By the twelfth century there were in Greenland a bishopric, two monasteries, a nunnery, and fourteen churches. The colony was in a flourishing condition, and cannot have had a population of less than three thousand; the actual number may have been considerably more than that. They regularly paid their tithes to Rome, and we have papal records of the fact that in 1347 they even contributed in walrus ivory to the Crusades and to a Norwegian war expedition against Russia. The trade of the country was mostly with Norway, and besides ivory their exports were hides and thongs, oil, butter, wool, and other products of the farm. At first the Greenlanders used to sail their own vessels, and we have records of their making triangular voyages, going first from Greenland to the mainland of America to take on cargoes of timber, taking these thence to Iceland to sell them for house-building purposes, taking Icelandic wares in exchange, and returning with them to Greenland. Later on, however, bad times came upon the colony through the establishment of a trade monopoly by the Norwegian king, who in 1294 sold to a single firm of merchants in Bergen the exclusive right of trading with Greenland, and made it a statutory crime for the Greenlanders to build or sail their own ships, or to deal with any one not connected with this firm. In consequence the trade with Europe, which had been fairly brisk up to this time, gradually dwindled so that toward the end of the fourteenth century it was often several years between the sailings of ships to Greenland.

When the Scandinavians first settled southwest Greenland they found there house ruins and other remains which indicated that Eskimo had visited the country before its settlement. For some reason, however, these Eskimo had left the country again, and the

Scandinavians came in no contact with them during the early period of the colony. About the middle of the thirteenth century, however, they began to crowd down upon the colony from the north, apparently having come from the American continent by way of the Arctic islands, crossing thence to Greenland by way of Smith Sound. We have several accounts of the earlier fights between the Scandinavians and the Eskimo, and we know definitely that shortly after the year 1341 the most northerly Scandinavian colony was destroyed. The last reliable accounts of the southern portion of the Scandinavian settlement date from the first years of the fifteenth century, although more doubtful accounts take this story nearly down to the year 1500. At the time that Columbus sailed for America a bishop appointed by the Pope still had the nominal office of "Bishop of Greenland," although he never left Europe to assume his actual duties in the West.

It was a combination of circumstances that finally cut off all communication between Bergen and Greenland. The paralysis that fell upon Europe as a consequence of the Black Death was one of the influences; raids upon Bergen by ships of the Hanseatic League was another. When communications with Greenland were resumed, Norway had lost her lead in maritime affairs, and it was the sailors of England who rediscovered the country. In 1585 John Davis sailed up into the strait which bears his name, and the navigators that followed him brought to the attention of Europe the Eskimo, who were by that time the sole inhabitants of the districts in which the Scandinavian colony had previously flourished. It cannot have been much more than a hundred years from the disappearance of the Scandinavians from Greenland to the coming of Davis, and it is certain that had the people of that time taken the scientific interest that modern explorers do in the things they saw and heard, they could have cleared up the mystery which still envelops the fate of the colony. Historians have always considered it probable that it was no war of extermination that ended the Norse occupation, but that one of two things happened: either the remnants of Europeans may have intermarried with the Eskimo in Greenland, or, more probably, they may have migrated westward to the portions of America so well known to their forefathers. In

America they then either perished through starvation or by war, or became amalgamated with the population which they found in the country.

Shortly after the announcement last fall of our discovery of European-like people in southwest Victoria Island, General A. W. Greely undertook a survey of the entire mass of Arctic literature with the view of finding references to previous discoveries of a similar nature by the early voyagers. His thorough familiarity with the printed sources, and the possession of manuscript documents of great value, enabled him to bring together many things which had previously escaped notice, but which established a fairly complete historical chain of references to "Blond Eskimo" from the time of Davis to the present. The first, and perhaps the most interesting, reference is that to Nicolas Tunes, captain of a fishing vessel, who in 1656 sailed up into Davis Strait to 72° north latitude. He found the district which he visited occupied by two different sorts of people. He saw one kind which he described as very tall, well built, of a rather fair complexion, swift of foot; the other was much smaller, with an olive complexion, and short, thick legs. The latter of these two types is easily recognized as the Eskimo, while the former would fit well a people of mixed Scandinavian and Eskimo descent, in whom the Scandinavian was the predominating element. Coming to more recent times and to more westerly districts, we find on the road which any migrating people must have travelled between Greenland and Victoria Island numerous references by explorers at various times to people whom they did not consider to be typical Eskimo. Sir John Franklin, who was the first of the explorers to approach the region in which the European-like Eskimo now live, came in contact in 1824 with just one Eskimo, a decrepit old man, abandoned by his companions, who had fled at the approach of the exploring party. Of him Franklin says:

"The countenance [of this man] was oval, with a sufficiently prominent nose, and had nothing very different from a European face, except in the smallness of his eyes and, perhaps, in the narrowness of his forehead. His complexion was very fresh and red, and he had a longer beard than I have hitherto seen on any of the aborigines of America."

In the same district in 1837 Dease and Simpson came in contact with a small party of Eskimo, one of whom they described as of "a distinguished appearance," and as looking "much like a Scandinavian."

There is no reason for insisting now or ever that the "Blond Eskimo" of Victoria Island are descended from the Scandinavan colonists of Greenland, but looking at it historically or geographically there is no reason why they might not be. We have seen that the Scandinavians flourished for centuries on the west coast of Greenland. We know that at the time when communications between Europe and Greenland were cut off there were still large numbers of them living in Greenland in proximity to the Eskimo. We know that the habits of the Eskimo are such, as exemplified in their relations with the American Indian and the white man in recent times, that they are inclined to mix with any race with which they come in contact. Greenland is not far from Victoria Island. If there were any reason for doing so, I could go by sled in less than twenty-four months from the southwest corner of Victoria Island, where the "Blond Eskimo" now live, by way of Smith Sound, to the districts in Greenland which the Scandinavians inhabited, or by crossing from Greenland in a boat in summer I could go in one year thence by sled west to Victoria Island. As a matter of fact, the Eskimo who now winter on the ice west of Victoria Island start thence in March, and by August meet for trading purposes the Eskimo of the Hudson Bay, just above Chesterfield Inlet. There is, then, no more reason geographically than there is historically to suppose any barrier that could have kept the Scandinavians from moving west to Victoria Island had they wanted to.

If the reason that the Victoria Island Eskimo are European-like is that they are of European blood, then the Scandinavian colony in Greenland furnishes not only an explanation, but the only explanation. It has been suggested in print that there may be some connection between these blond tribes and the English explorers of the Arctic islands. A sufficient lack of information might make this supposition seem probable. It is true, however, that the literature of the Franklin expeditions not only is fairly complete, but also that the Eskimo themselves still remember such contact as they had

OUR CAMP IN THE INTERIOR OF VICTORIA ISLAND.

COMING HOME FROM A SUCCESSFUL BEARDED SEAL HUNT—EACH DOG DRAGGING
A SEGMENT OF THE SEAL.

with the explorers. Of all tribes visited by us only three were shown by our literature to have come in contact with the explorers, and in all these three tribes I found men still living who remembered the incident. The extracts already quoted show that when the first Englishmen came in contact with these people, they found already among them exactly the same blond traits that we find to-day, and secondly, the amount of contact was so slight that no physical change of whole tribes could have been produced. Had Franklin's entire ship's company of two hundred and thirty men survived in Victoria Island, and had they all married among and lived among the Eskimo, their descendants could not have been numerous enough to give us the condition we find there to-day. We have records, however, of the actual death of more than half of Franklin's men, and we feel certain that they had all perished before the year 1860 at the latest.

It is over a hundred years since the Eskimo of western Alaska came in contact with the early Russians. For half a century they have been in contact with the American whaling fleet, numbering at times as many as a thousand men. A good many of these whalers have married Eskimo women and have settled in the country, and their grandchildren are already growing into man's estate; yet all this mixing of races has produced in northern Alaska no such blond type as we find in Victoria Island. There are living in northern Alaska and the Mackenzie district perhaps a hundred individuals of mixed European and Eskimo descent. If this hundred were gathered together in one place, it would be found that many of them could not be distinguished offhand from full-blooded Eskimo, and the group as a whole would by no means present so north-European an appearance as would any of the three tribes in southwest Victoria Island. And then it is to be noted that if recent admixture of European blood were the cause of the blondness of the Victoria Island Eskimo, you would expect to find more blondness the farther east you go, because the European contact would have to be supposed to have come from the direction of Hudson Bay. The fact is, however, that the blond type is most pronounced farthest west, and gradually fades the farther east you go toward Hudson Bay. I have not myself seen the Eskimo of Hudson Bay, who have for more than a century been in contact with the Scotch and American whalers; but Captain

George Comer, of East Haddam, Connecticut, who has had dealings with them continuously for more than a quarter of a century, has told me that such European-like appearance of the people as I have described for Victoria Island and as my photographs show is quite beyond anything he has seen before even in those tribes which have been most intimately connected with the whalers.

As for the contact of the Victoria Island Eskimo with the American whalers, there is little to be said. Only one out of the thirteen tribes visited by my party had ever been seen by whalers, and they were first seen by the schooner *Olga* in 1906, when she wintered behind Bell Island near the southwest corner of Victoria Island. They were re-visited by the *Olga* in 1908, but by no other ship, and the total contact of the *Olga's* crew with the people did not amount to a whole week of continuous association.

Apart from the historical explanation, there are, of course, purely biological ones. It is possible that for some so-called "accidental" reason blond individuals may have been born from time to time in the past from parents of pure Eskimo blood, and that these may have perpetuated themselves. As to supposing that it is the climate that has made the Victoria Island Eskimo blond, the theory would be hardly tenable, for they live on the same food and under the same climatic conditions as do the Eskimo east of them and west of them, none of whom show the same European-like traits.

CHAPTER XIII

AS we proceeded east along Dolphin and Union Straits from Cape Bexley, we found here and there traces of Eskimo parties who were going in from their winter hunt on the sea ice to cache their clothing, household property, and stores of oil on the beach preparatory to moving inland for their summer caribou hunt. Some of these groups we never saw at all; the trails of others we picked up and followed until we overtook the parties, who were usually camped on the shore of a small lake, where they were fishing with hooks through holes they had made with their ice-picks in the seven-foot-thick ice. The caribou in this district are scarce in spring and difficult to get by the hunting methods of the Eskimo. Fish were not secured in large numbers, either, for these people know nothing of nets. Our archæological investigations have shown us that the knowledge of fishing by nets never extended farther east along the north shore of the mainland than Cape Parry, and the Copper Eskimo have no method of catching fish except that of hooks and spears. The hooks are, like most of their weapons, made of native copper. They are unsuited for setting, for there is no barb, and unless the fish be pulled out of the water as soon as he takes the hook he is sure to get off again.

West of Cape Bexley we had seen no traces of caribou for a hundred and fifty miles, but as soon as we came to where the straits began to narrow, east of Cape Bexley, we began to find more and more frequently the tracks of the northward migrating bands of cow caribou bound for Victoria Island. At first we did not see on an average more than ten or fifteen animals a day, but later on they increased in number; and with our excellent rifles we found not the slightest difficulty in supplying ourselves with plenty of venison and in having enough to spare to feed also the people at whose villages we visited.

In coming to the coast from the south, caribou take the ice without hesitation. It cannot be that they see land to the north of the straits, for half of the time, at least, the land is hidden in a haze, even from the human eye, which is far keener than that of the caribou. Neither can it be the sense of smell that guides them, for the northward direction of their march is not interfered with by change of wind. They will sometimes go ten miles out on the ice and lie down there, then wander around in circles for several hours or half a day, and finally proceed north again. Both at Liston and Sutton islands, in Simpson Bay, and farther east at Lambert Island, we saw caribou march right past without paying any attention to the islands, although there was food upon them, and they in some cases passed within a hundred yards or so. The bands would generally be from five to twelve caribou, consisting in the main of females about to drop their fawns, but also of yearlings and two-year-olds of both sexes. All of them were skin-poor and the marrow in their bones was as blood, but we had with us plenty of seal oil from seals killed farther west along the coast, so that the two together made a satisfactory diet. The skins at this season of the year are worthless, partly because the hair is loose, but also because they are full of holes, ranging in size from that of a pea to that of a navy bean, from the grubs of the bot-fly which infest the backs of the animals. When spread out to dry, the skin of the spring-killed caribou looks like a sieve.

In general, we tried to get a man from each party we came upon to accompany us to the next party or village so as to introduce us properly and guard against possible mishap, but when it happened that no one was with us when we came to a village, we always had to go through the formality of standing outside the house until some one could get a little blubber, cut it in pieces, and let each of us swallow one piece. This, as has been explained before, is the ordinary test to determine whether the visitor is human or a spirit, for it is a well-know fact that spirits will not swallow blubber. We found the people everywhere, when this formality was over, uniformly hospitable and glad to see us. They were especially glad we came at this time of year, for the fishing was precarious and most of them were on short rations. Commonly my Eskimo would pitch our camp, while I myself went a mile or two off in search of caribou. On hearing the report of my rifle a sledge would come from the village for the meat. Although the bands of caribou were small, by careful shooting I was in some cases able to save ammunition by aligning two and getting both in one shot. I found that if you get the animals in a line, the soft-pointed bullet of the six and one half millimeter Mannlicher-Schoenauer will, in spite of its mushrooming, still have killing force after going through the body of the first caribou. In some cases, however, the force of the bullet was completely spent against the vertebræ of large animals.

To get to Coronation Gulf two routes were open to us: one to follow Dolphin and Union Straits east around Cape Krusenstern, and the other to go south overland from the neighborhood of Lambert Island to Basil Hall Bay, the western arm of Coronation Gulf. We chose this latter method to save time, for spring was approaching. We knew by experience that in the Mackenzie district most of the snow is generally gone from the ground by the last week in May. Here, however, the season was so much later that there was scarcely a sign of thaw as we crossed overland, reaching Basil Hall Bay on May 28th. Some Eskimo whom we found here were living exclusively on tomcod and getting about half enough to eat, but all were in the best of spirits.

At this point I had hard luck in hunting. After assuring the village that it would be an easy matter for me to go out and get meat for them, I spent a day in climbing up and scrambling down basaltic precipices in a vain search for even the tracks of caribou in the fresh snow. Of course my inability to get food for them meant also our own inability to get food for ourselves, and Basil Hall Bay was therefore a place where we could not tarry. After a day's fruitless hunt, we accordingly hitched up our dogs and proceeded south upon the ice of Coronation Gulf to where there was promise of finding seals.

It was now daylight the twenty-four hours through, and early the next morning we simultaneously sighted Eskimo and a seal basking on the ice. It is a curious thing that the art of harpooning seals on the ice is practiced almost not at all by these Eskimo. Although they were short of provisions and the seal lay in plain sight, no one in camp thought it worth while going after him, for no one present had practice in that sort of hunting. In general, among the Copper Eskimo I should say that not more than one man in six knows how to hunt seals on the spring ice, and the ones who know are chiefly old men. The whole family, therefore, looked on with great interest as my Alaskan companion Natkusiak crawled up to within about twenty yards of this seal and shot him. At this season of the year the seals were lying on top of the ice basking in the warm sun. You see them here and there like small black dots sprinkled over the vast whiteness of the ocean. Each is lying beside a hole through which he has all winter been getting his supply of fresh air, which he has kept open all winter by continual gnawing, and which he has now enlarged from the two inches that were necessary to give air space to his nostrils in winter to perhaps a foot and a half in diameter, so that he can haul himself on top of the ice. He is lying on a slippery incline beside this hole, and the least twitch of his body will slide him into the water. He must, therefore, be approached and killed before he has suspicion of danger, and he must be killed instantly, for the quiver of a flipper would be almost as effective as the most energetic movement in sliding his body into the water.

The family whom we found here differed not at all from the generality of their countrymen in being more impressed with my companion's skill in stalking, which they thoroughly understood, than by the performances of his rifle, which to them were miraculous and therefore no more wonderful than ordinary miracles. There were three tents altogether, occupied by an old man with his wife and young son, and by his married son and married daughter. Eskimo differ exactly as we do, and this family was one of the most agreeable whom we had met. Later in the summer we fell in with them again and were together with them an aggregate of several weeks.

Proceeding south, we came in the night to a small village at the mouth of the Rae River. Every one was asleep, and the Eskimo dogs, as was their custom, came up to us with wagging tails, and never barked, giving their masters no warning. I let one of my men go up to the tent and shout from the outside that visitors had come, and in the excitement most of the men and all of the children came running out naked to see what it was all about. Although the season was advancing rapidly and I knew the snow would soon be gone

EKALUKPIK.

In 1848, when a boy of about six, he saw Richardson's party at Rae River.

from the land and make sled travel impossible, we stayed at this camp a day. I was especially anxious to make definite inquiries, for here at last we had come upon a tribe who should have some knowledge of white men, for I knew from the records of English explorers that Dease and Simpson had visited them in the thirties and Richardson and Rae in the forties of the last century.

After we had breakfasted together I therefore asked them what they knew of white men. Oh, they knew a great deal, they said. A few years ago a single Eskimo family of a tribe other than theirs had seen white men on a lake farther inland to the south. This lake I was easily able to identify as Dismal Lake, and the party of course was Hanbury's in 1904. But hadn't they themselves seen white men, I asked them. No, they never had, and were sure white men had never been in their country, but they knew a great deal about white men other than Hanbury by hearsay from tribes to the east. These that I questioned were all people under middle age. The one old man of the village did not happen to be present. A little later when he came to our tent I asked him the same question.

Oh, yes, he had seen white men. He had seen them when he was a small boy and he well remembered the occasion. He said that his parents and other people had been encamped exactly where we were now and that white men had come from the north without boats and wanted to cross the river; that the Eskimo had made rafts by lashing several of their kayaks together and had ferried the white men over. This coincided exactly with Dr. Richardson's account of his crossing the river in 1848. Further, the width at the point where we were camped coincided with that given in Richardson's narrative, whereas had the crossing been half a mile farther down or half a mile farther up-stream, the width of the river would have been entirely different. I then asked the younger generation why they had not told me this. Their answer was: "We did not know; we did not see it." "But didn't you hear?" Oh, yes, they had heard, but they had heard so many things.

This case illustrates well the difficulty of learning things from the Eskimo. In general, they are willing to tell, but nevertheless they don't seem to realize what it is that you want to learn. But the real explanation of the difficulty is that so many wonderful things

happen to them continually that all the different wonders take a
dead level and none stand out above the others. Suppose, for instance, that some of these people might (as they did not) have made
a five-hundred-mile journey east in 1903 to visit Captain Amundsen
at King William Island. They would have seen a ship in size quite
beyond their comprehension, and marvelous things without end;
and when they came back home they would have told about these
things and their stories would have been listened to with interest.
The men themselves would have been centers of attraction for some
time, but soon after their return some powerful magician would
have had occasion to visit the white man's land in a spirit flight,
and on his magical return would have told still more wonderful stories
than were told by those who had actually seen Amundsen's party,
and the stories would have been listened to with equal interest and
would quickly after have taken their places in the minds and memories
of the people. And then another shaman would have taken a journey
to the moon and on his return would have told about the curious
people he had seen and their strange customs. In his turn he would
have been believed and would have had his day, as people have their
day in the newspapers of our country. A few years later if I came
to visit these people and asked them to relate to me the important
things they knew, they would tell me of the journey to King William
Island, of the journey to the white men's land, and the journey to the
moon with equal impressiveness, putting them all on a dead level
and leaving me dependent entirely upon my own resources in deter-
mining which of the stories was fact and which fiction. Among
themselves the comparatively tame experiences of the people who
really saw Amundsen would soon be lost and forgotten in the wealth
of adventure and extraordinary detail of the miraculous journeys
that had since been made to stranger and more distant places.

We entered the mouth of the Coppermine River June 4th and
found the ice lying smooth, snow-covered, and white as in midwinter.
This all looked well, but the aspect of things changed suddenly
when we reached Bloody Fall. In itself this is one of the most picturesque spots in the Northland and historically it is the center of
the story of the North, for this is the point reached by Samuel Hearne
in 1771, when, accompanied by a horde of Chipewyan Indians, he

made this the turning-point of one of the most remarkable expeditions ever undertaken on the mainland of North America. It was here that the Chipewyans, cowardly in general but brave under the circumstances, attacked some tents occupied by a dozen or so Eskimo who were sleeping and killed them all. This gave the sinister name of Bloody Fall to the basaltic gorge through which the Coppermine was now rushing, open as though in summer except for a narrow, somewhat sloping ledge of ice, in places not more than two yards wide, that still clung to the rock along the west side of the gorge and gave us a doubtful footpath along a shelf overhanging one of the deadliest rapids in the world.

It was, perhaps, unwise of us to decide not to portage the six hundred odd paces around the falls and to attempt this ice ledge instead. I was not sure it was safe — I am now sure it was entirely unsafe — but we managed to get past without accident. Of course, if there had been an accident it could only have been a fatal one, because it would have consisted in the breaking down of the ice ledge along which we were sledging, and that would have been the last of us, for immediately below the falls the river plunges under the ice. It has often been the case with us, and so it was here, that at exciting moments we forgot all about our camera. When we had an adventure it took all of us to have it, and we could spare no one to stand aside and push the button.

We had agreed with the Rae River Eskimo that we would meet them on Dismal Lake, and it was therefore our idea to keep to the west side of the Coppermine, so that whenever we found further progress impossible on account of the approaching summer we should be able to leave our sled on that side of the river and walk overland southwest to Dismal Lake. A mile and a half above the fall, however, it appeared that the going was so much better on the east side of the stream that we crossed over and proceeded along that bank for three or four miles. It was a very warm day, the sun beat down incessantly from a clear sky, and about six miles above Bloody Fall we found progress on that side of the stream impossible on account of the increasing water on top of the ice and the absence of snow from the land. We then tried to cross over, but found that the water, which farther downstream had been flowing like a small

P

river on top of the ice, had here dug its way clean through the ice and had become an impassable open channel. On realizing this we turned downstream again, but found that a few hours had made so much difference that while our crossing to the east side had been safe in the morning, our return was impossible in the afternoon. The river was now open and uncrossable the whole six miles back to Bloody Fall. We were caught on the east side of the river in a district unfrequented at present by Eskimo, poorly supplied with game, and one in which we had no interest; while the promised hunting-land, the summer country of the Eskimo, lay across the river to the west, completely out of our reach, for the Coppermine River is practically a series of rapids, and during the spring freshets attempting to cross it by raft would be suicidal, as the strips of quiet water between the rapids are so few that a raft would be inevitably swept into the next rapid below before it could be paddled across.

We had not been able to quite reach the tree-line by sled. It had been my intention to hide the sled somewhere in a clump of trees for fear the Eskimo might find it during the summer and break it up to secure the iron runners. Of course I had no fear of those Eskimo with whom we had come in contact, for they would know whose sled it was and would respect it accordingly; but I had reason to think that wandering bands from the east might come upon our cache, and might consider it a windfall. The tree-line, however, was three miles away, so we merely portaged our sleds and our stuff to the top of the hill, and cached them in a small hollow where they could be seen from no great distance.

I left my Eskimo to do this work and struck out at once eastward to hunt. Tracks of caribou were found on every one of the few spots that were soft enough to preserve a track, — in the soft mud where there was mud, in the snowbanks where they still existed in the shelter of the hills, and on top of the ice in the creek bottoms; but in general the country is solid rock, which leaves no trace of the passing of man or beast. All the tracks led west along the Coppermine; few of them were less than two weeks old, and none were quite fresh. Under ordinary circumstances one of us went out to hunt and did not return without securing game, although sometimes that was a task that ran a good deal beyond the twenty-four hours; but

COOKING WITH HEATHER IN SPRING.

COOKING WITH DWARF WILLOWS IN SPRING ON THE SHORE OF FROZEN LAKE.

in this case I thought it best that we should proceed up the Coppermine to the forested area at once, for I considered the chances of finding caribou there a little better than out on the barren ground.

After a half-dozen hours of vain search, therefore, I returned. One of the Eskimo meantime had secured a few squirrels (*Spermophilus parryi*). Ptarmigan were fairly numerous, but our ammunition was too valuable to use it on them except in an emergency. We prepared for leaving behind everything except a portion of our ammunition and cooking-gear. I cached even my camera and my large diary, with the idea that in a few days we would have occasion to return to the cache, and I took with me only a small pocket note-book.

We started south late in the afternoon, and about two hours later we reached, in a driving shower which was the first rain of the summer, the most northerly clump of trees on the Coppermine, about eighteen miles south of the ocean. Under ordinary circumstances we should have proceeded farther, but a rain-storm is much more disagreeable than a snow-storm, so we pitched our tent and made in front of it a roaring wood fire that defied the rain.

The next morning Natkusiak and myself started out to look for caribou, while Tannaumirk and Pannigabluk remained behind to snare squirrels and ptarmigan. There are a great many small streams that flow into the Coppermine from the east that can well be forded in late summer, when most of them are not knee-deep, but at this season every one of them was impassable, so Natkusiak and I were limited in our movements rather strictly by the topography. I must have gone perhaps fifteen or eighteen miles northeast before I got beyond the head of most of these small creeks and was able to circle to the north and west. I saw no game, however, and after perhaps fifteen or eighteen hours of walking I had returned within four or five miles of camp when I saw an Arctic hare. These animals are really not so very rare on the barren ground, as one may see by their traces left on the snow in winter, but in my entire Arctic experience I have seen only four or five, and have never shot a single one. Where caribou are plenty, of course a hare is not worth the ammunition, but in this case I made up my mind to try to get the animal, and I followed him a few hundred yards.

I was about to shoot, and he was so near that there was no doubt of the result, when suddenly, almost in line with the hare, I saw a caribou disappearing over a ridge. He evidently had seen me while my attention was concentrated on the hare and while I was exposed against the sky-line on top of the rock ridge along which the hare was running. Of course I gave no further thought to the hare. Caribou, when they merely see a man and do not get his wind, ordinarily do not run far, and within an hour I had come up to this one again. It turned out I had seen only one of two animals, both of which I now found quietly feeding upon a level spot — so level, indeed, that it took several hours of careful stalking before I got within range. The animals proved to be two young bulls, skin-poor, with the marrow as blood in their bones. Nevertheless there was great rejoicing in camp when I returned, after being out about twenty-four hours, with a back-load of caribou meat. I have found that Eskimo in a strange country are typically sceptical of the possibilities of finding food, and my people had several days ago made up their minds that all the caribou had left the district and we were destined to have to live the whole summer on squirrels and ptarmigan.

Natkusiak had not yet returned when I got home, and it was nearly another twenty-four hours before he put in an appearance, but he had been more successful than I in securing three old bull caribou which were in fair condition at this season of the year, and best of all he had shot a wolf that was as fat as a pig. In summer we much preferred wolf meat to caribou, for it is usually tender and fat, and the caribou, all except the oldest bulls, are in very indifferent condition. We never ate venison when there was wolf meat to be had at this season; at least that was true of all of us except Pannigabluk, to whose family and ancestors the wolf is taboo.

As the caribou killed by Natkusiak were in a southeasterly direction, we brought into camp at once the meat of the two that I had killed, and then proceeded farther upstream to a point from which it was only seven or eight miles to where Natkusiak had cached the other meat. We learned that at this season the caribou in the Coppermine country were all bulls, and none of them were moving. In general singly, or by twos and threes, they had taken possession of some snow-bank protected from the sun by a northward-facing precipice, and there they stayed. They would feed for an hour or two on the grass or moss in the neighborhood, and then go back to lie on the snow, where they had a measure of protection from the clouds of mosquitoes, and where the intense heat of the sun was more bearable to them.

On an average the number of caribou was not more than about one for every hundred square miles of country, and we always had to go south to kill the next one. Occasionally either Natkusiak or myself would hunt back downstream twenty or thirty miles, with the idea that caribou might have moved in behind us, but with no result; and each time we killed a caribou to the south and moved up to get its meat we got that much farther from our sled cache and from my camera and writing materials; so that by the latter part of June it had become evident that we should never be able to go back to the cache during the summer, for to go back meant starvation. By killing the caribou as we went we had burned our bridges behind us.

Later on, after we had succeeded in joining the Eskimo, there was scarcely a half-hour when some picturesque or unusual scene in their lives during the summer did not bring back to me the absence of my camera. As for my diary for the summer, it was written in my small pocket notebook in so microscopic a hand that it is difficult to read without a magnifying glass, and even so I had to trust to my memory for many things that in ordinary course I should have recorded.

July was intolerably hot. We had no thermometer, but I feel sure that many a day the temperature must have been over one hundred degrees in the sun, and sometimes for weeks on end there was not a cloud in the sky. At midnight the sun was what we would call an hour high, so that it beat down on us without rest the twenty-four hours through. The hottest period of the day was about eight o'clock in the evening, and the coolest perhaps four or five in the morning. The mosquitoes were so bad that several of our dogs went completely blind for the time, through the swelling closed of their eyes, and all of them were lame from running sores caused by the mosquito stings on the line where the hair meets the pad of the foot. It is true that on our entire expedition we had no experience that more nearly deserved the name of suffering than this of the combined heat and mosquitoes of our Coppermine River summer.

By the last week in July we had proceeded upstream as far as the mouth of the Kendall River, which flows in from the west from Dismal Lake. We had continually been putting off the crossing of the river, hoping to find a better place, and also being in no hurry, for we did not think the Rae River Eskimo whom we wanted to join would reach Dismal Lake before early August. We finally selected for the crossing a strip of river where there is half a mile of quiet water between two strong rapids, built a raft from dry spruce growing near the river, and got across with all our belongings, including at that time about three hundred pounds of dry caribou meat. Immediately upon landing on the west side we cached the meat safely in a rock crevice, under huge stones, intending it for a store against some future emergency, but our fortunes that summer never brought us back to the place again; so doubtless it is there yet unless some wandering Eskimo may have happened to find it.

On the north shore of Dismal Lake, which we reached in a two-days march from the Coppermine, we ran completely out of food for the only time in our period of fourteen months of absence from our base at Langton Bay. Of course, in an extremity we could have gone back to where we had cached the dried meat two days before, but our general policy was never to retreat, for we knew well that the chances of food ahead were always a little better than behind. The morning of July 29th I broke the rule against shooting ptarmigan, and used one of my valuable Mannlicher-Schoenauer bullets to secure half a pound of meat. That half-pound was the breakfast for the four of us, and the dogs, poor fellows, got nothing. But our fortune was soon to turn, for when immediately after breakfast I climbed the high hill behind our camp I saw a caribou coming from the north and disappearing among some hills to the east in a way to make it uncertain in just what direction he was going. The three of us therefore started to meet him by different routes. It happened that I was the one to get sight of him first, and it turned out he had a companion that must evidently have preceded him into the hills a moment before I turned my field glasses that way. The two of them were in good flesh, so that by four in the afternoon both ourselves and our dogs had had a square meal of better meat than ordinary.

Dismal Lake is incorrectly given on the maps as three separate lakes, connected by rivers. As a matter of fact, it is one lake extending in a general east-and-west direction, with a length of about thirty-six miles, and the width varying from four or more miles down to a hundred yards or so. At the point where we struck the lake it is filled with willow-covered islands. Here we knew from Eskimo report that a ford existed, but the Eskimo who cross by it every year put up no guide-posts, and no trails are visible, so that it took me half a day of wading back and forth before the ford was discovered. I had chosen this job as rather more interesting than hunting, and expected it to take me only a few minutes, so I had sent the two Eskimo off to hunt while I looked for the ford. While I was at it and wading about nearly neck-deep in the cold water a sudden cold rainstorm came up which quickly brought the Eskimo back from their caribou hunt to our comfortable tent, while it of course did not restrain me from my search for the ford, as I was already soaked to the neck. It was rather a cheerless job, and one of which I was thoroughly tired both physically and mentally, when eventually, after perhaps four hours of wading, I found the ford. It turned out to be not more than waist-deep, but involved about half a mile of wading. The next day it took us several hours to make the crossing of the lake, for the dogs, which ordinarily carried a large part of our gear, of course were of no use in fording the channels from island to island.

This fording of the lake took place on the last day of July, and the 1st of August, a little east of the middle of Dismal Lake, we came upon a camp of those particular families of the Rae River Eskimo whom we had met in May. In their company we moved south to the headwaters of the Dease River, where the caribou hunting-camps of the Eskimo are scattered on every other hill. This is one of the most cosmopolitan communities of Eskimo in America, for they come here from great distances to secure wood for sled-making and for the wooden portions of their weapons. There were two or three families from Dolphin and Union Straits as far west as Cape Bexley; there were several families from Victoria Island, and two or three from the east coast of Bathurst Inlet. The gathering there represented people from a territory five hundred miles in length from east to west, and two hundred or more miles wide from north to south. Some of the camps were pitched within a few miles of the shore of Bear Lake, and the oldest men there told us a rather surprising thing: that from their infancy they and their countrymen had every year been in the habit of hunting down to the northeast shore of Bear Lake. This is extraordinary in view of the fact that Bear Lake has been a sort of Mecca for the explorers of the North for a hundred years, and the Hudson's Bay Company has had a station at Fort Norman for a century; and yet neither these explorers nor the Hudson's Bay Company, nor even yet the Bear Lake Indians, realized that a large body of Eskimo hunted on the shores of the lake every year. True, every few years frightened Slavey or Dogrib Indians would come to the Hudson's Bay Company's post with stories of having found traces of the dreaded Eskimo, but it was believed that these were but small wandering bands who had come a great way from their country, which was vaguely supposed to be at a vast distance to the northeast.

In 1908, Dr. Anderson and I had come down a portion of the Mackenzie River with the English travelers C. D. Melvill and John Hornby, whose guests we had been aboard their boat all the way from Fort Smith to Fort Norman, a distance of over eight hundred miles. They had told me that they expected to spend the winter of 1909–1910 on Bear Lake. I had intended to spend that same winter with the Copper Eskimo, and we had arranged to try to meet on the Coppermine River; but I had been delayed in my plans a year, and although I had seen traces of their encampments on the Coppermine River, I supposed them to be by now back in England. However, I thought it worth while to have a look to see if they might not still be on Bear Lake. With this in view, Natkusiak and I made the journey to the mouth of the Dease River. We found no human traces less than apparently a year old, but we left, nevertheless, a letter in a tin can suspended from a pole in a conspicuous place at the mouth of the river, hoping that some wandering Indians might pick it up and eventually carry it to the Hudson's Bay post at Fort Norman, three hundred miles away.

On our return journey from Bear Lake I was one morning surprised to see on the sky-line a party who evidently were not Eskimo. We hastened to intercept them, and found them to be Slavey Indians, one of whom spoke fairly good English. They had been to the northward hunting caribou, and with a vague notion that they wanted to go farther than usual on the chance of seeing Eskimo. Two days before we saw them, when they had found traces of Eskimo, they had completely lost their desire to see them. Their courage had suddenly given out, and they were now in full retreat. When they learned, however, that we had been spending several months with the Eskimo and had found them to be very friendly, the English-speaking Slavey, who gave his name as Jimmie Soldat, told me that he was in the service of my friend Hornby; that Hornby had told him to keep a lookout for me, and to assist me in every way he could, and that Hornby had further requested that I take Jimmie in hand and bring him in contact with the Eskimo, so that later Jimmie might be able to guide Hornby to the place where the Eskimo are.

Now I did not desire to bring my unspoiled Coronation Gulf people into contact with civilization, with the ravages of which among the Eskimo of Alaska and the Mackenzie I am too familiar; but it seemed that the thing could not be staved off for more than a year or two, anyway, for the fact of my living with the Eskimo was already well known, and both the traders and missionaries who operate through Fort Norman would be sure to make use of the information. While I regretted the event in general, I was glad to be able to do a service, as I thought, to my friends Melvill and Hornby; so next day I took Jimmie and two of his Slavey companions to within a mile or two of an Eskimo encampment, and left them there in hiding behind a hill while I went to the Eskimo to ask their permission to bring the Indians into camp.

At first the Eskimo refused flatly. They said that they themselves had never had anything to do with the Indians; that their ancestors had had but rare contact with them, and that this contact had never been friendly; that sometimes Indians had killed some of them and sometimes they had killed some Indians, and that now no doubt these Indians had treacherous intentions in wanting to be introduced into camp. Through our long residence with them, however, Natkusiak and I had their confidence so fully that we finally talked them into allowing the Indians to come, on the condition that they leave their weapons behind them.

When I returned to Jimmie with this ultimatum, the Indians in their turn said that the intentions of the Eskimo were clear: that they intended to get them unarmed into their clutches and murder them, and Jimmie would have nothing more of the adventure. His backing out at this stage, however, did not suit me, for the Eskimo were sure to take that as a sign of treachery, and it would not have been a day until every Eskimo party in the neighborhood was on its way to the coast in a retreat in which they would have abandoned their sleds, their skins intended for clothing, and through which we would lose prestige by having brought this calamity upon them. Natkusiak and I therefore took the Indians practically by force into camp, threatening them with all sorts of dire results if they backed out. The Eskimo's reception of the Indians was friendly. The Indians were dressed in white men's clothing, and were not at all what the Eskimo had expected Indians to be like; and in fact several of them said to me at once that had they known the Indians were like this they would not have been so frightened of them.

This was early September, and the nights were dark at midnight. We had brought the Indians to camp about sundown, and an hour later, when supper had been eaten, the Eskimo invited the Indians to come and sleep in their tents; but this the Indians would not do, saying that it was their custom to sit beside the fire. This seemed to the Eskimo a strange thing, but to me it was a self-evident fib. The Indians were simply too frightened to trust themselves in the dwellings of the Eskimo. Natkusiak and I therefore sat up with the Indians for an hour or two until all the Eskimo were sound asleep, and then finally, by lying down one on either side, we got the Indians to go to sleep between us. The next morning after breakfast the Indians invited the Eskimo to accompany them down to their lodges, where they had considerable quantities of smoked caribou meat, caribou fat, and marrow-bones. Seven of the Eskimo went, including two women, and much of the forenoon was spent in the commodious lodges of the Slaveys in feasting and in exchanging opinions, in all of which I had to act as interpreter.

Finally when the feast was over and the Eskimo were apparently in the best of spirits, Jimmie brought forward a package of pictures of saints and holy men, and made a little speech in which he asked me to tell the Eskimo that he was an ambassador of a bishop of the Roman Catholic Church, and that the bishop said that if they were good men and never killed any more Indians and abjured their heathenish practices, he would come and build a mission among them and would convert them to the true faith. This speech, which meant so much to the Indian, would of course have meant nothing to the Eskimo, for they had never heard of the good bishop or of the faith he preaches. Jimmie went on to say that he had a picture for each of them, and that if they would take them and wear them over their hearts, the pictures would protect them from all evil and be of the greatest value to them. Without translating any of these things, I took the pictures, which were the ordinary religious chromos, and gave them to the Eskimo.

It turned out that Jimmie had had no commission from Hornby, and that he had merely, from overhearing Melvill's and Hornby's conversation, found out that I was a friend of theirs, and he had used this knowledge in a confidence game of his own, the object of which was to become the first Indian who had been in friendly contact with the Eskimo, that he might thereafter pride himself on that fact, and might be able to represent himself to the bishop as having been a pioneer in the spread of the faith among the Eskimo. Apparently the results have been what he desired, for I have since heard that the Roman Catholic Church sent in missionaries at once, who arrived among the Eskimo soon after we left them, and whose work in that field will no doubt continue indefinitely.

Among other things, Jimmie told me that Melvill and Hornby were somewhere on Great Bear Lake. This was good news, and from that time I was continually on the lookout for some signs of them. Finally, on the 13th of September, it happened that the pursuit of a large band of bull caribou had taken me a long distance away from our camp, and when I finally shot three of the animals it was on a slope of a hill facing the southwest. While I was skinning them I happened to look in the direction of Bear Lake, which lay some fifteen miles distant, and there, not more than a mile away, was pitched a tepee. I took this for an Indian camp, but went up to it to make inquiries about my friends, and it turned out to be their camp. They had a day or two before heard from Jimmie about my presence in the country, and were also looking for me. They had been down on the Mackenzie River in the summer, and had some news of the outside world. King Edward was dead, and a heavier than air flying-machine had crossed the English Channel. This news, not half a year old, was fresh news indeed in that country.

CHAPTER XIV

THE summer spent with the Copper Eskimo between Bear Lake and the Coppermine River had passed pleasantly for me, and profitably. From the first they had accepted me as one of them — they had not known that I was a white man until I told them so. My life was exactly as theirs in that I followed the game and hunted for a living. Even my rifle did not differentiate me from them, because they looked upon its performances as my magic, differing in no way essentially from their magic. I spoke the Mackenzie Eskimo dialect and made no attempt to learn theirs, for it was not necessary for convenience' sake, and it would have thoroughly confused me to try to keep two so similar dialects separate in my mind. Sometimes in meeting an utter stranger I found a little difficulty; not that it was difficult for me to understand him, for he spoke very much like all the others that I had dealt with, but he at first would have some difficulty in adjusting himself to the sort of language spoken by myself and my companions.

By August the caribou skins were suitable for clothing. Up to that time we had killed only for food and had eaten each animal before moving to where the next was killed, so that our baggage had not increased; but now we had to begin saving the skins against the winter, and by the latter part of August we had a bundle of something like forty of the soft, short-haired pelts, so that our movements began to be hampered by the bulk and weight of our back-loads. We therefore chose a large dead spruce, the trunk of which was free of bark and limbs, and fifteen feet up it we suspended our bundle of skins. This we did for fear of the wolverines, for the Indians say that the wolverine cannot climb a smooth tree-trunk if the tree be so stout that it is unable to reach half around it with its legs in trying to climb. In this I have not much faith, because I have seen so many caches made which the Indians and Eskimo say are perfectly safe, and later when the cache is found to be rifled, the natives are invariably astounded and assure you that they never heard of such a thing before. We tied our bundle with thongs to the trunk of the tree, and three weeks later when we came back it turned out that the first wolverine had just that day climbed up and eaten some of the thongs. Apparently it was mere accident that protected our clothing materials, and had we come a day later we might have found the skins destroyed.

The summer had been one of continuous sunshine, but that changed with the month of September, and the mists and fogs were then almost as continuous as the sunshine had been. The rutting season had commenced, and the bull caribou, which were numerous in summer in all the wood fringe northeast of Bear Lake, had moved out in the open country, and the hunting had become more difficult. Finally, by the end of September the caribou had become very few in number.

The Eskimo had all summer been making sledges, wooden snow-shovels, bows and spear handles, and other articles of wood. All these things and a good supply of caribou meat were stored at a spot which we called the "sled-making place," but which the Slaveys of Bear Lake, who know the country well and visit it in winter, call "Big Stick Island." This is a clump of large spruce trees on the southeast branch of the Dease River. The Eskimo were now waiting for the first snow of the year so they could hitch their dogs to the sleds they had made, load their provisions upon them, and move north toward the coast where they expected to spend the winter in sealing. But starvation began to threaten, so that finally, on September 25, the last party started toward the coast, carrying their sleds on their backs, for the first snow had not yet fallen.

I wanted very much to accompany them, to become as familiar with their winter life as I already was with their summer habits, but it did not seem a safe thing to try, for their only source of food in winter is the seal, and these must be hunted, under the peculiar Coronation Gulf conditions, by methods unfamiliar to my companions and myself. Of course, we could have learned their hunting methods readily enough, but they told us that almost every winter, in spite of the most assiduous care in hunting, they are reduced to the verge of starvation. Frequently (and it turned out to be so that winter) they have to eat the caribou sinew they have saved up to use as sewing-thread, the skins they have intended for clothing, and often their clothing, too, while about one year in three some of their dogs die of hunger; a few years ago about half of one of the larger tribes starved to death. It was both fear of actual want and fear that if want came their superstition would blame us for it that kept us from going to the sea-coast with them. We decided, therefore, to winter on the head-waters of the Dease River, where the woodland throws an arm far out into the Barren Ground; to try to lay up there sufficient stores of food for the winter; to pass there the period of the absence of the sun; and to join the Coronation Gulf Eskimo in March, when abundance of hunting-light would make it safer to go into a country poorly stocked with game.

When we had decided upon this, I left my Eskimo to build a winter hut, while I walked alone down to the mouth of the Dease River, a distance of about thirty miles, to where my friends Melvill and Hornby were going to have their winter camp. I found there also Mr. Joseph Hodgson with his family, consisting of his wife, son, daughter, and nephew. Mr. Hodgson is a retired officer of the Hudson's Bay Company, who, through the many years of his service on the Mackenzie River, had had a longing to get out of the beaten track of the fur-trader. For many years, he told me, it had been his special dream to spend the winter on the Dease River, and he had now come to do it. The mouth of the Dease is a picturesque spot, and although the Indians told Mr. Hodgson that it was "no good" as a fishing place or as a location for hunting or trapping, he nevertheless stuck to his original intention and built his house there.

Both Mr. Hodgson and the Englishmen who lived about three miles away from him had a small store of white men's food, such as flour, sugar, tea, salt, and the like. But these were articles we did completely without, and even to the others they were merely luxuries, for they had to get the main part of their food-supply from the caribou of the land and the trout of Bear Lake. In spite of the little they had they offered me a share, a thing that I much appreciated, both because it shows the spirit of the North and because my Eskimo were immeasurably gladdened by a little flour, a thing they had not expected and without which they can get along very well, but the possession of which they feel marks them off definitely from the poor trash who cannot afford such things.

Melvill and Hornby had built their house on Bear Lake itself, about half a mile east of the old site of Fort Confidence, which had been built by Dease and Simpson in the thirties, and occupied again by Richardson and Rae in the forties of the last century. The fort was a group of log buildings, which stood until a few years ago, when some Indians set fire to them, and now only the huge stone chimneys are standing, like the monoliths of Salisbury Plain, monuments of a bygone time.

The firewood chopped by Richardson's men, and piled up methodically after the nature of Englishmen, looked as if it had been chopped last year — a striking proof of the fact that in the northern regions decay is very slow. Some months before on the Arctic coast west of Cape Bexley I had seen wood that had been chopped with sharp axes. Now we knew that no one with a sharp axe had been there since Richardson in 1848, and yet these chips looked nearly fresh. The weathering of wood seems greater in one season in the latitude of 45° north than in twenty years in the latitude of 70°.

I spent two weeks with my friends on Bear Lake, writing letters which it was expected some Slavey Indians would take to Fort Norman at Christmas-time. In ordinary years no Indians winter on the east end of Bear Lake, but this time a few families were there, attracted by the presence of the white men; and they would, of course, being good Catholics, have to go to Fort Norman to celebrate Christmas as well as to trade with the Hudson's Bay Company and with the "Free Traders." These two weeks passed very pleasantly for me, yet in a way I regretted them, for I missed seeing the one big herd of caribou that came into our territory in the year. I have often seen five hundred caribou in a band, and sometimes a thousand, but the herd that crossed the eastern head waters of Dease River, going south from the 10th to the 14th of October, certainly numbered a great many hundreds of thousands, and probably millions.

The two Eskimo had gone off on what they intended as a day's prospecting trip to the eastward from our camp in search of a fishing-lake. They took with them their rifles, of course; but, not having seen any caribou the last few days, they had now, as they had done

Photograph from J. E. Bernier, Courtesy of the Canadian Government

YEARLY MIGRATION OF THE CARIBOU

the previous spring, made up their minds that no caribou were coming into our country any more, and they had therefore taken with them only about twenty cartridges, saying as they started that they felt sure they would catch enough fish so that they would not have to shoot ptarmigan. When they got down to the fishing-lake, they saw, to their surprise, a few caribou near its eastern end. The wind was blowing from the north, and when they were approaching these caribou, they noticed a strange stench which they hardly knew how to interpret. The big herd must have been a few miles to the north, and they had smelled it as one might smell a barnyard on close approach.

That day they wasted most of the cartridges on the few caribou in sight, skinned half a dozen or so, and camped overnight. When the big herd came the next morning, they were nearly without cartridges. They were awakened by the tramp of caribou marching past in solid columns, two, three, or more abreast, and the columns anywhere from a few yards to a quarter of a mile apart. Sometimes the herd walked, but generally they proceeded on a trot. Such a sight as this had never been seen by my Eskimo, and it dumfounded them. Natkusiak, who always did the thinking for the two of them, decided immediately that he would, with the few cartridges they had, sit down and try to shoot two or three caribou with each bullet, while Tannaumirk was to go back the short eight miles to our camp to get ammunition.

Tannaumirk accordingly started, but when he got a mile or so on his way, he saw a place where the caribou were crossing the frozen river, coming down a steep cut-bank. As they did so it occurred to him that if he were to hide under the cut-bank, he would be able to stab the caribou as they passed. The animals were too quick for him, however; and although, according to his own story, he was several times able to touch them with the point of his knife, he was unable to kill any. He then went and cut down a stout willow and made a long spear-handle for his knife. He is very sure that had he done this in the first place he would have killed a good many caribou, but when he took up his position afresh under the cut-bank, the caribou had ceased coming over that spot. Nevertheless, he spent the entire day skulking under other cut-banks, trying to stab caribou as they

Q

passed. Finally, when he was pretty well tired out, there was only daylight enough left for him to reach home.

The next morning when he was about to return to Natkusiak with the ammunition, he saw a band of bull caribou near the camp. Of course, no one with brains would have done such a thing as he had done the day before, nor would any one have stayed to follow three or four bulls when he knew that the march of the big herd was in progress to the east; but Tannaumirk was never very bright, and he spent the entire day in stalking and shooting three bulls. While he was skinning them, he happened to see some wolves, and made up his mind that it was important that he carry the meat home to camp. This took him several hours of the third day, and it was nearly evening on that day when he finally got back to Natkusiak with the cartridges.

Meantime Natkusiak had used his four or five bullets so well that he averaged killing two deer with each one, but when Tannaumirk got back, the herd had passed and only a few stragglers remained. For two days the herd had been moving south, past the west end of our fishing-lake, and when I came home a few days later, I found a belt of country several miles in breadth so trampled down by the feet of the caribou that it might be spoken of as one continuous trail. Had I been there myself, I don't think there would have been any possibility of making even an approximate count of the herd. As it was, I merely agree with the Eskimo that the numbers were beyond comprehension. We got only twenty-nine animals out of it, however, while with any management at all we should have been able to kill at one spot enough meat to last us the whole winter.

It will be remembered that I had left Dr. Anderson and some of our Eskimo behind at Langton Bay, and it seemed to me wise now to try to connect with him, because I knew he would already be worrying about what had happened to us. His Eskimo, I felt sure, would take it for granted that we were long since dead, and I thought it likely — as, indeed, was the case — that Dr. Anderson would have in mind starting a search expedition for us. It seemed evidently much easier for us to find him (for we knew where he was) than for him to find us. Besides, the largest unexplored area on the continent lay between us on Bear Lake and his location on Franklin Bay, and

Scene crossing Victoria Island.

this I was anxious to explore. The previous winter had been spent by us on the lower reaches of Horton River. When Richardson first saw the mouth of Horton River in 1826, he gave it a name; he also gave names in that immediate neighborhood to two other rivers, — Ellice and Jardine, — and the charts in no way indicate that one of these is larger than the other. The mouths of all are set down, but nothing else is shown. Now we found in the winter of 1909–1910 that the rivers Ellice and Jardine were creeks that you could jump across and not over six miles in length, while we had that same year explored some two hundred and fifty miles of the lower reaches of Horton River, and we had found it to have all the earmarks of a big river. It seemed as wide at two hundred and fifty miles upstream as it was twenty-five miles from the sea, and it came from the direction of Bear Lake.

Now that we were on Bear Lake, I thought that by taking a course northwest true from the northeast corner of the lake for Langton Bay I should not only reach Langton Bay, but, incidentally, should probably find and be able to chart the upper reaches of Horton River. On this journey Natkusiak would of course go with me, while Tannaumirk and Pannigabluk remained behind on Dease River at our winter camp; but it seemed advisable to get also a Slavey Indian companion, for the Slaveys claim to know the country far to the north of Bear Lake, and one man in particular, known as Johnny Sanderson, said he knew all about it for a distance of several days' travel. Besides, we had no toboggans of our own, and our runner-sled was unsuitable on the tundra, so I hired Johnny with two toboggans and one dog-team.

On November 8, 1910, we started from the mouth of Dease River on our journey toward Franklin Bay; for two or three days before that we had been engaged in putting the finishing touches on our equipment, which meant making dog-harness and packing up dry caribou meat. Both at this time and on the two or three other occasions when we had come to Dease River Mr. Hodgson entertained us hospitably and helped us in every way. For the first forty miles after leaving his house we followed the shore of Bear Lake northwestward, and then struck inland, traveling west by compass, which here means northwest true. We had only about six days' provisions with us, for among other things Johnny had told us that there would be plenty of caribou as soon as we got away from the fringe of woods about Bear Lake.   I have often started upon a longer trip than the three weeks we anticipated for this one, with less than six days' provisions, but in this case we could easily have taken more, for Mr. Hodgson generously offered to supply us with as much as we wanted to haul.   Johnny regarded himself, apparently, as quite infallible, and succeeded in impressing me with the probability that he was nearly so; but few men I have dealt with have panned out so poorly as Johnny Sanderson.

Going in a northwesterly direction, it takes about forty miles of traveling to reach the edge of the Barren Ground, and for all this distance we saw plenty of caribou tracks, but Johnny told us it would not be worth while following them and delaying our journey by a hunt in the woods, because, he said, "the Indians call the treeless country the Caribou Ground, and that is because it is always covered with caribou."   A few miles after we had left the trees behind us and entered upon what we called the Barren Ground (but what Johnny called the Caribou Ground) we crossed the tracks of half a dozen or so animals, and after that for two hundred miles we never saw another track.

Johnny was proud of his varied experiences as a traveler, and told how this and that great man of the Hudson's Bay Company had employed him as head guide, and how they always placed implicit reliance in him.   He said there were few places he did not know, and that even where he was a stranger his judgment was so good that he was seldom at fault.

This confidence in himself had been so often justified in the past that the fact of its being seldom justified on the present trip evidently seemed to him an exception scarcely worthy of note.   We struck the Barren Ground on the morning of our fourth day, and toward evening we had a blizzard.   When it came time to camp, we searched for a small lake, because the ice at this season was not much more than a foot thick and fuel was scarce, so we wanted to get water for cooking.   When we got to the shore of a small pond, I stopped the sled. The selection did not suit Johnny, however; he said that no one who knew anything about traveling would ever pick such a place for a camp. Half a mile back, he said, he had seen a cut-bank under the shelter of which we could have pitched our tent, and even now he could see, only a little way ahead of us, a round hill with a steep slope to leeward that would be a fine place under which to camp, for the hill would break the wind.

Now my idea and Natkusiak's did not coincide with Johnny's, because to us it was clear that if we camped in the lee of an obstruction the drifting snow would in the night cover up our tent and place us in danger of being smothered even were the tent not to cave in with the weight of the snow. No man of any winter experience in the open will pitch his tent in a shelter where there is the possibility of a blizzard. Johnny's ideas were all gained in the forested country, where it is wise, of course, to choose the most sheltered spots, and it seemed to him that we were little better than insane. He announced, therefore, that he would take the matter into his own hands and pitch the camp in the shelter of the hill, and he told me incidentally that I was the first white man he had ever seen who did not know enough to understand that an Indian knows more than a white man about how to make camp. Of course, the obvious answer was that now that he had the opportunity he had better watch carefully people who had different ideas from his and see what the result would be.

Natkusiak and I had to take Johnny's own sled away from him by a show of force, and had the pleasure of listening to his comments while we, without any help from him, put up the tent. During that time, and at various other times thereafter, Johnny told us much of a party of the Geological Survey of Canada which had been commanded by a white man who was my superior in every way, and who, while he was inexperienced, had the good sense to defer to Johnny in everything. Among other things Johnny had said that we would all probably freeze to death during the night, but we banked up the tent so well, Eskimo fashion, that we had not been inside of it more than an hour or so before Johnny began to complain that it was too warm, and that he was getting wet, through the snow in his clothes melting and soaking in. He had been so sure that the tent was going to be so cold — nothing could melt in it — that he had not thought it worth while to brush the snow off his fur coat.

We made no fire, for Natkusiak and I agreed that digging heather for fuel from underneath the snow was not worth the bother; we ate frozen raw caribou meat and drank cold water, at all of which Johnny complained bitterly. We could, he pointed out, have used the ordinary forethought of sane men; we could have hauled a load of dry spruce wood from the Bear Lake woods and could have made ourselves comfortable with a fire and a warm meal. To this we answered that our dogs agreed with us in considering the sleds heavy enough without piling a cord of wood on top of them, and that there was no need for special effort toward making us comfortable, for we were comfortable already.

The next morning we started early. Fortunately for us, the blizzard was from the southeast, and, although it was still blowing a little, it only helped us on. But with the southeast wind in this district there usually comes a fog, and so it was now. We got into some very hilly country — mountainous it seemed — and although we made a long day, we had to camp without finding any trees or sign of a river. I was expecting to find Horton River about here, and hoping that if we found it we should find spruce, or at least willows, in the valley bottom. It turned out that on our second Barren Ground day we camped just a little too soon, for the next morning early we struck a river about one hundred yards wide coming in from the east and flowing sluggishly through level country with scarcely the vestige of a valley. We followed it west about six miles; then the conformation of the country began to indicate that the stream probably made a large curve, first southwest, and later west, north, and a little back again east. Anyway, our destination was Franklin Bay, which lay northwest true, so we abandoned the stream and struck northwest again about eighteen miles. Here we came upon the river again, and found it, much to our satisfaction, to be fairly well timbered with black spruce, while at the point where we struck it in the morning there had been nothing but willows.

From this point on for six days we followed the winding course of the stream. There were rapids here and there and stretches of open water, but we always found a thoroughfare past these difficulties along one bank or the other. In some places the valley is fairly wide; in others the river plunges through narrow limestone cañons, and everywhere it is crooked, but when you once commit yourself to the

away, with the woods stretching black and unbroken toward Bear Lake. But for the wisdom of Johnny Sanderson we might have camped in its shelter and escaped one of the most disagreeable camp-making experiences we ever had.

The next day we had traveled only a few miles before we came upon the tracks of caribou. Our thermometer had broken some time before, and so I speak without the book, but there is little doubt that the temperature was considerably below 50° Fahrenheit. There was not a breath of air stirring. While the other three proceeded with the sled I struck out to one side to look for caribou. First I saw a band that had been frightened by our main party. There were only a few clearings in the woods, but wherever the animals were you could discover their presence by the clouds of steam that rose from them high above the tops of the trees.

There are few things one sees in the North so nearly beyond belief as certain of the phenomena of intense cold as I saw and heard them that day. It turned out that the woods were full of caribou, and wherever a band was running you could not only see the steam rising from it and revealing its presence, even on the other side of a fairly high hill, but, more remarkable still, the air was so calm that where an animal ran past rapidly he left behind him a cloud of steam hovering over his trail and marking it out plainly for a mile behind him. When you stopped to listen, you could hear the tramp of marching caribou all around you. On such days as this I have watched caribou bands a full mile away whose walking I could hear distinctly although there was no crust on the snow; and as for them, they could not only hear me walking, but could even tell the difference in the sounds of my footsteps from those of the hundreds of caribou that were walking about at the same time.

My first opportunity to shoot came through my hearing the approach of a small band. I stopped still and waited for them. I was not nervous, but rather absent-minded. In other words, my mind was more fully occupied than it should have been with the importance of getting those particular caribou. I always carry the magazine of my rifle full but the chamber empty, and as the animals approached I drew back the bolt to throw a cartridge into the chamber, but when I tried to shove the bolt forward it stuck fast. This is the only time in four years of hard usage that anything has interfered with the perfect working of my Mannlicher-Schoenauer. The caribou were moving past without seeing me, and I became a bit excited. I knew the rifle was strong, and I hammered on the end of the bolt with the palm of my hand, but it would not move. When the caribou were finally out of range and when nothing more could be done, I for the first time took a good look at the rifle to try to discover the trouble, and saw that one side of the bolt had something frozen fast to it. It turned out that when I had drawn the bolt back to load the rifle I had carelessly allowed the palm of my bare hand to rest against the bolt, and a piece of skin about an inch long and a quarter of an inch wide had frozen fast to the bolt and been torn away from my hand without my noticing it. It took but a few moments scraping with my hunting knife to remove the blood from the bolt, and the rifle was in good working order again.

Three days later we reached the house of Melvill and Hornby on Bear Lake, thirty-three days after leaving Langton Bay. After a short visit with them and Mr. Hodgson we proceeded up the Dease River and found Tannaumirk and Pannigabluk well, although getting short of food, for Tannaumirk was not a hunter of much enterprise.

No caribou were just then to be found near our winter quarters, so Dr. Anderson, one of the Eskimo, and myself struck out south to look for them. On the second day we found them near the northeast corner of Bear Lake, but had hard luck that day on account of variable faint airs that continually gave the animals our wind. The next day, however, we got sixteen, and within the next twenty days thereafter fifty-two more, which was plenty of meat for the rest of the winter.

CHAPTER XV

ON March 22, 1911, we started for Coronation Gulf, leaving Pannigabluk behind to look after our house, to prepare dried meat for the contemplated overland journey to Langton Bay, and to protect everything against thefts from wolves and wolverines. We had two toboggans and nine dogs, and carried with us about four days' provisions of meat, besides a few trade articles, some of which we had brought with us overland in the winter from Langton Bay and some of which we had secured from Melvill and Hornby and from Hodgson. These consisted chiefly of butcher knives, needles, and empty tin cans. The tin cans, although of little value to us, were of inestimable value to the Eskimo. One tin such as we throw away, after emptying it of its contents of baking powder or salmon, will last a thrifty Eskimo housewife several years as a cooking pot for boiling small things over a seal-oil lamp. I remember one trade we made where we gave some carpenter tools, worth about three dollars, for a bow and quiver of arrows. The man later, with our permission, returned the carpenter tools and took in their stead a cubical tin which had at one time held about five pounds of Melvill and Hornby's dried onions.

On the northward journey we broke new ground, partly because we wanted to see the country farther west than we had seen it before, but also because we thought that by going straight north from our camp we would probably strike the west end of Dismal Lake. We wanted not only to see the lake but also to use the thirty-six smooth miles of its ice-covered length, because by doing so we were sure of just that much easy going.

The road north from our camp led us through granitic hills with plenty of tree growth on them and caribou tracks here and there, showing that we need have no fear for the securing of food. However, we saw no animals for the first two days, and on the third day, exactly as I had hoped, we came in sight of Dismal Lake.

The lake itself in its western part is devoid of tree growth, except that the river which flows into its extreme end is thickly timbered and sends out a fringe of trees along the lake shore for a little way on each side of the mouth. From there east for thirty miles there is nothing for fuel except some small clumps of willows, the tallest of which will not be over four feet in height. The lake has a width of from a mile to six miles or so, until about eight miles from the eastern end, where it narrows down to a width of ninety to two hundred yards for a space of about a mile. East of that it widens again and along the northern shore spruce begin to appear. These change to an abundant growth at the outlet of the lake, and Kendall River, which drains the lake southeast into the Coppermine, may be considered thickly forested.

When about four miles from the eastern end of the lake we left it, striking off on the north side to make a short cut along the southern side of some steep hills which run east towards the Coppermine. We were traveling now on high ground and could see south across the valley of the Kendall bands of caribou grazing about six miles away. We accordingly camped, for our meat had about run out and it seemed well to replenish our stores.

I happened at this juncture to be suffering from a chafed foot on account of having worn a badly made stocking the day we left home. Dr. Anderson and Natkusiak therefore undertook to hunt, and I stayed at home to give my foot a chance to recover. Tannaumirk, who was a fair seamstress, also stayed at home mending boots and stockings and incidentally telling me folk-lore stories which I wrote down in the original language as he told them. Tannaumirk could never be relied upon for an enterprise of moment, but he had many good qualities, among which were an unvarying cheerfulness and an inexhaustible fund of folk-lore tales, songs, and charms, which he had at first, like the rest of his countrymen, been loath to repeat to me on account of being used to having white men make game of him for doing so. But now that he had found that I had a real interest in such things he never tired of telling them.

In the evening when our hunters came home they reported having seen caribou in great numbers, but they had not had the best of luck. Dr. Anderson had shot two and Natkusiak had failed to get

ROUGH ICE ON COPPERMINE.

ESKIMO WEARING SNOW GOGGLES.

any. It had been a bright sunshiny day and Dr. Anderson had care-lessly gone without glasses, with the result that he was slightly snow-blind the following morning.

Seeing that the subject has been mentioned, it may be worth while to say that we have tried glasses of all colors and makes and have found the amber ones, made on the same principle as light filters for cameras, to be far superior to blue, green, plain smoked, or any other variety. The Eskimo goggles, which are made of pieces of wood with two narrow slits for the eyes, each about large enough for a half-dollar to be slipped through it, are satisfactory in that they do not cloud over and that they protect the eyes from snow-blind-ness; but the difficulty with them is that the range of vision is so restricted that it is as if you were looking out through a pair of key-holes in a door. This is especially troublesome on rough ice or un-even ground, where you keep stubbing your toe against every ob-stacle, for through the narrow slits you can see what is in front of your feet only by looking directly down.

As my chafed foot was not completely recovered yet, and as Dr. Anderson was snow-blind, it fell to Natkusiak and Tannaumirk to go for the meat of the caribou Dr. Anderson had shot. It was an-other cold, clear day as it had been the day before, and it furnished us with yet another example of the fact that Eskimo do not have com-passes in their heads, for although the caribou had been killed and cached only about seven miles away from camp, Natkusiak was un-able to find them in an all-day search and the two of them returned home after dark with an empty sled. This meant loss of valuable time, and worst of all, the consumption by us and our dogs of the few remaining pounds of dried meat we had brought with us from home. It is of course always wise to eat your green meat first and keep the light and condensed dried meat to the last.

The place where the two deer were cached was plainly visible with the glasses from our camp, so that it seemed likely that the next day Natkusiak and Tannaumirk would be able to find it, which it turned out that they did. We had delayed so long now, however, that two caribou were hardly sufficient meat to go on with, so that I went across the Horton River a mile or two east of where the Eskimo went to get the cached meat, and shot three caribou and a fine specimen of white wolf.   This wolf was not only fat and excellent eating, but its skin was of great value, either scientifically or commercially; — scientifically because the animal is rare, and commercially because the Eskimo of the Mackenzie district and therefore the members of our own party value the skin highly as trimming for their winter coats. A wolfskin of the type which the Eskimo most admire can, when cut into strips, be sold for as much as twelve foxskins, which being translated into dollars at the prices quoted in 1912 would mean from one hundred to one hundred and twenty dollars for each wolfskin.

Natkusiak and Tannaumirk heard my shooting when I bagged the three caribou, and after discovering the cached meat they came over and helped me skin, and took on their sled some of the meat. The next day we spent in hauling the rest of the meat to camp and in making a platform cache upon which to leave behind what we could not take with us.   Besides meat, we left also in this cache the valuable wolfskin and the skins of two caribou which we intended for scientific specimens.   We knew very well that this cache would not be safe from wolverines, but counted on the rarity of those animals in these parts for a chance to get back before everything had been destroyed.   The wolves and foxes, we knew, would be unable to steal from a seven-foot high platform.

We reached the Coppermine March 30th, five or six miles north of the mouth of the Kendall, and followed it thence north beyond Bloody Fall, or within about four miles of the coast.   The Coppermine was this winter, and probably is all winters, a rough route to travel. In summer it is a continuous rapid and in winter it gives you in places the impression of medium bad pressure ice at sea.   What apparently happens is this: the river freezes over in the fall while the water still stands at a fairly high level, and the ice gets anywhere from a few inches to a foot in thickness.   The water in the river then begins to settle lower and lower and an air space is left between the ice and the running water.   Eventually the thin ice roof breaks down with a crash into the open water, and for a little way the big cakes of ice are carried down-stream by the strong current until they are finally jammed in a heap to freeze fast a second time.

Although in summer the Coppermine carries a considerable volume of water, it flows through a narrow valley and is itself a narrow

TRAVELING ON THE COPPERMINE RIVER IN SPRING.

stream. About fifteen miles north of the mouth of the Kendall I measured it in several places, finding it about 135 yards in one spot, 130 in another, 125 in a third, and 230 yards in the widest place seen that day, which meant the widest place in a stretch of fifteen miles. A few days before I had measured the width of the Kendall River in two places at 92 and 135 yards respectively. Of course that does not mean that the Kendall is nearly so large a stream as the Coppermine. It is in fact a river across which a man can wade in many places in summer, whereas the Coppermine is everywhere deep, although its channel is so tortuous, its bed so full of rocks, and its current so swift that it can never become a river for steamboat navigation, although it may sometime furnish almost unlimited power if its rapids and falls are ever harnessed for commercial purposes.

Traveling northward along the bed of the Coppermine, we naturally had no opportunities of seeing caribou, for there are no feeding grounds within sight from the river ice and we knew from experience that their habits did not lead them to cross the river, even when they fed in considerable numbers along its very banks. April 1st our supply of meat had again begun to run low, so instead of following the river bed we ascended the hill on the east side and traveled north parallel to the river, a mile or two away from it. After half a day of this sort of travel we came upon some level land which had the summer before, when we were there, been entirely devoid of game, but which was now fairly covered with tracks of caribou, and soon we came upon the caribou themselves grazing in hundreds. Natkusiak went after them, got within range, and fired, but without effect, and the whole mass started moving southeast towards the high hills. This gave me a chance and by a run of about half a mile I headed them off and shot four, which was quite enough for our wants. Natkusiak later in the day shot a fifth.

It seemed to us that the caribou here were of a different type from any farther west. They were somewhat smaller. The bulls among them had very big horns, and all the animals were much lighter colored and had a differently shaped head from those we were used to. The caribou farther west have what might be described as clean faces, or faces reminding one somewhat of horses. These eastern caribou have fuzzy or donkey-like faces, with the eyes appearing deep set

R

through the length of the hair on the face, and with an appearance of thickness of the face below the eyes, caused no doubt largely by the growth of hair. Of course the cow caribou, as the ones we killed were, could not be expected to be in good flesh at this time of year, but still we did not find them quite so poor as might have been expected.

The next day after the deer killing we spent in making a cache in the form of a log cabin for the safe keeping of our meat. Of course this is not really a safe cache, but if the logs are big it will take the wolverines several days to gnaw through them. We also set and baited several dead fall traps, partly because we wanted wolverine skins and partly with the hope that if we were able to trap the first two or three that visited the cache, we might return to it before the fourth one had had time to gnaw its way through.

April 4th we reached the place at which we had the previous spring cached our sled and other belongings that we could not carry with us on the Barren Ground hunt. We found all of these safe, although both grizzly bears and wolverines had been there and had knocked things about a good deal. But there was nothing in the whole lot which they recognized as food, and everything was carefully packed in the strong oak boxes which had formerly held our small supply of malted milk. We found these boxes of scarcely less value than the milk itself had been, for they kept our diaries, writing materials, photograph films, and things of that sort safe through all weather and protected from all animals. We left behind here one of the toboggans and took the high sled instead, which was much better adapted for work on the coast.

Something like thirty miles south of Coronation Gulf there appear hills of the same peculiar formation which is found in the islands of the gulf itself. In other words, each hill consists of a gradual slope, say 15° or 20° upward from northwest to southeast, ending finally in a precipice of greater or less height facing southeast. In traveling southwest through this country in foggy weather in summer I had often found these slopes so gradual as to be unnoticed by me until of a sudden I was on the brink of a precipice down which it was often very difficult to scramble.

A comparison of these terraces with the islands in Coronation

Gulf brings out the similarity strikingly. The terraces are formed of columnar basalt, underlaid, in the case of the islands at least, by stratified limestone. The result of these formations in Coronation Gulf is that there are shallows and dangerous reefs running to the northwest from most of the islands, while deep water is found close up to the precipices which form the southeast ends of the islands.

The passing of Bloody Fall had been dangerous the preceding spring, but was a safe and simple thing at this time of year. It had some appearance of danger, which I think was an appearance only, for the ice must have been very thick. It was hanging ice, however, or in other words there was an air space between it and the water below, and a formation of that kind is always open to suspicion. If there is a break, the accident is certain to be fatal to any man or beast who happens to be on top of the ice when it breaks, for it would be but an instant until the cake that broke off would be swept under the rim of ice in the whirlpool below the falls.

On the evening of April 4th we abandoned the Coppermine two miles north of Bloody Fall and struck straight north about four miles to the seacoast, where we camped on finding a few sticks of wood. In the spring, when the snow has been melted away by the warm sun, fresh drift-wood (most of it, no doubt, from the Coppermine) may be found almost anywhere in Coronation Gulf, especially to the east of the Coppermine, and more abundantly on the islands than on the mainland itself. But at this time of year the finding of a stick of wood on any of the shores of the gulf is rare, so that we used to make it a practice whenever we saw a piece to put it on the sled and haul it along until camp time. We had with us also a *primus* stove and a gallon and a half of kerosene, which we had hauled all the way from Langton Bay. These we kept to use in an emergency, for at this season of the year seals from which we might have obtained blubber for fuel are not to be had in Coronation Gulf by any method of hunting except the one practiced by the local Eskimo, which depends partly on the ability of dogs in smelling out the breathing-holes of the seals and partly on the skill in that particular kind of waiting game which we have elsewhere described. It is a hunting method in its essence requiring long delays, and therefore not very well adapted to traveling parties that are in a hurry, and kerosene was therefore of great value to us. Had we not had the oil, we could of course have gone several days without any fuel at all, but that would have been a rather unpleasant experience, for the weather was very cold, going down to 50° below zero at night occasionally.

Naturally we examined every stick of drift-wood we saw. One of them told an interesting story. It was a cottonwood log, some twenty feet or more in length and fully eighteen inches in diameter at the middle. It was a part of the trunk of a large tree evidently, and must have come from the Liard River by way of the Mackenzie, for in no other place do we know of the growth of cottonwoods of this size. This stick must have come from the Mackenzie eastward through Dolphin and Union Straits, which shows that at times at least there must be a current sweeping in an easterly direction. Our own observations of Dolphin and Union Straits, both before this time and after, indicate that through the narrows of the straits and about Lambert Island these currents may run with the swiftness of a mill race in either direction. They are swift enough, in fact, to keep ice of any thickness from forming all winter. But although the currents alternate in direction, the prevailing winds are northwesterly, and where the current is slack a log of wood might be, and in fact often is, driven against the current.

We were on Coronation Gulf in search of people, and we had no idea where to look for them, except that we knew that they would not be anywhere near shore. We confirmed on entering the gulf a fact of which we had seen some indications the previous spring, that there are four times as many islands in it as the charts show us. Most of these islands occur in chains running about parallel to the south shore of the gulf, or tending somewhat offshore as you go east. It seemed to us the best plan, therefore, to follow one of these chains eastward and to spy from the tops of their high islands with our glasses for possible villages out on the ice. Although the snow houses themselves are not easily seen at a great distance, an Eskimo village on the ice in the spring presents as a whole a dark appearance, on account of the wet clothes that are hung up outdoors to be dried and because of the blubber bags and the other household belongings which are scattered about.

After traveling to the northeast for a day we found an old snow village, but this had been deserted evidently in the early fall and the trail that led away from it had been completely obliterated by the blizzards. We proceeded two days northeast after that, but found no other traces, and decided then to turn north towards Victoria Island. We had gone only about ten miles north, however, when we came upon a fresh trail of one sled and four people going east. It was to be taken for granted that this sled was coming from one village and going to another. We decided to follow its track east rather than to retrace it west, and that evening late we came to a commodious and clean-looking snow house which had evidently been abandoned by the party we were following not more than two days before. We had found no fuel that day, and to save ourselves the trouble of making camp we moved into the house, for it was quite big enough for us.

A new camp is warmer than an old one, for a new snow house is a snow house, but an old one is an ice house. This particular one had evidently been kept pretty warm by its former occupants, for the walls were solid, glistening ice. We were all warm from fast travel, and in our hurry to get the camp heated up we closed the door tightly. The bed-platform was just wide enough for three, and we were all sitting on the front edge of it, with the exception of Natkusiak, who was sitting on the floor. I was a little higher than the rest, for the cooking was my job that night, and I had set the primus stove on a block of snow and was on my knees cutting up snow into the kettle to make water. Tannaumirk and Natkusiak were talking and joking as usual. In the midst of one of his funny stories, which he told with a good deal of pantomime, Tannaumirk all at once threw himself backward upon the bed and made a sort of gurgling noise. Anderson was sitting next to him. All three of us thought that these actions and gurglings were a part of the pantomime accompanying the story; still I asked Anderson to look and see what Tannaumirk was up to, for he did not get up again as quickly as we expected. When Dr. Anderson turned to look, he fell down face forward on top of Tannaumirk. I knew then in a twinkle what the matter was and immediately extinguished the primus stove, for it was clear that we were being poisoned by coal gas, which is so insidious a thing that under ordinary circumstances one does not notice its presence.

Natkusiak, to whom the phenomenon was a strange thing, saw nothing to be alarmed at, and when I told him to immediately break a hole in the snow wall back of where he was sitting, he went about it with deliberation. Fortunately, in order to make the hole he had to get up to reach for his knife which he had stuck into the wall. When he tried to arise he found himself powerless to do so, and that scared him so that with his last strength he threw himself back against the wall and broke away the loose block of snow by which we had a few minutes before closed up the door. He then crawled outdoors on all fours, but was too weak to stand up. I followed him out and had strength enough to stand up after getting out, but that was only for a moment and I fell down beside Natkusiak.

It was a calm, starlit night, with the temperature about 45° below zero, and the situation was evidently serious, for all of us were lightly clad. My first thought was to try to get back into the house and drag Anderson and Tannaumirk out, and I crawled to the opening for that purpose, but was so weak that it was evident I could do nothing if I did go in.

It must have been fifteen minutes that we lay flat outside the snow house before Anderson's face appeared at the hole in the wall. His mind was clear apparently, but he had no realization of what had happened and asked us in a querulous voice what we were doing out there and why we had put out the stove and let the cold air into the house. Before I had time to answer him, however, he realized what had happened and crawled out and started walking about and drawing into his lungs as deep breaths of air as possible. He soon found, however, as I had found a few minutes before, that this was the worst possible thing to do, and he had to stretch himself out flat on the ground like the rest of us.

It must have been another ten minutes until Tannaumirk also came to his senses and crawled out. By that time I, who had been less affected from the beginning than any of the others, had strength enough to fetch from the house our sleeping bags, into which I helped Anderson and Natkusiak to crawl. Tannaumirk would not crawl into the bag, saying that if he did he would no doubt go to sleep in it and freeze to death. He had been much worse affected than the rest of us and while we seemed to be able to think clearly his mind

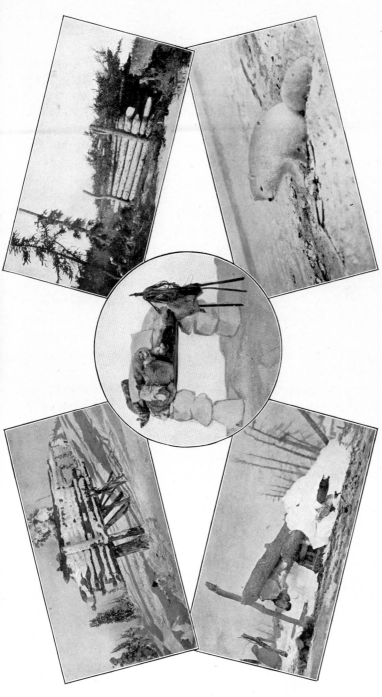

MEAT CACHES AND TRAPS SET TO GUARD THEM.

1. Bear Lake Indian cache of logs on stilts.　　2. Bear Lake Indian cache on ground.
3. Coronation Gulf platform cache on snowblocks.　　5. Fox in steel trap.
4. Deadfall trap of logs.

nation Gulf Eskimo had heard the Hudson's Bay Eskimo speak in this way of Hanbury, and the idea of a man being master of other men being entirely strange to them, they supposed that this was Hanbury's name instead of his title. But the fact that Hudson's Bay men called their commander *isumatak* (which becomes *ihumatak* in the Coronation Gulf dialect) made it entirely probable that this was the word which the King William Island natives had used of Franklin. Knowing this, it becomes possible to show with a degree of certainty that this is the word which Hall meant to write down.

In passing it may be said here that the great differences which at first appear to exist between an eastern Eskimo dialect written down by one man, and an Alaskan dialect written by another, are chiefly matters of phonography. To one who knows an Alaskan Eskimo dialect a word written by Thalbitzer for Greenland is clear as day in meaning, though Hall's phonography or Parry's would disguise it effectively.

Through our inquiries here we learned that a flourishing intertribal trade exists between Hudson's Bay and Kent peninsula, started by the Eskimo who accompanied Hanbury on his journey. Every winter now there arrives at the village of Umingmuktok on Kent peninsula a tribe known to the Coronation Gulf people as Pallirgmiut, named, as they say, from a branch river "Pallirk," which flows into the Akkilinik. In the winter of 1909–1910 there was said to have accompanied these Pallirgmiut to Umingmuktok a white man they call Kaksamina, who returned with them to the south again after a trading visit of a week or two. It seems possible that this may be a young white man who was lost from Hudson's Bay the year before, but it is by no means sure, for the Coronation Gulf Eskimo did not consider me a white man, but did consider white the Indians of Bear Lake, with whom, of course, they had had no dealings. It is possible, therefore, that the so-called white man may have been merely an Eskimo of another tribe than the Pallirgmiut, if not one of the Pallirgmiut themselves.

In this group we met some people who had evidently traveled farther abroad than any we had previously seen. Up to this time I had asked every one we met whether Victoria Island was an island or not, and they had invariably agreed that it was not an island;

in other words, that there was no other side to it or sea surrounding it, but in this village there were several people who
expressed themselves definitely as knowing that there was an east
side to the island. One of these, Iglihsirk, I questioned to see if he
knew anything about the loss of Franklin's ships. I asked him if
he had ever heard that a ship had been wrecked on the east coast
of Victoria Island, and what he knew about the fate of the men who
had been on the ship. He said so far as he knew no ship had been
wrecked *on the east coast*, but that in his father's time *two* ships had
frozen fast in the ice *a long way offshore*, beyond the east coast, and
the white men on them had evidently abandoned them and all died.
This was clear proof that they were familiar with Franklin's story.
Had the man answered my leading question offhand, saying that
one ship had been wrecked on the coast, it might have been considered
one of the cases of politeness among the Eskimo, who usually answer
any question in the way they think you would like to have it answered,
but he had corrected me exactly in accordance with the facts already
known to us, for Franklin's ships were not on the coast, but a considerable distance from it, and were abandoned before the ice broke up.

This was the very man whom Hanbury saw on Dismal Lake
and who, according to Hanbury's account, was familiar with the
Bloody Fall tragedy in which Samuel Hearne and his Chipewyan
were concerned in 1771, but when I asked him he said he knew
nothing of it. Evidently this is another case where Hanbury's
interpreters were at fault. I asked him whether his ancestors had
not been in the habit of fighting now and then with the Indians on
the Coppermine River. Oh, yes, they had, whenever they met.
But did they ever fight at Bloody Fall? No, not so far as he knew;
not in that particular place. He had never heard of Eskimo killing
Indians or Indians killing Eskimo at Bloody Fall. Long before he
was born his father had, he said, seen white men near the mouth of
the Rae River. This must no doubt have been Dease and Simpson's
party, for although Iglihsirk himself, as we learned from outside
sources, was a child of five or six at the time that Richardson visited
Rae River, he and his parents were not present at the time.

We had here a striking example of how easy it is to be misled by
native information. I had been led to believe in the spring that the

Coronation Gulf people never had had any knowledge of the killing of bow-head whales, although they were familiar with the carcasses of those that had drifted up on their beaches. Neither had they apparently ever seen a live one, which is not strange, considering the two facts that bow-head whales are not only no doubt very rare in these waters, but the people themselves are always inland in the summer time and are therefore not in a position to see the whales even if they might come into these waters in July or August. But here at this village and now for the first time, after vain inquiries all summer, we heard various stories of whale killings, most of them, however, centering about a single man whom they called Kaplavinna. They told how this person had on occasion even killed several whales in one day, and how he had a very large boat. This again was new information, for up to that time we had heard nothing about anything but kayaks. In the spring, in fact, the people had seemed to be unfamiliar with the very name of umiak.

I listened to several of these stories with great wonder and asked many questions which were readily answered, but which threw no great light on the subject, until it occurred to me to ask one of the narrators, "Who told you this story? Did you get it from your father?" The man said: "No, I got it from Natjinna." Now Natjinna had been a camp follower of ours all summer, and I had asked him specifically in the spring both about bow-head whales and umiaks and he knew nothing about either. It seemed strange to me that Natjinna should have misled me so in the summer, and I made up my mind to take him to task for it when I saw him. Two or three weeks later, when I happened to meet him, I asked how was it that in the spring he had been unwilling to tell me anything about whales or big boats and now he told long stories to others about them. "Oh, but those were the stories that Natkusiak told me," he answered.

It turned out on investigation that my own man, Natkusiak, was the fountain-head of all these stories, and that the redoubtable whaler Kaplavinna was none other than Natkusiak's former employer, Captain Leavitt of the steam whaler *Narwhal*. These were the local versions, changed to fit the circumstances and geography of Coronation Gulf, and translated into terms comprehensible to the Coppermine Eskimo. I had heard Natkusiak telling these stories the previous spring, but the versions that came to me a year later were so changed that they were not recognizable, and had been so thoroughly localized graphically that the narrators could tell me off just which Coronation Gulf headland the adventures had taken place.

When Natkusiak told these stories, as I noticed on many occasions, he never made any allowances for the fact that he was dealing with things entirely strange to the local people. He discussed davits, masts, sails, anchors, harpoon guns, dynamite bombs, the price of whalebone and the like, exactly as he would have done in his own home village at Port Clarence where these are all familiar topics and matters of everyday conversation. The very names of these things as well as the concepts behind them were absent from the vocabularies and the minds of the local people, and the ideas which they therefore got from Natkusiak's truthful stories were very far from those which would have been gained from the same narratives by a people whose everyday experiences made them comprehensible.

From the seeds sown here by Natkusiak there had grown up a local myth about Kaplavinna and his whaling adventures, — a myth which Natkusiak himself would have had fully as much trouble as I in recognizing, — just exactly as the discussion of the Christian religion by a missionary and of a strange social and political system by a school teacher gives rise to the most astounding ideas in the minds of the Alaskan Eskimo. Very likely it was thus from the preaching of an early missionary among them that some Indian originally evolved upon the model of Jehovah the Manitou idea, which people nowadays use to prove that the tribes of the New England wilderness were familiar with the conception of a single superior being.

Another story which we picked up at this time was that of the Imnait. These were vague and mysterious animals living in an unknown land to the west, which is also inhabited by the Kiligavait. This story did not give us nearly so much trouble in identifying it as did that of Kaplavinna, for the name of the monster was a correct reproduction of that used by my own Eskimo in the previous year in telling their adventures in mountain sheep hunting. Mountain sheep, of course, are found nowhere east of the Mackenzie River, and could not, therefore, be directly known to the Coronation Gulf Eskimo. These people were also unfamiliar with the dangers involved in the possible snow-slides and other peculiar conditions of mountain hunting. They had received from Natkusiak the general idea that mountain sheep hunting was dangerous, and being unable to ascribe any danger to the mountains as such, they had transferred the dangerousness of the snow-slides and precipices to the sheep themselves; and the hairbreadth escapes from death in snow-slides which Natkusiak had described became in their version hairbreadth escapes from the teeth and claws of the ferocious mountain sheep. The kiligavait, which they had associated with the mountain sheep in these narratives, were nothing but the mammoth, known to all branches of the Eskimo race by name at least, and known here also, according to what we were told, by the occasional finding of their bones. Of course Natkusiak had told nothing about mammoth hunting, but the mysterious mountain sheep naturally allied themselves in their minds with the also mysterious mammoth, and were therefore to be coupled together in recounting the same adventures. Thus we had a side-light, not only upon the origin of myths among primitive people, but also upon the startling rapidity with which they grow and change their form.

Along with these stories of Kaplavinna and the mountain sheep we were also told no doubt essentially truthful ones of the trading expeditions of certain men of this district to the lakes above the head of Chesterfield Inlet, as well as in all probability entirely fictitious accounts of how certain men had, during the last few years, made journeys to the moon. One of the local shamans had for a familiar spirit the spirit of a white man, and in séances spoke "white men's language." We were present at one of these séances; and when I said that I was unable to understand anything of what the white man's spirit said through the mouth of the woman whom he possessed, it was considered a very surprising thing, and apparently inclined some of the people to doubt that I was really a white man as I represented myself to be.

Not only does our experience here show how myths may originate, but it also shows how history and fact become mixed with fiction, and how facts are likely quickly to disappear, as in reality they do. It is impossible among the Eskimo, in the absence of extraneous evidence, to rely upon anything that is said to have happened farther back than the memory of the narrator himself extends.

As we have remarked elsewhere, the mind of the Eskimo is keen with reference to their immediate environment, although of course unable to grasp things that are outside of their experience. This keenness is shown especially in the use which they make of practically everything that can be turned to account in their struggle against Arctic conditions. Wood is not especially scarce in Coronation Gulf; still, substitutes for wood have to be found now and then. We saw here a sled which illustrated remarkably the resourcefulness of the Eskimo in this matter. A man named Kaiariok, who is the son of Iglihsirk and of whom Hanbury speaks as being temporarily absent from his father's camp at the time when he visited it on Dismal Lake, found himself in the fall in need of a sled and with no wood out of which to make one. He then took a musk-ox skin, soaked it in water and folded it into the shape of a plank, pressed it flat and straight, and carried it outdoors where it could freeze. It froze as solid as any real plank, and then with his adze he went to work and hewed out of it a sled runner exactly as he would hew one out of a plank. On the upper edge of the runner he made notches for the crosspieces as he would had it been ordinary spruce, drilled holes for the lacings and put in wooden crosspieces, and made a sled which I had seen several times without discovering that it was in any way different from the ordinary wooden sleds. It was only one day when I was thinking of buying a sled that I discovered the difference. There were two sleds for sale, and I was told that one of them was better than the other because when the weather got warm it would still be useful, while the other one would flatten out and become worthless in warm weather and was therefore for sale for half the price of the first one. This cheaper sled turned out to be the musk-ox skin one, for which as an ethnological specimen I would have been willing to pay much more than the other, had there been any possibility of transferring it unchanged to a museum. There was, however, involved the same difficulty that has prevented in such places as Montreal the preservation of ice palaces from year to year.

Of all things that these Eskimo told us, the one that surprised us most was the undoubtedly true statement that a ship manned by

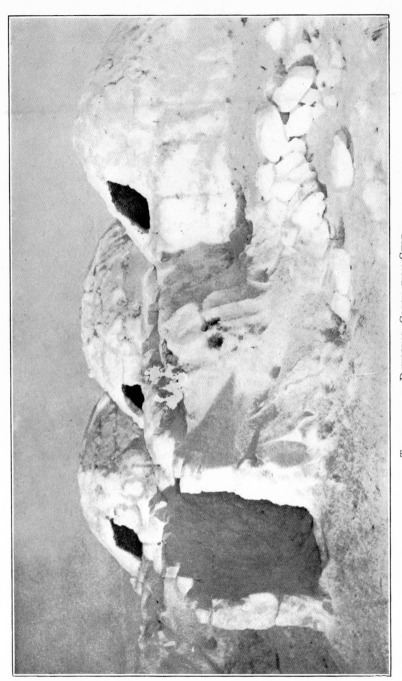

THREE-ROOMED DWELLING, CORONATION GULF.

Holes are not windows — they are broken in the wall for convenience in loading sledges at camp breaking.

white men and strange Eskimo was wintering in Coronation Gulf.
This we felt as the reverse of good news, for the natural feelings of
sympathy that had grown up through a year of association with
these people, who in their way were so infinitely superior to their
civilized brethren in the west, made me regret that civilization was
following so close upon our heels. We had come into the country
in May, and evidently this ship must have come the following September. She was wintering, they said, in the mouth of a small river
about half a day's journey east of the mouth of the Coppermine.
Seeing she was there, we would of course pay her a visit. We were
not in particular need of assistance from anybody, but still in a far
country like this one is always willing either to help or to be helped,
and there was no doubt that the meeting was likely to be both pleasant
and profitable to all concerned. In other words, now that the ship
was there we would make the best of a situation we regretted; we
would make what use of her we could and be of as much use to her as
possible, although had we had our way we should have wished her on
the other side of the earth.

After loading up our sleds with far more ethnological specimens
than our own dogs could haul, we purchased four more dogs to help
do the hauling and started off for the ship. The camp where we had
been trading was about twenty miles offshore from the mouth of
Tree River, and it was therefore about sixty miles southwest to
where we expected to find the vessel.

Our new dogs were of course homesick and we dared not unhitch
them near their homes for fear they would run away, so we traveled day and night, making about fifty miles before stopping, which
is a long march when one is freighting a heavy load, although nothing
particular if one has light sleds. At the end of the fifty miles neither
ourselves nor our dogs were in reality tired out, but still we had to
stop, for more than one of us had become so sleepy that it was literally impossible to keep awake. What finally stopped us was that
Dr. Anderson, who was a little way behind, stopped to fix his snow-
shoe and rolled over asleep on the snow. We had to turn back to
wake him up and then we went into camp.

It had been beautiful sunshiny weather, and even at midnight at
this season of the year it is not quite dark. But when we started

s

again for what we knew would be about ten or twelve miles of travel we had slept away our warm sunshiny day, and found ourselves traveling in a night which through clouds and fog was dark, although it would have been light enough had the sky been clear. We had, therefore, not gone more than six or eight miles when we considered it wise to camp again for fear of missing the ship, for we were able to see but a few hundred yards, and the darkness and the blizzards of the last few weeks made it uncertain that we would see any tracks, of which there would otherwise naturally be a good many in the neighborhood of the vessel. It was foggy still on the morning of the 19th of April when we pushed ahead again, but although the ship was lying in hiding in the bottom of a deep bight, we happened to walk right into her.

The ship was the *Teddy Bear*, a little gasoline schooner of thirteen tons register, from Nome, Alaska, and had on board but one white man, her owner, Captain Joseph Bernard, and a crew consisting of the Eskimo Tulugak, with his wife and their two children, a boy of fifteen and a girl of ten, as well as Tulugak's mother, and his young brother, a child of six or seven. The *Teddy Bear* had wintered the year before at Barter Island and had come east with the intention of getting to the west coast of Victoria Island, but when Captain Bernard had heard from Captain Wolki at Cape Bathurst that my party had gone into Coronation Gulf, he had changed his program and had followed us in. In the early fall he had met some Eskimo from whom he got hazy accounts of us as to where we were wintering (inland and on the Coppermine, they had told him, which was not true), and he had made an attempt to find us. He had been able to proceed only some thirty or forty miles up the Coppermine when he had been forced to return through a combination of circumstances consisting of bad going, scarcity of game, and the uncertainty of where to look for us. Having been in winter quarters here for over seven months without hearing anything further about us, he had naturally given up all hope of seeing us and was therefore almost as surprised when we turned up as we had been a few days before when we heard he was there.

We found Captain Bernard most kind and ready to do us any service possible. It took Dr. Anderson and me but an hour

or two to change all our plans, for now there presented itself
the new resource of a ship willing to coöperate with us. Instead
of making our overland trip from the Dease River to Franklin
Bay across country, as we had expected, and for which the season
was getting rather late anyway, we decided that Dr. Anderson,
Tannaumirk, and Pannigabluk should stay in Coronation Gulf,
where Dr. Anderson was anxious to carry forward his egg collecting
and other zoölogical work, and that I should, with Natkusiak alone
for companion, go north across Coronation Gulf and across the southwestern corner of Victoria Island to Prince Albert Sound and thence
to Banks Island, with the idea of spending the summer with the
Eskimo tribes which we supposed lived there. In the fall the *Teddy
Bear*, on her way west, would make an attempt to pick us up in
De Salis Bay, on southeastern Banks Island. If she should succeed
in that, all of course would be well, for she would carry us to Langton
Bay; but if she failed to find us, through fault either hers or ours,
we would simply spend the autumn months in Banks Island and
sledge across south to Cape Parry and Langton Bay the following
winter as soon as the sea ice got thick enough.

Captain Bernard undertook to carry for us the stone lamps and
stone cooking pots we had purchased from the Eskimo, while Dr.
Anderson and Tannaumirk were to take the remainder of our ethnological collection and the geological ones up to the mouth of Dease
River to hand them over either to Hodgson or to Melvill and Hornby,
who, we knew, would be willing to take them in their big York boat
to Fort Norman on the Mackenzie River, where they could be given
into the hands of the Hudson's Bay Company for shipment to New
York and Ottawa. All of this program was eventually carried out,
and our geological and ethnological collections, without the loss of a
single specimen, arrived at their destination in the civilized lands
about eighteen months after we gathered them in Coronation Gulf.

On the 30th of April Natkusiak and I accordingly started on one
of the longest and most difficult of the trips we have taken together,
although it did not prove quite so long as we had expected. There
were only the two of us, but we carried four rifles, for I had hopes of
being able to hire one of the Victoria Eskimo to accompany us
to Banks Island, and intended to use one rifle both for him to hunt

with while he was with us and to pay him for his services, for
the *Teddy Bear* had already commenced trading in rifles and it was
no longer possible, without the aid of such legislation as no government is likely to be wise enough to make, to confine the Eskimo to
their bows and arrows for hunting. The extra rifle we carried in
case one of ours should break, for Captain Bernard was both willing
and able to give us not only new rifles but also all the ammunition
we needed. Besides that he furnished us with about forty pounds of
trading materials, consisting chiefly of knives, files, and needles, with
which we expected to buy an ethnological collection in Banks Island.
We would have been able on this occasion to load our sled with as
many provisions as we liked, for Captain Bernard had an abundance,
but we preferred to travel light.

The ice was level and the sun was warm, so that our sleds glided
along easily. The season was already later than we would have
wished, so that we did not loiter much by the way, and on the first
day made something over fifty miles, taking turns in running ahead
of the dogs.

It may be well to point out here that our travels, whether they
were five miles or fifty per day, always meant so many miles of walking, for in my entire experience of over 10,000 miles of sled travel
I have never sat on the sled except when it was going down a steep
hill, with the exception of one or two occasions when I have been
suffering from chafed or blistered feet caused by improper footgear.
It is unfair to the dogs and unwise as a policy to ride on the sled.
If the dogs can haul you on top of the rest of the load twenty-five
miles a day, they could haul the load without you thirty or thirty-
five, and the same principle applies whether you make fifteen or
fifty miles in a day. The object is never merely to see how many
weeks and months you can stay away from home, but rather to see
how many miles you can cover while you are away, and consequently
you must do nothing to unnecessarily retard your progress. No
man should engage in Arctic exploration who is unable to walk as
many miles a day as his dogs are able to haul his sled and camp
gear.

It is to be said for a craft which has made great advances in recent
years that although many of the now dead and gone explorers whose

BOYS OF EIGHT AND SIX YEARS, CORONATION GULF.

names are engraved on the roll of fame as well as printed on ponderous volumes, have been little better than baggage hauled along by the common men of their expeditions (whose very names seldom find a place in the records), the explorers of to-day, the men of the type of Peary and Shackleton, are almost without exception both willing and able to do their own work in the field and to require of their subordinates no more than what they demand of themselves.

Our course was about due north for Cape Krusenstern, and we made it by full daylight, which now extended up to ten o'clock in the evening; but when we turned into Dolphin and Union Straits we were in the twilight, for there is in this latitude but a small arc of daylight in the north at midnight on the first of May. We knew that Lambert Island lies in the middle of the straits, and it seemed to me it would be a desirable camping place, for I knew from Eskimo report that there was some drift-wood upon it, and I thought I should find in this neighborhood the seal-hunting village of the Noahonirgmiut.

At night I always carry my 6-power Zeiss glasses, and with them I was able to see the land on either side of the straits although it was not visible to the naked eye, as well as the dark mass ahead which I knew must be Lambert Island. Besides this I saw scattered here and there over the ice little black dots that were a mystery to us, for none of them were near enough to be identified. One of them, however, was straight ahead and we were gradually approaching it. When we got within two or three hundred yards I turned my glasses on it again and found it to be a seal. Now it is not in the nature of seals ordinarily at this season of the year to lie on top of the ice in the dark of night. The thing was therefore a matter for speculation, as was also the large black patch on the ice, beside which the seal was lying.

Ordinarily a seal at this time of year hauls himself out through a hole that is barely large enough for the passage of his body. But the black spot besides this seal was no small hole, but was evidently many square yards in extent, and was therefore a mystery to me until the reflection of a star in it all at once made it clear to me that it was water. Things I had heard from the Eskimo about the strong currents in Dolphin and Union Straits came to my mind only then.

I should of course have remembered them earlier, before we entered the strait.

I was walking perhaps a hundred yards ahead of Natkusiak, who was following with the dog team. I immediately called to him to stop and simultaneously lay down flat on the ice, drew out my hunting knife, and stabbed it into the ice. There was practically no resistance and the knife went right through into the water; the ice was not much over an inch thick under about six inches of snow. I had only discovered this and turned around to crawl back when Natkusiak called out that the sled was settling, that it was already standing in a pool of water. He realized then as well as I did that we were on thin ice. Had the sled remained motionless for a few minutes, it would gradually have settled until the ice broke, sending it to the bottom. I therefore whistled to the dogs and crawling ahead of them made a slow circle and got around to our old trail again, and then commenced a retreat parallel to the old trail a half dozen yards away from it. Every few yards I tried the ice again with my knife and everywhere it seemed to be about an inch thick, while the sled tracks and footprints we had made going west were now black with the water that had oozed into them. Going carefully and continually testing the ice, we had to return several miles before the ice became two or three inches thick, which is a safe thickness. We then began working towards the mainland shore, but every now and then we came to thinner patches and had to turn back. It took us some hours at this rate to get ashore. When we eventually got there the sun was high in the sky.

This was another one of our adventures, brought on, as most adventures are, by incompetence. I had had positive information of the dangerousness of Dolphin and Union Straits, but I had allowed myself to forget it, and because the ice was everywhere smooth and white I had walked thoughtlessly into the danger from which had we broken through there would have been no escape, for the current flows like a mill race. When crawling back over the ice I had several times stopped to listen and could always hear the rustle of the water underneath the ice. Even if we had had no positive warning from the Eskimo, the fact that Dolphin and Union Straits at this point are shallow and less than twenty miles wide should have made it clear that it was dangerous ground, for they connect the open ocean to the west with the large and fairly deep Coronation Gulf to the east, and the tide currents are bound to be terrific.

The caribou migrations were now in steady progress. Both in Coronation Gulf and in Dolphin and Union Straits we crossed every half mile or so the beaten path of a band that had moved north ahead of us, and we saw marching bands on every hand. On the afternoon of the 1st of May, after our adventure with the thin ice, when it came time for us to cross from the mainland to Lambert Island, we waited an hour or so until a band of some twenty caribou passed us going north towards the island, and then we followed in their tracks with the idea that if they came upon weak ice they would fall through and by so doing give us ample warning. Their march was zigzag and took us considerably out of our way, but we followed their path rigorously and got across safely. As a matter of fact we passed over on very thin ice. I tested it frequently and found it nowhere over two inches in thickness.

CHAPTER XVII

JUST northeast of the east end of Lambert Island we found, as we had expected, the village of the Noahanirgmiut Eskimo, consisting chiefly of old friends and hunting companions of ours from the Bear Lake hunt of the summer before, but there were with them also a few families we had not seen. The Eskimo visit about a great deal, and although it is always possible for any one to say, "This is the village of such and such a people," still you are almost sure to find in any village members of one or more other tribes and generally of several. These visits are sometimes temporary, but commonly a family leaves its own tribe and joins another to be with it a period of a year, returning home at the end of that time, although sometimes the visit is only for a summer. A man who is in need of a new sled or a new bow, but whose own tribe hunts in a woodless country, may, for instance, join for the summer hunt a group that intends to go south to Bear Lake, in order to supply himself with the wood he needs.

The Noahanirgmiut were still living on seal meat and were making no attempt to kill any of the numerous caribou that were continually migrating past. I thought at first that there might be some taboo preventing them from hunting caribou on the ice, but this they told me was not so. It was simply that they had never hunted caribou on the ice and had not considered it possible. It would in fact be a fairly hopeless thing for them to try it; and while no doubt some of them might occasionally secure an animal, they would waste so much time that the number of pounds of meat they obtained in a week's hunt in that way would be but a small fraction of the amount of seal meat they might have secured in the same time. Besides that, this is the season which the Eskimo give up to the accumulation of blubber for the coming year. Fresh oil is not nearly so palatable or digestible as oil that has been allowed to ferment in a sealskin bag through the summer, and besides that it is difficult often to get seals in the fall. By getting seals in the spring, therefore, they secure an agreeable article of diet for the coming autumn and provide themselves as well with a sort of insurance against hard luck in the fall hunt. Each family will in the spring be able to lay away from three to seven bags of oil. Such a bag consists of the whole skin of the common seal. The animal has been skinned through the mouth in such a way that the few necessary openings in the skin can be easily sewed up or tied up with a thong. This makes a bag which will hold about three hundred pounds of blubber, so that a single family's store of oil for the fall will run from nine hundred to two thousand pounds.

To completely test the matter of whether there was a taboo or not, as well as to provide ourselves with fresh meat and our friends with a feast, Natkusiak and I intercepted one of the bands out of which he shot one and I shot three, two of the three, by the way, being killed in one shot as the animals were running past at a distance of about three hundred yards. The Eskimo immediately went at the skinning energetically, and I photographed them while they were at it. The meat was then cut up and divided equitably among all the families and the cooking began at once.

It is a theory which has been much in vogue among ethnologists that the fundamental reason back of the system of Eskimo taboos is that they are intended to keep the sea industries away from the land industries and the sea animals away from the land animals; the theory being that the Eskimo were once inland dwellers and accustomed only to land animals and hunting methods suited to the land, and that when they came down to the sea they found its requirements and its animal life so different from that of the land to which they were used that they conceived it necessary to keep the two rigidly apart and that taboos were therefore established. We have elsewhere pointed out that the western Eskimo consider that sudden death, pestilence, or famine will follow upon the sewing of caribou skin garments within a certain number of days after one of the large sea mammals has been killed. It is true among many tribes of Eskimo that caribou skin garments must not be made or mended on the sea ice. The flesh of caribou and of seals must not,

among some tribes, be eaten at the same time, nor must the flesh of
caribou be eaten on the sea at all. Under other circumstances
when both may be eaten, they will have to be cooked in separate
utensils and certain ceremonies have to be performed to cancel, as
it were, the evil effects that might otherwise ensue.

Here, however, everything was different. Not only did these
seal hunters engage in the cutting up of the animals, but the meat
was taken home and cooked in the same pots in which seal meat had
been cooked and eaten; and not only the same day that seal meat had
been eaten and the seals had been killed, but the seal meat and caribou meat were actually eaten at the same meal by the same individuals. One old man, however, said that he knew that it was not
right to boil caribou meat in the same pot in which seal meat had
been boiled unless you suspended the pot by a different string.
His wife therefore took off the old greasy string which had served
as a bale for the stone pot, braided a new sinew string, and swung
the pot by that over the lamp. These Eskimo have various taboos
relating to seal and to caribou, but none of those that I have seen in
use or heard of, except in the case of this one incident of the string,
had any tendency to keep the two apart.

There were in this village two brothers whom I much admired, and
one of them, called Hupgok, I had had in mind trying to engage along
with his family for the Banks Island journey. He would have been
very glad to go with us, he said, but a child had been recently born
in his family and he did not think it wise to go off on a long journey.
This was a great disappointment to me, for he was the only man I
knew who was likely to have the enterprise to pick up and leave his
own country to go to a distant land of which he knew nothing.

This party had come from the west, where they had been sealing
in Simpson Bay and trading with the Cape Bexley Eskimo of the
mainland and the Point Williams ones from Victoria Island, as
well as the Simpson Bay tribe proper, who are known as the Puiplirgmiut. By following their trail, they told us, we should come in a
short day's travel to the village still occupied by the Puiplirgmiut as
well as by a few members of other tribes, although the main bodies
had already moved ashore to the mainland or to Victoria Island,
according to their inclinations, for the summer hunt.

ESKIMO SKINNING THE FIRST CARIBOU THEY HAD SEEN SHOT WITH A RIFLE.

SPRING TENT OF ESKIMO, SOUTH SHORE OF CORONATION GULF, LATE APRIL.

When we started we followed the trail by which this party had arrived, and found eventually a village of five houses some six or eight miles east of Liston Island. Here we engaged to go with us to Banks Island a man whom we knew well and liked in a social way, but in whom we had no great confidence. He had, however, an excellent wife, which was the main consideration, for Natkusiak and I were well able to provide food and raw material for clothing, but we needed an able woman to do sewing for us and especially for making waterproof sealskin boots, without which a summer on the swampy tundra and more especially a spring on the water-covered spring ice were very disagreeable things to face. I was a little surprised to find Kirkpuk and his wife willing to go with us, for they had a baby not more than six or eight weeks old, but they told me that they would leave the child with its grandmother, and that the arrangement was one that they had contemplated anyway; for had Kirkpuk not gone with us, he would, he said, have gone on a long hunt to Bear Lake, upon which journey the child would have been a burden, especially as he had another one, a boy of five or six. It was necessary, Kirkpuk told us, that we wait a day or two while his wife finished cutting up blubber and putting it in bags for the summer. Most of these he would give to his wife's father to cache on the mainland, but one bag we were to take along with us to cache on Victoria Island, with the idea of his using it next fall when he was returning from Banks Island to his own country.

In order to put the people in as good humor as possible, I told Natkusiak to go out and try to get one or more bearded seals, of which there were great numbers in this neighborhood. Dolphin and Union Straits, wherever they are narrow enough so that the current keeps the ice thin, are stocked with seals beyond any part of the Arctic Ocean known to me or to our Eskimo. And not only are there plenty of seals, but most of these are of the valuable bearded variety (*Phoca barbata*), one of which is easily equal to four common seals (*fœtida*) either in blubber or in meat. Curiously enough the eastern Eskimo do not use the bearded seal skins for boot soles, as do those farther west, but employ them entirely as material for ropes.

On the morning when we crossed from the mainland to Lambert

Island I had, standing at sea level, counted with the naked eye over forty seals within a radius of two miles, basking in the sun, and more than three fourths of these were bearded seals. In this locality the bearded seal cannot be taken by the ordinary Eskimo method of hunting, which is to approach him by crawling up and playing seal and finally harpooning him. To try this would here be equivalent to an attempt at suicide by the hunter, for the ice is so thin that in order to pass over it safely at all the Eskimo in many places have to crawl on all fours or wiggle along on their stomachs, so as to distribute the weight of the body over a large area of ice; if they stood up, they would break through. If on such ice a man were to harpoon a big seal or even a small one and try to hold him, there could be but one result. The ice would be broken by the struggle into small cakes, and the man would be pulled into the water. With a rifle this is all different, inasmuch as you can shoot your seal dead, then attach a line to him and carefully crawl away to a distance before you commence pulling, because the ice is always even thinner than elsewhere in the immediate vicinity of the seal's hole.

Although bearded seals are common enough in many districts inhabited by the eastern Eskimo, their taking is a rare thing. It is seldom or never attempted in the spring when they are basking on the ice, and only rarely in winter, when it is done by the ordinary waiting method described elsewhere, and with two men working together. Occasionally a man will spear a bearded seal thinking it is an ordinary one, in which case, if he be a stout hunter, he sometimes gets the beast and is considered a hero for it by all his countrymen. But sometimes the harpoon line proves too weak and the valuable harpoon head is carried off by the animal. Occasionally, when the line does not break, the man is not strong enough to hold the seal and the line and all are carried off.

Among a tribe whom we visited at another time a boy of fourteen unknowingly harpooned a bearded seal through a breathing-hole, and in order to hold him he wrapped the line around his waist. Only one thing could happen, for the seal was as strong as several boys of that age, and he drew the young fellow crosswise of the hole, which at that season was only four inches or so in diameter, and held him there a prisoner for several hours, until a man finally went

CORONATION GULF HUNTERS WITH BOWS AND ARROWS.

PALAIYAK.   NOGASAK.

out to look for him, and found him lying there across the hole. The boy and man together were able to enlarge the hole, haul the animal up through, and kill him. An adventure of this kind does not happen often, and no doubt will be told by that boy and his relatives as long as he lives.

There was great rejoicing in the village when it was learned that Natkusiak was going seal-hunting, and all the men were anxious to go with him, partly to secure their legal share of the booty and partly to see hunting with a rifle. Only three of those in the village had been with us the previous summer, and they were the only ones who had ever seen an animal killed with a bullet.

As a matter of local law there were two or three hunters who would not have needed to go along in order to get a share of the game, for in the division of the spoils only one piece of the seal goes to each household, irrespective of how many hunters representing it are present. The rule is that when a bearded seal is killed, the man who does the killing takes his stand in a conspicuous place near the dead animal and makes signals, usually by swinging out his arms at right angles. All those hunters near enough so they can see the sign come running up. Then the animal is divided into as many segments as there are families represented by the hunters present; and when the cutting up has been done, the most influential person present has the first choice, which means that he takes the biggest and best piece, while the hunter himself, irrespective of his standing in the community, takes the last and therefore the poorest piece; but he has the honor, which is no small thing among them, for not only is the deed considered one of prowess but the man who provides so much food for the community thereby becomes a public benefactor, and gets a valued reward in the consciousness of increased public esteem.

While the other hunters were away I passed the time in writing up my diary and in the occasional pursuit of bands of caribou that were passing. They were however more than usually wary that day for some reason, and I secured only two. Late in the evening the sealers came home successful. Natkusiak had shot two bearded seals, although one of them had been on such thin ice that they had been compelled to approach it slowly and carefully after it was shot, with the result that the warm blood from the wound made the place in which the body lay so slippery that the carcass slid of its own weight into the water and was lost.

When one shoots seal on solid ice, the ordinary procedure is to drop one's gun immediately after it is fired and to run at top speed to the seal. It has happened to me many a time that after a fifty-yard sprint I have barely caught the animal by his hind flipper as he was beginning to slide, and it has happened oftener yet that I have been too late and have merely seen the splash as the animal disappeared in the water. Running of course was not to be thought of on the thin ice upon which Natkusiak hunted that day. The other seal had not slid from where he lay when shot, and had accordingly been saved and cut in six segments for the six native families represented, for Natkusiak had told them that as we were the guests of the village at the time and were not doing our own housekeeping, he did not consider we were entitled to a share.

Although it was blowing a stiff breeze the next day we started off north, for I was beginning to fear that the spring currents might break up the ice between Victoria and Banks Islands and make our proposed crossing to Banks Island impossible. I was anxious, nevertheless, to see as many as possible of the natives through whose country we were passing, so that we camped that evening earlier than usual because of coming to a crossroads where one new trail led northward to Victoria Island and another on eastward, both having been made within a day or two. We expected in the morning to be able to see one or more camps if the weather was clear.

The next morning the weather had changed, but so, unfortunately, had Kirkpuk's mind. During the night he and his wife had had time to think of many things : how badly they would miss their baby if they did not see him for a year, and of how they might never see him again for all they knew, going as they were with us into a dangerous and mysterious country ; and anyway, Kirkpuk now recollected he had promised So-and-so that he would meet him that summer at Bear Lake. After breakfast he presented to me these and other reasons of the same sort without end which made it imperative that he should break his agreement with us and return. I was a little unreasonably annoyed at this change of mind. There was nothing wrong about it from the Eskimo point of view. These people know nothing among themselves except absolute social equality. The relation of master and man is an unknown thing among them and therefore inconceivable. A promise according to their way of thinking means merely that a man tells you what he feels like doing at that particular moment, and so long as his mind does not change he will be willing to carry out that intention; but whenever he does change his mind there is nothing to be done but to inform you that his mind has been changed, and the explanation is considered satisfactory and the agreement dissolved. Yesterday Kirkpuk had intended to go with me to Banks Island and he had told me so; this morning he intended to go to Bear Lake and accordingly informed me of that fact. The Eskimo individually behaves like a sovereign state. The laws of others do not bind him, and he makes new laws for himself whenever he likes.

There was nothing for it but to bid farewell to Kirkpuk and to continue on the journey north. Before we parted that morning two families of the Puiplirgmiut came up to our camp, traveling eastward along one of the trails at the intersection of which our camp was pitched, and they visited with us a few hours — long enough to tell us the names of several conspicuous landmarks visible from where we were, which indicated how we might find the next village north without following the trail, which would be circuitous. They also had their photographs taken and their heads measured, as did nearly every one whom we saw during our entire year in the east.

We did not have to go over eight miles till we came to a camp of five houses, pitched on the ice about ten or twenty yards from shore, at the northeast corner of Simpson Bay. We were engaged with the help of some of the local men in pitching our tent about two hundred yards from the village when we noticed a man, evidently stone blind, come walking towards us, feeling about with a long cane as a blind man does. Two or three children stood watching him and kept warning him of the tide cracks, which were numerous here in the ice as they are everywhere near shore. The children kept shouting to him: "Turn to the right! Turn to the left! Again to the left! Now watch out for a tide crack!" These cracks are dangerous to a man who walks carelessly, for they are often covered with snow so as to be invisible and are wide enough for a man's foot to slip in, with considerable danger not only of a bad fall but of breaking a bone. With skill acquired through long blindness he avoided the tide cracks dexterously and walked straight up to where the children's voices told him that I was standing beside our sled, unloading it.

When he got near he told me that he knew already who I was, and that very likely I knew who he was, for he was a man so much more unfortunate than other men that the story of his misfortune had traveled to distant places. No doubt I had heard the story, he said, but nevertheless he would tell it to me himself so that I might know it from his own lips and take warning from it and tell my friends to do the same.

Many years ago his house had been standing by itself some distance from the village, but from where he stood beside the seal-hole watching for the seal to come up he could see several other hunters out sealing. The seal, when it came, proved to be a bearded one, but being a strong man he had been able to hold it and to kill it. Without any assistance he had with his ice pick enlarged the breathing-hole enough to pull the animal out. (It was no mean feat, seeing that a bearded seal will weigh from six hundred to eight hundred pounds.) Up to this time he had not thought of the other hunters, but now he looked around and saw that they were all far away, and while distinctly visible he felt sure that none of them had any idea what kind of a seal he had caught. (The hunters' law does not require that the hunters within sight be summoned to share at the cutting up of a common small seal.) When a bearded seal is killed all the hunters within view must be called in to share the prize.

It had occurred to him that by keeping the thing secret (by pretending this was a common seal), he might keep the animal to himself, and especially the skin, for he knew that he could sell pieces of it to a neighboring tribe who seldom catch bearded seals, for numerous articles of value. Accordingly he secretly cut the animal up, gave out the story that he had killed only a small seal, and pledged his wife to secrecy; but the story leaked out as such stories will. People came to him and took away from him both the skin and the

On Sea Ice.

meat and reproached him bitterly. He now repented his act and felt crushed by the disapproval of his people, but his punishment was to be made even heavier, for within a year he began to lose his eyesight and in another year he was stone blind. Since then he, poor miserable man, had been blind and a charge upon the community. Thus it was sure to go with those who did wicked things; and while he felt sure that I was a good man, nevertheless to know his story would do me no harm, and he wished I would pass it on to others, warning them to avoid selfish ways.

I had never heard this tale before, but Natkusiak told me later he had heard it from the Eskimo we had been with the previous summer. After this occurrence, whenever we told that we had visited this particular village, we were always asked whether we had seen the blind man, and then the story would be repeated to us, exactly as the blind man had told it, to illustrate how punishment comes to those who break the law.

The blind man and his companions told us that we had come ashore just in the right place for beginning our overland journey across the mountains to the foot of Prince Albert Sound, for farther to the west the mountains are high and difficult to cross, and farther to the east we would have had a longer distance to go as well as a more difficult road. Right opposite where we now were, they said, was the pass they used once every few years when they had occasion to go to trade for copper with the Prince Albert Sound people.

The commodities which they carry on these trading journeys, they told us, were tent poles, sleds, ready-made bows, and the materials for arrows, as well as now and then a stone pot or a stone lamp which they had secured from the Utkusiksaligmiut. I inquired also where they got the wood to trade, and they said that some of it they either picked up themselves on journeys to Cape Bexley or purchased from the Cape Bexley Eskimo; but that the best of it, and especially the tent poles and the material for bows, they got when now and then a family of their tribe went on a summer hunt to Great Bear Lake. This confirmed what we knew already — that the Victoria Islanders hunt habitually at Bear Lake, and that the presence of a few families of them there the summer that we were with them was no accident.

On May 7th, when we started for our crossing of Victoria Island,

T

three of the men accompanied us in the hope that we might meet
caribou and shoot some, in which case we should of course give them
some of the meat.   Sure enough, after traveling a mile or two and
before leaving the sea ice for the land, we saw a small band and
Natkusiak went in pursuit of them.

While he was gone I looked around carefully with my glasses and
about half a mile away I saw what looked to me like a stone house.
I asked the men about it, but they said no, it was merely a rock;
and on my pressing the inquiry they said they were sure of it; there
were no houses in that neighborhood and they had often seen this
rock and knew that it was no work of man.   The direction in which
the caribou ran when they went inland made it natural for us to
pass right by the rock in question.   I was about to pass it within
something like twenty yards when I became convinced that it was no
single rock, but a pile made by man.   I accordingly went up and
examined it.   The men then admitted that it was a house, but they
said it had not been built by human beings and it would be a bad
thing to have anything to do with it.   I would have liked to examine
the house carefully, but this was scarcely possible, for the many blizzards of winter had covered it up so, and evidently filled its interior
so solidly, that it would have been the work of a day or two, even
with good shovels, to clean it out so as to get an idea of the interior.
Unfortunately we had no shovel with us and neither did the Eskimo
have one.   I felt sure too that if they had had one they would not
have lent it to us for any such purpose as that of prying into this
house.   All the information I could get from them about it was that
it had been built by the spirits before the human race inhabited the
land.   I happened to be familiar with the fact that in Baffin Land and
elsewhere in the east there were stone dwellings said to have been built
by a race of men who were named with a name that differs but slightly
from the name for spirit.   The name given me here was identical
for that used locally for the familiar spirits of the shamans, and on
specific inquiry they told me that the spirits who built these houses
were identical in kind with those employed by the shamans.

When I asked what the house was like inside, they said first that
no man who has any sense ever goes inside; but later on they told me
that sometimes foolish children in the absence of their parents would

CROWD AT OUR TENT, JUNE 14, 1913.

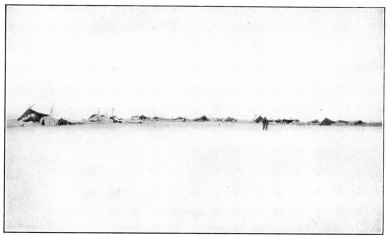

THE LARGEST COPPER ESKIMO VILLAGE WE EVER VISITED — TWENTY-SEVEN SNOW
HOUSES AND TENTS.

enter such houses in play; they in fact had done so themselves when they were children. The door, they said, was in the same position that an Eskimo house door ordinarily is. In other words, it was two and a half or three feet high, on the ground level, and just big enough for a man to crawl through it on all fours. The house was dome-shaped inside as well as outside and there were no rafters. They specifically denied that sods, sticks, or anything else but stones appeared in the walls. I asked this question with special reference to the manner of constructing stone houses used by the Icelandic colony in Greenland, for in Icelandic stone houses sod often is employed to fill in the chinks between the stones. On the beach here there are any number of flat and angular pieces of rock, and of these exclusively the house had been built. One could not tell very well about its dimensions because of the mass of snow covering it, but it seemed to be not over seven feet high, and very probably had an oval floor with transverse diameters no greater than five by seven feet.

After photographing this house as well as the circumstances would admit, we proceeded to follow Natkusiak and found that he had killed two caribou, one of which I gave as a present to the Eskimo while we made use of most of the other.

Our course in crossing Victoria Island from Simpson Bay, near the mouth of Forsyth Bay, was 310° Magnetic, so nearly as the formation of the land allowed. The elevation gets greater and greater constantly as one goes north until one gets within five or six miles of the shore of Prince Albert Sound, where there is an abrupt descent to sea level.

We discovered on this crossing, which, by the way, is the first crossing by a white man of any part of Victoria Island, a good many natural features of importance which are best indicated on the map, while the geology is indicated in the appendix on that subject. There is a mountain range, the western end of which was seen first by Sir John Richardson's party in 1826 from across Dolphin and Union Straits, but which was nevertheless named by Rae in 1851 on his journey along the southwest coast. These mountains (the Colville Mountains) come to an end in the low stretch where we crossed the land, but farther east again they rise to considerable height and one

peak is especially conspicuous. As we did not discover any Eskimo
name for it we called it Mount Bumpus, in honor of Dr. Herman C.
Bumpus, director of the American Museum of Natural History,
who had been the first man to take an active interest in the pro-
motion of our expedition.

We had had many opportunities to observe the migrations of
caribou, but never a better one than now; or perhaps a better way
of putting it may be that the phenomenon had never impressed
me so much. There were no tremendous herds such as those which
had passed our camp in October of the previous year, which led me
to speculate on the why and wherefore of the fundamental difference
of that migration from this one. I can never for a long time remain
of the same mind as to the reason for the almost unbelievable mass-
ing of animals shown by such a herd as the Dease River one of 1910,
described in a former chapter. If some one else were to advance
the theory I am about to present, I should no doubt immediately see
more than one way of demolishing it, but still we shall set it down
here.

It is a fact known to us through the statements of the Eskimo,
as well as deducible on *a priori* grounds, that the caribou in Victoria Island begin to move south when the approach of autumn
changes the conditions of the food. Many of them consequently
reach the sea on the south side of the island before the ice is thick
enough to afford them a bridge to the mainland. Accordingly they
crowd up on the south shore waiting for the chance to cross, the
numbers each day being augmented by the arrival of fresh bands from
the north, whose feeding ground has been farther back on the island.
Eventually, in case of a late fall, you would have all the caribou
of the entire island massed in a few places, either where the feeding
was good or where a point jutted out to the south. Then as soon
as a night or two of hard frost bridges the sea over, the entire vast
army moves across.

The chief flaw in this argument is that the caribou that passed
us in October did not seem to be, as a matter of fact, the same kind
of caribou as those which we later killed on Victoria Island, but rather
a larger variety and darker. The Victoria Island caribou seemed
chiefly of the kind which we had killed in early April east of the

THREE WOMEN OF PRINCE ALBERT SOUND.

Coppermine. It is probable, therefore, that while our explanation really does explain the occurrence of certain herds that move south, it does not explain the origin of the particular herd which crossed the Dease in October, 1910. Some other causes may have brought them together in the land uninhabited either by Eskimo or Indian which lies between Coronation Gulf and Horton River.

As we saw the migration now, it consisted of innumerable small bands. There were seldom less than three caribou and never more than forty. They were chiefly cows, but there were also young bulls and a few old ones, although I do not think the proportion of old bulls in Victoria Island in summer can be nearly as high as it is between Dismal Lake and Great Bear Lake, for the woods northeast of Bear Lake are literally full of them in summer.

These bands seemed in general to be heading fifteen or twenty degrees more to the east than we were, and therefore grew fewer and fewer as we proceeded north diagonally across their line of march, for comparatively few caribou cross Dolphin and Union Straits west of Liston and Sutton Islands. They traveled with speed slightly less than ours (we were making about two and a half miles per hour). They would occasionally feed for a few minutes and even lie down for an hour or two, but when they traveled they sometimes moved at a trot, although more commonly at a brisk walk. Sometimes they traveled in single file, especially in the rare places where the snow was deep; often, if the band was large, they would travel in four or five columns. Animals that got our wind were considerably frightened thereby, but behaved with fair uniformity. When they winded us, they usually ran ahead in the direction in which they had been going. A few, however, turned back or ran off before the wind and some came up to inspect us, approaching to within two hundred yards in many cases and now and then to less than a hundred.

The sight of the animals that came up from leeward and the smell of those traveling to windward kept our dogs continually excited, so that we made better progress than usual. At first the dogs were eager for a chance to pursue the caribou, but after a day or two they became so used to the appearance of caribou near them that they eventually got over their desire to break away from the sled and start out on a hunt of their own.

The wind was usually easterly airs and we commonly traveled in the afternoon, so that unfortunately in the few instances when caribou came very near us they were directly towards the sun and therefore difficult to photograph. They were never much nearer than a hundred yards, and the few snapshots I took of them show up as pin points. My films were not too abundant, and our time was too precious to make any delays for a photograph of an animal which is so common as the caribou, and of which we had numerous properly taken scientific specimens (skins with antlers, bones, and measurements), which would be much more valuable than photographs.

When the caribou travel in solid masses they do not mind a man at all, either the sight of him or the smell, but these bands were as wary as caribou ordinarily are. Nevertheless we found it quite safe not to bother with hauling any meat along with us. When it came time to pitch camp in the evening, one of us would put up the tent and do the cooking (for which on this trip we used the primus stove and some kerosene given us by Captain Bernard), and the other would shoot a caribou and skin it. Then after supper we would fetch home to camp enough meat for the dogs and ourselves for the evening and the morning meal and carry with us only thirty or forty pounds, which would give us supper the following day, but nothing for breakfast the next morning should we fail to get caribou. This did not mean wasting much meat, for we had picked up an extra dog and now had a team of seven. Between the seven of them and the two of us we got away in two meals with a hundred pounds of meat, which is the larger part of a caribou.

May 12th we reached Prince Albert Sound at a point where the charts show a conspicuous peninsula jutting out from the south shore just east of the middle of the sound. This, it turned out, is not a peninsula at all, but a long and narrow island known to the Eskimo as Walliraluk. For the last day or two caribou had not been so numerous — they were evidently heading more to the east of the sound. Accordingly we killed two, instead of the usual one, out of a band that came to Walliraluk Island that evening. There was no point in killing more than two, for we could not have hauled the meat.

A Village of Twenty-seven Deserted and Three Occupied Houses.

From the top of the island the next morning I could with the glasses see a native village on the ice ten or fifteen miles to the northwest, approximately in the middle of Prince Albert Sound. When we approached it we saw this to be the largest village of our whole experience. It turned out that there were twenty-seven dwelling houses in it. We had, of course, seen the ruined trading village at Cape Bexley, which had over fifty dwellings, but these had been the houses of traders from half a dozen or more different tribes, while this turned out to be the one tribe of the Kanghirgyuargmiut, and they were not all at home either, for later on we visited another village of three houses of the same people, and a third village of four houses we never saw at all.

Some of the other tribes visited had a special interest in that they had never before been seen by white men, either they or their ancestors; these had an interest of their own in being the one tribe which have oftener than others been visited by white men. It was the last of the tribes to be visited by us, and it was therefore especially interesting to me that we should come upon them on the 13th of May, which was the anniversary of our discovery of the Cape Bexley Eskimo of the year before.

When we approached the village and were about two miles south of it we came to a group of three men who had been sealing in different places but who had converged and come to meet us. They were a little timid at first. They seemed to be surprised not so much by the fact that we were white men, for this they recognized at once, but by our coming from the southeast, from the country, as they said, where they knew of no one except their friends, the Puiplirgmiut, who were now and then in the habit of arriving by the same route as ours, and at this season of the year, for purposes of trade. They were glad to see us, however, and assured us that we would be welcome in the village.

When we got within about half a mile of the houses, our companions began to communicate with their fellows in the village by the use of one of the few examples of sign language in existence among these Eskimo. The signs consist in one member of an approaching party running a few yards to one side of the sled and stopping, and then running across the trail until he is as many yards on the other side and stopping again. This is repeated several times and signifies that friendly strangers are coming. This sort of signaling, they told us, is never done by the strangers themselves, but always by local people who have joined the party of the strangers, just as these three people had joined ours.

The sign was quickly understood in the village, which in its entirety came running to meet us, — men, women, children, and about half the dogs, while the other half that happened to be tethered howled loudly and plaintively. It was a crowd that I later estimated at considerably over two hundred. The village was large, and as each came from his own house and some were fleeter of foot than others, they did not come upon us in a crowd, but it was only a few minutes until we were completely surrounded so that further progress was impossible. Most if not all of them shouted, talked loudly, and ran holding their arms higher than their heads, opening and closing their hands continually to show they carried no weapon, and saying, "You need not be afraid of us," "We have no knives," "We are glad you have come," and things of that sort.

We had been stopped too far away from the village to suit us, and after I had pointed this out to one man he jumped on top of our sled and shouted to the men to give us an opening so that we could get nearer to the village and have a chance to pitch camp. This was done with the greatest good will, but our dogs were so excited that they refused to pull, upon which some one suggested that we unhitch them, for there were plenty of people around for pulling our sled. The dogs were accordingly unhitched and used their first opportunity to get into fights with the local dogs, adding their growls and snarls to the shouting and cheering of the people as they tumultuously pushed and hauled our sled up to the village.

This was perhaps the most vociferous welcome we had ever received. What with dogs barking and howling and people laughing and talking it was difficult to make oneself understood. We were immediately asked whether we desired to put up a snow-house, in which case they offered to build one for us; but we had our own tent and the season of the year had now come when a tent is preferable to a snow-house. So we preferred to pitch it as we ordinarily did. Some of the dwellings of the people themselves were still of

PRINCE ALBERT SOUND YOUNG WOMEN.

snow, but most of them had had the snow roofs replaced by ones of caribou skins, and a few families were living in caribou skin tents.

One of the first things we learned here was something which changed our plans for the summer completely. We were told that there were no people on Banks Island in summer. Our informants themselves, they said, had spent the winter there at various points on the southeast coast between what we identified as De Salis Bay and Nelson Head, and were the only people who did live anywhere on Banks Island. They had all left there in what we understood to be the latter part of March, and were now bound for the eastward. The majority intended to ascend the River Kagloryuak, which flows into the east end of Prince Albert Sound, and rises near the center of the island. Another river, they told us, the Ekalluktok, also rises near the center of the island, but flows east into what we identified as Albert Edward Bay. Up this river would come to meet them the tribe of the Ekalluktogmiut, who hunt on Dease Strait in winter, but who frequent the same caribou hunting-grounds in summer as do the Prince Albert Sound people, partly on account of the caribou, but also for trading purposes.

These were the people whom Lieutenant Gotfred Hansen of Amundsen's expedition found in Dease Strait on his journey to Victoria Island and whom he misidentified as the Coppermine River Eskimo. His account of how he identified them as the Coppermine River people is naïve and deserves quoting:—

"When we came up to each other he (one of the Eskimo) said something about 'Kilnermiun Innuit,' the name of his tribe. I understood that, because I already knew the name, and I replied that we were 'Kabluna,' or white men. Then we embraced and rubbed our cheeks together. When you are in Rome you must do as Rome does. He was my friend for the two days that we remained there, and during that time he certainly thought I understood everything he said, merely because I had said that we were 'Kabluna' when he mentioned the name of his race, but *of course I did not understand a word.* As our Norwegian-Eskimo language was of no use to us, we could not get any information about the land further ahead, and any conversation which had a definite object had to be carried on by signs." (The North West Passage, Vol. 2, p. 327. London, 1908.)

It is true, as Lieutenant Hansen says, that there are people not very far from the Coppermine who are called the Killinermiut. That fact prompts a digression. Central northwest Alaska was occupied by numerous tribes, perhaps the smallest and least significant of all of which are the Nunatagmiut. Northwest of them live the Otur-kagmiut, south of them live the Noatagmiut, east of them live the Kangianergmiut — all of these far more important tribes and larger than the Nunatagmiut. But for some reason the name " Nunatag-miut " was applied by various distant peoples to all the country oc-cupied by all the above-named and numerous other tribes. The way it seems to have happened is this : If you approach from the south or the southwest at Kotzebue Sound and ask any one, "Who are the people that live northeast from you ?" the answer would be: "First come the Kuvugmiut, then come the Napaktogmiut, then the Noatamiut and *beyond them live the Nunatagmiut.*" In other words the people of Kotzebue Sound knew these tribes, and the last tribe they knew was the Nunatagmiut, and they knew the names of none beyond, so that approaching from the southwest the infor-mation always ended by saying "Beyond them live the Nunatagmiut." Similarly should you come to the mouth of the Colville River and ask, "Who are the tribes that live southwest from you ? " the answer would be, "First come the Killirgmiut, then the Kagmallirgmiut, then the Kangianergmiut, and *beyond them live the Nunatagmiut.*" In the Colville River you would hear nothing about the tribes which had been enumerated to you at Kotzebue Sound, for they are not so well known to the Colville people, and their information would end with the phrase, "beyond them live the Nunatagmiut," because they occupy the divide of land and on the other side of the divide everything was mysterious. The general result was that the impres-sion gained ground along the sea-coast that all the people who occu-pied the interior were called Nunatagmiut, although it is a matter of fact that when you once penetrate the interior, while you find some real Nunatagmiut you find that they are few compared to the mul-titude who are not Nunatagmiut. The whole interior population of Alaska thus became known to the coast people by the name not

PRINCE ALBERT SOUND WOMEN AND ONE MAN.

of the most important inland tribe, but by that of the most distant. So it seems to have been in Coronation Gulf. The people who hunt on the south coast of Victoria Island, east of Lady Franklin Point, the Killinermiut (called also, and most commonly, Nagyuktogmiut), are as a matter of fact known in folk-lore and song to the Mackenzie River Eskimo, and they seem to have been similarly known to Amundsen's King William Island Eskimo, while the names of all the other equally large or larger tribes are unknown.

Now the Ekalluktogmiut, whom Lieutenant Hansen saw, live so far east from the Coppermine that in all probability all the tribes more than a hundred miles west of them, or in other words all the tribes between Kent Peninsula and the Coppermine, would by them be grouped under one name. It is not conceivable that any tribe except the Killinermiut proper would have designated themselves as Killinermiut, but it is also unlikely that the Ekalluktogmiut would introduce themselves as Ekalluktogmiut. The Ekalluktogmiut would be far more likely to inquire about the Killinermiut, as the Killinermiut might about the Ekalluktogmiut. Any one familiar with Eskimo customs will know that it is the last thing that an Eskimo is likely to do to repeat the name of his own tribe. He is much more likely to volunteer unasked the information that such and such a tribe lives next beyond him, or to ask of the stranger, "Do you belong to Such-and-such a tribe?" or, "Have you been visiting that tribe?" After all, that is our own way. We seldom have occasion, if we are stay-at-homes, unless we happen to live in tourist centers, to explain to any one our own nationality, while the nationality of every foreigner who comes within our sphere of observation is a matter of interest and is continually on the tip of our tongue. That the man to whom Lieutenant Hansen listened pronounced the name of Killinermiut, among a thousand other non-understandable words which he also pronounced, cannot be looked upon as proving that he was a Killinermiut or that he had any intention of saying that he was. More likely he was giving Lieutenant Hansen information about a distant tribe or inquiring of him as to his knowledge of that tribe.

Perhaps this has been a rather complicated and lengthy digression, but it seems justified as a needed explanation of why it is that ethnologists and others are so prone to call a primitive people by a name to which those people themselves are entirely unwilling to subscribe, and also as explaining how it was that Lieutenant Hansen when among the Ekalluktogmiut of Albert Edward Bay thought he was among the Coppermine Eskimo.

One of the first things I did at the village of the Prince Albert Sound people was to inquire about their knowledge of white men. This group is not only the most prosperous as well as the most numerous of all the Copper Eskimo, but they are also remarkable for the extent of their seasonal migrations and for their consequently greater amount of information in regard to their own country and other countries and their general broad-mindedness. With them as with us, extensive travels have had their important effect upon the mental outlook and the character of the people. I found therefore that they were familiar not only with the presence of the exploring vessels to the west of their country during the time of the Franklin Search, and with the location of the Bay of Mercy and the abandonment of M'Clure's ship there, but they also knew about King William Island far to the east, and about the frequent visits of white men to it, and they even had information about the distant island of North Devon, as we could tell not only by the geographic description they gave of the country, but also by their reporting correctly the name of the people who inhabit it, the Tununirohirmiut, which is also the name recorded by Dr. Franz Boas and others from information gathered in Baffin Land and elsewhere in the east.

But most remarkable of all was the variety of countries they had seen with their own eyes. During the middle of winter they occupy the southeastern coast of Banks Island from De Salis Bay to Nelson Head, and it has always been so in the past so far as they know. About March each year they start east, and towards the middle of May, as we could tell from our present experience, they get to the eastern end of Prince Albert Sound. On the Sound they split into various parties. A few go north to hunt, between the Sound and Minto Inlet; in some years a few go south to meet the Eskimo of Point Williams, halfway between the Sound and Dolphin and Union Straits. A considerable number go southeast to meet the people of Simpson Bay (the Puiplirgmiut), and a considerable number also go northeast from the northeast corner of the Sound about forty

HITKOAK. ALUNAK. PAMIUNGITTOK.

A CORONATION GULF FAMILY.

miles to hunt caribou and to get, from the copper outcrops there, material for the making of implements for their own use and for sale to other tribes.   The largest body of all goes east, as we have already said, to meet the people of Albert Edward Bay (the Ekalluktogmiut) near the center of Victoria Island.   But most years two or three sleds will detach themselves from the main body in Prince Albert Sound, hurry east ahead of the others up the Kagloryuak River and down the Ekalluktok River to Albert Edward Bay, and thence south across the Straits to the Ahiagmiut, who inhabit the coast in the neighborhood of Ogden Bay, where they abandon their sleds, for summer has overtaken them, and proceed south with pack-dogs, the people themselves also carrying packs, until they reach the shores of Back River, where the Back River people, known to them as the Haningayogmiut, make rafts of their kayaks and ferry them to the south shore of the stream.   Resuming their overland travel, they eventually reach Hanbury's Arkilinik River in its wooded section, probably early in August.   The chief object of this journey has been to get wood and wooden articles of all kinds, which they obtain partly by cutting the trees and shaping the wood to their own desires, and partly by barter in exchange for copper implements and such things from the Eskimo of the Arkilinik, whom they call the Pallirgmiut.

Once only, they told me, had two or three families of their people seen white men on the Arkilinik, and their description of the party made clear that it was Hanbury's in 1903, for their account coincides quite with his.   Further, they knew the names of all of the members of Hanbury's party, and although those of the three white men were not recognizable, the names of those Eskimo whom Hanbury names as his companions are identical in his book and in the account given by the Victoria Islanders.   They name also several Eskimo whom Hanbury does not name (for Hanbury nowhere gives the entire roll of his party), including Panningaiyak, the daughter of Atangalak (whom Hanbury calls Utungerlah and whom Amundsen speaks of as Atangala).   There was only one man in Prince Albert Sound (named Hitkoak) when we were there of those who had seen Hanbury.   The others, he said, had some of them died since and some were now living among other tribes.

CHAPTER XVIII

WE stayed three days in this, the largest village of the Copper Eskimo. On account of the number of individuals gathered together, their social life tended a little more to complexity than was the case in any of the other districts, but still it can hardly be said that there was a semblance of government. Certain individuals appeared, however, to have a preponderating influence, based apparently on individual prowess and to some extent on their records as travelers. The men who had been down in the vicinity of Chesterfield Inlet, and who had visited numerous tribes other than those with which the tribe as a whole comes in contact, were apparently looked up to for that reason.

One of the more prominent men was named Kitirkolak. He gave me varied information about distant sections of Victoria Island, but told me that if I wanted to be really well informed I must visit his father, Pamiungittok, who lived in the next village to the westward and who was the only man now living of those who had seen Collinson in Walker Bay (1852). Kitirkolak volunteered to guide us to his father's village, and on the evening of May 15th he accompanied us west along the trail by which the party had come from Banks Island. In sixteen or so miles of travel we came to a village of the twenty-seven deserted snow-houses which had up to a week before accommodated the party we had just left. At the outskirts of the village were three houses still occupied by Pamiungittok, his son, Alunak, and his son-in-law, Hitkoak, with their families.

Before leaving the large village we had purchased a complete ethnological collection of hunting implements, clothing, cooking gear, and household utensils, with all of which our sled was now heavily loaded for its journey to our base at Langton Bay. We therefore added at this last village practically nothing to our material collection (for we could carry no more), but we did add considerably

286

to our stock of information, for Pamiungittok knew many things and was ready to tell all he knew. Perhaps I could make a clearer summary by re-writing the information secured from him, but it seems possible that the reader may be interested to see the way in which I made hasty note of the new information given me at this village. I will therefore set down here a few pages from my diary without editing, but merely adding in brackets what appears necessary to make the meaning intelligible. Matter inclosed in ordinary parenthesis marks is as it appears in the diary.

There are two reasons for the brevity and fragmentary character of my diary entries at this period: one that time was always scarce, and the other that writing-paper was even scarcer than time; for the one diary book in which all my entries had to be made was so nearly run to its close that everything had to be written in an almost microscopic hand, in many cases over fifteen hundred words to a page of eight inches by nine.

Tuesday, May 16. [Taking] cephalic measurements, etc. Caribou are crossing here [going] north but not in such numbers as farther east. This village — three tents [standing at one edge of a deserted snowhouse village] which once housed the whole tribe. [This village] seems about in the middle of the Sound from north to south (but farther west than middle probably?). Two families of the tribe seem to have hunted bears on the point south of the Sound [Cape Baring] but the rest [were in] Banks Island last winter. Those in Banks Island found no whale [carcasses] "this year" [which implies they usually find them], but those on Cape Baring found one with the meat mostly gone but the head bone [baleen] still there — the bears had eaten all the meat. When the wind blows either east or west [there is] open water at Nelson Head and off southwest Victoria Island as well.

Pamiungittok tells: He was about 8 years old when [in 1852] he visited Collinson's ship [in Walker Bay] with his father. The white men were excellent people and paid well for water boots, etc. They threw away much valuable stuff which the people picked up. At that time there were numerous people beyond [north of] Minto Inlet. He has never heard more than one name for these people —

Ugyugligmiut. He has heard that they attacked a ship (what ship?) and killed some white men. The white men then shot them down with guns and killed the last one. This he has heard; what he knows is that there are no people now beyond Minto Inlet — they are all dead, for one reason or another. Of the Minto Inlet people (Kan-hiryuatjiagmiut or Naperagvigmiut) there are now only four families, though they were once numerous, and one of these four families is really a Prince Albert Sound family moved over [to Minto Inlet].

There were numerous people once resident in Banks Island sum-mers, and on the ice near it winters. These are all dead — some of hunger in (or near) Banks Island and the last party on the ice of the mouth of Prince Albert Sound — these last died "because they had no food for their stomachs and because they had no oil [for fuel] to make water with." There are many stone houses here and there, chiefly between the Sound and Minto Inlet. These were not built by "the forefathers of our countrymen," but by the *turnnrat* [spirits] long ago.

The Prince Albert Sound people never heard from the Ekalluk-togmiut whom they see most summers, of ships being lost [Franklin's] or of white men starving on the east coast of Victoria Island. (Pa-miungittok's son, Kitirkulak, will make inquiries for me next summer of the Ekalluktogmiut [with regard to the loss of Franklin's ships].) He has never heard of any white men having Eskimo wives [or living in any part of Victoria Island — this question I asked with reference to the blond traits of many members of this tribe]. It is "in the nature of Eskimo to have light hair and blue eyes" [he told me, and all his countrymen agreed with him].

Range of the Kanghirgyuargmiut. In summer some of them (a few) hunt towards Minto Inlet; some hunt southeast and meet the Puiblirgmiut; most, however, hunt east and meet the Ekallugtogmiut and Ashiagmiut who live "on the east coast of our country, which is not far from here overland, and good sledding because we go by the rivers." Some join the Ekallugtogmiut for a time and with them visit the Arkilinik [near Baker Lake above the head of Chesterfield Inlet] "where there are trees, and where the people have guns and white men's clothes." (Have seen many metal articles, one shirt, one red knit woollen hood, etc., brought from these trips.) They

never met the Nagyuktogmiut. One man at least — Hitkoak —
has been both to the Akilinik and to Umingmuktok.

In the fall they [the Kanghirgyuargmiut] come to Prince Albert
Sound and proceed to Banks Island where in winter they live chiefly
on bears (some entirely; others partly on seals) off Nelson Head
and east of it. When bear hunting they often see Cape Parry [on
the mainland to the south]. Nelson Head can be seen from Parry
only from the hill tops, and that rarely, and it is much higher than
Parry, so they must hunt almost to the middle of the strait.

They usually have houses on or by the shore when in Banks Island. They often see caribou but "do not know how to hunt them
in winter." They know there are musk-oxen inland but they do not
go after them. In spring they return to the Sound and soon scatter
to the various hunting places. Those going to the Ekallugtogmiut
are already on the way (intended starting the day after we came to
the village and delayed for us). Those going north towards Minto
do not leave the sea till "the snow gets soft on the ice."

Wednesday, May 17. Have given up going farther in direction of
Banks Island, as there are no people that way. Started 3:30 P.M.
heading for Cape Back about true southwest. Camped 7:30 P.M.
to get chance to write up some of my briefer notes before the fillings-in
are forgotten or misremembered.

Game. No seals seen on top the ice — *ugrug* (bearded seals) are
to be expected nearer land and seals are not up yet. Crossed about
400 or 500 caribou tracks, ¾ of them over a week old. Migration
seems over, or at least there is a lull. Saw three bands of eight, seven,
and three. The latter two Natkusiak tried but got shot at last only
— three misses on the run at 200 yards. Ptarmigan seen every day,
mostly (or all?) rock ptarmigan. Crows every day. No snow-
buntings since leaving Walliraluk. Dist.[ance traveled] 12 [miles].

Pamiungittok tells: The Banks Island people used to be well off.
They killed so many deer and [musk] oxen that their dried meat
sometimes lasted the year round. They got to killing each other.
One man killed had relatives in the Sound. For this reason (*i.e.*
because of witchcraft practised by the dead man's relatives in the
Sound) food became scarce [in Banks Island]; there were no seals
for food or fuel and the people died of hunger — those that had not

U

been murdered in the feuds. This happened some fifteen years ago
— *i.e.* when Agleroittok [who is now about twenty-five] was a boy but
[after] his two brothers [were] grown up.

Population. In the village first visited (May 13) there were 27
dwellings. These were on the average much larger than among other
groups (because skins are more plentiful?). In one house there
were 9 persons and this was probably not the largest number. There
were 41 married women — none single — as I found out in giving
one needle to each tattooed woman. I was told there were many un-
married men, and children seemed numerous. This village therefore
had over 150 persons. That of May 16 had 11. There are 4 houses
that we did not see — that have moved to shore about north of the
May 16 village. Estimate these at 15. This gives 176 for Prince
Albert Sound group [as a minimum estimate — the true number is
probably higher.] There are four families in Minto Inlet, or about
fifteen to twenty more; [there are therefore] about 195 or 200 [people]
north of Cape Baring. The Ekalluktogmiut are about the same
number as the Prince Albert Sound people. There are said to be
the Tununirohirmiut north or northeast (?) of the Ekalluktogmiut.
(*Turnunirohirmiugok nunam turnuani inmata*).[1] I could get no
idea of how many they are; my informants are not even sure that
they are on Victoria Island. These are said to have no bows and to
dress only in seal. (They may be a fabulous people though I think
not.) Besides these groups there are the people from the Nagyuktogmiut east, for whom I have no data. The west coast north of
Minto Inlet and the north coast where the same [Prince Albert
Sound] people sometimes reach it (Collinson Inlet?) are said uninhabited. This sea to the north is said not to thaw all summer, but
the coast has caribou and there are seals on the ice. People sometimes reach it by sledding through rough country, "but when the
snow is hard yet" in a generally northern direction from the foot of
Prince Albert Sound.

Shamanism. May 15 we missed our primus stove "needle" —

[1] Translation : They are called " the People of the Back Side " (of the land)
because they are at the far end of (their) land (from the point of view of the
rest of the people). In other words: " People of the End of the Earth.",
The name probably refers to the north end of Prince of Wales Island.

it may have been taken by someone or it may have got lost. A woman angatkuk [shaman], I-ku-tok [by name], offered to get it for us (by witchcraft) if I paid for the performance. This I refused to do unless it were a success — in which event I would give her a small file. That suited her, and the performance began. As Natkusiak understands them [the shamanistic performances] somewhat better than I, it was arranged he should act in my part and "say yes" for me. There were about 15 persons in our tent and 50 or 60 outside listening. The woman got a free floor space about $1\frac{1}{2}$ by 3 feet in the middle of the tent, where she stood up. She began at first quietly, saying in an ordinary tone and manner that she would first look for the lost articles "apkuota"[1] — the "road," I suppose, by which it was taken away when stolen. Where was it when it was stolen? In that box? Where was the box? In what part of the box was it? Was she to find the thief? Was she to get her spirit to find the "road" of the thief? (to 19 out of 20 at least of her questions the answer was "yes").

Most of her questions [the shaman] asked of me, but some she asked of others. Not only the person asked but half a dozen others would answer "yes" in chorus, or else [they answered] by other affirmatives and urgings to "go on," "describe the thief," etc.

Gradually [the shaman] became more excited and little by little she narrowed her eyes till they were finally held closely shut. Then of a sudden she changed her tone of voice, evidently now trying to imitate an old man both by tone of speech and by hoarse laughing. She now announced that she was so-and-so (the name escaped me — it was no doubt the name of the spirit that now possessed her). "Ha, I see the road! It did not go out by the tent door; it went out by that corner of the tent! (As a matter of fact, our visitors used to come and go under any but the back side of our tent.) She goes to the village! It is not a man; it is a woman. She has hidden the needle in her boot. She has on a pair of 'fancy' boots." (Here followed a detailed description of [the thief's] costume, but as most women dress alike, no one could recognize the description.)

[The listeners now commenced asking eager questions of the shaman.] "Tell us, is she old or young? Is she a big woman?"

---

[1] Apkuota = its path; thoroughfare or channel by which it traveled.

etc. [But the sorceress kept on as if she did not hear.] "Oh, now I cannot see clearly; there is a fog coming over me. But I see one thing. She goes to a house a little east of the middle of the village. ([The audience:] 'Which house? which house?') The house has snow walls and a tent roof (nine-tenths of all the houses had) — it has a peaked tent roof (three-fourths of the houses had) (audience: 'What sort of gear is outside the house? Tell us and we will recognize the house'). There is a bag full of clothes (every house had one or more). There is a seal spear; there are two seal spears (a common number — most houses had two families). I cannot see more, the fog darkens. (Here she became more quiet. After being possessed by the spirit she spoke in hoarse shrieks. By now she was out of breath and tired.) I am now myself again, I am now no longer so-and-so."

Of a sudden the shaman staggered as if to fall backwards, then regained herself and began to mutter rapidly and not harshly. It was now said she was possessed by a *Kablunak* (*turnnrak*).[1] There were apparently no real words in this muttering (*i.e.* no Eskimo or any other speech), but it was said she was now speaking Kablunat (white men's) language. There were constant repetitions of -a-tji, -la-tji, -ta-tji, etc., reminding one strongly of Athabascan Indian speech, and almost exactly like our Tannaumirk's alleged imitations of Loucheux talk.

When all was done (about ten minutes of mutterings), the woman announced that the thief had left the village. She then assumed her natural voice and the performance was over. As two or three families had left that morning, starting east towards the bottom of the Sound, it was concluded one of the women [of those families] was the thief. A man offered to go get the needle [from them]. No one seemed to doubt he would get it. I offered the man the file if he would go, as the woman acknowledged she had failed to get the needle for me. She was, however, to get some pay also if the man succeeded. The man was gone about six hours, and came back unsuccessful. With him came back the whole suspected party, apparently to assert their innocence.

A man angatkuk now offered to try. His performance consisted

---

[1] Kablunak = white man, European; turn-nrak = spirit.

PRINCE ALBERT SOUND MEN AND ONE WOMAN.

in "ceremonially" removing from the primus stove box every article it contained except the (glass) alcohol bottle. This he feared, and I had to take it out for him. Fearing this was considered by the rest to be a sign of great wisdom. None of them had known enough to fear it and several had touched it [for it had looked harmless to them and it was only the supernatural wisdom of the Great Shaman that saw the insidious peril of this transparent thing that looked like ice but wasn't]. He then stuck his head into the box and kept it there three or four minutes, lifting and setting down the top several times meanwhile (his head all the time in the box). He finally emerged and announced he could not see the road by which the needle went. He said he had not been looking for the thief, merely for the "road" of the needle.

General [Comment]. The Sound people are evidently the most prosperous Eskimo we have seen; they are the most "travelled" and the best informed about their own country (Victoria Island) and its surroundings. While they have been to the Bay of Mercy on north Banks Island and west beyond Nelson Head on south Banks Island they do not seem any of them to have been across the [Dolphin and Union] straits to the Akuliakattak summer hunting grounds [near Cape Bexley on the mainland], or to the sea anywhere on south Victoria Island except among the Haneragmiut and Puiblirmiut. Those who have been to a little west of Uminmuktok have come from the east to it as visitors of the Ahiagmiut in most cases (Hanbury's *Arctic Coast Huskies?*). Hitkoak, about the most travelled of any, has been at the Bay of Mercy, well west of Nelson Head, to Uminmuktok and into Bathurst Inlet, and to the Arkilinik [near Chesterfield Inlet]. He looks not over thirty-five. He says he has ceased travelling, for he has seen "many places and none are so good as the [Prince Albert] Sound country." He told us that he and some other families with him killed not a single seal last winter — lived on polar bears alone. They got seal oil to burn from others in trade for bear fat and meat. Honesty seems on a higher level among them than among any other people we have seen except the Akuliakattagmiut and Haneragmiut. Their clothes are far the best, their tents the largest. They use far more copper than any other people — doubtless because it is more abundant [in their country].

The Kogluktogmiut [of the Coppermine River] are very eager for
metal rods for the middle piece of the seal spear. They never make
any of copper, no doubt because copper is too scarce. Their ice picks
are small: their seal hole feelers are all of horn or iron. In the
Sound [on the other hand] the copper ice picks are in some cases three-
quarters by one and a quarter inch and fifteen inches long. Most
seal spears have middle pieces of copper — the rest have iron [from
M'Clure's ship ?]. The seal hole feelers are most [of them] of copper.
Some of their tent sticks are of local driftwood, some are round young
spruce which they get from the Puiblirmiut who get them from our
neighbors of last August. Some sleds come from Dease River;
some from Cape Bexley, but in either case they have been bought of
the Puiplirgmiut or the Haneragmiut. Their stone pots are said to
be all from the Utkusiksialik or Kogluktualuk (Tree River). Some
they got from the Puiplirgmiut by the road Natkusiak and I came
last week, some around the point [Cape Baring] from the Haneragmiut by the road we are taking now. Their fire stones [iron pyrite
for striking fire] are some from the Haneragmiut, some picked up in
the mountains north of the Sound. The copper is all from the
mountains northeast of the bottom of the Sound. They say some
[detached] pieces of pure copper [in those mountains] are as high as
a man's shoulder and as wide as high; others project out of the hillside and are of unknown size. East of Prince Albert Sound [on the
Kagloryuak River] they use willows chiefly for fuel in summer —
these are four to five feet high in places. Heather [for fuel] is also
abundant. The musk oxen are confined to the unpeopled sections of
north and northeast Victoria Island and to Banks Island. They
think there are a few deer in north Victoria Island in winter but none
in south Victoria Island. The charms that starved the Banks Island people [see above] deprived that country (sea and land both) of
food animals for a time, but these have gradually increased and are
now numerous — Banks Island has again become a good country.
Nevertheless people never hunt there summers. There is plenty
driftwood along the south shore of Prince Albert Sound, some along
the north shore. There is plenty [drift]wood northwest of Nelson
Head [Banks Island] and considerably east of it, but it is hard to
find in winter. There are plenty of macu roots [polygonum biston-

tum] [1] on the Peninsula between the Sound and Minto [Inlet] — and elsewhere. People eat plenty of them. Many good fishing places here and there, but they do not live to nearly such an extent on fish as do the Ekalluktogmiut, who eat fish all winter, as well as seal.

Superstition. "Superstition" is perhaps more in evidence here than anywhere else. At the large village I could get no single individual to be photographed. An attempt to get a sample of "auburn" hair was futile and caused much [unfavorable] comment and suspicion. I tried first to trade some of my hair for it [a sample of the hair of a European-looking Eskimo], then to buy it. There were continual requests that I should next summer "think away" sickness from them and "think them" plenty game and good fortune. There have been requests of this sort at all villages, but nowhere so serious, insistent and often repeated. Pamiungittok gave me a pair of breeches and an arrow to make me "think good" for his son who was sick—Agleroittok [is his name]. He asked repeatedly that I give him nothing in return, for he feared if I paid for the breeches I would not "think good" for his son. The blind man, Avranna, in Clouston Bay (there is also a blind man at Prince Albert village — old man — about 60) told us the reason of his blindness was that he had killed a large *ugrug* and when the people came wanting to cut it up he grudged to let them help themselves, therefore he became blind. I could not make out if the grudging of itself caused the blindness, or if some "doctor" [shaman] was angered by it and made him blind — I believe the former. Natkusiak says it is no doubt true, for he knows of parallel cases in his own country. Usually there, however, it was this way: some one committed a bad deed (grudged to give something, stole, etc.) in secret. The "doctor" would then so ordain "magically" that the guilty person would in some way suffer — then not only was the guilt punished but also people found out who was guilty (*e.g.* if an article had been stolen).

At the first Nagyuktogmiut village in April some noise was heard outside our snowhouse. Our visitors of the time decided it was our

[1] These roots form on the mainland the chief food of the marmot and the grizzly bear, both of which are absent from Victoria Island. All Eskimo known to me use this root as food — the Alaskans extensively, but the Victorians to a negligible extent only.

(or my) *turnnrak* [familiar spirit] and forthwith started a chorus of requests and prayers to me (*not* to the *turnnrak*) to have the *turnnrak* provide plenty seals, good weather, good health, the safe birth of expected children, etc. As we were leaving there was a concerted request by all present that we intercede with the *turnnrak* for two women, Arnauyak and Anaktok (both young, though only Anaktok recently married — other two or three years) that they might have children born to them. At last village (May 16) I staid over a day to see if a few lead and opium pills would do Agleroittok any good — he had had chronic diarrhœa since the summer 1908. They did seem to do good, but they were not satisfied with that — I must "pat" his stomach before going. Hitkoak made for me and bound on me a charm sash (usual type) so that I should remember and "keep thinking that his wife should have safe delivery of a healthy child" — event about a month distant.

Natkusiak says the *angatkuk* performances are very different here from [those among] his people — he does not seem to think Victoria people are very powerful *angatkuk* [shamans] but has firm faith in all the claims of his own people's *angatkuk*.

The woman's performance [described above] was very similar to that of Ovayuak [a Mackenzie River shaman] in January, 1907. The Sound people would not do cats' cradles for me because it is now in the long days — they play them only when sun is away — cf. Akulia-kattagmiut as well as Ilavinirk's account of [cat's cradle customs in] Kotzebue Sound.

Natkusiak tells: Some or all children are *turnnrak* [spirits] before birth. A few people can remember the things they knew when they were (prenatally) *turnnrak*. These are powerful *angatkuk* and can tell people many things they must not do (*i.e.*, [these shamans] impose taboos). He has known one such man. He came as a *turnnrak* along the coast from the east and north, following every curve of the coast. Like other *turnnrak* of his class he was looking for a mother through whom to be born. He found her at Prince of Wales. The man when he grew up could tell many wonderful things that he knew before incarnation. Among other things, he told that the reason people don't see these *turnnrak* that are looking for mothers is that they *iglaurut tautugnaittuagun* (literally: travel through, or by,

Prince Albert Sound Group, all of whom show Blond Tendencies.

unseen regions). Natkusiak does not know just how this is — he has merely heard the expression. "Perhaps it means they travel underground," he says. He learnt in Prince Albert Sound [that there are there] some men who remember their prenatal existence.

Friday, May 19. Started 3 : 30 P.M. and camped 10 : 30 P.M. Dist. 20 miles. The ice is a little rough on getting near shore and [there are] a few cakes of ground ice on shore. At camp all looks smooth to north and northeast as seen from fifty foot elevation, but rougher [ice] ahead of us. Our camp is at the farthest point that has ever been visible to us — a cape at about a 20° angle of the coast. Numerous small fragments of wood [seen along the beach; they are] good [because they have been kept from decay by lying on a rocky beach. Driftwood decays quickly on sandy beaches].

The land so far as I have made out everywhere west of Walliraluk Island rises abruptly from the beach line (in less than a mile) to a height of 300 or 400 feet. There are plenty ravines but these do not give a serrated appearance to the skyline, which is about as even here as it is in the Melvill Mountains in Franklin Bay. Near Walliraluk, as near Langton Bay, there is a strip of 3 or 4 mile width of hilly low-land between sea and mountains. The rock *in situ* at camp (no solid edges exposed, but flat chipped rock of all sizes and of one kind chiefly) is the same as Walliraluk Island [of which we took specimens — limestone]. East of Walliraluk lowland widens and the foot of the Sound is everywhere low. This lowness extends across the entire island [from Prince Albert Sound to Albert Edward Bay], I under-stand, for it is all river valleys (the Kagloryuak and the Ekalluktok). The [Wollaston] peninsula (the people say, and it looks so too) is not practicable for crossing by sled anywhere except near where we crossed it. In communicating with the Haneragmiut winters they [the Sound people] always go west around the point [Cape Baring].

Caribou tracks as numerous as ever but mostly old. The height of the migration here was probably the first week of May. Tracks all [heading] between north and northwest true. Plenty fox tracks, one wolf [track]. No bear [polar] signs yet. A wolverine was shot (bow and arrow) on the ice of the sound (somewhere west of where we found people the other day) in the spring a year ago. I got both the skin and the phalanges bones, etc., from the man who shot it. [This wolverine probably became lost; otherwise it seems unlikely a forest animal would go a hundred miles north of the true line.]

Saturday, May 20th. Started 1 : 10. Camped midnight. Dist. 25 miles. The ice became rough inshore after travelling about ten miles to-day. At one time we lost three-quarters of hour making with axes a road to get inshore of a 40 yd. strip of broken ice. [Seen] from a 50 ft. elevation [on shore] it seemed that outside of a half-mile belt along shore the ice is fairly smooth north across the sound, though here and there small strips rough ice [appear]. [There was a] snow haze however so we could not see far. From "land sky" [1] ahead it seems we are nearing Cape Baring — the land sky curves south a little west of us. Tide cracks very numerous along shore. May 18th we crossed two tide cracks about four miles apart running perpendicular to the land, or north and south. These were about three feet [wide] and showed no pressure ice — looked like new cracks. Just east of Cape Back we crossed the third similar crack.

[Drift]wood everywhere when we approach close enough to see, but small pieces only. Have not seen one as large as four feet long. At camp the largest piece we found would go well in a kitchen stove. There is in sight perhaps a cord of wood for say 3 or 4 miles of beach, but no doubt the snow hides $\frac{2}{3}$ of what there is.

The land has in general an even skyline, though in places rounded hills show. Towards camp time [we passed] some precipices (of stratified limestone?). Elevation of skyline about 100 feet $\frac{1}{4}$ mile to $\frac{1}{2}$ mile from beach. Beach partly gravel, partly slate — cloven and somewhat waterworn (limestone?).

Caribou tracks fewer — three or four dozen all day, the last five or six just before camping. I fancy if they come to the coast here the rough ice turns them back [from crossing the Sound]. One *ugrug*, but weather not suited to their being out. Two cranes

---

[1] When clouds of a uniform color hang low there is reflected in them a map of the earth below them. Snow-free land and open water are shown in black on the clouds; the pure white sea ice appears in white, and land covered with snow soiled by blown sand, etc., is reflected darker than the sea but lighter than snowless land. This sky map is of the greatest use to sledge travelers always, and especially in crossing wide bays from headland to headland; where the landmarks themselves are below the horizon their position is accurately indicated by their reflection in the clouds.

flying east high over the coastline. Cold, cloudy, [wind] N W 20 [miles per hour] and a little snow [falling] all day.

Seeing the white men at Point Barrow living in frame houses would of itself have been sufficient to induce the Eskimo to do likewise, for the white men are well-to-do and powerful, and therefore become leaders of fashion in the matter of houses as in other things. The Eskimo have not had the means to build houses as well constructed as those of the white men, and even had they had the houses they would not have had the resources to keep them supplied with fuel, for coal is naturally expensive.

But the pernicious practice of building frame houses has had more than the passive encouragement of the resident whites. Active steps have been taken by various well-meaning persons to try to get the Eskimo to quit what the white men consider their "native hovels" in favor of the frame house. It is the natural tendency of the thoughtless white to assume that his ways are the best ways. Even the Department of Education has not been guiltless, for officers in Washington have issued,' presumably on the basis of their experience of the climate of Virginia and Maryland, instructions to the school teachers in Alaska to encourage the Eskimo in general to adopt white men's ways. My friend Mr. J. E. Sinclair, who for a year taught the government school on Wainwright Inlet, told me that he had specific instructions to encourage the Eskimo to dig coal in the coal mine there with the double idea that they might use the coal for heating their houses, and that they might earn money with which to buy flour to eat instead of the seal meat and walrus which was their ordinary diet. It is hard for me personally to get the point of view of a man who thinks that coal mining is a more desirable occupation than seal hunting. It would be a safe bet that he himself has never either hunted seal or dug coal.

But during the last few years there has fortunately come a change, largely, I believe, through the influence of Mr. Lopp and Mr. Evans, the present superintendent and assistant superintendent of the government schools of northern Alaska, who are men of considerable experience in the country, and who have come to see clearly that the white-man style of frame house is one of the most serious evils which they have to fight. Mr. Evans told me, the autumn of 1912, that he was doing everything he could to get the Eskimo to refrain from building frame houses and to induce them to go back to the building of houses of the old type. Any one who has the welfare of the Eskimo at heart will wish Mr. Evans success in his enterprise; but any one who understands the Eskimo will fear that success will come with difficulty, if at all. For the frame house has unfortunately become fashionable. It is not easy to get our own people to refrain from certain habits — of dress, for instance — on the ground that they are unhealthful. Neither will it be easy to get the Eskimo to avoid the frame house on the ground that it is dangerous to life. My experience of the Eskimo is that they are even more inclined than the white race to eat, wear, and use things on the ground that they are expensive and fashionable rather than on the ground that they are excellent in themselves.

PRINCE ALBERT SOUND—SPRING HOUSE, SLED, AND DOGS.

CHAPTER XIX

MAY 17th we had said good-by to these the last Eskimo whom we saw in Victoria Island. As mentioned above, their camp lay a little west of the middle of Prince Albert Sound. Although it must have been nearly two months since they started with loaded sledges on the eastward journey from their winter hunting district on the southeast shore of Banks Island, they were still living chiefly on supplies of polar bear meat brought with them; but the time had come for them to start the caribou hunt. Some of their friends had already moved into the mountains to the north that separate Prince Albert Sound from Minto Inlet, and it was the intention of these last three families with whom we had been visiting to follow them northward the day after our departure. As a matter of fact they would have gone even sooner had it not been for our visit.

I think it was Cape Back for which we headed on leaving the Eskimo village. The charts were not very accurate here, any more than anywhere else in the Arctic, and it is only the most conspicuous points that one can certainly identify. After traveling for about four hours we camped to give me a chance to enter in my diary more fully the varied information of which I had taken only hasty notes during our stay with the people.

In something like twelve miles of travel this day we must have crossed at least five hundred caribou tracks, but most of them were over a week old. The general direction in which the trails led was approximately northwest. We saw only three bands of eight, seven, and three animals respectively. All of them were too wild to allow us a close approach, although Natkusiak fired two or three vain shots at one of the bands. We saw no seals either. It was as yet too early for the common seal (*fœtida*) to appear on top of the ice, and the bearded seals frequent in general only the neighborhood of

301

land. We expected that to-morrow on our approach to land we should see some of them.

Our sled was so heavily loaded with the ethnological specimens purchased and the geological ones picked up on Victoria Island that it was impossible for us to haul much meat with us. Our second day therefore found us nearly out of food, when, according to expectations, on approaching within about seven miles of Cape Back we saw a bearded seal lying beside a tide crack out of which it had hauled itself. It was an especially wakeful animal and it took Natkusiak over two hours to make a successful approach. As neither the dogs nor ourselves had had quite enough to eat in the morning, we camped near where the animal was killed and allowed the dogs to gorge themselves.

From Cape Back until we rounded Cape Baring we had rougher ice than we were used to and our heavy and bulky load made the going somewhat difficult. Here and there we were forced to use an axe which we had along with us for the purpose of road-making, and it sometimes took us an hour to make fifteen or twenty yards. Between Cape Baring and what the Admiralty chart calls "Cape Kendall" the ice was also rough, and moreover the weather was so thick with falling snow and fog that we could seldom see more than a few hundred yards.

When we reached "Cape Kendall" we had come to the point from which our traverse of the western end of Dolphin and Union Straits had to be begun. Following the coast around toward Point Williams might have been the safer thing to do at this season of the year, for spring was approaching and the ice in the open sea could be expected to break up with a strong wind at any time and to float to the westward, carrying us off with it. But following the coast any farther was very much out of the way, and besides, I had a special reason for wanting to cross the Straits just at their western end where the charts place "Clerk Island." On our way east along the coast of the mainland the year before we had kept a keen look-out for Clerk Island, but had failed to see it. According to the account of its discoverer, Sir John Richardson, it is a good-sized island lying not more than twelve miles off the mainland shore. It happens that on this part of the mainland the Melvill Mountains are near the coast, and it had therefore been an easy thing for me to climb a few hundred feet into their slopes for the purpose of sweeping the sea ice with my glasses. The weather on this portion of our eastward journey had fortunately been clear, and although the mountains of Victoria Island itself, sixty miles away, were clearly visible, there was no sign of Clerk Island, although under the conditions of visibility which we had I should have been able to see an Eskimo camp had it been no farther offshore than Richardson describes Clerk Island as being. I had for a year been fairly clear in my mind that Clerk Island did not exist, and I was anxious to put the matter beyond doubt by crossing now in a direct line from "Cape Kendall" to Point Tinney, which should take us across the site of Clerk Island.

As the common seals were not yet out, we decided that if we took to the ice of the Straits with our sled empty of meat (as it already was, for we had finished all we had taken with us of the seal killed two days before), we should probably starve, for none but common seals could be expected anything over five miles from shore. We were sailing so close to the wind in the matter of provisions, on account of the weight of our load, that any untoward circumstance such as bad weather was sure to bring us to grief. It happened here that the weather remained unfavorable, cloudy, and with snow squalls. We camped for two days without being able to secure anything to eat. Of course we knew the tide was bound to turn soon, and the matter caused us no anxiety except that the season was advancing and each day the crossing of the Straits would become more and more dangerous.

The third day dawned bright and clear and by nine o'clock in the morning the snow was thawing all around us. This was the first thaw we had seen in Victoria Island, although on the south shore of Coronation Gulf the thaws had already begun when we left the *Teddy Bear* three weeks before. With the coming out of the sun the seals came out also and Natkusiak and I soon had one each. By the middle of the afternoon (May 26) we were on the road to the mainland heading direct for Point Tinney and taking our course from a conspicuous mountain on the mainland which we knew from the year before.

It is possible more than half a century after the event and long after the death of the distinguished explorer-naturalist who first described the mainland shore of Dolphin and Union Straits, to read his psychology, to an extent, as though the man himself were with us, by comparing his printed account with the facts. He was evidently rigorously truthful in matters of fact, but "conservative" in his judgments. If he says the formation is red sandstone, one may be sure it is sandstone, and red; if he were to say he measured a stratum and found it ten feet thick, I should feel sure it was ten feet thick; but if he says he estimated the stratum at ten feet, I should feel sure it was more than ten feet, and anything from fifteen to forty feet in all probability. That is "conservatism" — to be sure you always underestimate everything. In crossing Dolphin and Union Straits we had one of the many striking examples of this that have come to our notice. Richardson estimates the height of the Melvill Mountains on the mainland at about five hundred feet. We could see them from Victoria Island to the vicinity of Point Dease Thompson, though we stood on the sea ice. In other words, the higher sections of the mountains must be from 1500 to 2000 feet high.

During our stay at "Cape Kendall" we found that it was not a cape at all but an island. This surprised me not so very greatly, for while the Admiralty charts of this region are good enough to sail by, one is accustomed to finding them unreliable in the details of the coast. Indeed they cannot well be anything else, for most of them are made from ships of great draft standing along well offshore. From the masthead of such a ship even in clear weather there is much difficulty in seeing the true character of the coast line, and bad weather of course makes this impossible.

The interesting thing about our discovery that "Cape Kendall" is an island is not that we discovered it, but the fact that Dr. John Rae had discovered it long before, as I have since learned from consulting his contribution to Vol. 22 of the Proceedings of the Royal Geographical Society. In his excellent journey in 1851 he had found here an island which he had named Bell Island, and he had located it correctly off the mouth of a bay which in reality exists exactly as he portrays it on his sketch map. Collinson, when he sailed past this point a year or two later, made observations to the effect that, true enough, at a distance this looks like an island, but on close approach he found it to be a part of the mainland and he therefore struck out the name of Bell Island and called it "Cape Kendall," and his "correction" was adopted by the makers of the Admiralty charts. We camped at the spot for several days and hunted seals all around the island and found it to be shaped as Dr. Rae indicates in his chart, to be located with reference to the bay exactly as he locates it, and to be separated from the mainland by a fairly deep channel, as is shown by the presence everywhere of ice cakes, which must draw at least twelve or fifteen feet of water.

This is but one of the many instances of which I am aware that show the excellence of the work of John Rae, a man exact and truthful and in his methods of travel a generation ahead of his time, for while his countrymen were still using the (in many ways absurd) methods of travel which handicapped them so greatly and led to so much needless suffering and to so many deplorable tragedies, he had put into effect the only sound principle of the traveler — that of doing in Rome as the Romans do, which in the Arctic means using methods of travel which the forces of evolution have taught to the dwellers of icy lands, instead of methods which men, some of them ingenious and energetic, have evolved from their inner consciousness and from the limited experience of half a dozen years.

It is a striking thing that John Rae wintered in Repulse Bay, using only the food and fuel which nature has provided at Repulse Bay, and that he did this within a decade of the time when Sir John Franklin's entire company of able-bodied Englishmen, equipped quite as well as Rae's party, starved helplessly and died to the last man in a country as well supplied with food and fuel as was that where Rae spent his winter in comfort. That the country where Franklin's men starved is sufficiently provided with means of subsistence is shown by the fact that it was peopled by Eskimo both before and after that great tragedy. At the very time when these Englishmen were dying of hunger there were living all about them Eskimo families who were taking care of their aged and bringing up their children in comparative plenty, unaided by the rifles and other excellent implements which the Englishmen had in abundance.

When we parted with Dr. Anderson and Captain Bernard I had

x

told them it was our intention to proceed to Banks Island and spend the summer there. It was arranged that the *Teddy Bear* would come along whenever the ice cleared off and would pick us up in the neighborhood of Nelson Head, but in case anything occurred to change our plans we were to build conspicuous beacons at one or more of half a dozen designated points on the shore of Victoria Island. The *Teddy Bear* when she came along would keep a keen lookout for these beacons and would get any information we had left in them. We had now made up our minds not to go to Banks Island because of learning that it was uninhabited in summer, and as Bell Island ("Cape Kendall") was one of the proposed beacon sites, we built on its southwest corner a tall cairn of stones and left there a short account of our doings and plans, inclosed in one of our airtight malted milk tins. We had long ago consumed the last of the malted milk, but we still kept a few of the cans with us, for they were excellently made and ideal receptacles for matches or anything else that must not be dampened or affected by the weather. Of course this can would have been plunder to the Eskimo had they found it, but we knew that none of them were due to visit "Cape Kendall" until the spring of the following year, and we felt sure the *Teddy Bear* would come along before then, as she eventually did.

I learned later from Dr. Anderson that it was on July 30th, or a little more than two months after we built the cairn, that they sighted it with their glasses from the schooner eight or ten miles out at sea and came in to pick up the message. Incidentally they verified in summer what I had seen clearly enough in winter, that the place is really an island and not a cape.

We learned from the Eskimo of Prince Patrick Sound that it was behind this island that Captain Klinkenberg wintered in the *Olga* the season of 1905 and 1906, which he himself thought he had spent in Banks Island. On his return to Herschel Island in August, 1906, he had told us that looking southwest from his wintering place he was able to see land, and we had decided then that he must have wintered in Victoria Island near Minto Inlet and must have seen Banks Island across Prince of Wales Strait; but we now found that the land he saw to the southwest had been really the mainland of America, seen across Dolphin and Union Straits.

BEACON BUILT ON BELL ISLAND.

CORONATION GULF ESKIMO MEN'S STYLES IN DRESS.

CHAPTER XX

DURING the two or three weeks that followed our crossing south from Victoria Island, our progress westward along the mainland coast was slow on account of frequent troubles in getting around the open spaces in the sea ice created by the mouths of small rivers, each of which was bringing its quota of warm inland water to help thaw out the sea. We had now and then to make a considerable detour to seaward through rough ice to avoid these river deltas. We lived during this time entirely on seals; for the grizzly bears, which had been numerous here a month earlier in the season the year before, had now all moved inland. The small seals were out in numbers, basking on the ice. Although white men agree in general in preferring the flesh of the bearded to that of the small seal, my tastes are in that matter, as in most other things, with the Eskimo, so we shot only common seals, though the bearded variety were also abundant.

I neglected to say that on our way from Bell Island across the Straits to Point Tinney Natkusiak killed a polar bear which was the largest animal of its kind I have ever happened to see, although not quite so large as others the skins of which I have seen among the Eskimo. I measured it with a common string, for my tape did not happen to be convenient at the moment, and then of course I lost the string before the measurements got recorded. I suppose the animal would have weighed in the neighborhood of eight hundred pounds. According to our custom we carried with us only about two days' supply of this bear meat. This was our only change in diet from the time we left the Victoria Island Eskimo, May 17th, until about a month later, when we shot some sea gulls near Cape Lyon. Otherwise we lived entirely on seals.

One of the first things we did on landing near Crocker River was to climb a hill several hundred feet high to have another look for Clerk Island. As was the case a year previous, we had clear weather

311

and could see Victoria Island plainly enough, but there were no signs of Clerk Island, which should, according to the chart, have lain between us and Victoria Island and less than half as far off. Every five or eight miles or so on the way west from this point I had another vain look to seaward. Clearly the island was not there.

In this connection it is worth noting that Richardson himself did not see the island on his second voyage through the Straits in 1848, nor did Collinson see it when he passed that way aboard the *Enterprise*. I told Captain Bernard, when I visited him in Coronation Gulf, of my suspicions in the matter and I learned later that the following August (1911) he and Dr. Anderson cruised backward and forward over the site without discovering even a sign of a shoal or sand bank. On the other hand I have spoken with American whalemen who say they have seen the island. Captain S. F. Cottle of the steam whaler *Belvedere* is sure not only that he has seen it but that it is in the location where the chart puts it. But I have also learned since that Captain Amundsen in the *Gjoa*, in 1906, sailed near the supposed location of the island, if not quite over it, without seeing any sign of it.

We found on landing every indication that spring had been on the mainland over a month. Dr. Richardson remarks in his "Arctic Search Expedition" that there is a month's difference in the season between the mouth of the Mackenzie and the eastern end of Dolphin and Union Straits. My own experience of two different years goes to confirm this observation, and also to show that the dividing line between the colder and warmer districts is more sharply drawn than would have been suspected. In other words, although Crocker River may be considered to be at the western end of the Straits, nevertheless the difference in season between it and the eastern end of the Straits is nearly as great as Richardson assigns for the difference between Mackenzie River and their eastern end. The same difference holds between the mouth of the Crocker River and the southwest corner of Victoria Island, as we have already remarked. There are probably few other places on the earth's surface where it is possible by traveling sixty miles south, without changing from one altitude to a lower one, to pass from winter into summer in a day. We left Bell Island on May 26th, which was the date of the first thaw

Skinning a Large Bear.

The Part that went to Waste because our Party was too Small to Eat or Haul the Meat.

of the year at that place, as we could tell pretty certainly from the appearance of the snow and ice. We landed on the mainland at Crocker River May 29th, to find nearly all of the snow gone and the season in every way at least four weeks in advance of Bell Island.

The ground was now bare of snow where everything had been covered with it as we journeyed east the year before. This was my opportunity to find out what traces of human habitation there were on the land. Unfortunately I could not do this thoroughly, for there were only two of us, which is the minimum number for successfully managing a sledge on rough ice. There should never be less than three in a sledging party, so that two can travel ahead with the sled and the third can be free to hunt, whether it be for game or for scientific evidences of one sort or another. At our landing at Crocker River, however, we found the remains of ancient dwellings which were, so far as we could tell without excavating them, of the same type as those around Cape Parry.

Apropos of the statement implied in the previous paragraph, that we did not stop to excavate these interesting ruins, it is worth pointing out that the conditions under which excavation can be done in the Arctic are different from those that prevail in any other part of the world. Had the climate been a more southerly one, we might have probed each mound or ruin the day we discovered it, for it would not have taken long to dig at least a narrow trench down to the bottom of one of the ruins. Such things cannot be done in the North, where the frost is never but a few inches below the surface. To do in the Arctic regions archæological excavating of any account one should commence immediately after the spring warmth arrives, by taking off the grass sward from the entire surface of the ruin to be excavated. This will mean removing only two or three inches at first, but that leaves a black surface upon which the sun can work rapidly. The result will be that on each ordinary summer day a layer of earth will thaw out at least two or three inches thick. No excavation of great depth can be accomplished within a few days, for each three or four inch layer of thawed ground has to be removed before the sun gets a good chance to thaw out another layer. This is the only possible method, and it will be seen that it does not lend itself to a casual dipping into the problems of every mound one happens to pass on a journey. Besides, we had only a sledge, and it was necessary for us to reach Langton Bay before the sea ice had gone, else we could not cross the deep bays and swift rivers that intervened, and then we should be unable to do near Cape Parry the archæological work which would help so materially to change to an accomplished fact what had been up to now but the scientific program of the expedition.

On the entire westward journey, whenever we camped or went ashore for any reason, I always took long walks in the search for archæological remains, leaving Natkusiak to do the cooking and camp work. The result was that we established the fact that a continuous chain of human habitations of the general western wood-and-earth type runs at least as far east as Crocker River, and we know no reason to suppose that it ends there abruptly. More probably it will be found to extend to the vicinity of Cape Krusenstern, although the Dolphin and Union Straits people of the present day never make permanent dwellings of any kind, nor use anything that can be called a house, except the snow house. The Cape Bexley people told us that some of them were descended from people who had lived farther along the coast to the west beyond Crocker River, and who had dwelt in earth-and-wood houses. I am inclined to think, however, that either the story is entirely untrustworthy or else it is a very old one and has undergone considerable change, for they told us that those ancestors of theirs used to live in snow houses in the winter time, "as all men do of course," and that they lived in these earth-and-wood houses in the summer time.

That story seems to me essentially absurd on the face of it, for no Eskimo on the north coast of North America ever lived in earth-and-wood houses in summer, or indeed in anything except in tents, so far as I know. It is the nature of the Eskimo style of house that it begins dripping in the spring as soon as the sun begins to thaw the snow on the roof, and must therefore be abandoned even before the ground is bare of snow. The water forms in a puddle on the floor so that the interior of every Eskimo house is like a little lake all summer, and the dwelling is unfit for occupation until a week or two of hard frost in the autumn has solidified everything, when people can go in with adzes or picks, chop out the ice, and cover the floor with some dry

THE STORY OF A FORGOTTEN TRAGEDY.

The owner left this sled on the shore before proceeding inland in summer, weighted
it with stones, and never came back to take the stones off.   Finally
the sled collapsed with age.

SKINNING A SEAL FOR SUPPER.

covering. That is the Mackenzie River way at least. On the north coast of Alaska wooden floors are sometimes so constructed that the water does not cover them, but nevertheless there is continual damp and dripping whenever it rains, so the essential fact remains that the house is uninhabitable the entire summer through. These remarks, of course, have no reference to the modern "civilized" dwellings of the north Alaskans.

A thing of some ethnological importance is that we found numerous fragments of sledges all the way from Crocker River west, and they are all of the same type, which is the short Mackenzie River type, and not the long sledge now in use on Victoria Island and Coronation Gulf and everywhere to the eastward to King William Island and beyond. The longest of the runners of these sledges were never six feet, while in the east they run from twelve feet to over twenty. This, of course, is not for the reason that timber is more abundant in the east and of greater size—driftwood is scarcer the farther east you go. The short sledges are made in a district where logs of all sizes and dimensions up to eighty feet are found lying strewn thick along the beach.

Dr. Richardson, in his account of his boat voyage past this coast in 1848, concludes that whaling was not carried on systematically farther east than Cape Lyon, and he justifies that belief by the statement that villages of earth-and-wood houses are not found farther east than Cape Lyon. Standing well offshore generally, as he did in his boats, he of course had no means of telling certainly that the villages did not extend farther east. We found not only that they did extend to the eastward of Cape Lyon, as above stated, but also that the evidence furnished by the bones of whales scattered here and there along the beach, especially in the neighborhood of some of the ruined villages, indicates that whaling was carried on. That, together with the short sledge and the earth-and-wood house, connects the population of the entire mainland coast from Cape Parry east, as far at least as Crocker River, with the Mackenzie River people, rather than with those of Coronation Gulf.

West of Crocker River to Langton Bay and beyond, the Melvill Mountains are almost everywhere less than ten miles from the coast and must be in general well over a thousand feet in height, but east of Crocker River they are farther inland and may be lower, although there are certain conspicuous high peaks. West of Crocker River the foot-hills generally come down to the water's edge. From near Point Pierce the mountains run diagonally southwest towards the southeast corner of Darnley Bay, leaving a comparatively low but hilly triangle of land running out to a tip at Cape Lyon, which is farther from the mountains proper than any other point on the coast.

West of Point Dease Thompson we have one of the most picturesque sections of the long coast line along which we were traveling, although the whole of it is varied and in many places striking. It is here that Sir John Richardson gives us a sketch of what he calls "Torso Rock" and of the natural bridge behind it. We reproduce his sketch here along with photographs of the same features to show that the pencil has certain advantages above the camera in the illustration of one's travels, for it is impossible to select any position on sea or land from which the Torso Rock and the larger natural bridge can be seen both at once, although the smaller one, which is about a hundred yards from the larger, can be seen from the neighborhood of Torso Rock.

On the entire coast from Crocker River westward there is plenty of driftwood for fuel wherever there is a beach upon which the waves can lodge it. It is an interesting thing, though not quite so noticeable here as it is towards the Mackenzie and west of it, that the driftwood is always found in greater abundance and sometimes exclusively on westward-facing beaches. The explanation is of course simple. "Low tides" occur with easterly winds and "high tides" with westerly ones. Consequently, if a stick is thrown ashore by an easterly wind the next westerly one will, with its higher level of water, float it off again; while the westerly wind with its high tide will lodge the driftwood well above the reach of the most violent easterly gale — indeed the more violent the easterly gale the lower the tide. The easterly wind can therefore never take away what the westerly wind has brought.

It is worth pointing out here, too, that the prevailing direction of the wind in Dolphin and Union Straits and western Victoria Island influences the distribution of driftwood on the shores of Prince Albert

RICHARDSON'S DRAWING AND THREE PHOTOGRAPHS OF THE SAME PLACE.

Sound and the Straits themselves. The prevailing winds are north-westerly, and for that reason driftwood is found in some abundance on the south shore of Prince Albert Sound, although there is very little on the north shore. This we know from hearsay from the Eskimo, for we have not had occasion to follow the south shore of the Sound except between Cape Back and Cape Baring. On this stretch we found only a few little sticks, but that was no doubt because deep snow covered the wood of which the Eskimo had told us.

It is also by hearsay that we know that there is little wood on the southwest coast of Victoria Island from Bell Island east to Lady Franklin Point. We found a considerable straggling of small sticks on the beach near Forsythe Bay, at the foot of Simpson Bay, but nothing like the quantity which is found on the opposite mainland coast everywhere from Lambert Island west. Even on the mainland coast, however, large pieces of driftwood are rare east of Inman River.

That driftwood is found on any of the coasts of Victoria Island and the narrow portions of Dolphin and Union Straits is due to the fact that the Eskimo do not use wood for fuel. They consequently have for the present enough wood for their implements and for such articles as sledges. One of the effects of civilization will be that when they learn to use sheet-iron stoves they will in the course of two or three years burn all the wood that centuries have stored on the beach, exactly as the people in the vicinity of Point Barrow have done, and they will then, like the Point Barrow people, be under the necessity of importing wood when they need it to make the things that they can now make out of driftwood which they find on the beach.

In passing Point Pierce the year before we had noticed nothing particular about it except the magnificent vertical cliff of stratified limestone, the finest of the entire Arctic coast of America west of the Coppermine River. Now, on closer approach, we found that in the very tip of Point Pierce is one of the finest ship harbors, so far as we could judge, of the entire Arctic coast. Judging from the large cakes of drift ice which had floated in, there must be an entrance here for ships of over twenty foot draft (very likely over forty), and there is shelter from all winds. There is, however, an evidently dangerous line of reefs running in a curve convex to the shore from Point Pierce to Cape Lyon. A ship wishing to enter the Point Pierce harbor should therefore keep well offshore until directly off the high-cut cliff which forms the point, and should then stand directly south, entering the harbor at right angles to the line of the coast, running between the 200-foot high-cut cliff of the point proper on the west and the 50-foot high knoll of basaltic rock to the east. When we discovered this harbor, we were traveling along after midnight through a heavy rain and we were soaking wet, so that we felt disinclined to stop to measure the width of the entrance of the harbor or the dimensions of it; but I should say the entrance is over two hundred yards wide and there is room in the harbor for ten or more ships of the ordinary whaling vessel type.

We had previously discovered other harbors, though apparently none as good as this — one of them behind a small island southwest of Liston and Sutton Islands. This harbor is so hard to find that I doubt if I myself could find it again in rough weather, for the island which nearly closes the little bay looks as if it were a part of the mainland until you are right in the channel which separates it from the coast. At Point Keats is another harbor, which might perhaps more properly be called a shelter. Point Keats is T-shaped, so that a ship can get shelter from any wind by merely rounding it when necessary. In neither of these two places did we have such conclusive evidence of deep water as we did at Point Pierce. In fact it is probable that the harbor southeast of Liston Island is shoal.

Both at the Torso Rock and at various other points along the coast we had found gull rookeries chiefly inhabited by glaucous gulls, although there were also a few of the glaucous-winged and California gulls. The first really large rookery we came to was in the cliffs of Point Pierce, and there were others in the pillar rocks which in three places rise out of the reef that runs from Point Pierce to Cape Lyon. We would not have done so earlier in the season, but now we were so near home that we felt we could afford to use a few rifle cartridges in getting some gulls for a change of diet. At a more critical stage of our journey we should have followed our ordinary policy of never using bullets for anything smaller than a seal or a wolf.

Cape Lyon, better than any headland I have seen, deserves the name of a cape. With most capes it is difficult to tell just where the tip of them is because you round them so gradually and there seems to be no conspicuous sharp angle. The angle of Cape Lyon is

as sharp as that of the Flatiron Building; the direction of the cliff
front turns more than a right angle in the space of a fathom or so.
The sea is evidently very deep right up to the foot of the cliff. One
of the most difficult things we have ever done was to round Cape Lyon
on the slanting ice ledge that was not in some places more than two
yards wide between the cliff face and an open lead twenty feet in
width.   A pouring rain made the task not only more disagreeable but
also more difficult, and the sled more than once barely missed sliding
into the water. A few yards farther on, where the ledge had widened
again so there was no longer danger of our sliding off into the water,
the sledge upset. The load was so heavy and so high on the sled, and
Natkusiak had been trying so hard to keep it from upsetting, that
it fell on top of him and pinned him in the soft snow so completely
that he could scarcely move a finger and would have been entirely
unable to extricate himself without assistance. As it was it took
what strength I had to lift the load enough to allow him to get from
under it. The snow had been soft and no injury was done.

CHAPTER XXI

MORE than a year before, when I parted from Dr. Anderson near Langton Bay, I had asked him to make a cache for us in a little bight five miles south of Cape Lyon, in case we had not returned during the summer of 1910. Dr. Anderson and Ilavinirk had accordingly made the cache in October, 1910.

It was on the morning of June 9th that, soon after rounding Cape Lyon, we got to the site of this cache, to find that it had been torn down by polar bears. A rifle that had been left on an elevated platform constructed of driftwood on shore we found a hundred yards or so out on the sea ice. There had also been some bearded seal meat, but that the bears had naturally eaten. By a letter which I found here from Dr. Anderson it appeared that they had left for us, besides the meat and some blubber, fifty pounds of flour, five pounds of rice, two pounds of tea, one package of matches, a tin of salt, a sheet-iron stove and stove pipes, and some ammunition. The flour we found in several heaps on the ground where it had been scattered by the bear when he tore the bag open. We found a pile of rice at the bottom of a small rivulet; the tea, tobacco, and matches were all wet, and the only things quite safe were the cartridges and the tin of salt. Of course Dr. Anderson had expected when he made the cache that we should come for all these things the winter of 1910–1911; had we done which we might have found everything in order. That we should come in winter was the whole idea of caching these stores, for in the summer we should of course be in no straits for food.

It is one of the admirable qualities of flour that water will not penetrate a pile of it, so that although it had been raining heavily and repeatedly for a month we found a little dry flour at the center of every heap and were able to make out of it some pancakes. We had been so long without salt that the desire for it was quite gone, and I do not remember now whether we took the salt can or left it behind.

We tried at first to follow the shore around the foot of Darnley Bay, for the bay has never been mapped and we were desirous of making a survey of it. We made a geographical discovery almost immediately, however, which was interesting in itself but prevented a further exploration of the bay, for there are two good-sized rivers that come into it from the southeast and they had brought down so much warm water that all the ice in the southeast corner of the bay was so eaten up with holes and cracks that sledging had become impossible. We were therefore forced to cross the bay, which was indeed the shortest and simplest thing to do. Here and there on our way across we found open leads, but in every case by following them for a few miles we found cakes of ice which had broken loose from one bank of the lead or the other, which were oblong in shape, and which had turned around so that their ends nearly or quite touched both sides of the lead. These gave us bridges on which to cross. Most of them were so uncertain, however, that we did not have the nerve to delay on them while the process of crossing was being photographed. The best I could do was to photograph one of the cakes just after we had crossed.

Seals, like caribou, have certain favorite feeding grounds. The most remarkable place for bearded seals ever seen by us is the narrow portion of Dolphin and Union Straits east and west of Lambert Island, but the common seal (*fœtida*) we never saw anywhere in such numbers as on Darnley Bay. Standing on the sea ice at one time, for instance, I counted over four hundred within a radius of three miles or so. Most of them had come up through open leads and were lying strung along their edges like strings of black beads, but here and there away from the course of any lead there were sprinkled broadcast others that had come up through their enlarged winter breathing-holes and were lying beside them.

On June 16th, at the southwest corner of Darnley Bay, we left behind us all our geological specimens and everything we had with us which water and the animals would not be likely to destroy, and commenced the difficult undertaking of hauling the sledge loaded with Eskimo skin clothing and other ethnological specimens of a perishable nature across the twenty miles or more of land that separated Darnley Bay from Langton Bay. Had we been a week or so

Y

earlier this would not have been difficult, for although the land had been bare longer than that, there were numerous lakes on this neck of land so that at least fifteen of the twenty miles could have been negotiated over ice. But now the lakes were breaking up.

I do not think we have ever been in greater danger of our lives than we were in crossing a lake about five miles wide, which we reached after laboriously dragging the sledge over a ridge of hills perhaps a hundred feet high and half a mile wide that separates it from Darnley Bay. We knew the ice was not safe, but the sledging had been so hard that the smooth surface of the lake was a great temptation; and besides, if we did not cross the lake, we had to go a good many miles out of our way to round it, and we would have had to ferry in some place or other across more than one deep river.

Fresh-water ice, when it thaws in the spring, behaves in a manner fundamentally different from salt-water ice. No doubt this is a matter of common knowledge among physicists and a few others, but it was first brought forcibly to my attention the summer we spent on the Coppermine River. In the spring freshets huge blocks of ice had been left stranded on the bottom lands of the river well in among some trees. I remember one morning passing one of these and noticing that it was quite as high as I was myself. In the evening when I returned over the same ground I was astonished to find the bowlder of ice missing. A little search showed me, however, a flattened-out heap of crystals, some of them a foot or more in length. The whole cake had divided into separate crystals and all of a sudden the forces of cohesion had given way and the whole thing had settled down into a loose pile. Later on I used to walk up to these stranded bowlders of ice and give them a smart blow with a stick or something. It happened now and then that one of them would crumble at a touch into exactly such a heap as that into which the first big bowlder had degenerated.

When after crossing the half-mile wide ridge from Darnley Bay we entered upon the ice surface of the first of the lakes which in summer furnish a portage route to near Langton Bay, I noticed that all the ice was breaking up into needles or crystals in the manner of the bowlders of ice on the Coppermine River. I had with me a sharp pointed pole and by jabbing it into the ice I was able to force it be-

WATER ON TOP SOLID SEA ICE IN JUNE.

LOOSE ICE CAKE FORMING BRIDGE ACROSS LEAD.

tween the ice crystals clear through the ice into the water below, although the ice was at least three feet thick. When we discovered the sort of condition the ice was in we decided to wait a few hours, for, although the season was well advanced, we usually had a little frost after midnight. We waited until two or three in the morning, hoping for the usual frost which would cement the ice needles together a little and make the crossing safer, but unfortunately this proved to be the first night of the year (June 14th) when it did not freeze at all.

We made the crossing, nevertheless, going carefully as possible and with our hearts in our mouths the whole way. When we got within about fifty yards of the other shore, we found that the land was separated from us by a channel of open water. We unhitched the dogs with the idea that we would fasten together all the ropes we had, take the dogs ashore somehow, hitch them to one end of the rope on land, while the other was made fast to the sled out on the ice beyond the lane of shore water, and drive off at a sharp run, hoping that the ice would not break until the sled was so near shore that it would plump down into shallow water only.

The first dog we unhitched was eager to get ashore, and as soon as his harness was removed he started off on a brisk trot for the land; but while he was yet as much as ten feet from the edge of the water that separated him from the land, the ice, which was more than a foot thick at that place, suddenly crumbled to pieces under him and he fell into the water. This scared him, and he turned around and tried to climb back on to the ice again; but as fast as he tried to climb upon it it crumbled into separate crystals, and as he swam towards us he made with his pawing a channel through the ice up to within about ten feet of where we stood, where the ice finally became solid enough for him to haul himself out.

Evidently we were in a dangerous place. With my long pole I punched a hole in the ice and found that the water was over six feet in depth. It was therefore hopeless to try to land at this point. Fortunately, about a half a mile to the south was a cut bank in the shelter of which a thick snowdrift extended out upon the lake ice, and we found that underneath the snow of this drift the ice had not decomposed into crystals. We therefore hitched up the sled again, drove around to this point, and were able to get the sled into less than three feet of water before the ice broke down. Even at that we got the larger portion of our load pretty well soaked, but the weather was fine and by spreading the skins and clothing out to dry in the evening we had them in fit condition against the next morning. I have not mentioned it before, but this had been our routine work every day since we landed at Crocker River, for there was scarcely a ten-mile stretch where we did not have to cross some channel of water so deep that the larger portion of the load got soaking wet. Had we allowed the things to remain undried, the beautiful skin clothing of which our load partly consisted would have rotted to pieces before we got to Langton Bay.

It took us ten days of the hardest toil to cover the twenty miles that separated us from Langton Bay. We ventured on the ice of no more lakes, and in fact most of the lakes were already open. We had been living on seal meat up to this time, but now we lived on geese and swans. The neck of Cape Parry is one of the great swan breeding grounds. The birds themselves are not difficult to shoot with a rifle, and the nests are among the most conspicuous objects in the animal life of the Arctic. A swan's nest is the size of a bushel basket and is usually built on the barren shore of a lake. The dun color of the nest itself and the spotless white bird on top of it can be seen with the naked eye much farther than either the caribou or the grizzly bear. There are often six eggs in a nest, and as they are more than twice the size of the egg of a goose, half a dozen of them would make a square meal for a fairly hungry man. There were also some caribou in this district, and one day while Natkusiak was cooking lunch I secured three of them and two days later another two besides.

By June 20th, while we were still making the overland crossing, the mosquitoes had become so numerous as to make sleep almost impossible, for we had no mosquito nets with us. This made us struggle all the harder, for our base camp at Langton Bay was now less than twenty miles away, and we knew that we would find there not only our Eskimo companions and a comfortable camp, but best of all and most important, mosquito nets under which we could get a comfortable night's rest.

Early on the morning of June 23d we reached the sea ice near the

SLEDGING ACROSS BARREN GROUND IN JUNE IS HOT WORK.

northeast corner of Langton Bay. It was fifteen miles from this spot to the Langton Bay harbor where our permanent camp was situated, and the ice was smooth and level in front of us so that we expected to be home within four hours. But although the ice was white as if in winter, near the shoal east end of the bay where there are no strong currents, it gradually became worse and worse as we got over deeper water, and when we approached the harbor where the tide currents are strong at all times of the year we saw that to reach land on the harbor side of the bay was going to be impossible. Three miles from shore the water channels on top of the ice had become so deep that the dogs had to swim in crossing them and our sled was half under water.

A little less than three miles from shore progress with the load became impossible, and I had to leave Natkusiak with the sled and to work my way carefully as near to the Langton Bay sand spit as possible. With my glasses I could see our Eskimo in camp on shore. Smoke was rising, showing that they were awake and cooking breakfast. As I worked my way cautiously toward shore I had several narrow escapes from falling through holes in the ice. Salt-water ice when it thaws never disintegrates into separate crystals as does fresh-water ice, and it is always tough and reliable. In the spring there is little danger of falling through it unless one steps into an open hole, and in the fall we much prefer an inch and a half of salt-water ice to two inches and a half of fresh, for fresh-water ice cracks like the breaking of a window pane, but salt-water ice bends before breaking and always gives you warning. However, in this case, while I was still a mile and a half from shore I came to a place where there was no more fast ice in front, but only big cakes floating back and forth in the deep current-swept ship channel that separates Langton Bay harbor on the south from the low sand spit three miles north of it.

There was nothing for it but to stop, for a channel of ice-water a mile and a half wide and ten fathoms deep is scarcely easier to swim across than it would be to wade over. I could do nothing but alternately fire my rifle over the heads of the people ashore and wave my coat for a signal. They neither heard me nor saw me until Mamayauk, following a characteristic habit of hers, came out of the

tent with her husband's spy-glass to sweep with it the ice for a
possible polar bear or seal.   Through my field glasses I could see
her take her seat on a log outside the tent and begin her survey of
the horizon at the west, her glass methodically sweeping the ice eastward.   It was then a question of only a few minutes until she was
bound to see us, for I knew her to have a keen eye from which few
things escaped.   No sooner had she brought her glass into line with
where I stood waving my coat than she dropped it on the beach and
ran towards the end of the sand spit where I now noticed for the first
time the head of her husband Ilavinirk, where he was sitting behind
a log, apparently watching at the end of the sand spit for seals that
might swim past.   Five minutes later Ilavinirk and Palaiyak in
two kayaks were coming out towards me, alternately paddling across
open water and climbing on to cakes of ice which they had to cross
before they could launch their kayaks again.

It was a happy home-coming for all of us.   Natkusiak and I were
tired of traveling, cold and hungry from much wading, and they at
home had been lonesome, for they had seen no stranger for half a
year.   They had long been worrying over our prolonged absence
and had begun to think we were never going to return.

We found it impossible to get our sledge ashore at the harbor
and had to land it on the sand spit three miles directly north of our
home camp.   We left Natkusiak and Palaiyak there to take care of
the dogs.   Palaiyak had brought with him a shotgun (Natkusiak
and I had on our long trip carried nothing but rifles, for shotgun
ammunition is too heavy to carry on such journeys as ours had
been), and there was an abundance of ducks and geese for them to
hunt.   I took Palaiyak's kayak, and Ilavinirk and I paddled ashore
to spend hours on end in talking about the varied things that had
happened both to them and to us since we last met, and then we
went to sleep peacefully under the protection of our good mosquito
nets.

Ilavinirk, like most of the western Eskimo, was not of much account as a traveling companion because of general timidity and
particular fear of new places.   He was always afraid of starvation,
always afraid that if we went into any place where none of his countrymen had been before we should find no food animals to live on.   This

DRYING CLOTHES AND ETHNOLOGICAL SPECIMENS AFTER TRAVELING OVER WATER-COVERED ICE.

THE CACHE.

was his weak point — that was why we had to set him to the work of taking care of our base camp, for which task he was admirably adapted. He not only took excellent care of everything, but his memory was so good that he always knew not only exactly where everything was, but also how much there was of it and in what condition it was. He was conscientious about everything and never idle. We had particularly impressed him with the scientific value of the grizzly bear and with the importance of taking the appropriate measurements of the animal before it was skinned. He had accordingly secured for us three excellent specimens, which were not only properly skinned and preserved, but of which by means of knotted strings he had also taken the necessary measurements. He had, too, during the winter shot a silver fox, which is an animal common enough in the fur markets, but almost absent in the scientific collections of museums. Besides these two most important things he had taken and preserved the skins of various animals and birds, but best of all, from my point of view at least, he had made an important archæological discovery.

I remember well, when I was in college listening to lectures on North American archæology and ethnology, that our professor told us substantially the following about the occurrence of pottery among the Eskimo. Pottery, he said, was fairly abundant among the Eskimo south of the Yukon River of Alaska, and there was a little also north of the mouth of the Yukon, but it was very crude. He considered the northern limit of the art of pottery making to have been at the foot of Kotzebue Sound. True enough, Murdoch had brought back in 1882 two or three fragments of pottery from Point Barrow, but it seemed likely to our lecturer that these might have been brought to Point Barrow as articles of trade from Kotzebue Sound, and that the real knowledge of pottery making did not go quite so far. In any case this was, our professor considered, evidence of the fact that the Eskimo had come into Alaska from the east along the coast. They had come ignorant of the potter's art, and the advance guard of them when they met the Indians in the neighborhood of or south of the Yukon had learned the art from the Indians, and it had begun to spread eastward (upstream, as it were, against the current of migration) but had never penetrated farther east than

Kotzebue Sound, or to Point Barrow at the utmost. So much for the knowledge of pottery among the Eskimo as I acquired it in my university days. Practically this was the state of information on the subject among anthropologists, although I believe Murdoch himself considered the pottery he had found at Point Barrow had really been made there.

Ilavinirk was a native of Kotzebue Sound and had often seen his own mother make pottery. He now told me that some twelve or fifteen miles northeast of Langton Bay, at the mouth of the river located behind what is known to us as Point Stivens, he had seen in the mud along the river some fragments of pottery of the same kind that his mother used to make in Kotzebue Sound.

I will here anticipate the results of our summer's work by saying that we eventually found pottery both at the place where it was first discovered by Ilavinirk and at other places in the same neighborhood and that we found it in great abundance. Not only was it abundant, but it was found as deep down as any of the human remains we uncovered and was therefore evidently of equal antiquity with the earliest of them. In other words, the Eskimo when they came here (from the east no doubt) knew pottery making as well as they did at any later time. They had not learned it in Alaska in recent times, as the anthropologists had been thinking. Neither did this art until recently fall into decay among the Mackenzie River or Baillie Islands Eskimo (as we learned from inquiries), for there are still living at the Baillie Islands a few people who themselves have helped to make pottery, and many who can remember their parents making it.

I was of course anxious to begin the work of archæological excavation at once after our arrival at Langton Bay, but the season was still a little early. The most promising place was the one discovered by Ilavinirk behind Point Stivens, and this we could not reach for some time because the ice prevented our launching our umiak. I therefore occupied the first week after our return home in writing letters and reports to forward to the Baillie Islands with our Eskimo, whom I decided to allow a little vacation. They had been so long without seeing any of their countrymen that they were anxious to make the trip to the Baillie Islands ninety miles to the westward to visit their friends for a few days, and to wait there for the hoped-for coming in of whaling vessels. This suited me very well, for while we did not expect any supplies we hoped for mail, and I was anxious to send letters out with information of what our work had been the year before and what our intentions were for the future.

There are a number of old house ruins on the sand spit which forms the outer wall of the Langton Bay harbor. Although wood is abundant enough in these parts, most of the houses seem to have had their walls made of the bones of whales, especially of the vertebræ and skull bones. Although we did a considerable amount of work in digging out these dwellings, we found but few things of importance except pottery fragments, which were so numerous that they showed conclusively that the clay pots of which these were the remnants could not have been imported. They must have been made in the neighborhood.

It turned out that in all our digging during two summers, both near Langton Bay and Point Barrow, we never found an unbroken clay pot. I hoped for such a find at first, but it is easy to see on careful thought that a buried clay pot could not possibly remain whole in damp ground (and all ground up here is damp), for frozen earth, like ice, keeps cracking in cold weather; and when the earth in which a pot is imbedded cracks, the pot will have to crack with it. The only fairly complete specimens we ever secured were surface finds — cooking vessels that had been placed by the mourners beside the grave of some dead woman.

CHAPTER XXII

BY June 30th the ice had been driven out of sight from the main body of Franklin Bay, although Langton Bay itself to the east of us was still ice-covered. Not until July 8th did we feel sure the bay behind Point Stivens was clear of ice, and it was then we set out in our skin boat to visit it, for here the archæological work of the summer was to be done. We reached on the evening of July 9th the site of the ruins discovered by Ilavinirk and at once began digging.

Although we learned later that some of these houses had been occupied about the time of the childhood of a woman still living at the Baillie Islands (who was about fifteen years old when Richardson came there in 1848), yet they had every appearance of great age, and the best-preserved rafters that were found in the earth near the surface could be picked to pieces with the fingers, so decayed were they. Farther down, the ground was frozen and everything was better preserved.

It is one of the elements of uncertainty one has to face here that the degree of decay of a wooden, bone, or ivory object gives no idea of its age except one take careful account of many circumstances, only one of which is how deep down in the earth it was buried. I remember especially the finding of a spear shaft which was embedded in the earth at an angle of about 45°. I must have dug away some of the end of it without noticing anything at all, and lower down I found what resembled a bundle of wet brown paper that could by no means be made to hang together. Farther down still the shaft was like a partly decayed stick of wood, and below that it was but slightly decayed, while the lower end of it was so well preserved in the perpetual frost that it looked as if it might have been made a year or two ago. This shaft had been buried by the caving in of a house, evidently. Had I taken samples of the upper and the lower end of this shaft and exhibited them together, without comment, any one would have thought that there might have been a difference of from one to several centuries in time between the two pieces.

I have no reason to doubt the accuracy of the story which places the latest occupation of this village site at something like eighty or ninety years ago, but I am inclined to think that the house ruins which actually exist are much older than that. The river on the banks of which they are located is gradually meandering southward and has cut away already a portion of the village site. It is not improbable that it may have carried away entirely the recent houses of which our informants told us, and that these which we excavated are really much more ancient ones. I am inclined to this view especially from the fact, as stated elsewhere, that I have seen wood chopped by Richardson's party in 1848 which looks for all the world as if it might have been chopped only three or four years ago, while every stick in this site was thoroughly rotten unless it was deep in the frozen earth.

I have omitted mentioning that when we returned home from Langton Bay we found there not only the four Eskimo who constituted Ilavinirk's family, but also a young man by the name of Mangilanna, a younger brother of the Tannaumirk who was working for us and whom I had left in Dr. Anderson's party at Coronation Gulf. The day after reaching the river mouth at Point Stivens I sent Ilavinirk, Natkusiak and this Mangilanna with the umiak up the river towards Darnley Bay to fetch the goods which we had cached there two weeks before. This is a little river about thirty miles long, the mouth of which occupies the same place as the fictitious four or five hundred mile long River La Ronciere of the maps. The stream rises in the Melvill mountains south of Darnley Bay and flows through the lake of which we have spoken as the one over which we had made such a dangerous crossing immediately after leaving Darnley Bay. This river therefore furnishes a water route from Franklin Bay to within half a mile of Darnley Bay. It was only a matter of two or three days until the umiak had returned to us again, bringing the stuff we had left behind.

For about two weeks we worked energetically at the task of excavating this old village site which to the Baillie Islands Eskimo is known by the name of Kugum Panga, which being translated means merely "the mouth of the river." Besides finding a bushel or so of pottery fragments we found missile points, knives, and other articles of slate and "flint," pieces of iron pyrite that had been used for fire making, and various articles of whalebone, antler, and ivory. The ivory was very rare, for in that day no doubt as well as in this it had to be imported from Point Barrow or beyond.

Besides showing us that pottery had been commonly used, these excavations threw many an interesting side light on the character of the people who had once occupied the land; but nothing perhaps was so striking as the complete absence of fish-nets and all other articles associated with the art of netting fish. There were not any floats or sinkers and none of the peculiar tools which the Eskimo use in Alaska for regulating the size of the mesh.

Using these facts as a basis of inquiry, we later on found that the same Baillie Islands woman (Pannigiok) whom we mentioned above as having been about fifteen when she saw Richardson in 1848, told us that she had been born near Langton Bay and had never seen nets in her own community, though she had heard some talk about their being in use to the westward. She had seen the first fish-net when at the age of eight or ten years she moved with her parents to the Baillie Islands. This was at a time, she told us, when the people of Langton Bay had for several years suffered from scarcity of food, and the community to which she belonged had divided up, some moving east along the coast while she and her people moved west. Since then, she said, the people who went east have never returned or been heard from. This is probably an accurate, truthful account of the breaking up of the continuous chain of habitation that once stretched eastward along the coast to Coronation Gulf and of which we had found evidences everywhere along that coast in the shape of house ruins and graves. In ancient times it had been in a way necessary that people should occupy the whole coast for the purpose of trading, bringing the valuable stone lamps and stone pots and copper implements from the east and (in later days at least, and possibly even long ago) receiving from the west iron and other white men's or Asiatic wares that came by prehistoric trade routes across Bering Straits and eastward along the coast.

By July 23d we began to fear, because the sea had been open so long, that whaling ships might arrive at the Baillie Islands any day;

BRINGING ASHORE A BEARDED SEAL AT LANGTON BAY.

and we accordingly set sail from Point Stivens for Langton Bay with
the archæological plunder we had been able to secure. Of course
we had been able to dig up but a small portion of the very rich
village site on which we had been working, but our "finds," such
as they were, had in more than one way their aspects of great
significance.

On the way south we happened to pick up a polar bear that
was wandering about on shore. A day or two before that Palaiyak
and Mangilanna had secured a young grizzly bear, and a day or two
after Palaiyak got another one in the Melvill Mountains south of
Langton Bay. In general, however, at this time we lived on the
meat of the bearded seal, which the boys Palaiyak and Mangilanna
secured by paddling out to sea in their kayaks and shooting the
seals as they slept on floating cakes of ice.

July 27th Ilavinirk, Natkusiak, and Mangilanna with our umiak
started west to the Baillie Islands, while I remained behind doing
archæological work around Langton Bay with the intermittent
assistance of Palaiyak, Mamayauk, and Nogasak. In general, as I
have had many occasions to point out, Nogasak was a very lazy and
useless sort of person; but scratching around in the ground with the
prospect of finding spear points or knives was something that appealed to her, and she really was my most valuable assistant throughout the entire summer in the work of excavating. I am inclined to
think the main reason may have been that I discouraged her from the
first, for fear that she might damage through carelessness some important find that she made. She was therefore very careful, and
whenever she found a sign of anything she would come to me and
tell me about it before she finally dug it up. It would no doubt
have been more desirable had I had the means of employing expert
diggers who would have done everything according to the book,
but as it was it seemed to be much more useful that Nogasak should
find things in the wrong way than that they should remain buried
and probably unfound forever.

The time had now come when the caribou might be expected to
have a little fat on their backs and the skins were becoming suitable
for clothing. Altogether, myself and various members of our party
had killed only half a dozen or so caribou since we came back to

Langton Bay, and the skins of all of them had been of little use, for they were full of large holes made by the escaping grubs of the bot-fly which had been growing under the hides of the poor animals' backs all winter and which had now just come out of their warm quarters and taken wing. The hair also is rather too short until towards the end of July, but from that time until the 20th of September it is in excellent condition for clothing, after which it becomes too long.

It is not only the length of hair which is right in the month of August, but also the thickness of the hide itself. From Christmas time until May the skin is as thin as parchment and there is very little strength to it. In June it begins to thicken, but is as yet full of bot-fly holes. Towards the end of July these holes heal up and the skin becomes of the right thickness, while by October it has become too thick and unpliable for use as clothing. For that reason we use the hides of ordinary animals taken in September and October for clothing only in emergencies, and otherwise utilize them for bedding only, except the skins of the old bull caribou, which have often the thickness of sole leather and which we accordingly use for boot soles for our winter footwear.

It was because we knew the caribou were getting into condition and because we had to "take thought for the morrow" in the matter of clothing for winter that we set out on July 30th southward to look for caribou.

The Endicott Mountains look like mountains true enough as seen from the sea, but when in the three-mile walk inland you have climbed up two thousand feet or so you find yourself on a fairly level table-land, although within three miles from the sea the streams begin to flow inland towards Horton River, which lies about fifteen miles away, parallel to the coast.

Soon after I reached the top of this plateau and about five miles from camp I came upon a grizzly bear accompanied by two small cubs. I did not realize how small the cubs were at first and shot the old animal and one of the cubs. On closer approach I saw that the living animal was but the size of a wolverine and showed no fear or concern of me whatever. It occurred to me then that it would be a very interesting thing to take the thing alive; but unfortunately I did not have any string with me or other means of taking the cub along to the coast. I therefore returned home and immediately hitched our dogs to a sled, with which and an empty box we started to fetch the bear. It was a matter of eight or ten hours until we got to where I had left the cub behind; but although he had not been afraid of me then, the poor fellow had by now evidently realized the death of his two relatives, and we were at least half a mile away when he saw us and took to his heels. I followed him a considerable distance while the others skinned the two dead bears, but I never got anywhere near him.

With me the matter of big game hunting is another case of "swords sticking to hands that seek the plow." I am afraid I am not a true sportsman. It is impossible for me to get enjoyment out of the killing of animals (and as for that, if I did I should get a job in the Chicago stockyards rather than follow poor frightened wild things around with a rifle). It is mere nonsense to talk of wild animals (in the case of those on the continent of North America at least) having a chance for their lives against the hunter. They all give us as wide a berth as they can; their only desire and hope of safety is in hiding or in flight. None of them, so far as my experience goes, will fight unless wounded or cornered, or in the defence of their helpless young. No matter how well they are provided by nature with claws and teeth and stout muscles, they have no more chance against a man with a modern rifle than a fly has against a sledge hammer.

Unfortunately the Barren Ground grizzly is a priceless thing scientifically. There are practically none of them in museums and one of our avowed objects in coming North was to get some. I never allowed any to pass, therefore, and I shot altogether thirteen, but somehow the killing of these poor animals affected me more than that of any others. They are provided by nature with a fighting equipment second to no animal on the continent, and yet they try their best to live peacefully and inoffensively. They feed on roots almost entirely, and whenever they discover the sign of a human being, whether they see or smell his footprints, or see him or get his wind, they immediately use every means in their power to get out of the way. But they are dull of sight and not very quick of hearing and when the hunter once sees them there is no escape.

August 8th Palaiyak hunted to the south also and shot three deer about five miles away from camp.   We were about to set out to fetch the meat of them when a sail appeared to the north which our glasses told us was Captain Bernard's *Teddy Bear*.   It was reasonable enough she should arrive just then, although we had not expected her for a week or so yet.

The *Teddy Bear* dropped anchor in the harbor late in the afternoon of August 9th, bringing Dr. Anderson, Tannaumirk, and Pannigabluk, all safe.   Spring had been very early in Coronation Gulf, and they really could have come out sooner than they did.   Cruising up along the southwest coast of Victoria Island they had found our beacon on Bell Island and had thereby, as we intended, been saved from the trip to Banks Island to look for us.

I was very confident that we would be able in the neighborhood of Langton Bay to kill caribou and grizzly bears enough for our food the coming winter, but our Eskimo knew very well that their countrymen at the Baillie Islands, less than a hundred miles to the westward, would have plenty of flour, tea, and things of that sort, and we felt they would not be content with us unless they had it also.   Captain Bernard had a considerable stock of these things and kindly furnished us with a supply.   Dr. Anderson and I are not particular about such luxuries as flour and sugar, but our Eskimo had no scientific interests to keep them in the country, and, like servants everywhere, wanted as high wages and as good food as possible.   So of course we had to supply them with what we could get in the way of imported food.

It is not really so much that these Eskimo regard baking powder bread as such excellent food, but it is rather that they know it is expensive and they are human enough to want to have their neighbors know that they can afford to have this and that to eat even if it does cost money, differing not so much from the rest of humanity in that matter.   They judge things chiefly by price, and desire them in proportion to their current market value.

Dr. Anderson was anxious to communicate with the whaling ships if possible for the purpose of sending out mail and for other reasons, and so he continued west with the *Teddy Bear* toward the Baillie Islands with the intention of returning thence with Ilavinirk and Natkusiak in our umiak, while Tannaumirk and Pannigabluk came ashore

THE "TEDDY BEAR."

and joined us.   As the caribou season was now at its best we stayed around Langton Bay only a few hours after the *Teddy Bear* left and then started inland in the search for game.

As we have pointed out elsewhere, the caribou hunt is not merely to secure meat.   A supply of dried venison to tide you over the sunless days helps you to face the season with confidence, but the main consideration is to secure skins for clothing against the winter.   Our method of hunting is in general that we travel from one high hill to another high hill, pause on each hilltop and with our field glasses and telescopes carefully examine every inch of visible ground in the hope of seeing caribou.

On these summer hunts the dogs are equipped with pack saddles, consisting essentially of two big pouches that nearly reach to the ground on either side of the animal when the pack is in place.   These pack saddles are loaded with the heaviest and least bulky things we have to carry.   A fifty-pound dog will carry a forty-pound pack or even a heavier one, and he will carry it all day, although his walking gait is rather slow, perhaps not much over two miles an hour.   The people of the party will carry on their backs the bulky things, such as the bedding, tents, and cooking utensils.   A man does not carry more than thirty or forty pounds, although under special conditions he may carry as much as a hundred and fifty or even two hundred.

When caribou are discovered, the women and children, if there are any in the party, stop and make camp, while the men secure the caribou, skin them, and cut them up.   Usually long before the skinning is done camp has been made ; and if the caribou are located so near that the women know the killing has actually taken place, they come with the dogs to help bring home the meat ; or if a considerable number of caribou are killed, it may be easier than moving the meat to camp to move the camp up to the scene of the slaughter.   The meat is then cut up into thin strips and spread out on the ground or on stones to dry ; or if there are sticks available a frame is made over which the meat is hung up.   The skins too are spread out to dry.   The process of drying meat delays camp moving, so the men go out and hunt for more caribou in all directions from the camp ; and if they secure any they usually bring home the meat, unless indeed they make a big killing, in which case it is easier to transport the half-dried meat

z

and the camp gear to the deer kill than to bring home the fresh meat to camp. Then whenever the meat is dried and if no more caribou are likely to be found in that immediate vicinity, the meat is cached in the safest way possible, usually by stones being piled on top of it, and the party moves on, carrying with it the dried caribou skins, for they are too precious to leave behind to the uncertain safety of a cache. The same kind of traveling as before is resumed as soon as all the meat killable in any locality has been turned into dry meat, the party marching from hilltop to hilltop and continually looking for game, which is finally found. And then the same process repeats itself.

On the particular hunt under discussion the caribou were not very numerous. First we went about fifteen miles south from Langton Bay to the head of a small wooded creek that runs into Horton River from the north, and here during the course of a week we killed about a dozen caribou and three grizzly bears. The Eskimo generally merely wind-dry the meat, but personally I rather prefer the Indian method of smoke-drying it, and so we built a spruce bough lodge in the Indian style and dried the meat that way. This has an additional advantage, for when you want to leave for another hunting camp you can with tolerable safety cache anything you want inside of the abandoned lodge, for the smoke smell, while it is at all fresh, will keep beasts of prey at a distance. Eventually, of course (in a fortnight or so), some wolverine will become contemptuous enough of the fire smell which it at first dreaded, and will venture into the deserted house to steal.

We remained about a week in the camp on the wooded creek-head where we had made our first kill, and then we were forced to leave it on account of the absence of caribou in that neighborhood, and by the fact that I one day happened to kill four animals a long way to the eastward in a country where game signs were more numerous. Moving to these better pastures was a matter of nearly a day's walk, for we traveled heavy laden with the caribou fat and skins that were too precious to risk leaving behind with the meat. Traveling at this time of year is particularly pleasant, for while the days are still warm, the placid nights are cool and the power of the mosquito has been broken. There are few things in one's experience in the North

The March across Barren Ground.

Camp Breaking and Preparing Packs for Travel.

that are so pleasant to remember as these autumn hunts, when the camp is pitched among a clump of spruce trees at the bottom of some ravine, and when at the end of a day's hunt you can gather around a crackling fire in the enveloping darkness, for the four-months' summer day is just over. The occasional howl of a wolf in the near shadow lends an additional romance, especially if, as not seldom happens, the wolves are so numerous and near that the dogs become frightened and gather in a close circle around the fire. Few meals can be more satisfying, either, at the end of a hard day's work, than a caribou head that has been rotated continuously before the fire until it is roasted through, even to the base of the tongue and the center of the brain. The dreams of boyhood seldom come true, but I am not sure that there is not sometimes as much romance about the reality of such evenings as there was about the dreams of Crusoe-like adventures on desert islands.

As the nights grew longer and the weather colder we gradually worked our way south to the place where in December, 1910, I had hoped to find Dr. Anderson and his companions when Natkusiak, the Slavey Indian, and I were on our way north from Great Bear Lake. My parting injunction to Dr. Anderson in March, 1910, had been that he should if possible winter on the head of Coal Creek; and when we came from the south and found that he was not there, it had been a disappointment not only because the fear of starvation was upon us, but also because it seemed to me such a picturesque spot in which to spend the winter — so promising in the comfort of the deep spruce-wooded valley and in the resources of the fishing lake at the head of the creek, where we had always found the caribou plentiful whenever we sought them the winter before (1909–1910). Since Dr. Anderson did not settle there when he was in charge in 1910 I was going to see to it now that in 1911 we should; and accordingly on September 16th we moved camp down into the bottom lands of Coal Creek, about half a mile east from Horton River, at a place where I intended we should build our winter house. The following day, September 17th, Dr. Anderson and Ilavinirk arrived from Baillie Islands, so that we now had a force of men sufficient to build a house in a hurry.

CHAPTER XXIII

DR. ANDERSON brought the news that Natkusiak had left our service. It seemed that a man at the Baillie Islands named Kutukak had made up his mind that Natkusiak would be a desirable son-in-law (about which there could be no reasonable doubt, for a more competent man in everything which concerns making a living in the Arctic could not possibly be found in that community). Natkusiak had accordingly joined Kutukak's family as his son-in-law, and they had gone off to Liverpool Bay, where they intended to spend the autumn. This was a very disappointing piece of news, for in all my long travels and in everything of difficulty which I had had to undertake in the past three years, Natkusiak had always been my mainstay and in many cases the only man on whom I could rely. But while this about him was disappointing intelligence, news of another sort quite took it out of my mind.

When Dr. Anderson told it to me first, the thing seemed quite beyond belief. He had learned at the Baillie Islands that Inspector Fitzgerald and three mounted policemen under his command had starved to death on the ordinarily very simple journey from Fort Macpherson south to Dawson with the winter mail. Fitzgerald and two of his companions, Kinney and Carter, I knew personally. The news struck me like a blow. There were many aspects of it, but the most personal one was that the last conversation I had had with Fitzgerald was one in which he told me his thorough disapprobation of my methods of travel, and that if I tried to follow them I should surely come to grief. And here were we in comfort and in plenty listening to the story of his tragic death.

He had been a man of great courage, as were all of his companions; but they had failed through the essential weakness of their system of travel, which was to take with them all the food which they thought they could possibly need on the journey, without making any preparations for gathering more from the country when their stores should become exhausted. The result was in that case, as it has been in so many others, that when unlooked-for circumstances stretched the time of the journey beyond the limit reckoned on at first, supplies ran out; the dogs were eaten, then the men's skin clothing and the harness of the dogs; and then came death through cold and starvation.

It is always easy to see when a tragedy has happened how it could have been avoided, but it has always seemed to me that so long as you are traveling in a country supplied with game, you are safer to start with a rifle and with the resolution to find food (but without a pound of food on your sled), than you would be in starting with a sled heavily loaded with food and with no provision made for getting more when the sled load has been eaten up.

But perhaps more startling than this story of death among harsh circumstances was the further news that Sergeant Selig, whom both Dr. Anderson and I knew personally and a man from whom we had received much kindness, had been left in good health and comfort by Inspector Fitzgerald at Herschel Island and had died there from sudden illness long before the news reached him of Fitzgerald's death. Five out of the six policemen whom we had left at Herschel Island a little more than a year ago, comfortably housed amid plenty, were now all dead; and new men had come to take their places.

Various other items of news Dr. Anderson brought also, such as these: the *Teddy Bear* was going to winter at the Baillie Islands and so was Captain Wolki's whaling schooner, the *Rosie H.* Three or four whaling vessels had either touched at the Bailie Islands or had been seen to pass in the offing, and one of these, the *Belvedere*, under Captain Cottle, was going to winter at Herschel Island.

Another piece of news which did not then bear the aspect of tragedy was that an Englishman, Hubert Darrell, had not reached Fort Macpherson after having visited the Baillie Islands in the fall of 1910. When Dr. Anderson repeated this piece of news to me we discussed it and agreed, as we still do, that Darrell was a man who would not have starved under ordinary circumstances, and we therefore felt sure that he had turned up alive and well somewhere or other unless sickness or accident had overtaken him. Darrell was a man who understood thoroughly the principle of "doing

in Rome as the Romans do," and he had on many occasions, to
my knowledge, in the past applied that principle so well that he
was as safe as an Eskimo in his wanderings about the country;
and really safer by far, for he had learned all the Eskimo had to teach
him, and added to that knowledge the superiority of the white man's
trained mind, and a natural energy and resourcefulness that are rare
among men of any race.

Although it was not until a year later that we became certain
that the travels of Darrell over the northland of Canada had come
to a tragic ending, I shall insert here a brief sketch of the man and his
work. He was one that did not advertise, and although some of the
most wonderful journeys ever performed in Arctic lands were done by
him, the world would probably never have heard much of them even
had he lived a longer time.

Darrell had come from England as a young man and owned a farm
in Manitoba. I think it was the gold rush to the Yukon that first drew
him thence to the North, although at that time he did not go much
beyond Great Slave Lake, where he spent some time with the half-
caste and Indian hunters and travelers. He had already learned
their ways when David T. Hanbury came there in 1901 and induced
Darrell to join him on a trip eastward from Slave Lake to Chesterfield
Inlet.

After spending the winter near Hudson Bay, a party consisting of
Hanbury, Darrell, a third man named Sandy Ferguson, and about
twenty Eskimo went inland, crossing north over Back's Great Fish
River to the Arctic coast, following the coast west to the Coppermine
River and ascending it to Dismal Lake, and there crossing over the
divide which separates the waters of the Arctic Ocean from those of
Great Bear Lake. Here the Eskimo turned back in August, and on
their way home incidentally paid a visit to Captain Amundsen
when he was wintering on King William Island, while the three
white men proceeded by canoe across Great Bear Lake to the Mackenzie River. This was a journey of more than seven months in
which the entire party had lived wholly on the country. It was
Hanbury's last trip, but not so with Darrell.

I met Darrell first at Shingle Point on the Arctic coast, just west
of the Mackenzie River, when I was spending my first winter among

the Eskimo (1906–1907), and when he was on his way guiding a party of mounted policemen from Herschel Island to Fort Macpherson. That was always his way. He was about as new to that country as the policemen were, but still he was a competent guide, for he never lost his head, and after all, in most places in the North it is not difficult to find your way if you keep your wits about you.

It was the winter before I saw him that he had made one of his most wonderful journeys. That winter Captain Amundsen with the *Gjoa* was wintering at King Point, halfway between the Mackenzie River and Herschel Island. In the fall of 1905 Captain Amundsen, as the guest of some whalers, traveled south in their company across the Endicott Mountains to the Yukon. The whalers and Amundsen had several sleds, and Eskimo to do the housework and camp making, and they traveled over a well-known road, where it is only a matter of three or four days from the time you leave the last Eskimo camp on the north side of the divide, where you can any time purchase deer meat, condensed milk, flour, or any such article you think you may need, up to the time you come to the first Indian camp on the south side of the divide, where you can supply yourself with dried fish, venison, and other articles of food. Amundsen has of course never said a word to indicate that he considers this Alaskan journey he made a difficult one, which as a matter of fact it is not; but the world at large insists upon considering it a marvelous feat, and the story, which the telegraphs and cables flashed all over the world, of the arduous road over which Amundsen had come to Eagle City, keeps echoing and reëchoing in the speech of men and in the pages of magazines.

That same winter Darrell also made a trip south from the Arctic Ocean to the Yukon. Instead of having whalemen for companions and Eskimo for guides, he went alone. Instead of having several teams and sledges, he had no dogs and only a small hand sledge which he pulled behind him; and on that sledge he carried sixty pounds of mail. He made his way from Fort Macpherson over the mountains by a more difficult road than that followed by Amundsen's party. Although he traveled alone he had no adventures and no mishaps (adventures and mishaps seldom happen to a competent man), and when he arrived on the Yukon the telegraph despatches recorded the simple fact that mail had arrived from the imprisoned whalers in the Beaufort Sea, and not a word of who had brought it or how it had been brought.

On the Yukon Amundsen happened to meet Darrell. He recognized the feat for what it was — one of the most remarkable things ever done in Arctic lands. "With a crew of men like that," Amundsen says, "I could go to the moon." Although he no doubt never expected to see him again, Captain Amundsen invited Darrell to visit him on the *Gjoa* at Shingle Point. Darrell does not seem to have agreed to this at once, and Amundsen returned with his party north to the coast, leaving Darrell behind on the Yukon. But one day towards early spring Darrell turned up at Amundsen's camp at King Point. He had come alone again over the mountains by a new route, and without adventure, as always.

From the time I saw him guiding a party of mounted police in November, 1906, I did not see Darrell again until the summer of 1908, when I met him at Arctic Red River, the most northerly Hudson's Bay post on the Mackenzie River proper. In the meantime he had been making his quiet journeys alone, here and there through the north, and that fall I believe he crossed the mountains again to the Yukon. I do not know what his movements were from that on until the fall of 1910, when he appeared at the Eskimo village at the Baillie Islands, without dogs as usual, and dragging his sled behind him. The schooner *Rosie H.* was wintering there at the time, but Captain Wolki was away and the ship was under the command of her first officer, Harry Slate.

To travel alone and without dogs is an unheard of thing even among the Eskimo, and both they and Mr. Slate tried first to get Darrell to stop over and next offered to give him some dogs to haul his sled, but both without avail. He was used to traveling that way, he said, and it would be too much bother to hitch up the dogs in the morning. He told them further, truly, that nothing would go wrong so long as no accident happened, and that to have dogs with him if an accident did happen would be of no particular use.

Darrell had been with a canoe up Anderson River the previous summer and had left his camp near the mouth of the river at the foot of Liverpool Bay. In order to return there he started southwest from the Baillie Islands, and a few days later he met some Eskimo by whom he sent a letter to Mr. Slate. At first Darrell had intended to come and visit me (for our base at Langton Bay was only ninety miles east of the Baillie Islands), but Slate had told him that I would not be at home, and only Ilavinirk's family were keeping the camp for me. He had therefore decided not to come. The letter he wrote Mr. Slate, which contains some messages to me, is the last positive thing we know of Darrell. In it he says, as he had already told Slate, that he intended to go the three hundred miles or so to Fort Macpherson and thence across the mountains to Dawson, and intended to return the next year. Eskimo information makes it clear that he left his camp in Liverpool Bay, but in what direction he went we do not know. Personally, in making such a journey, I should have traveled along the coast; but Darrell was used to the woodlands, and certainly the woods are an advantage in a way, although the snow is soft among the trees. It may be that he tried to go straight overland through the forested area from Liverpool Bay to Fort Macpherson. It is also possible that he may at the last moment, because of approaching sickness or for some other reason, have taken to the ice of the Anderson River with the idea of reaching a camp of the Fort Good Hope Indians, who may be expected at one place or another after you get a hundred miles up the Anderson.

The only thing discovered since Darrell was last seen that may possibly be a clew, is that some Eskimo told me at the Baillie Islands in March, 1912, that the previous summer they had been in a boat up the Anderson River and had seen a blazed tree with some writing upon it. As a good many of the Fort Good Hope Indians can read and write, the chances are that this is some of their scribbling. Nevertheless I advised the Eskimo if they went up to the place again to cut down the tree and bring the piece containing the writing down to Captain Wolki at the Baillie Islands.

It is not likely we shall ever know what the ultimate end of Darrell was; but whatever it was, those who knew him feel sure that he met it bravely and without heroics.

When Dr. Anderson and Ilavinirk arrived, they came carrying pack loads from Langton Bay, for the snow had not yet come; but before they had been with us more than a day or two we had a heavy fall of snow which seemed to indicate that winter had begun. Some of the party therefore had to return the thirty or so miles to Langton Bay to fetch from our base there the sleds which we should need in our hunt for caribou in the early winter, while others had to work at the building of our house.

Dr. Anderson volunteered to go get the sleds from the seacoast, and it was decided that all but two of the Eskimo should accompany him, for there was heavy work involved. But before they started we all put in two days in building a house frame and in sodding it over roughly. The sodding was so poorly done that we later on had to do it all over again. The building was a simple affair. There were a pair of vertical posts about twenty feet apart and nine feet high, across the tops of which a ridgepole was laid. An essential feature of the walls was that they were not vertical, but sloped in, so that earth, no matter how carelessly it was thrown against the house, would fit in and not cave away as commonly happens when you try to build vertical walled houses in white men's fashion.

It is hard to say why it is, but some white man seem to feel there is something vulgar or degrading about a house wall that is not vertical, and everywhere on the Arctic coast you find white men trying to build warm houses by sodding up the outside of a vertical wall. The thing always fails, for the sod is sure to leave an open space between itself and the wall — a thing that need not happen in the prairie provinces of Canada (out of the sods of which I have seen warm houses built), but which is bound to happen in the Arctic where "sod" is but another name for loose earth.

When our house was built it was comfortable enough and a cheerful place. We left a square hole in the roof and under this we built a fire. Dr. Anderson and I would have preferred that this should be our heating system for the whole winter, for to white men there is something cheerful and homelike about a crackling fire. Not so with the Eskimo. For thousands of years their ancestors before them have never built any big fires, and it seems that the charm of a fire, so instinctively felt by a white man, is an incomprehensible idea to the Eskimo. They knew about sheet-iron stoves, one of which we had down on the seacoast, and it was beyond their comprehension

1. Frame of Coal Creek House, 1911–12.
2. Dease River House, February, 1911.

3. Dease River House, May, 1911.
4. Ruins (1910) of House occupied in 1908–9.

how any man could want to have an open fire if he could have a sheet-iron stove. I explained to them that the high and mighty of our land, who could perfectly well afford sheet-iron stoves, much prefer open fires. In connection with this I think they had an opinion of me to the effect that while I was fairly reliable in everyday matters, I had a sort of amiable weakness which led me to misrepresent my countrymen and to make them out far sillier than they really are.

When the house had been built and the sleds fetched from the sea-coast we gathered together, from the various places where we had left them behind, our stores of dried caribou and grizzly bear meat. We also prospected the country about in search of fishing lakes, and found that the most promising was the one in which Coal Creek heads, and which lies about six miles east of Horton River. This lake was five or six miles long and perhaps two miles wide at the widest part, and seemed to be well supplied with fresh-water trout and fresh-water cod. In the summer it had also been full of Back's greyling, bluefish, or Arctic trout (as they are variously called), but all of these seemed to have run out of the lake through Coal Creek to Horton River, about the time of the freeze-up.

The freeze-up, by the way, was far slower the fall of 1911 than in other years which we have spent in the Arctic. The earliest coming of frost experienced by us was the fall of 1908, when small lakes were thickly covered with ice on September 6th and the freezing of the sheltered portion of the sea began on that date. In 1911 we had a heavy rain as late as the 21st of October. Shallow lakes had been frozen before that, and also the quieter strips of Horton River; the rain was heavy enough to break the ice off the river, although it did not destroy the thicker ice of the small lakes. The deeper lakes had not been frozen at all before the warmer spell of which this late October rain was but one feature, and it was the beginning of November before the deepest of them were finally frozen over. We learned later that at various points on the coast it was late in November before the ocean was finally frozen, which was two months later than ordinary.

It seemed the first part of October that the caribou, which had been so numerous around Coal Creek in 1909–1910, were now not going to come at all. We made long hunts in various directions in vain.

There were not even any tracks to be seen. The ptarmigan were numerous, however, and we shot a good many of them, for our camp was this time so near our base at Langton Bay that we could afford to haul shotgun ammunition to it. The fishing was also turning out fairly well. We had three short nets in which we took from twenty to seventy-five pounds per day. This was not quite as much as we were eating, of course, for there were ten of us and fifteen dogs, so our dry meat stores from the summer began to dwindle.

I quite agree with Hanbury when he says that there is no way of telling about caribou migrations — when they will come or just where they will pass. It is a certain thing, however, that the time at which the freeze-up of the lakes and rivers occurs with reference to the first coming of the autumn has a marked influence on the direction of migration. It is no doubt the change in the quality of food, brought about by a change of weather, which makes caribou restless where they are and induces them to start out in search of better pastures; and when they have once started migrating they will cross a lake that they find frozen over and be deflected to the right or left by another which they find open. The result is that an exceptionally early or an exceptionally late freeze-up may throw the migration into a track this year that is far removed from the track of last year. We supposed, and no doubt it was true, that the lateness of the autumn of 1911 was in part responsible for the caribou not turning up as early as we had expected.

On October 27th our luck turned. During previous years I had been in the habit of doing most of the shooting for our party, but this year there were so many other able-bodied hunters in camp that I had decided to leave the hunting to them and devote my time to linguistic work, to the recording of Eskimo folk-lore in the original language, and the writing up of grammatical notes. It therefore fell to Tannaumirk to make the first discovery of caribou. He had gone eight or ten miles southeast and had seen one bull, but had decided not to approach him because of the absence of wind and the probability of being heard before he had come within shooting distance. The following day Palaiyak and Tannaumirk together went to look for this bull, but found instead a band of eight cows and calves, of which they were able to secure only one cow. After the shooting they followed the band for ten or more miles east and saw a great many tracks of caribou apparently moving south.

This was a time for letting linguistics go by the board for a day or two, for the fall caribou migration seemed to be beginning, and so all of us hunted the next day. Dr. Anderson went southeast, saw eight caribou and got five of them — two cows, two calves, and a young bull. I hunted first northeast, then east, and later southeast, a distance of perhaps twenty miles, and finally saw about a hundred caribou, but too late in the day to be able to do much about it. When I saw them first it was about an hour before sundown, and it was a good eight miles to go to reach the neighborhood of where they were, so that it was already half an hour after sundown when I got my first shot. I got four animals only, for it was getting dark and I could not follow them up. The next day Dr. Anderson and Tannaumirk fetched the meat of the five deer Dr. Anderson had killed and succeeded in getting two more. Palaiyak and I went to get the meat of those shot by me and killed three on the way. Ilavinirk went to tend the fish-nets and near the lake saw some caribou of which he secured two.

On the face of it, this seemed a good beginning, but it was really a wrong beginning; for the caribou apparently were coming from the southeast in a direction straight for our camp and had we waited a day or two they would have been all around us. As it was we had gone to meet them so far that we had seen them only towards dark each day and had not been able to make a good killing at any time, while the few we had killed were scattered in a semicircle ten or twelve miles in extent, which blocked the further advance of the migration towards us; for when the main body of the caribou got that far, the ground was crisscrossed with our snow-shoe tracks and the air was everywhere tainted with the smell of the animals that had been killed and cut up. This fence of disagreeable sights and smells turned the migration so that it never came any nearer to us. We did not fully realize at once that it was not coming nearer, and we did not therefore hunt as energetically as we might. We kept getting a few stray animals, however, until a total of about forty had been secured.

The year before on our journey up Horton River we had been forced to abandon one of our sledges and about a hundred pounds of

gear up Horton River, half way between Langton Bay and Great
Bear Lake. We now decided to go to fetch these things, partly because we wanted the sled, and also because we were anxious to make
a geological collection along the river. We had, true enough, picked
up specimens here and there on the way south the year before, but
the difficulties of transportation had limited us both in the number
and the size of the specimens, and we saw our chance now to supplement them. Accordingly on November 9th, Dr. Anderson, Tannaumirk, and I started up the river, and on December 15th we
reached the place where the sled had been abandoned.

On the way south we saw, about twenty miles southeast of our
camp, a considerable number of caribou and a great number of
tracks, but we made no special effort to get them. In the same
district on the way home we again saw a few tracks, though not so
many as when we went south. Evidently the caribou were keeping pretty well to the east of us and chiefly, as I have no doubt, for
the reason assigned above, that we had stopped their westward
migration by the line of deer kills which were a line of danger signals
that beckoned them away from the neighborhood of our camp.
November 20th we were home at our base camp again from this brief
up-river excursion, with a sled load of articles cached the year
before, and with a representative collection of rock specimens from
the various precipices and gorges along Horton River.

The chief interest in life among the civilized Eskimo in winter
is trapping fur. This was an interest of ours also, because we
were anxious to secure wolf, wolverine, and fox skins for museum specimens. It had accordingly been our arrangement on
hiring our Eskimo that we pay them not only $200 a year in money
or its equivalent (for the North Alaskans well understood the use of
money), but we had also agreed with them that whenever we had
nothing else for them to do they were to be free to trap, and half of
what they got should belong to them. Trapping around Coal
Creek had been poor and only something like thirty skins altogether
had been secured of foxes (white, red, and cross), wolves, and
wolverines. There was a firm belief in our party that foxes were
abundant down on the seacoast, and a strong desire therefore to move
to the sea for the purpose of trapping. This did not suit me at all.

I much preferred living in the wooded and well-sheltered creek bottom where our house stood to trapping foxes along the barren and shelterless coast of Langton Bay, but in order to keep peace in the family I finally agreed that some of our party should go down and try the trapping. Accordingly Ilavinirk's family and myself crossed the Melvill Mountains to Langton Bay, leaving the others behind on Horton River.

The same whale carcass which had been so useful to us the year before was still lying stranded on the beach west of Langton Bay. It had been about two miles west of the harbor the year before, but the past summer the waves had moved it about a mile nearer to our storehouse. Within a day or two from getting down to the coast we caught six white foxes near this carcass, but after that no more; and there was not a track to be seen.

This failure of our trapping even in the neighborhood of a stranded whale gives us the text for discussing the peculiar habits of the Arctic fox. In summer the white fox is a land animal, but in winter ninety per cent of them probably go off on the sea ice and live parasitically, as it were, upon the fruits of the labor of the polar bear. Whenever you see the tracks of a bear in winter you are likely to see following them the tracks of anywhere from one to a dozen foxes. Here and there on the ocean seals and fish that died from natural causes are thrown up and are found by the keen scent of the foxes. Here and there also when the ice is being crushed up into pressure ridges a few fish are caught and killed by the tumbling blocks, and these the fox also tries to find. But this supply depends upon accident and is not what the fox really relies upon. His main dependence is the skill and energy of the polar bear as a seal hunter. If the bear has hard luck and kills only a seal in a great while, he may devour the whole animal, and the fox which follows behind will go hungry. But if the bear has any ordinary luck at all, he will kill off more seals than he needs and will eat only a small part of what he kills, leaving the rest. When he has dropped asleep near the remains of his feast or has gone ahead about his business, the foxes that have been dogging his footsteps come up and eat whatever is left.

The polar bear can get seals only along the edge of open water. Certain years the winds are such that in the neighborhood of Cape

Parry, and elsewhere on the north coast of America, lanes of open water are only a few miles offshore. Those years there are plenty of polar bears around and consequently plenty of foxes also. The winter of 1911–1912 was exceptional apparently in ice conditions. None of our party ever went far out on the ice and I know of no one on the thousand-mile stretch between Cape Parry and Point Barrow who did, but knowing the habits of the bears and the foxes, it seems to me evident that there could have been no open water anywhere near shore, for the year was remarkable above all others to which the memory of the Eskimo in Alaska and the white traders extended, in the almost complete absence from the whole coast line from November until late March of both polar bears and foxes. At the Baillie Islands, for instance, energetic Eskimo trappers that habitually get two hundred foxes in winter had caught less than ten by the end of March. This was a universal calamity, comparable to a drought in a farming district, for the game upon which the Eskimo formerly lived has been destroyed throughout this entire district by the bringing in of firearms and the wanton destruction of food animals that followed, and the Eskimo now depend for their food and clothing in a large part upon the provisions which they can buy from the trading ships in summer in exchange for furs.

We spent between two and three weeks on the coast at the Langton Bay ship harbor without succeeding in getting any more foxes. Finally, December 11th, we started back south and December 13th we arrived home.

CHAPTER XXIV

WHETHER I was traveling about or staying at home, I was always devoting every available hour to the recording of folk-lore and linguistic material. While Ilavinirk, as we have said before, was not much good as a traveling companion (through a quality which he no doubt looks upon as conservatism and good sense, but which we diagnose as timidity), he possessed, besides other good qualities, as already mentioned, a vast store of the lore and religions of his people and was the most patient narrator of them whom I have ever found among Eskimo men. But as good an informant as willingness made him, he was under the disadvantage, from my point of view, of having, during the forty years or so of his lifetime, lived among people who spoke so many and various dialects that his own speech had become a mixture of a dozen or more, and I could never tell when he was pronouncing a word in the manner of Kotzebue Sound, when in the manner of the upper Noatak, and when after the fashion of the people of Point Barrow. He had also in his speech a strong flavoring from the Mackenzie district, but this did not trouble me so much, for by now my ear had become fairly familiar with the peculiarities of that dialect.

It has been my experience, like that of most other ethnologists, that women are better sources of information than men, for several reasons. Among primitive people, as among the uneducated of our own race, it is much easier to get straightforward answers and intelligent ones from the women than from the men; and although Ilavinirk was as an informant one of the best Eskimo men I have known, he was not nearly so good as his wife Mamayauk, who further had the advantage of speaking the Mackenzie dialect fairly pure. True, she was in the habit in her daily speech of using certain forms which did not belong to her own people, but she had been in the habit of doing this only for the last seven or eight years and was still conscious of the fact that these were foreign words, and she could, by watching herself, avoid them in giving information to me.

There was no danger of the winter becoming tedious to me, for in my linguistic and folk-lore investigations I had a field of inquiry as full of scientific interest as are researches in any other science, and full of human interest besides. There were unsuspected things coming up continually. One day I discovered an adjective that in Greenland has ceased to be an adjective and has become a suffix, and this threw light on the processes by which the language had grown to become the complicated and sensitive medium of expression that it is. Another day I would find a word of the everyday speech of Greenland to be reproduced in some ancient and barely understood charm or rigmarole of the Mackenzie district. This likewise threw its light on the history of the language. In the folk-lore I would come upon stories that were told at the Mackenzie mouth almost exactly as Rasmussen had heard them in Smith Sound, and there were even elements which might be construed to show European origin, or at least common origin with some of the folk-lore of Europe.

The days were never long enough and the patience of my Eskimo never sufficient to make me tire of the day's work before it was over. It was different with Dr. Anderson, who had now practically nothing to do, for winter is not favorable to zoölogical investigations, so far as land animals are concerned at least. No doubt he as well as I might have found the Eskimo folk-lore of interest, but he had never acquired the language well enough to be able to follow the narrators in the original (and neither did our Eskimo know English well enough to be able to express themselves sufficiently clearly or gracefully to give him much of an indication of what the character of their thoughts really was), for the Eskimo language is a very difficult one to learn. The grammatical structure is fundamentally different from English, and one has really to learn a different method of thought before one can acquire versatility in expression.

It is commonly believed that many white men who in one part of the world or another have associated with the Eskimo, have learned the language of the Eskimo, but this is not the case. I have known in Alaska white men who have been married to Eskimo women for over thirty years and whose grandchildren are now growing up, and yet they have acquired so little of the Eskimo language that when their own wives talk to their own children they have no idea what they are saying. The women usually, and the children commonly, know scarcely a word of English, and the white man knows scarcely a word of Eskimo; but there has grown up in their intercourse a sort of jargon analogous to "pigeon" English, or the so-called Chinook which is spoken in certain parts of the western United States and Canada. This Eskimo jargon in Alaska consists of a few English words, a few from the South Sea Islands (and especially the Hawaiian), a word or two from Spanish and from Danish, and a number of Eskimo words. The jargon vocabularies of different men vary from probably three hundred to five hundred words. There being no inflection, this language is easy to learn. It can be picked up in a week and will serve for the expression of the ordinary simple ideas concerning the everyday life of the North. The jargon is, however, quite incapable of expressing any fine shades of thought, and those who know it only, get the impression of the Eskimo that their minds are more impoverished and their thoughts cruder than is really the case.

Perhaps the chief stumbling-block in the way of the ordinary white man in an attempt to learn the language is that his mental habits incline him to deal in nouns modified by adjectives. If there were no adjectives in Eskimo, the white man would soon discover the fact that adjectives cannot be used to modify nouns. There are, however, as a matter of fact, a good many adjectives, but they are not used in the manner of ours, except on extraordinary occasions. When the typical white man begins to learn Eskimo, he will find some Eskimo who knows a little English and will cross-question him, writing down as a result a vocabulary which he proceeds to learn. Taking an object in his hand to make sure that he is not misunderstood, the white man will ask: "What is your word for knife?" and the Eskimo will reply "Savik"; "And what is your word for 'big'?" will be the next question; and the answer in the Mackenzie River dialect will be "angiyok." "Now," thinks the white man, "I know how to say 'big knife'"; but as a matter of fact he does not know how to say "big knife" at all, for the Eskimo does not say "big knife" by attaching the adjective for "big" to the word for "knife." He has an entirely different word for a big knife from the word he uses for a small knife. We, in speaking of a small horse, have the option of calling it a small horse or calling it a pony; practically speaking, in everyday life, the Eskimo has no option. If he does not have an entirely different word for a "small horse" or a "small knife" he will nevertheless not use an adjective, but will use a suffix to indicate smallness as we can do in a few isolated cases, as in "hill" and "hillock" and "river" and "rivulet."

The system of suffixes to modify the meaning of words is far more developed with the Eskimo than with us, and is a very useful thing in the expression of shades of meaning and in the clear statement of new ideas. We can say *hill* and *hilly* and *hilliness* and possibly we may say *hillocky*, but we can never say *hillockiness*, although it seems to me that it would be an excellent thing if we could, for I have found by experience that the principle lends itself well to the expression of the most finely shaded meanings. The Eskimo can not only say "hillockiness," or things analogous to that, but he may go on and add six or eight or even more suffixes to a single word, each suffix carrying its clear meaning that modifies the fundamental idea of the statement. There are over a hundred and sixty suffixes in the Mackenzie dialect, and the meanings which they express are far more than that number. About the only suffixes which cannot be tacked one on to the other are those of contradictory meanings, such as those implying longness and shortness or quickness and slowness.

To illustrate how the principle works when applied to nouns, we will take the word *iglu*, which in those Eskimo dialects where it is used at all means a dwelling place of any kind, and in some places may apply to the den of an animal or the nest of a bird, although in our common dictionaries and works of travel it appears only as the word for snow-hut. Attaching appropriate suffixes to the stem of *iglu*, we have *iglupûk*, a large house; *iglunguak*, a make-believe house or a play house, something which is not really a house but you pretend it is; *iglorak*, a wooden house; *iglukuk*, a ruined house; *igluliak*, a house that some one built; *iglulianga*, the house that he built; *igluliakpuk*, the house that the two of us built; *iglulik*, that which contains houses (used for instance for an island which is inhabited); *iglutun*, like a house. All of these suffixes and a great many others are used in addition to the declension endings, which are analogous to those of Latin or Anglo-Saxon, for instance. These run as follows for the singular:

NOMINATIVE	*iglum*	
ACCUSATIVE	*iglu*	
TERMINALIS	*iglumun,*	to the house
ABLATIVE	*iglumin,*	from the house
INSTRUMENTAL	*iglumik,*	by means of the house
VIALIS	*iglukun,*	through the house
LOCATIVE	*iglumi,*	in the house

This is but the beginning. The nouns are used in the singular, dual, and plural; and their use is of course idiomatic, so that you can never tell for certain from the English meaning what case you must use in the Eskimo. But the noun is simple, compared with the verb. "Sum" in Latin was the ordinary form for "I am." The pronoun "ego" was used rarely and chiefly for emphasis. Similarly in the Eskimo, in the case of transitive verbs, not only is the subject incorporated but the object also, and either the subject or the object may be in the singular, dual, or plural number. Besides, there are inflections for tenses, and then come the suffixes proper, which have a nature peculiar to themselves; and most confusing of all to the ordinary white man is the fact that these suffixes undergo certain euphonistic and other sound changes, so that when you have learned to recognize the suffix in one word, you may fail to recognize the same suffix in the next.

No man has ever worked out the number of possible different ways in which a single Eskimo verb may be used, but it is undoubtedly up in the tens of thousands, if not in the hundreds of thousands. At first glance it may seem that you could take an Eskimo verb and find out how many suffixes could be used with it, and that you could then by the laws of permutation and combination arrive at the number of different possible combinations by multiplying $1 \times 2 \times 3 \times 4$ and so on up to 16, or 23, or whatever the number of usable suffixes may be; but the case is not so simple as that, for some of the suffixes are really identical in meaning and should not therefore be used together, and others, while apparently identical in meaning, may nevertheless be used together ; so that it is only by the method of trial and error that the result can be arrived at, and then only by an Eskimo or by some white man who through a lifetime of study has acquired the "feeling" of the language.

It is common to hear the assertion that the Eskimo is a simple language and easy to learn, and you may meet in any town in America or Europe some person who says to you, "I had a friend who lived in Alaska (or Labrador, or Hudson's Bay) and he learned to speak Eskimo in three months." That idea of course is based on the supposition that the jargon which the white men use in dealing with the Eskimo is in reality the language of the Eskimo ; but it is not, nor anything like it.

In a book such as this it is hopeless to attempt giving an outline of the grammatical principles of the language. Any one who is sufficiently interested and who happens to know German can get them fairly laid down in the grammar of Samuel Kleinschmidt. It may, however, be worth while, for purposes of illustration, to give a few verb forms that show how suffixes (or infixes, rather) may be joined on to a verb to modify its meaning.

We shall take the verb in the third person, intransitive, which in the Mackenzie dialect has the form *tikitok* (Greenland form : tikitpok), he has arrived. Without giving any formal conjugation we set down the following at random :

tikitpit	have you arrived ? (singular)
tikitpetik	have you arrived ? (dual)
tikitpisi	have you arrived ? (plural)
tikitga	he arrived at it, he reached it.
tikinngitga	he did not reach it.
tikiniakpa	will he arrive ?
tikiniakpiung	shall you arrive at it ? shall you reach it ?
tikiniakpaunggiak	will he probably reach it ?
tikiniakpalungniakpaung	will he probably reach it ?
tikiniaksungnakpaunngok	he said : would he be likely to reach it, one wonders.

We have stretched this word out now by joining to it suffixes (or as they may preferably be called, infixes), until it may seem to the reader in all conscience long enough, but this is not half what a skillful Eskimo could do with it. Perhaps the example will suffice, however, to incline us to the idea that the conjugation of the Eskimo verb is not a very simple matter.

What we started out to show here, and it may be hoped that we have succeeded, is that the Eskimo is not only an exceedingly complicated language, but also very different from English. To put it roughly, there is no doubt that for an Englishman it would be much easier to acquire Russian, Swedish, French, and Greek than to acquire Eskimo alone. To take the only actual case the circumstances of which are fully known to me, which is of course my own, it may be said that I had a book knowledge of the Eskimo before going to the North and I have lived for five years in houses where nothing but Eskimo was spoken. I listened to every word with all my ears, for to acquire the language has been both my chief work and my chief pastime, and yet it was only the last of the five winters that my command of the language had become such that I could follow without effort the ordinary conversations going on in the house.

This has turned into an extensive digression on Eskimo linguistics, although it was meant in the beginning only as an explanation of why it was that I found no difficulty in passing the long winter days, while it was a tedious and endless time for Dr. Anderson. He used to lecture me on the consolation that a smoker can get from his pipe, but I noticed that the atmosphere of the house got fairly thick with smoke before he got any noticeable consolation out of it. Finally, shortly after Christmas, he made up his mind that he would like to make the 150-mile trip to the Baillie Islands, partly to pass away the time and also to begin now the transportation to our shipping point of some of our more valuable scientific collections.

Dr. Anderson accordingly set out December 27th for the Baillie Islands with two sleds and accompanied by Palaiyak, Tannaumirk, and Pannigabluk, the last named of whom had made up her mind to sever her connection with our party. They went by way of Langton Bay to pick up provisions for the journey, for we had there considerable quantities of flour and other "civilized" foods which we had bought from the *Teddy Bear*. We made it a principle to live on the country when we were anywhere else than at Langton Bay, and to live at Langton Bay on the stores we had purchased and which we kept there, for indeed there was nothing else to live on at the place except the whale which had now been two years dead (thawed two summers and frozen two winters), and was therefore not so palatable as it had been the year before. By this I do not mean to say that it was unfit for food. We did, as a matter of fact, cut up some of it to eat, and that by choice rather than through necessity. The Eskimo found it an agreeable change of diet from the fish, venison, and baking powder bread, and I found it not particularly distasteful, although I preferred the monotony of the venison to the change to rotten whale.

While Dr. Anderson was gone we at the home camp altered in no way our ordinary habits of life. There was not much daylight for hunting, so Ilavinirk merely tended his traps and the fish nets. Tending fish nets is not, by the way, the most pleasant occupation imaginable in an Arctic January. The nets were set underneath the ice, which had now become about four feet thick, and it took considerable work with a pick every day to make a hole so that the net could be hauled out, and when it was hauled out the fish had to be disentangled from the meshes with the bare hands. Sticking your hands into ice water when the weather is something like 40° below zero, and especially if the wind is blowing, is as unpleasant a job as one can well undertake. We have to use the bare hands also in skinning the caribou which we kill in winter, but that is not nearly so serious a matter, for whenever your hands get cold you can warm them by sticking them inside the body of the animal you are cutting up.

The fishing was gradually getting poorer and poorer. The outlet of the lake had frozen to the bottom early in the fall, so that we knew the fish were still in the lake, but somehow the three kinds other than the fresh-water cod seemed to get sleepy and sluggish towards midwinter and to cease swimming about. Possibly they were, in a way, hibernating in the deepest parts of the lake. The "ling" (as I believe the fresh-water cod is called) seemed to get more active as winter advanced, so that while in the fall these cod had been no more than ten per cent of the catch, by Christmas a single net would frequently contain a dozen cod and only three or four of the other kinds of fish. Finally towards the middle of January

Coal Seam, Coal Creek.

Smoking Mountains (Burning Coal Mines), Franklin Bay.

the ice had become so thick and the fish so few that I agreed with Ilavinirk in thinking it was scarcely worth while to continue.

Of course it is only after having tried it that one can learn how best to do such a thing as to winter under the conditions which we had to face. During the few days while we were building our house in the fall we noticed that Back's greyling were running down the creek past us in continuous streams day and night. Had we not been in such a hurry to build the house and had we put up a fish trap instead, we could have taken tens of thousands of fish at our very door; but when the house had been built and we turned our attention to the fishing, the run was already over. Had we to winter again in Coal Creek we could, on the basis of this knowledge, rely on putting up tons of fish in the few weeks immediately preceding the freeze up. It took us some time also to find the best fishing places in the lake. With plenty of nets, ranging from a $2\frac{1}{2}$-inch to a 5-inch mesh, a large quantity of food could be gotten together while the ice is thin the first few weeks after it forms, by setting the nets in the right places.

Although Ilavinirk had found out in the fall that there were no white foxes around Langton Bay, he was by the middle of January thoroughly convinced that now there must be lots of them everywhere on the seacoast and especially on the promontories, such as Cape Bathurst. I was bound to put my entire time on the linguistic work and he was bound that nothing at Coal Creek should succeed in keeping us there any longer than until Dr. Anderson returned, so although he hunted every day, I was as sure as I know he was that he would find no game. "I knew in my heart" that had I cared to make a good day's hunt to the eastward I should have been able to find something, but after all, my only concern this winter was to keep my Eskimo in good humor and to follow them around, writing folk-lore from their dictation whenever they were in the house. Accordingly, when Dr. Anderson returned, January 30th, we began making preparations to move to the coast.

He brought back from the Baillie Islands such news as was in a measure to be expected. Captain Wolki and his ship's company were wintering there, and so was Captain Bernard of the *Teddy Bear*. There had been sickness as always and people were dying now and then.   One of those who had died was Natkusiak's wife.   He had also become a bit tired of his association with the Baillie Islanders, and consequently had decided to return to us with Dr. Anderson. Tannaumirk, on the other hand, had been picked up as a desirable son-in-law by one of the Baillie Islands families and had therefore left our service.

Although Natkusiak reported that all winter the people of the Baillie Islands had caught no foxes, still he agreed with Ilavinirk in thinking that surely there must be plenty of them out at Cape Parry.   Temperamentally it seems difficult for Eskimo to imagine that things can change.   Natkusiak had found plenty of foxes on Cape Parry in January, 1910, and he could not see why there should not be plenty also in January, 1912.   But I felt certain that the same condition, namely the distance from land of the open water, that kept the foxes away from Cape Bathurst must also be keeping them away from Cape Parry.

As my chief object was to keep the Eskimo in good humor, and as even Dr. Anderson seemed a bit anxious to move (for when he stayed in camp there was nothing for him to do), we started on February 15th, hauling our belongings towards Langton Bay.   For the first fifteen or eighteen miles of this journey we had to follow the river, but when the time came for leaving it and striking across over the mountains to Langton Bay, we camped for a few days at the last trees, so that while some of us advanced part of our gear halfway from the river to Langton Bay and cached it there, Dr. Anderson, with Natkusiak for company, was able to make a short trip down Horton River in search of bush rabbits, the skins of which he wanted for scientific specimens.   In ordinary years rabbits abound among the large willows north of the spruce tree line towards the mouth of Horton River.

When Dr. Anderson returned, all of us struck across country for the sea; and on February 20th we reached Langton Bay to find there encamped in our storehouse the Baillie Islands Eskimo Alingnak with his wife Guninana and their adopted daughter.   At first it seemed a nuisance to find them there, for I had heard much of the contagious sickness from which Alingnak suffered, and of the laziness which white men and Eskimo alike seem to have found his chief characteristic. We found him, however, to be a cheerful and good companion and not at all lazy, although incapable of hard work through ill health. But his wife Guninana proved to be so valuable a find for my linguistic work that no matter what the rest of the family might have been, I should have been glad to keep them. Up to this time my chief informant had been Mamayauk, but I found that Guninana was far better versed in the ancient lore of her people, spoke the Baillie Islands dialect with undoubted purity of accent, and was the most cheerful and long-suffering person I have ever encountered in answering what must necessarily be tedious questions because of the great sameness about them and their (to the Eskimo mind) complete lack of point; for naturally the Eskimo can see little importance in the laws of sound change between dialects, or in the modifications of sounds through association with other sounds within a word.

My experience of two years before had shown that at this season of the year there was a probability of finding caribou in the low hills between Langton Bay and Darnley Bay. It suited everybody that Dr. Anderson and most of the able-bodied men should go down there (which they did on February 25th) looking for the caribou and with the hope of trapping foxes, while the rest of us remained at Langton Bay, I writing folk-lore at Guninana's dictation while the others kept house.

Guninana was not only well informed, but was also, fortunately for me, not such a good Christian as the rest of her countrymen. She had not yet learned that the native lore of her people was essentially wicked and needed to be forgotten, and she told me of how diseases were controlled, how famines were averted, how people were killed or cured by magic, how the future could be foretold and the secrets of the past uncovered, how people could see through hills and fly to the moon, and various things of that sort of which the Christian Eskimo pretend an ignorance and of which they will either tell you nothing or else half truths and untruths. Personally I have always been unable to see why the creations of the Eskimo's imagination should be any more wicked than our "blue-beards," or why the knowledge of the Eskimo method of reading the future should be any more likely to lead to damnation than our palmistry or the reading of the grounds in the bottom of a teacup; but so it seems to be. And if there are only some of the missionaries who think the native lore wicked, that minority have impressed their views so completely on the Eskimo that no Eskimo who values his immortal soul (and most of them value their immortal souls extravagantly) will defile himself or endanger his eternal welfare by telling the things which they still believe quite as much as they ever did, but which they now consider to be wicked, and which they have abjured on the principle of its not profiting a man to gain the whole earth if he lose his own soul. Most of the Eskimo are a bit regretful over having surrendered the familiar spirits which formerly served them and did their every bidding: changed for them the winds, cured their children when they were ill, and brought caribou to be killed at the very front doors of the houses. Many of them express freely their regret that the use of such useful magic should be incompatible with salvation.

While Dr. Anderson and his party were hunting caribou east of the bay, one or another of them paid us a visit every two or three days, and the whole party finally returned March 10th. They had killed eleven deer and seen a good many others and had trapped two or three foxes. The idea of going to Cape Parry had been quite given up because shortly before we came to the coast Alingnak had been out there and had seen no tracks of either polar bear or fox.

At the place where they had been hunting caribou, which was, by the way, the lake of which Natkusiak and I had made such a hazardous crossing the previous June, there is an excellent fishing place, well known to the Baillie Islands Eskimo, where Alingnak in the fall had put up several hundred pounds of fish; and although the killing of eleven caribou in two weeks was in itself nothing much, still the meat amounted to a good deal when they brought it home because they had lived in part on the fish cache and had not been compelled to feed the caribou meat up so fast to the dogs, as they otherwise would have had to do.

On March 12th visitors from the Baillie Islands arrived. They were the Mackenzie River couple Kommana and Ituayok, with their little daughter Siksigak, and Alingnak's father, Iyituaryuk. They had come in seven days from the winter settlement of Nogarvik, which is about twelve miles east of the Baillie Islands. On the way they had secured only two seals and had consequently been on short rations. They told further stories of illness and death at the Baillie Islands, and a woman well known to us, named Inonngranna, had gone permanently insane. We learned later that Captain Wolki and the other white men at the Baillie Islands were inclined to blame the insanity to a violent religious revival in which the woman had been one of the chief participants. There may be something in that theory, for the fear of hell is among the newly Christianized Eskimo an obsession such as we can scarcely comprehend; but I think it more likely that the insanity may have had some deeper organic cause, although the woman had apparently been in the best of health up to the time of the outbreak.

Kommana, in order to buy my favor, brought me a present which he knew I would appreciate: a knife of ancient pattern and with a well-attested history. There had been a man in the Point Atkinson community some forty years ago who became intolerable to his fellows, and three of the most energetic and public-spirited men volunteered to execute him. This matter had the complete approval of the community, and was the knowledge of every one except the victim. One day the three men took him aside and of a sudden the most resolute, the owner of the knife, stabbed the man in the back with this very knife. The Eskimo system of government, which is really no system at all (or in other words a communistic anarchy), has but this one punishment, except that the power of public opinion is so much stronger with them than with us that the mere knowledge of having displeased the community would be severe punishment in itself. It seems then, on the face of it, that removing an intolerable man in the manner just described is not a bad way of dealing with a difficult situation; and it would not be if the story ended there. But the weak point of the system is that no matter if the man's relations may have been loudest of all in denouncing him and demanding that he should be killed, still the moment that any one kills him it becomes the duty of his relatives to take blood revenge on some member of the family of those who helped do the killing. Some one has to be killed, though it need not be the man directly responsible — it may quite as well be his decrepit mother or his little niece; and even that does not square things, for as soon as the relation has been killed in revenge for the execution, it becomes the duty of the executioner and his family to take revenge again upon the family of the man originally executed, so that there commences a blood feud which has no ending until the tribe divides in two sections, one of which moves to a distant place quite out of the reach of the other. This is the general way things run, but it seems that in the particular case with which our story of the knife is concerned, the relations of the executed man made it known that they intended to kill all the executioners, and within four or five years they had succeeded in killing two of them. But the third man, the owner of the knife, had been so watchful and had carried this long knife around with him so constantly that he had not yet been killed when a severe epidemic of measles swept off most of the family of the avengers, with the result that the owner of the knife lived for many years and finally died a natural death.

After telling the story of the knife, Kommana handed it to me. I immediately asked him what he wanted in payment for it, but before he had named his price some one remarked that the owner of the knife was the father of Guninana, the woman who for the last three weeks had been a member of our party. I asked Kommana then how he came by the knife, and he said that just last fall, on the way from the Mackenzie River to the Baillie Islands, he happened to pass the grave on which the knife was lying and he thought to himself he would pick it up and give it to me. It seemed to me that Guninana might have a word to say about the matter; and it throws an interesting light on their habits of thought that she replied that the knife had belonged to her father and not to her, and that if Kommana dared to take the risk of removing it from the grave it was no concern of hers, and if any one got a price for it it should be Kommana, for he had brought it, and he and his family were running all the risks (of supernatural punishment). Kommana's comment on this was that surely he was the man to be paid; and as for being afraid of taking the knife from the grave, that was a matter which did not worry him very much, because wherever he went he carried a prayer book and hymnal with him and never neglected saying his prayers at night and grace before meals, and he felt sure therefore that nothing evil could harm him. Guninana did not seem to feel the least resentment in the matter, but apparently was not quite so certain as Kommana that no supernatural punishment would follow the offense; it was a matter entirely between Kommana and the supernatural powers and she had no concern in it, nor wished to have.

After the arrival of this last party I devoted my inquiries for some days, not to the folk-lore and linguistic side, but to the actual history of the people at the time, some fifty years ago, when Iyituaryuk was a boy, with special reference to what they knew about the relations between the Baillie Islands Eskimo and the Fort Good Hope (Hare) Indians. The details are too complicated for setting down here, but the net result was to show that the relation had been semi-friendly with occasional trade intercourse; that there had been killings now and then (in the way of murders); that on both sides captives had now and then been carried off and had been allowed to live by their captors; and that in one case an Eskimo child had been sold for a definite price to Indians, among whom she is said to be still living.

My informants went into much detail willingly about the various customs of man-killing. They agreed that in general to kill a man was about the equivalent of killing a whale, though they were a little doubtful whether the killing of an Eskimo was to be considered quite so much of an achievement as the killing of whale; but an Indian was quite up to a whale. In either case the one who did the killing was entitled to two tattoo lines across his face. If a whale was killed, the man had a line tattooed from the corners of the mouth to the lobes of the ears; but if an Indian had been killed the tattoo lines were from the nose to the ears. On the other hand, Iyituaryuk had seen Indians tattooed around the roots of the hair and had been told that those were Indians who had killed Eskimo. In the case of the killing of either a whale or an Indian the Eskimo who did it had to refrain from all work for five days and from certain foods for a year. Notably he must not eat the intestines of any animals nor their heads.

CHAPTER XXV

WE had already at Langton Bay done archæological work upon which we had been able to base certain important conclusions with reference to the Eskimo of that district. The transportation problem, the matter of hauling our finds from Langton Bay to the Baillie Islands, was so serious that it had long seemed unlikely we could accomplish much more the coming spring than the mere hauling to the Baillie Islands of the materials which we had already. Dr. Anderson's specimens of caribou skins, grizzly bears, and polar bears were especially numerous, heavy, and bulky. As for the linguistic and folk-lore investigations, they could of course go on without end. Guninana alone could have told me stories, she said (and I suppose it to be true), that it would have taken me years to write down.

It had always seemed to me that important results were to be looked for from archæological work done at Point Barrow, the most northerly point of the western half of the continent of America, and anything we could find at Point Barrow would be easy of transportation to civilization, for whaling ships, freighters, and United States revenue cutters call there each year. Dr. Anderson and I therefore talked the matter over, and for the reason already mentioned (and others which need not be entered into) I decided to make the thousand-mile trip to Point Barrow by sled. On the way I intended to visit for ethnological purposes every Eskimo settlement along the coast. I could do that, travel slowly, and yet get to Point Barrow in plenty of time to put in the season at archæological work before taking the ship for home. Dr. Anderson and our Eskimo could take care of the transportation work from Langton Bay to the Baillie Islands, and if they had any spare time they could do a little digging in the house ruins at the mouth of the Horton River or elsewhere, while Anderson would of course concern himself with zoölogical collecting.

After this plan had been decided upon it took us but a few days to get ready, and on March 20th we started towards the Baillie Islands with three sledges loaded with scientific specimens. On March 22d we arrived there, or rather at the Eskimo settlement at the tip of Cape Bathurst, where the *Rosie H.* and the *Teddy Bear* were also wintering.

After a week spent pleasantly in visiting Captain Bernard and Captain Wolki, Natkusiak and I started April 1st for the west on one of our longest journeys together, leaving Dr. Anderson and the rest of the party to return to Langton Bay. The boy Palaiyak accompanied us with the intention of going as far as Herschel Island to visit his relatives and to return to Langton Bay in the summer aboard the *Belvedere*.

The journey towards Point Barrow, although a long one, is very simple, for it is never much over two hundred miles between houses and there are four points at least where one can count on securing provisions — from Captain Anderson of the *North Star* trading schooner at Point Atkinson, from Mr. Young and Mr. Fry at the Church of England mission on the eastern edge of the Mackenzie delta, from Captain Cottle of the *Belvedere* and the mounted police at Herschel Island, and from Mr. Leffingwell, where he was carrying forward his geological studies on the north coast of Alaska at Flaxman Island. And then at Point Barrow we were sure of a welcome from old friends and of walking into an abundance of almost everything that a man could wish for to minister to his comfort in the Arctic.

After crossing Liverpool Bay in two days we came to the house of Mr. John Anderson, near Cape Dalhousie, where he had been trapping alone all winter, visited once a month or so by his brother, Captain Matt Anderson, whose winter quarters were at Point Atkinson, about fifty-seven miles to the west. When I told Mr. Anderson of the things we had been doing the past two or three years, it seemed to him that we had gone through many hardships and had done difficult things; but it seemed to me that living alone as he was doing and monotonously visiting the same circle of traps day after day, with nothing to look forward to but the monthly visits of his brother, was a thing I was less eager to try than to repeat our own experiences.

2 B

He had not even any dogs for company or to help him with his work, and the day we spent with him we helped him haul to the house a load or two of firewood from the beach about half a mile away. This is so near the mouth of the Mackenzie that in favorable locations there are hundreds of cords of driftwood to the mile of beach.

Although we learned that Captain Anderson with his wonderful team of dogs (trained after the manner of the Alaskan sweepstakes racers that go the four hundred miles from Nome to Candle in three days) was in the habit of coming from Point Atkinson to his brother's trapping camp in seven hours, it took us nearly three days to make the same distance, for this is a gameless coast and our sled was heavy with seal and whale meat for dog food. We could no doubt have made the distance in two days, but certain deserted Eskimo houses in which it was convenient to camp induced us to divide the journey in three sections.

At Point Atkinson April 5th we found not only Captain Matthew Anderson and the village of Eskimo who had gathered there around the wintering place of the *North Star*, but also Rev. Mr. Fry, a Church of England missionary to the Eskimo of the Mackenzie district, who was on his way to the Baillie Islands. Mr. Fry, although young in the service, brought a good deal of enthusiasm to the work and had linguistic ability evidently beyond the ordinary, for he had already in two years picked up a smattering of the Eskimo which was considerably in excess of that commonly acquired by whalemen in an entire lifetime.

I was especially interested in meeting Mr. Fry, because I wanted to learn from him his attitude with reference to certain matters which I had often discussed with various Eskimo, most often with our own employees, notably the form which certain Christian doctrines have taken in their minds, as described by me in Chapter XXVII of this book headed "On the Conversion of the Heathen." I found, as I had expected, that although Mr. Fry's ideas of Christianity were more those which one might have expected forty years ago than those in vogue in our enlightened churches of to-day, still he is in no way intentionally responsible for most of the curious ideas which the Eskimo hold of his teachings and those of his senior, Mr. Whittaker.

In the village near Captain Anderson's ship was, among others, a young boy who had been for several months in Mr. Fry's house for the purpose of learning English as well as mastering the elements of Christianity. Mr. Fry and I had various talks while he was with us about whether the Eskimo still retained the doctrines of their old system, my point of view being that they believed now everything which they had ever believed, and all the doctrines and facts of Christianity on top of that. Mr. Fry felt certain that this young man at least had quite relinquished all the old beliefs.

The day before I left Captain Anderson's place Mr. Fry left for the Baillie Islands. It was unfortunately not until after he had gone that Captain Anderson and I got into a talk with the young man who had so long lived with Mr. Fry in his house and who was therefore considered by the rest of the Eskimo to be an authority on the doctrines of the Church. I asked him whether he believed his countrymen were able to fly to the moon, or from one village to another, magically. He said, and there were half a dozen other people in the house at the time who agreed with him, that the fact of many people being able to fly to the moon was a matter of common knowledge, just as their ability to walk on snow-shoes or to snare ptarmigan was a matter of common knowledge. We asked the boy to specify some of the people who could do this, and he named among others Alualuk, at whose house I would sleep on my way west the first day after leaving Captain Anderson's place. He also specified a young man whom I knew well, named Kublualuk, who had long been in the employ of the mounted police at Herschel Island. Alualuk, he said, had unfortunately embraced Christianity and had since then ceased to fly, but Kublualuk, he thought, had not yet been converted and would still have his old powers. There were others who could do it too, some of them right in the village beside us; but he thought that perhaps none of them would fly even if I asked them to, because they now understood that to employ familiar spirits is wicked and that a man cannot employ them without endangering his prospects of salvation.

After he had given us all the information he had with regard to flying, the boy asked me what I would give any one who would perform the magic flight for me, and I suggested my rifle and field glasses, both of which were of a kind and quality much coveted by the Eskimo.

The young man thought he would very likely be able to find some one who would fly for me in order to get these articles, although he said that the risk of offending God was considerable and the pay small in proportion to the risk. Upon hearing this, Captain Anderson volunteered to give any of them the schooner *North Star* with her entire cargo, suggesting at the same time that the risk of damnation was not very great, especially if some young man did the flying, for he would no doubt have ample time in which to repent of his wickedness before he died. Of course nothing came of the conversation, for the boy canvassed the village without finding any one who would weigh the prospect of gaining a schooner against the prospect of losing his soul. Captain Anderson said, however, he would be sure when Mr. Fry returned to inform him in exactly how far his favorite disciple and housemate had renounced the beliefs of his Eskimo forefathers.

I stayed at Captain Anderson's several days merely because there was no hurry, for all I had to do was to reach Point Barrow within two months. There was always interesting information to pick up from talking with the old people of the village, and incidentally I was able to be of some slight use to Mr. Fry in explaining certain things to the Eskimo and in assisting at a ceremony of vaccination. There was a rumor that smallpox was prevalent among the Indians in the interior of Alaska, and it goes without saying that an attack of this disease upon the Eskimo of the Mackenzie district would probably carry off most of the few whom the measles have allowed to survive until now.

On the morning of April 11th early we started on our westward march again. By fast travel we reached the eastern edge of the Mackenzie delta proper at eight in the evening and lodged at the house of an old friend of mine, Alualuk (mentioned before), whom I had known on my first expedition in 1906. Alualuk had then been a shaman in possession of half a dozen familiar spirits which enabled him to cure diseases, wake people from the dead, and perform various miracles with the greatest ease. He told me now that since I saw him last he had become a Christian, had renounced all his familiar spirits, and was now as powerless as I or any other man in dealing with the things of the other world. He told me that not only had he found it an inconvenience to be without the assistance of the spirits which had served him so long and efficiently, but he also missed them as one misses a friend who is dead or who has gone away, for his association with them had been so intimate. Also, he said, the spirits grieved at having been separated from him and he pitied them in their loneliness. Some of them had been moved to anger rather than to grief at being cast out; one or two of them, in fact, would lose no opportunity of doing him harm if they could, so that he had to be very watchful in saying his prayers and keeping the commandments of the Christian Church in order to assure himself of the protection of Jesus from the wiles and meditated attacks of these his former servants. He reminded me that, as I no doubt knew, he had waked Taiakpanna from the dead when he had died a few years ago. That was while the spirits served him. Now Taiakpanna had died again and this time he (Alualuk) had been powerless to wake him from the dead. He could now only weep for the loss of his friend and pray that his soul might have found salvation.

We were entertained for a day most hospitably by Alualuk's family. They were living comfortably for the present, with an abundance of fish to eat, but they complained much of prospective poverty, for they had been able to get very few foxes and would have little with which to buy tea and tobacco the following summer.

Living as a neighbor of Alualuk's in a tent a mile or two away was an old acquaintance of mine, a Swiss-American named John Gruben, who had been on the north coast of Alaska for a good many years and whom I first knew at Flaxman Island in 1907. He was now traveling about among the Mackenzie Eskimo representing Captain Cottle and trying to do some trading for him, a thing that was impossible in the nature of the case, for the people had nothing with which to pay for anything they might want to buy.

April 13th we left Alualuk's, and in a day's journey of something over forty miles we reached the Church of England Mission at Kittegaryuit, on the mainland opposite Richard Island. Here we were received with the greatest hospitality by Mr. Young, an old worker in the mission field. We stayed with him several days, partly because we enjoyed it and there was no reason for hurrying, and partly also to give me time to write out a list of Eskimo inflections and suffixes for the use of Mr. Fry in his work of acquiring the language.

After spending five pleasant days with Mr. Young in his comfortable house we resumed our journeying again, and went on about eighteen miles to another camp of Eskimo whom I had known when I wintered in this district in 1906, and the day after that we reached a village of four or five houses at Tununirk, the south point of Richard Island. It was on Friday that we came there. This was the home of my old friend Ovayuak, who had entertained me so generously at his house for several months six years before on my first visit to the country. I had therefore to stay for several days to talk over old times. There was so much rejoicing in camp over our visit that although the main occupation of the community was rabbit hunting and although there was nothing to eat except the rabbits shot by the men and the ptarmigan snared and the fish hooked by the women, still all these occupations were suspended in honor of our coming, and we feasted so energetically that by Saturday night we had eaten up all the food that was in camp. This did not seem serious to me in the evening, for there were ptarmigan on every hillside and rabbits in every bush, and doubtless a good many fat fish under the ice right in front of our tent door. But on Sunday morning, as I might have known would be the case had I thought of the matter, nobody was willing to do anything toward getting food, for it was now the Sabbath and the Sabbath must not be broken. I felt a bit hungry myself. There were on our sled little provisions beyond a few delicacies which Mr. Young had given us to help along on the journey to Herschel Island, and I was stingy of these, so instead of bringing them out at once I informed the community that I also was well versed in the Scripture and proceeded to tell them the story of how the ears of corn had been gathered on the Sabbath. The consensus of comment was that while to take flour off the bush in the country where it grows might not be wrong, they had had specific instructions that it was wrong to hunt rabbits or to fish on Sunday, and they would therefore prefer to go hungry rather than risk the displeasure of the Deity.

I thought it would be too much of a task for me alone to go out with the idea of getting rabbits for the whole crowd, so I took out of my sled and shared with them what was not nearly enough food to satisfy our hunger, but it was all we had to do us over Sunday. Monday morning bright and early every one was out hunting and fishing, and long before noon we had plenty to eat. This entire community had been heathen to a man when I lived with them in 1906.

It is said sometimes about the people of New England that they consider cleanliness next to godliness. It is true of the Mackenzie River Eskimo to-day that they look upon washing as a part of godliness. Soaps, towels, and the wash-basins are with them concrete means of grace. Although Christianity had not yet obtained hold among these people as a confession of faith when I first lived with them (in 1906), the idea was even then prevalent that washing was a thing of magic value, likely to promote good fortune and turn away evil influences. I tried then and later to counteract this idea as much as possible by seldom washing, but this deterred them in no way, for they knew from my frank avowals that I was not a shaman and knew nothing of the occult forces.

I found now on Saturday night in Ovayuak's house that things had gone much farther in the matter of washing and towels than they had when I lived with them five years before. Just before bedtime Ovayuak got out a tub filled a quarter full of water and took a bath. Although he had been an apparently healthy man when I first knew him, both he and other members of his family now have sores on various parts of their bodies which I have no doubt are of syphilitic origin. After bathing he wiped with a towel, rubbing it into all these sores. When he was through bathing, his wife took the towel, and after bathing wiped with it also. It was then passed on to the other members of the family, and when everybody had bathed the towel was hung up beside the stove to dry. Next morning when we woke up all the family washed their faces and wiped with the one towel. Several visitors also came in to have breakfast in our house, and, as the custom is among these people now, they all washed their hands and faces in their host's wash-basin and wiped with his towel. I expostulated with Ovayuak, explaining to him by analogies with certain vermin with which they were thoroughly familiar that the germs which inhabit the sores that accompany contagious diseases get on the towel when it is rubbed into the sores, and will later on be transferred by the towel to the eyes and other parts of the bodies of people who wipe with it. Notably would these invisible vermin enter any sores which the person who used the towel might happen to have on his body and would make them sick in turn. By much explaining I was able to make these things thoroughly clear to my Eskimo friends, and it was evident not only that they believed me but also that they were much impressed with the danger they were in.

When I saw how clear an impression I had made I said: "Now you must not do these things any more. You must promise me that you won't take any more baths unless you each wipe with your own towel, which you allow no one else to use or unless the towel can be boiled between times." But they answered regretfully that they could not follow my advice because they had so few towels. God had commanded them that they must wash all over their bodies every Saturday night and must wash their hands and faces before every meal and on waking up in the morning. Their first duty was, they considered, to obey God lest they fail to attain salvation, for they considered that the health of the body was of small consequence beside the welfare of the soul.

The point is, of course, as we have explained elsewhere, that they look upon the missionary as the spokesman of God, and anything which he tells them they consider he tells them as the direct commandment of the Lord. For that reason, although they were much exercised over the gruesome picture which I had painted of the effects of the promiscuous use of towels, they felt themselves unable to do anything because the commandments of God in the matter had to be obeyed at all costs. They explained to me, as others have done on similar occasions, that when I first knew them and lived among them they had not been Christians, but that they had since learned about heaven and hell and considered that nothing else is of vital importance except the avoiding of eternal punishment; for after all, they said, a man has to die sometime anyway and it makes comparatively little difference when he dies, but if he observes the commandments of God while he lives, his soul will when he dies go to heaven and dwell there in joy forever.

The best I could do was to make these people promise me that the next time the missionary came their way they would ask him; and that if it was true, as I said, that they had misunderstood him and that he had had no intention of telling them that washing was necessary to salvation; if he were to confirm my statements in this matter and they were to learn that washing was really merely a matter of cleanliness and had nothing to do with the soul's welfare, then they would quickly stop washing unless they could get towels. They said that, as far as that went, they did not see why they might not stop washing altogether, because their ancestors before them had been healthy and well without washing, and it was only because of the desire to keep all the commandments of the Lord that they were washing now.

I pointed out to them my own example and showed how I much preferred to go unwashed rather than use towels which others used. I told them that I was not the least bit afraid of eternal punishment in consequence, and asked them whether they did not think I would know about it if eternal punishment were the punishment of the unwashed. But they explained to me that they considered my information might be deficient, for the missionary had told them that in matters of religion, in many cases, the foolish knew the things which were hidden from the wise.

April 22d we said good-by to these old friends of ours and started west across the delta. We were now in a thickly settled district and met people or passed their camps every day. April 24th we got to Escape Reef, where there were some Eskimo houses and where there was also living Mr. Storkerson, who had been a member of our party for a short while the fall of 1908. That night there arrived also at Escape Reef Mr. Charles H. Burt, a miner, of San Francisco, California, accompanied by a Loucheux Indian, Enoch Moses, and by Mr. Louis Cardinal. Mr. Burt with three white companions had been engaged in some mining operations on the westernmost channel of the Mackenzie delta and was now on his way to Herschel Island to visit Captain Cottle. The evening of the following day I started for Herschel Island in company with Mr. Burt and the others, and we got there early in the morning of April 26th.

During my stay of about a week at Herschel Island I was the guest of the Royal Northwest Mounted Police at the barracks. The detachment was in command of Inspector Beyts and consisted of three men besides him.   But while I was formally staying at the barracks I spent much of my time aboard the *Karluk* with my friends Captain and Mrs. Cottle.   Several of their visitors and some members of their crew I knew also from former years, and I had now a pleasant opportunity of renewing old acquaintances.

We stayed at the island a week as it was, but we might have stayed longer had it not been that every one there was firmly impressed with the idea that this was going to be an exceptionally early spring and that the rivers might be expected to come out on the ice at any time. Of course we did not desire to be caught by the spring thaws four hundred miles short of our destination (Point Barrow) and so on May 4th, late in the evening, we pulled out, but travelled only about twelve miles, half around the island, and camped on the "Sou'west Sandspit," as it is known to the whalers.   Natkusiak and I were now alone, for we had left Palaiyak, as intended, with his relatives at the island.

Herschel Island is apparently of alluvial formation and is about five hundred feet above sea-level at its highest, is irregular in shape, with its longest diameter about eight miles, and has three sandspits running out of it.   The shortest, and under present conditions the most important, is one of not over half a mile near the northeast corner of the island, which by an elbow curve forms between itself and the main body of the island one of the finest harbors in all the Arctic waters, and one that has been used by the whaling fleet ever since the first ship of them wintered in this part of the Arctic in 1889.   This sandspit was, before the white men came, the site of an Eskimo village, and so was the sandspit at the southeast corner of the island, known now to the white men as Flanders Point.   The longest sandspit of the three is at the southwest corner of the island, for which reason it is known as "Sou'west Sandspit."   It is about five miles long, thickly covered with driftwood, and carries, as well as the others, the ruins of former Eskimo dwellings.

There is nothing much to tell of our journey west from Herschel Island until we reached Collinson Point.   We passed here and there on the way ancient ruins which we had often seen before (for I had made this same journey twice by sled and twice by boat in previous years), and now and again also more recent habitations, constructed within the last year or two but now abandoned.

At Collinson Point we found the trader E. B. O'Connor, known in Nome and elsewhere in Alaska as "Duffy" O'Connor. He and his stores of trade goods had been brought in from Nome the previous summer and landed here, while the ship returned to Bering Straits. As any one could have told him who knew the conditions, this was not the place for trading, for it is not a country rich in foxes. The Eskimo of the neighborhood are few and indolent, and besides that, Mr. Leffingwell's trading establishment at Flaxman Island was only sixty miles to the west. It never seemed possible to me that even Mr. Leffingwell alone could make expenses by trading in that country, and certainly there was nothing to divide between him and O'Connor. These things Mr. O'Connor had found out long before we arrived there, but to have found them out even the day after his ship left would have been already too late, for when a man is once set down so far from civilization with an outfit of trade goods he can do nothing but stay and see it through. Mr. O'Connor was staying and seeing it through. He was as hospitable as every one else is in that country, and really more so. He treated us with the greatest possible kindness and urged us to stay as long as we dared. When we left I think he was sorely tempted to hitch up his dogs and accompany us, for he was clearly homesick for his family and friends at Nome.

From Collinson Point it was but a day's journey to Flaxman Island. This was a place where I had lived for several months in 1906, at the time of its occupation by the Anglo-American Polar Expedition commanded by Leffingwell and Mikkelsen, and I had revisited it many times since. There was still at Flaxman Island Mr. Ernest de Koven Leffingwell, who had returned there in 1909 with an ample supply of the comforts and the conveniences of civilization for the purpose incidentally of trading, but primarily of carrying on geological researches in the neighborhood to complete investigations which he had begun in 1906–1907.

Mr. Leffingwell was doing work on an intensive scale, it may be said, for he had confined most of his activities to the district between the Colville River eighty miles west of Flaxman Island, and Barter

Island fifty or sixty miles to the east of it, and to the Endicott Mountains to the south. To put in three years on an area more than a hundred and twenty-five miles long by forty or so wide may not seem very "intensive" to those used to geological work in lower latitudes, but it means closer investigation probably than has been carried out by any one else in so high a latitude on the North American continent. An especially valuable part of his work, from the point of view of the whaling and trading vessels which enter this region, is his careful charting by double triangulation of the lagoons which run most of the way from the Colville to Flaxman Island, and his sounding of the various channels; with the result that ships which formerly had to keep entirely outside of the chain of low islands which here flanks the coast, can now in many cases go between the islands and the coast protected by them from the danger of heavy ice that lies outside. The ships can thus now make their way through the open water of the lagoon, where in former times, before the lagoon was sounded, they would have had to remain tied up to an ice cake outside, unable to proceed and exposed to the dangers of the pack.

There was with Mr. Leffingwell at Flaxman Island Mr. "Scotty" McIntyre, an old miner and whaleman, who had been assisting Mr. Leffingwell in his work and who intended the following year to take Mr. Leffingwell's yawl *Argo* eastward to Victoria Island, where he hoped to make their joint fortune in trading with the Eskimo of Prince Albert Sound.

After spending several days pleasantly at Flaxman Island we proceeded a short half day westward to where there was camped with his family Mr. Ned Arey, prospector, whom we also knew of old and who has been in these parts for the better portion of the last twenty years. He also was planning to go to the eastward, a thing which is really true of practically every white man on the north coast of Alaska, for Arctic Alaska has the last ten years become "poor country" through the depletion of its resources by the extermination of the caribou.

I have always enjoyed visiting Ned Arey, and now I had a special reason for lingering at his camp as well as at Flaxman Island, because my only companion, Natkusiak, had been taken with a felon of the left hand, which prevented him from doing any work with it (and that meant practically inability to do work at all, for he happens to be left-handed). The hand had for some days been so painful that not only was he unable to do anything, but he suffered great pain in walking or in sitting on the sled even where the going was exceptionally smooth. By the time we left Mr. Arey's, which was in the course of two or three days, he had so far improved as to be able to walk along without it paining him much.

Mr. Leffingwell at Flaxman Island had offered us as much of everything in the way of provisions as we cared to haul with us, but the season was not advancing with anything like the rapidity predicted for it at Herschel Island, and I rather preferred to go slowly so as not to arrive at Point Barrow while all the population were still off on the ice, whaling. It would suit us best, I thought, to get there about the time that every one would be returning from the ice, and if we meant to loiter by the way we might as well spend part of the time in hunting, so I decided to prefer hunting seals for food on the way westward to taking a large amount of provisions from Leffingwell. I never liked hauling more food than was necessary, and we knew there were bound to be seals on the ice.

I had often shot seals before, of course, but this was really the first experience I had in having to do the whole thing; that is, not only to kill the animals but also to cut them up, feed the dogs, boil the meat, pitch the camp, and everything. When we travelled together, Natkusiak and I alone, it often fell to me to pitch camp, but the cutting up of seals and the feeding of the dogs had always been his portion of the work.

When we came to the crossing of Harrison Bay I decided to strike straight across from Jones Islands to Cape Halkett. This was a wider crossing than we had ever made before and one quite beyond the practice of the Eskimo, who always follow the land around the foot of any big bight, although it is farther. In fact, Natkusiak was considerably worried. I never knew him to show timidity in the matter of going into an unknown country where the game conditions were uncertain, but on this occasion as well as on the previous one of our crossing of Dolphin and Union Straits (in May of the year before) he had been plainly worried. On this present crossing we used no compass, but depended upon the snow-drifts made by the southeasterly winds, crossing them all the way approximately at an angle of 45°, doing which would, I knew, bring us across to Cape Halkett in the course of three or four days.

We travelled slowly (it was thick weather and there were plenty of seals for food), so it was on the fifth day from the Jones (sometimes miscalled Thetis) Islands that we sighted land again. It turned out that our course, had the weather been thicker so that land could not have been seen at a distance, would have taken us only about three miles outside of Cape Halkett, which was pretty good for travel by dead reckoning across a sixty-mile bay in thick weather, and shows that the drifted snow makes a fairly good compass. There would have been no harm in missing the cape by a few miles, except that had fog or a blizzard hidden the land from us for a long time we should, had we kept our course, have been compelled to travel through some rough ice, whereas it would have been smoother over the shallow water near shore. Of course it is true that had we not sighted land at the time we did we should have turned inshore anyway soon after, for our reckoning of the distance was about right and I felt sure we must be abreast of the Cape or beyond it.

Spring was coming on with fair rapidity, and geese and ducks were beginning to fly. We had, contrary to our general custom, taken with us a shotgun from Herschel Island, for this was an easy trip and we could afford to carry heavy and comparatively inefficient ammunition. It was easy enough for us to get as many seals as we wanted any day at this season, but we preferred a change of food, especially as geese were even easier to get than seals.

At this season (first part of June) and on this particular coast-line the sea ice is of course snow-white and so is the land back from the shore, but the cut banks along the beach are dark. The migrating geese coming from the west follow the dark line of the cut bank as cows do a winding trail. If there be a very narrow bight, they may fly across it; if there be a slender point of land sticking out to seaward, they may cross over; but in general they follow the coast so closely that you can sit down almost anywhere and rely on it that three flocks out of every four will pass within gunshot. This is especially true in thick or foggy weather. The geese we saw were chiefly the

American white-fronted. This is the commonest variety at Point Barrow. The Hutchins goose, which is fairly common about the Mackenzie and east of it, almost never comes to Point Barrow. In all his stay there since 1884 Mr. Brower has seen only three specimens, one of which was brought in at a time when I happened to be present.

When we came to Pitt Point we had a better opportunity than ever before of seeing the curious formation of "ground ice." The cut bank here is anywhere from five to twenty or more feet in height, and in many places the face of the cliff shows a series of what appear to be boulders of ice imbedded in the wall of the cut bank somewhat as stones are in earth in other places. These may vary in size from that of a walnut to that of a load of hay. Sometimes the boulders look "dirty," but usually they are of ice that is clear white. Where the cut bank is as much as sixteen feet in height the base is always exposed, for this ice does not seem to go deep down. If a particular boulder goes within twenty inches or so of the surface, the top of it is flat, apparently through thawing, but otherwise it may be any shape. Overlying the ice there is always a certain amount of earth (anywhere from eight to twenty inches).

It is scarcely worth while to theorize much about how these boulders of ice came to be imbedded in the earth of the Alaskan coastal plain. Similar formations have been described by Dr. Bruce from Spitzbergen, Tyrell from the plains back of Hudson Bay, and Leffingwell from Flaxman Island, and no doubt by a great many others, although photographs showing the ice in position are, I believe, rare. It is probable that the method of formation was not the same in all places. There is a natural temptation to call upon the "great ice age" for an explanation, for it seems to be a sort of universal solvent of geological mysteries. It may be worth while, however, to describe certain activities which are seen at work on the north coast of Alaska to-day which are by themselves competent, apparently, to produce such conditions as are shown by our photographs.

In the autumn, if the weather is calm, the sea freezes over near the coast line level as a pond. If an offshore wind blows, this level ice is carried off to seaward at any time during the winter, and so soon as the next calm comes it is replaced by a fresh layer of level ice; but if an onshore wind blows, the ice is crushed against the beach by the force of the wind and forms in what are known as pressure ridges far out to sea. Each hummock of ice sticks above the general level, and each pressure ridge acts as a sail, under the combined wind-driven force of which the sea ice is, in a landward storm, forced against the beach with a power incomprehensible. Under such conditions tongues of ice may slip up on the beach and be shoved inland two or three hundred feet beyond the limit of high tide and thirty or forty feet above sea level. This is a common phenomenon. A rather less common one, but by no means rare, is that the tongue of ice is stabbed like a dagger into the ground. When the ice thaws the following summer and drifts away to seaward, these daggers are broken off in the wound, as it were, and left behind, covered with more or less earth according to the circumstances of the case. I have seen this happen on the gravel beach between Cape Smythe and Point Barrow and on the first sandspit east of Pitt Point. At Point Barrow the covering of the ice chunks was of gravel, through which the summer rains easily trickled, with the result that in the course of two or three years the ice melted within the gravel, which may still be seen there in heaps on the beach. But on the sandspit east of Pitt Point the covering was partly peaty earth, and a half dozen inches of it will prevent any ice underneath from thawing forever.

The north coast of Alaska is at present a wasting coast, so that though a piece of ice be left imbedded in the earth and protected by it sufficiently from the heat of the sun to keep it from thawing, it is nevertheless a question of but a few years until the waves will break away that part of the beach and carry off the ice as well as the earth that covers it. But if the coast were a growing coast instead of a wasting one, if it were now in the process of upbuilding, then it may be said to be a certainty that the ice dagger left behind on the beach east of Pitt Point would remain there imbedded in the earth until the geological cycle of upbuilding had ceased and the sea finally uncovered it again in a new cycle of aggressiveness.

There is no doubt, too, that in an analogous way underground ice may be formed by a meandering river. Let the ice first form and then be covered by a spring freshet with a few inches of earth, to be added to next year by a few more inches. As the river meanders to the left so as to leave behind it on its right bank chunks of ice, they

SECTIONS OF UNDERGROUND ICE BOWLDERS EXPOSED IN CUTBANK, PITT POINT.
Icicles complicate the outlines somewhat.

ONE METHOD OF FORMATION OF UNDERGROUND ICE.
A dagger of ice is stabbed into bank and broken off, leaving ice covered by a heap of dirt.

are here and there imbedded in the earth, exactly as sticks of wood are nowadays, and exactly, no doubt, as the mammoth were in their day covered, to be preserved to our time so that their flesh is still flesh in the earth after unknown thousands of years.

By the time we reached Smith Bay many kinds of Arctic birds had become fairly numerous. We saw the first jaegers May 31st, and while coming across Harrison Bay we had seen old squaw ducks three days before that. The first plovers were seen June 4th coming landward from what had no doubt been a short excursion out over the ice. All the rest of the birds were coming from the west along the coast. The first eider-ducks appeared June 4th and the first sandpipers June 5th. The brant appeared in large flocks June 2d. The first American white-fronted geese were seen May 31st and waveys two days later. No swans or cranes were seen at any time.

June 9th Natkusiak was taken with a bad case of snow-blindness. In general the Eskimo seem far more susceptible to snow-blindness than white men. Doubtless this is not a racial question. The reason is pretty clear — a man who has never had snow-blindness does not easily get it, but when you have had it once you get it more easily the next time and so on indefinitely until middle age. Men who have been exposed to it from childhood are very prone to the affliction.

It would be natural to suppose that the light most trying to the eyes would be the intense glare on spotless snow when the sun stands high in a cloudless sky. This is not the case, however. The most trying is hazy weather when the sun shines through thin clouds. This is the sort of weather that makes it very difficult to gauge the distance of objects or to discern inequalities in the surface over which you are walking, for the light is so uniformly diffused that no shadows are cast. Doubtless it is the extra strain on the eye in its effort to see things clearly under difficulties which brings on snow-blindness quickly under these conditions.

It is extremely important, in trying to avoid snow-blindness, not only to wear goggles (as discussed elsewhere) that properly protect the eyes in the daytime, but also to sleep in a dark place at night. Apparently that is because the light penetrates to the eyes through the closed eyelids. A tent of such material as white balloon silk, for

2 c

instance, is very trying. We were using such a tent on the present journey. As soon as Natkusiak became snow-blind we not only ceased traveling, but covered the tent outside with blankets and skins so as to make it dark. With this treatment he recovered almost completely in two days.

On the last week of our journey toward Point Barrow we had fresh evidences of the food prejudices of dogs. Most of our team came from the Eskimo of Coronation Gulf, and in that country, where even the bolas is unknown, geese, naturally, are seldom killed. Since before reaching Pitt Point we had had no meat except geese, and all of the Coronation Gulf dogs at first refused to eat. One of them, Ivarluk by name, went for a week without eating, and prowled around looking for rags and ropes to swallow when pieces of goose were scattered all about. Finally, on the seventh day, he ate the bill of a goose and a portion of the front part of the head, although he refused even then the meat proper. I meant to starve him into submission, but we got to Point Barrow too soon, for there seal meat and whale abounded, while the few geese we had with us when we arrived were too much in demand as man food for any attempt to force them on an unwilling dog.

It was on June 13th that we arrived at the house of Tom Gordon, three miles north of Cape Smythe. We had miscalculated the whaling season. The whalers had all been back for more than a week. There is scarcely need to say that we were in a way glad to get to Cape Smythe, which to our eyes was the heart of civilization. Really it was not so much that we had been hungering for the comfort and softness of the civilized man's rather tame existence — it was rather that we had two months ago already turned our backs upon the serious work of the North. Our task, in a way, was completed, and it seemed as if we now were home and had a right to rest. Many of the people of Cape Smythe were old friends and some were good friends though not very "old," for friendships seem more easily made and less easily outgrown here on the ragged edges of the world than in the crowded and distracted cities.

I should have liked to stay with Mr. Gordon for the day at least, but he said, and I knew it was true, that Mr. Brower and the rest down at Cape Smythe village would expect me to look them up without delay. We accordingly left Natkusiak and the dog team behind, and Mr. Gordon walked with me down to Cape Smythe, where I found at the whaling station not only my old friends, Mr. and Mrs. Brower and Mr. John Hadley, but also Mr. James Clarke, who, although not a stranger in the Arctic, had come to Cape Smythe after my leaving it in 1909. At the Presbyterian Mission, too, were friends of earlier years, Dr. and Mrs. Marsh and their family. Mr. and Mrs. Hawkesworth I was sorry not to see. They had left the government school for more southerly fields of work and their places had been taken by Mr. and Mrs. Cram. The Eskimo girl, Koodlalook, who had helped me so materially with my work four years before, had gone south with the Hawkesworths, and her place in the school had been taken by another young Eskimo woman, Alice.

There were two months to be spent at Cape Smythe, for the revenue cutter *Bear*, with which I intended to take passage for the outside world, could not be expected to arrive before August. I knew that as the guest of Mr. Brower I would find this time pass pleasantly and quickly, but I was anxious to turn it to profit also, and this I was able to do with Mr. Brower's assistance.

The people of the two villages of Cape Smythe and Point Barrow, nearly five hundred in number, had had a rather unprofitable winter. Few foxes had been caught and only six whales all together in the spring whaling season, and the price of whalebone was lower than it had been for years. The day has long gone when the Point Barrow people are economically independent. There was a time when they got from their own land and ice-covered sea all their food, clothing, fuel, and the other necessities of life; but now they import tea, clothing, phonographs, jewelry, chewing gum, perfumeries, and a hundred other things of which they formerly knew no need. They must therefore have money with which to buy these things, and the money they get only from foxskins and whalebone. Just now they were in great need of many things which they were used to doing without; notably there was a chewing gum famine, and men, women, and children were willing to do anything to get a little gum. When therefore Mr. Brower put at my disposal the unlimited credit of his firm and the resources of his storehouse, and when I announced that I was willing to pay in chewing gum for the excavation of the native village sites of the neighborhood, every one from the children to the most decrepit turned out to help me in the work.

It was a small army that turned out to dig wherever there was a ruin or a kitchen midden, and they worked energetically and well. While the excavations were not done as methodically and scientifically as could have been wished, still we were able to get from them a collection of over 20,000 archæological specimens within the space of six weeks. This collection (which is now safely stored in the American Museum of Natural History) brings out many significant and some revolutionary ideas with regard to the prehistoric history of the Eskimo. My method was to dig as much as possible myself, and to go around as best I could to see the others at work. In many cases I was able to see the exact position from which the important finds were taken.

Not only Mr. Brower's whaling station was put at my disposal in which to assort, pack, and label the specimens, but also the government schoolhouse and Mr. Cram's residence, which was for several weeks littered with archæological finds and the dirt and débris which crumbled from them. Such time as I had free from these archæological activities I devoted to linguistic work with the useful and able assistance of Dr. Marsh, who in thirteen years of residence among the Eskimo at Cape Smythe has acquired a mastery of the Point Barrow dialect.

July 24th the first ship of the season arrived, the *Elvira*, owned by Schroder and Arliss, both of whom were aboard, and under the command of Captain C. T. Pedersen. The weather was favorable for getting to the eastward, and as she was anxious to reach the Beaufort Sea for the summer whaling she did not drop anchor at all at Cape Smythe, although she stopped for a few hours at Point Barrow. The *Elvira* brought us the news of the wreck of the *Titanic*. As for that, I was getting fairly well abreast of the times, for there are three mails a year at Point Barrow and Mr. Brower keeps fairly well informed of what is going on in the outside world.

The *Elvira* told us that she was the only whaling ship going into Beaufort Sea this year on account of the low price of whalebone (due to the discovery of the satisfactory commercial substitute hitherto mentioned). It was supposed, however, that one or two ships might

SEARCHING FOR ARCHÆOLOGICAL SPECIMENS AT CAPE SMYTHE.

come up as far as Point Barrow, and a few days later one of these, the *John and Winthrop*, hove in sight.   She was commanded by another old whaleman friend of mine, Captain Joseph.   There are no whales around Point Barrow this season of the year, and the *John and Winthrop* merely cast anchor a few miles offshore and stayed there for the entire remainder of my visit at Cape Smythe.

A small gasoline trading schooner also came up and passed to the eastward.   She was under the command of and owned by Captain Chris Sten, one of the oldest whalers in these waters and a man at whose camp I had several times visited during the winter of 1906–1907, when he was living at Shingle Point, about twenty miles west of the Mackenzie River.   This is the same Mr. Sten whom Amundsen mentions in his "Northwest Passage" as wintering at King Point the same year as the *Gjoa*.

August 12th the revenue cutter *Bear* arrived off Cape Smythe, and the evening of the 13th she set sail back towards Nome, carrying me with her.   The voyage, which ended at Nome August 18th, was rendered especially pleasant for me through the kindness of Captain J. G. Ballinger and his officers.   They were not only courteous, as one would expect gentlemen of the revenue service to be, but they put themselves out especially in many ways in my service.   An especially good fortune was that through the kindness of Lieutenant Philip H. Scott I was able, in a stay of a few short hours at Point Hope, to obtain there archæological collections which form a useful supplement to those I had secured at Point Barrow.   Lieutenant Scott had for many years taken an interest in such matters, and through his acquaintance with the natives I was able to secure many valuable specimens which it would otherwise have been impossible for me to get.

When we dropped anchor off Nome, August 18th, it was in the dark of night ; and the lights of the city flickering on the hillsides and reflected against the sky gave this famous gold mining camp a metropolitan appearance which struck my imagination much more forcibly than did the great city of Seattle when we landed there from the passenger steamer some three weeks later.

CHAPTER XXVI

ON THE RELIGION OF THE ESKIMO

ONE often hears the statement that there never have been discovered people so low that they do not have some form of religion. This is stating a true thing in such a way that it implies an untruth. The case is put rightly and the exact facts are truly implied, in saying that the lower you go in the scale of cultural development the more religion you find until, when you get to the people that are really toward the bottom of the scale of social and intellectual evolution, religion begins to cover practically all the activities and phenomena of life. There is a religious significance in every act and accident and a religious formula for every eventuality in life.

The Eskimo are people whose intelligence is keen with reference to the facts of their immediate environment; but that environment is so monotonous, the range of possible experiences is so small, that no matter what the fiber of their minds may be at bottom, the exercise is wanting that might lead to a broad mental development.

There was a time when I used to think I knew what the word "savage" meant. Since then I have associated with people who dress in skins, who live largely on raw meat, who had never seen white men until they saw me, who were as strange to our ideas and ways as any people on this earth can be to-day; and the net result is that the word "savage" has quite lost its meaning. Like the word "squaw," or "half-breed," the word "savage" is reprehensible because it carries a stigma which the facts do not justify. I should prefer to describe the peoples ordinarily referred to as "savage," as "child-like," because the word is truthfully descriptive and not odious. It is the purpose of the present chapter to describe some phases of the religion of one of the child-like peoples.

To begin with, the Eskimo are very unclear in their religious thinking, a fact which does not, however, differentiate them abysmally from our own race. Scepticism in religious matters is unknown. If they are acquainted with my private character and find me in the ordinary relations of life reliable; if I don't tell lies concerning the number or the fatness of the caribou I have killed, nor about the distance at which I shot them, nor the difficulty I had in stalking them, they will believe anything I say about any subject. They will assume as unquestioningly the truth of any metaphysical statement I make if they have once learned to rely on my statements regarding the thickness of the back-fat of the bull caribou I shot during the summer. On the other hand, if I told them there were ten caribou in a band I saw and they later on discovered there were only five, they would be disinclined to believe me if I told them there was but one God. The reasoning would simply be this: he did not tell us the truth about the number of caribou, therefore how can we rely on the truth of his statements about the number of the gods?

There are among all Eskimo certain persons whom we call "shamans" and they call "angatkut." These persons hold communion with the spirits and are familiar with the things of the other world; they are the formulators of religious opinion. The days of miracles are not yet past among any primitive people, and new miracles happen on the shores of the polar sea daily, but more especially in the dark of winter. The miracles usually happen at the behest of the shamans, and invariably it is the shaman who tells about them; but while new revelations are frequent, they are always revelations of the old sort. There is little originality in the minds of primitive people; their daily experiences are uniform, and their thoughts are uniform, too.

The most fundamental thing in Eskimo religion is that all phenomena are controlled by spirits and these spirits in turn are controlled by formulæ, or charms, which are mainly in the possession of the medicine-men, although certain simple charms may be owned and used by any one. It follows from this fundamental conception that nothing like prayer or worship is possible. Supplication will do no good, for why should you beg anything from spirits that you can command? All spirits can be controlled, and in fact are controlled, by charms; but certain spirits are especially at the service of certain men, and these men are the shamans. They may be male or female, and in fact some of the greatest shamans known to me are women.

As we have said, the religious thinking of the Eskimo is unclear. There seems no agreement, and in fact no settled opinion on the subject of whether there are spirits, of the class susceptible of becoming familiar spirits, which are not already in the service of some shaman. The general feeling seems to be that every one of these spirits has its master. For that reason, among the Mackenzie River people, at least, when a young man wants to become a shaman he must, in one way or another, secure a spirit from some one who is already a shaman, or else secure a spirit that has been freed by the death of a shaman.

The ordinary Mackenzie River shaman has about half a dozen familiar spirits, any of which will do his bidding. When engaged in some such thing as the finding of a hidden article, the shaman will summon these spirits, one after another, and send them out separately in search of the lost article. Evidently a man may be able to get along fairly well with five familiar spirits, though he may be in the habit of employing six, exactly as we can dispense with an extra servant. A shaman may be old and decrepit or for some other reason may be what we should call "hard up." This is a propitious occasion for some ambitious young man to obtain a familiar spirit. He will go to the old shaman and some such conversation as this will take place:

"Will you sell me one of your *keyukat?*" (that being the Mackenzie River name for familiar spirit).

"Yes. I don't see why I might not. I am getting to be an old man now and shall not need their services much longer; besides, I have had my eye on you for a long time and shall be glad to have you for my successor. I think I might let you have my Polar Bear spirit."

"That would be kind of you, but don't you think you could spare your Tide Crack spirit?"

"Well, no; that is the one that I intend to keep to the very last. It has been very faithful to me and useful, but if you don't like the Polar Bear spirit you might have my Indian spirit."

And so the bargaining goes on, until finally it is decided that the

young man buys the Raven spirit for an umiak freshly made of five
beluga skins, twenty summer-killed-deer skins, two bags of seal oil,
a green stone labret, and things of that sort without end — giving
a new boat, in fact, loaded with all sorts of gear.

The young man now goes home, and presently, using the appropriate formula given him by the shaman, he summons his familiar
spirit, but the familiar spirit refuses to appear. The young man then
goes back to the old shaman and says to him: "How is this? The
spirit which you sold me has not come." And the old man replies:
"Well, I cannot help that; I transferred him to you in good faith,
and if you are one of those persons with whom spirits refuse to associate, that is a thing which I cannot help. I did my part in the
matter."

That is the consensus of opinion in the community. The shaman
has transferred the spirit in good faith and has kept his part of the
contract and consequently keeps the boat and everything else with
which the young man has paid for the spirit. Further, when it
becomes noised about that this young man is the sort of a man
with whom spirits will not associate, he loses social standing, for
it becomes evident not only that he will never become a great shaman, but also that he is lacking in those essential personal qualities
which commend him to the spirits, and which therefore commend
him to his fellow-countrymen also.

In our hypothetical case we have supposed the young man to go
back to the shaman to complain over the non-arrival of the spirit.
As a matter of fact it is only once or twice in a generation that such
a thing takes place. When he has once publicly paid for the spirit,
the young man has everything to lose by admitting that he did not
receive it. He cannot get back what he paid for it; he cannot have
the advantage of being considered a shaman; and he will lose social
standing through the publication of the fact that the spirit refuses
to associate with him. As a matter of practice, therefore, the pur-
chaser will pretend that he received the spirit, and he will announce
that fact. Some time later sickness occurs in a family or a valuable
article is lost. The young man is appealed to, and in order to keep
up the deception which he has begun by pretending to have received
the spirit, he goes into as good an imitation of a trance as he can

manage, for he has from childhood up watched the shamans in their trances. If he succeeds in the cure or whatever the object of the seance may be, his reputation is made; and if he does not succeed nothing is lost, for it is as easy for an Eskimo to explain the failure of a shamanistic performance as it is for us to explain why a prayer is not answered. It may have been because some other more powerful shaman was working against him, or it may have been for any one of a thousand reasons, all of which are satisfactory and sufficient to the Eskimo mind.

In general, among the Mackenzie Eskimo there are two main theories of disease: either a man's soul has been stolen, in which case the symptoms are chills, shivering, and a general lassitude; or a spirit may have been sent by an ill-disposed shaman into another person to make him sick. In this latter case the symptoms will be anything at all and the treatment is exorcism, to drive out the evil spirit that has taken possession — or not really an evil spirit, for according to Eskimo ideas the spirits are neither good nor evil in themselves, but merely perform the good or evil bidding of those who send them.

There are various methods of exorcism, usually including chanting, drum-beating, conjuring tricks, ventriloquism, and the like, on the part of the shaman, and the observance of taboos on the part of the sick man and his relatives, and occasionally on the part of an entirely unrelated person arbitrarily designated by the shaman. A child will be eventually cured if its mother refrains from changing her socks as long as the illness lasts, or the disease will be aggravated if the sick man's brother should eat any portion of the left side of caribou.

The procedure in the case of a soul being stolen is a simpler one. The problem is merely to find the soul and restore it to the sick person, and all the shaman has to do is to summon his familiar spirits and send them out over all the earth in search of the place where the soul has been forcibly confined. Eventually one of the spirits will find the soul, unless indeed it has been craftily placed in some cavity or hole the mouth of which has been greased with seal or whale oil, for in that case neither will the soul be able to pass out of such a confinement nor will the spirit which is searching for the soul be able to enter in order to find it.   When a shaman steals a man's soul and wants to be sure that no other shaman shall be able to recover it for him, the favorite hiding-place is one of the foramina of the lower maxillary bone of the bow-head whale.

Most travellers who have visited the Arctic lands have commented upon the fact that Eskimo children are never punished, or, in fact, forbidden anything.   The explanations offered have been various, and usually such offhand ones as the "common sense" of the observer has suggested to him.   In dealing with primitive people, however, "common sense" is an exceedingly dangerous thing.   It is a frail reed indeed to rely upon, for scarcely anything that the primitive man does is done without a religious motive, and we in these later days are so prone to neglect the religious aspect of things that the chances are necessarily small of the right reason being divined.   We count it as one of the chief triumphs of the four-year expedition of the American Museum of Natural History to the Eskimo that we discovered why it is that children are not punished — for such immaterial things is the money of scientific institutions expended !

One family of Eskimo were the servants of the expedition for its whole four years and I had known them also on a previous expedition. This family consists of the man Ilavinirk, his wife Mamayak, and their daughter Noashak.   When I first knew Noashak I formed the opinion that she was the worst child I had ever known and I retained that opinion for over six years, or until she was a young woman of perhaps twelve years.   (Some Eskimo girls are fully developed at the age of twelve or thirteen.)   In spite of her badness Noashak was never punished.

The two stock explanations of why Eskimo do not punish their children are : first, that the children themselves are so good that they do not need being punished (but that scarcely applied to Noashak's case) ; or that the Eskimo are so fond of their children that they cannot bear to punish them, which is not true, either, for they show in many ways that they are no fonder of their children than we are.

During the entire time that Noashak's family was with us she was the undisputed ruler of our establishment.   My plan of work was such that I could not get along without the help of Eskimo, and I had continually before me the choice of doing as Noashak wanted or else losing the services of her parents.   They were both excellent people of whom I was personally very fond, and they were more useful to me than any one else whom I could hope to secure in their places ; besides, most Eskimo families have children, and to dispose of the family of which Noashak was head would only have compelled me to engage some other family of which some other child was master.   True, I was allowed to decide upon the broad policy of the expedition, but any little details were liable to change without notice at Noashak's option.

It was during the absence of the sun in December, 1909, that this family and I were travelling up Horton River.   We had been several days without anything to eat except sea-oil ; our dogs were tired and weak from hunger and had ceased pulling.   Ilavinirk and I were harnessed to the sled on either side, breaking our backs to pull it forward, and Mamayak was walking ahead breaking trail for the sled.   Noashak, then a fat and sturdy girl of eight, was on top of the load, which was heavy enough in all conscience without her.   Whenever we stopped to rest she would immediately jump off the sled, run up some cut-bank and slide down it, run up again and slide down again, and so on as long as we stayed.   The moment we started she would jump on the load and ride.

One day when her father and I were more tired than usual and getting weaker from long fasting, I asked Ilavinirk whether he did not think it would be a good idea if Noashak got off and walked a little (we had, by the way, saved food for Noashak so that she had something to eat when the rest of us did not).   He put the matter to her, telling her that it was his opinion that walking would really do her good ; he told her how tired he and I were getting, and wanted to know if his dear daughter was not willing to walk now and then so as to enable us to travel a little farther each day and to reach our destination, where plenty of food waited for us, that much sooner. But she said she did not feel like walking, and that ended the discussion.

Later on when we stopped to rest again and Noashak started her old tactics of running uphill and sliding down, I again suggested to her father that she might rest while we rested and then she would no doubt feel like walking when we started travelling again.   He put the case to her as before. Evidently his sympathies were on my side and he was as anxious to have her walk as I was, but her curt decision that she would rather slide downhill than walk beside the sled settled the matter.

I am unable to remember now whether I had any theory by which I explained to myself why it was that Noashak was never forbidden anything and never punished, but I know now that if I had a theory it must have been a wrong one. As a matter of fact, I do not think I had one. I am afraid I took Noashak for granted, as a sort of necessary evil, like mosquitoes. It was only in February or March, 1912, that I got the key to the situation, and I found it then to involve also that most interesting question of how it is that Eskimos get their names.

I had noticed ever since I knew them that Mamayak in speaking to Noashak always addressed her as "mother." When one stops to think of it, it was of course a bit curious that a woman of twenty-five should address a girl of eight as "mother." I suppose, if I thought about the matter at all, I must have put this practice of theirs in the same category with that which we find among our own people, where we often hear a man addressing his wife as "mother."

One day another Eskimo family came to visit us, and strangely enough, the woman of the family also spoke to Noashak and called her "mother." Then my curiosity was finally aroused, and I asked: "Why do you two grown women call this child your mother?" Their answer was: "Simply because she is our mother," an answer which was for the moment more incomprehensible to me than the original problem. I saw, however, that I was on the track of something interesting, and both women were in a communicative mood, so it was not long until my questions brought out the facts, which (pieced together with what I already knew) make the following coherent explanation, which shows not only why these women called Noashak "mother," but shows also why it was that she must never under any circumstances be forbidden anything or punished.

When a Mackenzie Eskimo dies, the body is taken out the same day as the death occurs to the top of some neighboring hill and covered with a pile of drift-logs, but the soul (*nappan*) remains in the house where the death occurred for four days if it is a man, and for five days if it is a woman. At the end of that time a ceremony is performed by means of which the spirit is induced to leave the house and to go up to the grave, where it remains with the body waiting for the next child in the community to be born.

When a child is born, it comes into the world with a soul of its own (*nappan*), but this soul is as inexperienced, foolish, and feeble as a child is and looks. It is evident, therefore, that the child needs a more experienced and wiser soul than its own to do the thinking for it and take care of it. Accordingly the mother, so soon as she can after the birth of the child, pronounces a magic formula to summon from the grave the waiting soul of the dead to become the guardian soul of the new-born child, or its *atka*, as they express it.

Let us suppose that the dead person was an old wise man by the name of John. The mother then pronounces the formula which may be roughly translated as follows: "Soul of John, come here, come here, be my child's guardian! Soul of John, come here, come here, be my child's guardian!" (Most magic formulæ among the Eskimo must be repeated twice.)

When the soul of John, waiting at the grave, hears the summons of the mother, it comes and enters the child. From that time on it becomes the business of this acquired soul not only to do the thinking for the child, but to help in every way to keep it strong and healthy: to assist it in learning to walk, to keep it from becoming bow-legged, to assist it in teething, and in every way to look after its welfare, things which the child's own soul with which it was born could not possibly do for the child, on account of its weakness and inexperience.

The spirit of John not only teaches the child to talk, but after the child learns to talk it is really the soul of John which talks to you and not the inborn soul of the child. The child, therefore, speaks with all the acquired wisdom which John accumulated in the long lifetime, plus the higher wisdom which only comes after death. Evidently, therefore, the child is the wisest person in the family or in the community, and its opinions should be listened to accordingly. What it says and does may seem foolish to you, but that is mere seeming and in reality the child is wise beyond your comprehension.

The fact that the child possesses all the wisdom of the dead John is never forgotten by its parents. If it cries for a knife or a pair of scissors, it is not a foolish child that wants the knife, but the soul of the wise old man John that wants it, and it would be presumptuous of a young mother to suppose she knows better than John what is good for the child, and so she gives it the knife. If she refused the knife (and this is the main point), she would not only be preferring her own foolishness to the wisdom of John, but also she would thereby give offense to the spirit of John, and in his anger John would abandon the child. Upon the withdrawal of his protection the child would become the prey to disease and would probably die, and if it did not die, it would become stupid or hump-backed or otherwise deformed or unfortunate. John must, therefore, be propitiated at every cost, and to deliberately offend him would be in fact equivalent to desiring the child's misfortune or death and would be so construed by the community; so that a man is restrained from forbidding his child or punishing it, not only by his own interest in the child's welfare, but also by the fear of public opinion, because if he began to forbid his child or to punish it, he would at once become known to the community as a cruel and inhuman father, careless of the welfare of his child.

We can see here how much there is in the point of view. On the basis of this explanation it is easy to understand how a man, tired and hungry and at the limit of his strength, would still haul his daughter on top of the sled load rather than compel her to get off and walk, for to compel her to do so would have been equivalent to desiring to bring upon her serious misfortune, if not death, through giving offense to her guardian angel.

Among the Mackenzie River Eskimo, if you see a man who is bow-legged, or hump-backed, or whose ears are big, and if you ask any one why he is bow-legged or hump-backed, the answer will usually be: "It is because his parents forbade him things when he was young and offended his guardian spirit."

As the child grows up the soul with which he was born (the *nappan*) gradually develops in strength, experience, and wisdom, so that after the age of ten or twelve years it is fairly competent to look after the child and begins to do so; at that age it therefore becomes of less vital moment to please the guardian spirit (*atka*), and accordingly it is customary to begin forbidding children and punishing them when they come to the age of eleven or twelve years. People say about them then: "I think the nappan is competent now to take care of him and it will be safe to begin teaching him things."

In the case of Noashak the transition period arrived in February, 1912. For four or five months before that it had been known to her parents and to all of us that she was beginning to chew tobacco. She used to steal it wherever she could find it. Her parents and I moralized with her on the subject; we told her that the white people were now increasing in number in the community, that white men did not approve of girls chewing tobacco, and that she would be looked down upon for doing it. But she said she did not care what white men thought of her. The matter gave her parents a good deal of concern; they tried in every way to hide the tobacco so that she could not find it; but she was ingenious, and considered it a personal triumph whenever she was able to assist any one toward the apparently accidental discovery of tobacco stains on her lips, for that was an evidence that she had outwitted her parents again.

One day her parents discussed the matter with me, saying that I understood their point of view and that they therefore wanted my advice. I refrained from interfering much, however. They eventually decided that Noashak's *nappan* was now approximately fully developed (Noashak was as big as her mother already) and so they thought they would try punishing her. The next time that she was caught chewing tobacco her father gave her another lengthy talk, urging her to stop the practice, but she only laughed at him, upon which he slapped her. To be struck was an undreamt-of thing in her philosophy. At first she was speechless with astonishment and then she started crying with rage and kept on crying all day, at the end of which she seemed to have thought the matter over carefully and to have realized that she was no longer ruler of the family. She accordingly stopped chewing.

The natural consequence of the fact that it is the spirit of John that does the thinking and talking for the child is that the child is addressed as a relative by all the relatives of John (for it is indeed to John that they are talking). If John was my father and your uncle, then I speak to the child as father and you speak to it as uncle, irrespective of the child's age or sex.   There was, for instance, a couple I knew who had for a child a boy of seven years, whose father called him stepmother and whose mother called him aunt, for those were their respective relationships to the woman whose soul was the boy's guardian, or *atka*.

As Eskimo communities are small and the people are necessarily usually related in one way or another, it is common to find a child addressed as a relative by every person in the village.   It is one of the child's earliest tasks to learn to recognize all these people and to address them by the proper terms of relationship, dealing with them in this matter entirely with reference to their relation to his guardian spirit.

Still, as in other matters, the thinking of the Eskimo is unclear here, and there is no absolute mutual exclusion of the two relationships — the child's relationship as we see it, on the one hand, and the relationship to the guardian spirit on the other, so that in speaking to you a man will say, "This is my daughter," although in speaking to her he may call her "nephew."   He may also call her "daughter" and "nephew" alternately.   A boy may therefore find himself in the position of being at once his father's son and his father's mother, which relationship he will of course find perfectly natural, being the one he has been brought up to recognize.

The fact that children address all the other people of a village by terms of relationship has often been noted and has usually been explained in a "common-sense" way by saying that Eskimo children are taught to be respectful to their elders and that as a sign of this respect they are instructed to address them by terms of relationship. This explanation is an eminently reasonable one to our minds, but does not happen to be true to the facts.

A person may continue through his entire lifetime to address certain individuals by the terms of relationship required by their position with regard to his guardian spirit, but as a usual thing the older a man gets the more this wears off and the more the real blood relationship begins to come forward.

It appears from the foregoing that every man has two souls, the one with which he was born and the one he acquired immediately after birth.   He may, in fact, have more souls than that.   If three

2 D

people, or thirteen, have just died before the child was born, then he gets three guardian spirits, or thirteen, according to the circumstances. But when he dies it is none of these acquired souls, but the soul that he was born with, which in its turn remains for four or five days in the house after death, which is then ceremonially driven out to the grave, and which waits there until it is summoned to become the second soul of a new-born child. No one knows what becomes of the guardian soul after the death of the persons whose guardians they have been. I have repeatedly asked about it, but no one seems to have ever heard the matter discussed and no one seemed to think the question was of great importance.

This answers, then, the commonly asked questions: "What is the Eskimo's idea of a future life?" "What has he that corresponds to heaven and hell?" He has nothing which corresponds to either heaven or hell. For four or five days after death the spirit remains in the house where the death occurred; from then on it remains by the grave until it is summoned to enter a new-born child; and from that time on until the death of the child the soul remains with it, unless it has been compelled to abandon it earlier, as would happen if the child were habitually punished. It is not known to the Mackenzie Eskimo what would happen to a soul in case it abandoned the person it was guarding. (As the guardian spirit is the *atka* of the child, so the child is the *saunirk* of the guardian spirit.)

It happens sometimes that between the occurrence of one death and the occurrence of the next several children are born. Each of them can and does receive the soul of the dead man as his guardian. This is another case of the Eskimo's unclearness of thinking, for they seem to look upon each child as being the abode of the soul of the dead. How a single soul of a single man can, after his death, become three souls or thirteen, inhabiting simultaneously three children or thirteen children, is a metaphysical question in Eskimo theology. They cannot explain the fact, but they know it is so, which, after all, allies their metaphysics to those of other and more highly developed races.

The fact that most things have a religious or supernatural explanation implies that few things have natural ones. The miracles of the Eskimo are like ours in being of supernatural origin, but they

differ from ours in being of more frequent occurrence. It would surprise most of us to see miracles happening all around us. It is not so
with the Eskimo. They expect them continually, and when any one
tells of having seen or heard of a miraculous thing, there is only un-
questioning belief, for it is but the narration of an expected occurrence
and an ordinary one.

Apparently miracles may happen at the instigation of uncon-
trolled spirits, but certainly over ninety per cent of them are directly
ascribed to the activities of a spirit controlled by some shaman.

The list of the different kinds and characteristics of miracles would
be too long to recite. We shall describe merely what, among Mackenzie River Eskimo at least, is the commonest of all miracles, the
best understood and most universally vouched for — the spirit flight
in which the actual body of the shaman flies to some distant place,
sometimes to a neighboring village, often to a far country, and most
frequently of all, to the sun, to the moon, or to the bottom of the sea.
There is also another kind of spirit flight in which the body remains in
its place and the soul alone goes abroad. These two sorts of spirit
flights differ essentially in this : that while the first must be performed
in darkness, the second can be managed in daylight.

The bodily shamanistic flight takes place usually at night in
winter and in the dark of the moon. The event is announced before-
hand and all those who desire to be present gather in the clubhouse or
the largest available private residence. As is always the case in the
Mackenzie River houses, there is one window at the peak of the
"cottage"-shaped roof, and directly under this, near the center of the
floor, sits the shaman, usually wearing no clothes except knee-
breeches, although he may be fully dressed. Two or three men who
are skilled in the manipulation of ropes take a long thong and tie
and truss the shaman until, humanly speaking, it is impossible for
him to move. Usually one feature of the tying is that a bight of the
rope is passed under his knees and over the back of his neck and the
rope drawn tight until his chin rests between his knees. When the
tying is done, there is always left over a loose rope-end about three
inches long to which is attached a stone or other heavy object, such
as a hammer or an ax-blade. Before the beginning of the performance the window has been covered with a thick skin or blanket. All

the people take their seats in a circle about the shaman as far away as possible from the center of the house, leaving him in an unoccupied circle of perhaps ten feet diameter. The lights are put out and the house is so dark that one can see absolutely nothing. Nevertheless every one leans forward and closes his eyes tightly. If there are any children present, an older person sits behind each child and holds his hands over the child's eyes.

The moment after the light goes out the shaman begins to chant a magic song. Presently he says: "I do not feel so heavy now as I usually do. Somehow it seems as if I were not sitting very heavily upon the floor. Now I am becoming as light as a feather. Now I am beginning to want to rise like a dry stick in water." All these things he says in a low and indefinite tone of voice, speaking well in his throat so that it is difficult to judge just how far away he is, but of course thus far every one knows exactly where he is, for he remains (by his own account) in the center of the circle where he was when the lights were put out.

The next stage of the performance is that the shaman, still speaking in the manner of a ventriloquist, says: "Now I am beginning to rise; now I am going to fly in circles slowly just above the floor; now I am flying fast; now I am flying faster." Presently the people begin to hear a whizzing noise. This is the stone or ax which was attached to the loose rope-end. The shaman is now flying in circles so fast that the centrifugal force makes the hammer on the rope-end produce a whizzing noise. If any one were to open his eyes even a little to try to see what was going on, the hammer would strike him in the head, killing him instantly. Consequently, the louder the whizzing noise the more tightly is every eye squeezed shut, and the more firmly are the hands of the parents held over the eyes of their children.

While the hammer still continues the whizzing noise the voice of the shaman is heard to say: "Now I am rising above your heads; now I am getting near the roof; now I am about to pass out through the window." Then the voice grows actually fainter and fainter as the shaman rises toward the roof and flies out through the window, and finally the whizzing noise dies away in the distance.

For half an hour or more the audience sits in absolute silence with eyes shut, and then is heard again the shaman's voice: "Now

I am coming in through the window; now I am settling down; now I am down on the floor; now you may open your eyes and light the lamps." The lamps are lighted, and, lo! there sits the shaman exactly where he was when the lights were put out three-quarters of an hour before.

Some one now unties the shaman and he relates to an attentive audience his adventures on the spirit flight. He went to the moon and approached the house of the man in the moon. He did not dare to enter, but waited outside until the man in the moon's wife came out, saw him, and invited him in. Shortly after, the man in the moon himself came home from a caribou-hunt, bringing with him a back load of meat and a number of marrow bones. A meal was prepared of caribou meat, and after that the three of them cracked marrow-bones until the broken bones lay in a large heap on the floor. The man in the moon said that last year the caribou-hunt had not been very good in the moon, but this year it was much better; the caribou in the moon this year were fatter than usual, which was no doubt due to the fact that the summer had been cool and there had not been very many mosquitoes. The man in the moon's wife also joined in the conversation, saying that they had already secured an abundance of skins for clothing for the coming winter, and that as for sinew with which to sew, they had enough already for two years. She inquired for the shaman's wife, whether his little boy had begun yet to kill ptarmigan, whether the people in the shaman's village carefully kept all the taboos, and who it was that had broken some, for she knew from the vapor rising from the village that something was amiss.

The shaman had answered her questions to the best of his ability. He regretted that a certain young woman had been very careless in sewing caribou skin soon after the killing of white whales, and various other things of this sort the shaman was compelled reluctantly to tell, for he was a truthful man and must speak out, although he was ashamed of his fellow-countrymen and would gladly have been able to conceal the facts from the moon people.

Time is not measured the same way in the moon as upon earth, the shaman tells, and really he had been in the moon a long time, although on earth it seemed but a short while that he was away. He had lingered, feasted, and talked, but finally his visit was at an end, and he started off, promising the man in the moon to visit him again next year.

When the shaman's narrative is over, a general discussion takes place, in which both men and women join, and finally when the crowd gets tired and sleepy they disperse to their own homes.

This that we have described is not one of the most wonderful miracles, but merely the commonest one and the best attested. Some miracles, such as the walking on water, are of rare occurrence, and only a few people have seen them. Raising people from the dead is also a seldom thing. But every man and woman you meet can attest the genuineness of the spirit flight, for they have all been present when it was done. Besides that, such things are a matter of common knowledge among the people. You might as well try to convince an Englishman that balloon flights have never been taken in the British Isles as attempt to persuade an Eskimo that spirit flights have never occurred in the Mackenzie delta.

One day when I was explaining to my Eskimo that there were mountains on the moon and going into details of the moon's physical characteristics, the account I gave did not coincide with the opinion held by my Eskimo listeners, and they asked me how I knew these things were so. I explained that we had telescopes as long as the masts of ships and that through them we could see the things on the moon's surface. "But had any white man ever been to the moon?" I was asked, and when I replied that no one ever had, they said that while they did not have any telescopes as long as ship's masts, yet they did have men, and truthful men, too, that had been to the moon, walked about there and seen everything, and they had come back and told them about it. With all deference to the ingenuity of white men, they thought that under the circumstances the Eskimo ought to be better informed than the white men as to the facts regarding the moon.

It may seem to you that these that we have described are extraordinary and untenable views, and that it ought to be an easy thing to undeceive the men who hold them, but if you have ever tried to change the religious views of one of your own countrymen so as to make them coincide with yours, you will know that the knowledge that comes through faith is not an easy thing to shake, and if you want to appreciate such an attitude of mind as that of the Eskimo and cannot find an analogy among your own neighbors, I would recommend the reading of Mark Twain's *A Yankee at the Court of King Arthur*. It is one of the remarkable things about Mark Twain that he understood the minds of the intellectually primitive as few others have done — even of those who have made a study of such things. Mark Twain's Englishmen of King Arthur's time think such thoughts as I have found the Eskimo thinking in our own generation, and justify them in the manner in which the Eskimo justify theirs. If you were to try to displace from the minds of the Eskimo such beliefs as we have described, you would find (as I have found upon occasion) that you would succeed no better than did Mark Twain's Yankee in his crusade against Merlin. But if you concern yourself not with the unteaching of old beliefs but with the teaching of new ones, you will find an easy path before you. The Eskimo already believe many mutually contradictory things, and they will continue believing them while they gladly accept and devoutly believe everything you teach them. They will (as the Christianized Arctic Eskimo are in fact doing) continue believing all they used to believe and will believe all the new things on top of that.

The belief in the spirit flight is as strong at Point Barrow after more than ten years of Christianity as the belief in witchcraft was in England after more than ten centuries of Christianity.

CHAPTER XXVII

ON THE CONVERSION OF THE HEATHEN

SOME friends of mine who travel in Africa are of the opinion that the greater part of black Africa is on the way toward becoming uniformly Mohammedan. They explain this by saying that the natives do not understand Christianity, but they do Mohammedanism; that Mohammedanism seems adapted to local needs, and apparently is in Africa the right thing in the right place.

A few years ago, when I was a student in a divinity school, I remember the professor of church history and allied subjects explaining how in Europe Christianity underwent local changes to suit itself to the environment and understanding of the different peoples as it spread northward during the early centuries of our era. It is, of course, a truism that every one of us must think in the terms of his own experience. "When I was a child, I thought as a child" applies also to the races who are really in the childhood stage of intellectual evolution. It ought to be self-evident, and really it is when one stops to think, that the Christianity of the cultured, club-frequenting, wealthy man of the city can never be quite the same as that of the farmer in the backwoods, for the thoughts of each and their outlook on life are colored by their associations; still it is apparently true that when the clubman writes out his check for foreign missions and the farmer drops his silver coin in the contribution-plate, each seems to think that the money is going to be spent to produce in the minds of distant savages exactly the type of Christianity which the giver himself holds or which he is in the habit of hearing from his own pulpit.

It has been my fortune at various times and in many lands to see several other religions besides Christianity in actual operation, and to see the operations of Christianity in a large assortment of environments. The religious phenomena among primitive races are in general as fraught with human interest as any of the phases of their lives, and the manifestations of the Christianity which they acquire from missionaries, or from already converted fellow-country-men of their own, should be quite as interesting to us as the native religion of these people — more interesting, in fact, through the circumstance that here we see familiar ideas in strange guise, and have before us phenomena which we are better able to understand than the purely native religions of races that differ antipodally from us in their outlook on life.

One of the races which just now is being converted to Christianity is that of the Eskimo. Those of us interested in missions may have at our fingers' ends the statistics of the work: In such a year the missionary went to this or that district; in so many years he made so many converts; religious services were regularly held; the results of the work are most gratifying. These things we can get out of the missionary reports, and we can hear them from lecture platforms and pulpits when in their sabbatical years the missionaries return to us to tell about their work and its results. I know of no case where there is any reason to doubt the accuracy of the report of these missionaries so far as outward facts are concerned. If they say that twenty-five have been baptized, you may take it for granted that twenty-five have been baptized. There is no reason to undertake an inquiry into these statistics. What we shall undertake — a thing which the missionary seldom attempts — is to examine the minds of the twenty-five converts and see just how much of a spiritual transformation the baptism has wrought, and under what form the teachings of the missionaries are now being treasured in their simple hearts.

I have lived with the Eskimo until they have become as my own people. I pass my winters in their houses and my summers in their tents; I dress as they do, eat what they eat, and follow the game across the tundra to get my food exactly as they do, and I have come to feel that I understand them as well as I do my own people. My footing among them is antipodal to that of the missionary — he comes to teach, but I to learn. He tells them, "Don't do this" and "Don't do that," and the people soon learn what it is he approves of and of what he disapproves; but I merely look and listen, with interest, but without comment. They will show him the characteristics which they know are likely to win his approbation, and they will keep from his knowledge the things he considers reprehensible; with me they take it for granted that I feel as they do — which, in fact, I do in many cases. In dealing with the missionary the Eskimo say "Aye, aye," and "Nay, nay," and they watch him out of the corners of their eyes to see whether they said "Aye" and "Nay" at the right time. The footing of the scientific student is also different from that of the whaler or trader who is not interested in their language or their lore. He laughs at their beliefs and calls them silly, exactly as the missionary frowns over them and calls them wicked. His interests are in fur and in whalebone, as the missionary's are in the teaching of doctrine and the enforcement of Sabbath observance, and the habits of the foxes are of greater interest to him than the habits of the people.

When Christianity came to Rome, the temples of the gods became the churches of God, but there was still the atmosphere of the temple about them. The feasts of the heathen became the feasts of the church. Yule became Christmas, and in German countries the gods Thor and Odin became devils, snarers of souls, and the enemies of the Kingdom. Just so among the Eskimo the missionary becomes in the minds of the people a shaman. His prohibitions become taboos; and as miracles could be wrought under the old system by formulæ and charms, so the Christian religion among them becomes not one of "works," but of ritual, and prayers are expected to have their immediate and material effect as the charms did formerly.

To illustrate one of the phases of the native religion of the Eskimo, we may consider the question of food taboos. In the mountains of Alaska, on the upper Kuvuk and Noatak rivers, and on the headwaters of the Colville, the prohibitions which applied to the eating of the flesh of the mountain sheep alone were as extensive as the entire dietary section of the Mosaic law. A young girl, for instance, might eat only certain ribs, and when she was a little older she might eat certain other ribs; but when she was full grown she would for a time have to abstain from eating the ribs which had been allowed to her up to then. After a woman had had her first child, she might eat certain other ribs, after her second child still others, and only after having five children might she eat all the ribs; but even then she must not eat the membranes on the inside of the ribs. If her child was sick, she must not eat certain ribs, and if two of her children were sick, she might not eat certain other ribs. If her brother's child was sick, she might not eat certain portions, and if her brother's wife died, there were still different prohibitions. The taboos applying to the ribs of the sheep had relation to the health of her children and of her relatives. They also depended upon what animals her relatives or herself had killed recently, and on whether those animals were male or female.

When all the compulsory taboos were remembered and complied with, there were still some optional ones. If she wanted her daughter to be a good seamstress, she would observe certain taboos with regard to the mountain sheep, and if her son was to be a good hunter, there was a different set of rules to be followed; when her son had killed his first game, there was still another variation, and so on. When people of different districts met at a meal, some one, perhaps the hostess, would recite all the taboos which she knew which were appropriate to that meal, and then would ask one of her guests whether he knew any in addition. He would then contribute such as his hostess had omitted; then a second guest would be appealed to, and when all the taboos which all those present knew of had been clearly called to mind, the meal would go on. Then the next day, if one of them had a headache, or if the cousin of another broke a leg, they would say to one another, "What taboo could it have been that we broke?" Some wise old man's advice would be called upon, and he would be told of all the taboos which were observed, and then he would say, "How did you break your marrow-bone?" Some one would volunteer, "I broke mine with a stone." "Yes, and which hand did you hold the stone in when you broke it?" "My right hand." "Ah yes, that explains it; you should have held the stone in your left hand. That is why your cousin's leg got broken. You broke the marrow-bone the wrong way."

It may be a little difficult for the average white man to enter into the frame of mind of those who live under such a complicated taboo system, but it is also difficult for us to sympathize with some of the beliefs held by our immediate ancestors; and if it is a little difficult for us to understand the frame of mind of these people, may it not be a little difficult for them to understand ours? Is it not likely that an elaborate and ingrained system such as this will affect their conception of our rather abstract teachings? A people brought up in the thought habits of a taboo system such as this are likely to continue thinking in the terms of that system after they have been baptized. They will fit the instruction of their teachers, be they schoolmasters or missionaries, into the molds of their ancestral lore.

Among the Eskimo the expression, "a wise man," being translated, means "a man who knows a large number of taboos." He is an honored member of the community always who knows more than any one else about the things that ought not to be done. To know these things is very important, for if they be done — if a taboo be broken — no matter how innocently and unknowingly, the inevitable penalty follows in the form of an epidemic or a famine or an accident or illness affecting some relative of the breaker of the taboo.

An Eskimo who is a great admirer of the white people (and some Eskimo are not) said to me once that some Eskimo foolishly maintained that white men were less intelligent than Eskimo are. But he said that he had a crushing reply to those who made this statement. He would say to them: "Our wise men have taboos on food and drink, they have taboos on clothing and methods of travel, on words and thoughts; but until the white man came, did we ever hear of Sunday? Did the wisest of us ever think of the fact that a *day* might be taboo?"

A shaman among the Eskimos is in his own person no wiser than you or I. In every-day life he is quite as likely to do foolish things, quite as liable to be wrong; but when he goes into a trance his own spirit is superseded by the familiar spirit which enters his body, and it is the familiar spirit which talks through the mouth of the shaman. It is only then that his words become wisdom, on which you may rely unthinkingly. When in a trance the shaman is the mouth-piece of a spirit, and at any time, by the use of the formulæ by which the spirits are controlled, he can get them to do his bidding, be it good or ill. For that reason the shaman is deferred to, irrespective of whether you like him personally or not, and without regard to what you may think of his character and natural abilities, except that the more you fear he may be disposed to evil actions, the more careful you are not to give him offense, and to comply with everything he commands or intimates, for (being evilly disposed) he may punish you harshly if you incur his displeasure.

Just as in Rome the priests of the new religion took the place of the priests of the old, so among the Eskimo the missionary under the new dispensation takes the place of the ancient shaman of the old régime. When he speaks as a missionary, he speaks as the mouth-piece of God, exactly as the shaman was the mouth-piece of the spirits. The commands he issues at that time are the commands of God, as the commands of the shaman were not his own but those of the spirit which possessed him. And as in the old days the evilly dis-posed shamans were the most feared, similarly that one of all the missionaries known to me who is personally the most unpopular among his Eskimo congregation is also the one whose word is the most absolute law and whom none would cross under any circumstances. "For," think the Eskimo, "being a bad man, he may pray to God to make us sick or do us some harm."

Our main purpose here is not to elucidate or to present conclu-sions, but rather to present facts which happen to be chiefly in the form of anecdotes; but the foregoing has seemed necessary to give the reader a point of view from which the evidence can be interpreted. To see the bearing of the facts clearly we must keep sight of the two things of main importance: namely, first, that the ideas which the Eskimo has of the new religion are dictated by his environment and colored by the habits of thought developed under the old religion; and, second (and most important), that he looks upon the missionary as the mouth-piece of God, exactly as the shaman was the mouth-piece of the spirits; bearing these things in mind, we shall glance at the history of the spread of Christianity in Alaska.

Most of the abstract and strange ideas of which the Eskimo of even the civilized north coast of Alaska have knowledge have been presented to them first by missionaries, who generally precede the school-teacher into distant fields, yet we shall draw our first case for consideration from an Alaskan public school. The winter of 1908, and for a year before that and a year after, the government school-teacher at Point Barrow was Mr. Charles W. Hawkesworth. Mr. Hawkesworth was a New Englander, a graduate of Bowdoin, a fine type of man of the sort that is rare even in New England and yet typical of New England. He said, and I agreed with him, that he thought the Eskimo boys and girls at Barrow had as much native intelligence as boys and girls of a similar age and the same grade in school in Massachusetts or New Hampshire. But I told him that, admitting all that, I did not believe they were getting from the books which they read and the lectures which he delivered to them the same ideas that pupils in a Massachusetts school would get, for their environment was so essentially different from that described in the books that many a thing which is a plain statement to a boy in Massachusetts must be to the boy' of northern Alaska a riddle without a key. Apparently Mr. Hawkesworth did not fully agree with me in this, but an examination in United States history which he held shortly after gave results which bore out my contention fairly well. He had been lecturing for several weeks on the causes of the war with England, and his pupils had in connection with these lectures read the ordinary assigned reading required of pupils of the eighth and ninth grades. Among other things, they had heard much of the "Boston Tea Party" and of the events that preceded and followed. One of the questions in the examination was, "Why did the American colonists go to war with England?" and one of the brightest Eskimo boys wrote the following answer: "It was no wonder that the Americans got angry at the English, for the English were so mean they put tacks in the tea they sold the Americans." The point is obvious. Had the lectures and reading been on the Pure Food and Drugs Act, every pupil in the Barrow school would have understood, because the adulteration of food by traders is to them a familiar thing; but taxation, with or without representation, was a foreign idea and essentially incomprehensible. And if taxation is incomprehensible when presented by a schoolmaster, our abstract religious concepts are no less so when expounded by a missionary.

The Christianity which exists in the minds of the missionaries being as essentially incomprehensible to the Eskimo as our abstract political and scientific ideas and complex social organization, the missionaries at first naturally accomplished little. At the mouth of the Mackenzie River, for instance, when I was there first in the winter of 1906–07, the missionaries of the Church of England had been already for more than a decade without making a convert. The people were still unconverted in September, 1907, when I left the district. When I returned in June, 1908, they had been Christianized to the last man.

I am not sure where Christianity started in Arctic Alaska, but I believe it to have been in Kotzebue Sound. So soon as the people here were converted, there grew up among them what might be called an Eskimoized Christianity, in other words, Christianity comprehensible to the Eskimo. The real Christianity had had great difficulty in taking root, but this new form spread like the measles. It went northwest along the coast to Point Hope, and northeast across the mountains to the Colville River, so that when I reached the Colville in October, 1908, every man there had become a Christian, although they had had no direct dealings with white missionaries.

* I was considerably astonished (in October, 1908), on entering the first Eskimo house at the mouth of the Itkillik, a branch of the Colville, to have set before me a wash-dish and towel, and to have my host recite a lengthy prayer over the wash-dish, in order, as he said, to make the water suitable for my use. According to my custom, I declined the use of the basin and towel, even after they had been consecrated, telling my host that a boiled towel would have been much more attractive to me than a consecrated one; for here, as everywhere else among the civilized Eskimo, one must be on his guard against the contagious skin and eye diseases of civilization that spread in no way faster than by the use of common towels.

After my Eskimo companions had washed (from ancestral custom they were inclined to accept every new taboo as a matter of course), another prayer was recited over the basin and towel, and then a lengthy grace was said over the food before we commenced eating, as well as a separate one over the teacups, which were brought in at the end of the meal. Finally, thanks were offered at the close. I asked my host from whence he got these prayers and these new ideas, and he said that they came over the mountains from Kotzebue Sound, brought by a man well versed in the new religion and the possessor of a great many efficient prayers. The best prayer of all

* NOTE: Various incidents in this chapter were previously related in a different context in Chapter VI.

which this man had brought, and the most useful, our host told us, was one for caribou. The Colville people had used it the first year with such success that they had killed as many caribou as they had any need for. This was three years ago, and last year the prayer had not worked so well, while this year it had seemed to be of no use at all. The hunting had been very poor indeed. By the gradually decreasing efficiency of this prayer our host had been led to suppose that prayers, like white men's rifles and other things which they bring, had their full efficiency only while new, and no doubt gradually wore out and finally became useless. (This, by the way, can scarcely be said to be in the terms of the old religion, for it was believed that the older a charm was the greater its power. They had apparently transferred their experience with the white man's shoddy trade goods to the realm of his religion.) Now that this prayer, after three years' use, had lost its power over game, our host inquired anxiously if we did not know a good one from the Mackenzie River missionary, of the general efficiency of whose prayers the Colville people had heard much. I knew no such prayer, and neither did Natkusiak, but Akpek announced he had a fairly good one. When this fact became known, the village lost interest in the two of us in large measure, and concentrated it on Akpek, who was fêted and invited about from house to house, always followed by a crowd of people eager to learn from him the new prayer to have it ready for the caribou hunting in the spring.

We settled down to live with these Colville people, and commenced making preparations for the winter. The only thing to do was to catch fish. Now it seems that in Kotzebue Sound, where the Christian doctrines of the Colville people had originated, fishing is by nets only. As fishing is no doubt practically the only work done there, or was so before the development of mining, the missionary had probably said to them, "Do not put out your fish-nets on Sunday," meaning thereby, "Do not work on Sunday" — there being no other work. However that may be, the prohibition came to our community in the form: "God has said you must not use fish-nets on Sunday." Accordingly the entire community pulled their fish-nets out of the river Saturday night, fished with hooks all day Sunday, and put the nets back into the water Monday morning.

The winter of 1908–09, while I was staying at the village of Cape Smythe, there arrived one Saturday about noon a man and his wife with a well-fed team of dogs and sled-load consisting partly of fresh caribou skins and caribou sinew, which latter has a high value on the north coast of Alaska as sewing-thread. Although this couple did not actually appear at the whaling station where I was staying, I learned about their coming immediately, for the news spread like wild-fire through the village that people had come who had caribou skins to sell. The couple said that they had spent the fall on the upper Colville River, had made a successful caribou hunt there, had stayed until all the meat was eaten up except what they could haul with them on their sled, and had then set out across country, heading northwest for Cape Smythe. This was the substance of what they told about their journeyings, until toward midnight, when they added the further detail that the man's sister and her husband had been with them on the upper Colville, that they had not succeeded so well in the caribou hunt, and that when they started, each family with its own sled, from the Colville, the sled of this second couple had been empty of meat. The family who had plenty had with great generosity fed the family which had none, but had refused to give any meat to their dogs, with the result that the poor animals became nothing but skin and bones. Then a severe blizzard struck them, and all the hungry dogs froze to death, while of course nothing happened to the well-fed dog team. When the one couple had no dogs with which to haul their sled, the other could no longer wait for them and had abandoned them about forty miles southeast from Cape Smythe.

The people who had been abandoned had some relatives in the Cape Smythe village, and even apart from them there were many who were ready to go to the rescue. The relief party was about to set out when some one pointed out that Saturday was just merging into Sunday and that no work must be done on the Sabbath.

Strangely enough, none of the white men at Cape Smythe heard anything of the abandoned couple, although we learned later that their case had been a topic of continuous conversation all day Sunday. The first any white man knew of it was after Dr. Marsh had conducted the regular evening services in the church, when he found, very

2 E

much to his surprise, that the people after the service did not leave the church as usual and go to their homes.   When he asked them why this was, they replied that they were waiting for Sunday to be over so that they could start out to the rescue of a starving couple that had been abandoned inland.   When Dr. Marsh knew about the case he of course did all he could to hurry things up, but it was already midnight when the searchers got started.   The weather had been fine on Saturday, and there would that day have been no trouble in following the trail of the couple who had arrived, but by Sunday night the wind had been blowing and the drifting snow had covered up the trail.   The search party was out two days, but returned to Cape Smythe without finding any one.

A day or two after this, Thomas Gordon, who was living about three miles northeast of Cape Smythe, heard a faint noise outside his front door.   He thought nothing of it at first, but a little later some one accidentally went out and found an Eskimo who had collapsed and fainted on the front-door step.   When this man had been revived in the warmth of the house, it turned out that he was the man of the couple abandoned.   Mr. Gordon sent a sled on the man's trail, and they soon found his wife encamped in a fireless hut, with her hands and feet slightly but not seriously frozen.   Half a dozen hours later she would no doubt have been maimed for life.

While I was in the Cape Smythe village, I never saw the man who had abandoned his sister and her husband to starve and freeze, but it happened a month or two later that my party was storm-bound on the southeast corner of Smith Bay, at the house of an old acquaintance of ours named Kunagrak, who was related to all the people concerned.   The man who had done the abandoning happened to be staying with Kunagrak.   I noticed that when we sat down to meals it was he who said grace; in spiritual matters he seemed to be an authority and the leading light of the place.   As a matter of curiosity I asked him if he had been long a Christian, and he replied, "About ten years."   He further volunteered the information that during all that time he had never eaten a meal without saying grace, and had never worked on Sunday, and had kept all the commandments of the Lord.   I asked him if he had never heard that to abandon people to starve was against the commandments of the Lord.   He had never heard that particular commandment, he said; but that might be because his Christianity had come entirely from some Kotzebue Sound Eskimo. He had never had the advantage of the direct instruction of a white missionary, and no doubt he might not have heard all the commandments of which those might have knowledge who had been better instructed than he. Just as a man who sits down to a meal of mountain sheep will adopt quickly a food taboo of which he is informed by any one who happens to be present, so this man seemed glad to learn that abandoning people to starve was against the desire of the Lord, and he would make a point of seeing that it did not happen again.

Many of my ideas as to the form which Christianity takes in the minds of the Eskimo I naturally get from the Eskimo with whom we most associated, the civilized Alaskans whom we employed to accompany us on our journeys of exploration. One of them, Ilavinirk, was a native of Kotzebue Sound, and had for over twenty years been fairly continuously in the service of white men, although, like the rest of the natives of Herschel Island, he had not been an avowed Christian more than four years.

During the summer of 1909, when we were traveling by boat east along the coast from Flaxman Island, there was in our party, but sailing his own boat, an Eskimo by the name of Oniyak. His old and decrepit father was also of the party, and it seemed to me that I had seldom seen an old man so badly treated, for every evening he was compelled to make his own camp separate from that of his son and family, although there was plenty of room for him in his son's tent. He was not allowed to take his meals with the rest of them, but was given a sort of "hand out." He was continually short of tobacco and matches, although his son was a trader and had more of both than he needed for his own use. The old man used to beg various things from us, which we of course gave him gladly. I did not understand at the time why he should have been so treated, and thought of it only as an unusual example of unfilial conduct. In general I have seen old people among the Eskimos remarkably well treated.

It was only one day at Langton Bay, two years later, that Ilavinirk asked me if I knew why it was that Oniyak treated his father in this way, and when I said I did not know why, he explained that it was because the son had just been converted to Christianity, and the missionary had told the converts not to associate with unbelievers. The old man and one old woman in the tribe were the only two who did not accept Christianity. The old man's son, Ilavinirk said, was in a great quandary, because he was fond of his father but did not dare to disobey the missionary's injunctions. He had found a sort of middle course, therefore, by compelling the old man to keep his own house and to eat by himself.

Continuing on this subject, Ilavinirk said that the old woman who would not accept Christianity was the most perverse old body he ever heard tell of. All arguments had failed to convince her of the truths of Christianity, and she kept saying that she had seen the spirits of her own belief cure disease, avert famine, and bring a change of wind, and she had yet to see that the new religion could do any better. It was of no avail to explain to her that the new religion did not claim to do any better in these things, but differed from the old in promising eternal blessedness to those who lived righteously, and threatened eternal punishment to those who did not. The old woman kept saying she would wait and see. She would not believe in either heaven or hell until she saw them.

Ilavinirk said that the old woman's son was greatly worried by this attitude of mind of his mother, and whenever he got new arguments and new facts from the missionary or from the converted Eskimo he would always present them to his mother with the hope of getting her to experience a change of heart. One day a missionary had preached to them in this way: If any of you believe that fire will not burn you if you stick your hand into it, then you may believe also that the things I tell you are not true; but if you believe that fire would burn you, then you must believe also that what I say is true. (Naturally, no missionary ever said any such thing. What he really said can only be guessed at. Extreme misunderstandings are, of course, common, due partly to the missionary's imperfect command of Eskimo, and partly to the fact that his ideas are essentially strange to them.) When her son presented this argument, Ilavinirk said that such was the old woman's perversity that she only laughed and ridiculed it, saying that she did not see anything convincing about that sort of reasoning. Hoping nevertheless to convince her by an actual test, her son waited until she was asleep, when he lit a match and held it under her hand, letting the flame play over her fingers. The old woman awoke screaming with pain. But so perverse was she that even this did not convince her, and so far as Ilavinirk knew she was still a heathen. Some people are that way, Ilavinirk philosophized. He supposed, however, that if the fire of a match was not hot enough to make unbelievers change their minds, perhaps the fires of hell would be more convincing.

I heard from Ilavinirk a good deal about the religious views of the Baillie Islands Eskimo, but knew little of them otherwise, for it has happened that I have never associated much with that particular group. The summer of 1911 I sent Ilavinirk and Natkusiak to the Baillie Islands with a boat, and they remained there for several weeks. At that time Ilavinirk told me there came from the Mackenzie River the report that God had said that you must not look at the sun. It is difficult to guess what the foundation of this story may have been. It is conceivable it may have been based on the story of how the Israelites fell away from the true religion and worshiped false gods, and how some people have looked upon the sun as a god. Possibly the missionary may have meant to tell his hearers that they must not look upon the sun, powerful and brilliant though it is, as a deity. But what they understood was that they must not glance at it. This commandment struck Ilavinirk as a little unreasonable, and he said that he had argued with the Baillie Islanders to the effect that no doubt God did not mean that they should be prohibited from glancing at the sun, but only that they must refrain from staring intently at it.

As an introduction to the narrative that follows it is necessary to point out that among the Eskimo, as among many other primitive people, notably in North America, a person who is under some sort of taboo must not follow in the trail made by other people, and if he makes a trail, then others must not follow it.

Apparently some missionary in Alaska, or it may possibly have been at Mackenzie River, had preached from the text : "Do not follow in the footsteps of the wicked." What some of the Eskimo thought of me, no less than how they understood the text upon which the missionary had preached, can be seen from the fact that one day I noticed that some Eskimo who were traveling behind me were not following in my trail.

Some of the things concerning which the Eskimo have received new ideas from the missionaries are of a somewhat fundamental nature; other things which Ilavinirk believed the missionaries to have taught his people are rather immaterial and make little difference one way or the other. He told me one day that he had often wondered why it was that the mammoth are all extinct. He knew now, however, for Mr. Whittaker, the missionary at Herschel Island, had explained to them how it was. After God created the earth and made the people and the animals in it, the people gradually became wickeder and wickeder, until God made up His mind to destroy them all by drowning. But one man called Noah was an excellent man. God went to him one day and told him to build a ship, and to take into it all his family, and to invite all the animals of the earth to enter the ship also. Noah did as he was directed and invited the animals to enter, and they all entered except the mammoth. When Noah asked the mammoth why they had not come into the ship also, they said they did not think there would be much of a flood; and anyway, if there were something of a flood, they thought their legs were long enough to keep their heads above water. So God became angry with the mammoth; and although the other animals were saved, He drowned all the mammoth. That is why the caribou and the wolves and foxes are still alive, and why the mammoth are all dead.

With reference to this story and others, I used to argue with our Eskimo, telling them that they must have misunderstood the missionary, and that he could not have said any such thing; but my arguing was without avail. While they considered that I was fairly reliable in every-day affairs, they had my own word for it that in spiritual matters I had no special knowledge. And anyway, they said, in the old days one man knew taboos and doctrines which another did not know, even though both were shamans, and so they thought it was perfectly possible that Mr. Whittaker might know things about God and His works of which I had never heard. Then, too, they said, "He tells us these things when he is preaching" (which being interpreted means that when he was preaching, Mr. Whittaker was the spokesman of God in the same sense that the shamans had been the spokesmen of the spirits under the old system. In other words, when they listen to a missionary preaching they hear the voice of Jehovah speaking through the mouth of a man).

I had many talks with Ilavinirk on religion, for he was communicative, and his mental processes, typical as they are of those of his people, were of the greatest interest to me. It was Dr. Anderson, however, who told me the following: It was when he and Ilavinirk and some other Eskimo in February, 1912, were hunting caribou east of Langton Bay. They had been sitting in the house for some time, and no one had been talking, when Ilavinirk all of a sudden remarked to Dr. Anderson that it was a pity they had killed Christ so young. Dr. Anderson made some non-committal answer, and Ilavinirk continued: "Yes, it is a great pity; for the missionary has told us Christ came to all the people of the earth, and He never came to the Eskimo. I suppose that must have been because He visited the other countries first, and had not yet found time to visit the Eskimo before He was killed." This shows pretty clearly what Ilavinirk's idea was of Christ's having come as a messenger not only to the Jews, but to the Gentiles also.

Another of our Eskimo, Tannaumirk, was considered by his countrymen, the Mackenzie River people, as exceptionally well versed in the truths of the new religion. He was, on the whole, a very sensible boy and a bit philosophical, although not very resourceful or self-reliant in every-day affairs. He liked to have long talks on the whys and wherefores of things. It was during the convalescence of Dr. Anderson from pneumonia at Cape Parry that Tannaumirk and I one day were discussing the religion of his people and mine. "Is it true," he asked me, "that Christ was the only white man who could raise people from the dead?" "Yes," I told him, "He was the only one; and some of my countrymen doubt that even He could." Said Tannaumirk: "I can understand how that might easily be so with your countrymen. If Christ was the only white man who could do it, and if you never knew of any one else who could, I can see why you should doubt His being able to do it. You naturally would not understand how it was done. But we Eskimo do not doubt it, because we understand it. We ourselves can raise people from the dead. You know that some years before you first came to the Mackenzie district Taiakpanna died. He died in the morning, and Alualuk, the great shaman, arrived in the afternoon. The body of Taiakpanna was still lying there in the house; Alualuk immediately summoned his familiar spirits, performed the appropriate ceremonies, and woke Taiakpanna from the dead, and, as you know, he is still living. If Alualuk could do it, why should we doubt that Christ could do it, too ?"

This Alualuk referred to by Tannaumirk is a Point Barrow Eskimo living among the Mackenzie people. I have known him for many years, and I also knew Taiakpanna during the winter of 1906–07. He was then an old man, possibly sixty years of age. The spring of 1912, on my way from Langton Bay to Point Barrow, I visited Alualuk's house and stayed there overnight. Among other things, he told me, about as Tannaumirk had related it, the story of how he had waked Taiakpanna from the dead a few years ago, and continued, with evident regret, to the effect that now Taiakpanna had died again last year, and that he had this time been unable to wake him from the dead because he (Alualuk) had now renounced his familiar spirits and had become a Christian. I asked him whether he could not possibly have summoned back his familiar spirits and awakened Taiakpanna. He said that possibly he might have; he did not know. The spirits had been rather badly offended by his having renounced them in favor of Christianity, and while they might have been willing to return to him again had he summoned them, it was more likely they would not have responded. But anyway, he was a Christian now, and he knew it was wicked to employ familiar spirits. For that reason he would not have been willing to undertake to revive Taiakpanna even had he been able. After all, he pointed out to me, Taiakpanna was an old man, and it was time for him to die. He had been converted and had died in the true faith, and no doubt his soul had been saved and was now dwelling in everlasting bliss; and why should he interfere to confer a doubtful benefit on Taiakpanna, especially when it was at the risk of his own salvation ?

This statement of Alualuk's puts fairly clearly the attitude of his people toward things of the old religion. When the Norsemen accepted Jehovah they did not cease to believe in Thor and Odin, but they renounced them in favor of the higher new God and the preferred new religion. Thor and Odin continued to exist, becoming in the minds of the people the enemies of the new faith and of all who professed it. Just so the Eskimo still believe in all the spirits of the old faith and in all its other facts, and they believe all the Christian teachings on top of that. They have not ceased to have faith in the heathen things, but they have ceased to practice them because they are wicked and lessen one's chances of salvation. The familiar spirits have been renounced, but they still exist, and are in general inimical to the new faith and angry with their former patrons who have renounced them.

Our first experience with the Sunday taboo was at Shingle Point, about fifty miles east of Herschel Island, in July, 1908. Dr. Anderson and I, with our Eskimo and two whale-boats, had arrived there at the boat harbor one evening. Each Eskimo family had its own whale-boat, and we were all bound for Herschel Island and anxious to reach it, because we feared that any day the whaling fleet might arrive from the west, put into the Herschel Island harbor for a day, according to their custom, and pass on to the east, and all of us were anxious to be there to meet the ships.

The morning after we reached Shingle Point and for several days after that it blew a steady head-wind, and we were unable to proceed. We were getting more impatient each day and more worried, for the wind that was foul to us was fair to the whaling-ships, and would bring them in and take them past without our seeing them, we feared. When our impatience to be moving had grown to a high pitch, we awoke on a Sunday morning early, to find a change of wind. It blew off the land, and the weather was therefore propitious for travel. Some of our Eskimo neighbors paid us an early morning visit, and inquired whether we were going to start for Herschel Island that day. My answer was that of course we were, at which they were evidently well pleased; and when we had eaten breakfast a good many of them had struck their tents and were loading the camp-gear into the boats. After our breakfast was over I said to our Eskimo that now we would start, but they replied that they could not do so unless some one started off first, in which case we could follow. Considerably astonished, I asked them why that should be so. They replied it was Sunday, and a person who led off in Sabbath-breaking would receive punishment. Accordingly, they said, if any one was found who was willing to start, they were willing to follow; but they would not lead off, for then the sin would be on their heads, and they or their relatives would be punished.

As many of the Eskimo boats were already loaded, I at first thought it would be a question of but a few moments until some one would start, for these people had all been heathen when I had lived with them the previous autumn, and I could not at once grasp the fact of the new sacredness of the Sabbath, which had been a neglected institution half a year before. But it turned out that of all our impatient party no one dared to start. I went around among them from boat to boat, inquiring whether they were not going to launch out. The answer of each boat crew was that they would not start out first, but they would follow me if I started.

After talking over with Dr. Anderson the necessity of doing something, I suggested to our own Eskimo servants that Dr. Anderson and I alone would sail one of our whale-boats and lead off, and they could follow in their boat; to which they replied that a subterfuge of that sort would avail nothing, for they belonged to my party now, and would (so long as they were of my party) have to suffer the penalty of any wrongdoing of mine. If I insisted upon sailing that day, they would have to sever their connection with us in order to escape the penalty of our desecration of the Sabbath. So we accordingly had the choice of losing the services of our Eskimo, which for the future were indispensable to us, or of letting the fair wind blow itself out unused, which we did.

I spoke to Ilavinirk about the fact that he and I, less than a year before, had traveled together on Sunday, to which he replied that at that time he was not a Christian, and although he had heard of heaven and hell, he had not then realized the situation or the importance of good conduct; but that now he realized both fully, as did all his countrymen, and not only did he not care to brave the Divine punishment, but also he was unwilling to become an object of the disapprobation of his countrymen. (I believe that in fact the latter reason was with Ilavinirk quite as strong as the former, for on other occasions when none of his countrymen were around he often followed my lead in breaking the Sabbath.)

The good wind blew all day, and there we stayed, all of us eager to reach Herschel Island, and each of us unwilling to be the first to break the divine law. Toward sundown the situation was changed by the arrival from the east of a whale-boat manned by Royal Northwest Mounted Police, a party of whom were on their way from Fort McPherson to Herschel Island. We signaled them to come ashore, and they had tea with us. Afterward, when they set sail, all of us followed them, for by landing and taking tea with us they had joined themselves to our party, and it was therefore they and not we who broke the Sabbath when they started off, with our boats close behind. By the time we finally got off the fair wind had nearly spent itself, and most of us had a good deal of trouble in getting to Herschel Island by beating and rowing, which is a detail.

The foundation of the next story we have to tell is no doubt a discussion by some missionary of a text the substance of which is that everything on earth, and all that men have, is from God. This the Eskimo have understood in a manner to make Christ practically the equivalent of the ancient culture hero. Just as Hiawatha gave mankind the Indian corn and taught us how to cultivate it, so Christ has given the white men everything they have and taught them everything they know. Consequently it is not such a wonderful thing, nor indeed one with which we ought to credit ourselves particularly, that we possess marvelous inventions and much knowledge. It is Hiawatha and not the ordinary Indian who deserves the credit for introducing the art of corn-growing; and so it is Christ and not any ordinary human being who deserves the credit for having taught white men how to raise wheat and grind it into flour. "All our knowledge is from God" they understand to mean that Christ, who represented God on earth, personally instructed us in all arts and crafts. Gunpowder and field-glasses are wonderful in their way, but the Eskimo does not see why he should be considered behind the white man just because Christ taught the white men how to make these things. He did not happen to teach it to the Eskimo, which is the misfortune of the Eskimo and not their fault.

In the winter of 1911–12 I met with a striking example of this belief among the members of my own party. There is in use among the Mackenzie River Eskimo for writing purposes an alphabet introduced among them by Rev. C. E. Whittaker, the missionary of the Church of England at Fort McPherson. This alphabet being based on English and being introduced by Mr. Whittaker before he had as yet acquired the same command of the language which he now has, is not very phonetic, and for my own use I had devised an alphabet on more strictly phonetic principles, where the ideal is that each letter shall represent but one sound, and that there shall be a separate letter for every sound. My own Eskimo, who knew Mr. Whittaker's system of writing, soon picked up mine and grew to prefer it. They were very enthusiastic about the new system, and commenced teaching it to their neighbors, for one of the most remarkable things about the Eskimo is their passion for such rudiments of learning as they have been able to lay their hands on.

One day there arose in our house a discussion of the various arts and inventions possessed by the white men, and the Eskimo, in a moralizing way, said that we had to be thankful to Christ not only for the spiritual blessings which He had bestowed upon mankind and the hope of salvation He had given them, but also for teaching them useful things, and especially for teaching them to read and write, for they considered reading and writing to be the foundation of all knowledge and of all the advancement of the white men. With reference to this, I said that they had evidently misunderstood the missionary. The missionary had no intention of telling them that Christ had taught us how to read and write. "Well," they asked me, "if Christ did not teach you, how did you first learn it?" I had to reply that I did not know how we first learned, but I did know that it occurred longer ago than the date assigned as that on which Christ lived on earth, and explained to them the fact that many books of the Bible much antedated the coming of Christ. That was as it might be, about the antiquity of the books of the Bible, they said in reply, but one thing they did know was that Mr. Whittaker had told them that Christ taught mankind to read and write, and as for them, they believed it. They did not know what I thought of Mr. Whittaker, but they believed that he was a truthful man. I told them that my regard for the veracity of Mr. Whittaker was quite as high as theirs, but I felt sure that they had misunderstood him, and then, in a joking way, I said to them that whoever it might have been who originated the alphabet which Mr. Whittaker gave them, it was I myself who had originated the alphabet which they were now using. No doubt, they replied, I knew whereof I spoke with reference to my alphabet; but so did Mr. Whittaker know with reference to his alphabet; Mr. Whittaker had told them that Christ had made it, and that being so, they were hereafter going to use Christ's alphabet and not mine. From that time on they ceased writing letters to their friends in my alphabet or in any way using it, going back entirely to Mr. Whittaker's alphabet.

Those who do not know any situation analogous to the one we are describing are likely to say that any such notions as those indicated by these scattered anecdotes can be easily eradicated by a missionary who understands the situation and sets himself to the work, but this is not so. [Fundamentally, the Eskimo consider themselves better men than we are. In the matter of Christianity they concede that we introduced it, but they do not concede that we know more about it than they do; just as many Christians concede that Christianity spread from Rome, but do not concede that Rome is nowadays the highest authority in religious matters.

A striking way in which this shows itself is in the belief in special revelations which come directly to the Eskimo, and the belief in the rebirth of the Saviour among them. Both in Alaska and in Greenland there have been, since the coming of Christianity, many cases of Immaculate Conception and the birth of heralded saviors of the race. In some cases the thing has been nipped in the bud through the fact that the child born happened to be a female, which was not according to the predictions. A sufficient number of these cases are on record in books, and instead of retelling them I shall therefore merely refer to the interesting accounts of Knud Rasmussen from Greenland, which can be secured in any bookshop or library.

There are also in every community Eskimo who are in the habit of visiting heaven and conferring there with Christ Himself, with Saint Peter and others, quite in the manner in which they used to visit the moon while still heathen and have discussions with the man in the moon. The man in the moon used to teach the shamans songs and spells, and now St. Peter teaches the deacons of the Eskimo church hymns and chants (which are, curiously enough, generally in the jargon language which the whalers use in dealing with the Eskimo).

There are also frequent and weighty revelations in the matter of doctrine. If the missionary should learn of any of these things and should disagree with them (but he is not likely to learn, for the Eskimo have found out that the missionaries do not approve of present-day revelation, and therefore keep it secret as much as possible), they might be respectful and polite about it to his face, as they always are, but among themselves they would say that while they had no doubt that the Lord spoke unto Moses, neither did they doubt that he also spoke unto this and that countryman of theirs; and if what God said to the Hebrews seems to disagree with what He has said more recently, then evidently it is only reasonable to accept the latter version.

One missionary whom I knew set himself seriously to combating the new and strange doctrines which he found springing up among his flock. This was Dr. Marsh, the medical missionary of the Presbyterian Church at Point Barrow. No doubt he knew some of these remarkable phases of Eskimo Christianity before, but certain things which he found astounding were brought to his attention in the winter of 1908–09, after living some time with the Colville Eskimo. In his next Sunday's sermon he took up two or three of the peculiar local beliefs I had called to his attention, and denied explicitly that there was any authority for them. I heard Eskimo discussions of these sermons afterward, and the point of view was this:

In the old days one shaman knew what another shaman did not know, and naturally among the missionaries one of them knew things of which another had never heard. In the old days they had looked upon a shaman who knew a taboo that another did not know as the wiser of the two, and why should they not similarly look upon him as the wiser missionary who knew commands of God of which another missionary had never heard? Was it not possible, was it not, in fact, altogether likely, that there were wiser missionaries than Dr. Marsh from whom these teachings might have originally come?

As a matter of fact, most of these peculiar beliefs we are discussing were supposed to have originated in Kotzebue Sound, and were credited by the Eskimo to the white missionaries there, who are held in high esteem in all of western Arctic America as authorities on religious matters. Dr. Marsh told me that every summer, after members of his congregation visited the Colville River, they brought with them large numbers of new doctrines which were entirely strange to him. At first I believe he imagined he could disabuse the minds of his congregation of these new beliefs; later he realized that he could not, and the net result of all his efforts was that the Eskimo became thoroughly dissatisfied with him as a religious teacher and asked to have him replaced by another.

The story of how Dr. Marsh eventually left his field of work at Point Barrow is of considerable interest. The way in which I tell it may not give the complete story, but I believe that such facts as I state are to be relied upon; at any rate, I give the version which is believed by the white men and Eskimo alike at Point Barrow.

The chief occupation of the people at Point Barrow and Cape Smythe is bow-head whaling, and the harvest season is in the spring. Throughout the winter the ice has lain thick off the coast, unless there have been violent offshore gales. In the spring a crack, known as a lead, forms a mile or it may be five miles offshore, parallel to the coast, from Point Barrow running down southwest toward Bering Strait. This lead may be from a few yards to several miles in width, according to the direction and violence of the wind that causes it, and this forms a pathway along which the bow-head whales migrate from their winter feeding-grounds in the Pacific to their summer pastures in the Beaufort Sea. About the first of May the whales will begin to come. At that time the Eskimo whale-men, and during the last few years the white men also, take their boats and their whaling-gear out to the edge of the land-fast ice (called the floe), which, as we have said, may be from a mile to five miles off shore, and on the edge of the ice along the narrow lane of open water they keep watching day and night for the whales to appear. There is no regularity about the migration; there may be a hundred whales in one day and then none for a whole week, and, according to the point of view of the white men, the day upon which the whales come is as likely as not to be a Sunday.

Dr. Marsh was stationed at Cape Smythe for something like nine

years, and then he went away for four or five, after which he returned
to Cape Smythe again (in 1908). When he was there before, the
Sabbath had not been kept, but upon his return he found that during
the whaling season the Eskimo whalemen would, at about noon on
Saturday, begin to pull their boats back from the water and get
everything ready for leaving them, and toward evening they would
go ashore and remain ashore through the entire twenty-four hours
of what they considered the duration of Sunday. They would sleep
ashore on Sunday night and return to their boats Monday forenoon,
with the result that they were seldom ready for whaling until noon
on Monday. This was wasting two days out of seven in a whaling
season of not over six weeks.

This seemed to Dr. Marsh an unwise policy, and he expostulated
with the people, pointing out that not only might the whales pass
while they were ashore on Sunday, but it was quite possible that
a northeast wind might blow up any time, breaking the ice and carrying their boats and gear away to sea, which, if it were to happen,
would be a crushing calamity to the community as a whole, for the
people get from the whales not only the bone that they sell to the
traders, but also tons of meat upon which they will live the coming
year. "But," they asked Dr. Marsh, "couldn't you ask God to see
to it that the whales come on week days only, and that a northeast
wind does not blow on Sunday while we are ashore?"

Dr. Marsh replied by explaining that in his opinion God has
established certain laws according to which He governs the universe
and with the operation of which He is not likely to interfere even
should Dr. Marsh entreat him to do so. We can tell by observation,
Dr. Marsh pointed out, approximately what these laws are, and we
should not ask God to change them but should arrange our conduct
so as to fit in with things as we find He has established them.

Thinking back to their old shamanistic days, the Eskimo remembered that some of the shamans had been powerful and others inefficient;
that one shaman could bring on a gale or stop it, while to another the
weather was quite beyond control. I have often heard them talk
about Dr. Marsh and compare him to an inefficient shaman. Evidently his prayers could not be relied upon to control wind and
weather, but that was no reason for supposing that other missionaries

were equally powerless. They inquired from Eskimo who came from the Mackenzie district and from others who had been in Kotzebue Sound or at Point Hope, and these Eskimo said (truthfully or not, I do not know) that they had missionaries who told them that whatever it was they asked of God He would grant it to them if they asked in the right way. Hearing this, the Point Barrow Eskimo grumbled, saying it was strange that other less important communities should have such able missionaries and they, the biggest and most prosperous of all the Eskimo villages, should have a man whose prayers were of no avail — that they were of no avail there was no doubt, for he himself had confessed it. They accordingly got an Eskimo who had been in school at Carlisle to write a letter to the Presbyterian Board of Home Missions in New York. This letter, no doubt, made various charges the details of which I do not know.

We have already discussed the foundation for the first two of these charges. The foundation for the third is that in extremely cold winter weather the only sensible and comfortable way of dressing, as I know as well as Dr. Marsh, and as every one knows who has tried it, is to wear a fur coat next to the body with no underwear between. This is the way the Eskimo always dressed until recently, and a man who dresses so has naturally to take off his coat as soon as he comes into their overheated dwellings. It was, until two or three years ago, the custom of both men and women to sit in the houses stripped to the waist. There was nothing immodest about it in their eyes. They did not know that the human body is essentially vile and must be hidden from sight, until they learnt that fact from white men recently. It seems it has been certain missionaries chiefly that have warned them against the custom, and they therefore consider "You shall not take off your coat in the house" as one of the precepts of the new religion, to be broken only at the peril of one's immortal soul.

Dr. Marsh several times spoke to me of these things, and remarked that when in college he had stripped a good deal more for rowing and for other exercises ; that the natural and unstudied taking off of one's coat for comfort in a house could not possibly be considered immodest, while there might be an opening for argument in the matter of the evening dress of our women, where the exact degree of exposure is

2F

studied and the whole complicated costume is planned with malice aforethought.

This he explained to the Eskimo also, and tried by his own example to get them to go back to the sensible way which they had practiced until a few years ago. But with them it was not a question of modesty or the reverse; it was merely that they understood that God had commanded them not to take off their coats in the house, and they meant to keep His commandments. If Dr. Marsh did not know that there was any such commandment, that was merely a sign that he was not well informed. On the other hand, if he really knew of the commandment and chose to break it for the sake of bodily comfort, then that might be a risk which he was willing to take, but one which they did not care to run.

These men who had come to me now explained that while they were still of the opinion that Dr. Marsh was not very orthodox and that there were other missionaries better than he, they had only now begun to realize what hard straits they should be in if they or their families became sick. They had been thinking, they said, of how much they had profited in the past by Dr. Marsh's care of their sick, and of how many of the lives of their women he had saved at childbirth. In reply to all of this I had to explain to them, of course, that Captain Ballinger had nothing to do with Dr. Marsh's leaving, and that all I could do was to go down to the office of the Presbyterian Mission Board sometime the following winter and have a talk with them about the situation.

If you ask the missionaries working among the Alaskan or the Mackenzie River Eskimo whether they have been Christianized, they will say yes; if you ask the Eskimo themselves whether they are Christians, they also will answer in the affirmative; and if you ask me, too, then so will I. But to supplement my answer I would like the privilege of explaining what kind of Christians they are, to explain which fact has been the purpose of this article.

I am so great an admirer of the Eskimo before civilization changed them that it is not easy to get me to say that civilization has improved them in any material way, leaving aside, of course, the question of whether it profiteth a man that he gain the whole earth if he lose his own soul. But although it is not easy to get me to admit that the present-day Eskimo are far better men than their forefathers, it is easy to get them themselves to admit it. In fact, they are of late years rather prone to assert that they are better men than their ancestors. To quote my man Ilavinirk again, he said to me one day: "The people of Kotzebue Sound were formerly very bad, but they are all good now. In my father's time and when I was young they used to lie and to steal and to work on Sunday." "But," I asked him, "don't they, as a matter of fact, tell lies now occasionally?" "Oh, yes, they sometimes do." "Well, don't they really, as a matter of fact, tell about as many lies now as they ever did?" "Well, yes, perhaps they do." "And don't they, as a matter of fact, steal about as frequently as ever?" "Well, possibly. But they don't work on Sunday."

REPORT ON THE NATURAL HISTORY COLLECTIONS
OF THE EXPEDITION

By Rudolph Martin Anderson, Ph.D.

ANYTHING more than a cursory discussion of the topographical and geological features of the regions visited [1] — from Point Barrow, Alaska, east to the middle portion of Coronation Gulf and southern Victoria Island — is impossible within the limits of this chapter. A fairly complete series of the various rock

[1] For the convenience of readers of these notes, the following record of routes traveled, with dates, is given:

April 15th–August 13th, 1908. New York to Edmonton, Alberta; Athabaska Landing, Athabaska River, Athabaska Lake, Slave River, Great Slave Lake, Mackenzie River, Mackenzie Bay, to Herschel Island, Yukon Territory, Canada.

August 14th, 1908–August 21st, 1909. Herschel Island, Canada, west to Flaxman Island, Alaska; Hula-hula River, and Endicott Mountains; Chandlar River (south side of Endicott Mountains), northeast Alaska, to Hula-hula River; Flaxman Island; west to Smith Bay, and east again to Colville River delta, Alaska; up Colville River to mouth of Itkillik River, and down Colville to Beeche Point; east to Flaxman Island, Alaska; Demarcation Point; to Herschel Island, Canada.

August 22d, 1909–March 14th, 1910. Herschel Island, Canada, east through Mackenzie River delta, to Richard Island, N.W.T., Toker Point, Cape Brown, Cape Dalhousie, Liverpool Bay, Nicholson Island, Baillie Island, Cape Bathurst, Franklin Bay, Horton River, Langton Bay, Cape Parry, Booth Island, and back to Langton Bay.

March 15th–December 13th, 1910. Langton Bay, along west coast of Franklin Bay, across the Smoking Mountains to Horton River, down Horton River to Franklin Bay, Baillie Island, Liverpool, across country to McKinley Bay, to east side of eastern estuary of the Mackenzie River, Richard Island, through east branch of Mackenzie delta, to Point Separation, Peel River, Fort McPherson; through west branch of Mackenzie delta, to Tent Island, Shingle Point, Herschel Island; on board S. S. *Herman* to Baillie Island, Cape Bathurst; Franklin Bay, Langton Bay; across Melville Mountains to Horton River; to Darnley Bay, Cape Lyon, and back to Langton Bay.

December 13th, 1910–April 14th, 1911. Langton Bay, N. W. T., Canada, across Melville Mountains to Horton River, up Horton River, across the Barren Grounds to Great Bear Lake, Dease River, Caribou Point, Dismal Lake, Kendall River, Coppermine River, and Coronation Gulf.

formations were taken for the American Museum of Natural History, of New York City, and the Dominion Geological Survey, of Ottawa, Canada, and is now being worked up in detail by the geologists and petrologists of the Survey.

The north coast of Alaska is a comparatively flat tundra plain, ten or fifteen miles wide, a little west of Herschel Island (in Canada), and seventy-five or one hundred miles wide at the Colville, the largest river flowing into the Arctic Ocean in northern Alaska. A number of fairly large and comparatively unknown rivers flow down from the Endicott range through this tundra plain, and lakes and ponds are numerous.

Although they have been nearly neglected by the cartographers, some of the North Alaskan rivers are large — the Colville with a delta forty miles across, and an innumerable maze of channels and islands. The Sharavanktok, east of the Colville, has a delta about fifteen miles wide, with the usual number of low, flat islands and mud bars outside of its mouth. All of these northern Alaskan rivers, being rapid, carry out considerable silt, sand, and gravel, which is deposited in flat alluvial islands, or shoved up by the heavy sea ice into long sandspits or bars outside of the mouths of the rivers. Two of these rivers, the Kū'gū-rak, flowing into the Arctic Ocean near Flaxman Island, and the Hula-hula and the Ōk-pī'lak, which come out near Barter Island, have been recently explored geologically by Mr. E. de K. Leffingwell, and his results here, as well as in charting

April 15th–December 31st, 1911. Coronation Gulf (about 75 miles east of the mouth of the Coppermine River), to Coppermine River, Dismal Lake, Dease River; back to Coronation Gulf (spring collecting around mouth of Kogaryuak River, about 18 miles east of Coppermine River); Duke of York Archipelago; Lady Franklin Point, Austin Bay, Simpson Bay, Dolphin and Union straits, Point Williams, Cape Kendall, Cape Baring (Victoria Island); Amundsen Gulf, Darnley Bay, Cape Parry, Franklin Bay, Langton Bay, to Baillie Island; to Booth Island, Langton Bay, Horton River, and back to Langton Bay.

January 1st–November 1st, 1912. Langton Bay, N.W.T., Canada, to Baillie Island, Cape Bathurst; back to Langton Bay, Darnley Bay, Horton River, Liverpool Bay, Harrowby Bay, the Smoking Mountains, Franklin Bay; on board S. S. *Belvedere* to Amundsen Gulf, around the southern end of Banks Island; Booth Island, Herschel Island; Point Barrow, Cape Smyth, Alaska; Herald Island, Bering Straits, Bering Sea, Unalaska, and North Pacific Ocean, to San Francisco.

a part of the hitherto very imperfectly mapped north coast of Alaska, will doubtless soon be made available through the publications of the United States Geological Survey and the United States Coast and Geodetic Survey.   My own expeditions up the Hula-hula River, into the Endicott Mountains, and on a branch of the Chandlar River (a northern tributary of the Yukon), were made in mid-winter, primarily for hunting, and under conditions very unfavorable for collecting geological specimens, or transporting heavy collections of any kind.

The great delta of the Mackenzie, over one hundred miles wide, is a maze of low, flat, alluvial islands, well timbered with spruce nearly as far north as the south end of Richard Island, and dense willow thickets which gradually diminish in height and luxuriance as the outer rim of islands is approached.   The steep bluffs at Tu-nun-irk, the southern tip of Richard Island, which are from one hundred to one hundred fifty feet high, with rolling hills behind, are apparently a continuation of the Reindeer Hills, which extend along the eastern side of the Mackenzie delta, and outcrop in the last stratified rock on the river's eastern bank some distance below the head of the delta.   From the eastern side of the Mackenzie delta to Liverpool Bay the country is low and flat with numerous small lakes and ponds.   The so-called Esquimaux Lake of the older charts is now known to consist of a chain of lakes extending from near the Mackenzie and running into the southeast corner of Liverpool Bay, west of the mouth of the Anderson River.   The Eskimo Lakes have long been used as a winter portage route by the Mackenzie River and Cape Bathurst Eskimo.   Another portage which I followed with a large Eskimo party in the spring of 1910 extends from the west side of Liverpool Bay, crossing a rather high ridge of rounded hills on the west side of Liverpool Bay, and thence westward along a chain of ten small lakes to a place on the coast called Nū-vō′rak (the Point Atkinson of Sir John Richardson).   These lakes are nearly elliptical in shape, with long axes approximately southeast to northwest, and separated by only narrow ridges not more than three or four feet high.   A range of low rolling hills to the southward separates this chain of small lakes from the larger Eskimo Lakes.

A conspicuous feature of the country east of the Mackenzie, near

Kittigaryuit (Point Encounter), Toker Point, Warren Point, and to a lesser extent east of this region, are large rounded hills of mud or clay, rising from fifty to one hundred twenty-five feet in height from the flat plain surrounding. These hills, called pi-ñok-tja'lū-it by the local Eskimo, are sometimes hemispherical, with either smooth or furrowed sides, and sometimes in the shape of a truncated cone, with a crater in the center, like an extinct volcano. One of the most typical "mud volcanoes" of this type is situated on the flat plain at the base of the Parry Peninsula between Langton Bay and Darnley Bay — a landmark for many miles. In summer this crater has a pool of water in its bottom.

Going east from the Mackenzie along the coast, the first indurated formations appear at Maitland Point (Ik-pi-sūg'yōk — "big bluff"), cliffs of gray shales rising nearly vertical for forty or fifty feet above sea level, breaking down into irregular-shaped fragments. At the eastern end of Harrowby Bay, which extends into the Cape Bathurst peninsula within four or five miles of the west side of Franklin Bay, much farther than the charts indicate, the ground on top and sides of the bluffs is light ashy gray clay, overlying small exposures of thin leaves of broken gray shales with yellowish efflorescence or inter-calations.

East of the Baillie Islands (Cape Bathurst), along the west side of Franklin Bay, are found the so-called "Smoking Mountains," or burning cliffs. These were noted as burning in 1826 and again in 1847 by Sir John Richardson. Within recent times, from our own observations, and information derived from whalers and Eskimo, we know that these fires may smolder for years in one place, then die down, and burst out in another place some distance away. Most of these smoke- and gas-emitting fire-holes are along the coast, but combustion is also going on in one or two places on Horton River, which runs nearly parallel with and only a few miles from the coast, behind the mountains on the southwest side of Franklin Bay.

In 1912, the most westerly smoking cliffs were about thirty miles east of Cape Bathurst, and fifteen miles northwest of the mouth of Horton River. Smoke was also seen oozing out of the cliffs at various points as far as thirty miles east of Horton River. I was never able to see live coals or flames, although the soil is often hot above the smoke-holes. In spring and early summer the clouds of vapor are much more dense, probably due to steam formed by melting snow-water percolating on the heated rock. The smell in the vicinity is always strongly sulphurous. The burning material is apparently a black carbonaceous shale which is much in evidence on the west side of Franklin Bay and on Horton River back of Langton Bay, and varying much in quality, according to the amount of clay it contains. The belief of the Cape Bathurst Eskimo was that these subterranean fires were kept alive by spirits (turn'rat) and they were accustomed to leave small offerings of food when passing with their sleds. Failure to leave these votive offerings was supposed to be followed by the death of the offending party within one year.

The sea-cliffs along the west side of Franklin Bay are usually steep, particularly at Whale Bluff (Kingak), a precipice of shale about eighteen miles east of Cape Bathurst. Still farther east are exposures of yellow dolomite near sea-level with leafy intercalations of gypsum. In many places the cliffs are washed down or caved in as a result of the fires smoldering below, and often the surface exposures show evidence of being residue of the burned cliffs. Some masses resemble vitrified brick or coal clinkers, others are yellowish, of clayey or cheesy consistency, or are composed of various shades of soft red ochraceous pigment, in many places of brilliant hue. These ochers make a very serviceable paint even when mixed with nothing more than seal oil. The water in ponds and rivulets all along this section of coast in summer is usually very bad and almost undrinkable, being strongly impregnated with alum or other astringent salts.

No coal is exposed along the shores of Franklin Bay itself, although I found two thin seams of finely crumbled bits of black lignite between layers of fine loose sand, in cut bank about forty feet above sea-level, in sea-bluffs about one and a half miles west of Langton Bay Harbor. Occasionally large, loose slabs of light, brittle coal, ranging from shiny, black, glossy, clean-fracturing lumps, to shapeless pieces of light brown lignite composed of little changed plant stems and roots, are found on the hills around Langton Bay. South of Langton Bay from fifteen to forty miles, across the Melville Range, coal outcrops in numerous places in the sides of deep gullies and valleys cut by

Horton River and its numerous tributary creeks — veins from one inch to two feet in thickness, alternating with strata of fine sand, friable sandstones, and shales. Some of this coal is of good quality, burns readily in a camp stove, and is readily accessible.

Associated with the coal veins on Horton River are carboniferous shales, which often have hard streaks of iron pyrites running through them. Spherical nodules of iron pyrites are very common in the soft sandstone banks of Horton River south of Langton Bay, and are numerous in places on the river's edge, weathered out from the banks. Short, thin strata of sharp, brad-like spicules are also found here. Farther upstream, Horton River passes through two long series of rampart cliffs — composed of finely grained limestones, with here and there patches of oölite, quartz crystals, and occasional masses of calcite.

The rock formations beginning on the east side of Franklin Bay are stratified limestones, often wave-worn into arches facing the sea. On the east side of Cracroft Bay, the upper surface of the limestone rock is planed perfectly flat and smooth, but scored with small but distinct striæ, overlain with fine yellowish clayey sand and rounded bowlders. Cape Parry and the west side of Darnley Bay show limestone of similar appearance, the limestone often weathering out into irregular cavities or pockets.

From Cape Lyon and eastward to about sixty-five miles east of the mouth of the Coppermine River, the sea-cliffs, where exposed, are dark-colored columnar basalt or diabase. Specimens from Cape Lyon and Point Deas Thompson are finer-grained than specimens from near the mouth of the Coppermine and the Duke of York Archipelago (Coronation Gulf), and specimens from farther east (seventy-five miles east of the Coppermine) are still coarser-grained. Mr. R. W. Brock, Director of the Dominion Geological Survey, who has had our collections painstakingly examined, informs me that only two out of more than fifty specimens of this rock formation failed to show traces of copper.

The rock formations on the north side of Dolphin and Union Straits (southwestern Victoria Island) are stratified limestone, and the columnar pillars of diabase which form most of the islands of Coronation Gulf sometimes show strata of limestone beneath them near sea-level. Sandstone is also found below the diabase in some places. About sixty-five miles east of the mouth of the Coppermine River red granitic rock appears at sea-level and forms many little barren rock islands near shore. In the bottom of Kogaryuak River, about eighteen miles east of the mouth of the Coppermine River, indurated shales of reddish and gray color are found in the bed of the river. Shales, slate, and limestone also appear along the banks of the Coppermine River above Bloody Fall. At Bloody Fall, the Coppermine River cuts a gorge through a mass of the dark-colored diabase rock. Overlying and fringing this mass of diabase just south of Bloody Fall on both sides of the Coppermine River are a series of high, steep hills, composed of a very fine, light-colored, homogeneous clay, like potter's clay. These clay hills extend some distance east of the Coppermine River, parallel with the coast.

The pot-stone, a talc chlorite schist, as described by Hanbury, and used by the Eskimo for making blubber-lamps and cooking-pots, appears, from all accounts, to be found only at and east of a point near the mouth of Tree River (Kōg-lūk-tū-ā′lūk), some seventy-five miles east of the mouth of the Coppermine River. Although this kind of stone is not known to be found in the Eskimo country to the westward, lamps of this peculiar stone have passed by barter as far west as Point Barrow, in early times, i.e. before the advent of white men. Owing to the great amount of labor involved in quarrying out slabs of stone of the proper size, and the time required to work them into utensils, with the very primitive tools which are used, these soft stone lamps and pots are valued rather highly by the people.

The whole region is apparently rich in copper, from at least as far east as Bathurst Inlet, where large masses were seen in situ by Hanbury. Natives of the Coronation Gulf region told us that they usually make their implements, such as knives, arrow-and-spear heads, and the like, from small pieces of float which they pick up on the coast of Coronation Gulf, along the Coppermine River, and in the region north of Dismal Lake and west of the Coppermine. Large masses of copper were less seldom used because of the difficulty of cutting out pieces of suitable size. From the greater amount of copper implements in the hands of the natives of Prince Albert Sound, southwestern Victoria Island, and from the information which

1. Columnar Basalt underlaid by Stratified Limestone.

2. A View of Two Islands, from the Southwest, the Nearer One a Half-Mile Distant.

they gave Mr. Stefánsson, it is probable that the surface deposits, at least of free native copper, are richer in western Victoria Island than they are on the mainland around Coronation Gulf.

Besides iron pyrites used for kindling fire iron is apparently unknown to the Eskimo of this region except as in implements or in fragments of iron or steel obtained directly or indirectly from white men. The art of smelting is unknown, and the only other metallic substances which we found in use were Galena, or Galenite (PbS), and red oxide of lead. The latter is often used by Coronation Gulf and Victoria Island Eskimo for coloring skins red. I was unable to find out where this mineral is to be found *in situ*, but the Eskimo say that they sometimes pick it up on the sea beach in Coronation Gulf. The Galenite is frequently used by the same Eskimo for blackening skins. Specimens of Galenite were found in old house ruins at Langton Bay, although this mineral was not otherwise observed west of Dolphin and Union Straits and none was seen *in situ*.

The most distinctive feature of the innumerable islands of Coronation Gulf is the fact that they lie in parallel series approximately east and west, or trending slightly to a northeast-southwest direction. These islands almost invariably have vertical sea-cliffs fronting to the south or southeast, and sloping down to the sea on the north and northwest, forming an angle of about fifteen degrees with the horizon. The same terraced formation of diabase rock is continued on the mainland west and southwest of Coronation Gulf, from around Cape Kendall to about thirty miles south of the Gulf on the east side of the Coppermine River. East of the Coppermine River the hills are in general more barren than farther west, even the most bleak uplands have little pockets and valleys of green, visible here and there, when surveyed from the higher vantage points in summer — vegetation enough to support small bands of Caribou in almost any locality.

TREES

The great northward extension of the tree line, or the northern limit of the growth of trees, in many localities far north of the Arctic Circle, is noteworthy. Our travels and observations enable us to extend the far-flung line of the conifers considerably beyond the limits assigned by previous maps, in many cases. In discussing "trees" we shall follow the vernacular of the North, and restrict the term to evergreen or coniferous trees, the White Spruce, *Picea canadensis* (Mill.) B. S. P., and Black Spruce, *Picea Mariana* (Mill.) B. S. P., excluding the numerous species of Willows (*Salix*) which, in their creeping or ground forms, struggle up to very high latitudes.

In Alaska, according to the consensus of reports from Eskimo hunters, there are no conifers found north of the Endicott Mountains except a few on one of the eastern tributaries of the Colville. Most of the mountain rivers, however, have large, scrubby willows growing in the deeper mountain valleys and gullies, enough to supply the scanty fuel necessities of Eskimo hunting parties, and in some places even large enough to supply material for the manufacture of snow-shoes and tent-poles. On the Hula-hula River, inside of the foot-hills, just at the foot of the high mountains, I saw one little bunch of Poplars five or six feet high, probably Aspen Poplar (*Populus tremuloides* Michx.), but no other Poplars were seen except in the Mackenzie delta, a few on the lower Horton River, and around Dease River, at the east end of Great Lake Bear.

In the Mackenzie delta, the great wilderness of low, flat islands is heavily forested with spruce, the timber extending in some places to tide water. At the mouth of the Peel River, far north of the Circle, tall, straight spruce of more than a foot in diameter grow densely. The Canoe Birch (*Betula papyrifers* Marsh) and the Aspen Poplar (*Populus tremuloides* Michx.) are also found in small numbers in the Mackenzie delta. East of the Mackenzie there is a little fringe of spruce on the Eskimo Lakes, and the forests come nearly to the coast on the Anderson River, south of Liverpool Bay. South of Langton Bay, the northernmost spruce trees come within ten or twelve miles of the coast on a large creek valley tributary to Horton River. Horton River has a pretty continuous fringe of spruce trees all along the bottom of its deep sinuous valley through the "Barren Grounds," from about forty miles of its mouth on the west side of Franklin Bay to within sixty miles of Great Bear Lake. Great Bear Lake is sur-rounded by a continuous belt of timber, the Dease River is well timbered, and trees are found along the banks of the Coppermine River up to within twenty miles of Coronation Gulf. The most northern bunch of spruce trees in this region is within six miles of the coast on a little creek valley several miles east of the Coppermine River, but these trees are scrubby and dwarfed. In a small, isolated grove of spruce near Kendall River, a few miles west of the Coppermine River, and not far from Dismal Lake, I measured one tree which was four feet and six inches in circumference, five feet above the ground and above the bench roots; the same tree was five feet in circumference, three feet above the ground. None of these trees were very high, but were mostly straight-grained, and not twisted spirally as are most of the spruce in this region.

NOTES ON PLANTS

Very few plants outside of the trees and woody shrubs are put to economic use by the Eskimo. North of the limit of trees, the various species of shrub and ground willows are burned, as is also the Northern Dwarf Birch (*Betula nana* Linn.). The latter, known as "partridge-brush" in the Great Bear Lake region, as ōk-r̂uk′tok by Alaskan Eskimo, and as av-al-lū′kret by the Coronation Gulf people, burns with a fierce heat, even when green, and can be used in a camp-stove if twisted into bunches. On the Barren Grounds, a species of heather, *Cassiope tetragona* (L.) D. Don., is much used for fuel, particularly in the summer-time. It burns either green or dry, and can even be dug from under the snow and burned in winter. This species, or one very similar to it, is common in various places — in the Endicott Mountains, Alaska; King Point, Yukon Territory; Langton Bay, Coronation Gulf, Dismal Lake, Dease River, and Great Bear Lake. It is called Ik-hlū′tit by the Coronation Gulf Eskimo; Pi-la-rau-ū′it by western Alaskan Eskimo (Port Clarence); and Tu-kak-shi-ū′uit by Mackenzie delta Eskimo. The inner bark of the Mountain Alder, *Alnus alnobetula* (Ehrh.) Koch., is often used to stain the inner side of tanned skins red.

The only roots which I have seen used as food by the Eskimo are the roots of a species of Knotweed — either *Polygonum bistortum* (Tourn.) L., *Polygonum viviparum* L., or *Polygonum fugax* Small. The roots of plants of this genus, known to the Eskimo as Mā′sū, or Mā′shū, are frequently dug and eaten in summer, but usually only when there is a scarcity of meat or fish for food. These roots are fairly edible, either raw or cooked, having a slightly sweetish taste, but are somewhat woody and fibrous. On the Colville River, Alaska, the Eskimo preserve the Masu roots in sealskin "pokes," and eat them in a somewhat fermented state. Several species of small ground-growing berries are often eaten by the western Eskimo, particularly a yellow berry called Ak'pek (the Cloudberry, *Rubus chamæmarus* Linn.), the' At'tsi-ak (Alpine Bearberry, *Mairania alpina* (Linn.) Desv.), and the paun'rat (Crowberry, *Empetrum nigrum* Linn.). These berries are eaten by the Coronation Gulf Eskimo, except the akpek, the use of which is unknown, although in the opinion of white men and of the western Eskimo it is the best of all local berries. They are eaten by the Mackenzie Eskimo, but they say they did not use them extensively until taught to do so by the Alaskan Eskimo (not more than twenty-five years ago). The leaves of *Oxyria digyna* (L.), a species of sorrel, are frequently mixed with seal-oil and eaten as a sort of salad by the western Eskimo. The plant is called Kō'na-ritj by Alaskan Eskimo. The partly digested stomach contents of the Barren Ground caribou are frequently eaten frozen in winter. Stomachs filled with reindeer-moss are considered much better than those from caribou which have been feeding on the coarse, woody fibers of grassy plants. As with most other viands, this dish is not considered complete without a liberal dressing of seal-oil.

The collecting of plants on the expedition was only incidental for the greater part of the time, owing to lack of facilities for preserving and transporting specimens. A collection mainly of flowering plants from the north coast of Alaska was completely lost. A small lot of plants which survived the vicissitudes of northern travel were turned over to the New York Botanical Garden, Bronx Park, New York City, and were very kindly determined by Dr. P. A. Rydberg, as follows:

Coronation Gulf. Mouth of Kogaryuak River, eighteen miles east of Coppermine River, Arctic coast, Canada, June 18th, 1911. *Salix arctica* Pallas. Rather small specimen.
Draba hirta L. Tall specimen.
Astragalus sp. An unknown species, somewhat resembling *A.*

alpinus, but more slender, with small, narrow, grayish, hirsute leaflets, purple only on the tip of the keel, black-hairy calyx shorter than in *A. alpinus.* No fruit is found, which makes it impossible to characterize the plant fully.

Lupinus arcticus S. Wats. A form more grayish-pubescent than the Victoria Island specimen.

Hedysarum mackenzii Richards. A low specimen.

Rhododendron lapponicum L. (This species is abundant on south side of Coronation Gulf.)

Cassiope tetragona D. Don. Luxuriant specimens. (Used for fuel.)

Pedicularis lanata Willd. Fair specimen.

Pedicularis arctica R. Br. Good specimen.

Southwestern Victoria Island, fifteen miles east of Point Williams, July 21st, 1911.

Salix phlebophylla And. Specimen with rather large leaves.

Papaver radicatum Rottb. In fruit.

Dryas integrifolia Vahl. Both the typical and the lobed-leaved forms.

Potentilla pulchella R. Br. Good specimen with rather narrow leaf.

Lupinus arcticus S. Wats. The typical form.

Mairania alpina (L.) Desv. In leaves only. It is probably the red-fruited form.

Androsace chamæiasme arctica Kunth. Excellent specimens.

Statice sibirica (Turcz.) Ledeb. Good specimens.

Chrysanthemum integrifolium Richards. Small specimen.

Cape Bathurst, Arctic coast, Northwest Territory, Canada, July 6th, 1912.

Salix anglorum Cham. Typical.

Oxyria digyna (L.) Compt. Good specimens. (Often eaten as a relish.)

Ranunculus nivalis L. Good typical specimens.

Draba glacialis Adams. In young flowers, small-leaved.

Cochlearis grœnlandica L. In flowers.

Androsace chamaeiasme arctica Kunth. Excellent specimens.

Primula borealis Duby. Just beginning to bloom, therefore pedicils rather short.

Phlox richardsonii Hook. Best specimens seen of this rare plant.

Pneumaria maritima (L.) Hill. Good specimens.

King Point, Arctic coast, Yukon Territory, Canada, August 27th, 1912.

Polygonum fugax Small. Out of bloom and spike gone, but probably
this form.

Vaccinim Vitis-Idæa L. Only a fragment.

Valeriana capitata Pallas. Rather small specimen.

INSECTS

While the Arctic regions cannot boast of the number of insects to be found in more southern latitudes, certain species are
found in numbers almost beyond belief. The mosquito, Kĭk-
tō′rĭ-ak of the Eskimos, is a weariness to the flesh during at least
two of the summer months in nearly all parts of the North. Immediately on the coast they may be kept down at times by cold
on-shore breezes, but a few miles from the coast will usually find
them in almost unbearable numbers. I have found it difficult to
shoot a rifle, and have seen dogs practically blinded by mosquito
stings closing up their eyes. Several species of small flies, blue-
bottle flies, and a large species of *Tabanus* are also common at times.
The larger flies are called Nĭv-ĭ-ō′wak by the Eskimo. The
Barren Ground caribou are much annoyed in summer by a species
of bot-fly which deposits its eggs under the skin. These eggs hatch
under the skin, and by the month of February the encysted grubs
are about the same size and appearance of a white navy bean. By
the early part of June, when the grubs drop out on the ground, they
are about an inch in length, with rough, encircling bands. Summer-
killed caribou skins are often almost worthless on account of being
riddled by the holes made by these grubs. The grubs of the caribou,
as well as lice and other parasites found on human beings and lower
animals, are indiscriminately classed together as Kō′mait (sing.
Kō′mak). Beetles and other small insects, as well as small water-
dwelling larvæ, are called Kō-pī′la-rok.

Bumblebees are very widely distributed, and fairly common in
many places. I observed them at a number of points on the north
coast of Alaska, the Mackenzie delta, Franklin Bay, Coronation
Gulf, and Victoria Island. A number of specimens of Bumblebees

were brought back somewhat the worse for preservation in alcohol, but Dr. Frank E. Lutz, Assistant Curator of the Department of Invertebrate Zoology of the American Museum of Natural History, who has been working them up, informs me that they seem to be as follows:

Bombus frigidus F. Sm.   Athabaska River, Alberta.
Bombus polaris Curt.   Mainland, east of Richard Island, Mackenzie delta.
Bombus sylvicola Kirby.   Langton Bay, N.W.T., June 15th, 1910.
Bombus sp.   Either a new species or variety of *B. occidentalis.* Coronation Gulf, June 10th, 1911.

Dr. Lutz also kindly furnished me with a list of the Coleoptera collected, so far as they have been identified:

Cicindela vulgaris Say.   Boiler Rapid, Athabaska River, Fort Chipewyan.
Cicindela hirticollis Say.   Boiler Rapid, Athabaska River.
Cicindela 12-guttata var. *oregona* Lec.   Fort Chipewyan.
Carabus vietinghovi Adams.   Mackenzie River delta.
Carabus baccivorus Fisch.   Richard Island, Mackenzie River delta.
Ophistomus richardsoni Kirby.   Boiler Rapid, Athabaska River.
Amara brunneipennis Dej.   Mainland east of Mackenzie delta.
Amara sp.   Richard Island, Mackenzie delta.
Hippodamia parenthesis Say.   Athabaska River.
Hippodamia sinuata var. *spuria* Lec.   Smith's Portage, Slave River.
Ceratomegilla ulkei Cr.   Mackenzie River delta, Richard Island.
Colymbetes sculptilis Harr.   Richard Island, Mackenzie delta.
Colymbetes sp.   Coronation Gulf.
Grynius sp.   Richard Island, Mackenzie delta.
Silpha lapponica Hbst.   Langton Bay, Coronation Gulf, Richard Island.
Dicerca divaricata Say.   Smith's Portage, Slave River.
Thanasimus dubius Fab.   Fort Chipewyan, Lake Athabaska.
Merium proteus Kirby.   Athabaska River.
Rhagium lineatum Oliv.
Acmæops proteus Kirby.   Smith's Landing, Slave River.
Disonycha alternata Ill.   Boiler Rapid, Athabaska River.
Entomescells adonides Fab.   Athabaska River, Alberta.

2 G

FISHES

Fish play probably a more important part than anything else in the domestic economy of the Eskimo of the western Arctic coast. The list of food fishes is not large, but the number of individuals is so great that a family supplied with a gill-net or two can travel in summer along practically the whole Arctic coast, and be reasonably sure of catching enough fish for themselves and dogs at nearly every camping-place. When all the food required for a family can be obtained by merely putting out a fish-net every night and clearing it every morning, making a living is not a difficult matter. The Mackenzie delta is preëminently a fish country, fish being the staple food throughout the year — fresh in summer, and usually in a tainted or semi-putrid state in winter. Fish taken early in the fall are stored away in large caches, and generally become more or less tainted before they freeze. The tainted fish are always eaten raw and frozen. As usual where game and fish are very easy to obtain in season, the natives generally underestimate their needs for the winter, and have a period of shortage in the early spring.

West of Franklin Bay the common method of fishing is by gill-nets, set along the shore or across the mouths of rivers and creeks, rigged with sinkers and floats, and set from a kayak or shoved out into the water with a very long pole made of driftwood sticks spliced together. In winter the usual method is by "jigging" through holes in the ice with barbless hooks of bone, ivory, or silver, although sometimes nets are set under the ice. Nets are set under the ice by cutting a series of holes through the ice, a few feet apart, and poking a line under the ice by means of long, curved willow poles, or by putting a long stick float with line attached under the ice and working it along from hole to hole with another forked stick. After a stout line has been passed beneath the ice, connecting the two holes at opposite ends of the line, the net is easily drawn under the ice and taken out and cleared of fish at will by merely chopping open the two end holes, the intervening holes being useless after the line has once been passed under the ice.

East of Dolphin and Union Straits, the Eskimo do not use fish for food so extensively as do the natives farther west. They have no

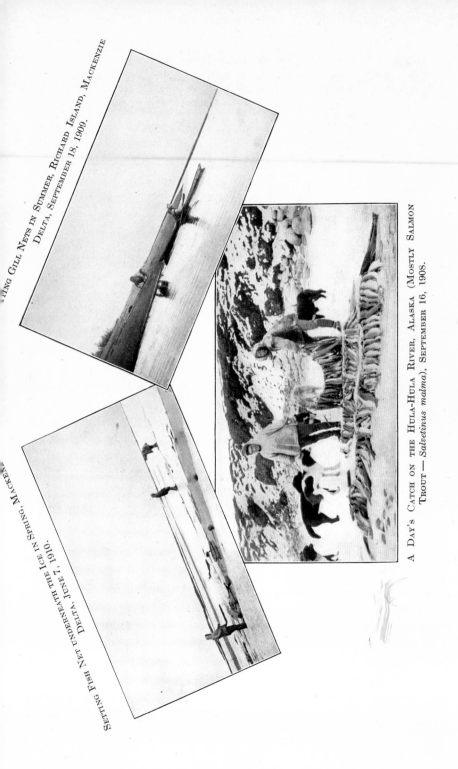

ING GILL NETS IN SUMMER, RICHARD ISLAND, MACKENZIE
DELTA, SEPTEMBER 18, 1909.

SETTING FISH NET UNDERNEATH THE ICE IN SPRING, MACKEN
DELTA, JUNE 7, 1910.

A DAY'S CATCH ON THE HULA-HULA RIVER, ALASKA (MOSTLY SALMON
TROUT—*Salvelinus malma*), SEPTEMBER 16, 1908.

fish-nets, and catch fish through the ice with crude copper and bone hooks, or spear them while ascending shallows or rapids in the streams during the summer.

Our collection of fishes is not at all complete, and although most of the important food fishes are represented, a few were unavoidably omitted. The specimens brought were kindly determined by Mr. John Treadwell Nichols, Assistant Curator of Recent Fishes, Department of Ichthyology and Herpetology, American Museum of Natural History, New York City.

Catostomus catostomus (Forster). Long-nosed Sucker. Mil-lū′i-ak — name given by Eskimo of northern Alaska and the Mackenzie delta. Mĭ′luk — milk; mil-lū′i-ak — he milks, or sucks.

Found commonly in parts of the Mackenzie delta; not valued very highly as a food fish by the Eskimo, and used only for dog-food when other fish are obtainable. Specimen taken in Colville River, Alaska, July 4th, 1909, identified by Nichols.

Argyrosomus tullibee (Richardson). Tullibee. Toolaby. No specimens of this fish were brought back, but from the general appearance of the fish, it is probably the species known to the Mackenzie Eskimo as pi-kōk′tŏk.

This fish is taken commonly in branches of the east side of Mackenzie delta, and we caught large numbers in nets set under the ice of a large lake south of Langton Bay. It resembles somewhat another fish called the An-ark′hlirk. The An-ark′hlirk is much more highly regarded by the Eskimo than is the pi-kok′tok, because the former species is usually fatter. The pi-kok′tok is usually without much fat, and the flesh is rather coarse and tasteless.

Leucichthys lucidus (Richardson). Great Bear Lake Herring. Kak′tak (pl. Kak′tat), the name given by all Eskimo from northern Alaska east to Cape Bathurst.

The most common food fish, found almost everywhere along the coast, and for some distance up into the larger rivers. We found the species common as far east as Coronation Gulf. It is generally taken in gill-nets, during the whole summer, but in early spring at the time when the ice-sea opens up into cracks (early in June, and later), large numbers are caught with hooks through holes or cracks, or from the edge of floating or grounded ice-cakes near shore. This fish is the species commonly spoken of as "Whitefish" by white men and English-speaking natives along the Arctic coast. Specimen from Herschel Island, Yukon Territory, identified by Nichols.

Clupea pallasii Cuvier and Valenciennes. California Herring.

Great numbers come into the Cape Bathurst sandspit during the latter part of August. Only occasional stragglers appear during the middle of the month. On August 3d, 1911, we ran one end of a 200-foot sweep-net out from the beach with a dory, and drew in about thirteen barrels of Herring (about 3000 fish) at one sweep. A very few *Leucichthys lucidus* were taken in this haul. Three days later, at the same place, two hauls brought in about a barrel and a half of Herring and about two barrels of "Whitefish." The Herring were very fat, one Herring being as satisfying as two much larger "Whitefish." The Baillie Islands Eskimo say that the Herring were never caught here before the white men came (a little over twenty years ago), and think that the Herring followed the white men in. The explanation seems to be that the Herring schools come in only periodically, and not often close inshore, while the Eskimo did not use long seines, confining their fishing operations to short gill-nets along the beach.

Stenodus mackenzii (Richardson). Inconnu. Connie. A-sjhī-ū′-rok, commonly called Shī (shee) by Mackenzie River Eskimos.

Common in the Mackenzie River, Great Slave Lake, and up the Slave River as far as the Grand Rapids at Fort Smith, 60° N. Lat. Found in brackish and salt water as far west of the Mackenzie mouth as Shingle Point, and occasionally as far west as Herschel Island, on the east side of the delta to Toker Point. I have seen specimens taken in the mouth of Anderson River, Liverpool Bay. Did not observe the species west of Herschel Island or east of Cape Bathurst. Large numbers are caught in gill-nets in brackish water at Shingle Point, Mackenzie Bay, in July and August, but the flesh is rather soft and flabby at that season. Eskimo catch many with barbless hooks through the ice on the east mainland side of Richard Island in October, November, and December. The Connies are fat and firm of flesh at that season. Not many are caught in midwinter, but they

bite better again after the sun comes back, later in the winter. The average weight here is eight or ten pounds, but I have seen a specimen taken at Fort McPherson, Peel River, weighing nearly fifty pounds. *Salvelinus malma* (Walbaum).   Salmon Trout. Ek-kal-lûk′pĭk,
name given by Eskimo from northern Alaska to Coronation Gulf.

Found in most of the larger streams where the water is clear. Not so common in salt water, but quite frequently taken at Herschel Island, Cape Bathurst, and Langton Bay. Specimens from Herschel Island and Hula-hula River, Alaska, identified by Nichols. While seining some pools in the Hula-hula River, in the foothills of the Endicott Mountains, Alaska, together with the common form we caught a large number of what may be a dark phase of this variable species, or perhaps another species. The common form seen near the coast has back dull grayish green, sides pale silvery green, with numerous round, pale pink spots, and belly silvery white. The others had back very dark olive, almost black, with very faint, small, obscure, pinkish spots, some irregular, some comma-shaped, etc.; sides bright olive-green, with brilliant vermilion spots; belly bright vermilion, sometimes inclined to crimson, slightly paler along median line, and fading to salmon color on breast and throat; pectoral and ventral fins with anterior border white. Females were duller colored, belly pink or rosy, sometimes with a yellowish tint, and the lower jaws were less strongly hooked; most of the fish were spawning at that time (September 11th, 1908), the large yellow eggs being about the size of No. 1 shot. These brilliantly colored Trout were seen only in the Hula-hula River, and no specimens were brought out.

Cristivomer namaycush (Walbaum).   Lake Trout.   Kal-ū-ak′pŭk,
Mackenzie River Eskimo name for fish brought from the Eskimo Lakes.   Also called Siñ-a-yō′ri-ak by Mackenzie River and Baillie Islands people.   I-shi-ū′mŭt, Coronation Gulf Eskimo name.

Found in most large inland lakes from Alaska to Coronation Gulf. At Great Bear Lake the people claim that they are often taken of forty pounds' weight, and occasionally run to sixty pounds. They are taken on set-hooks, or by "jigging" through the ice, or in nets. One specimen from northern foothills of Endicott Mountains, Alaska, and three specimens from lake at head of Coal Creek, Horton River, about forty miles south of Langton Bay, were identified by Nichols.

Thymallus signifer (Richardson). Arctic Grayling. Sū-lûk-pau′-rak (Alaskan Eskimo), or Sū-lûk-pau′yak (Mackenzie River Eskimo).

Observed the Grayling in the Hula-hula and Chandlar rivers, Alaska, in the Horton River and its tributaries, and in the Dease River. It was not observed in the delta of the Mackenzie River, as the water seems to be too turbid, but caught one and saw several in the Mackenzie at Fort Providence, where the river water is quite clear. The Grayling is commonly called Bluefish on the Mackenzie.

Osmereus dentex Steindachner. Arctic Smelt.

Very rarely taken along the Arctic coast. One specimen, taken at Cape Bathurst, was identified by Nichols, who says: "The smelt is *Osmereus dentex*, as it agrees pretty well with the type description of that species, and perfectly with specimens from Vladivostock, which is not far from the type locality. It is quite unlike the description of that fish from Alaska, but probably those descriptions are inaccurate. At any rate, it is the Alaskan fish, not our specimen, which may be different."

Esox lucius Linnæus. Pike. Jackfish. Shĭ-ū′lik, name given by Eskimo from northern Alaska to Cape Bathurst.

Found abundantly in the Mackenzie delta and other rivers, also in lakes as far east as Coronation Gulf. Specimens from lake near Horton River, south of Langton Bay, identified by Nichols.

Platichthys stellatus (Pallas). Starry Flounder.

Small Flounders were occasionally taken in our nets at Langton Bay only, and we did not find them very common. Specimens identified by Nichols.

Microgadus proximus (Girard). Tomcod. Ō′gak (pl. Ō′kat), by Eskimo as far east as Coronation Gulf.

At Toker Point, on the east side of the mouth of the Mackenzie River, the species is apparently rare. Locally common in Liverpool Bay. Tomcod are very abundant in certain spots near the eastern end of Langton Bay, and are very easily hooked through the ice all winter with almost any kind of hook. In Coronation

Gulf they are common in certain localities. The Copper Eskimo catch them with a very large, barbless, gaff-like hook which is "jigged" up and down. On the shank of the hook, two or three inches above the point, small bangles of white bone are suspended. When the fish come to nibble at these swinging bangles, the hook is jerked sharply up, usually catching the fish in the throat. A species of Rock Cod, growing to eighteen inches in length, is occasionally caught in the Tomcod fishing place at Langton Bay, and is called U-ga'vik. The Rock Cod was not observed elsewhere.

Cottus punctulatus (Gill).   Blob.   Miller's Thumb.

One specimen, taken in the upper portion of the Chandlar River, Endicott Mountains, Alaska, February 23d, 1909, was identified by Nichols.

Oncocottus hexacornis (Richardson).   Six-horned Bullhead.

This Sculpin was described from specimens collected at the mouth of Tree River near the Coppermine. Sculpins or "Bullheads" are found almost everywhere along the Arctic coast, but are only occasionally eaten by the Eskimo, at times when other fish are scarce. They are quite common as far up the Mackenzie delta as Kittigaryuit, but I did not notice any farther up the river. They are frequently taken on hooks while fishing in salt water for Tomcod and other fish. The common, universally distributed species is dull drab-colored, paler below. In Langton Bay we occasionally caught another species, averaging a little larger, and lighter colored, mottled with yellowish. Kā-nai'yūk is the Eskimo name for the Sculpin from northern Alaska to Coronation Gulf.

Lota maculosa (Le Sœur).   Ling.   Loche.   Known as Tĭ-tal'-
lirk by the Eskimo from northern Alaska to Cape Bathurst.

It is probably the favorite food fish of all these Eskimo, and is universally distributed in fresh and brackish waters, but seems nowhere to be taken in very large numbers. The very large, fatty liver is considered the best portion for food. It is caught both in gill-nets and on set-hooks on the bottom. Specimen from Horton River, about thirty-five miles south of Langton Bay, was identified by Nichols.

BIRDS

(7)   *Gavia immer* (Brünnich).   Loon.   Tūh′lik.

The Common Loon or Great Northern Diver occasionally straggles to the Arctic coast, both in Alaska and Canada.   It closely resembles the Yellow-billed Loon, which is pretty generally distributed, but the Common Loon is smaller in size and is easily recognized by the black bill.   I saw one specimen swimming in mouth of Kogaryuak River, Coronation Gulf, eighteen miles east of the mouth of the Coppermine, June 26th, 1911.   Captain Fritz Wolki showed me the head of one killed at mouth of Horton River, on the west side of Franklin Bay, the only one seen during several years' hunting in that region.   One was seen near Langton Bay in 1910.   Mr. E. de K. Leffingwell informed me that a *black-billed* Tuh-lik was killed near Flaxman Island, Alaska, the first specimen that the Eskimo there had ever seen.

(8)   *Gavia ádamsi* (Gray).   Yellow-billed Loon.   Tūh′lik.

The Yellow-billed Loon is found in most places on the Arctic coast in summer, from northwestern Alaska to Coronation Gulf, but does not seem to be very common anywhere.   Its note is a wild piercing whistle, quite unlike the note of either the Pacific or Red-throated Loons, and its light horn-colored or whitish bill can be recognized almost as far as the bird can be seen.   The species is well known to the Eskimo, who formerly used the head and bill as an ornament on ceremonial dresses and dance-caps.   I have never been able to find a nest of this bird or hear of any white man or native in the North who had ever done so.

(9)   *Gavia arctica* (Linnæus).   Black-throated Loon.

All specimens of Black-throated Loon in my collection (from northern Alaska, Mackenzie delta, Franklin Bay, and Coronation Gulf) were referred to the Pacific species, after consultation and comparison by Dr. Louis P. Bishop, Dr. Jonathan Dwight, Jr., and Mr. A. C. Bent.   Dr. Bishop states that he has specimens of true *arctica* from Franklin Bay.

(10)   *Gavia   pacifica*   (Lawrence).   Pacific Loon.   Mal-lē-rē′ (Alaskan Eskimo).   Kak′tjauk kak-hlū′lik, Hooded Loon (Mackenzie Eskimo).

Fairly common in most Arctic localities as far east as Coronation Gulf. My specimens from Coronation Gulf show a slight tendency towards an intermediate relation with *G. arctica*, but the *pacifica* characters seem to be more marked. Dr. Louis P. Bishop gives as the most valuable diagnostic mark that *G. pacifica* has much wider white barrings on the back than *G. artica*. Found nests with fresh eggs on July 5th, 1911, on south side of Coronation Gulf, and on June 22d and 28th, 1912, near Cape Bathurst. All nests on little semi-floating islands in shallow marshes. The Eskimo consider all Loons good game-birds, and I should call them as good eating as the average sea ducks. In the spring migration of 1910, on the east side of the Mackenzie delta, large numbers were shot by the natives as they passed over, singly and in pairs, flying straight northeast along the coast with rapid, regular flight. They usually rise from the water by flapping and splashing along the surface for some distance.

(11) *Gavia stellata* (Pontoppidan). Red-throated Loon. Kak-tjauk or Kak-sauk. Sometimes Kak-tjauk-pi-a'luk, "the ordinary Loon," to distinguish from *pacifica* (Mackenzie Eskimo).

Common everywhere along the Arctic coast; in most places more abundant than the Pacific Loon. On the wing its flight is rapid and regular, and I have seen the bird fly up directly from the water like a duck. On account of its prevalence and its large repertoire of loud, weird, and startling notes, which are heard at all hours of the twenty-four, the Red-throated Loon is in many ways the most notable summer bird of the Arctic. Sometimes a shrill staccato shriek, at other times like the distant wailing or moaning of a child, any uncanny or unaccountable noise can usually be correctly attributed to a Kak-sauk.

Like the Pacific Loon, the Red-throated Loon begins nesting a little later than most of the Arctic birds. Near the mouth of the Colville River, northern Alaska, I took one set of two slightly incubated eggs July 4th, 1909, on wet, boggy ground at brink of a pond. Another more advanced in incubation on July 13th, on a little flat-topped peat island about eight inches above water level. On south side of Coronation Gulf fresh eggs were taken on June 28th and July 11th, 1911, and downy young on the Duke of York Islands July 21st.

Near Cape Bathurst fresh eggs were taken on June 22d and 28th, 1912. Near Kay Point, Yukon Territory, we shot two juvenal specimens which were full-grown, although the sterna were entirely cartilaginous and the coracoids nearly so.

(31 a) *Uria lomvia arra* (Pallas). Pallas's Murre.

One specimen was taken at Herschel Island, Yukon Territory, and preserved by the late Sergeant J. A. E. Selig, of the Royal Northwest Mounted Police, in 1909 or 1910, and later presented to me. I did not observe any other examples of this species, or in fact any other birds which could be identified as belonging to the Auk, Murre, or Puffin group anywhere east of Flaxman Island, Alaska.

(36) *Stercorarius pomarinus* (Temminck). Pomarine Jaeger. I-shūng-ok. Kĭ-pĭ-yōk-tel'lik (Baillie Islands).

Rather more local in distribution than the two other species of Jaegers. I did not see any west of the Mackenzie or east of Cape Parry. Large numbers were seen on the east side of the Mackenzie early in June, flying to northeast, in company with the other species, usually in twos or threes. On the west side of Franklin Bay this species is most abundant. Its habits and flight are quite hawk-like, but it is a little more sluggish than either the Parasitic or Long-tailed species. It is readily distinguished from the others by the rudder-like middle tail feathers. The dusky phase is much less common than the white phase, about one to one hundred in the Franklin Bay region. The dusky phase of the Long-tailed Jaeger is much more frequent. One set of two eggs was taken on Baillie Islands July 3d, 1912, the nest consisting merely of a few leaves and bits of grass lining a little hollow in a small turf elevation in a wide flat of soft, wet tundra.

(37) *Stercorarius parasiticus* (Linnæus). Parasitic Jaeger. I-shūng'ok.

Fairly common and generally distributed. The Jaegers are the terror of the smaller birds, spending their time ceaselessly hawking back and forth over the tundra looking for eggs and young birds. Large numbers of eggs of Eiders and Gulls are destroyed in the rookeries by the Jaegers. Wherever the Arctic Terns are nesting, their neighbors are comparatively safe, as the belligerent little Terns speedily cause any marauding Jaeger to beat a hasty retreat. I have also seen Ruddy Turnstones drive a Jaeger away from their nests. I once observed a pair of Jaegers chasing a flock of Sandpipers. One Sandpiper flew out of the flock, the Jaegers in pursuit. They seemed to work together, one darting in while the other turned. The Sandpiper finally escaped by flying upward until almost out of sight, and the Jaegers finally gave up the chase. Found a nest and two eggs near Colville delta June 24th, 1909, on the tip of a little peninsula projecting into a small pond about half a mile from the coast. The female present was of the white, the male of the dark, phase. Some other birds will also attack the Jaegers, which are really cowardly birds when heartily opposed. I have on two or three occasions seen a Rock Ptarmigan fly fiercely at a Jaeger which came too near his nesting place, and put the Jaeger to ignominious flight.

(38) *Stercorarius longicaudus* Vieillot.   Long-tailed Jaeger. I-shūng-ok.

Generally distributed and probably the most common species in most localities. Habits identical with those of the Parasitic Jaeger, and the two species are rather hard to distinguish from each other in life. Nest usually a little depression in moss on upland tundra not far from the sea-coast. When the nest is approached, the parent birds usually make a great deal of fuss, screaming and darting down at the intruder's head.

(39) *Pagophila alba* (Gunnerus).   Ivory Gull.

Three Ivory Gulls were seen and one female shot by Stefánsson, October 7th, 1908, about fifteen miles east of Beachy Point, the eastern edge of the Colville River delta, northern Alaska. This species was not positively identified on any other occasion by members of our party.

(42) *Larus hyperboreus* Gunnerus.   Glaucous Gull.   Nau'yak (gull).   Nau-ya-vuk (big gull).

Fairly common in most localities on Arctic coast, nesting singly or in small colonies either on tops of rocky islands or ledges of sea cliffs or on small low islands in tundra lakes. Wandering gulls usually appear along the Arctic coast early in May, become fairly common by the end of May, and remain until October. All the gulls are considered game-birds by the Eskimo, and when young (in the gray or dusky plumage) are not bad eating.

(44) *Larus glaucescens* Naumann.   Glaucous-winged Gull.
Nau'yak.

Common at various points along the Arctic coast, but in life is
difficult to distinguish from other closely related species. Specimens from Barter Island, Alaska, and Langton Bay were preserved.
At Langton Bay in September large numbers of this species (mostly
juvenal) were seen in company with *L. hyperboreus*, feeding on carcass of a stranded whale.

(51) *Larus argentatus* Pontoppidan.   Herring Gull.

Common on Great Slave Lake. One female specimen taken at
mouth of Kogaryuak River, Coronation Gulf, June 10th, 1911.

(53) *Larus californicus* Lawrence.   California Gull.   Nau'yak.

Common species in Coronation Gulf.   Male specimen taken at
mouth of Kogaryuak River, June 10th, 1911.   Numbers nesting with
Glaucous Gulls on shelves of rock on Duke of York Archipelago,
Coronation Gulf, and near Point Williams, Victoria Island.   Probably equally abundant farther west, but the species was not distinguished from the other species and no specimens preserved.

(54) *Larus delawarensis* Ord.   Ring-billed Gull.

Common on Athabaska Lake. A few nesting on small, rocky
islands in the Grand Rapids of Slave River. Not seen on the Arctic
coast.

(55) *Larus brachyrhynchus* Richardson.   Short-billed Gull.   Nau-
ya-vat'kū-tjū-a'lik (Mackenzie Eskimo).

Fairly common in Mackenzie delta.   Our specimen taken on
mainland east of Richard Island, June 7th, 1910.

(61) *Rhodostethia rosea* (Macgillivray).   Ross's Gull.

This species was not observed on any of our journeys.   Whalers
say that the species occasionally is seen in some numbers near Point
Barrow in the fall, and that often large numbers used to come around
the ships while cutting in Bow-head Whales in the vicinity of Herald
Island and Wrangell Land late in the fall.

(62) *Xema sabini* (J. Sabine).   Sabine's Gull.   Ka-rĭ-ga'gū-ak
(western Eskimo).   Ĭk-kēg-gā'gĭ-ak (Baillie Islands Eskimo).

Observed in small numbers during the breeding season from the
Colville delta, Alaska, east to Coronation Gulf.   Downy young
were captured in Austin Bay, southern Victoria Island, July 23d, 1911.

FEMALE ROCK PTARMIGAN,
CORONATION GULF.

NEST OF ROCK PTARMIGAN, NEAR FRANK-
LIN BAY, JUNE 17, 1911. R. M. A.

Large numbers were found nesting on the edges of a large, marshy lake near Cape Bathurst, Franklin Bay, on June 22d and 28th, 1912. The nests were usually on a little low, wet, boggy peninsula projecting out into the water, but sometimes on flat, boggy ground over one hundred yards from water. The Gulls were often seen sitting on eggs, but flew up when a person came within thirty yards or more, circling about overhead screaming tsû-tsû-tsû-û (very rapidly and shrilly). They feed by walking over wet, boggy ground or over tide flats, picking up bits, or by swimming in shoal water and picking up minute particles from the surface in the manner of Phalaropes.

(70) *Sterna hirundo* Linnæus. Common Tern.

Numbers nesting in delta of Slave River, Mackenzie Territory, on low sand and mud-bar islands. I did not take any specimens on the Arctic coast, but Captain Joseph F. Bernard showed me several specimens of eggs which he had taken, with parent birds, on Jags River sandspit, near Barter Island, Alaska, July 7th, 1910. A small colony were nesting here, near to a larger colony of Arctic Terns.

(71) *Sterna paradisæa* Brünnich. Arctic Tern. I-mĭt-kō-tai′lak.

Nesting commonly in colonies all along the Arctic coast on sandspits and bars, or on islands in rivers and lakes near the coast. Nests are sometimes placed within two or three feet of a Black Brant's or Eider Duck's nest. This is an advantageous arrangement, as the pugnacious little Terns effectually keep off any predatory gulls or Jaegers which are always on the lookout for eggs of other birds. The Eiders suffer severely when nesting alone, but when Terns occupy the same rookery, the Ducks usually hatch their eggs unless disturbed by man or large animals.

(125) *Pelecanus erythrorhynchos* Gmelin. White Pelican.

In 1908 (June 9th), visited a rookery on a small, timbered island in the Grand Rapids of the Slave River 60° N. Lat., which contained ninety-seven nests, some with eggs and some with young birds, on an area of perhaps fifty feet in diameter. The Indian who accompanied me said that the Pelicans formerly nested on a small, barren rock about two hundred yards above the present rookery, but had moved to the larger island two years before. This is probably the most northerly nesting place of this species, which is unknown to the natives of the Mackenzie delta. Captain F. Wolki, who had a little trading station at the mouth of Horton River, on the west side of Franklin Bay, about 1903–1907, states that he saw White Pelican killed near the mouth of Anderson River at the southern end of Liverpool Bay, the only specimen the natives had ever seen.

(129) *Mergus americanus* Cassin. Merganser.

Observed on the Athabaska River, but not near the Arctic coast.

(130) *Mergus serrator* Linnæus. Red-breasted Merganser. Pai (Alaskan and Mackenzie Eskimos).

Fairly common in the Mackenzie delta in the deep, narrow creeks, grown up to the dense willow thickets. Occasional on the Arctic coast of Alaska. Shot five in the mouth of the Hula-hula River, September 5th, 1908. At that time the wing quills were nearly grown, but the ducks either could not or would not fly, and tried to escape by diving.

(132) *Anas platyrhynchos* Linnæus. Mallard.

I did not see any Mallards farther north than the lower part of Slave River, but Mr. H. W. Jones informed me that the species was found at Hay River at the western end of Great Slave Lake. His first 1908 record was May 1st, and he took a set of ten eggs May 28th, with incubation advanced.

(137) *Mareca americana* (Gmelin). Baldpate.

Observed this species in the Slave River delta June 21st, 1908. Mr. H. W. Jones reported it at Hay River, and Captain F. Wolki informed me that he had taken specimens once or twice at the mouth of Horton River on Franklin Bay.

(139) *Nettion carolinense* (Gmelin). Green-winged Teal. Sha-vĭ-lĭ-r̃a'lŭk (Mackenzie Eskimo). (Named from metallic luster on speculum.)

Found one nest in delta of Slave River June 23d, 1908, hidden in dead grass on a small hummock at roots of a clump of willows. Rather rare in Mackenzie delta, but several specimens taken on mainland east of Richard Island in June, 1910.

(142) *Spatula clypeata* (Linnæus). Shoveler.

Nesting in the Slave River delta in some numbers. A few seen in the Mackenzie delta in June. Captain F. Wolki says that he shot six Shovelers at the mouth of Horton River several years ago.

(143) *Dafila acuta* (Linnæus). Pintail. Kū'rū-ak (Alaskan Eskimo). Iv'ū-rak (Mackenzie Eskimo).

Rather common in fresh-water ponds along the Arctic coast of Alaska and Canada as far east as Coronation Gulf. In the Mackenzie delta the Pintail begins to nest early in June. At Cape Bathurst, on the 28th of June, 1912, female Pintails had shed quills and were unable to fly, while the males were flying around in flocks.

(146) *Marila americana* (Eyton). Redhead.

Did not observe this species, but Mr. H. W. Jones informs me that it occurs at Hay River, where he noted the first spring arrival May 17th, 1908.

(148) *Marila marila* (Linnæus). Scaup Duck. Kak-hlū-tok' (Alaskan and Mackenzie Eskimo).

June 9th, 1910. Shot a female Scaup from a bunch of four which flew over our blind on east side of Mackenzie delta, opposite Richard Island. The Eskimo here do not distinguish between this species and the Lesser Scaup.

(149) *Marila affinis* (Eyton). Lesser Scaup Duck. Kak-hlū-tak' (Alaskan and Mackenzie Eskimo).

Fairly common throughout the Mackenzie delta. July 22d, 1908, saw a flock in a reedy pond on a large island and killed three. Two had the primaries shed and one had wing and tail feathers still in place. Occasional specimens taken near Langton Bay and on south side of Coronation Gulf.

(151) *Clangula clangula americana* (Bonaparte). Golden-eye.

Common on the Athabaska, Slave, and upper Mackenzie rivers; known almost universally as "Wood Duck" in this region. The only Arctic occurrence which I have noted is of a few seen on the east branch of the Mackenzie delta, June 24th, 1910. These birds may have been Barrow's Golden-eye *Clangula islandica* (Gmelin).

(153) *Charitonetta albeola* (Linnæus). Buffle-head.

Observed on the Athabaska River in May, 1908.

(154) *Harelda hyemalis* (Linnæus). Old-squaw. A-har'lik. A-ha'lirx (Alaskan Eskimo). Ma-lǐ-ɼa'lūk (Mackenzie Eskimo).

The commonest duck found in the Arctic — everywhere along the coast and in fresh-water ponds and lakes. During the whole summer its "A-ha-ha'lik" call is almost as prevalent and character-istic as the wailing of the Red-throated and Pacific Loons. The nesting is rather late, at the end of June or early part of July. The nests are usually built on small islands or on the edge of a pond or lake, a little hollow in a clump of grass, lined with a mass of black down. In July and August, when the quills have been molted and the ducks are unable to fly, thousands are sometimes seen congregated in bays and large lakes, and when pursued, dive with great expertness. The Old-squaws often remain until October or November around some ice-hole or lead of open water.

(155) *Histrionicus histrionicus* (Linnæus). Harlequin Duck.

I never observed this species in the Arctic. Mr. H. W. Jones reported the first arrival at Hay River, May 16th, 1908.

(157) *Polysticta stelleri* (Pallas). Steller's Eider. Ig-nak-ĭ'rĭ — fire bird (Alaskan Eskimo).

One male specimen of this beautiful species was taken just west of the Colville River delta June 18th, 1909. Two females in fall plumage were taken at west end of Barter Island sandspit, Alaska, on August 28th and 31st, 1908 This is the most eastern point at which I have seen this species, but Captain F. Wolki told me (in 1912) that several years before he had shot one at Cape Bathurst. Steller's Eider is apparently only a very rare straggler east of the Alaskan boundary.

(158) *Arctonetta fischeri* (Brandt). Spectacled Eider. Kring-a'lik (western Eskimo).

This species was fairly common in fresh-water ponds west of the Colville River delta in June and also in the delta in July. Females killed June 12th had eggs in ovary about the size of a Robin's egg. On July 4th our dogs flushed a duck apparently of this species from a nest containing eight fresh eggs, on the ground in a little patch of scrub willows about one foot high, ten yards from river bank. On July 7th, while drifting down the river, the dogs flushed a Spectacled Eider from the willow brush, and, from the wrangling which ensued, I think they found a nest with eggs.

Several Spectacled Eiders were shot while drifting down through the Colville delta.

(161) *Somateria v-nigra* (Gray). Pacific Eider. ♂ A-mau'lik

(Mackenzie and Baillie Islands Eskimo.) ♀ Mi'tirk or Aî-na'vĭak.

Common everywhere along the Arctic coast during the eastward spring migration and westward fall migration. Breeds locally in large colonies on sandspits and islands along the coast, notably in Kuparuk and Jags river sandspits, Alaska; Cape Brown, Horton River sandspit, and in small numbers as far east as Simpson Bay, Victoria Island, where I found a nest containing eggs July 26th, 1911. The males begin to migrate west along the coast in large flocks shortly after the eggs are laid. At Cape Bathurst, in the summer of 1912, large flocks of male Eiders were going west nearly every day during July. From the 1st to the 18th of July the male King Eiders were largely in the majority, and after that date the Pacific Eiders were more numerous. Females and young migrate later, some remaining on open water until late in October.

(162) *Somateria spectabilis* (Linnæus). King Eider. Kau-ñik or Kau'-ñē-vik (Alaskan Eskimo). ♂ Tu-tĭ-ri-ā'lik. ♀ Mitirk or Ag-na'vi-ak (Mackenzie and Baillie Islands Eskimo).

Common everywhere along the coast during migration, and breeds locally in colonies on sandspits and islands as well as here and there near fresh-water ponds near the coast. Males migrate westward before the females. At Cape Bathurst in 1912 they began going west about June 30th, following a very regular course usually, but sometimes in V-shaped flocks like geese. On the morning of July 11th for about three hours a large flock would pass every few minutes, and sometimes four or five flocks were in sight at once. They were mostly King Eiders, about one flock of Pacific Eiders to ten of King Eiders. The Pacific Eiders were still quite fat at this time, but the bill was getting soft, flabby, and faded in color. By the 18th of July as many Pacific Eiders as King Eiders were flying, and occasionally a King Eider was taken with head finely streaked with brown.

(165) *Oidemia degland* Bonaparte. White-winged Scoter. Tŭrn-ra'vik (Mackenzie Eskimo).

Fairly common in the Mackenzie River delta. East of Richard Island the first appeared June 2d, 1910. Several flocks, all males, passed north about 2:00 A.M. on June 17th. On the evening of the

2 H

20th, several flocks passed, going north, and the same day one of the Eskimo killed a female with a hard-shelled egg in the oviduct. Did not notice this species far to the east or west side of Mackenzie delta. Both the White-winged and Surf Scoters are called Tŭrn-ra′vik by the natives of the Mackenzie delta. This is unusual, as species of much less apparent resemblance are usually distinguished from each other.

(166) *Oidemia perspicillata* [(Linnæus). Surf Scoter. A-vĭ-lūk′tjak (western Eskimo). Turn-ra′vik (Mackenzie Eskimo).

Rather common in the Mackenzie delta, but less so than the White-winged Scoter. At Herschel Island in August, hundreds of molting Scoters and Old-squaws frequented the large bay on the south side of the island. Most of them appeared unable to fly, and immediately swim out to sea or try to escape by diving when any one approaches.

(169) *Chen hyperboreus hyperboreus* (Pallas). Snow Goose. Ka-ngok′ (Alaskan and Mackenzie Eskimo).

Nests in small numbers at various points along the north Alaskan coast, in large numbers on Richard Island in the Mackenzie delta, and to some extent on the Cape Bathurst peninsula. Large numbers pass northeastward through the east branch of the Mackenzie delta, but only a few remain to nest on the mainland in this region. Captain F. Wolki, who lived at the mouth of Horton River for several years, told me that when the winter's snowfall was light and consequently melted away quickly, there was very little goose-shooting in the spring. If there is little snow on the ground when the geese arrive, they stay only three or four days and head out seaward to the northeast, apparently to Banks Land. If the ground is snow-covered, the large flocks sometimes stay for a long time, moving back and forth in the direction of Harrowby Bay and the Anderson River. The greatest migration route east of the Mackenzie seems to be down the Anderson River and along the east side of Liverpool Bay. Very few pass around Cape Bathurst, although formerly a few pairs nested on Baillie Islands. The main flight passes over Harrowby Bay (the eastern arm of Liverpool Bay) and either scatter out to nest on the tundra flats behind the Smoking Mountains or cross over to Banks Land. Very few pass Langton Bay in spring, and only occasional stragglers were seen in Coronation Gulf. In 1912 we took the first sets of fresh eggs on the Bathurst peninsula June 8th; nest on a little dry, grassy ridge between two ditches on a flat valley intersected by a network of small, shallow ditches about half a mile from a large ice-bound lake. The Eskimo often call up passing flocks by imitating their call Ka-ngok′! Ka-ngok′!

On the northwest side of Richard Island, before the gun and rifle days, the Eskimo used to kill thousands of Snow Geese in July and August when the birds were molting and unable to fly, large quantities of goose breasts being dried and stored away for winter use. At the present time few people ever visit this part of the Mackenzie delta, and there are no permanent residents. The few Eskimos remaining in the Mackenzie delta, however, live almost entirely on geese — about equal numbers of White-fronted, Hutchins's and Snow Geese and the Black Brant — for about three weeks in May and June, but as the natives nowadays find it necessary to make long boat voyages to Fort McPherson and Herschel Island to trade they seldom have time to visit the large rookeries in season. In the vicinity of Cape Halkett, Alaska, is also a famous hunting ground for killing molting Snow Geese, but it is seldom visited, except by an occasional traveling party of Eskimo.

(169, 1) *Chen cærulescens* (Linnæus). Blue Goose.

This species was not observed at all by our party. At Lake Athabaska, one of the greatest goose-shooting points in the North, large numbers of geese are killed and stored away for winter. Mr. Peter Loutit, Dominion Forest Ranger, told me that he killed one Blue Wavey, the first one he had ever seen, in the fall of 1907. Loutit and his father killed about 1200 geese, mostly "White Wavies" (Snow Geese) and "Gray Wavies" (White-fronted Geese) at Lake Athabaska that season.

(170) *Chen rossi* (Cassin). Ross's Goose.

Small numbers were seen on the lower Athabaska River in the latter part of May, 1908. At the western end of Lake Athabaska, Ross's Goose migrates late, after the bulk of the Snow Geese and White-fronted geese have gone north. They come in large numbers and are easily killed. Owing to their stupid habits, the birds have received the common name of "Galoots" in the Athabaska region. Numerous inquiries among the Eskimo of northern Alaska and the

Mackenzie River delta brought out the fact that no natives of the region west of Cape Bathurst had ever seen or knew of any name for a goose smaller than the Snow Goose. One was killed about fifteen miles east of Cape Bathurst in June, 1912, and Captain Wolki told me that some seasons he had killed a number at the mouth of Horton River. None were observed during the spring and summer which I spent on Coronation Gulf.

(171 *a*) *Anser albifrons gambeli* Hartlaub. White-fronted Goose. Ki'ri-yuk. Lirk'lē-vik (Alaskan Eskimo). Ting'mi-ak (Mackenzie River and Coronation Gulf).

In the Mackenzie region Tingmiat is the ordinary term for geese in general. Common in summer all along the Arctic coast and nesting in suitable localities. A nest found on an island in the Colville delta, Alaska, had four young goslings just hatched, — July 10th, 1909; color olive-greenish on back and crown, under parts and neck bright greenish yellow. The nest was on a little mound of dry earth (Spermophile's burrow) a foot or two higher than the surrounding land and about forty yards from the river. A nest with four slightly incubated eggs taken June 16th, 1911, on the south side of Coronation Gulf, was placed on a little peninsula at side of a small, fresh-water lake. The Eskimos can usually attract the attention of passing White-fronted Geese by imitating their note "Lirk-a-lik-lik-lik," and very often a goose or a flock wheels about to investigate and circles over the hunter. This species is usually fatter than the other geese (except the Black Brant) when arriving at the mouth of the Mackenzie in the spring, and accordingly is prized most.

(172) *Branta canadensis canadensis* (Linnæus). Canada Goose.

Fairly common as far north as Great Slave Lake, but replaced on the Arctic coast by *B. c. hutchinsi*.

(172 *a*) *Branta canadensis hutchinsi* (Richardson). Hutchins's Goose. Ex-rau-tel'lik (Alaskan Eskimo). Ū-lū-a-r̂o'lik (Mackenzie Eskimo).

Fairly common in most localities on the Arctic coast, nesting from the Colville River, Alaska, east to Coronation Gulf. A set of five slightly incubated eggs was taken June 30th, 1909, on a little island of peat, about six feet in diameter, top about one foot above water level — fifteen yards from mainland. A pair with four young were seen in the east branch of Mackenzie delta June 24th, 1910. One young gosling which we caught was covered with dark yellow down with a greenish cast — bill and feet black. The season was about a month further advanced here than it was fifty miles farther north (beyond the tree line). East of Richard Island the Black Brant and Longspurs had just begun to lay, about June 16th. Around Coronation Gulf a few Hutchins's Geese were seen during the spring and summer of 1911, but no nests were found.

(174) *Branta nigricans* (Lawrence). Black Brant. Nig'lirk-nak (Alaskan Eskimo). Nig-lir-na'lūk (Mackenzie Eskimo).

Common all along the Arctic coast, migrating east and west, breeding as far east as Coronation Gulf. Nests usually on small, flat islands in shallow tundra lakes not far from the coast, but often are found on the edges of lakes or on the ground in wet, marshy places. Nests commonly on tundra in northern Alaska, very abundantly on the low land east of the Mackenzie delta and on the Cape Bathurst peninsula. Less common farther east. The most eastern locality where I observed the species was on the Duke of York Archipelago in Coronation Gulf, where four adults and six young with light gray downy plumage were seen and all captured July 21st, 1911. The adults were molting quills and seemed able to fly only a few yards. Nests are usually composed of a few grasses and a large mass of thickly matted down pellets. When sitting on eggs, the female Brant often stretches her head and neck out, extending flat on the ground.

(180) *Olor columbianus* (Ord.). Whistling Swan. Kōg'r̄uk (Alaskan Eskimo). Kōg'yūk, -yōk (2), -yū-ĭt (3) (Mackenzie Eskimo).

Occurs in summer in suitable localities from northern Alaska to Coronation Gulf. Found one nest in the Colville delta, Alaska, June 25th, 1909, with five eggs, slightly incubated. Saw the Swan with field-glasses sitting on her nest on edge of a lake over a mile away, and after encircling an almost interminable labyrinth of connected lakes and ponds, finally got out to the nest on a narrow little peninsula. The nest was about ten feet from the water of the lake, and the base about four feet above water level. The lake was filled with solid ice, except 10–30 yards around the edge. Base of nest about seven feet across; about eighteen inches high and twenty-four inches across depression at top. The bulk of nest was composed of small blocks and chunks of moss, evidently broken up piecemeal by the Swans into bits about one and one half or two inches square and partially dried. On top of this foundation was laid a thick circular mass of grass and weed-stalks, mixed with a few feathers and white down. A considerable amount of down and feathers was lodged on grass stalks for fifteen to twenty feet to leeward of the nest. The Swan left her nest when I was about two hundred yards away, and was soon joined by her mate. The pair kept at about three hundred yards' distance all the time I was near the nest, feeding apparently unconcerned. Several nests were said to have been found near Camden Bay, Alaska, the same season, late in June and early in July. Most of the nests were on small islands in tundra lakes and could not be reached without using a kayak. Swans are fairly common on east side of the Mackenzie delta, but the most abundant nesting locality is probably on the lake-covered flat lands between Langton Bay and Darnley Bay. In the fall nearly every little lake in the Langton Bay region has a pair or brood of young Swans. Flying Swans are very often called back by Eskimo imitating their resonant call note. Sometimes the Swans will come very near to investigate.

(190) *Botaurus léntiginosus* (Montagu). Bittern.

One seen in Slave River delta, near Fort Resolution, June 20th, 1908. Mr. Harry W. Jones informed me that the American Bittern is often seen at Hay River, and he has observed it on the Mackenzie as far north as the mouth of Willow River.

(204) *Grus americana* (Linnæus). Whooping Crane.

I did not observe the species in the North. Mr. H. W. Jones reported the first 1908 arrival at Hay River (Great Slave Lake) on May 12th; three or four bands of five or six each being seen. Eskimo who are familiar with the whole Mackenzie delta up to Arctic River and Fort McPherson on Peel River, all say they have never seen a White Crane.

(205) *Grus canadensis* (Linnæus). Little Brown Crane. Ta-tĭ'gi-ak (Alaskan and Mackenzie Eskimo).

Several pairs apparently nesting near Fort Resolution; species is fairly common on the large flat delta islands of the west branch of the Mackenzie River, from the last trees north to Tent Island. Less common on east side of the delta and very rare on the Cape Bathurst Peninsula. One seen in the Colville delta, Alaska, July 4th, 1909, apparently nesting. Specimens killed at Kañian-nik, east of Richard Island on May 29th, 1910, were fat and had the whole alimentary canal stained purple with the juice of crowberries. The first arrival here was on May 11th, 1910.

(214) *Porzana carolina* (Linnæus). Sora.

Shot one male specimen in the Slave River delta, June 18th, 1908. H. W. Jones reports the first 1908 arrival at Hay River June 18th, and a male shot June 22d. Not observed north of Great Slave Lake.

(222) *Phalaropus fulicarius* (Linnæus). Red Phalarope. I-ma-rī'-a-r̂ŭk (Alaskan Eskimo). Kai-yat-r̂o-yōk'pok (Mackenzie Eskimo).

Generally distributed in summer from northern Alaska to Victoria Island, and locally common. In the Colville delta, northern Alaska, found a number of nests between the 20th of June and 10th of July; slight hollows in the ground in little clumps of grass, usually on wet, sloppy tundra near water. The male parent attends to the incubation. The Phalaropes feed principally by wading in shallow ponds. When feeding in deeper water, they have a habit of whirling around and around as if on a pivot. Later in summer they assemble in flocks and keep to the coast, remaining until September. When feeding at sea, they swim about, continually bobbing the head, and often picking up some tiny floating morsel with a motion so quick as to be difficult to detect. They are very adept at riding breakers, sailing over head-on, or skipping lightly over a curler. The red breast plumage is changed for the whitish fall coat by the middle of August.

(223) *Lobipes lobatus* (Linnæus). Northern Phalarope. Kai-yat-r̂o-yō-a'luk (Mackenzie Eskimo). Kū-yĭ-r̂o'tit (Alaskan Eskimo).

Generally distributed in summer from northern Alaska to Coronation Gulf. Rather rare and local in Colville region, Alaska; more common east of the Mackenzie, and the only species of Phalarope

observed on the south side of Coronation Gulf. Nests on low, flat
tundra, and the male bird sits on the eggs.

(230) *Gallinago delicata* (Ord.). Wilson's Snipe.

Not observed north of Hay River, Great Slave Lake, where the
species seems to be numerous.

(232) *Macrorhamphus griseus scolopaceus* (Say). Long-billed Dow-
ticher.

A few specimens seen in the Mackenzie delta, also downy young
near mouth of Kuparuk River, northern Alaska, July 25th, 1909.

(233) *Micropalama himantopus* (Bonaparte). Stilt Sandpiper.

One male specimen was taken June 30th, 1911, on a low, marshy
flat near mouth of Kogaryuak River, eighteen miles east of the mouth
of the Coppermine.

(239) *Pisobia maculata* (Vieillot). Pectoral Sandpiper. Nū-vak′-
e-ruk (Alaskan Eskimo). Pū-ĭ-jĭ-shūk′tok (Baillie Islands).

Nesting commonly on tundra flats from the Colville delta, Alaska,
east; abundant east of the Mackenzie delta and in the Cape Bathurst
region. Very rare near Coronation Gulf. Shortly after the arrival
of the Pectoral Sandpipers early in June, the male begins a succession
of soaring flights, with neck swollen up and hanging down lower
than the breast, at the same time uttering a dull, muffled "dthoo!
dthoo!" At this season the thick growth of loose, fatty, fibrous
tissue on the neck and breast of the male Sandpiper is much developed. The female Sandpiper has only a slight development of
this fatty tissue.

(241) *Pisobia bairdi* (Coues). Baird's Sandpiper. Lĭ-wā′lĭ-wak
(Alaskan Eskimo). Nĭ-vĭ-lĭ-vĭ-lā′luk (Baillie Islands Eskimo).

Fairly common, and breeding at various points along the Arctic
coast from Alaska to Coronation Gulf and Victoria Island. Nests
somewhat locally, usually on dry ground near the coast. Sometimes
the species is absent a certain point and abundant only a few miles
away.

(242) *Pisobia minutilla* (Vieillot). Least Sandpiper.

Specimen taken at Herschel Island, Yukon Territory, and occasionally observed near the mouth of the Mackenzie.

(243 *a*) *Pelidna alpina sakhalina* (Vieillot). Red-backed Sandpiper. I′lak-tel′lik — "It had a patch" (on breast) —
(Alaskan Eskimo).

Fairly common in the Colville River delta, Alaska, in June. One set of four eggs, incubation begun, taken from a slight hollow in the ground, lined with small dead leaves, and partially concealed by grass, on a gently sloping hillside. The black belly-patch was noted on specimens seen August 1st, but on August 30th, the fall plumage had been donned.

(246) *Ereunetes pusillus* (Linnæus). Semipalmated Sandpiper. Nū-wĭ-hlūk′ (Port Clarence). Lĭ-wa′-lĭ-wak (Colville). Nĭ-vĭ-lĭ-vĭ-la′ ūk (Baillie Islands).

Common, and breeding everywhere along the Arctic coast from northern Alaska to Coronation Gulf. No specimens referable to *E. mauri* (Western Sandpiper) were taken, all being typical *pusillus*. Nests were found almost anywhere on tussocks on wet, boggy land, in bunches of moss, or on dry, barren ground. Sometimes a Semipalmated Sandpiper will hover in the air like a big humming-bird, at the same time uttering a continuous twitter. At other times, while flitting about over the water, singly, in pairs, or in groups of three or four, their rapid motions reminded me of swallows.

(248) *Calidris leucophaea* (Pallas). Sanderling.

Fairly common on Cape Bathurst in August. Not found nesting.

(250) *Limosa lapponica baueri* Naumann. Pacific Godwit.

Shot one male, July 5th, 1909, in a wide, marshy flat in Colville delta, Alaska, about ten miles below the mouth of Itkillik River. The bird was alone, and kept uttering a loud, clear whistle, resembling the note of a Curlew.

(255) *Totanus flavipes* (Gmelin). Yellowlegs.

One specimen seen on the portage between Smith's Landing and Fort Smith, Slave River, June 2d, 1908. At Hay River, Mr. H. W. Jones noted the first arrival May 2d, 1908.

(262) *Tryngites subruficollis* (Vieillot). Buff-breasted Sandpiper.

Saw two Buff-breasted Sandpipers near Cape Halkett, Alaska, June 3d, 1909. Saw two flocks of six or seven each feeding on damp tundra near Cape Bathurst, July 6th, 1912, and killed two. This beautiful species is apparently very rare on the Arctic coast.

(263) *Actitis macularia* (Linnæus). Spotted Sandpiper.

Common everywhere along the Athabaska, Slave, and Mackenzie

rivers, about to the northern limit of trees. Not seen in northern Alaska or east of the Mackenzie.

(265) *Numenius hudsonicus* Latham. Hudsonian Curlew.

Saw one bird, probably of this species, on Herschel Island, August 4th, 1908. It was very noisy, and very wild, and I could not get within gunshot.

(270) *Squatarola squatarola* (Linnæus). Black-billed Plover. Tū'- lik (Alaskan and Mackenzie Eskimo).

Found in small numbers nesting in the Colville River delta, Alaska, near Cape Bathurst, and on southern Victoria Island. Nests are very difficult to find, as one Plover is always on the lookout, and gives warning when a person approaches. The incubating bird then slips quietly away from the nest until the danger passes. A nest with two half-incubated eggs was found on a flat, sandy island in Colville delta, June 27th, 1909. Another nest with four eggs, about one fourth incubated, was found July 9th, and four eggs just ready to hatch on July 20th. While we were near the nest, the Plover frequently uttered a mellow "Tū-lī-ū'" note, while trying to decoy us away. When migrating, the call note is a clear "Tū-lik'," the first syllable prolonged, the last one short. At Kittigaryuit, east branch of Mackenzie, the first spring migrates appeared May 24th. They were migrating westward at Barter Island, Alaska, September 2d, 1908.

(272) *Charadrius dominicus dominicus* (Müller). Golden Plover. Tū'lik (Alaskan and Mackenzie Eskimo).

Rather rare on the north coast of Alaska. The first pair posi- tively identified were nesting east of the Colville delta, July 15th, 1909, and three eggs taken, incubation advanced. The usual note resembles that of the Black-bellied Plover, but is perhaps a trifle less loud. The Eskimo have the same name "Tū-lik" (in imitation of the note) for both species. When the nest was approached, the Plover would approach with wings spread and slightly drooping, uttering a plaintive "peent," sometimes wailing out a mournful "Tu-lik" or a sharp "Cheep ! Cheep !" A few Golden Plovers seen July 21st–22d at mouth of Kuparuk River, and four east of Collinson Point, Alaska, August 8th, 1909.

Several pairs were nesting on Baillie Islands in 1912, and I found one slightly incubated set of four eggs while hunting nests in a slight snow-storm on the night of July 3d. On July 6th, I found four young Plovers just hatched near Cape Bathurst.

(273) *Oxyechus vociferus* (Linnæus). Killdeer.

Common as far north as Fort Chipewyan on Athabaska Lake.

(274) *Ægialitis semipalmata* (Bonaparte). Semipalmated Plover. Kō-lĭ-ka-lĭ-a'lok (Mackenzie Eskimo). Harl-r̃ug (Coronation Gulf Eskimo).

Common on sand-bars along the Slave, Mackenzie, and Peel rivers, nesting in the Colville delta, Alaska, in the Mackenzie delta, and rather commonly on the south shore of Coronation Gulf. A set of four fresh eggs was taken June 16th, and another set of four half-incubated eggs June 25th, 1911, near mouth of Kogaryuak River, Coronation Gulf. Downy young were taken on the west branch of the Mackenzie delta July 20th, 1910.

(283 *a*) *Arenaria interpres morinella* (Linnæus). Ruddy Turnstone. Tel-ĭ'gū-ak (Alaskan Eskimo).

Rather rare, and locally distributed. First seen near Cape Halkett, Alaska, May 29th, 1909. Several pairs seen in the Colville delta in June and July, 1909, and two sets of four eggs, far advanced in incubation, were taken June 27th on a low, flat, sandy delta island. The female Turnstone was very tame and returned to the nest several times to be photographed, the last time with the camera at a distance of two feet and eight inches. Turnstones were also seen at Cape Bathurst and on south side of Coronation Gulf in the spring, but none remained to breed. Several pairs were seen on beach at Austin Bay, Victoria Island, July 23d, 1911, and four downy young were captured. Old birds have the legs brilliant red and young birds dull red.

(298 *b*) *Canachites canadensis osgoodi* Bishop. Alaska Spruce Partridge.

I never met with this species personally in the Arctic, either in timber on the south side of Endicott Mountains, in the Mackenzie delta, or at east end of Great Bear Lake. Messrs. Joseph Hodgson, C. D. Melvill, and J. Hornby told me that Partridges, presumably this species, are fairly common around the western end of Great Bear Lake and at Fort Norman.

(300 *b*) *Bonasa umbellus umbelloides* (Douglas). Gray Ruffed Grouse.

One seen at Fort McKay on the Athabaska River, May 18th, and others heard drumming at other points. One female specimen, which was accompanied by two or three half-grown young birds, was taken at Fort Providence on the Mackenzie June 27th, 1908. The crop of this bird was full of the white buds and blossoms of the wild pea-vine. Not observed north of Fort Providence.

(301) *Lagopus lagopus lagopus* (Linnæus). Willow Ptarmigan. A-ka′gĭ-r̂ik (Alaskan Eskimo). A-krī-gī-a′lūk (Mackenzie Eskimo).

The two species of Ptarmigan are probably the most important game-birds of the Arctic for the reason that they are almost universally distributed, and are practically the only game-birds available during at least seven months of the year. The Willow Ptarmigan begins to change from the dark, mottled summer plumage to the white winter plumage early in September, and is usually nearly all white by the first of October. During the transition period no two birds are alike, being mottled and pied in the most bizarre patterns. In spring the males begin to molt first, appearing with dark brown head and neck early in May, and at this season are very noisy as well as conspicuous in appearance. The brown feathers on the back come out very slowly, and often the Ptarmigan do not get the full summer plumage before the end of June. Females usually attain the summer plumage by the end of May. The eggs are usually laid by the middle of June. In northern Alaska the great bulk of the Willow Ptarmigan go up into the mountain valleys in October, returning to the coast in April. They are found along the coast in summer from Smith Bay, Alaska, to Liverpool Bay. East of Liverpool Bay the Willow Ptarmigan come as far north as Harrowby Bay to the south end of Franklin Bay, Horton River, and are exceedingly abundant at the northeast end of Great Bear Lake. None were seen in the vicinity of Coronation Gulf. In winter the Ptarmigan feed chiefly on willow buds and in summer on buds of various kinds, seeds, the red bearberry, crowberry, etc. The Eskimo do not hunt them regularly, but kill a good many in the course of a year with guns, snares, and occasionally in nets, looking upon the Ptarmigan as an ever present resource in times of scarcity of other food.

The Ptarmigan are so abundant and generally distributed that the hunting of the Eskimo has very little effect upon the numbers of birds. Fifteen Willow Ptarmigan killed in October weighed twenty-two pounds. Rock Ptarmigan average considerably smaller.

(302) *Lagopus rupestris rupestris* (Gmelin). Rock Ptarmigan. Nik-shak′tūng-ŏk (Alaskan Eskimo). Nik-shak-tī-ra′lūk (Mackenzie Eskimo). Both species are commonly classed together as A-krī-gi-a′wit.

The Rock Ptarmigan is somewhat smaller than the Willow Ptarmigan and is further distinguished by having a well-defined black streak of feathers before the eye and an obscure streak in the female. The habits are similar, and the two species are commonly found together. In northern Alaska the Rock Ptarmigan are commonly found farther up in the mountains in winter, but come down to the sea coast in the spring. North of the tree line in the Mackenzie delta the species are about equally numerous, while at Cape Bathurst and on the Barren Grounds around Coronation Gulf and on Victoria Island the Rock Ptarmigan is found to the exclusion of other species. In spring the Copper Eskimo kill a good many with their bows and arrows. On the shores of Franklin Bay fresh eggs were found about the middle of June. Like the Willow Ptarmigan, the food is principally willow buds and leaves, but in the spring large quantities of berries are eaten, principally the black crowberries, and in many cases the breasts and bills of the Ptarmigan are stained purple by berry juice. Although the female Rock Ptarmigan changes to the summer plumage early in the summer, the plumage of the male remains unchanged until nearly the last of June. Male Rock Ptarmigan usually present a dirty, stained, and unkempt appearance during the month of June. While the female Ptarmigan is nesting, the male Ptarmigan is usually mounting guard on a little knoll near by. In the springtime the male Rock Ptarmigan frequently springs up thirty or forty feet into the air, dropping to the ground with a rattling, croaking sound.

(316) *Zenaidura macroura carolinensis* (Linnæus). Mourning Dove. Mr. Harry W. Jones informed me that a pair were seen and one secured at Hay River, Great Slave Lake, June 13th, 1908; very rare, and the species unknown to the natives there.

(331) *Circus hudsonius* (Linnæus). Marsh Hawk. Kĭ-la-rek (Alaskan and Mackenzie Eskimo).

Occasionally seen at various points on the Arctic coast east and west of the delta of the Mackenzie.

(334) *Astur atricapillus atricapillus* (Wilson). Goshawk.

Occasionally seen on the south side of the Endicott Mountains, Alaska, and on Horton River.

(337 *b*) *Buteo borealis calurus* Cassin. Western Redtail.

Observed on Slave River, near below mouth of Salt River, June 11th, 1908.

(347 *a*) *Archibuteo lagopus sancti-johannis* (Gmelin). Rough-legged Hawk. Kĭ-la-rek (Alaskan and Mackenzie Eskimo).

Nesting on mud bluffs at Herschel Island, along the west side of Franklin Bay, and very commonly on ledges of the diabase cliffs on south side of Coronation Gulf.

(349) *Aquila chrysætos* (Linnæus). Golden Eagle. Ting-miak'-puk (Mackenzie Eskimo).

Mr. H. W. Jones noted the first arrival at Hay River, April 30th, 1908. Rests regularly on steep bluff banks of Horton River about fifteen miles south of Langton Bay. Saw one specimen near Cape Bathurst June 28th, 1912.

(356 *a*) *Falco peregrinus anatum* Bonaparte. Duck Hawk.

Observed on the Hula-hula River, Alaska, at Escape Reef, Mackenzie Bay, Horton River, and Coronation Gulf. Specimen taken near Langton Bay, where a pair nested in Melville Mountains in 1911. Captain F. Wolki found a nest containing eggs April 18th, 1912, in a nest at top of a spruce stub near the northern limit of trees on Horton River.

(357) *Falco columbarius columbarius* Linnæus. Pigeon Hawk.

Small Hawks, probably of this species, were seen occasionally on Horton River, south of Langton Bay.

(364) *Pandion haliætus carolinensis* (Gmelin). Osprey.

Observed on the Athabaska River, Alberta.

(367) *Asio flammeus* (Pontoppidan). Short-eared Owl. Nĭ-pai-hlūk'tak (Alaskan Eskimo). Ni-pai-ngak'tak (Mackenzie Eskimo).

Found sparsely at all points along the Arctic coast. One set of four eggs taken by myself on Coronation Gulf, June 23d, and another set by J. F. Bernard, July 1st, 1911.

(370) *Scotiaptex nebulosa nebulosa* (J. R. Forster). Great Gray Owl. Na'tak (Alaskan and Mackenzie Eskimo).

One female specimen taken December 13th, 1908; another female January 5th, 1909, in spruce timber on south side of Endicott Range, Alaska. Another seen January 16th and still another on February 4th, 1909. After crossing to the north side of the Endicott Mountains and many miles north of the tree line, one of my Eskimos, a reliable man, said that he saw a Na'tak alighted on a rock quite near him as he was coming down a little creek gorge on March 26th. He was positive of its identity.

(371) *Cryptoglaux funerea richardsoni* (Bonaparte). Richardson's Owl.

Did not observe this species, but it was reported as being occasionally seen in winter in the heavy timber near the mouth of Dease River.

(376) *Nyctea nyctea* (Linnæus). Snowy Owl. Ug'pik (Alaskan and Mackenzie Eskimo).

Fairly common summer resident all along the Arctic coast and occasionally seen in winter. Varies much in numbers during different years, the number apparently fluctuating according to the abundance of mice and lemmings, which form its principal food. The Snowy Owl is considered one of the choicest of game-birds by the Eskimo, as it is usually fat and in good condition.

(377 *a*) *Surnia ulula caparoch* (Müller). Hawk-Owl.

This species was not observed by our party in the North. Mr. H. W. Jones gave his first spring record as May 1st, 1908, at Hay River, but thought that the species remained there all winter.

(390) *Ceryle alcyon* (Linnæus). Belted Kingfisher.

The only Arctic record which I have of this species is a single specimen seen near the mouth of Peel River, below Fort McPherson, July 18th, 1910.

(393 *a*) *Dryobates villosus leucomelas* (Boddaert). Northern Hairy Woodpecker.

A few specimens observed on the Athabaska River, Alberta, but none farther north.

(400) *Picoides arcticus* (Swainson).   Arctic Three-toed Woodpecker.

One seen on brulé on Smith's Portage, Slave River, June 2d, 1908. Captain J. W. Mills of Fort Smith told me that he shot one in the same place the autumn before, the only one he saw.

(401 *a*) *Picoides americanus fasciatus* Baird.   Alaska Three-toed Woodpecker.   Tū'yūk (Alaskan and Mackenzie Eskimo).

Mr. H. W. Jones gives his first 1908 record as May 4th at Hay River, and one specimen taken May 30th, 1908.   I saw one specimen December 20th, 1908, in heavy spruce timber on the south side of the Endicott Range, Alaska.   The species is fairly well known to the Eskimo of the Mackenzie delta, and I heard one calling in the timber on a wooded island on the east branch of delta.   One of our Eskimo also reported seeing a single bird in spruce timber on Horton River about fifteen miles south of Langton Bay early in October, 1910.

(402) *Sphyrapicus varius varius* (Linnæus).   Yellow-bellied Sapsucker.

Common and nesting as far north as Fort Smith on the Slave River.

(412) *Colaptes auratus luteus* Bangs.   Northern Flicker.

Fairly common on the Athabaska and Slave rivers.   Mr. H. W. Jones noted the species at Hay River in 1908.

(413) *Colaptes cafer collaris* Vigors.   Red-shafted Flicker.

Saw one pair on Smith's Portage, Slave River, June 8th, 1908; none others seen.

(420) *Chordeiles virginianus virginianus* (Gmelin).   Night-hawk.

Fairly common at Fort Smith, on the Slave River, in June, 1908. A specimen taken was of the typical dark-colored Eastern variety.

(456) *Saornis phœbe* (Latham).   Phœbe.

Common on Athabaska and Slave rivers and noted on the Mackenzie as far north as Fort Providence.

(457) *Saornis sayus* (Bonaparte).   Say's Phœbe.

Mr. H. W. Jones notes a pair seen and one specimen secured May 7th, 1908, at Hay River.   On July 8th, 1910, I saw a single bird on the willow-grown flats of Peel River at Fort McPherson.

(459) *Nuttallornis borealis* (Swainson).   Olive-sided Flycatcher.

Two or three specimens seen on Smith's Portage, Slave River, June 8th, 1908.

(463) *Empidonax flaviventris* (W. M. and S. F. Baird). Yellow-bellied Flycatcher.

Shot a female specimen at Smith's Landing on the Slave River, June 6th, 1908.

(466 *a*) *Empidonas trailli alnorum* Brewster. Alder Flycatcher.

Saw a few specimens in willow and alder thickets in delta of Slave River and shot one male June 23d, 1908. Mr. H. W. Jones notes the first arrival at Hay River June 5th, and one specimen taken June 9th, 1908.

(474 *k*) *Otocoris alpestris hoyti* Bishop. Hoyt's Horned Lark.

A-kū-lǐ-wak′shŭk. A-kū-lǐ-wak′shǐ-ō′wak (Mackenzie Eskimo).

Nesting in small numbers at Herschel Island, Cape Bathurst, Franklin Bay, and on the south side of Coronation Gulf. A nest with five eggs, taken June 15th, 1911, at mouth of Kogaryuak River, was like an ordinary *first* nest of the Prairie Horned Lark, a little hollow sunken in the ground, lined with a few grasses and feathers, on flat, dry, sandy soil, where vegetation was very short and scanty (not over half an inch high).

(484) *Perisoreus canadensis canadensis* (Linnæus). Canada Jay.

Kē′yūk (Mackenzie Eskimo).

Common along the Athabaska, Slave, and Mackenzie rivers as far north as the limit of trees in the Mackenzie delta. Mr. H. W. Jones told me that he had taken nests and eggs at Hay River, the earliest date being May 18th, the latest June 3d (the latter advanced in incubation). Sergeant J. A. E. Selig found a nest near Fort McPherson early in the spring of 1909, and Captain F. Wolki found a nest on the lower Horton River in early spring, when the weather was so cold that the Jay could scarcely be made to leave her nest. The Jays become very tame around camp and are a nuisance at times, as they come up to the meat-drying racks and pick away the choice bits of fat from drying Caribou meat, gorging themselves and carrying away large pieces. They do not seem to travel far from their own particular creek valleys in winter, and if the Jays are killed off around a camp, the locality is seldom visited by other Jays, even if they are common in another valley less than a mile away.

21

(484 *b*)   *Perisoreus canadensis fumifrons* Ridgway.   Alaska Jay.
   Kē′rūk (Alaskan Eskimo).

Several seen on the south slope of the Endicott Mountains on branches of the Chandlar River in 1909.   One seen in the willows several miles north of the last trees on the river.   They are as tame and inquisitive as the eastern representative.   One came up within fifteen or twenty feet of us while we were cutting up a Mountain Sheep.

(486 *a*)   *Corvus corax principalis* Ridgway.   Northern Raven.   Tū-
   lū′ak (Alaskan and Mackenzie Eskimo).

Generally distributed everywhere in the Arctic, but not very abundant anywhere.   Usually shy and wary, but I have seen Ravens so gorged with meat from a stranded whale's carcass that they would scarcely get out of the way.   Ravens often cause annoyance by springing Fox or Wolf traps or by eating meat left uncovered on the hunting field.   I have seen Alaskan Eskimo set up empty brass cartridges on sticks near a dead Caribou to keep Ravens from molesting the game.   Ravens on southern Victoria Island were very tame, allowing us to approach within twenty-five yards.   The only nest I found was on a ledge of black diabase rock in Bloody Fall gorge, nine miles from the mouth of the Coppermine, May 21st, 1911, but it was practically inaccessible.   The Raven left the nest, but came back to it while we were watching her at a distance of about fifty feet.

(488)   *Corvus brachyrhynchos brachyrhynchos* Brehm.   Crow.

Fairly common on the Athabaska, River du Rochers, and Slave River in 1908.   Mr. H. W. Jones reported it common at Hay River; the first seen there April 15th and eggs taken May 24th.

(495)   *Molothrus ater ater* (Boddaert).   Cow-bird.

A few seen on the Athabaska River.   Mr. H. W. Jones states that the species is rare at Hay River.

(497)   *Xanthocephalus xanthocephalus* (Bonaparte).   Yellow-headed
   Blackbird.

Shortly before noon on October 12th, 1912, on the Arctic Ocean, about one hundred miles west of Point Hope, Alaska, a female (or young male) flew all around the whaler *Belvedere*.   It seemed very tired, but afraid to alight as it fluttered about the rigging.   It rested a few times, and finally darted under the forecastle head.   I tried to catch it and touched the bird with one hand as it came out. Watched it within ten feet distance for some time and was sure of identity — rusty brown plumage; dull yellow (mixed with a little whitish) on throat and breast, and a little white on bend of wing. This species was not observed elsewhere in the North.

(498 *d*) *Agelaius phœniceus fortis* Ridgway. Thick-billed Redwing.

Fairly common and nesting on Smith's Portage in the Slave River delta in June. Mr. Harry W. Jones noted the first arrival at Hay River April 29th, 1908. Not observed north of this point.

(501, 1) *Sturnella neglecta* Audubon. Western Meadow-lark.

A few seen between Edmonton and Athabaska Landing. Not observed north of Athabaska Landing, Alberta.

(509) *Euphagus carolinus* (Müller). Rusty Blackbird. Tū-lū-ō'rak, the little Raven (Mackenzie Eskimo).

Common in the Mackenzie delta in summer, going some distance north of the northern limit of trees.

(511 *b*) *Quiscalus quiscula æneus* Ridgway. Bronzed Grackle.

Mr. H. W. Jones reported seeing one April 28th, 1908, at Hay River. I did not observe the species myself.

(515 *c*) *Pinicola enucleator alascensis* Ridgway. Alaska Pine Grosbeak.

Observed one or two specimens of this species in December, 1908, and January, 1909, on a branch of the Chandlar River, on south side of Endicott Mountains, Alaska. Pine Grosbreaks were not observed in any other locality.

(517) *Carpodacus purpureus purpureus* (Gmelin). Purple Finch.

Five or six males seen at the Grand Rapids of Athabaska River, Alberta, May 13th, 1908.

(521) *Loxia curvirostra minor* (Brehm). Crossbill.

Saw a number of specimens, both males and females, on Smith's Portage, Slave River, June 8th and 10th, 1908.

(522) *Loxia leucoptera* Gmelin. White-winged Crossbill.

Noted at various points on the Athabaska River in May, 1908. A juvenal female in streaky plumage taken at Fort Chipewyan, on Athabaska Lake, May 27th. Several were seen feeding on spruce cones. Several seen on Smith's Portage, Slave River, June 10th. The only place where I observed them north of the Arctic Circle was in spruce timber on Dease River, northeast of Great Bear Lake, in January and May, 1911.

(523) *Leucosticte griseonucha* (Brandt). Aleutian Rosy Finch.

Fairly common in Unalaska harbor, Aleutian Islands, Alaska, October 16th–17th, 1912, alighting on rigging of ships, and on docks and buildings.

(524) *Leucosticte tephrocotis tephrocotis* Swainson. Gray-crowned Rosy Finch.

One seen May 3d, 1908, near Athabaska Landing, Alberta, in a burned-out poplar thicket.

(527 *a*) *Acanthis hornemanni exilipes* (Coues). Hoary Redpoll. Sūk-sūng′ōk (Alaskan and Mackenzie Eskimo).

A few seen on both sides of the Endicott Mountains, Alaska, from September to January. Commonly nesting in the Mackenzie delta as far north as Richard Island. A number of nests taken in dense willow thickets near mouth of Kogaryuak River, eighteen miles east of the Coppermine River, Coronation Gulf, from June 16th to July 11th, 1911. Nests from one to three feet from the ground in small willows; composed externally of small dead grasses and equisetæ mixed with cottony substances, lined with willow cotton, and in some cases an inner lining of soft feathers (usually of Ptarmigan).

(528) *Acanthis linaria linaria* (Linnæus). Redpoll. Sūk-sūng′ōk (Alaskan and Mackenzie Eskimo).

Fairly common at the mouth of the Kogaryuak River, Coronation Gulf, nesting in willow thickets in company with the Hoary Redpoll. Nests identical in location and structure. Probably also occurs with the Hoary Redpoll in the Mackenzie region, although no specimens were taken there.

(533) *Spinus pinus* (Wilson). Pine Siskin.

A nest with three eggs, advanced in incubation, was found in a White Spruce tree, about fifteen feet from the ground on Moose Island, Great Slave Lake, June 24th, 1908. A few Siskins were seen here, but none elsewhere.

(534) *Plectrophenax nivalis nivalis* (Linnæus). Snow Bunting. A-mau′lik (Alaskan Eskimo).   A-mau′li-r̂a′lûk (Mackenzie Eskimo).

Fairly common everywhere along the Arctic coast in summer, but seldom seen far from the coast during the breeding season. In 1908 the last were seen September 20th, at the Hula-hula River, Alaska. The first spring arrival was April 1st, 1909, on the Hula-hula, but no more were seen until May 11th at Cape Halkett. In 1910 the first were seen April 9th on Liverpool Bay; in 1911 the first on April 19th on Coronation Gulf. On the north coast of Alaska and east of the Mackenzie the Snow Bunting usually builds its nest in cavities or crevices among old driftwood logs. Farther east, as in Coronation Gulf, where large driftwood is scarce, the birds apparently nest in crevices of rocks. At Baillie Islands nests were observed on jib-sheets of schooner, in cabin of schooner, in paint can on top of rack, under false bottom of whaleboat, and in Eskimo coffins (above ground). Around the settlements they are about as tame as English Sparrows.

(536) *Calcarius lapponicus lapponicus* (Linnæus). Lapland Longspur.

(537) *Calcarius pictus* (Swainson). Smith's Longspur.

Mr. H. W. Jones reported the first arrival of this species at Hay River, May 12th, 1908, and took one specimen. Saw a pair, male and female, near the mouth of Kogaryuak River, Coronation Gulf, June 30th, 1911, and shot the male. Saw a specimen here on one or two occasions.

(542 *b*) *Passerculus sandwichensis alaudinus* Bonaparte. Western Savannah Sparrow. Shak-shag-ĭ-ā'lŭk (Mackenzie Eskimo).

Fairly common everywhere in grassy situations, breeding in the Slave River delta, Colville River delta, Alaska, Mackenzie delta, and Coronation Gulf. Dr. Jonathan Dwight, Jr., Dr. Louis P. Bishop, and Mr. A. C. Bent examined all my specimens of this group and referred them all (Mackenzie and Coronation Gulf) to the slender-billed western form *alaudinus*.

(548) *Passerherbulus lecontei* (Audubon). Leconte's Sparrow.

Saw two specimens and shot one male on wet, marshy flats at west end of Athabaska Lake, Alberta, May 22d, 1908. Mr. H. W. Jones took a specimen at Hay River, west end of Great Slave Lake, June 23d, 1908.

(553) *Zonotrichia querula* (Nuttall). Harris's Sparrow.

Mr. H. W. Jones reports the first arrival at Hay River, Great

Slave Lake, May 14th, 1908, at which time several flocks were seen, and male and female specimens taken.

(554 *a*) *Zonotrichia   leucophrys   gambeli*   (Nuttall).   Gambel's Sparrow.

Common all along the Mackenzie River in summer nearly to the northern limit of trees in the delta. Very musical, singing at all hours of the day and night. Near the mouth of Kogaryuak River, Coronation Gulf, one was seen several times in a thick clump of willows June 19th, 1911, apparently with a nest in the vicinity. The bird was later (June 28th) taken for a specimen (the only Arctic record which I have for the species outside of the Mackenzie delta).

(558) *Zonotrichia albicollis* (Gmelin). White-throated Sparrow.

Noted on the Mackenzie as far north as Fort Norman at the mouth of Great Bear River.

(559) *Spizella monticola monticola* (Gmelin). Tree Sparrow.

Rather locally distributed on the Arctic coast, but fairly common in places north of the tree line, where willow thickets are found near the coast. Common on the south end of Richard Island and the adjacent mainland; a few near Demarcation Point and one on the west side of Franklin Bay. Nesting commonly on the south side of Coronation Gulf; three nests with six eggs each were taken June 16th, 1911 — nests all on ground in bunches of grass in open willow scrub and very artistically built of bits of green moss, a middle layer of grasses, and an inner lining of cotton and feathers. All the specimens in my series of skins from Coronation Gulf and Mackenzie are undoubtedly *S. m. monticola*. The only specimens observed in Alaska were a few in the Colville delta, where a nest with young birds was found July 6th, 1909. The Alaska birds may possibly be referable to *S. monticola ochracea* Brewster (Western Tree Sparrow).

(560 *a*) *Spizella   passerina   arizonæ*   Coues.   Western   Chipping Sparrow.

Fairly common at all the Athabaska and Slave rivers as far north as Hay River. Mr. H. W. Jones noted the first arrival at Hay River May 27th, and took male and female with four young June 23d, 1908.

(561) *Spizella pallida* (Swainson). Clay-colored Sparrow.

Mr. H. W. Jones took sets of four eggs June 19th, and five eggs fresh, on June 26th, 1908, at Hay River. Not observed north of this point.

(567) *Junco hyemalis hyemalis* (Linnæus). Slate-colored Junco.

Common on the Mackenzie River in summer, north nearly to the limit of trees in the delta. A set of four eggs with parent, incubation begun, was taken at Fort Chipewyan, Lake Athabaska, May 25th, 1908, on top of a granite ridge, imbedded in moss and covered with several branches of low spreading juniper. One specimen seen on Dease River, May 10th, 1911, but I am informed that the species is common at east end of Great Bear Lake a little later in the season. Shot a male near mouth of Bear River at Fort Norman, July 7th, 1908. A pair were evidently nesting near the river.

(567 *f*) *Junco hyemalis montanus* Ridgway. Montana Junco.

At Fort Chipewyan, Lake Athabaska, May 23d, 1908, I shot a female specimen with pinkish sides — ovaries not well developed. Near Fort Norman, July 9th, 1908, I took a female Montana Junco with nests and four eggs, advanced in incubation, near the summit of Bear Rock, the highest elevation in this vicinity, east of the Mackenzie River. The nest was placed in a hollow beside a lichen-covered rock, composed of coarse gray weeds and lined with fine yellowish grass. My specimens of Junco were determined by Dr. Jonathan Dwight, Jr., the well-known authority on this difficult group.

(581) *Melospiza melodia melodia* (Wilson). Song Sparrow.

Common as far north as the delta of the Slave River.

(583) *Melospiza lincolni lincolni* (Audubon). Lincoln's Sparrow.

Saw one bird on the Athabaska River May 15th, 1908, and took a nest and four young at Hay River June 25th, 1908. Mr. H. W. Jones noted the first arrival at Hay River May 12th, 1908, and took eggs June 17th–22d. The species breeds abundantly at Hay River. I saw quite a number at Fort Wrigley on the Mackenzie, but none north of this point.

(584) *Melospiza georgiana* Latham. Swamp Sparrow.

Shot one male specimen in the Slave River delta June 22d, 1908; not observed elsewhere.

(585) *Passerella iliaca iliaca* (Merrem). Fox Sparrow.

Mr. H. W. Jones noted the first arrivals at Hay River May 13th, 1908, and all apparently passed to the northward. Later he found a nest, June 6th, containing two eggs which were hatched June 7th or 8th. I saw one on east branch of Mackenzie June 22, near the mouth of Peel River June 28th, 1910. The only Fox Sparrows seen north of the tree line were two specimens on mainland east of Richard Island, where two were seen in willow shrubs two or three feet high, May 31st, 1910. One of these birds was in full song.

(612) *Petrochelidon lunifrons lunifrons* (Say). Cliff Swallow.

Common at various points along the Mackenzie River. Noticed large numbers building nests on sides of a steep granite island in Slave River, above Smith's Landing, May 29th, 1908. At Fort McPherson, June 30th, 1910, three or four pairs of Cliff Swallows were nesting under the eaves of the R.N.W.M.P. barracks and the Mission House. Rev. C. E. Whittaker said that the summer of 1909 was the first time that the species had appeared there. On the Dease River, northeast of Great Bear Lake, I saw a large group of the bottle-shaped nests on the side of a rocky gorge.

(614) *Iridoprocne bicolor* (Vieillot). Tree Swallow.

Noted on the Athabaska and Slave rivers. At Smith's Landing, Slave River, May 30th, 1908, the Tree Swallows were common on the water front. I found no nests, but people there said that the Tree Swallows built nests under the gable ends of houses.

(616) *Riparia riparia* (Linnæus). Bank Swallow. Tū-lū-āk-na'lŭk (Mackenzie Eskimo).

Abundant all along the Athabaska, Slave, and Mackenzie rivers, nesting everywhere in suitable sand-banks north nearly to the limit of trees in the Mackenzie delta. In some places the river banks are literally honeycombed with their nesting burrows. I did not see any Bank Swallows in northern Alaska, but saw a cut bank on the Hula-hula River, north of the Endicott Mountains, thickly perforated with holes.

(618) *Bombycilla garrula* (Linnæus). Bohemian Waxwing.

On Smith's Portage between Smith's Landing and Fort Smith on the Slave River, about a dozen Waxwings were seen, and three specimens shot June 8th, 1908. A nest with six eggs was found in a large Jack-pine (*Pinus banksiana*) June 10th, 1908. Mr. H. W. Jones noted the first arrival at Hay River May 7th, 1908. In the west branch of the Mackenzie delta I shot a well-fledged young male

July 20th, 1910; only one specimen was seen. The only other specimens seen in the Arctic were on the east branch of Dease River. On May 14th, 1911, several Bohemian Waxwings were seen in spruce trees around our house, one in the top of nearly every tree, uttering the peculiar lisping whistle so characteristic of the Waxwings.

(622) *Lanius borealis* (Vieillot). Northern Shrike.

The only specimen which I saw in the North was a single specimen which we saw near the northernmost spruce in the Mackenzie delta, between Tent Island and Richard Island, on September 11th, 1909. A single Northern Shrike alighted on our boat, clinging to the wire cable mainstay, but soon flew to the tip of the yard, then to the cross-stay of a schooner which was sailing alongside of us. The bird flew to land about a quarter of a mile away before I could get a gun ready.

(624) *Vireosylva olivacea* (Linnæus). Red-eyed Vireo.

Shot one male at Smith's Landing, Slave River, June 6th, 1908. Mr. H. W. Jones noted the first arrival at Hay River June 6th, and took a specimen June 9th.

(629) *Lanivireo solitarius solitarius* (Wilson). Blue-headed Vireo.

Mr. H. W. Jones noted the first arrival at Hay River May 23d, 1908; specimen taken.

(636) *Mniotilta varia* (Linnæus). Black-and-white Warbler.

Saw two pairs at Fort McKay, Athabaska River, May 18th, 1908; the first Warblers of the season.

(646) *Vermivora celata celata* (Say). Orange-crowned Warbler.

Mr. H. W. Jones noted the first arrival at Hay River May 25th, 1908; five fresh eggs were taken June 16th.

(647) *Vermivora peregrina* (Wilson). Tennessee Warbler.

Fairly common around Smith's Landing, Slave River. Shot a male June 6th, 1908, which was singing from a treetop; note much like the warbling Vireo. Mr. H. W. Jones noted the first arrival at River June 11th, 1908. At Fort Providence the species was common. One male was shot at Fort Wrigley June 30th — the most northern point at which I observed the species.

(652) *Dendroica œstiva œstiva* (Gmelin). Yellow Warbler. Ku-a-ra-luk (Mackenzie Eskimo).

Abundant all along the Mackenzie River and nesting as far north as the south end of Richard Island, and the mainland on east side of Richard Island, twenty-five or thirty miles north of the tree line.

(655) *Dendroica coronata* (Linnæus). Myrtle Warbler.

Mr. H. W. Jones noted the first arrival at Hay River May 13th, 1908; he shot one male May 16th. The birds all passed north and do not breed around Hay River. I did not observe the species at all in the North.

(661) *Dendroica striata* (J. R. Forster). Black-poll Warbler.

Shot one male in the Slave River delta June 18th, 1908, and found a nest with four eggs, advanced in incubation, on Moose Island, Great Slave Lake, June 24th, 1908. Mr. H. W. Jones noted the first arrival at Hay River June 2d, and took a specimen June 3d, 1908.

(672) *Dendroica palmarum palmarum* (Gmelin). Palm Warbler.

Two seen on Smith's Portage, Slave River, June 3d, 1908, but none observed north of this point.

(675 a) *Seiurus noveboracensis notabilis* Ridgway. Grinnell's Water Thrush.

Shot one specimen in the Slave River delta June 20th, 1908. Mr. H. W. Jones states that the species is rare at Hay River (Great Slave Lake), but abundant at Willow River, on the Mackenzie. June 23d, 1910, I found a nest containing four eggs, incubation begun, on an island in the east branch of the Mackenzie delta. Flushed the bird from a mass of old driftwood near the river. The bird was very wary and kept well out of sight in thick willow and alder brush. The nest was soon found on the ground under a projecting root, and I returned later and captured the bird.

(685) *Wilsonia pusilla pusilla* (Wilson). Wilson's Warbler.

While at sea on S.S. *Belvedere*, Mackenzie Bay, west of Pullen Island and east of Sabine Point, about 69° 50′ N. and 167° 15′ W., August 31st, 1912. While the ship's boats were lowered for whales, a female Wilson's Warbler remained on the ship for an hour or two, flitting about among the rigging and running gear, from one end of the ship to the other, never going higher than ten feet above the deck. She made several starts to fly away, but as the wind was strong, the sea rough, and no land in sight, always came back. Watched the bird at a distance of less than ten feet for a long time, but could not catch her, and shooting was not permissible when bow-head whales were around.

(687) *Setophaga ruticilla* (Linnæus). Redstart.

Mr. H. W. Jones says that species also is rare at Hay River, but abundant at Willow River, on the Mackenzie. Took one specimen at Fort Providence June 27th, and saw another at Fort Wrigley June 30th, 1908.

(696) *Budytes flavus alascensis* Ridgway. Alaska Yellow Wagtail.

Observed this species only in the Colville River delta, northern Alaska. The first glimpse of these beautiful birds was on July 4th, 1908, a little above the trading rendezvous of Nigalik. A nest containing five recently hatched young was found on a level place near the river, traversed with a network of little ridges from six inches to two feet high, sparsely covered with weeds and low ground willows. The nest was placed under the side of a heavy tussock of turf, completely covered by the turf and well concealed by long grasses on top of the tussock and around the sides; nest neatly cupped and composed of grasses, lined with fine grass and feathers. When flying against the wind, the birds pursued an up-and-down seesaw course. Several pairs were seen farther up in the delta, nowhere numerous, but probably at least one or two pairs were nesting every half mile along the river, near the willows. A short distance from the river, where the tundra is bare, no Wagtails have been seen.

(697) *Anthus rubescens* (Tunstall). Pipit. Shūng-ōk-shi'a-fĕk
    (Alaskan Eskimo).

Fairly common at various points along the Arctic coast, but somewhat local. Several seen on the Hula-hula River, Alaska, in September, a few at Herschel Island, and one nest taken on west side of Franklin Bay June 16th, 1912. Very common on the south side of Coronation Gulf, nesting in mossy hummocks at base of the numerous rocky cliffs. The males often sing while flying, soaring upward to a height of 40–50 feet in a gentle curve, then sailing down with wings and tail spread, usually alighting upon some flat-topped rock with a little run and with tail elevated. Note while soaring is a very quickly repeated *tweet-tweet-tweet-tweet-tweet;* sometimes *tweet-tweet-tsi-ū, tsi-ū, tsi-ū, tsi-ū, tsi-ū, tsi-ū.*

(735 a) *Penthestes atricapillus septentrionalis* (Harris). Long-tailed Chickadee.

Observed at various points along the Athabaska in May, 1908. Common at Grand Rapids of Athabaska, May 14th.

(739) *Penthestes cinctus alascensis* (Prazak). Alaska Chickadee. Mĭ-shī-ka'kak (Alaskan Eskimo).

A few specimens seen in November and December, 1908, and January and February, 1909, in the willows on Hula-hula River, north side of Endicott Mountains, Alaska, and in spruce timber on south side of the divide. On the south side of Richard Island in the Mackenzie delta, thirty or forty miles north of the tree line, we saw a single Chickadee singing merrily in the willows, September 18th, 1909. I followed him a long way, from bush to bush, but he finally flew up into the air and went across to the mainland. On Horton River, October 18th and 23d, 1911, we saw a Chickadee, probably this species, about fifteen miles south of Langton Bay, the only Chickadee seen east of the Mackenzie delta.

(740) *Penthestes hudsonicus hudsonicus* (J. R. Forster). Hudsonian Chickadee.

Several seen on the Athabaska River, and one seen at Smith's Landing, Slave River, June 2d, 1908. Mr. H. W. Jones noted the first arrival of this species at Hay River (Great Slave Lake) on May 12th, 1908.

(749) *Regulus calendula calendula* (Linnæus). Ruby-crowned Kinglet.

On the morning of September 24th, 1912, I picked up a dead male Ruby-crowned Kinglet, on the deck of S. S. *Belvedere*, fifteen to twenty miles offshore on Harrison Bay, east of Cape Halkett, northern Alaska. The night before I had seen a small bird flitting across the poop of the *Belvedere;* only a glimpse, and I could not see the bird again. He was probably picked up somewhere off the western side of the Colville delta.

(657) *Hylocichla aliciæ aliciæ* (Baird). Gray-cheeked Thrush.

Mr. H. W. Jones took a specimen at Hay River May 20th, 1908. Found one nest with three eggs in a spruce tree about four feet from the ground on a large, heavily wooded island in the eastern part of the Mackenzie delta June 24th, 1910. The eggs were greenish-blue with rich burnt sienna spots. Six or eight nests of similar construction were found in the immediate vicinity. The parent birds were very shy and nervous.

(738 a) *Hylocichla ustulata swainsoni* (Tschudi). Olive-backed Thrush.

In dense willow thickets in Slave River delta I found one nest containing two fresh eggs June 22d, 1908, in a clump of willows about two and a half feet from the ground. The nest was quite loosely built, composed of coarse grass and moss and lined with fine grass; eggs spotted. June 2d I found another nest containing one egg and three young birds, seven feet from the ground in a willow tree. The birds were very quiet and retiring.

(759 b) *Hylocichla guttata pallasi* (Cabanis). Hermit Thrush.

Mr. Harry W. Jones showed me a nest and four eggs taken at Hay River June 16th, 1908, incubation advanced. Eggs were plain blue color.

(761) *Planesticus migratorius migratorius* (Linnæus). Robin. Krē-kū-ak′tū-yōk (Mackenzie Eskimo). Shab′wak (Alaskan Eskimo).

Nesting commonly all along the Athabaska, Slave, and Mackenzie rivers, a little beyond the northern limit of trees. At Fort McKay, on the Athabaska River, found nest with two eggs May 18th; at Smith's Landing, Slave River, nest with young June 7th. At Fort Simpson, Mackenzie River, Robins were abundant; one nest with four eggs under steps of the Hudson Bay Company's museum and another on a fish stage. A nest containing four young birds was found June 22d, on the east branch of the Mackenzie delta. The first Robin of the season was seen on Dease River May 10th, and one specimen was taken June 19th, 1911, near the mouth of Kogaryuak River, on south side of Coronation Gulf; the only Robin which I have seen on the Arctic coast, although one specimen was seen at Herschel Island several years ago (according to accounts of the whalers). Robins are fairly common in the spruce timber on Horton River fifteen or twenty miles south of Langton Bay.

(763) *Ixoreus nœvius meruloides* (Swainson). Northern Varied Thrush.

Several adults were seen on low, wooded islands on the western part of the Mackenzie River delta, and one fully fledged young bird was found dead on the ground in a willow thicket on the edge of heavy spruce timber. This is one of the very few species of western passerine birds which comes over into the Mackenzie delta.

(765) *Saxicola œnanthe œnanthe* (Linnæus). Wheat-ear.

The only specimen of this rather noticeable species observed was a juvenal female taken at Herschel Island, Yukon Territory, July 31st, 1908. The basal half of this bird's tail-feathers being white made it very conspicuous. The bird was very wild, and I chased it for some distance before getting near enough to shoot it.

(768) *Sialia currucoides* (Bechstein). Mountain Bluebird.

Saw several pairs of this beautiful species along the road from Edmonton to Athabaska Landing, Alberta, but none farther north.

MAMMALS

Order CETACEA — Cetaceans.

Balæna mysticetus Linn. Arctic Bowhead Whale. Ak'virk.

Delphinapterus catodon (Linn.). White Whale. Kil-la-lū'ak.

Order UNGULATA — Hoofed Mammals.

Cervus canadensis (Erxleben). Canadian Wapiti.

Odocoileus hemionus (Rafinesque). Mule Deer.

Alces americanus Jardine. Eastern Moose. Tûk'tū-vŭk.

Rangifer arcticus (Richardson). Barren Ground Caribou. Tûk'tū.

Bison bison athabascæ Rhoads. Wood Bison.

Ovibos moschatus (Zimm.). Muskox. U'miñ-muk.

Ovis dalli (Nelson). Northern Mountain Sheep. Imp'nak.

Order RODENTIA — Rodents.

Marmota caligata (Eschscholtz). Hoary Marmot. Tjik-rik-puk.

Citellus parryi (Richardson). Hudson Bay Spermophile. Tjik-rik (W.). Tsik-tsik (E.).

Citellus parryi kennicotti (Ross). Mackenzie Spermophile. Tjikrik.

Citellus franklini (Sabine). Franklin's Spermophile.

Citellus tridecemlineatus (Mitchill). Thirteen-lined Spermophile.

Eutamias borealis (Allen). Liard River Chipmunk.

Sciurus hudsonicus Erxleben. Husdon Bay Red Squirrel. Nipaktam Tjik-rik.

Sciuropterus sabrinus (Shaw). Hudson Bay Flying Squirrel.

Peromyscus maniculatus borealis Mearns. Arctic White-footed Mouse.

Evotomys gapperi athabascœ Preble. Athabaska Red-backed Mouse.

Evotomys dawsoni Merriam. Dawson Red-backed Mouse.

Lemmus trimucronatus (Richardson). Back Lemming. Ki-lañmu'tak.

Dicrostonyx nelsoni Merriam. Point Barrow Lemming. A-viñ'-yak a-mirk-lirk.

Microtus drummondi (Aud. and Bach.). Drummond Vole. A-viñ-yak.

Microtus (species undetermined, from Arctic coast, probably *M. xanthognathus* (Leach), *M. macfarlani* Merriam.

Ondatra zibethicus spatulatus (Osgood). Northwest Muskrat. Ki-ŕa'luk.

Castor canadensis Kuhl. Canadian Beaver. Ki'gi-ak.

Zapus hudsonius (Zimm.). Hudson Bay Jumping Mouse.

Erethizon epixanthum Brandt. Yellow-haired Porcupine. Krēng-yā'lūk. I-lū-k̄ō'tak.

Lepus americanus macfarlani Merriam. Macfarlane Varying Hare. O-ka'lik.

Lepus arcticus canus Preble. Keewatin Arctic Hare. Ō-ka'-li-shūg'yuk.

Order CARNIVORA — Carnivores.

Lynx canadensis mollipilosus Stone. Northern Canada Lynx. Nī-tū'yak (Alaskan, Mackenzie River). Pi-tak'si-kok.

Canis occidentalis (Richardson). Gray Wolf. A'ma-rok.

Canis occidentalis albus Sabine. Barren Ground Wolf. (Discuss Preble on bases of color.)

Vulpes alascensis Merriam. Alaska Red Fox. Kai-yōk'tok (N. Alaska). Auk-pī-lak'tok (Mackenzie River).

"Cross Fox" variety — Krĭ-a-nŕok (N. Alaska). Kī-a-ser-ō-tĭl'ik (Mackenzie River).

"Silver" or "Black" — Ker-a-nek'tok (N. Alaska). Mag'r̂ok (Mackenzie River).

Blue Fox — Kai-a-nĭ-rak'tok (Colorado River). Ig-ra'lik (Mackenzie River).

Alopex lagopus innuitus (Merriam). Continental Arctic Fox. Ti-ra-ga'ni-ok.

Ursus americanus Pallas. Black Bear.

Ursus richardsoni Swainson. Barren Ground Bear. Ak'lak.

Thalarctos maritimus (Phipps). Polar Bear. Nan'nuk.

Mephitis hudsonica (Richardson). Northern Plains Skunk.

Lutra canadensis (Schreber). Canadian Otter.

Latax lutris (Linnæus). Gray Sea Otter. (Not observed.)

Taxidea taxus (Schreber). Badger.

Mustela vison ingens (Osgood). Alaska Mink. Tĭ-rĭ-ak'puk.

Mustela rixosa (Bangs). Least Weasel. Nau-li-ak'.

Mustela arctica (Merriam). Tundra Weasel. Tĭ'rĭ-ak.

Martes americana actuosa (Osgood). Alaska Marten. Ka-vi-a'-tjak.

Gulo luscus (Linn.). Hudson Bay Wolverine. Kap'rik (Alaska). Kap'vik (Mackenzie River). Kal'vik (Coronation Gulf).

Order PINNIPEDIA — Sea Lions, Seals, etc.

Callorhinus alascanus Jordan and Clark. Alaska Fur Seal.

Odobenus obesus (Illiger). Pacific Walrus. Ai'vuk.

Phoca hispida Schreber. Rough Seal. Na'tjirk.

Erignathus barbatus (Erxleben). Bearded Seal. Ūg-ŕuk (Alaska). Ug-yuk (E.).

Order INSECTIVORA — Insectivores.

Sorex personatus. I. Geoffroy St. Hilaire. Common Eastern Shrew.

Sorex tundrensis Merriam. Tundra Shrew. Ug-ŕū'nak (Alaska). Ūg-yū'nak (Mackenzie River).

Order CHIROPTERA — The Bats.

Myotis lucifugus (Le Conte). Little Brown Bat.

Order CETACEA — Cetaceans

Balæna mysticetus Linn. Arctic Bowhead Whale. Ak'virk (Alaskan Mackenzie, and Coronation Gulf).

The Bowhead Whale, the largest animal of the Arctic regions, if not directly the most important animal, on account of being the

chief means of support of a number of Eskimo communities, has,
through the large fleets of vessels engaged in the whaling industry,
indirectly been the most responsible agent for bringing the white
man's civilization into the western Arctic, with its concomitant effects
upon population and fauna.   Although whaling had long been prosecuted in the Bering Sea and the Arctic Ocean west of Point Barrow,
the first ship wintered at Herschel Island in 1889–1890.   Later other
ships wintered at Baillie Island, Langton Bay, Cape Parry, and two
small schooners even wintered as far east as Victoria Island.   Whaling was prosecuted independently by Eskimos from Cape Prince of
Wales, Point Hope, to Cape Smyth and Point Barrow, Alaska, and
east of the Mackenzie, at Warren Point, Baillie Islands, Langton Bay,
and other points, before the advent of white men.   The Eskimos were
accustomed to pursue the whale from their skin-covered umiaks and
kill them with stone-headed lances, valuing the whale for its meat and
blubber and not for the "whalebone" or baleen.   Nowadays there
is no Eskimo whaling east of Point Barrow, and the western Eskimos
use modern weapons.   The whaling industry by white men has become practically dead within the past few years.   One ship and one
gasoline schooner, the only vessels which whaled in the Beaufort Sea,
killed twelve whales apiece during the summer of 1912, but the
voyages were considered unprofitable on account of the unsaleability
of bone.   The largest number of ships which wintered at Herschel
Island at one time was fourteen in 1893–1894.   The largest catches
are said to have been 69 whales by Captain Smith in the *Narwhal*,
1893–1895; 67 whales by Captain Norwood in the *Balæna* in 1893–
1895, and 64 whales by Captain Bodfish in the *Beluga* in a two-year
voyage about the same time.   At that time whales were frequently
killed near Herschel Island and Baillie Islands, but now they are
much less seldom seen inshore.   A good many Bowhead Whales are
killed in the spring by the Siberian natives at their whaling stations
at Indian Point, Plover Bay, and East Cape.   Whalers say that in
the spring the Bowheads do not follow the Siberian coast farther than
East Cape, but strike across from there to Point Hope, Alaska, and
follow up the American coast around Point Barrow, passing Point
Barrow, going to the eastward from about April 20th to June 1st.

After the Bowheads pass Point Barrow in April and May, little

2 K

is known of their movements. Whalers are apt to be met with anywhere in Amundsen Gulf in July and August, as early as ships can get
out of winter quarters. Whales are sometimes seen spouting offshore in Franklin Bay early in June. In August, in the region between Cape Parry and Banks Island, the whales usually seem to be
coming south along the west side of Banks Island, and going west,
although they often are seen in Franklin Bay until September.
Following them up, the whalers usually find whales most abundant
on the "offshore" or "pea-soup grounds" off Capes Dalhousie and
Brown, where the water is rather shoal, eighteen to thirty fathoms.
The whales often remain here for some time and if scared away, soon
come back. Whales killed here sometimes have mud on their backs
as if they had been rolling on a mud bottom, *i.e.*, whales which are
killed without sinking. A dead whale which sinks to the bottom
often brings up mud as a matter of course. Bowheads have been
chased into fresh water three fathoms deep near Pullen Islands, off
the mouth of the Mackenzie River. No parasites are found on Bow-
head Whales, like the barnacles and "lice" found on Right Whales
and Humpbacks.

The method of Bowhead whaling is to cruise about under sail,
keeping a sharp lookout from the masthead during the whole twenty-
four hours. Bowhead Whales are very easily frightened and are
very seldom if ever seen from a steamship while the propellor is working. Furthermore, after a whale is struck by a bomb, it is extremely
infrequent for another whale to be seen in the same vicinity for an
hour or more, even though there may have been many in sight before.
When a whale is "raised," the ship lowers all its available whale-boats.
Each boat usually has a ship's officer as boat header in the stern-sheets,
a boat-steerer (harpooner) in the bow, and a crew of four oarsmen.
A whale usually stays below the surface for a regular period, from
twenty minutes to an hour or more, according to his individual
peculiarity. When up, the whale moves slowly along, the top of
back just above the water, sometimes just below, making a wake,
every minute or two blowing up a white column of vapor to a height
of from eight to twelve feet. After spouting several times the whale
usually "turns flukes," raises his tail out of water, and dives down.
After two or three risings, the boat-header can usually tell the rate

of speed at which the whale is traveling, the direction of his course, and the time he is apt to stay below. The boat heads for the place of his probable reappearance, keeping a little to windward if possible. When the whale spouts again, the boat-header tries to run the boat directly across the top of the whale's head, the most favorable chance. As the boat passes over, the boat-steerer (harpooner) in the bow thrusts one or two tonnite (or sometimes black-powder) bombs into the whale's neck with the darting-gun. The darting-gun is a heavy lance-shaft with set-gun at tip. When the point of the harpoon enters, a stiff parallel wire explodes the eight-gauge cartridge which shoots the bomb into the whale. The handle is immediately disengaged, the barbed harpoon-head remaining in the wound, and attached to the lance-warp (rope), of which ten fathoms are kept in a box in the bow and one hundred or more fathoms in a tub in the boat. Sometimes a shoulder-gun is used after the darting-gun, if opportunity offers. The shoulder-gun is a heavy eight-bore, shooting a long feathered tonnite bomb with no warp attached. If struck fairly in the neck vertebræ, a whale is sometimes killed instantly with one shot, but sometimes eight or ten shots are required. The whale often tows a boat a long distance if only slightly wounded, and is sometimes lost by going under a large ice-field. As soon as the whale is "struck" by one boat, the other boats come up as soon as possible, and as the whale rises he is struck as often as possible. On small ships the whalebone baleen from the upper jaw is sometimes cut off in the water, but on the larger ships the upper portion of the whale's skull is cut off and hoisted on deck entire, and the bone removed later. Ordinarily the practice of the Bowhead whalers in recent years has been to remove only the baleen, turning the carcass with its fifty or more barrels of oil, adrift. This is a most wasteful practice, but when "bone" was high in price, a single whale might be worth $10,000 in bone, and the captains preferred not to spend a day saving a thousand dollars' worth of oil, and perhaps lose a possible second whale. The meat of the Bowhead is good, the young whale's flesh in particular being much like beef. The "blackskin," or *muk-tok*, as it is called by the Eskimo, is considered a great delicacy, being usually eaten raw by the Eskimo, and boiled fresh or pickled by the white whalers. At Point Barrow, Alaska, the "floe-whaling" is done principally in

Eskimo skin-umiaks, and the whalebone is cut out at the edge of the floe. A male which I saw killed August 23d, 1910, in Franklin Bay, was about 57 feet long, flukes 18 feet 4 inches across, and right fin or flipper 10 feet 4 inches around outer curvature. The whale yielded 2100 pounds of whalebone, the longest slabs (from middle of jaw) being about 11 feet in length.

Delphinapterus catodon (Linn.).   White Whale.   Kil-la-lū'ak (Alaskan and Mackenzie Eskimo).

The White Whale or Beluga, commonly called "White-fish" by white men in the North and Killaluak by the Eskimo, occurs somewhat irregularly at various points along the Arctic coast. It is generally pursued by the Eskimo only, who value the flesh and blubber highly and use the skin for making boot-soles, rawhide thongs, etc., and formerly for covering umiaks. One of the best hunting-grounds for the white whale is in the estuary of the Mackenzie, east of Richard Island, where the whales appear in large schools in July shortly after the ice breaks up. Eskimo from the whole Mackenzie region assemble here in July for the Killaluak fishery, and about two hundred were killed in July, 1909. The next year, 1910, only a small number appeared. The whales are pursued in whale-boats. The harpooners first strike the whale with a hand-iron, and after making fast in this way, the boat endeavors to get alongside the whale so that it can be shot in the head with a rifle. The water is shoal in this region, and the backs of the whales can usually be seen as they plow up the river. Eskimo say that sometimes the Beluga may be killed with a rifle, but the body always sinks as soon as killed. Another well-known hunting-ground is at the north end of Richard Island, and still another at the "Whitefish Station" between Tent Island and Escape Reef, Mackenzie Bay. In 1908 the fishery was unsuccessful at the latter place, and only two were caught. Beluga are said by the Eskimo to sometimes enter the Eskimo Lakes from Liverpool Bay. In the latter part of July and in August they are usually seen going steadily west, often plunging and splashing, showing half of the body out of water.

Order UNGULATA — Hoofed Mammals

Cervus canadensis (Erxleben).   Canadian Wapiti.   Elk.

Mr. Pierre Mercredi, the Hudson's Bay Company trader at Fort Chipewyan who has lived in the country many years, says that the Elk never ranged farther north than Fort McMurray on the Athabaska River.

Odocoileus hemionus (Rafinesque).   Mule Deer.

Mr. Wm. Briggs, the Dominion Forest Fire Ranger from Athabaska Landing to Fort McMurray, says that the Black-tailed Deer have come into this country during the last few years.

Alces americanus Jardine.   Eastern Moose.   Tûk′tū-vûk (Alaskan, Mackenzie, and Coronation Gulf Eskimo).   Ko-gon (Slavey Indian).

The Moose is common throughout the timbered country all along the Mackenzie River, and has occasionally been seen north of the timber line near Richard Island. According to the opinion of old residents and to data collected by the expedition, the Moose is increasing all through the northern country as well as extending its range rapidly and noticeably. Owing to its solitary habits and the nature of its habitat, the Moose cannot be slaughtered wholesale as can the Caribou and the Musk-ox, and the northern Indians have decreased in numbers at such a rapid rate as to more than compensate for the increased killing power of their more modern weapons. Moose venture very rarely into the region of the lower Horton River. Mr. Joseph Hodgson, one of the oldest of Hudson Bay traders, says that in the early days, up to less than fifty years ago, Moose were very rarely seen east of the Mackenzie, and told us in 1911 that it was only within the past half-dozen years that Moose had been seen on the east side of Great Bear Lake. Moose are now fairly numerous on Caribou Point, the great peninsula between Dease Bay and McTavish Bay, Great Bear Lake, and on the Dease River, northeast of Great Bear Lake. A Coronation Gulf Eskimo from the region near Rae River (Pal′lirk) told us that he had seen two Moose (which he thought cows, from their small antlers) near the mouth of Rae River in 1909 or 1910. These Eskimo often hunt in summer down to Great Bear Lake and know the Moose from that region. Rae River flows into the southwestern corner of Coronation Gulf, and the Moose undoubtedly wandered here from the region around Great Bear Lake. *Rangifer arcticus* (Richardsons).   Barren   Ground   Caribou. "Tûk'tū" (universal Eskimo name).   Adult bull, Pag'nirk. Adult female, Kūl'la-vŭk.   Fawn, Nō'wak.

With the possible exception of the Bowhead Whale, the Caribou is without doubt the most important animal of the Arctic.   There is scarcely anything manufactured which can equal Caribou skin as an article of clothing; in many districts the natives live for long periods almost exclusively upon the meat of the Caribou, while there are many vast sections of the land which could with difficulty even be explored without relying upon finding the herds of Caribou.   The Caribou were formerly universally and abundantly distributed over all parts of Arctic Alaska and Canada, but the numbers have been enormously decreased nearly everywhere within the last twenty years.   Until a few years ago the coastal plain of Arctic Alaska, from Point Barrow to the Mackenzie, was the pasture of vast herds.   Only an occasional scattered band is now seen.   As a consequence most of the Eskimo have been compelled by starvation to move out, notably from the Colville River region.   The Caribou are practically extinct around Point Barrow, and our party in the year 1908–1909 found only a few between Cape Halkett and the Colville.   We saw a herd of perhaps four hundred in the Kuparuk River delta (the only large band seen by anybody in northern Alaska that season) and other small bands as far west as Demarcation Point.   Around the mouth of the Mackenzie the Caribou have practically disappeared, although stragglers are occasionally seen on Richard Island and in the Eskimo Lakes region. Few are now found on the Cape Bathurst peninsula, and only small numbers around Langton Bay and Darnley Bay.   There are places in the interior of Alaska which are more favored.   In the southern foothills on the Endicott Mountains, on one of the northern tributaries of the Yukon, beyond the ordinary range of the Indians or the white prospectors, I saw in 1908 as many as one thousand Caribou in a single herd.   Farther east, the Caribou are much more plentiful.   Victoria Island pastures great numbers in summer. These herds cross to the mainland south of Victoria Island as soon as Dolphin and Union Straits and Coronation Gulf are frozen over in the fall (in 1910, about November 8th–10th), returning north over the ice in April and May.   Some Caribou are found all summer around Great Bear Lake and the Coppermine River.   Large numbers winter on Caribou Point, the large peninsula between Dease Bay and Mc-Tavish Bay at the eastern end of Great Bear Lake.   Here on the cold, calm days of midwinter the steam from the massed herds often rises like a cloud over the tops of the scattering spruce forests.   Although a large number of Caribou come down into the Bear Lake woods, and go out on the Barren Grounds in spring, not all the Caribou seek the shelter of the woods in winter.   Some Caribou are found in midwinter on the most wind-swept barrens and occur on almost any part of the Arctic coast at any season of the year.

The Eskimo of the Coronation Gulf and Victoria Island region have no firearms and kill Caribou by driving a herd between long rows of rock monuments into an ambush or into lakes where the Caribou are pursued and speared from kayaks.   Two or three stones or a bunch of turf placed on top of a rock two or three feet high, or even less, to resemble persons, form these little cairns, often extending for miles and converging in some valley or gulch.   The Caribou ordinarily pay no attention to these monuments, but when alarmed by the sight of people, seem to become confused and do not venture to cross the lines of mounds.   The custom is to have a person stationed here and there along the line, while others surround the herd of Caribou and start it moving towards the line.   As the Caribou approach, the people along the line of rock monuments display themselves, throwing the herd into a panic and as the herd rushes along between the converging lines into the ambush where concealed bowmen have an opportunity to shoot the Caribou at very short range.   On the Barren Grounds around Coronation Gulf these *inuktjuit* (inuk[man]-like) Caribou drives are found everywhere.   But even in this most favorable Caribou country the older people say that in their youth the Caribou were much more abundant than at present.

The hunting of the Barren Ground Caribou, as it is practiced by white men and the Eskimo who use firearms, is in theory a very simple matter.   The prime requisites are unlimited patience and much hard work.   The field-glass or telescope is almost as necessary as the rifle, since the Caribou should be discovered at a distance.   The herd is spied out from the highest knolls or elevations, and if the country is rough enough to afford even a little cover, the approach is comparatively easy by hunting up the wind, as the Caribou do not see very far. Their powers of scent and hearing are very acute, however. On a broad, flat tundra plain, where there is no cover, and there are not enough hunters to approach from several sides, obviously the proper thing to do is to wait for the Caribou to browse slowly along and move on to more favorable ground for stalking. During the short days of winter this is often impossible and under any circumstances is trying to the patience. The reputed superiority of the Eskimo hunter over his white confrère seems to be mainly in the former's willingness to spend unlimited time in approaching his quarry. The Great Bear Lake Indians often take advantage of the Caribou's frequent habit of circling around the hunter until certain of the danger. They will sneak up as far as practicable, then come out into the open and run directly at the Caribou, which often stand stupidly until the hunter is very near or else circle blindly around until they get the scent of the hunter and make off. I have always found it much easier to approach a small herd than a large one, because there is always a straggler or two on the flanks of a large herd to give alarm before the main body is approached.

For the purposes of making clothing, the skins of the Caribou are at their best from the 1st of August until about the 10th of September. Later than that the hair becomes too long and heavy. Towards the end of winter the hair begins to get loose, and by the last of April is so very loose that the skin is practically worthless. During June and July the Caribou usually have a more or less patchy appearance, due to bunches of loose, faded, old hair remaining in places. Summer skins are often badly perforated by the grubs of a species of bot-fly. Caribou skins are exceptional non-conductors of heat. When a number of Caribou are killed during the short days of midwinter, the Eskimo often skin only the legs, double the legs under the body, and pack soft snow around the carcass. I have seen many Caribou left out overnight at a temperature of $-45°$ Fahrenheit, and lower, and the heat retained by the skin so that the body was warm and readily skinned the next day.

The fawns, seldom more than one in number, are born between

the 1st and 15th of June. Two young fawns taken near the Colville delta, Alaska, June 16th, 1909, were quite different in color, one being decidedly brown, with short, sleek coat; the other was whitish gray with very little "fawn" color, and hair longer and softer, more woolly in texture. No traces of spotting on either specimen. The Caribou seen east of the Coppermine River and on the south side of Coronation Gulf seemed to average much lighter in color than the Caribou found on Great Bear Lake or on the Arctic coast west of Cape Parry. With very few exceptions the Coppermine Caribou were very light, with legs nearly white. The heads of these Caribou appeared to be much shorter than those of the Great Bear Lake Caribou, with a noticeable fullness or convexity between forehead and nose, reminding one in some degree of the profile of a rabbit. The difference is not very noticeable on the skulls, the fullness of the face being largely due to the fuzziness of the whorl of hair on front of face.

The old bull Caribou begin to shed their antlers by the first of January or earlier, and most of them have dropped them by the month of February. The young bulls and cows retain their antlers until May. On Caribou Point the old bulls herded together in winter, and in their antler-less condition presented a pitiably tame and defenseless appearance, in contrast to the bull Caribou's belligerent-looking autumn attitude. By the 10th of May the new antlers of the old bulls are about a foot long, with blunt, knobby ends.

Many Eskimo claim to be able to pick out the fat Caribou from a herd by observing the shape of the horns. This is probably merely the ability to distinguish between the sexes in a herd at the different seasons. At Great Bear Lake in the fall, before the rutting season, the old bulls had the greatest quantities of fat. In midwinter all the bulls were poor, while the cows often had considerable fat. Towards spring the young bulls began to pick up a little fat, while the cows seemed to fall away as the calving season approached. The cows can usually be distinguished from young bulls by the relative slenderness of their antlers. Old bulls seldom have much fat before the end of the mosquito season. When the antlers are full grown, then they begin to pick up rapidly. The largest slab of back-fat which I have seen taken from a Caribou on the Arctic coast was from a bull killed near Langton Bay early in September, the fat weighing 39 pounds.

A large bull killed by Mr. Stefánsson on Dease River in October had back-fat 72 mm. in thickness ($2\frac{7}{8}$ inches). Comparing the thickness of this with the Langton Bay specimen, the back-fat of the Dease River bull must have weighed at least 50 pounds. The thicker the back-fat of a Caribou is, the richer it is in proportion — the amount of connective tissue remaining the same, and the additional weight consisting of interstitial fat.

Bison bison athabascæ Rhoads. Wood Bison.

According to the estimates made by Major W. H. Routledge, R.N.W.M.P., who was in charge of the Buffalo protection at Fort Smith in 1908, there are probably not more than three hundred left. The number of Buffaloes in the region is difficult to estimate, as they range in small scattered bands west of the Slave River, from Salt River on the south to Hay River on the north. This remnant of the once great herds is pretty thoroughly protected now, although the wolves are said to kill a good many.

Ovibos moschatus (Zimmermann). Musk-ox. Ū-miñ-mŭk (Eskimo). Et-jir-er (Slavey Indian, Great Bear Lake).

No living Musk-oxen have probably been seen in Alaska at a later date than 1860–1865, although horns, skulls, and bones in a good state of preservation are to be found in various places from Point Barrow to the Colville River. None have been seen west of Liverpool Bay within the past twenty-five years. Around Franklin Bay, Langton Bay, and the lower part of Horton River, Musk-oxen were fairly common until about 1897.

The first vessel that went into Langton Bay to winter (fall of 1897) saw Musk-oxen on the hills, looking from the deck of the ship. During 1897–1898 four ships wintered at Langton Bay, and over eighty Musk-oxen were killed, mainly by Alaskan Eskimo hunting for the ships. Some of the meat was hauled to the ships, but most of the animals were killed too far away for the meat to be hauled in, and the bulk of the robes were left out too late in the spring thaws, so that very little use was made of anything. Since that time no traces of living Musk-oxen have been seen in the region, either by natives who occasionally hunt there, or by our party during nearly three years. In March, 1902, a party of Alaskan Eskimo made an extended journey to the southeast and east of Darnley Bay and killed twenty-seven. This was without doubt the last killing of Musk-oxen by Eskimo west of Dolphin and Union Straits.

In the summer of 1910 Mr. Stefánsson and his Eskimo found numerous Musk-ox droppings of the previous winter around the Lake Immaërnrk, the head of Dease River. We spent the greater part of the winter of 1910–1911 on the east branch of Dease River and eastern end of Great Bear Lake, but saw no recent signs of Musk-oxen. That same winter the Bear Lake Indians made an unsuccessful hunt to the northeast of Great Bear Lake. Two or three years before they had made a big hunt in this region and killed about eighty. In February or March, 1911, the Indians killed three Musk-oxen near the end of Caribou Point, the only specimens seen in the whole region that winter. Apparently the Musk-ox is seldom if ever found in the region of western Coronation Gulf around the mouths of Rae River, Richardson River, or the lower portion of the Coppermine River. Quite a number of Eskimo hunt in this region, and they say that the Musk-oxen are all farther to the east. Some old men in the Rae River region had never seen a Musk-ox. The number of Musk-oxen now living west of the lower Coppermine River is very small and probably confined to the rather small area of high, rocky barrens comprised in the triangle whose apices are Darnley Bay, Coronation and the north side of Great Bear Lake. From all the information we could get from the Coronation Gulf Eskimo, Musk-oxen are seldom if ever seen near the mainland coast less than seventy-five miles east of the mouth of the Coppermine River. It seems probable from information which Mr. Stefánsson received from numerous groups of Eskimo in Coronation Gulf, Dolphin and Union Straits, and Prince Albert Sound, that no Musk-oxen at all are found in either the southern or central portions of Victoria Island (i.e. Wollaston Land, Victoria Land, Prince Albert Land). Some of these Eskimo remember of the former occurrence of the Musk-ox around Minto Inlet and Walker Bay, but say there are now none in that region. It is their belief, however, that Musk-oxen are still found near the north coast of Victoria Island. Musk-oxen are said to be still common on Banks Island. The Musk-oxen are so readily killed, often to the last animal in a herd, that the species cannot hold its own against even the most primitive weapons, and the advent of modern rifles means speedy extinction.

Ovis dalli (Nelson).   Northern Mountain Sheep.   Imp'nak (Alaskan
    Eskimo).   Lamb, during the first year, No'wak.   Two-year-
    old, with short horns, Kĭ-rū-tai'lak.   Adult female, Kūl'la-vŭk.
    Adult male, Ang-a-tī-shūg-rŭk (literally big male).   Slavey
    Indian name, Thō.

    The White Sheep probably never ranged east of the Mackenzie,
although they are said to be still fairly common in the mountains
on the west side of the river from Fort Norman to the west side of the
delta.   The Endicott Mountains, or that branch of the northern
Rockies which runs northwest from the western edge of the Mackenzie
delta, form a divide ten or fifteen miles from the coast west from the
coast at Herschel Island and seventy-five or one hundred miles from
the coast at the Colville, the largest river flowing into the Arctic
in northern Alaska.   Sheep were formerly quite numerous on the
heads of nearly all the rivers on the Arctic side of the divide, at least
as far west as the Colville.   It is probable that until comparatively
recent times, before whaling ships began to winter at Herschel Island
in 1889, the sheep were not much hunted in this region.   The population was sparse, and the Caribou were larger, more abundant, and
more easily taken.   The gradual extermination of the Caribou in
northwestern Alaska, combined with other causes, has for many
years induced Eskimo from the rivers at the head of Kotzebue Sound
to move across to the Colville, at the same time that many Colville
Eskimo have gradually moved eastward, occupying one mountain
valley after another until the sheep became too scarce to support
them.   A considerable number of sheepskins have been sent west
each year with the Cape Smyth natives who came east each year to
barter white men goods for Sheep and Caribou skins.   In my expedition into the Endicott Mountains from October, 1908, to April, 1909, I
hunted sheep with the Eskimo on both sides of the Endicott Mountain divide, and found sheep much more common on the north side
of the divide than on the south side, although the south side of the
mountains is an uninhabited wilderness.   On the Hula-hula River,
which has a course of about forty-five miles in the mountains and
about the same distance across the central plain, we found two
families of Eskimo sheep-hunters.   One of these Eskimo had in this
small river valley killed thirty or thirty-five sheep from June to Au-

gust, 1908, and thirty-seven from September, 1908, to May, 1909, subsisting with his whole family almost entirely on sheep meat. This man's clothing from head to foot was made of sheepskins, his tent of sheepskins, and even his snowshoes strung with sheepskin thongs. Many people in the north prefer the skin of the Mountain Sheep to Caribou for clothing. Although the outer hair of the Sheep is brittle, only the ends of the hairs break off, and the sheepskin never becomes wholly denuded, while the Caribou skin garment becomes bare in spots on very slight provocation.

Although the rocky slopes where the sheep feed look pretty barren, the sheep manage to find enough to eat. The stomachs usually contain grass, and sometimes moss. The natives say the sheep do not browse on willows, although they often descend to the willows in the summer time. In winter the sheep usually keep to the higher ridges where the snow is less deep. They do not appear to paw the snow away, as it is seldom crusted hard, but browse through the snow, pushing it aside with the nose. Sheep are singularly unsuspicious of danger from above, although they are continually on the alert for enemies from below. Their eyesight is almost telescopic, the scent and hearing equally acute, and it is practically impossible to approach them from below. The hunter therefore always endeavors to work around some adjoining ridge or ascend some creek valley and approach them from above. In this manner, the native hunters sometimes approach within fifteen or twenty yards and kill several out of one band. The lambs are said to be born very early in the season, much earlier than the Caribou, while the snow is still on the ground. The natives told me that in summer the sheep sometimes go up on the ice-capped mountains when the mosquitoes get very bad on the lower ranges, but that they come down again towards evening, as there is no grass on the high mountain tops. Although the numbers of sheep have been greatly reduced, I believe that a few are still found near the head of every mountain river from the Colville to the Mackenzie. The natives hunt strictly for meat and skins, and the habitat of the sheep prevents the hunters in this particular region from picking up sheep as a side line to other game hunting and trapping. When a local influx of hunters cuts down the number of sheep beyond a certain limit in some mountain valley, pressure of hunger soon causes the people to move out. Word is passed along that the said river is starvation country, and an automatic close season affords the sheep a chance to recuperate. The Eskimo in the Endicott range occasionally capture a sheep by setting rope nooses or snares in the paths which the sheep make through the willow thickets while crossing from one side of a river valley to another. A few wolves are found on the sheep range, and I have seen wolf tracks following sheep's tracks high up into the mountains, so that probably a few are killed by Wolves.

Order RODENTIA — Rodents

Marmota caligata (Eschscholtz). Hoary Marmot. Tjik'rik-pŭk, "big marmot" (Alaskan Eskimo).

Common in the Endicott Mountains north to the edge of the foot-hills. A few skins are taken by the inland Eskimo, and sold under the name of "Badger." Eskimo east of the Mackenzie say that the animal is not found in their country, but know the species by name, from garments brought in by western Eskimo.

Citellus parryi kennicotti (Ross). Mackenzie Spermophile. Tjik'-rik (Alaskan Eskimo). Tsik-tsik (Mackenzie Eskimo).

Common all along the northern coast of Alaska, in the Mackenzie delta, and east to Franklin Bay. Less common in the more rocky and stony country east of Franklin Bay. These Spermophiles are particularly abundant in sandy, alluvial river bottoms where the ground thaws earlier and to a greater depth, allowing the animals to dig their favorite roots and excavate their burrows more readily than on the frozen, moss-covered tundra. They feed principally upon the roots of various species of *Polygonum*, the "masū'" roots of the Eskimo, and are very fat in the fall, and for a short time after coming out of winter quarter. The bulk of the Spermophiles go into hibernation in the latter part of September, but a few are occasionally seen until the middle of October. They come out again about the middle of April. The flesh is eaten by the Eskimo, and the skins make very good warm garments. The males fight viciously among themselves, and most of the old males are badly scarred from their numerous battles.

Citellus parryi (Richardson). Hudson Bay Spermophile. Srik-srik (Coronation Gulf Eskimo).

Mr. E. A. Preble (N. A. Fauna, No. 27, p. 160) has conventionally placed the line between the habitats of *C. parryi* and of *C. p. kennicotti* as the watershed between the Coppermine River and Great Bear Lake. The appearance and habits of the two varieties are similar, *kennicotti* being described as paler in color. The Spermophiles are very abundant in the sandy clay hills around the mouth of the Coppermine, and at various places along the south side of Coronation Gulf, and form a large part of the food of the Copper Eskimo in May and June, in the interim after they abandon sealing and leave their snow houses on the ice, and before they go inland for the summer Caribou hunt. We saw no evidence of the presence of Spermophiles on southern Victoria Island, and the Eskimo say that they are not found on the island.

Citellus franklini (Sabine). Franklin's Spermophile.

This species was not observed farther north than the Edmonton and Athabaska Landing trail.

Citellus tridecemlineatus (Mitchill). Thirteen-lined Spermophile.

Number seen on the trail a few miles north of Edmonton, Alberta, but none farther north.

Eutamias borealis (Allen). Liard River Chipmunk.

Observed at various points as far north as Smith's Portage, on the Slave River.

Sciurus hudsonicus Erxleben. Hudson Bay Red Squirrel. Nipaktam Tsik-tsik, "Spruce-tree Spermophile" (Mackenzie Eskimo).

Noted at various points along the Athabaska, Slave, and Mackenzie rivers, as far north as the mouth of Peel River below Fort McPherson. Rather rare at the northeast end of Great Bear Lake. Saw one in a spruce grove near the Dease River, March 9th, 1911; very active and noisy in spite of the cold weather.

Sciuropterus sabrinus (Shaw). Hudson Bay Flying Squirrel.

Mr. Harry W. Jones had in collection two young Flying Squirrels preserved in formalin, captured June 8th, 1908, in a nest in a spruce tree near Hay River, Great Slave Lake. They were apparently only a few days old, with hair very short, and eyes not yet opened. No other specimens were observed in the North.

Peromyscus maniculatus borealis (Mearns). Arctic White-footed
   Mouse.

This species is very common on the Athabaska, Slave, and Mackenzie rivers, as far north as Fort Norman. Specimens were trapped
at nearly all stopping places, usually in runways near fallen logs just
within the line of Spruce and Balsam Poplar, above the line of Willows and Alders on river banks. At all of the trading-posts they enter
the dwellings and warehouses and become as great a nuisance as the
common House Mouse does in civilized countries.

Evotomys gapperi athabascæ Preble. Athabaska Red-backed Mouse.

One specimen caught at Fort Chipewyan May 24th, 1908, in a run-
way on a ledge of rocks near the shore of Lake Athabaska.

Evotomys dawsoni Merriam. Dawson Red-backed Mouse.

Eight specimens trapped at Fort Norman July 4th–8th, 1908, most
of them in an old log house near the R. C. Mission. The species was
not taken elsewhere.

Lemnus trimucronatus (Richardson). Back Lemming. A-vī-ñka
   (the generic name for mouse, among Alaskan as well as the Mackenzie Eskimo).

In the Mackenzie delta and eastward this species is properly
designated "A-mirk-lirk," or "Auk-pi-lak-tok a-mirk'lirk." Specimens which are apparently referable to this species were taken at
various points along the Arctic coast from the Colville delta, Alaska,
to Coronation Gulf, but the species was not very common anywhere.

Dicrostonyx nelsoni Merriam. Point Barrow Lemming. Kī-lañ-
   mū'tak, "one out of the sky" (Alaskan and Mackenzie Eskimo).

The Eskimo have a common belief that the White Lemmings
fall from the sky. The animals in the dusky summer pelage, with
darker dorsal stripe, are called A-vi-ñat or mice. Specimens were
occasionally taken at various points from Flaxman Island, Alaska,
east to Coronation Gulf, but were not seen in numbers at any time.

Microtus drummondi (Aud. and Bach.). Drummond Vole.

Specimens taken in house at Fort Norman, also occasionally
in runways in the tall grass and spruce shrubs near the northern
limit of trees south of Langton Bay; also on the west side of Franklin
Bay.

Microtus macfarlani Merriam. Macfarlane Vole. Little Meadow

Mouse. A-vĭ-ñak (Alaskan and Mackenzie River Eskimo). A-vi-ña-ȓa'lūk (Mackenzie River Eskimo).

A large number of Mice were taken at Langton Bay from 1910 to 1912. The sandspit at the harbor was covered with a mat of wire-like grass, which was intersected by a maze of mouse runways, and the Mice also extended their depredations into the provisions and skins which we stored in the old whalers' storehouse. These Mice have not been thoroughly examined and compared with the types, but at least two species were found here, one of which is undoubtedly *macfarlani*. Specimens apparently referable to *macfarlani* were also taken on the mainland east of Richard Island. A few specimens of Mice in the collection from northern Alaska are still undetermined. During the year 1908–1909 Mice of all kinds were unusually scarce all along the coast of northern Alaska, while two years before they were said to have been excessively abundant. On that part of the coast, where stranded carcasses are rare, Mice seem to form the chief food of the White Foxes. The year when the Mice were scarce was also marked by an abnormal scarcity of Snowy Owls.

Ondatra zibethicus spatulatus (Osgood). Northwest Muskrat, Ki-ȓa'-lûk (Mackenzie Eskimo).

Common throughout the whole Mackenzie basin. Observed Muskrats in the west branch of Mackenzie delta nearly to Tent Island, and in the east branch up to Toker Point, both points being well north of the tree line. On the southeast end of Richard Island, September 17th, 1909, I killed twelve Muskrats in a grass-bordered slough channel. Several rat-houses here were built of heaped-up grass-stems, moss, and mud on the edge of open water; all houses rather small, not over eighteen inches above water and two and a half or three feet across.

Muskrats were fairly common in small lakes near Horton River, from ten to forty miles south of Langton Bay. In October, I saw several muskrat holes in the ice, two or three inches in diameter. They were covered by little bunches of grass on top of the ice encircling the hole, and were kept open all the time. I saw only one rat-house near shore built up with top about one foot above water. Muskrats have become fairly common on the east side of Great Bear Lake within the past few years, according to Mr. Joseph Hodgson,

2 L

a well-informed trader of the Hudson Bay Company. The Muskrat apparently does not go much east of the Coppermine River along the Arctic coast. Throughout the Indian and Eskimo country the Muskrat is considered delicious eating. Mr. Maxfield Hamilton, the Hudson Bay Company's agent at Smith's Landing, obtained an albino skin in the spring of 1908, the second one he had seen out of one or two hundred thousand rat skins handled.

Castor canadensis Kuhl. Canadian Beaver. Kĭ′gi-ak (Mackenzie Eskimo).

I saw specimens taken in the east branch of the Mackenzie delta, nearly as far north as the tree line, and also near the mouth of Peel River. The Eskimo consider the broad, flat tail of the Beaver a great delicacy; it is somewhat fatty, and when boiled has a soft, gelatinous structure. Mr. Joseph Hodgson says that the Beaver have greatly extended their range east of the Mackenzie during recent years, in the region around Great Bear Lake.

Zapus hudsonius (Zimm.). Hudson Bay Jumping Mouse.

The only specimen observed in the North was picked up dead on the edge of the Indian village at the foot of the hill at Fort Norman, July 6th, 1908.

Erethizon epixanthum Brandt. Yellow-haired Porcupine. Krēng-ya′lūk, I-lū-kō′tok (Alaskan Eskimo, names used by the same people indiscriminately).

Three specimens were killed in spruce timber on south side of Endicott Mountains, Alaska, in December, 1908, and February, 1908. The Eskimo say that Porcupines are very seldom seen north of the divide. One was said to have been killed on the Hula-hula River long ago, and another at Icy Reef, Alaska. They are seen more often on Firth River (near Herschel Island), but are not known by Eskimo east of the Mackenzie.

Lepus americanus macfarlani Merriam. Macfarlane Varying Hare. O-kal′lik (Alaskan and Mackenzie Eskimo).

During certain years the Varying Hares or Rabbits are very numerous, while during other years they are almost lacking. During the winter of 1908–1909 only a very few scattering tracks were seen on either the north or south sides of the Endicott Mountains. In 1909–1910, rabbits were very abundant in the willows of the northern

Mackenzie delta, and numbers were seen on the low delta islands in June, 1910. Rabbits are said to have been very abundant near the last trees on the lower Horton River several years ago, but during three years, 1909–1912, which members of our party spent on this river, only two or three specimens all together were seen. Not observed east of Franklin Bay.

Lepus arcticus canus Preble. Keewatin Arctic Hare. O-kal'lĭ-
    shūg'yuk (Mackenzie Eskimo). O-kal'lik (Coronation Gulf).

None observed west of Langton Bay, where an occasional specimen was shot on the barren hilltops. Hares were more common at Cape Parry, where they seem to hide out on the rough sea ice in the daytime, and only go up on the land in the night-time to feed. We regularly saw numerous signs of Hares on the rocky, lichen-covered hilltops, but almost never saw any Hares. Tracks were fairly common on the barren uplands on both sides of Horton River. Winter pelage white except for black-tipped ears. A specimen shot near Coronation Gulf, May 31st, 1911, had considerable gray on head and shoulders. One killed June 8th had bluish gray patches on head and neck, where the white hair had been shed, and another on June 17th had white only on back, ears, tail, and legs.

Order CARNIVORA — Carnivores

Lynx canadensis mollipilosus Stone.   Northern Canada Lynx.
    Nĭ-tŭ'yak (Alaskan Eskimo). Pĭ-tak'sĭ-kok (Mackenzie
    Eskimo).

The winter before I visited the Mackenzie delta Lynx were very abundant down to the coast, and the Mackenzie River Eskimo traded about two thousand of them. The next winter, 1908–1909, very few Lynx were seen in the Mackenzie delta, and in the Endicott Mountains, northern Alaska, we saw only a very few tracks. During the winter of 1909–1910 we were around Langton Bay and Cape Parry, out of the Lynx country, but the Mackenzie River Eskimo got only two or three skins that winter. None were seen around the east end of Great Bear Lake during the winter of 1910–1911, and we saw none in the timber on Horton River, where we spent most of the winter of 1911–1912.

Canis occidentalis Richardson.   Gray Wolf.   A-ma-rok (Alaskan and Mackenzie Eskimo).

The wolves of the Barren Grounds have been described as a separate form, the Barren Ground Wolf (*Canis occidentalis albus* Sabine), on account of the supposedly lighter color of Wolves from that region.   My experience has been that Wolves of every shade of color from black to almost white are found together on the Arctic coast from Alaska to Coronation Gulf.   Wolves of anything near a pure white color are very rare.

The typical Arctic wolf is light tawny yellowish in color, with a few black hairs intermingled along the median line of the back.   The common Eskimo belief is that the white wolves are old wolves, but we have observed a dark old female wolf with white cubs.   A specimen taken on the Hula-hula River, Alaska, was nearly pure black — head and face jet-black, tail somewhat fulvous, belly grayish.   Other "black" wolves were seen at Langton Bay, Horton River, Great Bear Lake, and Coronation Gulf.   An unusual specimen, a decrepit old male, was shot near Dease River — a sort of silvery gray, with white and black hairs mingled, like a "good" Cross Fox or "poor" Silver Fox.   The "good wolf" of the particular shade prized by the western Eskimo for trimming clothing must be well-furred, with the hair long, the median portion of each hair whitish, and each hair black-tipped.   When cut into strips, it should show: first, a dense layer of "fur" next to the skin, then a band of whitish, and a peripheral band of black or dusky.   Such a skin is prized more highly than any other, even more than the most fashionable shade of pale-yellow Wolverine fur.   Wolves are found in greatest numbers where the Caribou are most abundant, and follow the herds continuously. A compact herd is seldom attacked outright, but stragglers are cut off and run down.   The Caribou are swifter for a time, but the Wolf is tireless and seldom loses a Caribou which he has started.   Large packs of Wolves are seldom seen in the regions we visited, four or five being about the limit.   About fifty miles east of Coppermine I saw a female wolf which had been killed by Eskimo at her den with four cubs, June 3d, 1911.   The cubs' eyes were still unopened. The old wolf was yellowish colored, the cubs umber brown.   One cub was a runt, not much bigger than a Spermophile (*C. parryi*), the other three were much larger.

Vulpes alascensis Merriam. Alaska Red Fox. Red Fox — Kai-yōk'tok (Alaskan Eskimo), Auk-pī-lak'tok (Mackenzie Eskimo). Cross Fox — Krĭ-a-nr̂ok (Alaskan Eskimo), Kī-a-ser-ō-til-lik (Mackenzie Eskimo). Silver or Black Fox — Ker-a-nek'tok (Alaskan Eskimo), Mag'rok (Mackenzie Eskimo).

The Red Fox in its varying phases is only rarely found north of the northern limit of trees. A good many Cross Foxes, a few Silver-grays, and occasionally a Black Fox are taken in the Mackenzie delta. Occasionally a Silver Fox comes out on the coast; a good specimen was caught near Cape Bathurst in 1911. Every possible shade of intergradation in color is found from the bright rufous Red Fox, through various shades of dusky cross markings on back, shoulders, and hips; specimens with only traces of fulvous on shoulders; backs with silvery and black intermingled, and very rarely the jet-black. All phases have a prominent white tip to the tail. Very few "colored" foxes are found around the eastern end of Great Bear Lake, and practically none around Coronation Gulf.

Alopex lagopus innuitus Merriam. Continental Arctic Fox. Tĭ-ra-ga'nĭ-ok (Eskimo from Bering Sea to Coronation Gulf).

Common almost everywhere along the Arctic coast, but seldom goes far inland in any numbers. The White Foxes are found to a large extent on the salt-water ice in winter, and Polar Bear tracks are very commonly followed by Foxes, which pick up a living from offal of Seals killed by the Bears. A stranded whale's carcass will usually attract large numbers of foxes. An Eskimo man and boy in our employ caught about one hundred and forty during the winter of 1910–1911 around Langton Bay, and another Eskimo at Cape Bathurst caught one hundred and ninety six White Foxes the same winter. The next winter the latter caught only two, nobody caught more than twenty, and few over six. The White Fox is the staple fur of the Arctic coast, and the common medium of exchange everywhere west of Cape Parry. In summer the White Foxes are bluish gray, maltese color on back, head dusky mixed with silvery white, belly dirty yellowish white. Skins rarely become "prime," *i.e.*, pure white with long fur, before December 1st, and the hair usually begins to get loose by the last of March. The Eskimo frequently eat White Foxes, and consider the meat very good, particularly when it is fat. The White Foxes are fairly common at the edge of the Barren Grounds near east end of Great Bear Lake, and an Eskimo of our party caught about thirty during the winter of 1910–1911. An Alaskan Eskimo trapping near the mouth of the Coppermine River the same winter caught nearly one hundred. The Hudson Bay Company's agent informed me that one White Fox skin was taken during the winter of 1907–1908, at Smith's Landing, and one at Fort Chipewyan. Several skins are usually taken at Fond du Lac (east end of Lake Athabaska) every winter.

The Arctic Fox is much less suspicious than the Red, Cross, or Silver Foxes, and will enter almost any kind of trap. The common method of trapping is to cut a shallow hole in the snow, just deep enough for the open steel trap to lie below the level of surrounding snow. Then a slab of lightly packed snow, just hard enough to lift without cracking, is cut just large enough to cover the trap. This slab is laid carefully over the trap, and then shaved and smoothed with great care. The snow slab should be just thick enough to support its own weight and brittle enough to be easily broken when an animal steps on it. A few chips of blubber, fish, or meat are shaved off, and scattered loosely and carelessly over and around the vicinity of the trap — just enough to give a scent and cause the fox to hunt around until the trap is sprung. If a fox is caught by both feet, he is usually frozen to death by morning, or even if caught by one foot, if the night is cold. Foxes sometimes gnaw off a trapped foot, but only below the place where caught, and then probably after the foot is frozen and insensible to pain. Sometimes a little box-like snow-house is built over a trap, usually of four blocks of snow, three sides and roof, leaving one side open to the leeward. The bait is placed at the further end of the house so that the fox must step directly over the trap to get it. The White Foxes are said to have seven, eight, nine, or ten young at a birth. I examined one female which had ten embryos April 20th, 1910. The young become very tame if taken at an early age, and are extremely active and playful.

Blue Fox — Kai-a-nĭ-rak'tok (Colville River Eskimo). Ig-ra'lik (Mackenzie Eskimo).

The blue phase of coloration of the White Fox, known as "Blue

1. Leaving our Winter Sheep-Hunting Camp, Hula-Hula River, Alaska, March, 1909. 2. Male Barren Ground Bear, Horton River, N.W.T. 3. Head of Northern Mountain Sheep (Ram), Hula-Hula River, Endicott Mountains, Alaska, 1909. 4. Polar Bears Swimming at Sea near Cape Parry, August, 1911.

Fox," is pretty rare east of western Alaska. During the winter of 1910 four Blue Foxes were taken in midwinter near Cape Parry. Two of the skins were maltese gray with ends of hairs washed with brownish; the other, considered the "best" skin, was dark brown, almost black, with scanty traces of bluish color. A specimen taken by one of our Eskimo off Cape Parry in February had back light slaty gray, fading posteriorly; tail nearly white above, darker below; head dark slaty blue; under parts darker, washed with dull brownish. One taken near Toker Point, April 25th, was a very pale specimen, head and shoulders light brownish, sides slightly bluish, and tail nearly white; in general, much like a midsummer White Fox.

Ursus americanus Pallas. Black Bear.

The Black Bear is very common along the Athabaska River, and we saw eight Bears in less than four hours of drifting on the river below the Grand Rapids, May 14th, 1908. This part of the Athabaska has the reputation of being the best place for Black Bears in North America. They are seen most abundantly just after the ice goes out in the spring and they come down to the edge of the river to look for dead fish which have been pushed up by the ice. In the fall the tangled brushy slopes along the Athabaska are said to be much frequented by Black Bears which feed largely on blueberries at that season. It is, however, more difficult to see the Bears in autumn on account of the thickness of the underbrush. Black Bears are said by the Indians to be fairly common around Great Bear Lake and occasionally north to the Mackenzie delta.

Ursus richardsoni Swainson. Barren Ground Bear. Ak'lak (Eskimo name for Brown Bear from Bering Sea to Coronation Gulf).

Brown Bears, or Grizzlies, are found sparingly throughout the Arctic mainland from western Alaska to Coronation Gulf. There are undoubtedly two or three races or species in this region, but, owing to lack of specimens from important localities and lack of time for critical examination of the material at hand, I am obliged to nominally refer to the Arctic Brown Bears under the above heading. In northern Alaska they do not appear to be very common on the north side of the Endicott Mountains, and seldom, if ever, come out on the coastal plains. The inland Eskimo occasionally kill specimens and often use the skin for a tent door. I saw the skins of two which were killed on the Hula-hula River, in October, 1908, by a Colville River Eskimo named Auktel'lik. Auktel'lik told me he had killed forty-four Aklak in his time, and that only two of the lot came towards him and tried to attack him. From what I could learn he had not hunted very far west of the Colville or at all east of the Mackenzie. Most Eskimo, however, speak with much greater respect of the pugnacity of *Aklak* than of *Nannuk* (the Polar Bear) and are much more cautious about attacking him. On July 3d, 1912, Mr. Frederick Lambart, Engineer on the Alaska-Yukon Boundary Survey, shot a Brown Bear on the Arctic slope of the mountains on the 141st meridian, about forty-five miles from the Arctic Ocean at Demarcation Point. From three photos of the dead Bear, it appeared to be of the long-nosed type, with a pronounced hump on the shoulders. Mr. Lambart informs me that this bear has been examined by Dr. C. Hart Merriam and declared to be a new species hitherto undescribed. In the Mackenzie delta tracks of Brown Bears are occasionally seen, but the bears are seldom killed, owing to the impracticability of hunting them through the dense underbrush on the islands in summer.

I have been warned many times by natives against shooting at a Barren Ground Bear unless from above — as a wounded bear has greater difficulty in charging uphill. So far as our experience goes, however, the Barren Ground Bear is an inoffensive and wary brute, preferring to put as much ground as possible between himself and human society. I saw but one unwounded bear come towards me, but as he did not have my scent his advance was perhaps more from mere curiosity than from hostility. As the bear was on the uninhabited coast between Cape Lyon and Dolphin and Union Straits, and he had probably never seen human beings before, this inference seems plausible. Wounded bears are another story, of course, and it is generally admitted that the Barren Ground Bears are tougher or more tenacious of life than the Polar Bears.

We found the center of greatest abundance of the Barren Ground Bears in the country around Langton Bay and on Horton River, not more than thirty or forty miles south from Langton Bay. One was killed at Cape Lyon, and another on Dease River east of Great Bear Lake. In this region our party killed about twenty specimens, most of which were obtained on our dog-packing expeditions in early fall.

The Bears here showed two very distinct types, which for convenience we designate as the long-snouted and short-snouted types. The skulls are readily separated on this basis. It is rather hard to distinguish them by color, as late summer skins are usually much bleached out. In general the long-snouted Bears were inclined to a reddish brown cast of color (sometimes almost bay color), while the others were often very dark — dusky brown, with tips of hairs on dorsal surface light grayish brown on fulvous, sometimes with tips a faint golden yellowish tint. The Barren Ground Bears go into hibernation about the first week of October and come out early in April while the weather is still very cold.

While ascending the Horton River we saw at intervals the nearly fresh tracks of three Barren Ground Bears on December 29th, 1910, and January 1st, 1911, going along the river and over the shortest portages, at least forty miles in approximately a straight line. Neither the Eskimo or the Slavey Indian who were with us had ever before seen evidences of Brown Bears out of their holes in midwinter. They seem to be nearly as fat on their first emergence from their long sleep as in the fall, but speedily lose weight, and early summer specimens are invariably poor. This is natural from the nature of their food, which is to a large extent vegetable. Although the Bear's native heath is often conspicuously furrowed in many places by the unearthed burrows of Arctic spermophiles (*Citellus parryi* or *C. p. kennicotti*) I believe that the Bear's search is more for the little mammal's store of roots than for the little animal itself. The Bear's stomach is much more apt to contain *masu* roots (*Polygonum* sp.) than flesh. A bear must needs be very active to catch enough spermophiles above ground in spring and early summer, and if carcasses are not to be found, the Bears evidently suffer most from hunger at this season, when they can neither dig roots for themselves in the frozen ground nor dig out the spermophiles and their caches. One specimen was killed by an Eskimo of our party on Dease River, east of Great Bear Lake, after the Bear had gorged himself on a cache of Caribou meat, having more than fifty pounds of fresh meat in his stomach. A few Bears were met with in the Coppermine country, but throughout the Coronation Gulf region they are apparently rare. The Eskimo say that the Aklak is not found on Victoria Island.

The fact that the Barren Ground Bears seem to always have at least two cubs at a birth, that old bears are often seen followed by two young cubs and one yearling cub, and that we never saw more than one yearling cub accompanying its mother, is evidence that there must be considerable mortality among the cubs in the first year, probably during the second spring. The new-born cubs, of course, are nursing in the spring, while the older cubs presumably have to depend upon their own foraging. Otherwise these Bears have practically no enemies besides man. As there is little market for their skins, neither Eskimo nor Indians make any special effort to hunt them, the specimens obtained being in general upon summer Caribou hunts.

Thalarctos maritimus (Phipps). Polar Bear. Nan'nuk (all Eskimo dialects).

The Polar Bear or White Bear is a circumpolar cosmopolitan, although seldom found very far from the sea ice. In winter these bears are apt to appear anywhere along the coast, but in summer their occurrence depends largely upon the proximity of pack ice. Along the Arctic coast of Alaska, east of Point Barrow, the species is not very abundant, and the same may be said of the coast east and west of the Mackenzie delta. Numbers are annually killed near Cape Bathurst. The Polar Bears seem to be most abundant around Cape Parry and the southern end of Banks Island, very rarely passing through Dolphin and Union Straits, into Coronation Gulf. Around Cape Parry, in August, 1911, we saw fourteen Bears within two days roaming about the small rocky islands, evidently marooned when the ice left the beach. They are often seen swimming far out at sea. While whaling about twenty miles off Cape Bathurst (the nearest land) and about five miles from the nearest ice mass, we saw a Polar Bear which paddled along quite unconcernedly until he winded the ship, then veered away, heading out toward the ice pack. Shortly before Christmas an officer from the schooner *Rosie H.*, with a party of Eskimo, killed a female and two newly born cubs in a hole in the snow near the mouth of Shaviovik River, west of Flaxman Island. It was said to be unusual for a Polar Bear to have cubs so early in the winter.

Mephitis hudsonica (Richardson). Northern Plains Skunk.

In 1908 I saw one skin traded from Indians at Point Brule below Fort McKay on the Athabaska River, but did not notice skunk skins farther down the river.

Lutra canadensis (Schreber). Canadian Otter.

A few skins are taken annually around Fort McPherson. Mr. Joseph Hodgson informed me that the Otter is fairly common at the west end of Great Bear Lake and is occasionally taken at the east end of the lake. Johnny Sanderson told me that he had seen Otter "slides" near the east end of Great Bear Lake in the winter of 1910.

Taxidea taxus (Schreber). Badger.

Mr. Prudden, the Hudson Bay Company's trader at Calling River on the Athabaska River, Alberta, had skins of two Badgers. He told me that he killed one Badger himself near the river. The natives say that the Badger is very seldom seen north of there.

Mustela vision ingens (Osgood)   Tĭ-rĭ-ak′puk, "big weasel" (Alaska
   and Mackenzie Eskimo).

A few Mink tracks were seen on the Hula-hula River near the entrance to the north side of Endicott Mountains. Large numbers are taken by the Eskimo who winter in the Mackenzie River delta pretty well inside the northern limit of trees. We took no specimens anywhere.

Mustela arcticus (Merriam). Tundra Weasel. Ermine. Tĭ′rĭ-ak
   (Alaskan and Mackenzie Eskimo).

Generally distributed along the Arctic coast from Alaska to Coronation Gulf, but not very common anywhere. More common inland, particularly in the Mackenzie delta. A large number of the Eskimo of the Coronation Gulf region habitually wear an ermine skin suspended from the back of the coat, as a charm against sickness or for luck in hunting.

Martes americana actuosa (Osgood). Alaska Marten. Ka-vĭ-ā′tjak
   (Alaskan and Mackenzie Eskimo).

A few skins are taken by the Eskimo in the Mackenzie delta every winter. The Marten is very variable in numbers from year to year at the various northern posts, its abundance depending largely upon the relative abundance of Mice, Rabbits, etc., upon which it feeds. The winter of 1910–1911 was said to be a poor year at Great Bear Lake. The best catch was made by a white trapper who caught thirty. Very few Marten are ever caught at the east end of Great Bear Lake. Mr. Timothy Gaudetts, Hudson Bay Company's trader at Fort Wrigley, told me that at old Fort Wrigley in 1896–1897 he traded four hundred Marten skins from forty-six Indians. In 1908 only about twenty Indians were trading at the post.

Gulo luscus (Linn.). Hudson Bay Wolverine. Kap'rik (Alaska
    Eskimo). Kap'vik (Mackenzie Eskimo). Kal'vik (Corona-
    tion Gulf).

The Wolverine is rather rare in northern Alaska, but is occasionally seen in the mountains. In northern Canada the Wolverine is found everywhere up to the northern limit of trees and in many localities goes far outside of the trees. Wolverines frequently come out on the coast of Franklin Bay, and they are fairly common on the south side of Coronation Gulf. Mr. Stefánsson brought back part of a Wolverine skin from Victoria Island, which the owner said was taken near the east end of Prince Albert Sound. The western Eskimo, from Cape Bathurst to Bering Sea, consider Wolverine fur to be an essential part of the trimming on their garments, particularly a fringe of Wolverine fur around the rim of the hoods of both men and women. The skins, which are of the fashionable shade with a large area of light yellowish or straw-colored hair, long hair with thick under fur, are very highly prized and command a price in the local Eskimo trade many times its fur value in civilized markets. The dark-colored Wolverine skins are not very highly valued by the Eskimo. The Coronation Gulf and Victoria Island Eskimo do not use Wolverine skin to trim their clothes, and the skins are usually made into bags. The Wolverine is universally execrated throughout the North as an inveterate and tireless cache-robber. Hardly any kind of cache can be made strong enough to keep out a Wolverine if he has plenty of time to work undisturbed; for the animal is strong enough to roll away heavy stones and logs, gnaw through timbers, climb to elevated caches, and excavate buried goods. The pestiferous brute also has a penchant for lugging away and hiding articles which he has no apparent use for. Members of our party lost a shot-gun which was hung on a tree and a spy-glass and other things from a cached sled-load, all carried away by Wolverines. At Langton Bay a Wolverine ate a round hole through two plank doors to get into meat which we had stored in the old ice house. On attaining entrance to a food cache the animal will often remain until all the food is consumed. The most nearly Wolverine-proof cache I have seen was constructed by an Indian near Great Bear Lake. It was constructed by finding four trees in suitable position to form upright posts at the corners of the cache and cutting them off ten or twelve feet from the ground. The posts were notched on the inner sides to support horizontal beams, and logs laid across to form a floor, projecting two or three feet beyond each end. The logs forming the sides of the box were notched to receive end pieces of short logs. When filled up, the cache was roofed with a layer of heavy green logs three or four deep, too heavy for a Wolverine to move and too deep to gnaw through if he succeeded in getting on top. The uprights are stripped of bark and made as smooth as possible. If a Wolverine succeeds in climbing the upright posts, the projecting ends of the floor timbers prevent him from getting around to the top of the cache. Having no foothold, he cannot work at the bottom or sides of the cache, and consequently one thickness of timber suffices for these.

The Indians and Eskimo and most white men residing in the North generally come to look upon a certain amount of the depredations by Wolverines as unpreventable, fated, and like the annoyance of mosquitoes are taken as a matter of course The ordinary method of capture is by heavy steel traps, but log or stone dead-falls are commonly used.

Order PINNIPEDIA — Sea Lions, Seals, etc.

Callorhinus alascanus Jordan and Clark. Alaska Fur Seal.

There are various reports current of Fur Seals having been occasionally seen or captured to the east of Point Barrow years ago, but I was not able to verify any actual places or dates. The occurrence of the species in the Arctic Ocean is certainly only casual.

Odobenus obesus (Illiger). Pacific Walrus. Ai'vuk (Alaskan and Mackenzie Eskimo).

The walrus is fairly common to the westward of Point Barrow, but only casually comes east to that point. A walrus was killed several miles inland at Point Barrow during the winter of 1908–1909.

It had probably entered a lagoon and been stranded.   One was killed at Herschel Island in 1911, and Mr. E. de K. Leffingwell informs me that he found a walrus carcass on Cross Island, a little east of the Colville River, in 1910, and saw two live Walrus on a sandspit off mouth of Shaviovik River, west of Flaxman Island, Alaska, in 1911. Mr. Roderick MacFarlane records Walrus east of the Mackenzie, but recent records from east of the Mackenzie are rare and doubtful.

Phoca hispida Schreber. Rough Seal. Na'tjirk (Alaskan, Mackenzie, and Coronation Gulf Eskimo).

Fairly common everywhere along the coast from Bering Sea to Coronation Gulf. The western Eskimo occasionally catch seals in nets set under the ice, but by far the most common method is to shoot them with rifles from the beach or from boats in summer, or along the edge of the ice floe or tide cracks in winter. The Coronation Gulf and Victoria Island Eskimo live almost exclusively on seals in the winter. They find the seal's breathing-hole by the aid of dogs, and wait at the hole for the seal to come up to breathe, when they kill it with a spear. In all districts the Eskimo depend largely upon the blubber of the seal for their fatty food, even the inland Alaskans being obliged to trade for a few "pokes" of blubber oil annually. The summer water boots of the Eskimo are practically always made of sealskin, usually with soles of the large bearded seal's skin or the skin of the white whale. The seal oil is usually kept in pokes — bags made of the skin of the seal removed intact and turned so as to be impervious to oil. Seals killed in summer usually sink quickly, but after the last of September a majority of the seals shot float until they can be recovered. An average seal of this species weighs from 125 to 175 pounds. A very large male shot at Cape Parry, December 12th, 1910, measured 65 inches in length and greatest girth 54 inches, weight about 200 pounds.

Erignathus barbatus (Erxleben). Bearded Seal. Ūg'ᵣuk (Alaskan Eskimo). Ūg'yūk (Mackenzie Eskimo).

The bearded seal is considered to be quite rare along the north coast of Alaska, east of Point Barrow, although fairly common to the south and west of Point Barrow. We have observed the species rarely at Herschel Island, Baillie Islands, and Franklin Bay, but it is nowhere common west of Darnley Bay. Around Cape Lyon bearded seals were numerous, but the region of greatest abundance seemed to be in Dolphin and Union Straits. We saw numbers here in summer, and natives from this section say that they sometimes see ten at a single hole on the ice, basking in the sun in the warm spring days. Farther east in Coronation Gulf the Bearded Seals are less common. The Eskimo east as far as Cape Bathurst consider the skin of the Bearded Seal as almost indispensable for boot-soles and umiak-covers and for cutting into heavy rawhide rope. The skins of six or seven Ugyūk will cover an umiak (skin canoe) thirty feet or more in length. The animal may weigh from five to eight hundred pounds.

Order INSECTIVORA — Insectivores

Sorex personatus I. Geoffroy St. Hilaire. Common Eastern Shrew.

Shrews, probably of this species, are reported commonly at many posts along the Mackenzie. Mr. Henry Frazer, a trader at Fort Norman, said that Shrews were very abundant in his storehouse and did considerable damage, gnawing into any animal substances, such as bacon, skins, furs, etc. Although I kept a number of traps set I could not catch any specimens along the river, although later I took specimens in the Mackenzie delta which appear to be *personatus*.

Sorex tundrensis Merriam. Tundra Shrew. Ug-rū'nak (Alaskan Eskimo). Ug'yū-nak (Mackenzie Eskimo).

This species is apparently generally distributed all along the Arctic coast, but is not common anywhere. Specimens were taken in the Endicott Mountains, Alaska, Mackenzie delta, Cape Bathurst, and Horton River, south of Langton Bay.

Order CHIROPTERA — The Bats

Myotis lucifugus (Le Conte). Little Brown Bat.

Among a few small mammal skins, collected at Hay River at west end of Great Slave Lake in spring of 1908, Mr. Harry W. Jones had one Little Brown Bat. We saw no Bats at any place on the Mackenzie River during the summer of 1908, or elsewhere in the North.

PRINCE OF WALES
ISLAND

FRANKLIN STRAIT

BOOTHIA

71°

Strait of James Ross

70°

C. Felix

MATTY I.

KING WILLIAM
ISLAND

69°

Terror Bay

Washington
Bay

Swatka Bay

UGYULIGMIUT

Douglas
Bay

NETJILIGMIUT

ADELAIDE
PENINSULA

68°

67°

Lake
Franklin

Lake
Macdougal

Haningayok R.

66°

Williams Engraving Co., New York

Mean Scale—1 : 4,500,000

INDEX

A

Adventures and incompetence, theory of, 43, 164–165, 343.

Agricultural products at Fort Providence and to the north, 26.

Akowak, Point Barrow Eskimo, 94.

Akpek, Alaskan helper, 70–71, 73, 81, 82, 83, 98, 99, 101.

Alaska, character of coastal plain of northern, 65–66.

Alexander, wrecked whaling vessel, 120.

Alingnak, Baillie Islands Eskimo, 362–363.

Alphabet, experience with Eskimo and the, 427–429.

Alualuk, ex-shaman, 371, 372–373, 424.

Alunak, Victoria Island Eskimo, 286.

Amundsen, Captain, meeting with, at Herschel Island, 3; relics of, at King Point, 37; tribute by, to Hubert Darrell, 344.

Anderson, John, trapper, 369.

Anderson, Matthew, 369, 370, 371, 372.

Anderson, Rudolph M., joins author in expedition to the Eskimo, 5–6; arrival of, at Fort Macpherson, 33; investigations carried on by, in Alaska, 69; experiences of, in Arctic Alaska, 70; rejoins author at Flaxman Island, 101; mentioned, 113, 114, 258, 259, 305, 306, 312, 320, 336, 339; suffers attack of pneumonia at Cape Parry, 144–146; makes trip back to Herschel Island, 153 ff.; junction with author, at Langton Bay, 233; makes Bear Lake trip, 233–236; work of, about Coronation Gulf, 259; at Coal Creek camp, 339, 354, 359; left by author at Langton Bay, 368; report by, on natural history collections of the expedition, 436–527.

Anderson, Thomas, Hudson's Bay Company official, 33–34.

Archæological excavations, difficulties attending, 313–314; at Langton Bay, 328–329, 330–332; at Cape Smythe, 387–388.

Arctic R—d River, Fort, 29.

Arey, Gallagher, 117.

Arey, Ned, 68, 100, 117, 380–381.

Arkilinik River, 250, 251; Eskimo of the, 285.

Athabasca Lake, arrival at, 16.

Athabasca Landing, 7.

Athabasca River, voyage down the, 7 ff.; running rapids on the, 8–10; Grand Rapids of the, 12, 14–15; size of, 16.

Atkinson Point, visit to, 370–372.

B

Back, Cape, 301, 302.

Baillie Islands Eskimo, 362–363, 364–367.

Balæna, whaling vessel, 497.

Ballinger, Captain J. G., of revenue cutter *Bear*, 389.

Banks Island, 3, 4; possibility of existence of Eskimo on, 4; trip to, abandoned on account of uninhabited state in summer, 281; death of people once resident in, 288, 289–290; musk-oxen on, 507.

Barren Ground, caribou hunting in the, 135; crossing of, on round trip to Franklin Bay from Dease River, 228 ff., 234–236; caribou of the, 502–506; wolves of the, 516; bears of the, 519–522.

Basil Hall Bay, visit to, 205.

Bathing, customs as to, among Christianized Eskimo, 375–377, 415.

Bathurst, Cape, visit to, 369.

Bats, absence of, in the north, 527.

Beachy Point, 64.

Bear, revenue cutter, voyage to Nome on, 389.

Bearded seals, 267–269, 526–527.

Bear Lake. *See* Great Bear Lake.

Bear Rock, in Mackenzie Valley, 28.

Bears, signs of, near Athabasca Lake, 16; in Eskimo folklore, 57–58; hunting of, along Colville River, 74; adventures with polar, 126, 165–167, 311; Barren Ground grizzly, 127, 335; grizzly, at Langton Bay, 127, 129, 333, 334–335; Dr. Anderson's notes on, 519–522.

Beaver, the Canadian, 514.

Bell Island, Rae's, 304–305, 306, 307, 312.

Beluga, whaling ship, 47, 497.

Belvedere, whaling ship, 47, 119 n., 312, 341.

Bent, A. C., 456, 485.

2 M   529

Bernard, Captain Joseph, 258, 259, 260, 305, 312, 361, 369.
Bexley, Cape, deserted village at, 168, 279.
Beyts, Inspector, 378.
Birds, Arctic, 385; Dr. Anderson's notes on, 456–494.
Bishop, Louis P., 456, 457, 485.
Blind man, story of, at Simpson Bay, 271–273; at Clouston Bay, 295.
Blizzard, course to follow when caught in a, 155–156; hunting caribou in a, 163.
Blond Eskimo, discovery of, 173; first meeting with the, 190–192; description of, 192–194; form of heads of, 194–195; early references to existence of, by Arctic explorers, 199–200; possibility of descent of, from Scandinavian colonists of Greenland, 200–201; futility of various explanations of, 201–202.
Blood feuds among Eskimo, 365–366.
Bloody Fall, Coppermine River, 208–209; passage of, on ice ledge, 209; return passage of, 243.
Blue fox, the, 518–519.
Boas, Franz, facial indices for Eskimo by, 194–195; cited, 284.
Bodfish, Captain, 497.
Boulders of ice, formation of, 383.
Bowhead, whaling ship, 47, 48.
Bowhead whale, taking of a, 119.
Bowhead whales, 496–500.
Brabant, Hudson's Bay Company official, 34.
Bray, Herbert, 12–13.
Bremner, fellow-voyager on Athabasca River, 12.
Briggs, William, 501.
Brock, R. W., 441.
Brower, Charles D., 45, 46, 387; proficiency of, in Eskimo tongue, 85.
Brown, Jessie, 33.
Buffalo, west of Smith Landing, 19–20; destruction of caribou compared with that of, 49; number of, and range, 506.
Bumblebees, notes on, 448–449.
Bumpus, Dr. Herman C., 4.
Bumpus, Mount, Victoria Island, 276.
Burning cliffs, east of Cape Bathurst, 439.
Burt, Charles H., 377.

C

Cameron, Agnes Deans, at Fort Macpherson, 33.
Canadian Northern Railway, extension to Edmonton, 6.
Cape Bexley Eskimo. *See* Dolphin and Union Straits Eskimo.
Cape Smythe, village of, 45; population of, 66; two months' stay at, 85–94; visit to, on return trip, 386–389.
Cape Smythe Whaling and Trading Company, 45, 85.
Cardinal, Louis, 377.
Caribou, about Bear Lake, 29, 219, 221–222, 236; practical extinction of, in Arctic Alaska, 48–49, 502; band of, at Oliktok, 64–65; skins of, sent to American Museum of Natural History, New York, 65; depopulation of northern Alaska due to disappearance of, 66, 67; hunting in Colville River district, 73, 74, 114; Eskimo prayers for, 81–82; large herd of, east of Kuparuk River, 116; at Langton Bay, 127, 128, 155, 156; in Horton River district, 130, 135, 138, 139, 141–142, 239–240; near Point Pierce, 163–164; stalking the, 164; fearlessness of, as to traveling on ice, 203–204; in Coppermine River district, 211–213; vast herd of, to cross head waters of Dease River, 224–226; differences in appearance of eastern and western, 241–242; migrations of, 263, 276, 502–503; observation of migration from Victoria Island, 277–278; worthlessness of summer-killed skins of, 333–334, 448; description of summer hunt of, 337–338; wind-drying and smoke-drying the meat of, 338; uncertainty of migrations of, 348; contents of stomachs of, as food, 446; parasitic insects on, 448; Dr. Anderson's notes on the Barren Ground caribou, 502 ff.
Caribou skins, prices of, 62.
Cascade Rapid, Athabasca River, 10, 15.
Challenge, whaling schooner, 48, 84, 94, 103, 118.
Chandlar River, 438.
Chewing gum, demand for, among Cape Smythe Eskimo, 387.
Children, exposure of, among the Nagyuktogmiut, 160; beliefs of Eskimo concerning guardian spirits of, 395–403.
Chinook speech, 355.
Chipewyan, Fort, 16.
Chipewyan Indians, with Hearne at Bloody Fall, 208–209.
Chipman, C. C., 7.
Christianity, spread of, among Eskimo, 37–39; among Colville River Indians, 81–83; strange developments of, among the Eskimo, 89 ff., 415 ff.
Christie, Hudson's Bay Company official, 7, 12.
Church of England missionaries in the Mackenzie Valley, 24–25.
Clarke, James, 387.
Clerk Island, 302–303, 307, 311–312.

Clothing, for Arctic climate, 77; eating of one's, in Arctic regions, 133; misguided views of Christianized Eskimo in regard to, 433–434.

Clouds, use of, as a sky map, 298 n.

Coal Creek, camping on, 339 ff., 345–362.

Coal gas, experience with, in snow house, 245–247.

Coal outcrops, 440–441.

Collinson, 4; the "Cape Kendall" of, 304–305.

Collinson Point, 378–379.

Colored glasses, 239.

Colville Mountains, Victoria Island, 275–276.

Colville River, Eskimo living on the, 80 ff.; rise and fall of tide in the, 115; size of, 437.

Comer, Captain George, on Hudson Bay tribes and the "Blond Eskimo," 202.

Confidence, Fort, 224.

Conversion of Eskimo, effect of, 408 ff.

Cooper's Island, 51.

Copper, knife of, among Dolphin and Union Straits Eskimo, 177; use of, in hunting implements, 248; traces of, found from Cape Lyon eastward, 441, 442–443; in Victoria Island, 443.

Copper Eskimo, summer spent with, 203–222; on Prince Albert Sound, 279–285, 286 ff.

Coppermine River, arrival at, 208; journey along the, 211 ff.; heat during summer in district of, 213; size of, 240–241; return trip down, 240–243.

Coronation Gulf, 3, 121; moose seen at, 28; journey to, from Cape Bexley, 205 ff.; characteristics of islands in, 242–243, 443.

Cottle, Captain S. F., 48, 118, 119, 122; cited concerning Clerk Island, 312; visit to, at Herschel Island, 378.

Cram, Mr. and Mrs., 387.

Cranes, observations of, 470–471.

Crocker River, 307, 308, 309, 311, 312, 313.

D

Dalhousie, Cape, 369.

Dance, ceremonials attending an Eskimo, 87–89; among the Dolphin and Union Straits Eskimo, 185–187.

Darnley Bay, crossing of, 321.

Darrell, Hubert, loss of, and notice of achievements of, 341–345.

Davis, John, explorations of, 198.

Dease and Simpson, reference to "Blond Eskimo" by, 200; visit of, to Rae River Eskimo, 207.

Dease River, cosmopolitan Eskimo community at headwaters of, 215–216; trip to mouth of, 223; migration of caribou across, 224–226.

Dease Thompson, Point, 165, 316.

Deer, black-tailed, 501.

Demarcation Point, 31.

De Salis Bay, 281.

Dialects of Eskimo tribes, 251. See Language.

Direction, inferiority of Eskimo in sense of, 146–150.

Diseases among Indians of Mackenzie district, 22–24, 26.

Dismal Lake, 207, 209; arrival at, 214; experience in fording, 215; second visit to, 237; description of, 238.

Dogs, cruelty in treatment of, in the north, 11–12; food prejudices of, 111–112, 386.

Dolphin and Union Straits, 3; crossing of, to Victoria Island, 188 ff., 261–262; return trip across, 302–310.

Dolphin and Union Straits Eskimo, discovery of, 170–173; language of, 171, 174–175; first day among, 175 ff.; dances and songs of, 186–187; further consideration of, 188–202.

Driftwood along Coronation Gulf, 243–244; found on westward-facing beaches, 316; distribution of, on Dolphin and Union Straits and shores of Prince Albert Sound, 316–317.

Drums, the musical instruments of the Eskimo, 186.

Drying caribou meat, methods of, 338.

Duchess of Bedford, Leffingwell-Mikkelsen Expedition schooner, 1.

Ducks, Dr. Anderson's notes on, 461–466.

Dumbness, warding off of, in presence of a spirit, 171.

Dwight, Dr. Jonathan, Jr., 456, 485, 487.

E

Edmonton, arrival at, on way north, 6.

Eider-ducks, 385, 464–465.

Ekalluktogmiut Eskimo, 281, 287 ff.; Hansen's misidentification of, 281–283.

Ekalluktok River, 281.

Elk, range of, 501.

Ellice River, 227.

Elvira, whaling and trading vessel, 388.

Endicott Mountains, 334; crossing of, by Amundsen and by Hubert Darrell, 343–344.

Equipment for expedition, 6.

Eric the Red, discovery of Greenland by, 195–196.

Escape Reef, 377.

Eskimo, first experience in living with, 2; language of, 2; question of there being, on Victoria Island, 3, 4; possibility of existence of, hitherto undiscovered, 4; meeting with, at Fort Macpherson, 31, 32; spread of Christianity among, and effects, 36–39; effect on, of introduction of whaling industry, 39–40; folk-lore of the, 56–58; employed by whaling firms at Point Barrow, 60–61; notes of temperamental qualities of, 62–63, 207–208; disappearance of native, from northern Alaska, 66–67; compared with white men as to ability to stand cold, 75–79; winter houses of, 80; acquiring the language of the, 85–86; traces of early, about Cape Parry, 123; inferiority of, to white men, in sense of locality, 146–148; so-called "instinctive" qualities of, 149; fear of, for the Nagyuktogmiut, 159, 163–164; discovery of Dolphin and Union Straits Eskimo, 170–173; "Blond," 173, 190–194; references to Blond Eskimo by early explorers, 199–200; possibility of descent of Blond Eskimo from Scandinavian colonists of Greenland, 200–201; improbability of various theories regarding derivation of Blond Eskimo, 201–202; cosmopolitan gathering of, on Dease River, 215–216; meeting of Slavey Indians and, at Bear Lake, 217–219; disregard for promises among, 271; discussion of religion of the, 390–407; discussion of effect of conversion on, 408 ff.

Eskimo Lakes, 438.

Eva, Hislop and Nagle's steamer, 17.

Evans, Assistant School Superintendent, 299, 300.

Excavation of ruins, 313–314; at Langton Bay, 328–329, 330–332; at Cape Smythe, 387–388.

F

Ferguson, Sandy, 342.

Fires, in Canadian forests, 10; Eskimo views of, in houses, 346–347.

Firth, John, 31.

Fishes, Dr. Anderson's notes on, 450–455.

Fishing, among Copper Eskimo, 203; methods followed in, 450.

Fitzgerald, Inspector, views of, on living on the country, 41; death of, from starvation, 340–341.

Flaxman Island, 44; Leffingwell's headquarters at, 68, 379–380.

Flies, notes on, 448.

Folk-lore stories, study of, 56–58, 354, 363–

364; writing of, in original Eskimo, 85–86; by the Eskimo Tannaumirk, 238.

Food, shortcomings of lean meat as, 136–137, 140–141; of Dolphin and Union Straits Eskimo, 178–179.

Food supplies of trading posts in Mackenzie district, 27.

Food taboos, 151, 212, 410–411.

Foot-wear of Eskimo, 79.

Forests, waste of Canadian, by fire, 10; natural wealth of, in Mackenzie Valley, 10–11.

Forsythe Bay, 317.

Fort, explanation of term, as applied to trading stations, 29.

Foxes, Arctic, 157, 517–519; practice of, of following polar bears for game, 351–352.

Franklin, Sir John, reference to "Blond Eskimo" by, 199; memories of, among Coronation Gulf Eskimo, 252; needless starving of expedition of, 305.

Franklin Bay, round trip to, from Dease River, 227–236.

Frazer, Henry, 527.

Freezing, precautionary measures against, 75–79.

Frost bites, treatment of, 75–79.

Fry, Rev. Mr., Church of England missionary, 370–372.

Fuel problem about Point Barrow, 86–87.

Fur, trapping for, among Eskimo, 350–351.

Fur industry, 513–527.

G

Game, traces of, near Athabasca Lake, 16; conditions as to, at Fort Norman, 28; scarcity of, on Smith Bay, 55; near Point Dease Thompson, 165; remarks on killing of, as a sport, 335. *See* Bears, Caribou, Mountain sheep, etc.

Gaudetts, Timothy, 524.

Geese, at Cape Halkett, 382–383; Dr. Anderson's notes on, 466–469.

Giroux, Father, missionary at Fort Providence, 26.

Glasses, for Arctic use, 239; importance of wearing, 385.

Gordon, Thomas, home of, in America's farthest north, 45; sloop lent to author by, 49; story of the rescued Eskimo and, 96–98, 418; visit to, on return trip, 386.

Grand Rapids Island, Athabasca River, 8.

Grand Rapids of the Athabasca, 12, 14–15.

Great Bear Lake, game conditions about, 28–29; hunting by Eskimo along, 216;

visit of author to, to meet Melvill and Hornby, 216–220; Joseph Hodgson's winter camp at, 223; hunting by Victoria Islanders at, 273.

Greely, General A. W., researches of, in connection with "Blond Eskimo," 199.

Greenland, discovery of, by Scandinavians and contact between Europeans and Eskimo in, 196–198; possibility of descent of "Blond Eskimo" from Scandinavian colonists of, 200–201.

Grizzly bears, 127, 129, 333, 334–335, 519 ff.

Ground ice, 383–384.

Grouse, 476.

Gruben, John, 373.

Gull rookeries west of Crocker River, 318.

Gulls, Dr. Anderson's notes on, 459–461.

Guninana, folk-lore stories of, 363–364, 368.

H

Hadley, John, 46, 85, 387; adventure of, on an ice floe, 104–105.

Halkett, Cape, 63, 381–382.

Hall, Charles Francis, 250.

Hamilton, Florence, 31.

Hamilton, Maxfield, 20, 514.

Hanbury, David T., 72; usefulness of work by, 249–250; errors of, due to poor interpreters, 250–251, 252; traces of, among Prince Albert Sound Eskimo, 285; Hubert Darrell with, 342.

Haneragmiut, tribe of the, 190.

Hansen, Lieutenant Gotfred, 72; mistake of, regarding Ekalluktogmiut Eskimo, 281–283.

Harbors west of Crocker River, 317–318.

Hare, the Arctic, 211, 514–515.

Harrison Bay, crossing of, 381–382.

Hawkesworth, Mr. and Mrs. Charles, 46, 85, 94, 413–414.

Hawks, notes on, 478.

Hay River, mission at mouth of, 22–25; trading station at, 27.

Hearne, Samuel, expedition of, at Bloody Fall, 208–209.

Herring, taking of, in nets, 452.

Herschel Island, 2; arrival at, 37; visit to, on return trip, 377–378; formation and contour of, 378.

Hills, in Coronation Gulf region, 242–243, 443; in country east of Mackenzie River, 439.

Hislop and Nagle Trading Company, 32, 34.

Hitkoak, Victoria Island Eskimo, 286, 289.

Hodgson, Joseph, 21, 223, 227, 237; on

habitat of moose, 501; on muskrats, 513; on the otter, 523.

Hopson, Fred, 46.

Hornby, John, 20; at Bear Lake, 216, 220, 223, 236.

Horton River, 126; discovery of a branch of, 129; size of, 227; trip down, on journey to Franklin Bay, 230–232; coal veins on, 440–441; minerals along the, 441.

House, stone, on Victoria Island, 274.

Houses, of Eskimo about Point Barrow, 86–87; new and old, of snow, 245; pernicious practice of building frame, by Eskimo, 299–300; nature of modern Eskimo snow houses, 314–315; sodding of, 346.

House ruins, prehistoric, along Dolphin and Union Straits, 314; at Langton Bay, 329, 330–332; at Cape Smythe, 388.

Hudson's Bay Company, 7, 19; present conditions at posts of, compared with past, 26–27; "fish posts" and "meat posts," 27; so-called "forts" of the, 29; able handling of problems of the North by, 30.

Hulahula River, 437, 438, 508.

Hupgok brothers, 266.

I

Ice, break-up of, in Athabasca Lake, 18; break-up of, in Slave Lake, 24; duration of, in Mackenzie River, 28; movement of, in Arctic Ocean north of Alaska, 47; quality of freshness of old salt-water ice, 115–116; action of fresh-water, on melting, 322–323; action of salt-water, 325; formation of ground ice, 383–384; formation of underground, by rivers, 384–385.

Ice crystals, fresh-water, 322–323.

Icy Cape, Eskimo dance at, 87–89.

Iglihsirk, Coronation Gulf Eskimo, 251–252.

Iglorak, sandspit of, 51.

Ilavinirk, Eskimo employee, 35, 52, 60, 64, 70, 98, 101, 106 ff., 117, 131 ff., 150, 151, 326 ff., 353; exposition of religious views of Eskimo by, 419–423, 435.

Indians, improvidence of northern, in clothes and food, 18–19; language, customs, and religion of, along Mackenzie River, 20–21; tuberculosis among, due to misguided missionary teachings, 22–24; questionable effects of education on, 25–26; divergent views concerning in the South and in the North, 30; attitude of Colville River Eskimo

toward, 114; meeting between Eskimo and, at Bear Lake, 217–219.
Insanity, case of, at Baillie Islands, 365.
Insects, notes on, 448–449.
Instinctive qualities, so called, in primitive peoples, 149.
Introductions among Victoria Island Eskimo, 172, 190–191.
Iron pyrites, Horton River district, 441.
Itkillik River, 80, 115.
Ivory, articles of, found in archæological excavations, 330, 332.
Ivory gulls, 459.
Ivy, whaling schooner, 103.
Iyituaryuk, Baillie Islands Eskimo, 364, 367.

J

Jaegers, observation of and notes on, 385, 458–459.
Jardine River, 227.
Jarvis, Major A. M., 31, 32.
Jays, observations of, 481–482.
Jeanette, whaling vessel, 47, 48.
John and Winthrop, whaling vessel, 389.
John the Sailmaker, 158.
Johnson, missionary at Slave Lake, 24.
Jones, H. W., cited on birds, 462, 463, 464, 470, 471, 473, 477–483, 485, 493; flying squirrels in collection of, 511.
Jones Islands, 381, 382.
Joseph, Captain, 389.

K

Kagloryuak River, 281.
Kaiariok, musk-ox skin sled made by, 256.
Kanghirgyuargmiut Eskimo, Prince Albert Sound, 279.
Karluk, whaling vessel, 40, 42, 43, 44, 45, 118, 119, 378.
Keats, Point, harbor at, 318.
Kendall, "Cape," 302, 304, 305, 306.
Kendall River, 214, 238; measurements of, 241.
Killinermiut tribe, 281–283.
King Point, relics of Amundsen at, 37.
Kirkpuk, Puiplirgmiut Eskimo, 267, 270–271.
Kitirkolak, Victoria Island Eskimo, 286, 288.
Kittegaryuit, mission at, 373–374.
Klinkenberg, Captain Charles, 3–4, 103, 306.
Knife, gift to author, of a historic, 365–367.
Kommana, story of knife given to author by, 365–367.
Koodlalook, Annie, assistant to missionary at Cape Smythe, 46, 85, 94, 387.

Kotzebue Sound, spread of Christianity from, 38, 415.
Kugum Panga, village site known as, 331.
Kugurak River, 437.
Kunaluk, Eskimo helper, 49, 50, 52, 53, 54, 64.
Kunasluk, father of Pikaluk, 131, 133, 136.
Kuparuk River, herds of caribou at, 67, 116.
Kutukak, father-in-law of Natkusiak, 340.

L

Lambart, Frederick, 520.
Lambert Island, crossing Dolphin and Union Straits to, 261–262; Eskimo on, 264.
Lamps of stone, 248, 249.
Langton Bay, description of, 125–126; defects as a wintering place, 126; start from, for the unknown east, 159–161; journey to, from Bear Lake, 223–233; difficulties of return to, after Victoria Island trip, 320–326.
Language, of the Eskimo, 2, 250–251, 354–359; of Indians along Mackenzie River, 21; study of Eskimo, at Cape Smythe, 85; of Dolphin and Union Straits Eskimo, 171, 174–175; study of the Eskimo, during winter of 1911–1912, 353 ff.
Leavitt, Captain George, 48, 253.
Leffingwell, E. de K., 49, 68, 102, 369, 379; meeting with, at Flaxman Island, 44; work done by, in geology and in cartography, 379–380, 437–438.
Leffingwell-Mikkelsen Arctic Expedition, 1.
Leighton, first mate of the *Olga,* 84, 98.
Limestone, deposits of, 441, 442.
Lindy, faithful dog, 75.
Ling, favorite food fish of Eskimo, 455.
Liverpool Bay, crossing of, 369.
Locality, Eskimo lacking in sense of, 146–150.
Loons on Arctic coast, 456–458.
Lopp, Superintendent of Schools, 299.
Loutit, Peter, 467.
Lutz, Frank E., 449.
Lynx, the Northern Canada, 515.
Lyon, Cape, 161, 311, 316, 317; sharp angle of, 318–319.

M

MacFarlane, Roderick, 526.
McIntyre, "Scotty," 380.
Mackenzie River, comparison of Yukon and, 17–18; trip down the, 20 ff.;